THE SOCIOLOGY OF HEALTH AND HEALTH CARE IN ISRAEL

Studies of Israeli Society

Volume V

THE SOCIOLOGY OF HEALTH AND HEALTH CARE IN ISRAEL

Studies of Israeli Society

Volume V

Editor
Aaron Antonovsky

Series Editor
Ernest Krausz

Publication Series of the Israel Sociological Society

Transaction Publishers
New Brunswick (U.S.A.) and London (U.K.)

Sponsored by the Schnitzer Foundation for Research on the Israeli Economy and Society—Bar-Ilan University.

Library of Congress Catalog Number: 79-93045
ISBN: 0-88738-308-4 (cloth) 0-88738-824-8 (paper)

Printed in the United States of America

Library of Congress Cataloguing in Publication Data
(Revised for vol. 5)

Studies of Israeli society

Publication series of the Israel Sociological Society.
Vol. 2: Editor, Ernest Krausz; assistant editor, David Glanz.
Vol. 5: Editor, Aaron Antonovsky.
Includes bibliographies.
Contents: v. 1. Migration, ethnicity, and community—[etc.]—v. 3. Politics and society in Israel— —v. 5. Health and health care in Israel.
1. Kibbutzim—Israel. 2. Israel—Social conditons. 3. Israel—Emigration and immigration. 4. Israel—Ethnic relations. 5. Medical care—Israel. I. Krausz, Ernest. II. Glanz, David. III. Title. IV. Series.

HN660.A8S83 306′.095694 79-93045
ISBN 0-878455-369-X (v.1)

Contents

Preface

The Sociology of Health and Health Care in Israel is the fifth volume of *Studies of Israeli Society*, published under the aegis of the Israeli Sociological Society and Transaction. The series is designed to make available to the international community of sociologists, as well as to others interested in Israel, some of the fruits of the research conducted in Israel. Previous volumes have been devoted to ethnicity, the kibbutz, political sociology, and education. All four were issued under the editorship of Ernest Krausz, who continues to serve as general editor of the series.

As in the case of the preceding volumes, the selection of the overall topic for the collection has been guided by two principal criteria: first, that the subject be specifically directed to a better understanding of Israeli society and generally contribute to the larger world of the social sciences; and second, that a critical mass of literature be available to provide a comprehensive review of "the state of the art" in the field under review.

The reader should be aware of the criteria for selection of papers included in this volume, for they tell something about the character and history of medical sociology in Israel. The first—that only papers published in English be included—is not unduly restrictive. English in Israel, as elsewhere, is the predominant language of scientific publication. The not inconsiderable research reported in Hebrew monographs and reports is largely oriented to the needs of particular clients and seldom framed in theoretical terms of interest to the sociologist. The second criterion—inclusion of the work of anthropologists—extends the scope, suggesting that the professional (as well as the personal) boundary between the sociological and anthropological fields, in a small society, is unclear and not of great significance. The third criterion, requiring that the paper deal with some aspect of Israeli life, led to the omission of a number of significant papers which are contributions to the sociology of health but shed no light on Israeli society in particular.

The two final criteria are indeed restrictive, but were judged to be essential, given considerations of space and the desire to have the volume be representative of the work of the entire community. No papers are included which were published prior to 1980. To have gone beyond this arbitrary date would have meant facing severe problems of selection. Finally, no colleague is represented more than once as first author (with the exception of one paper). Medical sociology in Israel is, as elsewhere, about a generation old. And, as elsewhere, for the first years the initiators, who continue to be active in publishing, were few in number. A more representative sample of published papers would have led to the exclusion of many of the growing number of colleagues who have begun to publish more recently.

It is to be hoped that the bibliography, designed to include all references to work omitted because of these restrictive criteria, will meet the needs of the reader whose appetite has been whetted.

I should like to express my thanks for support and advice to Ernest Krausz, general editor of the series, and to his colleagues on the editorial board; to Bilha Mannheim and Shlomo Deshen, who served as careful readers and consultants; and to the Schnitzer Foundation for Research on the Israeli Economy and Society, Bar-Ilan University, whose generous grant made the publication possible. Finally, we gratefully acknowledge the generous cooperation we have received from all the authors and publishers who permitted us to reprint their works.

Aaron Antonovsky
Beer-Sheva
September 1989

Acknowledgments

We wish to gratefully acknowledge the permission to use copyrighted material granted by journals and publishers.

Our first debt is to Dr. Peter J.M. McEwan, Editor-in-Chief of Social Science & Medicine, *and to its publisher, Pergamon Press (Headington Hill Hall, Oxford, U.K.), for permission to reprint the following papers:*

Lewin-Epstein, Noah. 1986. "Employment and Ill-Health among Women in Israel." *Social Science & Medicine* 23:1171-79. © Pergamon Press.

Kremer, Yael. 1985. "The Association between Health and Retirement: Self-Health Assessment of Israeli Retirees." *Social Science & Medicine* 20:61-66. © Pergamon Press.

Leviatan, Uri and Jiska Cohen. 1985. "Gender Differences in Life Expectancy among Kibbutz Members." *Social Science & Medicine* 21:545-51. © Pergamon Press.

Mansbach, Ivonne, Hava Palti, Bella Pevsner, Helen Pridan and Zvi Palti. 1984. "Advice from the Obstetrician and Other Sources: Do They Affect Women's Feeding Practices? A Study among Different Jewish Groups in Jerusalem." *Social Science & Medicine* 199:157-62. © Pergamon Press.

Shuval, Judith T., Rachel Javetz and Diana Shye. 1989. "Self-Care in Israel: Physicians' Views and Perspectives." *Social Science & Medicine* 29:233-44. © Pergamon Press.

Honig-Parnass, Tikvah. 1982. "The Effects of Latent Social Needs on Physician Utilization by Immigrants: A Replication Study." *Social Science & Medicine* 16:505-14. © Pergamon Press.

Yishai, Yael. 1982. "Politics and Medicine: The Case of Israeli National Health Service." *Social Science & Medicine* 16:285-91. © Pergamon Press.

Carmel, Sara, Ilana S. Yakubovich, Leah Zwanger, and Tsila Zalcman. 1988. "Nurses' Autonomy and Job Satisfaction." *Social Science & Medicine* 26:1103-07. © Pergamon Press.

Ben-Sira, Zeev. 1986. "Disability, Stress and Readjustment: The Function of the Professional's Latent Goals and Affective Behavior in Rehabilitation." *Social Science & Medicine* 23:43-55. © Pergamon Press.

Ichilov, Orit and Mirit Dotan. 1980. "Formation of Professional Images among Israeli Student Nurses." *International Journal of Nursing Studies* 17:247-59. © Pergamon Press.

The following two papers are reprinted by permission of Kluwer Academic Publishers (Dordrecht, The Netherlands):

Basker, Eileen. 1983. "Coping with Fertility in Israel: A Case Study of Culture Clash." *Culture, Medicine & Psychiatry* 7:199-211. © D. Reidel Publishing Company.

Minuchin-Itzigsohn, S.D., R. Ben-Shaoul, A. Weingrod, and D. Krasilowsky. 1984. "The Effect of Cultural Conceptions on Therapy: A Comparative Study of Patients in Israeli Psychiatric Clinics." *Culture, Medicine & Psychiatry* 8:229-54. © D. Reidel Publishing Company.

The following two papers are reprinted by permission of Israel Scientific Publishers Ltd. (Jerusalem):

Javetz, Rachel and Judith T. Shuval. 1982. "Vulnerability to Drugs among Israeli Adolescents." *Israel Journal of Psychiatry & Related Sciences* 19:97-119. © Israel Scientific Publishers Ltd.

Soskolne, Varda. 1984. "The Effect of Ethnic Origin on Personality Resources and Psychophysiological Health in a Chronic Stress Situation: The Case of Spouses of Dialysis Patients." *Israel Journal of Psychiatry & Related Sciences* 21:137-50. © Israel Scientific Publishers Ltd.

We also gratefully acknowledge permission to use the following copyrighted material:

Zuckerman-Bareli, Chaya. 1982. "The Effect of Border Tension on the Adjustment of Kibbutzim and Moshavim on the Northern Border of Israel." Pp. 81-91 in C. D. Spielberger and I. G. Sarason (Eds.). *Stress and Anxiety Vol. 8*. © McGraw-Hill Publishing Co.

Palgi, Phyllis. 1983. "Mental Health, Traditional Beliefs, and the Moral Order among Yemenite Jews in Israel." Pp. 319-335 in L. Romanucci-Ross, D.E. Moerman, and L.R. Tancredi (Eds.). *The Anthropology of Medicine*. © J.F. Bergin Publishers, Inc.

Baider, Lea and Henry Abramovitch. 1985. "The Dybbuk: Cultural Context of a Cancer Patient." *Hospice Journal* 1:113-9. © Haworth Press.

Tzuriel, David and Leonard Weller. 1986. "Social and Psychological Determinants of Breast-Feeding and Bottle-Feeding Mothers." *Basic and Applied Social Psychology* 7:85-100. © Lawrence Erlbaum Assoc., Inc.

Datan, Nancy, Aaron Antonovsky and Benjamin Maoz. 1981. "The Age of Transition." Pp. 108-16 in *A Time to Reap: The Middle Age of Women in Five Israeli Subcultures*. © Johns Hopkins University Press.

Deshen, Shlomo and Hilda Deshen. 1989. "Managing at Home: Relationships between Blind Parents and Sighted Children." *Human Organization* 48:386-410. © Society of Applied Anthropology.

Antonovsky, Aaron and Talma Sourani. 1988. "Family Sense of Coherence and Family Adaptation." *Journal of Marriage & the Family* 50:79-92. © National Council of Family Relations.

Shuval, Judith T. 1985. "Soviet Immigrant Physicians in Israel." Pp. 119-50 in Rita J. Simon (Ed.). *New Lives: The Adjustment of Soviet Jewish Immigrants in the United States and Israel.* © Lexington Books, D.C. Heath & Co.

Levav, Yitzhak and Yoram Bilu. 1980. "A Transcultural Review of Israeli Psychiatry." *Transcultural Psychiatric Research Review* 17:7-36. © Department of Psychiatry, McGill University.

Bernstein, Judith and Sara Carmel. 1986. "Trait-Anxiety Differences among Medical Students." *Psychological Reports* 59:1063-68. © Psychological Reports.

Izraeli, Dafna N. and Netta Notzer. 1983. "Sex Differences in Persistence and Alternative Occupational Choice of Unsuccessful Applicants to Medical School." *Journal of Occupational Behavior* 4:229-35. © John Wiley & Sons.

Introduction: The Sociology of Health in Israel: A Critical View

Judith T. Shuval and *Aaron Antonovsky*

This chapter provides a backdrop for the papers in this volume. It presents the reader with a picture of what has been going on in medical sociology in Israel and where the focus has been placed in terms of research. Following a brief description of the structure of the health care system, a number of dominant themes are noted; these have served as focal points of content around which much of the work in the field has been done. Some, termed "Israeli themes," are intimately linked to special features of the social structure or culture of Israeli society: ethnicity, immigration, stress, and health care utilization. Other themes are more general and use Israel as an additional case study that augments the body of knowledge in the field: studies of professional socialization, gender differences, drug and substance use, and consumer and professional roles in health care. Finally, the community of medical sociologists has been scrutinized in terms of its structure and the kinds of research it has pursued. We have pointed to some important gaps in the content of research undertaken to date and have indicated a number of critical questions which could fruitfully be addressed in the future.

This volume includes twenty-five papers regarding the sociology of health and health care in Israel. All were published during the 1980s. They represent a broad spectrum of topics and social scientists, both sociologists and anthropologists, working in this field.

The material presented is most fruitfully viewed against the wider structural and cultural context of Israeli society. This is because health and health care are intimately linked to broader sets of values and social processes; there is a dynamic, interactive process in which health and health care are influenced by and in turn influence the social system as a whole.

Rather than attempting to summarize the papers in this volume, we will

---

General references in this chapter are given in the usual form and appear at the end of the chapter. Numbers appearing in parentheses refer to the papers included in this volume. See Contents page.

view them in a more general context regarding the sociology of health in Israel. Considerable research in this field and in fields related to it has gone on before the 1980s. The 1960s saw the beginnings of a small group of social scientists who viewed the sociology of health (or medical sociology, as it was then called) as their principal focus for research. This group has continued to grow and to expand its areas of interest; their earlier research serves as the backdrop and in some cases as the impetus for the research reported on here. We will, therefore, draw on such material to provide the reader with a general picture of the central themes and some of the findings which serve as the background for the papers in this book.

The basic structure of the Israeli health care system, which in itself reflects broader social values and processes, sets the stage on which the health scene is acted out; it needs to be kept in mind when the papers are read. Thus, the first goal of the present chapter is to present a brief outline of the basic structure of this health care system.

Our second goal is to examine the subarea of sociology known as the sociology of health in its Israeli setting. What have been its principal areas of substantive interest? Rather than attempting to summarize over twenty years of research in the field, we will point to a number of central themes on which most of the research in the field has focused. The first set to be considered are "Israeli themes" placed on the research agenda by the particular character of Israeli society. The second set consists of themes reflecting more general social processes.

The third goal of this chapter is to consider the community of social scientists engaged in research on health and health care in Israel. Some comments on this professional community and on factors that have influenced its structure and its selection of substantive areas for study will be presented.

Structure of the Health Care System

By all common criteria, Israel is without question a Western society. Its GNP, labor force structure, mortality and morbidity patterns, predominance of chronic rather than infectious diseases, organization of formal health care, and training of practitioners are all similar to those found in European and North American countries. But as in all societies, the health care system, serving 4.3 million people, includes formal and informal components. The latter include networks of lay caretakers—traditional practitioners such as the Bedouin dervish and the wonder-working rabbi—as well as a wide array of health-related specialists and groups outside the framework of the formal structure.

Taken together these provide the population with most of its health care. This general balance is not noticeably different from that seen in other societies, although, as will be noted below, the Israeli population is characterized by high dependence on the formal health care system.

The structure of the formal health care system has been described as a pluralistic, politically linked system in which there is considerable fragmentation and duplication as a result of competition among the unequal components and little coordination among them (Cohen 1986; Halevi 1980; Shuval 1989b). The formal health care system may be described schematically in terms of three components.

- *Four voluntary sick funds* of which one, the General Sick Fund (Kupat Holim Klalit) has always been dominant in size and influence as a result of its political affiliation with the powerful trade union, the General Confederation of Labor (Histadrut), and with the Labor Party. In addition, there are three small sick funds: Maccabi, Meuchedet, and Leumit. Together these sick funds provide prepaid, comprehensive health care, including ambulatory, hospital, drug, convalescent, and other services to 95.4 percent of the population through networks of community services spread throughout the country in both rural and urban areas.

  In 1986 the General Sick Fund insured 3,303,072 persons, or about 80 percent of the insured population. It operates 1,282 ambulatory clinics, fifteen hospitals, and numerous laboratory and convalescent homes as well as other facilities. It employs 27,804 persons, of whom 5,146 are physicians and 9,181 are nurses (General Kupat Holim 1986, 1987). The three smaller sick funds provide similar services to almost 17 percent of the insured population.
- The *Ministry of Health* took over the role of the Department of Health of the British Mandatory authority in 1948. As a result it inherited and perpetuated the anomalous dual role of the latter, acting simultaneously as a provider of health care—through its network of hospitals, care for the homebound and chronically ill, and preventive services, particularly mother and child-care clinics—and as a supervisor and coordinator of health services. Both of these functions have been expanded considerably over the years. The Ministry now runs thirty hospitals and includes a wide range of departments dealing with such public health areas as health education, licensing of health professionals, road safety, sanitation, pest prevention, epidemiology, food control, nutrition, and pharmacology as well as planning and operations research (Bilski 1980; Tulchinski, et al. 1982).

  There is widespread consensus that this dual role, in which the Ministry is simultaneously a provider and a supervisor-planner of health services, is dysfunctional for the system and involves complicated political overtones. These are most evident in competition for resources among various components of the health care system, when political affiliations assume critical importance in the negotiating process.
- A *"voluntary" component* which, like the others, has its roots in the pre-independence period. It includes a variety of institutions such as Hadassah,

religious and missionary hospitals, and several small organizations geared to provide care to special groups. It is noteworthy that institutional fee-for-service care is limited to a few small private hospitals and nursing homes.

Almost all physicians and most other health care personnel, with the prominent exception of dentists, are employed in salaried positions in one of the public health care organizations. Wages are controlled by universal pay grades and have been the subject of ongoing controversy and unrest.

A private sector of health care appears to be growing (Rosen 1989). While most of those providing health care are employed full-time either in hospitals or ambulatory care settings in one of the public health care organizations, many supplement their incomes from part-time, fee-for-service practice. Some hospitals have established formal structures enabling salaried physicians to accept private patients on a controlled fee-for-service basis. However, there is an unresolved debate over the optimal balance between public and private health care in a society with a strong, deeply rooted commitment to the former.

The formal health care system in Israel is intimately linked to the overall political structure. Historical factors, predating independence, set the stage for this pattern which has persisted over the years and has developed a deeply entrenched political reality.

There is as yet no national health insurance. The sick funds are financed by incremental monthly premiums paid by employees (for those served by the General Sick Fund, payments take the form of trade union dues), employer contributions, and government allocations. The latter are apportioned to each of the sick funds on a basis which has been the subject of intense political negotiation since 1950 (Halevi 1980). Israel has always had a coalition government, composed of numerous parties joined in a tenuous balance dominated by the Labor Party until 1977. This has frequently led to bargaining among the partners which focused on the health care system. In particular, the powerful General Sick Fund has served the interests of the Histadrut and the Labor Party so that decisions concerning its financing and operation have been guided in no small measure by political considerations.

It is therefore not entirely surprising that proposals for national health insurance have been supported by the more conservative political parties, while the Labor Party and its affiliates have opposed it except for a version which would guarantee its operation through the existing sick fund structure. The latter groups have blocked a number of efforts to pass such a bill in the Knesset (Halevi 1980; Cohen 1986). Indeed, one of the anomalies of health politics in Israel has been the fact that the right supports national health insurance while the left for the most part opposes it.

Major Themes in the Sociology of Health and Health Care

Like the broader community of scientists in Israel, the social scientists in this field have always viewed themselves as part of the larger scholarly community which crossscuts geographical boundaries. The themes around which research has clustered are therefore partly reflective of more general themes which have interested scholars in other countries. Indeed, because of Israel's small size and fear of isolation, its scholarly community has always made special efforts to promote its network of professional reference groups in other countries and to link its own theoretical and substantive work to this broader context. At the same time, the substantive themes vary in their emphasis: some are more focused on Israel while others are more general.

Certain of the themes on which research in the sociology of health and health care has focused are a function of idiosyncratic cultural or structural elements in Israel's society. While one may assume that few social phenomena are unique in a pure sense, some are so intimately linked to special characteristics of the society that they may be said to represent "Israeli themes" in the sociology of health and health care. The "Israeli" quality of a theme stems from its intimate relationship to structural or cultural features of the society, either in the sense that it relates substantively to a situation that is unique to Israel or that Israel provides a specially conducive setting to research it. Some of these themes have counterparts in other societies, but the form they assume in Israel has a quality of its own. This does not mean that the concepts and principles by which they can be understood are not cross-cultural.

Other themes which have served as the substantive focus of research in the sociology of health in Israel share the interests of research carried out in other societies. These studies view Israel as a testing ground for theories and empirical findings reported elsewhere. Findings from such research often show patterns in Israel which are not very different from those observed elsewhere. On the other hand, familiar patterns may take on a special Israeli form, or their appearance may be timed differently—i.e., before or, more commonly, after their appearance in other societies. However, the "local" quality of a pattern need not obscure our recognition of its familiarity and the satisfying sense that it provides replicative evidence for the generality of processes observed elsewhere. From this point of view, familiar patterns are not uninteresting but rather encouraging in a discipline known for its discrete, frequently noncumulative findings.

The distinction we have drawn between Israeli themes and more general ones is a heuristic one and far from absolute; like many categorizations, it is partly in the eyes of the beholder and simply a helpful method to organize the substantive themes on which research has focused. The first group is not purely local nor is the second group purely non-Israeli in its relevance. Because of their intimate linkage to the general professional community, both contribute to the general store of knowledge in the field; because their research has been carried out in Israel, both provide better understanding of the sociology of health in that society.

"Israeli" Themes

Immigration and Ethnic Heterogeneity

Since 1948 the population of Israel has come to include large groups of Jewish immigrants from a variety of traditional settings in North Africa and the Middle East as well as groups stemming from a broad spectrum of European countries and other parts of the Western world. These groups have been characterized by wide diversity in cultural patterns and have differed considerably in the extent of their exposure to processes of modernization. A wide array of substantive research issues, of which health is only one, have been explored in Israel over the years. These have been referred to as studies in "ethnicity", the reference being to the different groups of Jewish immigrants or, more recently, to their children (Ben Rafael 1982; Krausz 1980; Shuval 1989a; Smooha 1978; Weingrod 1985).

The papers in this volume reflect a continued interest in this focus. Despite the fact that over 60 percent of the Jewish population is native-born, and a high proportion of the foreign-born population has been exposed to many years of life in Israel, the findings show that certain types of health behavior and health attitudes are tenaciously conditioned by orientations anchored in cultures imported by immigrant groups. Since immigration from many of the more traditional societies has been infrequent in recent years, informants are often of relatively advanced age. Nevertheless, several of the anthropologists represented in the volume have captured these patterns in studies of Yemenites (3), Kurds (4), North Africans (10), Persians, Ashkenazis, Moroccans (17) and Middle Eastern groups (22). Their findings document the continuing power of traditional orientations to structure, attitudes and behavior regarding issues such as mental health, infertility, cancer and abortion. Concepts of etiology, diagnosis, treatment and relations with health care experts, both physicians and traditional practitioners, are conditioned by these orientations.

Traditional ethnic healers continue to practice in Israel, although many encourage their patients to utilize modern physicians as well. One of the papers (22) notes the functionality of this simultaneous usage pattern which has been reported in other societies: traditional healers are an important recourse mechanism for some patients when modern medicine fails or is unsatisfactory (cf. Ronen 1989).

The anthropological studies are not the only ones to highlight the role of ethnicity in health behavior. Several of the sociological contributions focus specifically on this variable and many include it as a central background characteristic. In the former category is the study comparing five groups of women, from Central Europe, Turkey, Persia, North Africa and a group of Israeli Arab women, on their responses to menopause (7). While the findings indicate certain differences among the ethnic groups, the response patterns did not line up in terms of the modern-traditional continuum proposed but, rather, pointed to a different ordering in which the groups characterized by stability of culture context showed higher levels of health, adaptation and satisfaction than the groups still undergoing processes of culture change. Furthermore, there are important similarities among the groups which in many cases override their differences and point to transcendent patterns which cut across broad cultural differences.

Ethnicity is a central variable in determining response to stress. This is shown in studies of the psychophysiological health of spouses of dialysis patients (16) and of response to border tension (2). While all spouses show some decrease in their personality resources as a result of the prolonged stress of ongoing dialysis, the style of coping seen in persons of European origin differs from that of Easterners: with the latter there tends to be greater passivity, more negative self-perception and more frequent somatic symptoms than with the former, whose pattern of coping is more externalized and expressed in psychological rather than physiological symptoms. Exposure to border tension results in greater anxiety and lower morale among settlers of Eastern origin who are less identified with their communities and generally less educated than Europeans.

Patterns of social change and acculturation sometimes cause reversals in expected patterns as traditional groups strive to conform to what are perceived as the appropriate norms in a modern society. Although more women of North African and Asian origin decided to breast-feed their infants immediately after childbirth (6), another study of similar mothers shows that they breast-feed their infants for a shorter period of time than mothers of European origin, who are more exposed to contemporary social movements emphasizing the importance of natural processes. The former appear to view breast feeding as a "primitive" pattern which is better given up in the effort to become "Israeli" (11). Here is an additional example of the dysfunctional effects of modernization on well-founded traditional patterns.

Ethnicity and socioeconomic class are juxtaposed to a considerable extent in Israeli society, and the correlation between them makes it difficult to disentangle the separate effects of each. Many social scientists are of the opinion that differences attributed to ethnicity are to no small extent social class differences; in the long run it is the latter that are meaningful and are likely to be of relevance in the future (Ben Rafael 1982; Krausz 1980; Shuval 1989a; Smooha 1978; Weingrod 1985). For broad segments of the population this trend can already be discerned. There has been little evidence in Israel of self-conscious ethnic movements seeking to preserve traditional patterns or to assert their identity in the spirit of "ethnic is beautiful."

Ethnic diversity is a function of immigration, which has been an ongoing process in Israel during its entire history including the period predating independence. A formal open-door policy accepts virtually all Jewish immigrants and views their arrival as a symbolic reaffirmation of the fundamental raison d'etre of the society. Pragmatic considerations of economic need or job availability have not served, as in other countries, as criteria for admission. The assumption has been that the society and its economic structure must be adapted to the economic and social needs of the immigrants rather than the reverse.

Physicians have figured prominently among immigrants to Israel. Numbers have varied at different periods depending on the countries of origin from which populations were emigrating. During the years 1939-45, when many German Jewish doctors escaped from Nazi Germany, the ratio of physicians to total immigrants was as high as 1:120 (Sicron 1957). In more recent years, large numbers of physicians arrived in Israel from Eastern European countries, the most recent ones from the Soviet Union.

These immigrant physicians augmented the population of graduates of the four Israeli medical schools and the group of Israelis who went abroad to study medicine, producing what is one of the highest ratios of physicians to population in the world: 330/100,000 (World Health Organization 1988). Although there is no evidence to suggest that this ratio is related to excessive health problems (Tulchinsky et al. 1982; Shuval 1989b), in recent years the annual rate of increase in the number of practicing physicians has been three times the rate of growth of the population (State Controller's Office 1986).

Dovetailing into the ideological commitment to an open-door policy for Jewish immigrants has been the commitment to full employment, which has been a central goal of the government since 1948. In fact, unemployment has been kept relatively low: in 1987, 5.6 percent of the labor force was unemployed and this figure rose to 7 percent in 1988. Major efforts have been invested in finding employment for the large physician population and, in fact, almost all have been employed in their profession in the health care system. This remarkable goal has been achieved by means of a number of social mechanisms described in one of the papers in this volume (21), which discusses the integration of recent Soviet immigrant physicians into the health care system.

One of these mechanisms has been the unique structure of the licensure process, which reflects an effort to reconcile two major societal needs: to provide employment for immigrants and prevent emigration while simultaneously protecting the population by controlling the quality of health care. To this end, basic employment in general practice has been provided for virtually all immigrant physicians once their formal medical school credentials have been established, while quality control has been focused more stringently on licensure for specialty status. More rigorous quality control was applied to the first level of licensing in 1987 by requiring physicians trained outside Israel to pass qualifying examinations for general practice.

The translation of this ideology into practice has been made possible by a stratified allocation of medical manpower differentiated by the locus of practice. Immigrant physicians, especially those without specialty status, are largely employed in the primary care clinics. The uneven level of training of doctors from a wide variety of medical schools in different countries has compounded the chronic structural problems concerning the quality of primary care.

Graduates of the Israeli medical schools, who are generally comparable in level to graduates of the better Western schools, have almost invariably entered specialty practice and work in the hospital system which is structurally separate from the primary care clinic system (Shuval 1980).

There is an invidious status differential distinguishing the two loci of practice, with the hospitals enjoying considerably more prestige than the clinics in the eyes of both professionals and lay persons. This distribution of medical personnel has caused serious questioning of the differential quality of health care at the two levels, but it has been functional in keeping unemployment among immigrant physicians to a minimum (State Controller's Office 1986).

In an effort to remedy this situation, the General Sick Fund has undertaken a program to train specialists in family medicine whose natural locus of practice is the primary care clinic. Interest in this field is growing, partly in response to constraints in other residency options and partly because there is increased awareness of the importance of the psychosocial aspects of health which are a major focus of family medicine. Whether the differential quality of primary and hospital care will be seriously affected by this development remains to be seen.

There are a number of other mechanisms that have been utilized to minimize unemployment in the large population of Israeli physicians. There is underemployment of physicians in the primary health care sector, evidenced by a relatively short work day—especially for older physicians who are permitted to put in fewer hours, particularly during the summer months (Ministry of Health 1964). Primary care clinics also employ a high proportion of women physicians, who tend on the average to work fewer hours (General Kupat Holim 1987). Furthermore, the Israel Medical Association has helped provide employment for its members through a stringent set of professional requirements which minimize the substitution of nurses or other allied health personnel for physicians in the performance of tasks which in other countries have been delegated to such personnel. For example, the ratio of nurses to physicians is relatively low in Israel (3.3:1), as is the nurse-to-population ratio (1:154 in 1980) (Bergman and Hen 1976; Cohen 1986).

Stress

Israelis are frequently asked by non-Israelis how they can possibly live reasonably normal lives in a social context fraught with stress: frequent wars and threats of additional war, terrorism, Holocaust memories, reserve military service for men up to age 55. And all of these come on top of the everyday stressors of life experienced by people in all societies. Another way of phrasing the question is to ask if there is any evidence that health is demonstrably influenced by the extra and unique stresses characterizing life in Israel.

A systematic answer requires comparative analysis of health parameters in other societies. Such comparisons are tricky, not only because other societies have their own unique forms of stress but also because of the ecological fallacy. In fact, international comparisons of health indicators do not show Israel to be dramatically high on most parameters describing infectious and chronic diseases (Rosen 1987). However, such data provide only a partial answer to this question, especially in light of the fact that morbidity records and, especially, hospitalization data are notorious for revealing only the tip of the iceberg. This is particularly true for data regarding mental health and other aspects of well-being.

There has been increasing interest in Israel and in other countries in the problems faced by Holocaust survivors and their children. The psychiatric emphasis of this work has caused it to be individually focused so that it has not generally dealt with the potential effects of a collective memory on persons for whom the latter is the critical experience. For example, Israeli schools devote considerable curricular time to the Holocaust, so that young people in the society are systematically exposed to the historical facts and implications, but little is known concerning the effects of such exposure.

It is probably not coincidental that Antonovsky's seminal research regarding stress and coping was developed in Israel (Antonovsky 1979). While the principal relevance of this work is to broader theories of stress, it has been empirically examined in Israel and it is fair to suggest that the special social context of that society gave it some impetus. Indeed, the "sense of coherence" concept which is so central to this work may well be associated, if indirectly, with the collective solidarity that characterized Israeli society during its pioneering stages and has invariably surfaced during periods of crisis.

The paper included in this volume seeks to broaden the sense of coherence concept from an individual to a group context by shifting the focus to the family (13).

Of course, the most general answer to the basic question posed focuses on coping mechanisms. As in all societies, response to stress is a function of the meaning attributed to stress, the kinds of individual and collective resources available to cope with it, and the skills to activate resources when need arises. Retirement from work, for example, is not necessarily a stressful experience (8). In this regard, despite the frequency and intensity of stress in Israel, a number of important coping mechanisms may be noted. Although it is changing, family structure is generally more traditional than in many Western societies, thus providing social support in everyday life and at times of crisis. There are also important institutional support systems that play a role even though they may not always be sufficient. The paper on gender differences in life expectancy among kibbutz members indicates that differences between males and females are smaller than elsewhere because of the particular life style of the kibbutz, which reduces role differentiation between genders and maximizes social support in a small collective community (9). Nevertheless, it is probably true that ongoing stress takes its toll. We have already noted that one paper in the book deals directly with the effect of border tension on the emotional and social adjustment of kibbutz and moshay members located on the northern border of Israel (2).

Utilization and Primary Care

As noted, the structural and status differentiation of the hospital and primary care systems, combined with the concentration of immigrant physicians in the latter, have made primary care a unique issue that has justifiably been an Israeli theme for research. This is particularly true because Israel has been characterized for many years by one of the highest rates of primary care utilization in the world. The average annual number of physician contacts per insured persons is 12.3 and the number of prescriptions per year is 24 (Barell and Zadka 1984; Central Bureau of Statistics 1986).

Over and above the high value traditionally placed on health by Jews (Antonovsky 1972; Mechanic 1962; Zborowski and Herzog 1952; Suchman 1964; Twaddle 1969) and the large population of physicians in Israel, research has pointed to the importance of certain latent functions of the health care system which encourage utilization of primary care services in a society characterized by immigration and ethnic heterogeneity (Shuval et al. 1970). These latent functions answer people's need for psychological support, legitimation of failure through the sick role, and formal certification of illness in order to utilize sick leave benefits. Physicians often play a critical role in decisions concerning distribution of scarce resources such as cars for the disabled, sheltered housing, special jobs, telephones, and other benefits.

One of the papers in the volume undertakes to replicate earlier research concerning the latent functions of primary health care (15). Replication is a rare phenomenon in social science research and is therefore in itself worthy of note, especially, as in this case, when more sophisticated techniques of analysis are utilized and the findings are cumulative. It was found that with the passage of time immigrants no longer utilize the physician to gain support and sympathy, but rather seek other agents of support in the social system. The author notes that this pattern could be a result of changes in the health care system, which is increasingly bureaucratized and therefore less attractive as a provider of social or psychological support—despite widespread need for such support.

A considerable volume of research has developed on the problematic aspects of primary care in Israel, with much of it focusing on the structure of physician-patient relationships. A distinction between the doctor's instrumental and affective role has proved useful in distinguishing between technical functions and emotional-supportive functions, each of which plays a different role with respect to provider and patient satisfaction (Ben-Sira 1985, 1986). As in other countries, it is possible that power enhancement is in effect a latent goal of many physicians, an issue which is explored from the viewpoint of disabled persons in one of the papers (20). It is also discussed in the context of physicians' responses to increased independence and autonomy of consumers which result from self-care initiatives of lay persons (14).

The 1980s were characterized by considerable unrest in the health care institutions reflecting widespread dissatisfaction with working conditions and wages in the clinics and hospitals. A four-month physicians' strike took place in 1983 and work stoppages, slowdowns, and other strikes since then have been frequent. There was an almost constant process of negotiation over working conditions and wages among the bodies involved: the ministries of health and finance, the Histadrut, and a variety of occupational groups in the health care organizations such as physicians, nurses, administrative personnel, and maintenance staff. As noted, the health care system is intimately linked with the political structure, so that these negotiating processes reflected the broader political context and its ongoing conflicts as much as they expressed problems intrinsic to the health care system.

One of the papers took advantage of the physicians' strike to examine a number of issues which came into focus through that event. Here is a case of serendipity in which discerning social scientists organized their research expeditiously to take advantage of a unique situation. In a study dealing with one of the traditional women's occupations, nursing, light is shed on the way women perceive their role with particular reference to its expansion beyond traditional definitions (19). We have noted that the Israel Medical Association has been conservative in delegating tasks traditionally controlled by physicians to other health care personnel. During the four-month physicians' strike in 1983, the nurses remained on their jobs and were the most qualified professionals available. During that period, some of the traditional limits on autonomy were removed: nurses could regulate their own allocation of time for routine work and could initiate new tasks previously performed exclusively by doctors. The research examined the perceptions and job satisfaction of nurses in primary care clinics where the expansion of autonomy could be expected to be greatest.

The findings point up the conservative character of Israeli society in general and of the health professions in particular. In looking back on their recent experience during the strike, most nurses reported that they had in fact increased their routine activity and expanded their autonomy; both of these were associated with increased job satisfaction. Despite this, they did not seek increased autonomy in the wake of the strike, rather viewing their expanded role as a temporary challenge that had to be met during an emergency. It is our impression that such a stance is congruent with the way most Israeli women are viewed and perceive themselves at this time: they are willing and frequently pleased to undertake nontraditional roles for prescribed, limited periods, especially in the case of special need or emergency. Indeed, the willingness to do that is in itself a traditional female norm, for example, taking over nonfemale tasks when a husband is ill. But most women in Israel, with some exceptions, are not actively concerned with basic changes in female roles—despite the fact that a high proportion of them are employed outside their homes and serve in the army. Change in this area is distressingly slow but certainly inevitable.

Themes Reflecting General Social Processes

Professional Socialization

Medical and nursing education have been studied by Israeli social scientists, who have generally followed the research traditions developed in other countries, principally the United States. Two of the papers in the book are concerned with various aspects of professional socialization (23,24), but the greater part of the work done in this field does not appear in this volume, given the restrictions referred to in the preface (Shuval 1980).

Undergraduate medical education in Israel is structured as a six-year program followed by a year of internship. Most students, both men and women, enter medical school after completing army service. They are therefore somewhat older when they make their occupational choice than comparable students in other countries. Of the four medical schools now functioning, three have followed fairly conservative, traditional styles of professional education following the curricular models of medical schools in the United States. The newest medical school, founded in 1974 at the Ben-Gurion University of the Negev in Beersheba, is innovative in the general style of the medical schools at the University of New Mexico in the United States, Mastricht University in the Netherlands and McMaster University in Canada. What particularly characterizes these schools is the utilization of an integrated, community-oriented curriculum which is geared to channel a significant proportion of students to careers in primary care and community medicine and to provide all students with increased sensitivity to their importance (Prywes 1983).

The two papers included here both focus on patterns internal to the professional socialization process, one at a medical school and the other at a school of nursing. The first examines the level of students' anxiety during six years of medical education at the Ben-Gurion Medical School. It demonstrates that anxiety declines over time as students gain confidence during their progress through medical school, but that women consistently show higher anxiety than men (24). A study of a similar genre explores the development of professional images among students in nursing school and the manner in which the teaching staff serves as role models (23).

Gender Studies

There is a growing interest in gender studies in Israel, but only a few have focused systematically on health issues. Considering the large number of women in the health occupations and the number of gender-linked health issues, this area should undoubtedly be expanded in the future.

The two papers included in this volume reflect different research strategies. One considers gender differences in choice of occupation (25), while the other focuses on the health of women characterized by different occupational status (1). Both provide Israeli findings regarding issues that have been studied elsewhere.

A comparison of men and women who have been unsuccessful in their initial application to medical school shows that men are more persistent than women in reapplication. However, men were more likely to drop their interest in medicine in favor of other high-status occupations outside the field of health, while women showed a stronger commitment to health-linked occupations and to careers in traditionally male-dominated or mixed-sex occupations (25). In more ways than one, these highly qualified women show behavior which differs from the widespread conservatism that characterizes the predominant majority of Israeli women.

The other paper concerns the health effects of employment on married women and uses Israel as an additional case study to examine a variety of hypotheses that have been advanced in the literature (1). In a carefully designed multivariate analysis, the author finds that employed women are characterized by better health than housewives on a variety of measures. The differences are largely, but not entirely, explained by younger age, better education, and the relative infrequency of chronic conditions in the employed group. While the "fixed role obligation" theory gains some support, the paper shows that the major explanatory factors reside in the population composition of the two groups.

We have already noted the widespread conservatism of Israeli women with specific reference to the nursing population, which showed little interest in increased autonomy or role expansion on a long-term basis even after their experience during the physicians' strike. Further evidence of this general pattern is provided by another paper in this volume, which suggests that women physicians tend to be less accepting than their male colleagues of innovative notions such as increased self-care by lay persons (14).

Drugs, Substance Abuse, and AIDS

Drug use, substance abuse, and, more recently, Acquired Immune Deficiency Syndrome (AIDS) are examples of major health problems on which considerable sociological research has been carried out in many countries; Israeli social scientists have been active in this field, although research on the social aspects of AIDS is just beginning. One of the papers in this volume provides data on stability over a decade of secondary school students' reported consumption of drugs, almost entirely marijuana. While the overall prevalence is low as compared to some other countries, this does not mean that there is no cause for concern: in specific subgroups of the population considerably higher rates of drug use are reported (5). Ongoing monitoring of this problem is essential, as is documentation concerning the apparent increase in the use of hard drugs in all age groups.

Consumer and Professional Roles

Many Western societies have been characterized by growing criticism of medico-centrism and sensitivity to overdependence on the biomedical model in health care. This has generally been accompanied by a growth in consumer groups focusing on the quality of health care and on the augmented role of lay persons in providing it. These patterns have been slow to develop in Israel, as have more general patterns of consumer awareness regarding quality of products and services. On the more general level, this has been the result of a prolonged inflationary economy which induced widespread, uncritical spending in a seller's market. The structure of the health care services has encouraged user passivity and dependence on professional personnel, not least because of the comprehensive insurance system which in effect grants little power to consumers in the provider-patient relationship. While there is a pro forma supervisory committee at the national level of the General Sick Fund, its role is recognized to be predominantly ritual; in practice members have very little real input into the system and a minimum of control over the service provided.

The self-care movement, which encourages initiatives and autonomy of lay persons regarding their own health, has barely begun to show the kind of viability in Israel that has been seen in other Western societies. The women's movement, which in other countries has included autonomy in health care as one of its central concerns, is making its presence felt to an increasing extent. Needless to say, people do care for their own health and that of their families, but conscious awareness of the importance of self-reliance and the possibility of substitution of self-treatment for professional care for many less threatening or chronic health problems is still not widespread.

One of the papers in this volume analyzes Israeli physicians' views concerning lay self-care and reports considerable reluctance to encourage lay initiatives and autonomy (14). While many doctors recognize that increased self-care by lay people could reduce the burden of high utilization and costs that currently trouble the health care system, most are unwilling to redistribute the power and responsibility for care which is at present concentrated in their hands (14).

There is some research to indicate that allied health professionals in Israel, the largest proportion of whom are women, are more positive than physicians in their encouragement of lay initiatives and self-care in health (Shye et al. 1989). Research on lay attitudes and practices in this area is currently under way.

Medical Sociologists in Israel and Their Work

In contrast to the situation in some European countries, where medical sociology originated in policy and practice areas, Israeli sociologists, following more closely in the American pattern, were originally, and to a considerable extent still are, university-based. Some came to the field after considerable research in other fields of sociology and not a few continue such work. However, in recent years, as academic training programs in the field have developed, more researchers have started their careers directly in this field while still in graduate school. Academia is the major locus of work for the majority of such social scientists but an increasing number are based in practice-oriented or policy-making settings.

Thus it is not surprising that virtually all consider it important to link their research to theories and empirical findings accumulated in Israel and in other countries. There is no single, dominant theoretical tradition guiding research in this area; social scientists concerned with research on health are no more homogeneous in their theoretical leaning than is the wider community of Israeli professionals from which they are drawn. While there was a tendency for functionalism to prevail in the 1950s and early 1960s, Israeli sociologists generally followed the critical theoretical reappraisals of the later years, so that the present community of social scientists adheres to a broad gamut of theoretical orientations.

In contrast to the above heterogeneity, there is a predominance of sociologists who utilize quantitative methods to analyze their data, and a growing group who are skilled in sophisticated, multivariate techniques of analysis. The qualitative tradition is represented by a small but important group of anthropologists; there are few qualitative sociologists in this field.

The anthropologists concerned with health focus almost exclusively on beliefs and practices of traditional ethnic groups and practitioners. Only one paper contributed by an anthropologist utilizes that discipline's skills to study a subject outside the ethnic area (12). The concentration on ethnicity reflects a general trend of the anthropological community in Israel, which seeks to utilize the "natural" ethnic heterogeneity to study problems which cannot be investigated in more homogeneous settings or in settings where Western values and processes of modernization are more dominant. Furthermore, there is a sense of urgency which encourages that focus in view of the ephemeral quality of traditional ethnic patterns and the paucity of immigrants stemming from traditional settings. The Ethiopian community is an exception to this generalization and, in fact, there is ongoing research regarding this group.

There are other groups and social contexts on which additional anthropological studies of health behavior could be carried out—Arabs or Orthodox Jews, for example. It would also be useful to have an anthropological perspective on a variety of other health issues on which qualitative analysis is lacking. A useful example in this volume is the paper which expands Goffman's sociology of stigma to a previously unstudied group: blind parents and their sighted children (12). In this unique context, the handicapped, stigmatized person is confronted by ongoing interaction with an able-bodied person who is structurally subordinate in status and power by virtue of generational position but who is part of an overall social system that stigmatizes the blind. The research considers the ambiguity in the parent-child relationship which stems from this reversal in the power structure among the actors.

Sociologists of health cover a wide array of subjects which reflect many topics in the general literature. To a large extent, the substantive areas actually dealt with have reflected the individual curiosity and interests of this particular group of social scientists during the late 1970s and first half of the 1980s. At the same time, the luxury to follow those proclivities is constrained by the resources available to undertake research and by structural factors associated with occupational settings. For example, certain topics may be given priority for research by bodies which provide funding, medical and nursing schools may offer captive populations or ready data for social scientists, and certain topics become "hot" at certain times. As in all countries, research resources are scarce and competition to gain access to them is often formidable.

An important additional constraint on the content of the research stems from the applied implications of research in the field of health. While theoretical issues abound, the apparent immediacy of policy implications is in many ways more compelling than in other areas of sociology. This tends to press for applied research. Policymakers often direct practical questions to researchers whose work is then designed to seek meaningful answers. Most Israeli social scientists seek to anchor such research in an appropriate theoretical framework that links it to other research in the field. However, pressure for quick findings regarding applied issues combined with sparse funding often prevent full utilization of data for the kind of analysis that most social scientists consider appropriate and professionally rewarding.

While Israeli sociologists and anthropologists began research on health behavior and health care as early as the 1960s, there is not much evidence for cumulative findings. This problem is far from unique to Israel, but in a small country with limited resources it is especially unfortunate. One reason for this phenomenon is the strong other-directedness of Israeli social scientists to professional reference groups in other countries. Many prefer to continue or develop a line of research initiated outside Israel rather than pursue research on a problem on which some findings already exist in Israel. In fact, these two options are not incompatible.

Despite the considerable variety and diversity of research concerning the sociology of health in Israel, there are a number of important content areas which are conspicuously weak or absent. Some of these are "Israeli themes," in that they are unique to the society, while others are more general.

The most evident gap concerns research on the sociology of health in the Israeli Arab sector of the population. In part, this paucity of research stems from political constraints and logistical problems (access, language, cooperation, etc.). On the other hand, it has been noted that the Jewish majority has tended in the past to be "blind" to most issues and problems concerning Israeli Arabs, preferring to ignore a complex set of topics that go well beyond the field of health. In the latter area, epidemiological research has in fact documented mortality and morbidity rates in the Arab sector, but sociologists concerned with health have generally adopted the prevailing "blindness" and have not come to grips with the many important and interesting research issues that are an integral part of their overall social context. Studies based on population samples rarely include the Arab population. While anthropologists, seeking traditional health patterns, have shown an interest in Bedouin groups, such efforts have been somewhat sporadic and have not captured the interest of major segments of the professional community. Israeli Arab social scientists could well make a contribution in this broad field; it is ripe for collaborative efforts with Jewish colleagues.

The kibbutz has served as a principal Israeli theme for social science research for many years and a considerable body of sociological findings has accumulated on a variety of topics related to this unique way of life (Krausz 1983). It is therefore somewhat surprising that it has not attracted much research regarding the sociology of health. This volume includes one such paper (9). Here is an area in which issues such as the health effects of different lifestyles, social support systems, a changing work ethic, shifting levels and forms of ideological commitment, and other uniquely structured social issues can be studied. Most of the more general kibbutz research has focused internally on specific small communities or on the kibbutz movements. It would be useful to pursue this tradition with a focus on health-oriented research, but even more fruitful to introduce comparative analysis of kibbutz and non-kibbutz settings.

Another area which has hardly been studied concerns alternative health care. Virtually all of the research carried on to date, with the exceptions noted above regarding the anthropologists, has focused on the established health care system. However, like many societies, Israel shows an increasing proliferation of practitioners and groups which base their approaches to diagnosis, treatment, and prevention of illness on non-Western values and theories. Some of these draw on Chinese or other Eastern traditions, while others are based on a wide variety of practical and theoretical orientations which are outside the biomedical system. These include various approaches to birthing, holistic medicine, biomedical feedback, homeopathic medicine, many types of dietary and nutritional approaches to health, body consciousness, relaxation, and physical exercise, and a wide variety of self-help groups which focus on health or health-related problems. None of these are formally recognized as part of the health care system, nor are their users covered by the health insurance schemes; some are overtly denigrated by the formal medical establishment. Physicians differ in the extent to which they are aware of the usefulness and effectiveness of such practices and practitioners; little if any reference is made to them in medical school curricula. In a strongly medicocentric system, there is little awareness of their potential to play a constructive, sometimes critical, role in the health care system, and the possible dangers to health that might result from their use have frequently been exaggerated. Furthermore, the proliferation of alternative health care practitioners and practices cannot help but raise questions regarding consumers' confidence in the quality and effectiveness of the formal biomedical health care system as presently structured. This is a rich area for research that has hardly been touched by the sociological community (Ronen 1989).

There has been a paucity of research on the macro level of the health care system and this lacuna is reflected in the contents of the present volume. Only one paper (18) considers the health care system in its broad political context. Like other societies that have sought to provide a broad array of welfare services to their populations, Israel finds itself facing major crises in the costs of providing such services. The frequent work stoppages referred to above provide only a surface indication of the multitude of serious problems faced by the health care system, as does growing consumer dissatisfaction. Some research on these problems has been undertaken by political scientists or by specialists in health system analysis (e.g., Arian 1981; Baruch 1973; Bilski 1980; Cohen 1986; Ellencweig and Grafstein 1986; Halevi and Ever-Hadani 1979; Halevi 1980; Yishai 1979), but sociologists have been conspicuously absent to date.

Sociological research could be a useful means of gaining further understanding of the complex problems involved and examining the options available to address them. Thus far, the preferred response to most of these problems has been to appoint governmental or other public committees to investigate the issues and propose solutions (e.g., Trainin, Van Leer, Netanyahu, and others). As noted, the health care system is intimately tied to political interest groups which are generally reluctant to direct a nonpartisan, in-depth look at their own domain. Furthermore, many social scientists are not anxious to stick their necks out in studies of these macro issues, if only because some are employed by health care organizations and others may be future applicants for research funding from some of the same bodies. An undue concentration on microprocesses has been the result.

Rather than continue to nibble around the edges of the central, critical health care problems that trouble the society, medical sociologists in Israel should in fact stick their necks out to address these issues directly with the best tool at their disposal: research. This should be both theoretical and applied—and the two need not be structurally separate. The Israeli experience can be used to elucidate any number of basic theoretical issues in sociology and some will prefer to concentrate on these, continuing a dominant tradition of the profession. Others will be drawn to research on policy issues. This is as it should be, and serves to promote the creative process.

A good deal of mythology surrounds the Israeli health care system and this needs to be distinguished from the reality. Probing questions should be asked of a health care system that has prided itself for over sixty years on its pioneering accomplishment of bringing comprehensive health care to almost the entire population in all parts of the country, including the most isolated settlements. Some of these questions are:

- Is health care in fact allocated on an equitable basis?
- What can be said about the quality of health care in various segments of the system: primary care, hospital and community care for acute and chronic illness, prevention, and health promotion?
- How would the introduction of symbolic fees for health care affect utilization rates and health indicators?
- What are the implications for the health care system of growth in the private sector? How can the private sector be structured to prevent deterioration in the public sector and avoid gross differentials between the two in the quality of care?
- How can the sick funds learn from each other and from experience elsewhere to improve their organizational structure?
- Could more competition within and between subsegments of the health care system improve quality and reduce costs?
- How can the dysfunctions of medical bureaucracy be minimized to improve patient care and reduce costs?
- Is more humane medical care really possible in the 1990s?

This list of questions is far from exhaustive. Neither are they relevant only to Israel. But the troubled Israeli health care system is in urgent need of a critical reevaluation that would examine it from many points of view. Imaginative sociologists who do not flinch at looking beyond the rhetoric and the mythology could make a real contribution to that process.

References

Antonovsky, A. 1972. "A Model to Explain Visits to the Doctor: With Special Reference to the Case of Israel." *Journal of Health and Social Behavior* 13:446-54.

Antonovsky, A. 1979. *Health, Stress and Coping*. San Francisco: Jossey-Bass.

Arian, A. 1981. "Health Care in Israel: Political and Administrative Aspects." *International Political Science Review* 2:43-56.

Barell, V., and Zadka, P. 1984. "Health Care Systems in Israel." In *Proceedings of the International Collaborative Effort on Perinatal and Infant Mortality*, Vol. 1. Washington, D.C.: U.S. Department of Health and Human Services.

Baruch, N. 1973. *The Institutional Organization of Health Services in Israel*. Jerusalem: Center for Policy Research.

Ben-Rafael, E. 1982. *The Emergence of Ethnicity: Cultural Groups and Social Conflict in Israel*. London: Greenwood.

Ben-Sira, Z. 1986. "The Plight of Primary Medical Care: The Problematics of 'Committedness' to the Practice." *Social Science and Medicine* 22:699-712.

______. 1985. "Primary Medical Care and Coping with Stress and Disease: The Inclination of Primary Care Practitioners to Demonstrate Affective Behaviour." *Social Science and Medicine* 21:465-98.

Bergman, R., and Hen, R. 1976. "Nursing Personnel in Israel" (in Hebrew). *Bitachon Soziali* (July).

Bilski, R. 1980. "Planning in Israel's Public Health Services." In *Can Planning Replace Politics? The Israeli Experience*, ed. R. Bilski, 217-58. The Hague: Martinus Nijhoff.

Central Bureau of Statistics. 1986. *Statistical Abstract of Israel 1986*, no. 37. Jerusalem: Government Printer.

______. 1983. *Statistical Abstract of Israel 1983*, no. 34. Jerusalem: Government Printer.

Cohen, R. 1986. "The Israeli Health System: Power, Politics and Policies." Ph.D. dissertation, Faculty of Medicine, University of Toronto.

Ellencweig, A.Y., and Grafstein, O. 1986. *Inequality in Health: A Case Study*. Jerusalem: Department of Medical Ecology, Hebrew University-Hadassah Medical School.

General Kupat Holim. 1987. *Kupat Holim—Institutions and Services, 1987*, publ. no. 125 (in Hebrew). Tel Aviv: Research and Medical Economics Department.

______. 1986. *Manpower Planning in Kupat Holim*, publ. no. 123 (in Hebrew). Tel Aviv: Research and Medical Economics Department.

Halevi, Ḥ.S. 1980. *The Bumpy Road to National Health Insurance: The Case of Israel*. Jerusalem: Brookdale Institute of Research on Aging and Adult Human Development.

Halevi, H.S., and Ever-Hadani, P. 1979. "Health Expenditures under Multiple-Priority Pressures: A Case Study of Israel." *Israel Journal of Medical Sciences* 15:43-54.

Krausz, E., ed. 1983 *The Sociology of the Kibbutz: Studies in Israeli Society*. New Brunswick, N.J.: Transaction.

______, ed. 1980 *Migration, Ethnicity and Community: Studies in Israeli Society*. New Brunswick, N.J.: Transaction.

Mechanic, D. 1962. "Religion, Religiosity and Illness Behavior: The Special Case of the Jews." *Human Organization* 22:202-8.

Ministry of Health. 1964. *Report of the Commission for Clarifying the Problem of the Shortage of Doctors, 1963-64* (in Hebrew). Jerusalem: Ministry of Health.

Prywes, M. 1983. "Aimes of the Medical School in Relation to Motivation: Practice, Not Preaching, Creates Motivation." *Medical Education* 17:69-71.

Ronen, M. 1989. *Alternative Health Practitioners: Functional Equivalents in Health Care*. Ph.D. dissertation, Hebrew University, Jerusalem.

Rosen, B. 1989. *The Public-Private Mix in Israeli Health Care*. Jerusalem: Brookdale Institute for Research on Aging and Adult Human Development.

______. 1987. *The Health of the Israeli People: An International Comparison Based on the World Health Organization's "Quantitative Indicators for the European Region"*, research report no. 4-87. Jerusalem: Brookdale Institute for Research on Aging and Adult Human Development.

Shuval, J.T. 1989a. "The Structure and Dilemmas of Israeli Pluralism." In *The Israeli State and Society: Boundaries and Frontiers*, ed. B. Kimmerling, 218-36. Albany: State University of New York.

______. 1989b. "Medical Manpower in Israel: Political Processes and Constraints." In *The Political Dynamics of Physician Manpower Policy*, eds. I. Butter, M. Field, and M. Rosenthal. London: Kings Fund Press.

______. 1980. *Entering Medicine: The Dynamics of Transition: A Seven-Year Study of Medical Education in Israel*. London: Pergamon.

Shuval, J.T., Antonovsky, A., and Davies, A.M. 1970. *Social Functions of Medical Practice*. San Francisco: Jossey-Bass.

Shye, D., Javetz, R., and Shuval, J.T. 1989. *Patient Initiatives and Physician-Challenging Behaviors: The View of Israeli Health Professionals*. Jerusalem: Brookdale Institute of Research on Aging and Adult Human Development.

Sicron, M. 1957. *Aliyah to Israel: 1948-1953* (in Hebrew). Jerusalem: Falk Institute for Economic Research in Israel and the Central Bureau of Statistics.

Smooha, S. 1978. *Israel: Pluralism and Conflict*. London: Routledge and Kegan Paul.

State Controller's Office. 1986. *Annual Report*, no. 37 (in Hebrew). Jerusalem: Government Printer.

Suchman, E.A. 1964. "Sociomedical Variations among Ethnic Groups." *American Journal of Sociology* 70:319-31.

Tulchinsky, T.H., Lunenfeld, B., Haber, S., and Handelsman, M. 1982. "Israel Health Review." *Israel Journal of Medical Sciences* 18:345-55.

Twaddle, A.C. 1969. "Health Decisions and Sick Role Variations: An Exploration." *Journal of Health and Social Behavior* 10:105-14.

Weingrod, A., ed. 1985. *Studies in Israeli Ethnicity: After the Ingathering*. London: Gordon and Breach.

World Health Organization. 1988. *Indicators for Monitoring Progress toward Health for All: Selected Quantitative Indicators for the European Region*. Copenhagen: European Regional Office.

Yishai, Y. 1979. "Interest Groups in Israel." *The Jerusalem Quarterly* 11:128-44.

Zborowski, M., and Herzog, E. 1952. *Life Is with People*. New York: International Universities Press.

Part I

Structural and Cultural Factors in Health and Illness

1

Employment and Ill-Health among Women in Israel

Noah Lewin-Epstein

One of the noticeable outcomes of research on gender differences in morbidity is its contribution to the emergence of the study of illness among working and non-working women. Recent work, in particular, had focused on differences between employed and non-employed women, using much the same propositions applied earlier to the comparison between men and women. The few studies that specifically set out to examine the health status of female populations used a variety of measures to represent respondents' health status, and employed a number of statistical approaches aimed at identifying the effect of being employed (vs non-employed) on female morbidity. Some studies used additive models [1, 2] while others specified more complex interaction affects [3, 4]. Practically all studies, however, found that housewives reported more symptoms, more days of disability, and greater anxiety than employed women [1–5].

The present study follows previous research in the area and aims to contribute to our understanding of the phenomenon in a number of ways. The first goal is to more accurately specify propositions that relate the employment of women to various dimensions of illness and illness behavior so that alternative hypotheses concerning the differences between employed and non-employed women may be evaluated. A second purpose of this study in addition to evaluating the effect of employment on female health, is to examine the extent to which employed women differ from non-employed women in their socio-demographic characteristics and how each of these characteristics is related to health. In addition, the data examined were collected in Israel and hence provide an opportunity to assess the generalizability of previous findings all of which were based on research conducted in the United States.

PREVIOUS RESEARCH AND FINDINGS

A number of explanatory approaches have been advanced in the literature and utilized in explaining the higher levels of morbidity generally found among housewives as compared to employed women. Following the proposition that illness is less stigmatizing for women than for men [6, 7], Nathanson hypothesized that "... if illness is a culturally acceptable form of expression for women, then women for whom it is more acceptable should report more illness" [8, p. 61]. This implies, of course, that women in more traditional female roles, such as homemakers, are expected to report more symptoms, to seek medical care more frequently, and to report greater incidence of disability.

A second approach, developed by Gove and his associates [9, 10] in their studies of differences in morbidity between men and women, proposes that higher morbidity reports among women are not merely a reflection of their enhanced awareness and greater willingness to enter the sick role. Rather, the differences between men and women are real and are derived from social psychological factors associated with the roles they occupy. When applied to different groups of women, the argument suggests that employed women will experience better health than homemakers since a job outside the household presents a more attractive role and a source of gratification other than the family. The activities of employed women are likely to be more structured and to provide a sense of purpose and accomplishment. These features contribute towards a more positive self-identity and are conducive to emotional stability and a sense of well-being, which in turn produce better health [8]. This indeed was the interpretation given by Welch and Booth [1] to their findings that females employed full-time reported less psychiatric impairment and incidence of stress than non-employed housewives, even though no differences were found in the number of diseases identified during a medical examination, nor in the number of bed-ridden days experienced by the two groups. In a similar vein, Nathanson [3] found that employment was postively associated with self-appraised health status, and that the association was strongest among women with least access to alternative sources of gratification and social support.

A third perspective on the difference in morbidity between employed and non-employed women derives from the 'fixed role obligations' framework. According to this approach, differences in morbidity are associated with the extent of compatibility between the sick role and other role obligations which a person has [5, 11, 12, 13]. When applied to subgroups of the female population this approach states that if illness and illness behavior are a function of time constraints and role demands, then women with fewer and less structured role obligations should engage in this behavior more frequently [8]. A major implication of this perspective is that women who occupy work roles in addition to familial roles will be less likely to adopt the sick role and to engage in illness behavior. This perspective was central to the work of Verbrugge [4] who found that employment, marriage, and parenthood were all related to infrequent adoption of illness behavior and that they had additive effects.

Findings reported by Nathanson [3] and by Woods and Hulka [2] lend additional support to this explanatory approach. They found that employed women, in accordance with their denser obligations, had fewer days of restricted activities. According to Woods and Hulka, however, the same was not true for illness symptoms. They found that a large number of role obligations added, in fact, to the likelihood of reporting symptoms. They argued that conflicting demands originating in the home and at work are likely to cause strain and fatigue and lead to higher levels of morbidity. Indeed, this point is akin to the 'nurturant role' hypothesis originally advanced by Gove and Hughes [14] to explain gender differences in morbidity, and which proposes that too many role obligations can interfere with self-care, and will have a negative effect on one's health.

Overall, then, there exists systematic findings on differences between employed women and housewives in their self-assessed health status as well as some aspects of illness behavior. These findings seem to support the role-correspondence hypothesis and the fixed role obligations approach according to which employment both provides social support and allows less free time so as to limit the need and opportunity of engaging in illness behavior. The findings, however, are also consistent with a less prominent though provocative explanation which reverses the causal order. The 'healthy worker effect'—as it is often referred to—maintains that poor health may cause many women to leave or remain out of the labor force, and consequently working women are found to enjoy better health [4, 15]. This hypothesis, while plausible, has not been adequately tested and would probably require longitudinal data in order to determine the extent of selection and its contribution to explaining the association between employment status and health. It should be noted, however, that a review of the literature revealed no systematic differences in chronic illness or other physical conditions between employed women and housewives and hence no obvious basis for the preselection.

DIMENSIONS OF ILL-HEALTH

The fact that findings often varied when different measures of ill-health, such as chronic conditions, restricted activity, medical visits, or self-appraised health, were examined, suggests that these outcomes should not be taken simply as interchangeable indicators of morbidity, but rather as representing various dimensions of illness which are unequally related to employment. Consequently, it is necessary to specify more precisely what the dimensions are, and how they are hypothesized to be affected by employment.

For this purpose it will be useful to distinguish between illness and sickness; illness behavior and sick role behavior. These concepts are related, of course, but they represent different levels of action and different degrees of social identification and role taking. *Illness* is often defined as experiences such as pain, weakness, anxiety or related feelings reported by individuals which can result in others defining them as unhealthy [16]. Illness is assumed to be caused by disease but it is essentially a psychological state. *Sickness* is defined in an interaction process with others. It is a socially institutionalized role type. It is generally characterized by incapacity to fulfill normally expected tasks or act in accordance with prescribed norms. What is of interest here however is the individual's perception of the role. When people are defined by others or "... they publicly define themselves as unhealthy, a shift in social identity takes place" [16, p. 97]. Sickness is usually presumed to reflect disease (the biological dimension) or illness, although it can occur independent of both.

Illness behavior and *sick role behavior* are action oriented manifestations of illness and sickness and allude to specific interactions and structured activities in addition to subjective identities. "Illness behavior is any activity, undertaken by a person who feels ill, to define the state of his health and to discover a suitable remedy" [17, p. 246]. In most cases it involves seeking consultation and advice from various sources. Sick role behavior is the activity undertaken by those who perceive themselves as sick, for the purpose of getting well. It often includes receiving treatment from professional sources, extra rest, or other actions succeeding the identification of a problem. It presupposes a role identity of 'sick' and refers to the normative actions associated with the role. While illness and sick role behavior assume the states of illness and sickness respectively, they are often affected by non-medical determinants such as conflicting norms, role constraints, and personal attributes. Previous research has shown that various social and psychological factors such as perceived threat, social and economic barriers, and tolerance of pain and disability, intervene in the process and effect the decision of whether or not to engage in particular behaviors [16–20].

In line with these distinctions and to the extent that employment and non-employment affect women's health, it is expected that the most significant differences will be found with respect to illness behavior and—to a lesser extent—sick role behavior since it is here where the amount of discretion is greatest and where social interactions are required which are likely to conflict with other role obligations associated with work. The differences in behavior between employed and non-employed women would be congruent with all explanatory approaches outlined at the outset since it may derive from either real differences in symptoms and illness or unequal tendencies to engage in actions to define and treat illness.

In order to evaluate the relative merit of the different approaches it is necessary to examine additional dimensions of health. For instance, the 'role correspondence' hypothesis which proposes that sickness is more congruent with traditional female roles implies not only less illness behavior among employed women, but also a weaker tendency for self-perception of sickness; that is identifying oneself as sick. According to the gratification approach or to the nurturant role hypothesis, employed and non-employed women should exhibit different levels of minor disease and illness. The lack of gratification or self-fulfillment, as noted earlier, is expected to hinder psychological well-being and to eventually result in physical symptoms. The nurturant role hypothesis asserts just the opposite, that multiple role obligations are likely to cause stress which in turn may lead to symptoms of illness. In any case both approaches emphasize the effect of employment on illness and disease not only on behavior. In the absence of such differences these approaches may be forsaken for simpler and more parsimonious explanations. In the present study, then, several dimensions of ill-health will be examined among employed and non-employed women in order to further our understanding of the way in which the two phenomena are related. In the process, the differences between employed and non-employed women will be decomposed into that part which reflects the different socio-demographic composition of the two groups, and that part which reveals the impact of the work situation.

METHODS AND PROCEDURES

Sample

Data analyzed in this report were obtained by means of a survey of 1000 non-institutionalized adults 26–65 years old, during the last two months of 1984. The target area for the survey was the two adjoining cities of Holon and Bat-Yam located just south of Tel Aviv. Holon has a population of approx. 135,000 and Bat-Yam has 130,000 residents all of which are Jews [21]. Multistage area sampling was used to select individuals.

Sample figures indicate a balanced gender representation of age groups—61% between the ages of 25 and 44, and 39% between the ages of 45 and 65 [22]. The interviews included mostly closed-ended questions concerning health status, life style, employment, and socio-demographic background, and took approx. 40 min to complete. Of the targeted 1000 interviews, 994 schedules were completed. The sample studied in the present report consists of 416 married women [23], 206 of which were employed and 210 were not employed at the time of the survey.

Variables

Four dependent variables are employed in order to gauge perceived illness and illness behavior. The first—health status—measures self appraised health on a five-category scale in response to the question: 'How would you define your health condition?' the possible responses ranged from very good (lowest score) to very poor (highest score). This came closest to measuring sickness—the state of perceiving onself as sick. The second variable—somatic complaints—measures symptoms of illness which are generally mild and not life-threatening. They are often viewed as psychosomatic in nature [24, 25]. It is a composite scale of eight items weighted according to scores obtained from a varimax rotated factor analysis [26]. A third variable—medical visits—gauges illness behavior measuring the number of visits the respondent made to a physician during the year prior to the survey; and treatment—the fourth variable—determines whether the respondent has recently been under medical care, in which case he receives a score of 1, and a score of zero otherwise. An additional variable—chronic—which enumerated diagnosed chronic conditions, the respondent reported suffering from, was added in order to partly control for self selection of individuals with different health conditions into employment and non-employment status (see [3] for use of a similar procedure).

The social attributes included in the analysis are ethnicity, age, education, spouse status, children, density, and work. Ethnicity refers to whether the woman was from Asian or African origin, or European/American origin. The former received a value of 0 and the latter a value of 1. Age measures respondents' age at their last birthday. Education measures the number of years the respondent attended school. Spouse status is the occupational status of spouse and is used here as proxy for the socio-economic standing of the family. Children is the number of children living in the household, and density is the number of persons in the household per room. The former variable gauges role obligations of the women whereas the latter is viewed as source of stress [27] which may differentially 'affect' housewives and women who spend a large portion of the day outside the home. The variable work distinguishes between women currently working outside the household (a value of 1) and those not employed (a value of 0) [28].

Method of analysis

Analysis of the data will involve a number of stages intended to successively determine the extent of reported illness and illness behavior among women, to evaluate the relationship of health and illness to employment status, and to probe into the characteristics of working and non-working women which contribute to the differences in reported aspects of ill-health. Following a short descriptive overview of the interrelationships among various dimensions of illness and their prevalence among women, OLS regression models will be utilized in order to assess the unique effect of employment status on illness while statistically controlling the effect of other important attributes of the respondents. In the final stage I intend to carry the analysis a step further and examine how much of the difference in illness between employed and non-employed women is due to the different composition of the two groups in terms of their age, education, household composition and other social attributes, and what portion of the difference results from different effects of these attributes in the two groups. It is expected that such a decomposition of the differences in reported illness and illness behavior will provide additional insight into the relationship of work and illness among women.

ANALYSIS AND FINDINGS

Ill-health among Israeli women

Intercorrelations among several indicators of illness and illness behavior are presented in Table 1 along with the mean values for the employed, non-employed, and total female populations. The correlations vary in magnitude but are generally moderate suggesting that different dimensions of illness are indeed being tapped. The correlations between health status and medical visits, and health status with treatment ($r = 0.42$ and $r = 0.37$, respectively) illustrate that along with some systematic relationship, there is still much indeterminacy so that women reporting similar levels of self-appraised health display different patterns of behavior.

Turning to the mean values on the measures reported by employed and non-employed women it is observed that non-employed women have consistently *higher* average scores indicating *more severe* levels of illness. On a scale of 1 to 5 of self appraised health where 1 represented excellent health, employed women had a mean score of 1.9 and non-employed women had a score of 2.18. Non-employed women had a slightly higher average level of illness as measured by somatic complaints. They also had an average of over 2.5 more visits to a physician in the past year and were more likely to be under treatment.

In order to examine whether the differences in scores between the two groups of women were actually associated with employment status and not merely a result of socio-demographic characteristics of the respondents, multivariate least squares regression was employed. The four measures of illness were individually regressed on employment status (employed or non-employed) and a set of additional variables used here as controls. The results of the analysis are presented in Table 2. The four dependent variables are displayed across the top of the table.

Table 1. Means, standard deviations, and correlations among indicators of ill-health for married women ($n = 416$)

	Means (standard deviations)			Correlations			
	Total population	Non-employed	Employed	Health status	Somatic	Medical visits	Treatment
Health status	2.05 (0.76)	2.18 (0.79)	1.90* (0.69)				
Somatic	0.15 (0.48)	0.21 (0.48)	0.13† (0.44)	0.27			
Medical visits	4.87 (7.09)	5.93 (9.23)	3.23* (4.02)	0.42	0.12		
Treatment	0.27 (0.44)	0.31 (0.46)	0.22* (0.42)	0.37	−0.06‡	0.35	
Chronic	0.83 (1.01)	0.92 (1.04)	0.75 (0.96)	0.48	0.34	0.27	0.24

*The difference in means between employed and non-employed women is statistically significant at $P < 0.05$ (one-sided test).

†The difference in means between employed and non-employed women is statistically significant at $P < 0.1$ (one-sided test).

‡This correlation is not statistically significant at $P < 0.05$, all others are.

Table 2. Unstandardized regression coefficients predicting various aspects of ill-health (standard errors in parentheses)

	Health status	Somatic	Medical visits	Treatment
Ethinicity	−0.01 (0.08)	−0.11 (0.10)	−0.73 (1.29)	−0.02 (0.05)
Density	0.02 (0.02)	−0.02 (0.03)	0.01 (0.04)	−0.01 (0.01)
Chronic	0.32* (0.04)	0.33* (0.05)	2.74* (0.59)	0.09* (0.02)
Children	−0.03 (0.02)	0.09* (0.04)	0.39 (0.47)	−0.02 (0.02)
Spouse status × 10^{-1}	−0.06* (0.02)	−0.02 (0.03)	−0.91* (0.38)	0.01 (0.01)
Age × 10^{-1}	−0.12* (0.04)	−0.06 (0.05)	1.19* (0.51)	0.07* (0.03)
Education	−0.01 (0.10)	−0.04* (0.02)	0.15 (0.21)	−0.01 (0.01)
Work	−0.09* (0.04)	0.12* (0.05)	−2.16* (1.07)	−0.05 (0.05)
Intercept	1.63	0.49	1.13	−0.01
R^2	0.34	0.18	0.12	0.10

*Signficant at $P < 0.05$.

For each model unstandardized coefficients are presented as well as the total amount of variance explained by the model (R^2). In general the amount of variance explained was not very high, but similar in magnitude to levels reported in previous studies [2–4].

The first model on the left gives self appraised health as a dependent variable. Employment status had a negative and significant effect on health status ($b = -0.09$). Since the measure of employment status received a value of zero if the women was not employed, and a value of one otherwise, the negative coefficient means that when controlling for all factors included in the model women, who were not working, had a more negative assessment of their health situation. Other factors in the model also displayed a statistically significant effect on health status. Both the number of diagnosed symptoms and age had a positive effect as one would expect. The older the person and the more disease present, the more likely she was to view herself as sick. Socio-economic score of spouse has the opposite effect where by higher status was associated with a more positive perception of health.

Turning to the additional models, we observe that employment status had statistically significant effects on the psychosomatic complaints and medical visits; once again in the expected direction. Working women had lower scores on the somatic symptom scale (indicating better health) and fewer visits to the physician. There was no effect of employment status, however, on the likelihood of being under medical treatment at the time of the survey. The figures indicate, then, that working women were less likely to perceive themselves as sick, had fewer mild illness symptoms and less frequently engaged in illness behavior as compared with non-employed women with similar average attributes of age, chronic disease, education, and socio-economic status. These findings are essentially similar to those reported by Nathanson for women in the United States and seem to lend support to the role correspondence, fixed role obligations, and the work gratification approaches.

Decomposing differences between working and non-working women

From the analysis reported thus far it is evident that employment status of women had a significant effect on the various measures of illness. This held true even when social and demographic differences between the two women populations were statistically controlled. The analysis that follows attempts to uncover the sources of differences in illness and illness behavior by taking into account both the distinctive social and demographic attributes of working and non-working women, and the effect these attributes have on illness in each of the two groups. The purpose, then, is to evaluate the extent to which the higher scores among non-employed women resulted from their particular social and demographic characteristics (e.g. their older age, lower education, or higher incidence of chronic conditions), and how much was due to the differential effect these characteristics had on health among employed and non-employed women (e.g. a different impact of every year of age, or every unit of household density, etc.).

Decomposition techniques will be applied in order to examine these different elements. As noted by Kessler [29], this procedure is particularly useful for studying differences in outcomes between two groups since it permits one to simultaneously evaluate the relative importance of the *differential distribution* of attributes related to illness, and of the *differential impact* of these attributes in each group. The present analysis follows Iams and Thornton's [30] method according to which the difference between two groups on a given attribute is decomposed into four separate components as illustrated in Appendix A. The four components are: the difference in illness due to differences in the composition of the groups ($\Sigma b_{iw}(x_{in} - x_{iw})$), difference in illness due to differences in the impacts of the social and demographic attributes ($\Sigma x_{iw}(b_{in} - b_{iw})$), difference in the intercepts which represents starting points of the two groups ($b_{on} - b_{ow}$), and a shared component which represents the joint change of mean values and regression coefficients ($\Sigma(X_{in} - X_{iw})(b_{in} - b_{iw})$). This interactional component can be interpreted as the additional effect of changing means and regression coefficients together, over the effects of changing them one at a time.

Results of the decomposition procedure for each of the four indicators of ill-health are presented in Table 3 (the calculations are based on regression coefficients and mean scores given in Table A1 in Appendix A). The components of the differences between employed and non-employed women are presented at the bottom of the table along with the portion of the total which each component accounts for [31]. The separate contributions of the independent variables are given in the upper part of the table. In Table 1 we noted that the mean value of health status among non-working women was 2.18, and the value for employed women was 1.90. The difference between the two groups was 0.28 points. Of this, 0.15 points were attributed to the population composition of the two groups; 0.06 points resulted from different effects of the social characteristics in the two groups; and 0.07 points were attributed to the interaction term. We see then, that social composition accounted for more than half (58%) of the gap in self-appraised health. In other words, most of the difference in favor of working women would disappear if the two groups had identical populations. In the upper part of Table 3 we find the contributions of separate variables where positive values indicate advantage in terms of health for employed women and negative values indicate advantage for the non-employed. In the case of self-appraised health status, chronic symptoms, age, and education had the strongest impact—all in favor of employed women. The fact that working women tended to be younger, better educated, and had fewer chronic symptoms accounted for most of the advantage they experienced in terms of health.

Only 20% of the gap in self-appraised health status was accounted for by the impact component. When we look down the column we find mostly negative values indicating advantage to non-working women in converting their social attributes into better health. Taking education for example, the value of −0.11 indicates that each additional year of schooling contributed more to improved perception of health

Table 3. Decomposition of the difference in measures of reported ill-health between employed and non-employed women

	Health status			Somatic			Medical visits			Treatment		
	Composition	Impact*	Interaction	Composition	Impact	Interaction	Composition	Impact	Interaction	Composition	Impact	Interaction
Ethnicity	−0.01	−0.04	0.01	0.04	0.09	−0.02	−0.14	−1.65	0.45	−0.02	−0.15	0.04
Density	0.01	−0.05	−0.01	−0.01	0.05	0.01	0.11	−0.86	−0.20	0.00	−0.05	−0.01
Chronic	0.05	0.08	0.03	0.05	0.03	0.01	0.12	1.07	0.24	0.01	0.01	0.00
Children	−0.00	−0.05	−0.00	0.00	−0.52	−0.00	0.01	0.02	0.00	−0.00	0.03	0.00
Spouse status	0.02	−0.04	0.01	−0.03	−0.03	0.08	0.27	−4.19	0.63	0.01	−0.01	0.00
Age	0.04	−0.06	−0.00	0.01	−0.98	−0.04	0.03	4.55	0.20	0.01	0.10	0.02
Education	0.04	−0.11	0.03	0.06	−0.28	0.04	−0.04	4.53	−0.75	0.01	0.02	−0.00
Intercept		0.33			1.52			−1.70			0.09	
Column totals	0.15	0.06	0.07	0.12	−0.12	0.08	0.36	1.77	0.57	0.02	0.03	0.05
(Percent of total gap)	(58)	(20)	(22)	(162)	(−172)	(110)	(13)	(67)	(21)	(22)	(27)	(51)

*The intercept component is included in the total of this column so that the sum of column totals equals the gross difference between employed and non-employed women (see Ref. [31]).

among non-working than among working women. This is true for other attributes as well, and seems to indicate that the work situation comes to be the central determinant influencing employed women's perception of health and illness to the exclusion of other sources that seem to operate among the non-employed.

Turning to somatic complaints we find that while population composition of the two groups adds 0.12 points to the gap between employed and non-employed women, the impact component operates to the advantage of the non-working women and reduces the gap by 0.12 points. The interaction component accounts for a smaller portion of the gap than the other components, but still in favor of working women. These results indicate that one important reason that working women, as a group, experience less somatic symptoms is their socio-demographic attributes. Working women tend to be younger, better educated, and are generally from higher status households. All these factors reduce the likelihood of illness. The negative value of the impact component, however, indicates that working women are at a disadvantage in converting personal attributes into better health. Apparently, factors which pose a greater risk to health, age and number of children in particular, have a stronger effect among working women. In contrast factors that contribute to better health, such as education or occupational status of spouse, have weaker effects among working women. The conjunction, then, of work with other attributes and responsibilities appears to be strenuous and leads to mild disease as illustrated by somatic symptoms.

Turning to illness behavior as exemplified by visits to the physician we encounter yet another pattern. The positive values indicate that all components contribute to fewer visits among employed women. Two thirds of the gap, however, are due to the impact effect and only 14 and 21% are contributed by group composition and the interaction component, respectively. This appears to reflect the fact that the work situation constrains behavior so that employed persons are less likely to visit a physician than are non-employed persons with similar characteristics. These findings are consistent with conclusions advanced in a number of previous studies [3, 8]. They support the proposition of fixed role obligations in explaining differences in behavior between working and non-working women and seem to indicate that these differences are uniquely related to the social structuring of work which provides limited opportunities for engaging in additional activity.

Finally, decomposition of the likelihood of being under treatment resulted in three components all of which contributed to the gap in favor of working women (favorable meaning less treatment). Composition accounts for 22%, and the impact component contributes 27% of the gap; but the major effect is that of the interaction component which accounts for half the gap. There is no unambiguous way of allocating this component between the composition and impact factors. Indeed the interaction represents the magnitude of the joint effect of composition and conversion beyond their individual effects. In the present case the interaction effect is due primarily to the contributions of ethnicity and age.

Their means covary with the coefficients so that the group with higher mean age and higher proportion of women of European/American origin is also characterized by a stronger effect on treatment. We cannot conclude with any certainty the degree to which the lower likelihood of treatment among working women can be attributed to the work situation itself, but it is clear that at least part of the gap is due to the work situation either separately or in conjunction with the composition of the populations. What this means is that equalizing the characteristics of the two groups would eliminate much of gap in treatment, though approx. 27% of the observed differences would still remain (since they are uniquely attributable to the impact component).

SUMMARY AND DISCUSSION

The purpose of this study was to elaborate on the relationship between employment status and different dimensions of illness among women. In the main, our findings indicate that employed women in Israel enjoyed better health than women who were not employed. This was true with respect to self-appraised health, somatic complaints, and visits to the physician. Non-employed women also reported more chronic conditions and were somewhat more likely to be under medical treatment. In this respect patterns found in urban settings in Israel confirm previous conclusions which were based on research in other western countries. It should further be noted that ethnic origin, a central factor in much social research in Israel, had no direct impact on ill-health, and the same is true for household density.

The choice of indicators of ill-health was meant to tap various aspects of the phenomenon in order to try to evaluate certain propositions concerning the significance of employment for health. The decomposition procedure was utilized so that we might evaluate what portion of the difference in reported levels of illness, between employed and non-employed women, resulted from the women's different characteristics, and what portion reflected the effect of the employment situation *per se*. The results demonstrated that employment status was differently related to the various dimensions of ill-health. Although employed women had more positive values on all measures of ill-health, only in the case of illness behavior was most of the gap uniquely attributable to the work situation. Employment obligations evidently hinder frequent visits to the physician, and more generally constrain illness behavior. These findings confirm the conclusions of Nathanson [3] and Verbrugge [4] and seem to support the 'fixed role obligations' hypothesis [5, 9] more directly than other approaches which focus on actual disease, or perceived sickness.

This, however, does not negate the additional conclusion that work also impacts on illness *per se*, at least as measured by somatic complaints. Although working women reported fewer symptoms, the decomposition analysis led to an important qualification. The unique component estimating the differential impact of personal attributes on illness actually operated in favor (less symptoms) of non-employed women. Conversely, age, education and household characteristics produced more symptoms among employed women. These symptoms are often associated with mild psychiatric impairment or physical weakness originating in stress or deferment of care [15, 18]. Indeed, Haynes and Feinleib [32] demonstrated that working women did experience more stress, and argued that dual roles of employment and family responsibility may involve excessive demands on working women. Hence, these particular findings lend support to the 'nurturant role' hypothesis though similar patterns were not observed for medical visits and self-appraised health status.

The findings concerning self-appraised health status indicated that differences in the perception of sickness were largely a result of population composition and were not due directly to the work situation. Had adjustments been made for the socio-demographic attributes of the two groups, most of the gap in self-appraised health would disappear. If, then, we take the 'role correspondence' hypothesis [8] to mean that the sick role is more compatible with the traditional female role (as in the case of homemakers) than with 'typically masculine' roles (work outside the house), we may argue that our findings provide only weak support for this proposition. The study, then, demonstrates that the current explanatory approaches are not necessarily mutually exclusive since, by and large, they address different dimensions of ill-health. By directing attention to a number of distinguishable aspects we were able to better evaluate the impact of employment and to infer in what areas current explanatory approaches are most useful.

Finally, it should be noted that this study did not directly test the 'healthy worker' hypothesis which reverses the direction of the relationship and places health status as causally prior to employment status. To the extent that our measure of chronic disease captured one's physical health situation we might argue that serious illness operated, to some degree, as a selective factor *vis-à-vis* employment, as we found a higher prevalence of chronic disease among women who were not employed. But employment, in turn, affected the variation in illness behavior and mild symptoms even after controlling the differences in chronic disease. It is possible that the measure used is a poor indicator of health, or alternatively, that we need to estimate a recursive system. Unfortunately, this could not be achieved with the data at hand. In terms of future research, then, a more complete and definitive investigation of the causal direction of the relationship should probably utilize panel data where time-sequencing of the events and their impact can be more clearly determined.

Acknowledgements—This study was made possible by financial support from the Pinhas Sapir Center and Tel Aviv University fund for Basic Research obtained in collaboration with Ephraim Yuchtman-Yaar. I would like to thank Aida Dynia and Naomi More for their assistance in data preparation and analysis; and Judith Shuval, Avi Gottlieb, Giora Rahav and two anonymous reviewers for their helpful comments.

REFERENCES

1. Welch S. and Booth A. Employment and health among married women. *Sex Roles* **3**, 385, 1977.

2. Woods N. F. and Hulka B. S. Symptom reports and illness behavior among employed women and homemakers. *J. commun. Hlth* **5,** 36, 1979.
3. Nathanson C. A. Social roles and health status among women: the significance of employment. *Soc. Sci. Med.* **14,** 463, 1980.
4. Verbrugge L. M. Multiple roles and physical health of women and men. *J. Hlth soc. Behav.* **24,** 16, 1983.
5. Marcus A. C. and Seeman T. E. Sex differences in reports of illness and disability: A preliminary test of the 'fixed role obligations' hypothesis. *J. Hlth soc. Behav.* **22,** 174, 1981.
6. Philips D. L. and Segal B. E. Sexual status and psychiatric symptoms. *Am. Social. Rev.* **34,** 58, 1969.
7. Broverman K. L. *et al.* Sex role stereotypes and clinical judgements of mental health. *J. Consult. clin. Psychol.* **34,** 1, 1970.
8. Nathanson C. A. Illness and the feminine role: a theoretical review. *Soc. Sci. Med.* **9,** 57, 1975.
9. Gove W. R. and Tudor J. Adult sex roles and mental illness. *Am. J. Sociol.* **78,** 812, 1973.
10. Gove W. R. and Geerkin M. R. The effect of children and employment on the mental health of married men and women. *Soc. Forces* **56,** 66, 1977.
11. Marcus A. C., Seeman T. E. and Telesky C. W. Sex differences in reports of illness and disability: a further test of the fixed role hypothesis. *Soc. Sci. Med.* **17,** 993, 1983.
12. Mechanic D. Sex, illness, illness behavior, and the use of health services. *J. Hum. Stress* **2,** 29, 1976.
13. Verbrugge L. Sex differences in morbidity and mortality in the United States. *Soc. Biol.* **23,** 275, 1977.
14. Gove W. R. and Hughes M. Possible causes of the apparent sex differences in physical health: an empirical investigation. *Am. Soc. Rev.* **44,** 126, 1979.
15. Jennings S., Mazaik C. and McKinlay S. *Women and Work: An Investigation of the Association Between Health and Employment Status in Middle-Aged Women.* Cambridge Research Center, Cambridge, Mass., 1983.
16. Twaddle A. C. and Hessler R. M. *A Sociology of Health.* Mosby, St Louis, Miss., 1977.
17. Kasl S. V. and Cobb S. Health behavior, illness behavior, and sick role behavior. *Archs Environ Hlth* **12,** 246, 1966.
18. Anderson R. and Newman J. F. Societal and individual determinants of medical care in the United States. *Milbank Mem. Fund. Q.* **51,** 95, 1973.
19. Becker M. H. The health belief model and sick role behavior. *Hlth Ed. Monogr.* **2,** 409, 1974.
20. Becker M. H. Psychosocial aspects of health-related behavior. In *Handbook of Medical Sociology* (Edited by Freeman H. E., Levine S. and Reeder, L. G.), 3rd edn. Prentice-Hall, Englewood Cliffs, N.J., 1979.
21. Approximately 50 percent of the combined population were between the ages of 25–65.
22. These figures correspond closely to the latest published figures on the age distribution of the population in the two cities, published in 1979. According to those figures 62% were in the 25–44 age group, and 38% were in the 45–65 category.
23. Currently unmarried women comprised only 13% of the sample of women due to the high marriage rate among females over 25 and the low divorce rate characteristic of Israel. About one-quarter of the currently unmarried women were never married and the rest were neither widowed nor divorced. Such small frequencies rendered the inclusion of marital status as a control factor in the analysis impracticable and only married are therefore included in the present report.
24. LaRocco J. M., House J. S. and French J. R. P. Social support, occupational stress and individual well being. *J. Hlth soc. Behav.* **21,** 202, 1980.
25. Langner T. S. A twenty-two item screening score of psychiatric symptoms indicating impairment. *J. Hlth Human Behav.* **3,** 269, 1962.
26. The items measure the frequency in which respondents experienced body pains, cramps, lack of energy, headaches, unexplained perspiring, unexplained nervousness, difficulty concentrating, fatigue and general weakness. As a group the items had a reliability coefficient of alpha = 0.79.
27. Gove W. *et al.* Overcrowding in the home: an empirical investigation of some of its possible pathological consequences. *Am. Sociol. Rev.* **44,** 59, 1979.
28. The occupational distribution of working women was quite varied, ranging from professionals to unskilled workers. The jobs differ, of course, in their rewards, responsibilities, and time demands. The present analysis, however, focuses on employment vs non-employment. This distinction is qualitative rather than quantitative. It is not simply a matter of hours outside the house, but a basic orientation of social roles and priorities. Nonetheless, a fuller understanding of the antecedents of illness among women would require closer attention to the dissimilarities in work roles and environments. Such an undertaking would require a somewhat different research strategy as well as additional data.
29. Kessler R. C. A strategy for studying differential vulnerability to the psychological consequences of stress. *J. Hlth soc. Behav.* **20,** 100, 1979.
30. Iams H. M. and Thornton A. Decomposition of differences. *Soc. Meth. Res.* **3,** 341, 1975.
31. For the purpose of the present analysis the intercepts component was combined with the impact component since the former cannot generally be uniquely interpreted except when dealing with ratio-level variables. For further discussion of this point see Jones F. L. and Kelley J., Decomposing differences between two groups. *Soc. Meth. Res.* **12,** 323, 1984.
32. Haynes S. G. and Feinleib M. Women, work and coronary heart disease: prospective findings from the Framingham Heart Study. *Am. J. publ. Hlth* **70,** 133, 1980.

APPENDIX A

Starting with a separate regression equation for each of the two groups being studied, the difference in the means of a given attribute is decomposed into four separate components by means of the following basic equation:

$$\bar{Y}_n - \bar{Y}_w = (b_{on} - b_{ow}) + \sum_{i=1}^{k} \bar{X}_{iw}(b_{in} - b_{iw}) + \sum_{i=1}^{k} b_{iw}(\bar{X}_{in} - \bar{X}_{iw}) + \sum_{i=1}^{k} (\bar{X}_{in} - \bar{X}_{iw})(b_{in} - b_{iw}).$$

According to the standard regression format:

$\bar{Y}_n$ = the overall mean of the dependent variable for non-working women;

$\bar{Y}_w$ = the overall mean of the dependent variable for working women;

b_{on} = the regression constant (intercept) for non-working women;

b_{ow} = the regression constant (intercept) for working women;

b_{in} = the partial regression coefficient for the *i*th explanatory variable for non-working women;

b_{iw} = the partial regression coefficient for the *i*th explanatory variable for working women;

$\bar{X}_{in}$ = the mean of the *i*th explanatory variable for non-working women;

$\bar{X}_{iw}$ = the mean of the *i*th explanatory variable for working women.

Appendix Table A1 on facing page (p. 1179)

Table A1. Means of independent variables for employed and non-employed women, and unstandardized regression coefficients predicting ill-health in each of the groups

	$\bar{X}$		Health status		Somatic		Medical visists		Treatment	
	Employed	Non-employed	Employed	Non-employed	Employed	Non-employed	Employed	Non-employed	Employed	Non-employed
Ethnicity	0.57	0.41	0.06	−0.03	−0.25	−0.10	0.94	−1.95	0.14	−0.13
Density	1.39	1.71	0.04	−0.00	−0.03	0.00	0.33	−0.28	0.06	−0.02
Chronic	0.75	0.92	0.24	0.35	0.29	0.33	0.75	2.18	0.01	0.08
Children	1.91	1.94	−0.04	−0.07	0.08	0.06	−0.28	−0.27	−0.04	−0.02
Spouse status × 10^{-1}	4.83	4.10	−0.03	−0.04	0.04	−0.07	−0.40	−1.27	−0.01	−0.01
Age × 10^{-1}	3.86	4.02	0.13	0.11	0.07	−0.02	0.16	0.13	0.07	0.01
Education	11.03	9.21	−0.01	−0.02	−0.03	−0.06	0.02	0.43	−0.01	−0.00
Constant			1.51	1.84	−0.19	1.33	3.24	1.54	−0.01	0.07
R^2			0.18	0.37	0.15	0.20	0.12	0.11	0.09	0.16

2

The Effect of Border Tension on the Adjustment of Kibbutzim and Moshavim on the Northern Border of Israel

Chaya Zuckerman-Bareli

This study deals with the effect of bombing and terrorist attack on the way of life of six settlements–three kibbutzim (communal settlements) and three moshavim of olim (non communal settlements founded by non-western immigrants after 1949 and based on cooperative supply and marketing)–near the Lebanese border and investigates the cultural, social, and personal factors that strengthen or weaken resistance to stress and the ability to carry on with a regular way of life. The study is limited to relatively mild social and emotional disturbances that reflect the suffering of the individual in responding to stressful situations–disturbances that may lead to breakdown and illness. It investigates the interrelationship of two sources of stress in addition to border tension: (a) migration to and acculturation in Israel and (b) the social and economic struggle to make a living. The effect of stressful events is presumed to be additive and cumulative, with multiple contemporary sources of stress threatening to overwhelm the individual more than stress from a single source.

The fact that exposure to stressful events makes some people psychically or psychologically ill although others remain in good health suggests that certain stress-resistant factors varying from one person to another may strengthen the ability of some to mitigate stress and to reduce their susceptibility to illness (Antonovsky, 1974; Hinkle, 1974).

THE RESEARCH VARIABLES

The dependent variables of this research were (a) emotional disturbances defined as the emergence and persistence of fears and insomnia following terrorist activity and (b) social disturbances defined as the curtailment of adult

This research was partly financed by the Israel National Academy of Science. The research was done within the framework of the Institute for the Study of Ethnic and Religious Groups as part of a project under the direction of Professor E. Krausz.

evening entertainment outside the home and the prohibition of children playing freely outdoors. These poststress events were regarded as disturbances only if they constituted a change in behavior compared to prestress habits.

The independent variables consisted of (a) the intensity and cumulative effect of the three stresses referred to earlier, (b) stress-resistant factors inherent in the social and cultural character of the community (kibbutz versus moshav), and (c) factors in the subjects themselves–their level of anxiousness, age, sex, education, and sense of belonging to and identification with their community. The background to and explication of the various independent variables are discussed below.

Bombing and Terrorist Incursions

Since 1967, the inhabitants of the settlements located on the northern border of Israel have lived with the knowledge that border incidents can occur at any moment without warning. The intensity of these incidents was rated according to the following criteria: frequency, duration, extent of property damage, and the number of casualties. Six settlements were then selected so as to fall in three categories–heavy, moderate, and mild intensity–with a kibbutz and a moshav paired in each category. The hypothesis was that people in the first settlement category, where there is greater threat to life and property, would manifest greater disturbance than people in the last two categories.

Country of Origin as Stressor

Studies on immigrants to Israel after the establishment of the State in 1948 (Eisenstadt, 1954; Hartman & Eilon, 1975; Smocha & Peres, 1974; Weintraub, 1963) suggest that immigrants from Arab-speaking countries in Africa and Asia (henceforth called Eastern) had more adjustment problems than immigrants from Europe and English-speaking countries (henceforth called Western) as a result of the gap between the traditional sociocultural background of the Eastern immigrants and the modern Western-oriented society developing in Israel. In the present study, duration of stay in Israel also corresponded to the Eastern-Western division, with the Western group arriving before the establishment of the State and the bulk of the Eastern group after. As one example of the failure of the Eastern group wholly to adapt to Israeli society, at the time of the research the executive manager in two of the three moshavim was an outsider, a veteran in Israel, hired by the moshav; and in the third settlement a moshav resident had only just replaced a hired veteran manager for the first time. The appointment of an outsider and an oldtimer to the major position of authority in the moshav for organizing and managing the socioeconomic life was due to the difficulties the moshav residents still had in adjusting to Western organizational and managerial methods. Such a problem did not exist in the kibbutzim, whose population was of longstanding in Israel and was of Western background.

At least two aspects of the sociocultural traditions associated with country of origin can be singled out as resources for resisting stress. First, in the traditional Eastern culture there are a greater uniformity of norms, roles, and subcultures and fewer possibilities for class and cultural mobility than in Western culture; according to Weintraub (1963), this makes it more difficult for Eastern immigrants to adapt effectively to new and changing situations in Israel. Second, to a large extent the Eastern-Western dichotomy is paralleled by a dichotomy between lower class and middle class. In the Eastern group, lower-class norms prevail, including uncontrolled discharge of emotion under stress and in the face of personal calamities, a characteristic that weakens resistance to stress and drives people to panic. For these reasons, we hypothesized that the stress of border incidents would result in a higher frequency of disturbance in Eastern than in Western settlers.

Kibbutz versus Moshav

A third set of variables also contributes to the difficulties Eastern settlers have handling the stress of border incidents, namely that they constitute the bulk of moshav olim settlers and a minority of kibbutz settlers–88 and 7%, respectively in the present study and comparable proportions throughout Israel. The kibbutzim in this study were founded with the establishment of the State and one of them even before. They consist largely of people of Western origin and have created a sound economic base for their livelihood. By contrast, the moshavim were established 10–15 years later by people of Eastern background and are still subject to economic crisis when one industrial venture fails and the community must seek a new source of employment for its members. In addition, however, the collectivist social structure of the kibbutz guarantees the identity of some of the goals and values of individuals with those of the collective; it provides for close daily interaction between members at work, in the communal dining hall; and in ideologically planned social and cultural activities–all features largely absent in the moshav. Moreover, in the kibbutz all property is collectively owned so that if a member's house or means of likelihood is damaged by terrorist attack it is replaced by the kibbutz and the individual does not suffer a private loss. By contrast, in the moshav most property is privately owned, so that the losses are private and affect the members' ability to make a living. Individuals must seek compensation for war-related damage from the government on their own. Given the greater vulnerability of the individual in the moshav and for all of the earlier reasons given, it was hypothesized that moshav members would show greater disturbance associated with border incidents than kibbutz members.

Specific Stress-resistance Resource Factors

The remaining variables presumed to affect adjustment to border incidents are anchored within the individual and are quantifiable: anxiousness, age, sex, education, satisfaction, and identification with one's community. *Anxiousness* refers to the degree of apprehension about terrorist attack even when terrorist attack has not occurred for some time and to the degree of apprehension about other stressful events as well. The greater the anxiousness, the greater the disturbance in relation to border incidents. This variable is regarded as a comprehensive mental attitude that precedes the actual response to stress and hence in part determines the responses to border incidents.

Age is also regarded as a stress-resistance resource factor; the younger the person, the fewer the disturbances because of the greater reservoir of energy at the disposal of young people. So too with level of *education*. The ability to recognize the existence of alternative solutions for resolving stressful situations and to choose among them depends in part on one's educational level, so that the higher the educational level, the fewer the disturbances.

Sex can be analyzed on similar lines. The social norms prevailing in Israeli society define women as the "weaker" sex in need of masculine protection. Even in the presumably egalitarian kibbutzim, only the men receive special training to use weapons in defense of the settlement and only they participate in guard duty; this was certainly true in the six settlements of the present study. Because people specially trained how to behave in stressful situations show less panic when they actually confront such situations (Gregory, 1978), one might expect women to show more disturbance than men, both in kibbutzim and moshavim, in response to border incidents.

Durkheim has pointed to the significance of a sense of belonging to and identification with the group as providing meaning to the individual's life, especially in time of stress. Therefore the extent to which a person derives *satisfaction* from life in the community (in the economic, cultural, and social spheres) and identifies with the community and its goals should be associated with the extent of disturbance; the greater the satisfaction and identification, the less the disturbance. Satisfaction and identification should also be treated as stress-resistance resources.

HYPOTHESES OF THE CONNECTIONS BETWEEN THE VARIABLES: THE PATH MODEL

The three stress factors—country of origin, kibbutz versus moshav, and intensity of border incidents—are presented in the path model as exogenous factors, that is, factors unaffected by one another or by other factors in the model but affecting other factors. The rationale is that border incident stress is not influenced by the other two, although there is the possibility that country of origin with its associated cultural tradition may affect the social structure of kibbutz and moshav.

Of the stress-resistant resource factors, age and sex are regarded as exogenous, whereas educational level appears to be influenced by country of origin, with the Western group higher in education than the Eastern. Education and kibbutz versus moshav are presented, however, as causally unrelated because there is no evidence of causal relationship of the two in either direction: education determining the sociocultural structure of the settlement or the reverse.

Country of origin is presumed to affect directly anxiousness on the one hand and satisfaction and identification with the community on the other. The Eastern group, who unlike the Western are relative newcomers and whose immigration crisis is severe, will be more susceptible to anxiousness than the Western group and will be less satisfied socially, economically, and culturally with their settlement. Similarly, the collectivist social structure of the kibbutz and its stable economic situation will provide its members with more support than the more individualistic and unstable economic situation of the moshav. On this ground we expect that there will be greater anxiousness and less satisfaction and identification with the moshav than with the kibbutz.

If we combine the foregoing and ask under what conditions border incidents increase anxiousness and reduce satisfaction and identification with one's community, we would reply: when the residents are still struggling to cope with the stresses of immigration, acculturation, and economic instability in an individualistic community structure. Under these circumstances, the greater the intensity of border incidents, the greater one's anxiousness and the less one's satisfaction and identification with one's community. Path analysis of the variables should clarify whether the intensity and accumulation of stressful events influence social and emotional disturbances directly, indirectly by affecting intervening attitudes that directly affect the degree of disturbance, or both.

It is presumed that the younger the age and the higher the level of education, the less the anxiousness. One might hypothesize the same relationship for extent of satisfaction and identification with the community, namely that the younger the age and the higher the education, the higher one's ability to adjust to one's surroundings and to derive satisfaction from one's community. On the other hand, these very variables, youth and education, may reduce one's satisfaction with one's community precisely if the community does not permit one to fulfill the high aspirations associated with youth and education. (But more of this later.) The various studies done in Israel give no evidence that sex affects anxiousness.

Anxiousness; overall satisfaction; economic, cultural, and social satisfaction; and identification with the community are presented in the path model as endogenous variables, and their possible interconnections are discussed below. Various studies in Israel (Guttman, Levy, & Mann, 1970; Kremer, 1978) have found that overall satisfaction is determined by specific sources of satisfaction; hence our measurement here of both overall satisfaction and satisfaction in economic, social, and cultural spheres. Statistical evidence suggests, moreover, that overall satisfaction is determined by degree of identification with the community rather than the reverse. In our regression analysis with identification as an independent variable and satisfaction as a dependent one, the beta coefficient was higher (.31) than in the reverse (.21).

Finally, anxiousness occupies a central position in the path model, as the most proximal variable to the ultimate dependent variables, disturbance in emotional and social spheres. It occupies the position of a factor that might carry over the effects of other endogenous and exogenous variables to the final dependent variables. Anxiousness is both (a) a deeply rooted disposition that has been formed by previous stressful situations and other personal and social stress-resistant resource factors and (b) a major factor affecting one's subsequent responses to present and future stress situations.

METHOD

Subjects

Our sample consisted of 100 kibbutz members and 100 moshav members randomly selected from the 740 members of the six settlements. The interview consisted mostly of close-ended questions with almost no refusals. The executive secretary and the security office of each settlement were also interviewed, and written data on the settlement were obtained.

Measures

Emotional disturbance was measured on a 3-point scale (high, low, medium) in four questions on fears and insomnia during the first month following a border incident. Social disturbance was measured on a 3-point scale (no change, some restriction, total restriction) in two questions referring to adult evening activity outside the home during the same interval. In one question on children's play outside the house, replies were scored on a 2-point scale (play resumed as usual or curtailed for from 2 days to 1 week). The division of disturbance into emotional and social was supported by factor analysis.

Anxiousness was measured by two questions about whether individuals were apprehensive about border incidents in the future and by two questions about their apprehensiveness about other undesirable events in the future. Given intercorrelations of the four questions in the .46–.60 range, they were combined with a minimum anxiousness index of 4 and a maximum of 12. Age was scaled according to three categories: 15–29, 30–34, and 45+. Education was scaled according to five categories with none as the lowest and 13+ years as the highest. Overall satisfaction was examined on a single 5-point scaled question. Identification with the community was measured by obtaining reasons for choosing to live in the community and for remaining there. Ideological, value-oriented reasons were scored 3; social-familial reasons, 2; and instrumental-economic reasons, 1. Given a correlation above .50 between the two questions, they were combined for an identification index with a minimum score of 2 and a maximum of 6. Finally, overall satisfaction and economic and sociocultural satisfaction were measured by one 5-point scale each.

The connections between the variables were analyzed by path analysis, a method that places the independent variables on different causal levels, both in relation to each other and in relation to the dependent variables.

Results

The method of path analysis according to which the material was treated provides an estimate both of the direct and of the indirect effect between independent and dependent variables as well as the paths of the additive effects of the different variables.[1] The relevant data are presented in Table 6-1 and Figure 6-1. The findings show that four variables directly affect emotional disturbance in descending order of importance: anxiousness, sex, country of origin, and economic satisfaction. When combined, these variables predict .38 of the dependent variable. Only the relationship of economic satisfaction to emotional disturbance was in the direction opposite to expectation. We found that the more satisfied economically a person was, the more upset emotionally he or she was following a border incident. This may be explained by the fact that such a person has more to lose in both private and community property damage. In a subsequent path analysis we also found that economic satisfaction had an additive effect that lowered emotional disturbance. In other words,

[1] Because of space limitations it was necessary to curtail drastically the presentation of the path model, its hypotheses, findings, and discussion. Readers are invited to write the author for the complete report.

Table 6-1 The Path Coefficients: Direct and Indirect Effect and Overall Correlation

Dependent variable	Independent variable	Path coefficient direct effect	*F*	Indirect effect	Overall correlation
Emotional disturbances	Anxiousness	–.38	33.12	–.08	.46
	Sex	.35	38.72	–.01	.34
	Country of origin	.23	12.00	.13	.36
	Overall satisfaction	–.15	6.23	.12	–.03
Social disturbances	Border incidents	–.27	18.01		–.27
	Anxiousness	–.22	10.43	–.09	–.31
	Age	.22	12.12		.22
	Sex	.19	8.82	–.09	.10
	Education	–.16	5.07	–.09	–.25
Anxiousness	Country of origin	–.21	4.53	–.29	–.50
	Kibbutz versus moshav	.18	3.98	.31	.50
	Education	.17	4.53	.26	.43
	Overall satisfaction	–.13	4.33	–.16	–.29
Overall satisfaction	Economic satisfaction	.33	63.06	.11	.44
	Identification with community	–.31	25.04	–.11	–.42
	Sociocultural satisfaction	.17	20.68	.13	.30
Sociocultural satisfaction	Education	.43	25.02	–.31	.12
	Kibbutz versus moshav	–.25	6.02	.06	–.19
	Country of origin	.26	4.89	–.04	.22
Economic satisfaction	Kibbutz versus moshav	–.39	30.98	.07	–.31
Identification with community	Kibbutz versus moshav	.32	12.24	.34	.66
	Education	.24			
	Country of origin	–.21	6.92	–.41	–.62
	Age	.13	3.80	.11	.24

Note. The symbol (–) is only technical in all cases, except for the effect of economic satisfaction on emotional disturbance. Whether a given relationship is positive or negative can be ascertained by consulting the text.

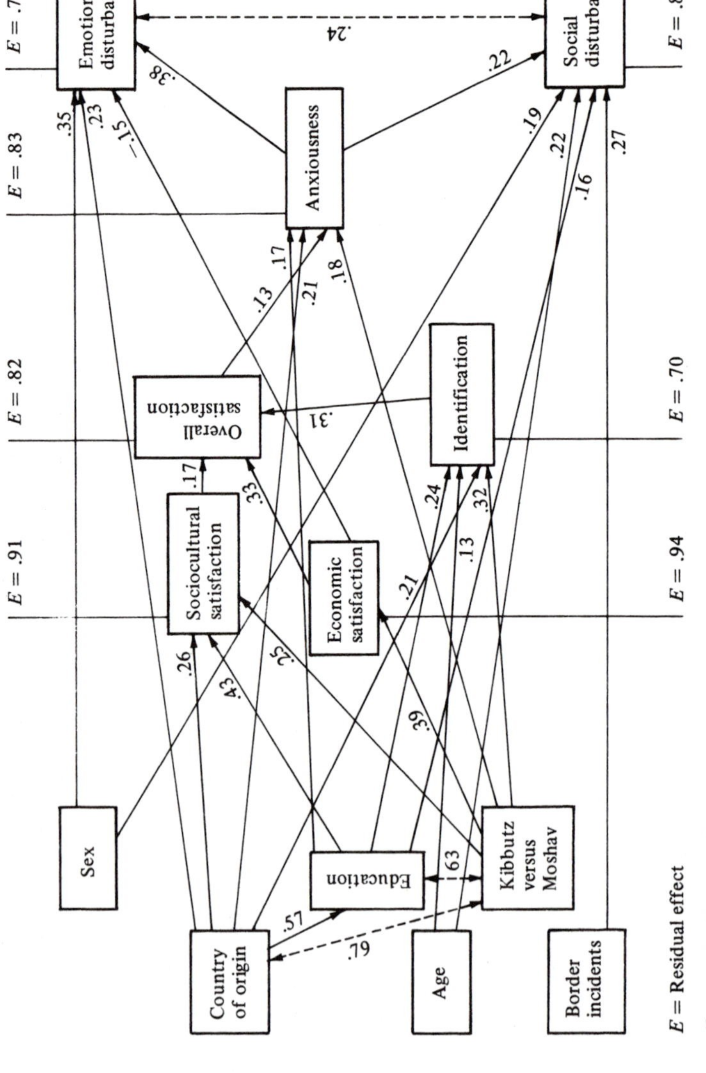

E = Residual effect

Figure 6-1 The path diagram.

economic satisfaction exercises opposite effects on emotional disturbance, its direct effect increasing it and its indirect effect reducing it. Contrary to expectation, a host of variables including age, education, kibbutz versus moshav, intensity of border incidents, satisfaction, and identification with the community did not directly affect emotional disturbance.

The variables affecting directly the second dependent variable, social disturbance, were, in descending order: anxiousness, age, border incident intensity, sex, and education. These variables together predict .25 of the dependent variable; all other variables were of inconsequential direct influence.

Turning to the paths of additive effect, we find that the additive paths to emotional disturbance and to social disturbance originate mainly in two variables: country of origin and kibbutz versus moshav. The paths that originate in country of origin are shown in Figure 6-2. These paths show that the Eastern-born (when kibbutz versus moshav is controlled) are more anxious than the Western-born, less satisfied with the sociocultural life, less identified with their community, and less educated. Similarly, the paths originating with kibbutz versus moshav (when country of origin is controlled) show that moshav members are more anxious and less satisfied economically and socioculturally than kibbutz members. Their identification with the moshav life is also lower than that of the kibbutz members with the kibbutz.

In path 4 and 5 in Figure 6-2, education had opposite effects. A lower level of education was associated with less identification with the community. Conversely, it was associated with greater satisfaction with the sociocultural life of the community. In other words, the lower level of education lowers individuals' sociocultural aspirations and in this way enables them to be satisfied. In the paths originating with kibbutz versus moshav, economic satisfaction had similar opposite effects.

These findings show that country of origin and kibbutz versus moshav affect directly those variables that from their side directly affect overall satisfaction. In this way, the additive effect of country of origin and kibbutz versus moshav was transmitted to overall satisfaction, which from its side carried it to anxiousness. Overall satisfaction is, then, the factor that transmits the sociocultural effects. Anxiousness, which emerged as the major proximal variable to disturbance in nearly all paths, received the sociocultural effects through overall satisfaction, and this additive effect is transmitted by it to the disturbances. Anxiousness is directly associated with the following variables in descending order of importance: country of origin; kibbutz versus moshav, level of education; and level of overall satisfaction. When combined, they predict .31 of the anxiousness. Anxiousness is not affected directly by border incidents.

Separate path analyses for kibbutz and moshav revealed that in the former there is a relationship between severity of border incidents and extent of emotional disturbance (beta = .19) but not in the moshav, whose members are equally emotionally disturbed whether living in a settlement with mild, moderate, or severe border incidents. This finding for the moshav seems to confirm Shuval's view (1963) that strong and extensive stressful events lower one's threshold for stress tolerance and induce one to respond to mild stress as if it were severe stress.

There was, on the other hand, a relationship between severity of border incidents and the extent of sociocultural satisfaction and identification with the

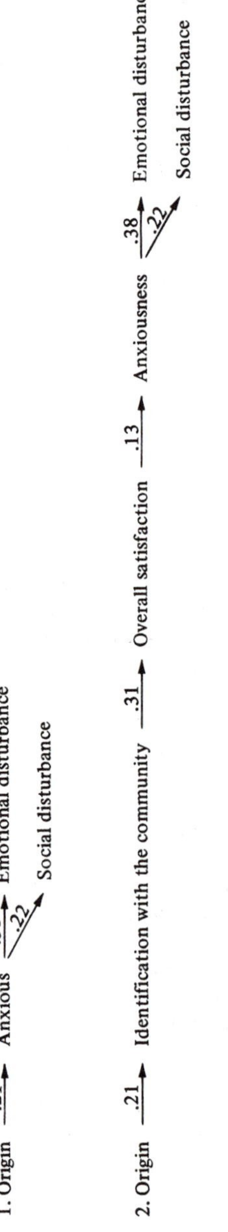

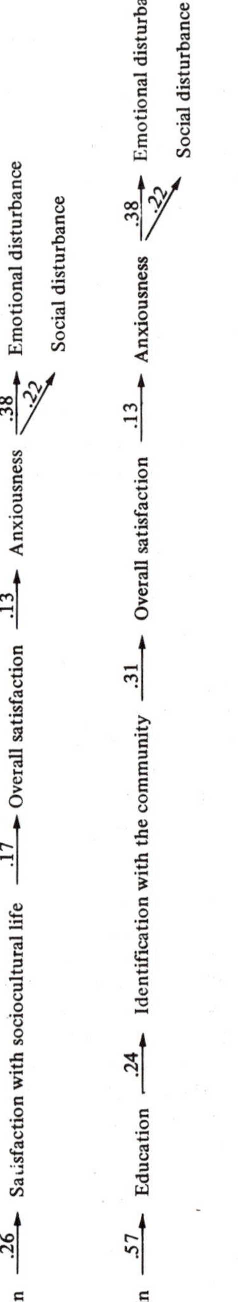

Figure 6-2 Additive paths for country of origin.

community in the moshav but not in the kibbutz. The greater the severity of border incidents, the lower the satisfaction (beta = .27) and identification with the moshav (beta = .18) and the greater the resulting emotional disturbance (beta = .18). In the kibbutz, by contrast, no such connections were found. The levels of satisfaction and identification were so high in the kibbutz that severity of border incidents made no difference.

CONCLUSIONS

We found that a Western as compared to an Eastern background directly raises the level of education, satisfaction, and identification with community and lowers anxiousness. These findings must be regarded with caution because our sample was representative only of a special section of the population. The same is true for the finding that kibbutz as compared to moshav background directly raises identification with the community and economic and sociocultural satisfaction and lowers anxiousness; whether these findings would apply to moshavim established before the State by Western members has yet to be investigated.

It is interesting to note that the severity of border incidents exercises a direct affect on social disturbance in both kibbutz (beta = .46) and moshav (beta = .21) but not on emotional disturbance. This difference in the consequences of border incidents to the two dependent variables may be explained by the fact the curtailing of entertainment of adults and the restriction of children's play following a border incident may be regarded as a normative and realistic response by members of these settlements, whereas their emotional adjustment is a more idiosyncratic response affected by the stress-resistant resources discussed above. Overall, the path analysis and other analyses reported provide support for the theoretical model proposed.

REFERENCES

Antonovsky, A. Conceptual and methodological problems in the study of resistance resources and stressful life events. In B. A. Dohrenwend & B. P. Dohrenwend (Eds.), *Stressful life events*. New York: Wiley, 1974.

Eisenstadt, S. N. *The absorption of immigrants*. London: Routledge & Kegan Paul, 1954.

Gregory, W. E. *Some aspects of personality related to coping with stress in war and peace*. Paper presented at the Second International Conference on Psychological Stress and Adjustment in Time of War and Peace. Jerusalem, June 1978.

Guttman, L., Levy, S., & Mann, K. J. *Adjustment to retirement* (Tech. Rep.) Jerusalem: Institute of Applied Social Research, 1970.

Hartman, M., & Eilon, H. Ethnicity and stratification in Israel. *Megamot*, 1975, *21*, 125–139.

Hinkle, L. E. The effect of exposure to culture change, social change, and changes in interpersonal relationships on health. In B. A. Dohrenwend & B. P. Dohrenwend (Eds.), *Stressful life events*. New York: Wiley, 1974.

Kremer, Y. *A sociological analysis of retirees' attitudes*. Unpublished doctoral dissertation, Bar Ilan University, Ramat Gan, 1978.

Shuval, J. T. *Immigrants on the threshold*. New York: Lieber-Atherton, 1963.

Smocha, S., & Peres, Y. Ethnic inequality in Israel. *Megamot*, 1974, *20*, 5–42.

Weintraub, D. *Patterns of social change in moshavim of new immigrants*. Unpublished doctoral dissertation, Hebrew University, Jerusalem, 1963.

3

Mental Health, Traditional Beliefs, and the Moral Order among Yemenite Jews in Israel

Phyllis Palgi

The purpose of this chapter is to demonstrate that in the field of health, particularly mental health, the Yemenite community in Israel draws from its traditional system as an accessory to the modern medical system, which in itself does not as yet satisfy the community on an emotional level.

According to the World Health Organization, health is a state of complete physical, mental, and social well-being, not merely the absence of disease and infirmity. This definition implies that one cannot understand the body without understanding the mind, and that body and mind have full meaning only in relation to society (Firth 1959). What does the word "health" mean both in concrete terms and symbolically to the Yemenites; what is its major connotation in their culture? The underlying philosophy and basic concepts of the Yemenite health system will be identified and presented as part of the configuration of their culture in general. An attempt will be made to narrow the area in which the relationships between health and other aspects of life are more closely bound together. The emphasis will be on the mutual relationship of basic health concepts and the Yemenite world view, which is dominated by an all-pervasive but rigid moral order. Furthermore, I will try to identify patterns of overt behavior during illness and the interpretation of the Yemenite view of causation, which will provide clues to both manifest and latent stress points in the culture.

Sources of the Traditional Yemenite Health System

All Middle Eastern Jewish communities have retained certain beliefs and practices stemming from early Babylonian, Egyptian, and Greek cultures—as well as from their own ancestral Hebrew culture. These beliefs and practices have become incorporated into evolving Middle East health systems, an integral part of which have been drawn from the more complex system found in the monotheistic religion of Judaism. The latter fact suggests that to learn about Yemenite traditional healing beliefs, a link between health and morality must be explored. From the classical anthropological point of view, the Yemenite health system may be characterized primarily as a folk system. Following the analysis of Saunders (1958), folk medicine differs from scientific medicine in that it is generally the common possession of the group, so that what one adult knows about illness and its treatment is usually known by all others.

> Although knowledge of the origins of folk medical practices and beliefs may have largely been lost, the practices and beliefs themselves are often so rooted in tradition that they seem a part of the natural order of things. . . . Folk medical law is transmitted from person to person and generation to generation by informal methods. . . . The expected attitude toward a given element of folk medicine is one of uncritical acceptance. Failure does not invalidate a practice or shake the belief on which it is based . . . If he [the patient] dies, the reason is not that the remedy was inappropriate, but that the patient was beyond help [p. 199].

The structure of the Yemenite health system includes preventive and curative aspects and is classified into diagnostic and therapeutic components. The Western dichotomy usually made between physical and mental illness, is much less applicable to the Yemenite system—although not totally inappropriate.

During the period in history when most of the Jewish communities were concentrated in the Muslim orbit, the body of knowledge of the famous medieval Arab physicians as well as the beliefs and practices of the local native folk societies became incorporated into the accepted Jewish system. In modern times, particularly during the second half of the present century, Western medicine has been introduced into the Middle East and was adopted on a selective basis and in varying degrees, according to the general technological level of the particular country or region. Thus, one may find that a partially developed modern medical system exists side by side with a well-developed time-honored folk system, or that the former has become an overlay upon the traditional system.

In Yemen, the Jews—who were entrenched for centuries in their isolated cultural niche and who had little or no contact with modernity—became very set in their ways and, on the whole, continued practices developed during medieval times. Modern medicine barely reached them except at a very minimal level in the capital town of San'a, where there were some hospital facilities. In fact, immediately upon arrival in Israel, in the first stage of resettlement, it was the confrontation with a modern medical system that became one of the most frightening aspects of the new life for the Yemenites. Israeli medical personnel were shocked by these immigrants' lack of knowledge regarding health matters. In particular, the high infant mortality rate among the Yemenites was an emotional issue even for doctors and nurses in a child-centered society like Israel.

Thus, in the first encounter between the Yemenite immigrants and the Israeli community, the health situation was a fertile ground for many mutual misunderstandings, tensions, and incriminations. Yet, significantly, the Yemenites, who during the past 25 years have clung to tradition in so many respects, have shown an unusual flexibility when faced with illness. It was the conservative, highly conforming Yemenites who eventually bridged the gulf between a folk system and a Western, scientifically based medical system. Today, Israeli Yemenites use both systems, either successively or simultaneously, the latter strategy being particularly common in cases of psychological problems or mental illness. This aspect will be stressed in this chapter.

As might be expected, after a quarter of a century of contact with modern medicine, the traditional system is not as intact and coherent as it was in the "old country." However, the successful traditional healers in Israel still have a large clientele. Apparently neither the healer nor the patient feels that there is a basic conflict in practice or in ideology between the old and the new system. True enough, visits to the traditional healers were not usually divulged by the patient during a visit to the "scientific" doctor, it being assumed that the latter would not understand the traditional system and might even ridicule it. Healers, on their part, prefer secrecy out of fear of being charged with the illegal practice of medicine, or are wary of some other official authority like the tax collector. More recently, as a result of the influence of anthropology in Israel, some psychiatrists have shown an interest in traditional therapeutic measures and have encouraged their patients to speak openly about their visits to folk healers. In fact, in certain circles, it has become almost chic to pay special attention to the opinions of the latter.

The body of medical knowledge comprising the traditional system, which had become crystallized into a coherent system by the medieval Islamic period, was drawn in the main from the following sources (Kepach 1961):

Jewish Sources

1. Rambam's writings in the twelfth century on medicine and Jewish philosophy had a major influence on Yemenite beliefs. His work, in turn, was heavily influenced by that of the Greeks. (The majority of his works were written in Arabic.) (*Encyclopedia Judaica* 1971:2: 778).

2. The other source, lesser known, but nevertheless important in medieval times, was the work of doctors such as Rabbi Yichia Al Tabib and the Yemenite doctor known as "Zacharia, the doctor." The latter was famous for the grasses and herbs he used for medicinal purposes. There were healers who linked their nature cures with astrology. For instance, Jacob Alkandi and Harara stressed the importance of the right day of the week or month or the right time of the day for healing treatment.

3. The Talmud spelled out very clearly specific health rules and regulations. It was also an important source of legitimation for recognition of the potentially dangerous nature of spirits as well as the power of the evil eye.

4. Kabbala and Zohar contributed, in the main, mystical aspects of diagnosis and treatment based on a combination of astrology and Jewish religious precepts.

The Yemenites seem to have had no problems in integrating Rambam's rationalistic approach with that of the mystics. They simply ignored the fact that Rambam, for instance, was against the use of amulets and cameos, which is basic to the Yemenite preventive medical practice. In other Jewish communities, a major controversy raged between the followers of these two opposing schools of thought, at one period even leading to violence. In the twentieth century, before emigration from Yemen, a small intellectual elite group among the Jews gave attention to the existence of a basic contradiction between the two main approaches. The controversy did not, however, touch the masses.

Arab Sources

1. Certain medical books reached Yemen, the most famous of which was *Zad Al Misasir* by Ibn al Hadad.

2. Prescriptions from the Kor'an and various Middle-Eastern folk beliefs became incorporated not only into the Jewish health system, but also into the Muslim legal system. Here, too, full support was given to the all-pervading influence of spirits, *jinns* as they were called in Arabic, which, it was believed, could enter into human beings or animals and take control of their behavior. The Muslim legal system accepted this belief as valid.

As Kroeber (1948) has pointed out, in all societies, cultural influences from different sources may become fused to form one coherent system. Linton (1936) has stressed the extent to which individuals are unaware of the origin of their customs and beliefs, most times assuming that they originated in their own tradition. When practices and beliefs are contradictory, dissonance may be resolved by regarding the disparate aspects as acceptable alternatives. In Yemen, as in Israel, Jews would turn to Arab healers, particularly when their own people failed to effect a cure, and vice versa.

In broad terms, one may say that Yemenite medicine was a subsystem within the total overall Middle-Eastern system of medicine. In Yemen itself the rigidity and religious fanaticism of Muslims and Jews alike, as well as the degree of isolation, enhanced the similarity of beliefs between the two ethnic groups. At the same time, the overall ethnic identities were kept scrupulously disparate. To understand this seemingly contradictory statement, one should know that the ethnic differences reasserted themselves whenever the medical beliefs merged into the religious system, which was the basic dividing line between the two communities. As has been pointed out earlier, whenever there was no obvious religious clash, Jews would easily consult Arab specialists and vice versa.

Fatalistic View of Illness

Yemenite Jews shared with both the Muslims and other Middle-Eastern Jewish communities the belief that, in the final analysis, illness and its cure was dependent on God's will. In a more direct way illness could be attributed to the work of some supernatural force like evil spirits or the evil eye; thus holy words and names of angels were involved in the curing process. The concept of natural disasters or some other external event causing illness did exist, but it was never quite clear whether affected individuals did, after all, bear some responsibility for bringing upon themselves the misfortune. This was the case even if the misfortune was regarded as the result of the evil design of other human beings, or through unfortunate combinations of events, which together combusted and produced a situation loaded with supernatural dangers.

The traditional system places no importance on the concept of awareness; on the contrary, at most times it strengthens the projective system and works towards cancelling out the evil effect of the alleged sorcery. However, the system is based upon the fact that there is almost invariably a recognition of the personal involvement between the victim and the persecutor.

On the basis of empiric experience, when the illness is brief or slight, a practical common-sense attitude is adopted: appropriate herbs, purgatives, or pastes are used, and little time is spent in discussing causation. Even a minimal ceremony might be performed to expunge the evil eye. All such techniques are comparable to minor surgery. Again, in view of the capricious nature of the evil eye, if the illness or mishap is temporary it is not considered necessary to search too deeply, or pinpoint the person who caused it. However, if the illness persists, and the patient suffers considerably and becomes unable to fulfill daily functions, then home remedies are no longer considered efficacious. At this point an expert in folk medicine will be consulted, and an explanation for the onset of illness will be sought as an essential part of the diagnostic and hence therapeutic process. It is suggested here that, in view of the all-pervasiveness of religion in Yemenite life, the explanation will invariably be found within the moral order. The nature of the Jewish religion—heavily dominated as it is by clearly expressed ethical principles referring to interpersonal human relations, as well as to religious precepts pertaining to behavior toward Almighty God—in itself helps support the moral approach.

Role of Spirits

In the Yemenite medical belief system, a very important role is attributed to spirits. Thus the nature and habits of spirits as viewed by the Yemenites warrant discussion in some detail. Yemenite beliefs about the spirit kingdom and spirit activity have persisted for centuries and are passed on from generation to generation. These beliefs, however, have been somewhat shaken since immigration to Israel, and some uncomfortable questions have been raised. However, the beliefs still linger on. The fact that the Talmud refers to the existence of spirits has strengthened the ideological connection between religion and health beliefs and contributed to the perseverance of the beliefs as well as their integration into life as a whole.

A visit to a learned Yemenite rabbi who holds an official position in the Israeli

Rabbinate confirmed this view. We sat in his study, which included an extensive library. When we turned to the subject of spirits, he rose from his chair, moved to the couch, sat upon it cross-legged, and pointed to the Talmud and some other ancient-looking books, saying "It is written there that there are *shedim* but how they came to Israel is something I cannot explain." He continued, "They should not be here. Israel is the Holy Land and they cannot live in the Holy Land. How did they cross the border?" He based his evidence that *shedim* did come to Israel on the fact that there are people in Israel who are mentally ill, which in itself is proof of possession by spirits. The rabbi was troubled and had no answer. "The doctors also have no answer," he said. "They lock people up in hospitals, and that solves nothing." The rabbi was trying to prove that it is not the "primitiveness" of the Yemenites that brings them to support the belief in spirits, but rather that the modern world is slowly beginning to understand the power of such supernatural creatures. However, he appeared puzzled and confused on the issue.

According to Yemenite Jews, the holiness of the Land should be strong enough to prevent spirits from crossing its frontiers. Furthermore, spirits do not like light, and since Israel is well lit, the spirits should be unable to function. Traditional Jewish Moroccan beliefs also support this contention. However, the fact remains that people display behavior considered to be a result of spirit intervention.

A psychotherapist reported a case to me regarding a husband and wife who were concerned that the disturbed mental state of the wife might be attributed to the work of a *shed.* This woman would fall into a trance-like state. While in the trance, she shouted, talked nonsense, appeared to be totally unaware of what was happening to her, and called for her dead sister. When she awoke she was perfectly logical and coherent. They consulted a *chacham* ("sage," in Mid-Eastern communities, "rabbi"), who diagnosed her situation as being one of spirit possession. According to the *chacham,* the woman bumped into a *shed,* and as revenge he came to take possession of her soul from time to time. The husband was a learned and religious man, and he too believed that *shedim* should not be found in the Holy Land. Both husband and wife felt helpless and in desperation they turned to psychiatric counseling for advice and treatment. The *chacham* apparently placed no blame on the possessed one, but located the encounter between the wife and the *shed* in her sister's home. According to further information, it appeared that the patient had guilt feelings about her anger and jealousy toward her late sister. The treatment of the *chacham* was a cleansing treatment to drive out the *shed,* which represented the badness in her. At the time of the report the patient continued to wear the cameo given to her by the *cacham,* and also continued to see the "official" therapist.

According to the Yemenites, the night is dangerous because of the spirits, and, therefore, one should never go out alone in the dark; three people should always be together. This suggests that humans have some capacity to ward off spirits. At night there may be more than ten thousand mischievious spirits lurking about, yet three human beings are enough to keep them away. A general concept of territorialism exists. Humans must be careful not to trespass in a blatant fashion or disturb the spirits unnecessarily. At the same time, a Yemenite must bear in mind that the spirits are expansionist in nature, and that there is a constant struggle on the part of the demons to extend the zone of their influence by means of marriage and inheritance (Kagan 1968). Thus, procedures must be established for humans to make contact and threaten the spirits or make compromises and conciliatory gestures toward them.

Basic Characteristics of Spirits

Spirits are more numerous than humans. Although they have the power to fly anywhere, they prefer to live in the house together with ordinary humans and are affected by the atmosphere of the home they inhabit.

All spirits like dark and damp places. The evil spirits prefer dirty and neglected places almost exclusively but may be found also near wells or springs or in forests and on mountain tops. In view of the nature and function of toilets, it is understandable that it was thought that toilets attracted spirits. Similarly, the Talmud cautions against exposure to dirty water and, for instance, advises against sitting under a drain pipe leading from the roof, because dirty water might drop down, inviting the evil spirits.

Spirits are good, bad, or neutral. Apparently they resemble human beings in this respect. Their degree of goodness is correlated positively with their degree of etherealness. Spirits combining fire and wind are the best, whereas spirits made of fire, wind, water, and dust are bad. The good are the most invisible; hence, if one feels or, in some form or other, sees a spirit, it is probably an evil one.

Yemenites have ways of evoking good spirits. If a powder is made from the placenta of a black kitten together with that of the kitten's mother, both of whom must be from the first litter, and the powder is rubbed on a person's eyes, good spirits may thereby be summoned. The tears of a donkey are also considered effective as a means of spirit revelation. Such techniques are not usually used by the ordinary person, but rather by the *mori,* who specializes in working out a person's fortune. The good spirits are important for the specialists who need information about the future. The specialists, however, are cautious; they claim that they can get information only about the near future.

Giridi (1945) claims that by studying the Talmud the Yemenites learned that spirits have three characteristics in common with angels and three with human beings. The spirits have wings like angels, their movement within the universe is unlimited, and there are no barriers to their hearing ability. Their human-like features are their mortality, their reproductive potential, and their need and desire for food and drink. They can reproduce, not only by sexual intercourse with their own kind, but also by cohabitation with humans. As a rule they are invisible, but they have various ways of making their presence felt or can appear in different forms, both human and animal. Rabbi Shmuel ben Yoseph Adani describes their basic constituents as various combinations of fire, wind, water and dust (Giridi 1945).

A Description of a Successful "Mori"

In Israel today there is a successful *mori* that the Yemenites suspect of being a charlatan. However, because of his ability to summon the spirits he has gained fame and power.

The *mori* lives not far from Tel Aviv in a neighborhood of immigrants from Middle-Eastern countries. The *mori*'s room is separated from the waiting room by a curtain. Children played, pushed, tusseled among themselves. The walls were dirty and the floor uncarpeted. I could see a lounge leading off the waiting room, which was shabby but better kept, and was obviously for family guests. The *mori*'s wife was in the kitchen cooking, and the pungent smell of food frying in oil filled our nostrils. The room the *mori* himself occupied was no sanctum. The children popped their heads in from time to time to ask the *mori* questions or to request small sums of money. The clientele included both sexes, most from Middle-Eastern countries but by no means exclusively Yemenite. Among them was a man of Rumanian origin accompanied by his teenage daughter. Talking with him, I concluded that the daughter had been diagnosed by a psychiatrist as suffering from schizophrenia.

This *mori* impressed me differently than the previously mentioned dignified rabbi. He, too, sat cross-legged on a bed and was surrounded by books, but the room was filled with bric-a-brac such as beads and dried beans. Next to him was a spittoon into which he coughed and spat loudly. From time to time he shouted to his wife and children. He was boastful of his powers over the spirits and his ability to diagnose and counteract sorcery. He smiled lasciviously when he spoke of sexual matters. In my presence he received a man who complained of a large number of vague physical and psychological symptoms. The *mori* said that he was not sure whether this client was possessed or not. He got up from his couch, walked to the door, lowered the blind, and, in the dark, behind the blind, on the verandah, he conducted his conversation with the spirits. He spoke in esoteric Aramaic terms. A second voice with a Yemenite accent was heard answering him. It was all done very quickly. The atmosphere in the room, where two other patients and I waited for the results, was tense. The *mori* returned tired but triumphant. He said that the spirits informed him that his client was not possessed by one of them; thus the *mori* concluded that the patient was ill because of the evil eye or some other sorcery. The *mori* dealt with the case accordingly.

Spirit Involvement with Human Beings

One of the outstanding features of the spirits is their deep involvement with human beings. The spirits could serve humans either for good or bad purposes, depending upon the character and motives of the humans with whom they were in contact, and also, of course, upon their own character. Usually, their evil intent dominates. A Yemenite explained to me how another Yemenite wished to harm him and was able to do so because the former cohabited with a female spirit, who served him as an "army of soldiers serves the general." The enemy had particularly strong evil powers and could perform sorcery with sperm that he obtained after intercourse with the female spirit. The family of the accused claimed that it was not true, because it was impossible to import his female spirit from Yemen to the Holy Land.

The spirits play a predominant role in the sexual aspects of human life. Various sexual dysfunctions, prohibited erotic behavior, and fantasies are closely associated with demon intervention. The evil spirits, sometimes called "angels of destruction," are more prone to reveal themselves, because of their malicious involvement with humans and their intent to harm them.

In Jewish demonology, Lilith is the most dangerous of all demons. She is not, however, the only female demon. Lilith is mentioned in the Talmud and also in the Kor'an under the name of Ziat Bint Silkes. Kagan (1968) traces the development of the idea of female demons, their behavior, and their characteristic traits. Like most Jewish traditional groups, the Yemenites attribute a number of disasters to Lilith's activities, such as possessing persons, terrifying them or making them mentally ill, and in various mysterious ways, Lilith is capable of causing a person's death.

From my own field experience, Lilith or other female demons became apparent in some kinds of forbidden sexual behavior or in fantasies. Kagan reports that in the early legends there were merely chance matings between human men and female demons and that only in the Middle Ages was the motif of marriage introduced. It is very common in Jewish communities of the Middle East to keep a 24-hour watch over the newborn child, particularly a male, for a period of at least one month. It is feared that the jealousy of a sterile female demon might drive her to strangle the child. One reason why men should not sleep alone, when in remote places far away from home, is that they are liable to be seduced by these female demons.

According to Kagan marriage to a female demon is punishment for a sin. However, Yemenites do not necessarily endorse this statement.

Case Studies on Spirit Possession

Case 1. The following is the account of Mrs. Yonah, a Yemenite woman suffering from severe anxieties and phantom pregnancy, who was hospitalized in an open psychiatric hospital. She no longer fulfilled most of her tasks as a wife and mother and claimed that some members of her husband's family were trying to harm her through magical means. It took intensive interviewing to discover what was worrying the woman. My knowledge about Yemenite spirits made it possible for me to build the necessary rapport with Mrs. Yonah so that she was able to admit to her terrifying secrets.

Mrs. Yonah, aged 30, was born in Yemen and came to Israel at the age of 16. She is illiterate and lives in a conservative Yemenite neighborhood. She works as a maid in an upper-middle-class modern home. At 20 she married a young man from her own neighborhood, despite opposition from her family, who claimed that they did not know the groom's family, and "he is not like one of us." They objected to his general behavior and his life-style. He was far less religious and less traditional than her family. When the future Mrs. Yonah insisted that she was in love with this man and would not give him up, her family finally consented to the marriage. However, soon after the marriage she realised that she had become an outsider in the eyes of her own kin, who looked upon her as being willful. Her husband's mother accepted her in a cursory fashion, but the rest of his family, particularly his siblings, openly rejected her, and she suddenly felt very much alone in the world. Because she did not become pregnant during the first three years of marriage, vague hints began emanating from her husband's family that he should divorce her. Out of desperation she did three things. She prayed incessantly to God, visited a *mori,* and finally went to a gynecologist. She now has three small boys and is not sure which procedure was the effective one.

Mrs. Yonah spent a great deal of time telling about the injustices, insults, and possible evil eye to which her husband's kin had subjected her. It seemed clear to her that misfortunes that befell her were a direct result of the evil eye given to her by her husband's siblings, who were jealous that she had given birth to another son.

Finally, in whispered tones, she confessed to what she believed was the major cause of her inability to function. Since the birth of her third child, her husband usually insisted upon anal intercourse, and on the rare occasions that they did have sexual relations in the accepted fashion, he practiced coitus interruptus, an act forbidden by Jewish law. Furthermore, he would insist upon approaching her before she was ritually clean; in other words, he would not wait out the prescribed number of days after she had completed her menstrual period, so that she could perform the ritual ablutions. Mrs. Yonah described these details sitting far away from any other patient or staff member. She had not previously been able to discuss these unmentionable details, because she was terrified about the punishment, and because she was so ashamed.

She began to understand her situation only after she had confided in a member of her husband's family, a practicing *mori.* Although he was not a very knowledgeable or skillful practitioner, because he did not have any secret books, he was an expert in Yemenite pharmacopoeia. This *mori* had dropped in to visit her after hearing that she had not been well, and had offered his professional services. She told him about her husband's demands, and also told him that despite the fact that she could not be pregnant and was menstruating regularly, she felt life in her womb.

The *mori* thought that she might have become pregnant by a *shed,* for, as he had explained, they swarm round spilled sperm. This meant that she was carrying an embryonic *shed* in her womb and might be possessed from time to time by a female *shed,* particularly at the time of coitus. Her confused thoughts supported the *mori's* thesis. For a rather large sum of money, the *mori* claimed that he could rid her of this undesirable supernatural pregnancy. She paid him eagerly, and he brought an ointment for her to rub over her body in a ritualistic fashion, particularly over her stomach. The ointment burned her skin, and brought on heavy vaginal bleeding, which the *mori* tried to stop by administering additional medicines. She felt desperately ill and began to suspect that he was practicing sorcery, especially since he was a member of her husband's family. She became desperate and neglected her housekeeping and the care of her children. This finally led to a serious row, when her husband came home one Friday afternoon and found that she had made no Sabbath preparations. When he threatened to beat her, she ran to her eldest brother, leaving the children at home. She waited for her husband to fetch her, but he refused to do so until there had been a full family council.

She was taken to the family doctor, who prescribed pills for her "pains and her nerves" and referred her to a psychiatrist. The psychiatrist hospitalized her in an open psychiatric setting. Her husband visited her often in the hospital. She described with some pride how he brought her slippers, food, and clean clothes.

Mrs. Yonah felt relieved after telling this story. She believed that she had been forced into committing a sin by her husband, even though he viewed life differently than she. Though he has become attentive to her, she does not trust him and does not know how to interpret his solicitous behavior.

She has two explanations for her husband's changed attitude toward her. He is either genuinely sorry for what he and his family have done to her, or he is guilty about his sexual behavior and wants to be sure that she does not tell any of the hospital staff.

In summing up the situation, she said that she felt abandoned by her own kin, ridiculed by her spouse's family, and contaminated by her husband's sinful behavior. Furthermore, she still feels uncomfortable with her husband's family and friends, who consider themselves an integral part of modern Israeli society, to which she knows she can never belong.

Case 2. The following story was told by Mrs. Simcha. Her grandfather, since deceased, was traveling alone through a mountainous area in Yemen, thought to be inhabited by *shedim.* A female demon entered his body and possessed him for the remainder of his life. She became in fact his "real" wife and was so jealous of his human wife that she would not allow him to have sexual relations with the latter. The wife accepted the situation when she realized that the she-demon was powerful, dangerous and capable of killing her out of jealousy. Mrs. Simcha explained that although her grandfather should not have gone alone into the mountains, he could not be blamed for what had happened. It was simply a matter of very bad luck. It was generally accepted that if a she-demon was passionately in love with a man, no one could remove her. As far as his human wife was concerned, she regarded her husband's impotence as a sickness inflicted upon him by supernatural causes. A subsequent meeting with the grandfather's widow revealed an extremely strong, independent, and domineering woman.

Case 3. Mr. Saadia, a dour, introverted man, owns a butcher shop in a Yemenite neighborhood. He is not well liked, but his wife is. Mrs. Saadia has a good relationship with her children, whereas their father is seen as a cold and distant figure. She is careful in the presence of her husband, but he is aware that she is the focus of the house.

One evening, Mr. Saadia returned home after a difficult day at the shop. He went to his room to rest. No other members of the family were at home. Suddenly, he felt a warm pressure on his back and had the feeling that he was being strangled. He went to see a *mori,* who said that a *shed* had come to plague him because he had not kept a promise. In addition, the *mori* suggested to him that he regularly chew *khat,** and then the *shedim* would no longer bother him.

There are three significant facts that led to the diagnosis and treatment prescribed by the *mori.* The first is that butcher shops, being spattered by blood and offal, are considered natural places for attracting *shedim.* The second is that *khat* is a mild toxicant widely used in Yemen, much like tranquilizers in Western society. Finally, that Mr. Saadia had made himself vulnerable to spirits.

Because of the taboo against masturbation, the admonition not to sleep alone was meant to protect men from temptation. It is expected that women are never alone. However, clinics report numerous cases of women who are fearful of the effect on their children of their own destructive or illicit sexual thoughts.

Almost invariably, bad thoughts are attributed to the interference of spirits or the evil eye. The person afflicted with bad thoughts considers himself ruled by the power of the spirits, the evil eye, or some other combination of supernatural forces. Here one sees the syncretism of both Muslim and Jewish folk beliefs to the basic Talmudic tenets.

Members of the family or friends of the afflicted one usually express their sympathy. However, these expressions may not be sincere. It is a cultural imperative that one must express sympathy for anyone who has met with misfortune. In any case, these expressions do not mean that the afflicted person may not in some way be responsible for his own misfortune. However, once a person is suffering, what brought the misfortune on is irrelevant.

Evil Eye

The ancient concept of the evil eye continues to have a strong grip on people throughout the Mid-East and North Africa. It is a phenomenon found in many different cultures, but the concept diffused throughout the present Muslim orbit and Christian Europe from ancient Mid-Eastern civilizations. During the Middle Ages it became an integral part of both Jewish and Christian life and became one of the daily fears throughout the *shtetl* of the Jewish Pale in Eastern Europe from

**Khat* is Arabic for the fresh or dried leaves of *Catha edalis, Celastraeae,* an excitant of the central nervous system widely used by the Yemenites.

the fourteenth until the early twentieth century. Lilienthal records over 80 anti-evil-eye practices among Eastern European Jewry (*Encyclopedia Judaica* 1971, 6: 1000).

In the Muslim world, when a person admires another and possibly adds a few words of praise, the danger of the evil eye is so great that he must utter *t'bark Allah* "May God be blessed" (Westermarck 1926:417). In contemporary Israel, when a compliment is given, particularly to a child, the expression in Hebrew, "B'li ayin harah" ("May there be no evil eye") is common in ordinary conversation, especially among the middle-aged foreign-born. The expression is also used when speaking to persons who have recovered from illness.

Much of the Yemenite view of the evil eye is shared by other Jewish communities that have lived for centuries in the Muslim orbit. According to Trachtenburg's (1939) historical data, the Jewish comprehension of the evil eye is a synthesis of two early versions of the phenomenon. The Babylonian view was that certain harmful properties were inherent in the evil eye, and that unfortunate men are born *jettarori* (endowed with these properties). They shed rays of destruction with every glance, frequently unaware themselves of their dread influence. Some *jettarori* may be recognized by the peculiar and striking cast of their eyes, but others pass unnoticed until an unfortunate experience unmasks them. They are to be found "in all stations of life" (p. 55). The ancient Palestinians viewed the evil eye as a temporary situation, which became effective only when the person feels envy or hatred. "We may see that this belief is a hypostatization of the evil which man discerns in invidiousness, a translation of a profound poetic truth into the language of superstition" (p. 56).

The literature refers to the magical power of the eye, which can work benevolent wonders for the entire community. The sage Shimon bar Yochai, venerated throughout the Middle East by all Jewish communities, was thought capable of transforming an evil person into a "heap of bones by the burning fire in his eyes" (*Encyclopedia Judaica* 1971:6: 998). Trachtenburg observes that several Talmudic rabbis were considered to possess such powers, but he stresses that this was a minor theme. If one accepts the idea that these pious and virtuous men were considered to be people born with destructive psychic power in their eyes but exercised it for good purposes only, then one may also accept Trachtenburg's view that the evil eye is a product of a synthesis of the two early versions of the phenomena.

The evil eye is considered by many to be a possible cause for a wide range of misfortunes that befall mankind. Westermarck (1926), referring to Muslim and Berber Moroccan society of which the Jews were an integral part, particularly in the sharing of magical beliefs, wrote: "It is said that the evil eye owns two thirds of the graveyard or that one half of mankind dies from the evil eye or that the evil eye empties the castles . . . and fills the graves" (p. 414).

The evil eye is usually, although not exclusively, attracted to a situation that manifests health, happiness, success or beauty. Children, in particular, are considered natural objects for the evil eye, and parents must never show either to the child or to anyone else that they are proud or pleased with them. Persons involved in an important happening are more susceptible than others. Brides and bridegrooms, pregnant women, or nursing mothers are all targets for the evil eye (Van Gennep, 1960).

When Israel first became a state one of the difficulties of getting mothers to come to infant clinics was that the mothers thought their babies could be exposed to evil eyes en route. Mothers would arrive at the height of summer with their babies fully wrapped up and covered from head to foot so that no one would see the child naked. However, mothers had no problem in breast-feeding their infants in public, for then only the mouth of the baby need be exposed. The breasts of the mother were not regarded as an erotic part of the body.

Bearers of the Evil Eye

From whom does the evil eye emanate? Potentially anybody and everybody can give the evil eye. This supports Trachtenburg's view that the Yemenites believe the evil eye is a natural human enmity that emerges under certain sets of circumstances.

On the basis of my empirical experience over a period of 20 years of contact with the Yemenites, I find that women more often than men have been suspected of being the bearer of the evil eye. This is apparently true for the Mid-Eastern and North African Muslims as well. Westermarck (1926) observed that in Morocco, "Women are allowed to eat first at feasts; otherwise they might injure the men with their evil eyes . . . it is believed that misfortune would befall any person or animal at whom a bride looked before she had seen her husband at her arrival at his house" (p. 420). Shiloh (1969) also maintains that women throughout the Middle East are more prone to possess the evil eye.

Since the presence and power of the evil eye is so commonplace, it is thought that most times the person does not intentionally cause harm. It is felt that it is simply in the nature of man, and apparently even more so in the nature of woman, to feel envious. Envy is aroused when one sees something he or she would like to possess, a material, nonmaterial, or human object. Thus, as moral principle, a person should fight envious feelings, although there are situations that trigger these feelings, and then, willy-nilly, the evil psychic power goes into action.

Case Studies on the Evil Eye

Case 1. Mrs. Mazal, a middle-aged Yemenite woman, tells how she inadvertently became victim of an evil eye. In Yemen, on her wedding night, a friendly young Arab woman entered the house to pay her respects. She looked at Mrs. Mazal, beautifully dressed, with envy in her heart but at the same time expressed her genuine admiration by saying, "What beautiful eyes you have." After the ceremony, Mrs. Mazal became almost blind and remained so for many months. She was taken to an Arab healer. She carried out his instructions, but it took many months before her eyesight was fully restored. (Mrs. Mazal was married very young, even before she began menstruating. She was emotionally unprepared for married life; this leads one to suspect that she was suffering from hysterical blindness.)

Case 2. Mr. Zaccariyah, a 45-year-old Yemenite, had been given the evil eye by both a male and a female. He fell from a ladder, broke his leg, and had to be operated on, and now, after many months he is still suffering from the effects of the fall. When I asked him how it happened, he explained that the ladder had suddenly split into two. The ladder was in perfect condition and Mr. Zaccariyah was always steady on his feet. While talking to me he became thoughtful and suddenly the explanation for his misfortune became clear. Some time before the accident, he was working in a nearby Muslim town. An Arab woman looked at him and admired how he could climb the ladder like a young man. Clearly, he said, she had given him the evil eye, for he had never before fallen from a ladder.

On another occasion, he was given the evil eye by an Ashkenazi Jewish worker who was jealous of his prowess as an electrician. This worker said he could not understand how a Yemenite who had not studied the trade and could not even read a plan could work faster and better than he. That night when Mr. Zaccariyah came home from work, he saw that a rash had spread over both his hands. The rash went away only when he stopped working on that particular job.

The evil eye can penetrate one's dreams. This is considered very dangerous and must be dealt with immediately. If not, the child of the person who had the dream might die.

Theories about the Evil Eye

Westermarck (1926), in his interpretation of the significance of the evil eye, introduced the element of fear, not only fear of the envy of others but one's own fears about the future. He wrote, "In accordance with one of the laws of the association of ideas, which generally play such an important part in magical beliefs, namely, the law of association by contrast, the praise or admiration of something good readily recalls its opposite—the more so as the future is always uncertain and fortune is not to be relied upon" (p. 418).

Freud (1917–1919) arrived at essentially the same conclusion as Westermarck. Freud's psychoanalytic approach is based on the premise that every person knows that envy is part of human nature, and, therefore, if someone has something very valuable, he will arouse envy in others, since, if he were in the place of the other, he would certainly feel envious.

According to the Yemenite view, the influence of the evil eye is enough to cause illness and misfortune but not severe mental illness, which is the work of the spirits. For protection, infants and children are provided with amulets, which are tied on their arms or hung around their neck as preventive measures. It is generally accepted that fearful and anxious persons are very susceptible and open to the evil eye, since fear is in itself a cause of ill health or misfortune.

Responses to the Evil Eye

In most families there is a grandmother, an aunt, or some other female who is competent to control the effects of the evil eye. If the situation becomes serious and the misfortune persists, a specialist is consulted. The treatment was and still is more or less standard. The healer interviews the afflicted person, learning all he can about the situation. After referring to the "books" he can inevitably reveal the name of the malevolent agent. A piece of cloth from a garment of the evil carrier must be obtained. This is burned in a metal box, and the afflicted one breathes in the smoke. Mrs. Mazal, for instance, said that she was cured in this way. She added that urine obtained from a small boy was thrown over the burning fire before she inhaled the smoke. Others have their heads covered while breathing in the fumes. Embedded in the cloth covering their heads are small pieces of paper on which the specialist has written the names of appropriate angels. All the specialists have knowledge derived from the Kabbala, which enables them to find the combination of names of angels that must be written on ritually clean paper or parchment and that is appropriate to the individual situation. Astrology is also involved, and the stars of the client and the client's parents are consulted.

There is a great similarity between the techniques used in the different Middle-Eastern and North African countries in handling the pernicious effects of the evil eye. However, there are some regional innovations. Moroccan Jewish women in Israel explain that if a woman who has had some known family problem arrives at a wedding, the mother or other female relative of the bride would run her tongue around her mouth and whisper prayers. An Egyptian Jewish woman who had only one child and was unable to bear another child went to a circumcision ceremony of the newborn son of one of her close friends. To her embarrassment, she was first ignored, and then she heard the whisperings of prayers, obviously designed to neutralize the evil eye which she might inadvertently give.

For the Yemenites, the evil eye mechanism serves several purposes. It is a means of expressing feelings as well as an instrument of social control. Rambam, in his demand for moderation based on Judaic principles, stressed the dangers of extreme emotions, such as anger, jealousy, or pride. Jealousy, for instance, is injurious both to the person who is the object of jealousy and to the jealous person. The Yemenites emphasize the sanctity of both the home and the community through the sexual purity and modesty of its members, who use supernatural means to help them cope both with their misfortunes and with their emotions. The key to understanding the role of the belief in spirits, the evil eye, or the power of forbidden obsessive thoughts within the Yemenite health system, lies in the Yemenite concept of the nature of humans and of the ideal moral order.

REFERENCES

Bialik, N., and Y.C. Rabnitzki. 1956. *Books of Legends Based on the Talmud.* (In Hebrew.) Tel Aviv: Dvir, 6:620–55.

Burton, A. 1974. "The Nature of Personality Theory." A. Burton, ed., *Operational Theories of Personality*. New York: Brunner–Mazel, p. 7.

Encyclopedia Judaica 1971. Jerusalem.

Firth, R. 1959. "Acculturation in Relation to Concepts of Health and Disease." I. Galdston, ed., *Medicine and Anthropology*. New York: International Universities Press, p. 132.

Freud, S., 1917–1919. *The Complete Psychological Works of Sigmund Freud,* vol. 17. London: Hogarth Press.

Giridi, S. 1945. *From Yemen to Zion*. (In Hebrew.) Tel Aviv: Massada.

Kagan, Z. 1968. "Marriages of Humans and Female Demons in Fable and Folklore." (In Hebrew.) *4th World Congress of Jewish Studies,* vol. 2.

Kepach, J. 1961. *Yemenite Customs*. (In Hebrew.) Jerusalem: Ben Zvi Institute.

Kroeber, A. 1948. *Anthropology*. New York: Harcourt Brace.

Linton, R. 1936. *The Study of Man*. New York: Appleton–Century.

Saunders, L. 1958. "Healing Ways in the Spanish South West." E. Jaco, ed., *Patients, Physicians and Illness*. Glencoe, Ill.: Free Press, p. 199.

Shiloh, A. 1969. "The Inter-Action of Middle Eastern and Western Systems of Medicine. A. Shiloh, ed., *Peoples and Cultures of the Middle East*. New York: Random House.

Trachtenburg, J. 1939. *Magic and Superstition*. New York: Behrman's Jewish Book House.

Van Gennep, A. 1960. *The Rites of Passage*. Chicago: Univ. of Chicago Press.

Westermarck, E. 1926. *Ritual and Belief in Morocco,* vol. 1. London: Macmillan.

Zborowski, M. 1969. *People in Pain*. San Francisco: Jossey–Bass.

4

The Dybbuk: Cultural Context of a Cancer Patient

Lea Baider and *Henry Abramovitch*

Until now, relatively little attention has been paid to the cultural context of the cancer patients. Although a tremendous amount of research exists concerning various psychosocial aspects of cancer, especially breast cancer, the literature is correspondingly sparse when it comes to the potential impact of cultural variation upon the coping style of such patients (American Cancer Society, 1984; Engelman and Craddick, 1984; Silberfarb, 1982.)

The nature of this influence involves the entire range of doctor-patient contacts such as the decision as to how or when to seek medical advice; traditional notions about the cause and course of specific illnesses, including folk taxonomies of illness; expected behavior of patients once they have entered the sick role; and expec-

---

The Dybbuk is an expression of possession by an evil spirit.

tations from healers, whether medical or traditional, including the nature of the relationship, taboos, or even remuneration (Kleinman, 1980; Rothschild, 1981). In this paper, we will show by means of a case study how traditional folk categories and theories of illness can and do play an important role in the treatment of cancer patients.

THE PATIENT: CULTURAL AND FAMILY BACKGROUND

The patient, Hana, was first seen in the Oncology Department of a University Hospital in Israel in 1980. She underwent a right radical mastectomy for stage I breast carcinoma. The patient did not receive adjuvant treatment and up to the time of writing (1984) there has been no evidence of recurrent disease. Hana was one of ten participants (5 couples) in group psychotherapy for post-mastectomy women and their husbands, led by the first author in 1981.

Hana was born in 1943 in Dahook, Kurdistan, in the mountainous region of northern Iraq, close to the Turkish border. She was the last child born to elderly parents. There was a seven year difference between her and a set of twins, and a 22 year gap between her and her eldest brother. She spent her early childhood in that remote region, but at the age of eight came to Israel with her family. (There are more than 100,000 Kurdish families living in Israel today.) Her move to Israel was also a move from a traditional patriarchal society to the social status of "new immigrant." In Jerusalem, the family lived in crowded and difficult conditions. Hana completed six years of schooling. At the age of 16 she was married to her first cousin, Abraham.

Many studies of Kurdish culture have emphasized the strong preference for close cousin, especially parallel cousin, marriage (Barth, 1954; Hansen, 1961; Leach, 1940). In Hana's parents' generation, cousin marriage was well represented: two brothers and a sister married two sisters and a brother. Marriage was a matter of family policy (Hansen, 1961), not an affair of personal choice. A girl might refuse a marriage proposal, but it was considered a great insult. Hana resisted initial attempts by her family to marry her to her cousin, who had become interested in her when she was only 14. Finally, at the age of 16, Hana submitted to the arranged marriage largely in order to leave the stifling atmosphere of her parental home.

Such an endogamous marriage pattern often produces close-knit and highly supportive family networks. In Hana's case, such a support network was disrupted for two reasons. First, although she and Abraham were first cousins, they had grown up in rival towns in Kurdistan, which led to intra-family tensions. Second, she failed to produce offspring, in a culture where the main function of marriage is the birth of many children.

In such patrilineal societies, the social position of a young bride remains insecure until she has presented her husband and his lineage with a son (Feitelson, 1959; Field, 1952; Sabar, 1982). In fact, the infertility problem clearly lay with Abraham. This was generally denied by the family despite their knowledge of his search for a cure. The Kurdish tradition of assuming the woman to be at fault in an infertile marriage led Hana to live with a double stigma: that of not having children and that of being blamed for her childless state. One symbolic illusion accompanied Hana's many years of hope that some day she would have a child; that despite what doctors might say, like Sara and Abraham in the Bible, she and Abraham would eventually have a child.

Shortly before the cancer was discovered, Hana finally decided to undergo artificial insemination by donor, against the dictates of Jewish religion. Although some rabbinical authorities do permit artificial insemination under certain conditions, masturbation or any spilling of the seed is ordinarily forbidden and even considered spiritually dangerous as it may cause disembodied "semen demons" to come into being (Epstein, 1981; Sabar, 1982). For Hana such a step would also cause stigmatization by and isolation from her family circle.

THE CANCER AND THE DYBBUK

One month before her final decision to undergo artificial insemination by donor (AID), Hana found a lump in her breast. She subsequently underwent radical mastectomy (Stage I, Breast Carcinoma N_0M_0), with no adjuvant treatment.

From that time she found herself "in a nightmare." Already stigmatized as infertile, the loss of a breast made her feel no longer a woman. Her husband had an affair with a neighbor while Hana was in hospital, and for several months afterwards. AID was postponed by her doctors for at least five years because of its threat to her life. It represented the loss of her last avenue of hope for pregnancy.

It was at this point that Hana's dybbuk made his first appearance. She described "him" as belonging to her, yet controlling her thoughts and deeds. She held dialogues with him, discussing future actions and their consequences, and became certain that the dybbuk would offer her the gift of impregnation. His domination of her will and desires was comforting. As ostracized as she felt herself to be from husband and family, she was now not alone. She ceased to communicate fully with others. In group psychotherapy, hers was more an internal monologue spoken aloud than a verbal interaction.

Hana viewed her cancer as divine retribution, believing that only sinners are punished by "such a disease."

"I remember all the rituals and rites that my family used to perform when they knew that someone of our village was punished by having this disease. We never said the word, and we never used to talk to that family again. Just the word could be contagious and the smell of it could penetrate into the nostrils or mouth. It was a disgrace and a punishment by God. And now, I have it and I feel proud, exhilarated and in a state of constant anxiety. I am waiting for what will come next to see finally how to create a child from my own sentence of death."

Hana's thoughts about death fulfilled her deep desire for both punishment and revenge. Not only would she be bringing a child into the world from her body's cancer, but she would be conquering death through life. The dybbuk would not kill her. Rather, she would exchange her current life for one more pure, healthy and beautiful. There was no one she could trust except the dybbuk—not family, nor friends, nor the medical staff—so she entered into an alliance with him, submitting to his control.

Hana was certain that she would conceive and deliver a child in spite of her illness, to show that she had not sinned and that she was finally able to be a woman. But she was also sure that her illness was the result of the rage of God at her impertinence and independence: "God showed me who was stronger."

Abraham, her husband, remained passive in the face of the dybbuk. He viewed himself as the outsider in the triad, unable to compete with the dybbuk. Hana, meanwhile, was content to wait. She sensed that the dybbuk was testing her patience and that she would fianlly be rewarded. The external world and time lost their significance. Her waiting became part of the state of internal delusion, as a compensation for her body's asymmetry and loss. Her delusion of possession by the dybbuk bore the resemblance of a "symbiotic relationship," replacing the emptiness of her tumor and serving as a "symbolic pregnancy" (Groddeck, 1954).

DISCUSSION AND CONCLUSIONS

Kotarba (1983) described how the process of coping with chronic pain most commonly involves both the search for medical and non-medical cures and the search for meaning for intractable suffering. Kotarba goes on to describe how various religious, philosophical and mystical belief systems may be employed by sufferers to come to terms with their condition. The search for meaning is not restricted to persons with chronic pain but affects those suffering from cancer and other dreaded diseases with variable and unknown trajectories as well (Kleiman, 1980).

Hana's use of her dybbuk as a means of coping with her suffering may be understood as a way of dealing with her two basic difficulties: (1) the cancer, which threatened her own life, and (2) her infertility, which threatened her most basic mode of symbolic immortality (Lifton, 1979). Hana faced many serious difficulties: the lack of social support, the threat of recurrence, the loss of hope for children and the loss of her honor in her family. Her dybbuk might be viewed as a "benign delusion" (Sachs, 1978) in the form of a culturally sanctioned internal object (Bilu, 1984).

The dybbuk not only fulfilled a long-standing desire for a child, but also transformed the negative anxiety and fears of her illness into a positive, adaptive mechanism of replacement. Hana could function and cope with the fact of her mastectomy because now her target of concern and emotional charge was localized in the dybbuk power of fertility inside her body. She no longer missed her lost breast, since she no longer saw her deformity or any empty space. Her body was now complete. The dybbuk had chosen her to compensate for something that was taken from her and unrecoverable. Klopfer (1957) suggested the existence of a symbiotic relationship between the patient and his or her cancer. The tumor may be as important to the integrity of the ego as is the use of any other ego defense mechanism (Engelman and Craddick, 1984).

Although Hana's story might be seen as extraordinary in statistical terms, it represents a common pattern of cultural differentiation. Those in the helping professions often misinterpret the meaning that a specific event has for an individual, and tend to view such an event from their own social and cultural perspective. Any event in the life of a person has personal, social and cultural relativity. When an event is charged with life and death implications, the psychological response of the individual and the surrounding network is much more extreme. Cancer, particularly, is still resonant with metaphorical connotations of punishment and self-inflicted suffering. Knowing the facts does not necessarily give us more possibilities to help. Helpers may feel like observers of an ancestral drama in which superstition and faith are more appropriate tools for guidance.

Moving from this particular case to more general principles, it seems possible to isolate a number of factors which influence the cultural context of the cancer patient:

1. Factors affecting the decision to enter into the sick role and the acceptance of "cancer" as a disease; e.g., the social stigma of the disease, the prohibition of mentioning the name "cancer," the role of pain in cancer.
2. Factors affecting the culturally derived explanations for the disease. In contrast to the impersonal worldview of scientific medicine, many traditional cultures are based on personal worldview in which the question "Why did this disease happen to me?" is of prime importance.
3. Factors affecting the course of treatment such as degree of compliance, compatibility of treatment with cultural roles and expectations and symbolic impact of "side effects."
4. Factors affecting the patient's coming to terms with the cancer and the search for meaning for his or her future fate and suffering.

From the medical point of view, these factors may help to determine whether the patient will: (1) enter into the sick role, (2) comply with the often severe medical regime, or (3) seek out alternative, non-medical, forms of help which may complement or conflict with the medical care. Finally, they will determine the nature of coping, daily functioning and the "dying trajectory."

Part of the tension between the patients and the medical staff may reflect conflicts between traditional conceptions of healing and care, and the more technological, institutionalized medical worldview. As a result, patients are often placed in a position where they feel that they must choose between options of their own cultural repertoire and those offered by the prevailing medical ideology. A greater awareness of the cultural context of the cancer patient on the part of the caregivers may allow them to translate practice into cultural idioms, so that traditional culture and medical practice might complement rather than conflict.

REFERENCES

American Cancer Society. (1984). Proceedings of the working conference on Methodology in Behavioral and Psychosocial Cancer Research. *Cancer, 53*, 2217-2384.

Barth, F. (1954). Father's brother's daughter marriage in Kurdistan. *South-West Journal of Anthropology, 10*, 11-17.

Bilu, Y. (1984). The taming of deviants and beyond: Analysis of dibbuk-possession and exorcism in Judaism. *The Psychoanalytic Study of Society, 11*.

Engelman, S.E. and Craddick, R. (1984). The symbolic relationship of breast cancer patients to their cancer, cure, physician and themselves. *Psychotherapy and Psychosomatics, 41*, 68-76.

Epstein, Sh. (Ed.) (1981). *The Jews in Kurdistan: Daily life, customs, arts and crafts* (Hebrew), Israel Museum, Jerusalem, Israel.

Feitelson, D. (1959). Aspects of social life amongst Jews of Kurdistan. *Jewish Journal of Sociology, 1*(2), 201-216.

Field, H. (1952). The anthropology of Iraq, Kurdistan. Papers of the Peabody Museum of American Archeology and Ethnology. *XLVI* (2) Part II. Cambridge, MA: Harvard University.

Groddeck, G. (1954). On the mental cause of cancer. *British Journal Medical Psychology, 27*, 210-215.

Halper, J. and Abramovitch, H. (1982). The Saharanei as a mediator of Kurdish Jewish ethnicity. Proceedings: Eighth World Congress of Jewish Studies (pp. 72-84). Jerusalem.

Hansen, H. (1961). *The Kurdish woman's life: Field research in a Muslim Society.* Iraq. Copenhagen: Nationalmuseet.

Kleinman, A. (1980). *Patients and healers in the context of culture.* Berkeley: University of California Press.

Klopfer, B. (1957). Psychological factors in human cancer. *Journal Projective Techniques, 21*, 331-340.

Kotarba, J.A. (1983). Perspective of death, belief systems and the process of coping with chronic pain. *Social Science Medicine, 17*, 681-689.

Leach, E.R. (1940). Social and economic organization of Rowanduz Kurds. *Monograph of Social Anthropology*, London School of Economics, *3*.

Lifton, R.J. (1979). *The broken connection: On death and the continuity of life.* New York: Simon and Schuster.

Rothschild, H.R. (Ed.) (1981). *Biocultural aspects of disease.* New York: Academic Press.

Sabar, Y. (1983). Belief in demons and evil spirits among Jews of Kurdistan. (Hebrew) *Yeda-Am, 8*, 8-27.

Sachs, O. (1978). *Awakenings.* London: Penguin Books.

Silberfarb, P.M. (1982). Research in adaptation to illness and psychological intervention: An overview. *Cancer, 50*, 1921-1925.

5

Vulnerability to Drugs among Israeli Adolescents

Rachel Javetz and *Judith T. Shuval*

Abstract. The study aims at providing a base-line for understanding the socio-cultural context and correlates of drug use among adolescents in Israel. Thus drug use is hypothesized to be a critical component in a more comprehensive behavioral syndrome of deviance from generally accepted social norms, phrased in terms of vulnerability to drugs. The population studied encompassed students in grades 7–12 in all types of schools in Israel, including working youth who study in part-time programs. The sample, 5,914 students, was drawn on a national basis by a multi-stage procedure. The data were collected in 1979 by means of an anonymous, pre-coded questionnaire completed by students in classrooms. The findings show a relatively low overall prevalence rate of drug use among Israeli high school students, when compared to most Western countries. Yet the data indicate that specific sub-groups of the population are characterized by rates well above the overall rates. From the pattern of correlations between drug use and social behavioral variables, it can be seen that illicit drug use is most highly correlated with exposure to drugs as well as with petty delinquency and use of legal substances such as tobacco and alcohol. Somewhat lower correlations are found between drug use and symptoms of strain in the home and school environments. Future follow-up of the phenomenon will indicate whether it develops in a pattern similar to that found in other Western countries; or, if the rates of drug use remain stable as they did in the previous decade, the phenomenon should be analyzed in terms of specific characteristics of Israeli society which work against the spread of drug use among young people.

Drug Use in Israel

Traditional use of hashish has been known for centuries in the Middle East. However, in recent years there has been evidence in Israel, though not systematically recorded, for increased use of various types of drugs among specific segments of the population such as criminal elements, the bohemia and lately in wider strata of the adult and youth population. Use of drugs, with the exception of alcohol, is illegal in Israel unless prescribed by a physician.

Public concern and scientific interest in contemporary patterns of drug use have resulted in a number of social and psychological studies in this area. Surveys carried out in Israel over the past decade have concentrated almost entirely on secondary school students and their findings give support to the relatively limited scope of drug use in this population: approximately 5% lifetime prevalence of use of any kind of drug (1–7).

The evidence concerning drug use reported in these studies carried out at different times during the last 10 years suggests that the scope of the phenomenon has remained fairly stable. However the full complexities of the social processes involved are yet to be clarified. Two alternative hypotheses need to be considered:

1. The phenomenon is at its early stage and may follow the growth pattern obseved in other Western countries.

2. Idiosyncratic characteristics of Israeli society and its socio-cultural system result in a unique social pattern of drug use which is expressed in the rates observed.

The paucity of research makes it difficult to confirm either of these hypotheses, since the studies carried out thus far have been sporadic, non-replicative and conducted by different research teams. What is more, the overall rates reported tell little about drug use patterns in sub-groups of the population. The data presented here are drawn from an encompassing study which aims at providing a base-line for understanding the socio-cultural context and correlates of drug use in Israel (8).

Theoretical Considerations

In an attempt to explain the behavioral patterns associated with drug use among high-school students in Western countries, studies have resorted to different theoretical approaches. Such explanatory attempts differ in their level of generality, or specificity. They can be regarded as neither exclusive nor exhaustive in creating a complete and valid explanation of this complex issue.

These approaches which may be grouped in the following categories, while not completely exclusive, indicate different theoretical emphases (1, 9–18):

1. Drug use and exposure to drugs as a function of differential association,

i.e. as an outcome of conformity or non-conformity to specific significant social others or groups of others. Historically, in some societies or in sub-groups of others, drug use has been accepted as a normative phenomenon.

2. Drug behavior as an expression of intra- or interpersonal problems of adaptation.

3. Use of drugs as a manifestation of a general tendency toward deviance on the behavioral as well as the perceptual levels. It reflects thereby a low commitment to values accepted in society, as shown by apathy and rebelliousness.

4. Use of drugs as a function of the special needs and characteristics of adolescents: sensation-seeking, need for independence, disengagement from home, and identification with peers, etc.

The current study draws on all of these conceptions and is based on a theoretical approach formulated in terms of levels of vulnerability. Drug use among teenagers is hypothesized to be a critical component in a more comprehensive behavioral and attitudinal syndrome of deviance from generally accepted social norms. *Vulnerability to drug use* is thus defined as an ordered composite of behavioral patterns and normative perceptions in the personal and environmental contexts which deviate from the generally approved social patterns.

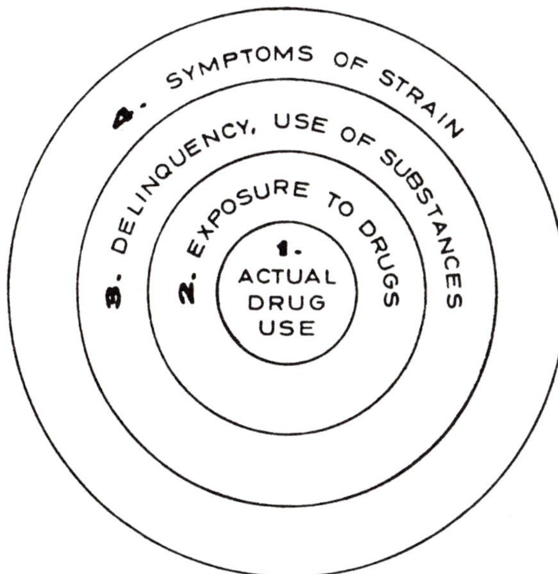

Figure 1. The model of vulnerability to drugs.

Operationally vulnerability to drugs is defined by four multi-variate sets which are hypothesized to form an ordered system described by four concentric circles as presented in Fig. 1. It may thus be seen that the multi-level approach proposed integrates theoretical conceptions of conformity and deviance, differential association, inter-personal strains, and maturation processes.

This model views adolescents who actually use illicit drugs as most vulnerable (circle 1). In addition it examines differential levels of vulnerability as measured by the extent of exposure to drug use (circle 2); tendency toward deviant behavior as expressed, for example, by petty delinquency and use of other substances not directly viewed as 'drugs' (tobacco, alcohol and psychoactive substances) (circle 3); and the extent to which various life areas are characterized by social and personal strain (circle 4).

It is hypothesized that the probability of *actual drug use* (1) decreases as an individual shows symptoms of vulnerability which are located in variable sets which are increasingly distant from the center of the model. This implies that persons *exposed to drugs* (2) are more likely to actually have used drugs (1) than are persons who are characterized by symptoms of *delinquency or use of substances* (3) but have not been exposed to drugs. Those with *symptoms of strain* (4) only are less likely than the former group to be characterized by *actual drug use*. Those with none of these symptoms of vulnerability are least likely to have actually tried drugs. Schematically $r_{12} > r_{13} > r_{14}$.* In other words, we hypothesize a probabilistic ordered set of vulnerability to drugs.

The order does not imply any necessary time series in the sequential appearance of vulnerability symptoms. The data refer to one point in time and therefore cannot shed light on the dynamics of the vulnerability syndrome. Yet we would hypothesize that no matter what the order of symptoms, they would be additive in predictive power.

It is the purpose of the present study to elucidate the empirical validity of this model and to explicate the nature of the relationships within the vulnerability syndrome.

Method

The study is geared to examine the vulnerability syndrome, described theoretically and operationally above, among students of the Jewish population in grades 7–12, in all types of schools in Israel.** The sample, 5,914 students, was drawn on a national basis by a multi-stage procedure and represents two principal sub-populations:

1. students in all schools under the auspices of the Ministry of Education (the sample comprised 2% of this population);

*r_{12} = the correlation between variables in circle 1 and variables in circle 2, etc.
**Arab-Israeli students were not included in the sample.

2. students in various part-time study programs for working youth under the auspices of the Ministry of Labor (the sample comprised 3% of this population).

The latter sub-population is generally from a lower socio-economic background than the former. Young people not in some school framework were not included in the study.* This population, including youngsters mostly in the age group 16–18, is likely in fact to include relatively high proportions of drug users. In view of the difficulty in sampling this sub-population, it was decided to focus the research on full and part-time students only. This distinction needs to be born in mind in considering the findings.

The data were collected during the 1978–79 school year by means of an anonymous, pre-coded questionnaire completed by students in classrooms. The questionnaire included items concerning various aspects of the student's family, leisure and school life as well as use of tobacco, alcohol and psychoactive substances and petty delinquency. In addition students reported on exposure to drug use, life-time prevalence of drug use, types of drugs used, age of first use and circumstances of drug use.

Satisfactory reliability is assured by low overall non-response rates for all items including those concerning illicit drug use: less than 1.5%. Furthermore there is high internal consistency among various items designed to measure similar conceptual dimensions (19). The Crowne and Marlowe Social Desirability scale (20) utilized as an additional tool for assessing reliability, does not change the basic relationships among the variables even in sub-groups showing high Social Desirability.

The purpose of the present paper is predominantly descriptive, and is geared to provide a general picture of drug use patterns in Israel. The data are thus presented in terms of bivariate tables and interaction among the independent variables is not considered in this paper.**

Findings

Eight discrete measures of drug use were utilized in the present research. These were first analyzed individually and subsequently combined in an overall Drug Use Index. We will first present findings based on the specific measures and then describe the Drug Use Index which will be used for the remaining analysis.

Overall findings by sex and age

Table 1 shows the distributions of the seven specific measures of drug use for the total population and by sex. Three principal findings emerge from these data:

1. The rate of drug use in general and of 'hard' drugs in particular is low in comparison to parallel data from other Western countries.

2. The two types of student populations, those in Ministry of Education schools and those in Ministry of Labor schools, differ in their rates of use. The former are consistently lower than the latter.

*This sub-population comprises approximately 15% of the age group concerned.

**Multivariate analysis of these data is presented elsewhere (8).

3. Boys show higher rates of use than girls consistently for all measures in both school systems. This finding parallels findings from other countries on which comparable data are available. For example, Table 1 shows that 3.3% of the boys in the Ministry of Education schools have ever used some kind of drug while among the girls in this population, only 1.3% report this behavior. The parallel findings in the Ministry of Labor schools are 8.4% and 4.1% respectively. Boys also show a greater tendency to use drugs frequently and a stronger proneness to experiment with 'hard' drugs. (All differences are statistically significant at the 0.001 level.)

It is worth noting the low rates of non-response as well as the consistency in the reported rates of drug use in Table 1. These patterns indicate a high level of reliability in the data reported.

TABLE 1. *Measures of drug behavior by sex (percentages)*

Drug behavior	Ministry of Education schools			Ministry of Labor schools		
	Males	Females	Total	Males	Females	Total
1. How many times have you used drugs?						
Never	95.1	98.1	96.7	88.5	96.0	90.2
Once	1.2	.7	.9	3.8	2.9	3.5
2–3 times	1.1	.4	.7	1.5	.6	1.4
4 or more times	1.0	.2	.6	3.1	.6	2.5
No answer	1.6	.7	1.1	3.1	–	2.3
2. At what age did you first use drugs?						
I've never tried	94.8	98.3	96.7	87.8	96.0	89.7
17 and after	.9	.2	.5	2.1	.6	1.7
Between 15–16	1.8	.7	1.2	4.1	2.9	3.8
Between 13–14	.4	.1	.3	1.7	–	1.4
Before I was 12	.6	.1	.3	1.0	.6	.9
No answer	1.5	.6	1.0	3.3	–	2.5
3. Have you used drugs during the past 6 months?						
Never	95.6	98.5	97.2	89.3	96.0	90.9
A long time ago	.8	.4	.6	3.8	1.2	3.3

(TABLE 1 cont'd)

Drug behavior	Ministry of Education schools			Ministry of Labor schools		
	Males	Females	Total	Males	Females	Total
Once or twice during the past 6 months	1.4	.2	.8	1.4	2.9	1.7
3 or more times	.9	.2	.5	2.6	–	2.0
No answer	1.4	.7	1.0	2.9	–	2.2
4. What type of drugs did you try?						
I've never used drugs	95.1	98.1	96.7	87.6	96.0	89.6
Hashish or marijuana	2.2	.8	1.4	4.7	2.3	4.0
L.S.D., opium or heroin	.6	.1	.4	1.7	.6	1.4
Other drugs	.1	.1	.1	.3	–	.3
Hashish and other drugs	.6	–	.3	2.2	1.2	2.1
No answer	1.4	.7	1.0	3.4	–	2.6
5. How did you obtain the drugs?						
I've never used drugs	94.8	98.0	96.6	87.6	96.0	89.6
From a friend or an acquaintance	2.6	1.0	1.7	5.7	4.0	5.2
I bought them from a supplier	.7	.1	.4	3.1	–	2.5
No answer	1.9	.8	1.3	3.6	–	2.7
*6. Where did you use drugs?**						
With a close friend	2.5	.8	1.6	5.2	3.5	4.7
In a small group	1.8	.5	1.1	4.8	1.2	3.9
At a large party	1.4	.3	.8	3.1	1.2	2.6
Alone	.9	.1	.5	2.4	–	1.8
7. Are you interested in trying drugs?						
Not interested at all	92.2	95.6	94.0	87.6	94.2	89.0
I've tried but I am not interested in continuing	1.5	.7	1.0	3.8	3.5	3.8

(TABLE 1 cont'd)

Drug behavior	Ministry of Education schools			Ministry of Labor schools		
	Males	Females	Total	Males	Females	Total
I am interested but have not tried drugs	2.8	2.6	2.7	1.2	1.7	1.3
I am interested and I have tried drugs	2.0	.5	1.2	4.0	.6	3.3
No answer	1.5	.7	1.1	3.4	–	2.6
8. Did anyone ever offer you drugs?						
No one ever offered me drugs	87.4	94.7	91.3	74.3	89.6	77.8
Yes, I've been offered but I refused them	8.0	3.7	5.7	15.7	6.4	13.6
Yes, I've been offered and I've tried them	3.1	.9	1.9	6.2	4.0	5.7
No answer	1.5	.8	1.1	3.8	–	2.9
The number of the pupils, total	2372	2775	5147	591	176	767

*In this item the percentages do not add up to 100% since only those using drugs in the specified setting are included.
Note: All questions in this and subsequent tables are translated from colloquial Hebrew, therefore, the English version may occasionally appear awkward. All differences are significant $P < .001$ by χ^2. This applies to all subsequent tables.

Table 2 shows the distribution of drug use by age. The prevalence increases systematically with age in both populations. These findings also demonstrate the dynamics of drug use among Israeli high school students: the pattern by which the phenomenon spreads from younger to older groups is clear. While the rate of lifetime prevalence among the 16–17 age group is five times as high as the rate in the 12–15 age group, Table 2 indicates that the rate among the 18-year-olds is only twice as high as the rate among the 16–17 age group (in the Ministry of Education schools). Thus we see that the main increase occurs around the age of 16 and subsequent growth is paced more slowly. Further research is needed to determine the developmental meaning of age 16 in the context of Israeli youth culture.

Table 2 also shows that prevalence among students in the Ministry of Labor schools at age 16–17 is roughly equal to that among the 18 age group in the Ministry of Education schools. We may therefore conclude that among the working youth in the Ministry of Labor schools, drug use is more widespread at an earlier age but is less correlated with age.

Even if prevalence of drug use in Israel is currently low, the potential of its spread may be discerned from data concerning students' personal and social exposure to drug use and users. Since exposure, of any form, to drugs can be regarded as a necessary condition to actual drug use, the exposure data underline potential trends of development of the phenomenon. Table 3 presents three measures of exposure by age.

The data indicate that on all three measures exposure to drugs is markedly greater than the scope of actual use. Thus 18.5% among the 12–14 age group personally know a person who has used drugs and 48% among the 17–18-year-olds report knowing such a person (item 1 in Table 3). Furthermore, 13% in the youngest group, 25% in the 15–16 age group, and 34% among the oldest have close friends who have tried drugs (item 2 in Table 3). Finally, 5% among the youngest have personally attended a gathering where drugs were used but close to 20% among the oldest group have had such an experience. In the Ministry of Labor schools exposure is more frequent but there is little variation among the age groups. This finding suggests that drug behavior is generally less deviant in the latter population.

Drug use index. In an attempt to construct a composite Drug Use Index which could serve as the principal predicted variable, the specific measures of

TABLE 2. *Number of times drugs have been used by age (percentages)*

	Ministry of Education schools (age)				Ministry of Labor schools (age)			
	12–15	16–17	18	Total	14–15	16–17	18	Total
Never	99.3	96.3	92.5	97.8	94.4	92.5	87.2	92.4
Once	.3	1.8	1.5	.9	4.5	2.8	5.8	3.6
2–3	.3	1.1	3.3	.7	1.0	1.3	3.5	1.5
More than 3	.2	.8	2.7	.6	–	3.4	3.5	2.5
Total %	100.0	100.0	100.0	100.0	100.0	100.0	100.0	100.0
N	3011	1737	333	5081	198	464	86	748

drug behavior were analyzed by means of a two-dimensional factor analysis. The results demonstrate the uni-dimensionality of the behavior measures. Table 4 shows the scores for the first and second factors and the percentage of variance explained by each. Thus we find the first factor explaining approximately 95% of the variance and the second factor explaining the remainder. Table 4 also indicates that the variance between the Factor 1 scores is small. In constructing the Drug Use Index we have therefore weighted them equally.

The score on the Drug Use Index is an arithmetic average of the respondent's scores on the specific measures shown in Table 4. For purposes of analysis the

TABLE 3. *Exposure to drugs by age (percentages)*

Exposure to drugs	Ministry of Education schools (age)				Ministry of Labor schools (age)		
	12–14	15–16	17–18	Total	14–16	17–18	Total
1. Personally acquainted with people who use drugs							
None	81.5	65.5	52.1	68.4	61.4	50.8	56.9
1–2	13.2	22.2	28.5	20.3	17.3	22.3	19.4
3 or more	5.3	12.4	19.3	11.3	21.3	26.8	23.6
Total %	100.0	100.0	100.0	100.0	100.0	100.0	100.0
N	1835	2144	1086	5065	423	313	736
2. Do you have close friends who use drugs?							
None	86.6	75.5	65.6	77.4	75.5	68.9	72.7
Don't know, possibly	11.6	16.7	14.9	14.4	12.9	13.0	13.0
Some have tried but don't use now	1.0	4.7	13.5	5.3	4.7	8.9	6.5
Yes, still using	.8	3.1	6.1	2.9	6.8	9.2	7.8
Total %	100.0	100.0	100.0	100.0	100.0	100.0	100.0
N	1837	2150	1084	5071	425	315	740
3. Have you ever been in a place where drugs were taken?							
Never	95.1	89.1	80.6	89.5	81.1	71.2	76.9
Once	2.9	6.3	10.7	6.0	9.5	14.7	11.7
More than once	2.0	4.5	8.7	4.5	9.5	14.1	11.4
Total %	100.0	100.0	100.0	100.0	100.0	100.0	100.0
N	1839	2145	1082	5066	423	313	736

TABLE 4. *Factor analysis of drug behavior measures**

Drug behavior measures	Ministry of Education schools		Ministry of Labor schools	
	Factor 1 weights	Factor 2 weights	Factor 1 weights	Factor 2 weights
Number of times drugs used	.94	.7	.94	.2
Age of first use	.91	.7	.92	.5
Use in past 6 months	.87	.4	.89	.4
Types of drugs used	.90	.19	.91	.17
How were drugs obtained	.87	.9	.93	.22
Interested in drugs	.73	.32	.85	.33
Has been offered drugs	.72	.26	.75	.14
Eigenvalue	95.7	4.3	96.3	3.7

*Item 6 in Table 1 was omitted.

continuum of the Drug Use Index was divided in terms of profiles defining three types of drug behavior. These referred to actual users, those who expressed an interest in using drugs or were offered drugs but did not report actual use, and the overwhelming group which declared that they had never used drugs and were not interested in trying. The distribution of these three groups in the two populations is as follows:

	Ministry of Education schools	Ministry of Labor schools
Drug users	2.4%	8.5%
'Tend' to use drugs	8.0%	13.8%
No use and no tendency	89.6%	77.7%

In the following presentation, the findings refer to the Drug Use Index in terms of its above categories.

Drug use and home characteristics

Four socio-demographic characteristics of the student's family will be considered in relation to drug behavior: father's education, ethnic origin, type of home community and religiosity.

TABLE 5. *Drug use by father's education**

Father's education	Ministry of Education schools		Ministry of Labor schools	
	%**	N†	%**	N†
0–4 years	1.8	703	9.9	202
5–8 years	2.2	1185	8.9	270
Incomplete high-school	1.9	1439	6.5	168
High-school matriculation	2.4	762	4.3	46
University	4.2	785	11.8	17

*'Drug use' refers to those scores on the Drug Use Index which indicate actual use of drugs. This applies to subsequent tables of the same form.
**Percentage of drug users in the cell.
†Size of cell.

Table 5 presents the relationship of drug behavior with father's level of education which may be viewed as a socio-economic indication. The data indicate that drug use among high-school students is not related to socio-economic background characteristics in any clear configuration. The findings show the following:

1. In the Ministry of Education sample, the distribution shows a generally positive, though not as strong, correlation between father's level of education and drug use.

2. In the Ministry of Labor schools the trend is reversed and the correlation is a negative one. (The rate of drug use among the last group whose fathers attained an academic education is based on a small number of cases and cannot be considered.)

Israel is characterized by a culturally heterogeneous population which has immigrated from a wide variety of countries of origin. For purposes of analysis these will be divided into three groups by father's country of origin: Asia–Africa, Israeli born, and Europe–America.* This variable will be referred to as ethnic origin.

Table 6 shows different rates of drug use in the two school populations by ethnic origin. The total distributions show that in the Ministry of Education schools the highest rates are among students whose fathers are Israeli born, and in the Ministry of Labor schools the highest rates are in the groups of both Israeli

*These are the groupings commonly used in social research in Israel.

TABLE 6. *Drug use by ethnic origin by sex*

Ethnic origin*	Ministry of Education schools						Ministry of Labor schools					
	Males		Females		Total		Males		Females		Total	
	%	N	%	N	%	N	%	N	%	N	%	N
Asia–Africa	3.9	1141	.3	1443	1.9	2584	10.8	399	3.4	118	9.1	517
Israel	4.4	433	1.9	482	3.1	915	10.9	55	–	10	9.2	65
Europe–America	2.9	715	2.6	773	2.8	1488	5.7	88	7.1	42	6.1	130
Total	3.7	2289	1.2	2698	2.4	4987	9.9	540	4.1	170	8.5	712

*Due to the large proportion of students born in Israel ethnic origin was defined by father's country of origin.

and Asian-African origin. In the Ministry of Education schools the lowest rates appear among those of Asian-African origin while in the Ministry of Labor schools the lowest rates occur among those of European-American origin.

A further differentiation appears in Table 6 when we consider the distribution by sex. Among males, the highest prevalence is, as noted above, among those of Israeli origin; among females, on the other hand, the highest rates occur among those of European origin in both sub-populations.

On the whole, it may therefore be said that ethnic origin of itself cannot be considered a clear-cut predictor of drug use in Israel.

In Table 7 which shows drug use by type of home community, we see that students who live in kibbutzim reveal the highest rates of drug use and tendency to use in the Ministry of Education schools. In this population differences among the other types of communities are insignificant. The high rates in the kibbutzim would appear to be associated with intensive peer interaction which is a function of common residence in dormitory settings. Other explanatory factors are undoubtedly relevant, and deserve separate in-depth investigation.* In fact, non-kibbutz students who live in dormitories in boarding schools also show equally high rates in both sub-samples of the population.

In the Ministry of Labor school, on the other hand, there are no students from kibbutzim and the highest rates of use appear among those coming from development towns. The latter are urban communities established after 1948. They are populated largely by immigrant settlers and are characterized by

*The large number of volunteers coming from Western countries to work in kibbutzim may provide one such explanatory factor.

TABLE 7. *Drug use and tendency to use by type of home community*

Type of home community	Ministry of Education schools			Ministry of Labor schools		
	% who used drugs*	% tend to use drugs**	N total	% who used drugs*	% tend to use drugs**	N total
Cooperative Village (Moshav)	1.8	7.2	346	4.4	13.3	45
Large Urban Community	2.3	7.7	3737	7.7	12.9	568
Development Town	2.4	8.7	412	18.6	14.6	75
Small Urban Community	2.6	8.3	390	5.8	17.3	52
Kibbutz†	5.6	13.2	196	–	–	–
Total	2.4	8.0	5081	8.5	13.4	740

*Based on those scores on the Drug Index which indicate actual use of drugs.
**Based on those scores on the Drug Index which indicate a tendency, i.e. expressed interest or were offered drugs.
†There are no kibbutz schools in the Ministry of Labor population.

numerous social problems. The remaining students in the Ministry of Labor schools demonstrate higher rates than comparable groups in the other population, but do not begin to approach those in the development towns. The latter segment of the population, in which 18.6% have actually used drugs, constitutes the most vulnerable group defined by any of the demographic variables examined. While young people in development towns are generally considered a relatively deprived group, it is of considerable interest to note that the comparable students in development towns studying full-time in the Ministry of Education schools, do not exhibit higher rates of drug use than groups in other types of communities. It would therefore seem that dropping out of the regular school system in the social context of a development town is associated with a particularly high level of vulnerability to drug use, or other factors in that context of which vulnerability is a part.

Religiosity affects vulnerability to drug use in Israel in a manner which parallels that found in other Western countries (11, 18). Table 8 shows that students from more religious homes are less vulnerable than those from non-observant backgrounds.* This pattern is systematic and clear-cut in all age groups in the Ministry of Education schools. In the Ministry of Labor schools, in which most students come from Asian-African background, religiosity carries a somewhat different implication: while a minority are truly orthodox, the majority define themselves as traditional so that differentiation by religiosity is less reliable. Therefore the distribution of drug use rate by religiosity is somewhat ambiguous.

Home characteristics. In addition to analysis by a variety of demographic variables, four of which have been discussed, drug use was examined in terms of the quality of inter-relationships in the student's home environment. Two dimensions of the family system were considered: structural and relational.

Structural characteristics of the student's family, such as broken homes, divorced or widowed parents or students living away from their parents, were found to account for only a small portion of the variance of drug behavior. On the other hand, variables describing the quality of relationships with parents and the atmosphere of the home were found to be stronger predictors of vulnerability. Table 9 which presents two of the principal variables considered, shows that students characterizing themselves as having strained family relations reveal relatively high rates of use and tendency to use drugs. For example, highest rates are found among those reporting poor relations with parents or who have run away from home. This pattern is seen among both males and females.

School characteristics

Here again, in the school, structural and relational variables were utilized to examine the effects of school life on vulnerability to drug use. In a general sense the pattern of findings concerning the school environment parallels that found with regard to the home. The structural variables such as type of school (e.g. academic, vocational, agricultural) are less related to drug use than variables describing the quality of the student's relationships with teachers and conformity to various school norms. In other words strain symptoms such as poor relationships with teachers, neglect of homework, cheating on exams, low motivation to excel in school work, cutting classes and truancy, are the principal factors associated with vulnerability to drug use. In Table 10 we see that the highest drug use appears among students who show the lowest level of conformity to a selected set of central school norms. It is also of interest that students characterized by poorer relations with their teachers more frequently report drug use. (The latter finding does not appear in Table 10.)

*See footnote to Table 8 for definition of religious observance.

TABLE 8. *Drug use and tendency to use by religiosity and age*

Religiosity*	12–15**			16–17			18			Total		
	% who used drugs	% who tend to use drugs	N total	% who used drugs	% who tend to use drugs	N total	% who used drugs	% who tend to use drugs	N total	% who used drugs	% who tend to use drugs	N total
Ministry of Education schools												
Orthodox	1.2†	2.8	498	2.0	6.0	300	2.7	5.4	74	1.6	4.1	872
Traditional	.3	3.9	771	2.4	10.8	462	4.7	17.6	85	1.3	7.2	1318
Observe some customs	.8	4.0	1423	4.9	13.3	691	6.7	22.0	118	2.4	7.8	2232
Not religious	1.6	8.5	316	6.4	21.7	281	20.0	23.6	55	5.3	15.5	652
Total	.8	4.2	3008	4.0	12.8	1734	7.5	17.5	332	2.4	8.0	5074
Ministry of Labor schools												
Orthodox	10.2	11.9	59	7.5	9.3	160	4.2	20.9	24	7.8	11.1	243
Traditional	2.2	8.7	46	8.9	17.7	113	10.0	25.0	20	7.3	16.2	179
Observe some customs	5.1	8.9	79	8.1	18.7	160	23.6	15.6	34	9.1	15.7	273
Not religious	7.7	7.7	13	13.4	6.7	30	25.0	12.5	8	13.7	7.9	51
Total	6.1	9.6	197	8.4	15.8	463	15.1	19.8	86	8.6	13.8	746

*The respective question in the questionnaire was phrased as follows: 'Is your home religious?', answers: '1. Strictly, orthodox; 2. Yes, traditional but not so orthodox; 3. We observe only some religious customs; 4. Do not observe any religious traditions.'

**In the Ministry of Labor schools, this group comprises 14–15 year-olds.

†The percentage of those who have used drugs among the respective age and religiosity categories.

TABLE 9. *Drug use and tendency to use by quality of family relations and sex*

	Ministry of Education schools						Ministry of Labor schools					
	Males			Females			Males			Females		
	% who used drugs	% who tend to use drugs	N total	% who used drugs	% who tend to use drugs	N total	% who used drugs	% who tend to use drugs	N total	% who used drugs	% who tend to use drugs	N total
Relationships with parents												
Excellent	2.0*	7.9	1464	.8	4.3	1430	7.7	14.1	362	1.5	7.4	68
Good	5.0	14.0	744	1.6	6.7	1069	12.5	17.9	168	5.3	1.3	76
Poor	19.6	21.6	97	1.4	12.0	217	21.4	21.4	28	7.4	22.2	27
Running away from home												
Never considered	1.9	7.7	1418	.7	3.6	1603	5.3	10.9	339	1.9	3.7	108
Considered, but did not carry out	4.4	13.8	749	1.5	7.3	992	11.7	21.4	154	7.5	7.5	53
Ran away once or more	18.5	20.7	135	4.1	22.8	123	28.4	23.9	67	–	40.0	10

*The percentage of those who have used drugs among the respective cell.

TABLE 10. *Drug use by conformity to school norms*

School Norms	Percentage of Drug Users**					
	Ministry of Education schools level of conformity*			Ministry of Labor schools level of conformity*		
	High	Medium	Low	High	Medium	Low
Preparing home-work	1.1	1.5	5.3	8.0	6.1	10.8
Honesty in exams	1.4	2.1	5.0	3.4	7.0	20.8
Excelling in school-work	1.5	2.5	6.4	7.6	7.2	19.7
Regular classroom attendance	1.0	3.3	8.5	3.8	12.5	21.1
Non-truancy	1.4	5.3	16.0	5.5	10.4	27.2

*The five variables measuring normative compliance in school had originally 3–5 response categories, ranging from high to low conformity to the respective norm. For comparative purposes, these ordinal scales were collapsed into three levels of conformity: high, medium, and low.

**The percentage of respondents reporting actual use of some kind of illicit drug, among all respondents showing the respective level of conformity to the respective norm.

In examining drug use in all specific classroom settings included in the sample (237 classes), the phenomenon was found to be highly dispersed rather than concentrated in a small number of schools or classes. In other words drug users, even though they are very few in number, are widely spread in many parts of the school system. Thus the potential for contact with users and exposure to drug culture is considerably greater than the low overall prevalence would indicate. However, only further research which will elaborate the dynamic aspects of the phenomenon could shed light on the issue of whether the 'drug culture' is socially 'contagious'.

Use of other substances and petty delinquency

While drug use is illegal in Israel, smoking cigarettes, alcohol consumption and use of tranquilizers, pep pills and sleeping pills (by prescription) are legal. The use of these substances, particularly tobacco, is more widespread than the use of illicit drugs in Israel. Thus in the Ministry of Education schools 12% smoke daily or occasionally, 2.4% consume alcohol 'quite often', and 4.3% report using some type of psychoactive pills occasionally or regularly. In the Ministry of Labor schools the corresponding percentages are 32.7%, 3.8% and 7.9%.

TABLE 11. *Drug use and tendency to use by use of other substances*

Frequency of the use of substances	Ministry of Education schools			Ministry of Labor schools		
	% who used drugs	% who tend to use drugs	N total	% who used drugs	% who tend to use drugs	N total
Tobacco						
Does not smoke and not interested in trying	.5	4.0	3940	2.1	5.2	420
Does not smoke, interested in trying	1.5	8.9	324	4.0	—	25
Smoked but stopped	4.8	21.4	229	11.9	22.0	59
Smokes occasionally	7.3	25.5	369	10.7	26.4	102
Smokes daily	25.0	33.7	232	25.2	28.0	143
Alcohol						
Does not drink	1.2	5.4	3583	4.9	10.1	508
Does not drink, interested in trying	2.8	10.2	108	10.0	—	20
Drinks rarely	4.5	14.0	1267	14.2	24.2	190
Drinks quite frequently	14.6	19.5	123	35.8	17.9	28
*Psycho-active substances**						
Never used	2.0	7.7	4686	6.6	13.5	688
Once or twice	3.0	10.4	163	28.9 (once or twice and occasionally combined)	11.1	45
Occasionally	4.0	9.4	149			
Quite frequently	13.9	25.0	36	42.9 (quite frequently and frequently combined)	21.4	14
Frequently	31.4	17.2	35			

*Respondents were asked to report on tranquilizers, sleeping pills or pep pills.

Table 11 shows the relationship of use of these legal substances to drug behavior. There is a clear and systematic patterning which shows a strong positive correlation in both sub-samples between use of the two types of substances. Those who use these legal substances, particularly on a regular basis, reveal rates of drug use which are several times higher than non-users of the legal substances. A similar relationship was shown in other studies as well (7, 21–24).

It is worth noting that 25% of those who smoke cigarettes daily have also used illicit drugs and in this case the rate of drug use among cigarette smokers in the Ministry of Education schools reaches the rates found in the Ministry of Labor schools. It will be recalled that in previous data reported there was a systematic difference between the two populations. Thus it would seem that regular cigarette smoking in the normative context of the Ministry of Education schools, where it represents stronger evidence of social deviance, is an indication of relatively high vulnerability to drug use.

Since drug use is practiced by such a small proportion of the population, such behavior is apparently anti-normative in the context of Israeli society. Hence, another set of anti-normative behavior patterns were considered in relation to drug use. These concern several forms of petty delinquency such as shoplifting, sneaking into movies and football matches, and stealing cars. In all cases, those reporting these behaviors also show a higher level of vulnerability to drugs. Among those in the Ministry of Education schools who engaged in shoplifting or car stealing more than once, some 20% have also used drugs. In the Ministry of Labor schools, among these sub-groups some 50% have used drugs.

Structure of the Vulnerability Syndrome

The principal hypothesis of the study states that the probability of drug use decreases as an individual shows fewer symptoms of vulnerability (see above and Fig. 1). The data in Table 12 provide evidence for confirmation of the ordered nature of the levels of the vulnerability syndrome as hypothesized.

It will be recalled that the four composite sets comprising the syndrome levels were: 1) actual drug use, 2) exposure to drugs, 3) delinquency or use of substances, and 4) symptoms of strain in the home and school environment. Each of these levels was measured empirically by several sets of variables examples of which have been presented above. In order to test the hypothesis, variables from syndrome levels 2, 3 and 4 were correlated with the Drug Use Index (level 1). Goodman-Kruskal's Gamma was utilized to measure the relationship.

Table 12 presents mean Gamma correlations between five sets of variables which represent the principal substantive areas investigated. The Gamma in

TABLE 12. *Average correlation (Gamma) between drug use and groups of vulnerability variables*

Groups of vulnerability variables	Average correlation (Gamma)	
	Ministry of Education schools	Ministry of Labor schools
Symptoms of strain in home and family	.33	.27
Symptoms of strain in school	.45	.32
Use of other substances	.61	.60
Petty delinquency	.60	.65
Exposure to drugs	.79	.74

Table 12 fall in three groups as follows: the lowest relationship to drug use appears with variables concerning the student's home and school environment (Gamma ranges from .27–.45); the relationship of use of substances and petty delinquency to drug use is somewhat stronger (Gamma ranges from .60–.65); the strongest relationship to drug use appears with variables concerning exposure to drugs (Gamma ranges from .74–.79). These findings support the hypothesis proposed.

Further confirmation utilizing more sophisticated analysis such as Logit (logarithmic transformational analysis) and Smallest Space Analysis appears in the full Hebrew report of the study (8).

Summary and Conclusion

Despite the relatively low overall prevalence of drug use among Israeli high school students found in this study, the data indicate that specific sub-groups of the population are characterized by rates well above the overall rates. While some of these sub-groups are numerically small, the rates of drug use and exposure to drug use within them are far from negligible. Examples of such sub-groups are the top grades of high school, students in boarding schools, part-time students in the Ministry of Labor schools, particularly those in development towns, and students in the kibbutzim.

In addition to the concentration of drug use in specific sub-groups, the research has shown that drug use is spread in many segments of the population. Since the vulnerability syndrome includes such symptoms as strain or problems in family and school contexts as well as use of legal substances, it is clear that vulnerability is relatively widespread and is not confined to special sub-populations. The wide dispersion indicates that no youngsters, even those presently lowest on vulnerability symptoms, can be considered insulated from the influence of what could be called a drug-using environment.

At this point neither of the two initial hypotheses can be clearly supported. The findings relevant to these hypotheses may be summarized as follows:

1. Low overall prevalence of drug use in Israel.

2. No evidence for change in prevalence of drug use in Israel during the decade ending in 1979.

3. A pattern of correlations between drug use and social behavioral variables which is similar to that found in other Western countries.

If future research reveals an increase in prevalence rates, this would provide support for hypothesis 1) which states that the phenomenon is at its early stage and may follow the growth pattern observed in other Western countries. If, on the other hand, future research shows continuation of the stable prevalence rates seen during the decade ending 1979, this would provide support for hypothesis 2) which indicates that specific characteristics of Israeli society work against the spread of drug use among young people. The nature of these social mechanisms is yet unclear and in-depth sociological research is needed to elucidate those features of the society which account for such stability.

Acknowledgements. The authors wish to thank the Ministry of Education and Culture, the Ministry of Labor and the Israel Foundation for Educational Research, Ltd. for their support.

References

1. Barnea Z. A multiple model of readiness to use drugs by adolescents. Soc Welfare 1978;1:359-83 (in Hebrew).
2. Peled Z, Schimmerling H. The drug culture among the youth in Israel: the case of high school students. Israel Institute of Applied Social Research, 1971.
3. Peled Z, Schimmerling H. Attitudes of school youth to the topic of drugs. Israel Institute of Applied Social Research, 1971.
4. Shoham SG, Geva N, Kliger D, Chai T. Drug abuse among Israeli youth: epidemiological pilot study. Bull Narc 1974;26:9-28.
5. Shoham SG, Rahav G, Esformes Y, et al. Differential patterns of drug involvement among Israeli youth. Bull Narc 1978;30:17-32.
6. Adler I, Kandel DB. Cross-cultural perspectives on developmental stages in adolescent drug use. New York: Columbia University School of Public Health, 1980 (mimeo).
7. Kandel DB, Adler I, Sudit M. The epidemiology of adolescent drug use in France and in Israel. Am J Pub Health 1981;71:256-65.
8. Javetz R, Shuval JT. Patterns of vulnerability to drugs among high school students in Israel. Jerusalem: The Hebrew University Medical School, 1980 (in Hebrew).
9. Braucht NG, Brakarsh D, Rollingstad D, Berry KL. Deviant drug use in adolescence: a review of psychological correlates. Psychol Bull 1973;79:92-106.

10. Ginsberg IJ, Greenley JR. Competing theories of marijuana use. J Health Soc Behav 1978;19:22-34.
11. Jessor R, Jessor LS. Theory testing in longitudinal research on marijuana use. In: Kandel DB, ed. Longitudinal research on drug use. New York: John Wiley, 1978: 41-71.
12. Kandel DB. Inter and intragenerational influences on adolescent marijuana use. J Soc Issues 1974;30:197-235.
13. Kandel DB, ed. Longitudinal research on drug use. New York: John Wiley, 1978.
14. Kandel DB, Kessler RC, Margulies RZ. Antecedents of adolescent initiation into stages of drug use: a developmental analysis. In: Kandel DB, ed. Longitudinal research on drug use. New York: John Wiley, 1978:73-99.
15. Lucas WL, Grupp SE, Schmitt RL. Predicting who will turn on: a four-year follow-up. Int J Addict 1975;10:305-26.
16. Miranne AC. Marijuana use and achievement orientations of college students. J Health Soc Behav 1979;20:194-9.
17. Smith GM, Fogg CP. Psychological predictors of early use, late use and non-use of marijuana among teenage students. In: Kandel DB, ed. Longitudinal research on drug use. New York: John Wiley, 1978:101-33.
18. Tec N. Grass is green in suburbia. New York: Libra Publications, 1974.
19. Amsel S, Mandell W, Matthias L, Mason C, Hocherman I. Reliability and validity of self-reported illegal activities and drug use collected from narcotic addicts. Int J Addict 1976;11:325-36.
20. Crowne D, Marlowe D. The approval motive. New York: John Wiley, 1964.
21. Goode E. Drugs in American society. New York: Knopf, 1972.
22. Johnston LD, Bachman JG, O'Malley PM. Drugs and the class of 1978: behaviors, attitudes and recent national trends. National Institute on Drug Abuse. Washington DC: US Government Printing Office, 1979.
23. Johnston LD, Bachman JG, O'Malley PM. Drug use among American high school students 1975-1977. National Institute on Drug Abuse. Washington DC: US Government Printing Office, 1977.
24. Kandel DB. Stages in adolescent involvement in drug use. Science 1975;190:912-4.
25. Goodman LA, Kruskal WH. Measures of association for cross-classifications. J Am Stat Assoc 1954;49:732-64.

6

Social and Psychological Determinants of Breast-Feeding and Bottle-Feeding Mothers

David Tzuriel and *Leonard Weller*

Our study examined the psychological and sociological factors of mothers who breast-feed and mothers who bottle-feed. Most of the data came from 124 Israeli mothers who had just given birth, but selective data were also collected on three additional samples – 108, 465, and 135 new mothers. The psychological measures included the Bar-Ilan Sex Role Inventory (Tzuriel, 1984) and body image as measured by the drawing of a dressed and a naked woman. None of the psychological factors distinguished between the two groups of women. Social factors, however, did distinguish between the two groups: Mothers who breast-fed were of Asian-African background; were less educated; held blue collar jobs or did not work; perceived their husbands, relatives, and friends as supporting their decision to breast-feed; and tended to be more religious. The discriminant function analysis – which predicted 73% of the cases – showed that the mother's education, her religiousness, and her perceived support of friends and relatives were the most important factors.

Our study focuses on the psychological and sociological factors pertaining to the mother's decision to breast-feed or bottle-feed. We are particularly concerned with (a) differences in breast-feeding practices of the two major ethnic groups in Israel (Jews of Asian-African descent and Jews of European descent), and (b) whether various social and psychological factors equally affect the two groups of mothers.

In the United States, from the beginning of this century to the 1930s, middle-class mothers were more likely than lower class mothers, to bottle-feed. In recent years, breast-feeding has become popular among middle-class mothers and bottle-feeding has become popular among lower class mothers, thus reversing the earlier trend (American Academy of Pediatrics Committee on Nutrition, 1974; Potter & Klein, 1957; Robertson, 1961). Although this phenomenon may be in response to medical and psychological reports, there is continuing uncertainty as to the importance of personality factors in determining the feeding method. Surprisingly, the literature on factors distinguishing between breast-feeding (BRSF) and bottle-feeding (BOTF) is relatively sparse.

With regard to personality, several researchers concluded that the decision to breast-feed or bottle-feed is little related to personality difference; it is related to the learning of information, practical considerations, and attitudinal differences (Bramble, 1978; Golub, 1978). Two studies, however, suggested that BRSF mothers have better psychological adjustment than BOTF mothers (Adams, 1959; Newton, 1951). Another finding was that BRSF mothers were more passive, but also more accepting of the feminine role and more interested in body contact than BOTF mothers (Brown, Chase, & Winston, 1961).

Several investigators have focused on the effects of family, friends, and health care professionals on the woman's decision to breast-feed. Not surprisingly, support from friends, medical personnel, and family members—as well as a supporting cultural environment—has been found to encourage breast-feeding (Bramble, 1978). Still, there are minor deviations on this major theme. Bramble (1978) reported that the influence of friends on feeding practice was negligible. Bryant (1982) found that for Cuban and Puerto Rican lower class mothers, the single most important source of information on breast-feeding was the maternal grandmother, in contrast to Anglo families in which the husband participated in decisions on feeding of infants.

Heath (1976), who was concerned with breast-feeding persistence, examined 54 mothers, both prenatally and postnatally, who planned to breast-feed their infants. She administered a monthly questionnaire for 5 months beginning with the ninth month of pregnancy. The findings indicated that women who continued breast-feeding more than 3 months had received significantly more accurate information about nursing and more social support than mothers who had weaned before 3 months. Also, the husbands of the long-term BRSF mothers were significantly more educated than were the husbands of short-term BRSF mothers. No other differences, however, were found between the two groups of mothers on either social, personality, or mental health factors. A multiple-regression analysis showed that the single most important factor in breast-feeding persistence was nursing information, which accounted for 57% of the variance. This result concurs with Golub's (1978) findings that the mother's knowledge about breast-feeding was an important determinant of her method of feeding.

In what is perhaps the study most similar to our own, Switzky, Vietze, and Switzky (1979) studied 42 BRSF and 42 BOTF mothers and found that all the mothers decided on their method of feeding before they entered the hospital. Unlike the results reported previously, the mother's own feeding history did not predict her feeding behavior. Furthermore, both groups perceived their husbands as approving their feeding behavior method.

Also examined in the literature is the question of why mothers give up breast-feeding. In a recent study, Bryant (1982) reported that the major reasons for not breast-feeding were the unavoidable public exposure of the breasts, apprehension by the mother that her own anxiety will spoil the milk, the need for a special diet, breast milk leaking between feedings, and the mother's concern that her figure will be ruined. This is consistent with a study by Brown, Lieberman, Winson, and Pleshette (1960) undertaken approximately 20 years earlier; they reported that BOTF mothers believed that breast-feeding caused breasts to be less attractive, inhibited their freedom, and in general was less convenient. In a theoretical, if not speculative vein, some authors suggested that avoidance of breast-feeding is related to a dislike of nudity and sexuality (Newton & Newton, 1967) and to fear and guilt associated with the expectation of erotic pleasure (Potter & Klein, 1957).

Unlike most other studies that have been concerned with factors relating to the persistence of breast-feeding behavior, our study dealt with psychological and sociological determinants of breast-feeding behavior of women who had just given birth—that is, while they were in the hospital (usually 3 days). In most hospitals in Israel, the women are pressured, directly or indirectly, to breast-feed. It is assumed that women who resist the nurses' and doctors' pressures will be different from the "conforming" women who choose to breast-feed at least while in the hospital.

We were particularly interested in two psychological factors: (a) psychological androgyny (Bem, 1974) and (b) body image as measured by the drawing of a dressed and a naked woman.

According to Bem, femininity and masculinity are two separate orthogonal dimensions rather than two end points of a single bipolar dimension. Psychologically androgynous persons who possess both feminine and masculine sex roles are considered to be more flexible and adaptive than sex-typed persons. Our hypotheses were (a) that feminine women would be more likely than masculine women to breast-feed and (b) that androgynous women would be more likely than undifferentiated (low on both masculinity and femininity) or masculine women but less likely than feminine women to breast-feed. Thus, we predicted the following order (from low to high) in terms of the relationship to breast-feeding: masculine, undifferentiated, androgynous, feminine.

We measured body image in this study by asking mothers in the maternity ward to draw first a figure of a woman and then a figure of a naked woman. We looked for how free or comfortable the women felt about their bodies and expected that the BRSF mothers would feel more at ease with their bodies than BOTF mothers would. Our expectations were that BRSF mothers would be more likely to draw the picture, particularly the naked one; would make less erasures (indicative of self-criticism); would elaborate more fully and portray the proportions of the body more adequately. For the naked picture, we also expected them to emphasize the breast and to draw the nipples as well as pubic hair.

The major sociological variables included in this study were country of origin, religiousness, occupation and education of mother and father, the mother's intention to return to work, the husband's presence at delivery, whether the baby was planned, and support of social network. Another factor was whether or not the marriage was ethnically homogeneous. Several of these social factors require explanation, as they are related specifically to Israeli society.

COUNTRY OF ORIGIN

Country of origin is the most important social variable in Israeli society. It is a socially defined category that forms a basis for group differentiation and identification. Following the proclamation of the state, Jews had to flee Arab countries, and some communities came in their entirety. Although there are important differences among the various communities (e.g., Yemenite Jews and Iraqi Jews), still as a group, the Easterners hailed from a fundamentally feudalistic and patriarchial style, their life style resembling that of the Moslems. The European immigrants were the pioneers who established the ideology of collectivism and egalitarianism and become the elite in the society. Although today, each ethnic group comprises about 50% of Israeli society, families of Asian-African extraction belong predominantly to a lower social class than families of Western origin.

In the country of origin, Eastern women were restricted to the traditional housewife/mother role, with little place left for the formal education of women. In Israel, at the time these women were of school age, education was "forced" upon them by a compulsory education law for the first 8 years of schooling. Because the Asian-African population is less oriented toward education for women and is not as well off economically, they are less likely to send their daughters to high school and college. Those of Asian-African background are more likely to be more religious, and religiosity further acts to restrict the amount of education they receive. Further, religious families in Israel have the option to send their children to religious schools, which tend more to prepare girls to be housewives than to engage in higher level occupations. Although Asian-African women have increased their participation in the labor force, they are still assuming the lowest jobs on the occupational scale.

RELIGIOUSNESS

People define themselves as to whether they are religious (which in Israel means orthodox), traditional (intermediate category), or nonreligious. This is one of the most important distinctions in Israeli society and is manifested (among other ways) by two parallel school systems, religious and nonreligious, which are both government supported. In the questionnaire and in the analysis, the women were asked to state with which of the three categories they were identified.

MOTHERS WORKING OR PLANNING TO RETURN TO WORK

All new mothers are allotted 3 months' vacation pay from the National Insurance Institute and their jobs are held for them for that period. It is also virtually impossible to fire a pregnant woman. It is assumed that mothers who planned to return to work were less likely to breast-feed than mothers who planned not to return to work.

"MIXED" MARRIAGES

We were also especially interested in mixed marriages in Israel—between Jews of Asian-African descent and Jews of European origin—which comprised almost 25% of the marriages in 1983. It should be noted that we were studying mothers and fathers born in Israel whose parents were for the most part born abroad. In fact, this was the impetus of this study because nurses' observation in one Israeli hospital reported that a higher percentage of the mothers who refused to breast-feed came from mixed couples, that is, the parents of the wife or the husband came from different areas of origin. These nurses reported that the preference for bottle-feeding was found even among primiparous mothers, who presumably would not have the excuse of having had past breast-feeding difficulties. It was further reported that some of these mothers were quite determined not to breast-feed; for example, they came to the hospital with medication to be taken after delivery to prevent lactation. The observation coincides with Entwistle and Doering's (1981) conclusion that a woman's feeding decision is almost always made before she enters the hospital. As the nurses' observations were most intriguing and not readily explainable, we decided that a more systematic investigation was called for.

METHOD

Subjects

Most of the data came from a sample of mothers who had just given birth (N = 124, Sample A) in a hospital located in the Tel-Aviv area. The sample included mothers who breast-fed their infants and mothers who did not. The mothers were randomly selected at the hospital within a 2-month period. Besides the background information (e.g., social class, country of birth, religiousness), all mothers were asked to complete the Bar-Ilan Sex Role Inventory (BI-SRI; Tzuriel, 1984) and to answer a questionnaire relating to various aspects of nursing (see Measures section for a description). In addition, all mothers were requested to draw both a woman and a naked woman, in that order.

Data on a second sample (N = 108, Sample B) were collected in another metropolitan Tel-Aviv area hospital. This sample was utilized mainly to collect information on the personality variables of sex-role typing.

Although virtually all the mothers in both samples who were approached agreed to participate in the study and answered the questionnaires, a large number refused to draw a woman.

In a third hospital located in the northern part of the country, information was available only on feeding mode and whether the marriage was homogeneous or mixed. One group of data consisted of 465 mothers (Sample C), and the other consisted of 135 primiparous mothers only (Sample D).

In the analysis, we have dealt with two major areas: social and psychological. The social area included parents' country of origin; religiousness; parents' occupation and education; husbands', relatives', and friends' support for breast-feeding or bottle-feeding; mothers' expectation to return to work after 3 months; husband's presence at the delivery; whether the baby was planned; and reasons given for bottle-feeding by BOTF mothers. The psychological factors included sex-role typing and body image.

The mothers in all samples were divided into two groups: breast-feeders and bottle-feeders. Several cases in which the mothers were unable to breastfeed for health reasons were eliminated from this study.

Measures

"Draw-a-Woman." Each woman was asked first to draw a woman and then a naked woman. Each drawing was categorized according to 10 dimensions: (a) draws or refuses to draw; (b) picture: frontal, back, or profile; (c) picture: full figure, lines, or impressionistic; (d) elaboration: full, medium, little, or very little; (e) sexy or not sexy; (f) erasures or no erasures; (g) breast emphasized: much, little, or none; (h) pubic hair emphasized in naked picture: much, little, or none; (i) proportions: good, average, or poor; (j) nipples appear in naked picture: yes or no.

Both investigators independently judged each picture for each of the 10 dimensions. With the exception of sexy or not sexy, there was a minimum of 90% agreement for each of the categories.

BI-SRI. The BI-SRI (Tzuriel, 1984) is similar to Bem's Sex Role Inventory (Bem, 1974) in structure and item-selection procedure. It was designed to fit Israeli norms and is composed of 20 masculine (M), 20 feminine (F), and 20 neutral items.

Procedure

Our assistant, dressed in a nurse's uniform, administered the aforementioned instruments and interviewed the mothers in the maternity ward during the first 3 days after delivery. She observed and recorded whether or not the mother breast-fed her baby before approaching her to answer the questionnaires. After completion of the interview and after completing the BI-SRI, the mother was asked to draw a picture of a woman and then a picture of a naked woman. When asked to draw a woman, the mothers did not know that the next task would be to draw a naked woman.

RESULTS

Personality Characteristics

Comparison of BRSF mothers to BOTF mothers on the personality factors in both Samples A and B revealed no significant findings. No category of "Draw-a-Woman," such as elaboration of breasts, drawing of pubic hair and nipples, figure elaboration, body proportions, not even refusal to draw a naked woman, distinguished between the two groups, both for the regular and the naked drawing of the woman (data not reported). It is interesting to note, however, that in both samples combined, 22% refused to draw both the dressed and the naked woman and another 9% refused to draw only the naked woman.

On the BI–SRI, median splits of the distribution of masculinity and femininity scales were performed to classify mothers into four groups: masculine (high M/low F), feminine (low M/high F), androgynous (high M/high F), and undifferentiated (low M/low F).

For both Sample A and Sample B, chi-square analyses of sex-role type by feeding mode failed to disclose a significant relationship (see Table 1). As shown in Table 1, not only did we not find the anticipated rank order of breast-feeding according to sex-role type, but even the simpler anticipation of feminine breast-feeders and masculine non-breast-feeders was not supported.

Social Characteristics

Table 2 shows the social characteristics of the BRSF and BOTF mothers.

Country of origin. The results for country of origin and mode of feeding are reported for both Samples A and B. As shown in the top part of the table, for both samples, mothers of Asian-African descent are more likely to breast-feed than are mothers of Western origin, who are more likely to bottle-feed. The results are significant for Sample A ($p = .10$) and for Sample B ($p = .08$). Taken together, we conclude that country of origin is related to method of feeding behavior.

Religiousness. Orthodox and traditional mothers were combined and compared with secular mothers. The results indicated that although BRSF mothers tended to be more religious or traditional than were BOTF mothers, the differences were not significant.

TABLE 1
Frequency Distribution of Breast-Feeding and Bottle-Feeding Mothers by Sex-Role Type in Samples A and B

	Sample A[a]		*Sample B*[b]	
Sex-Role Type	*BRSF*	*BOTF*	*BRSF*	*BOTF*
Masculine	14	6	18	7
Feminine	17	9	21	10
Undifferentiated	27	11	21	7
Androgynous	27	13	16	8
Total	85	39	76	32

[a]$\chi^2 = .27$, $df = 3$, $p > .05$.
[b]$\chi^2 = .58$, $df = 3$, $p > .05$.

TABLE 2
Social Characteristics of Breast-Feeding and Bottle-Feeding Mothers

Characteristics	*BRSF*	*BOTF*	χ^2	*df*	*p*
Country of origin (Sample A)					
Asian-African	45	15	2.72	1	.10
Western	34	22			
Country of origin (Sample B)					
Asian-African	38	10			
Western	30	18	3.23	1	.08
Religiousness					
Orthodox and traditional	42	13			
Nonreligious	33	19	2.12	1	.15
Occupation of father					
Blue collar	47	21			
White collar	29	17	0.46	1	ns
Occupation of mother					
Blue collar	28	9			
White collar	20	23			
Homemaker	33	5	16.48	2	.001
Plans to return to work					
Yes	34	26			
No	36	8			
Doesn't know	15	5	7.91	2	.02
Education of husband					
Partial high school or less	46	3			
High school	37	11			
More than high school	24	24	11.59	2	.01
Education of mother					
Partial high school or less	24	3			
High school	37	11			
More than high school	24	24	11.59	2	.01
Husband present at delivery					
Yes	33	23			
No	52	16	4.38	1	.05
Discussed breast-feeding with husband					
Yes	72	31	0.19	1	ns
No	15	8			
Husband is for or against breast-feeding					
For	63	10			
Against	1	6			
Not interfere	14	23			
No answer	7	1	39.63	3	.001
Discussed breast-feeding with friends/relatives					
Yes	56	23			
No	29	11	0.03	1	ns
Friends/relatives for or against breast-feeding					
Yes	46	11			
No	5	0			
Mixed	6	8			
Don't know	28	16	9.39	3	.05
Baby planned					
Yes	38	28			
No	28	11	2.12	1	.15

Note. Occasional missing data account for differences in number of cases in each variable.

Occupation. The husbands' occupations were divided into two major groups: blue collar and white collar. A significant difference was not found between the groups. However, when the women's jobs were likewise classified, with a housewife category added, it was found that a large percentage of the BRSF mothers did not work or were blue collar, whereas a larger percentage of the BOTF women were white collar ($p < .001$). Also, a larger percentage of BOTF mothers than BRSF mothers planned on returning to work ($p < .02$).

Education. The education of both the fathers and mothers was classified as to whether they had gone to high school, completed high school, or had more than a high school education (some had only 1 year above high school). As shown, the BOTF mothers and their husbands had significantly more education than the BRSF mothers and their husbands ($p < .05$, husbands; $p < .01$, wives).

Social support. Table 2 also shows that fewer husbands of the BRSF women were present at the delivery than were husbands of the BOTF women. Specifically, 38% of the husbands of the BRSF women were present at the delivery compared to 59% of the husbands of the BOTF women ($p < .05$).

The women were asked whether they discussed with their husbands the manner in which they would feed their babies and whether they thought their husbands were for or against breast-feeding. Table 2 shows that approximately 80% of both groups of women discussed with their husbands whether or not to breast-feed (no significant differences between the two groups). However, a majority of BRSF mothers claimed that their husbands wanted them to breast-feed, whereas a minority of BOTF mothers claimed that their husbands wanted them to breast-feed ($p < .001$).

With regard to discussing breast-feeding with friends or relatives, there were no significant differences between the BRSF mothers and BOTF mothers; 66% of the former group discussed it with their relatives or friends, as did 59% of the latter group. But again, the BRSF women reported that a larger percentage of their friends and relatives supported breast-feeding, as compared to 25% of the BOTF mothers ($p < .05$).

Finally, the women were asked whether or not the pregnancy was planned. A significant difference was not found, although there was a trend for more BRSF women to state that the baby was not planned.

The mothers who did not breast-feed were asked in an open-ended question why they decided to bottle-feed their babies. Their reasons were classified into three groups: physical discomfort (in most cases, mothers said that they were afraid of physical pain); emotional (breast feeding is considered "primitive," "ugly," "not pleasant"); intellectualization ("no control of how much milk is drunk," "cow's milk is just as good"). As shown in Table 3, the

TABLE 3
Reasons for Not Breast-Feeding

Reason	*Number*	*Percentage*
Fear of physical pain	16	41
Emotional (primitive, ugly, not pleasant)	17	43
Intellectual (no control over milk, regular milk just as good)	3	7
Other	2	5

replies were equally divided into the first two categories: fear of physical pain (41%) and emotional reaction (43%).

Homogeneous versus mixed marriage. The mode of feeding was investigated further in relation to ethnic homogeneity versus ethnic heterogeneity of the marriage. The data were classified as to whether the mother's parents were of the same country of origin (both of Western or both of Asian-African origin) or of mixed origin (one of Western and the other of Asian-African descent). Country of origin refers to the ethnic origin of the grandparents of the newborn infant, as virtually all the parents were born in Israel.

The results as reported in Table 4 show that for two Tel-Aviv metropolitan hospitals (Samples A & B), there were no significant differences. However, for each of the two groups of mothers of the northern hospital, large significant differences were found ($p < .001$). Most of the BRSF mothers came from homogeneous marriages, whereas most of the BOTF mothers came from mixed marriages.

In sum, the results showed that, in contrast to the women who bottle-fed, the women who breast-fed were much more likely to be of Asian-African origin, of lower educational level, and of lower occupational level (although there was no significant difference in the husbands' occupations). Their husbands were less likely to have attended the birth. The BRSF mothers also tended to be more religious or traditional and were less likely to have planned their pregnancies. They also perceived their husbands, relatives, and friends as approving breast-feeding.

Because many of these social factors overlap (those of Asian-African origin are more likely to be of lower social class and less likely to plan their pregnancies), we performed a discriminant function analysis where the criterion variable was feeding method, BRSF *versus* BOTF, and the predictors were the social variables. The discriminant function analysis revealed that the BRSF mothers were significantly different from their BOTF counterparts ($p < .001$). The canonical correlation was .52, and Wilks's lambda was .73. The discriminant function correctly predicted 73.17% of the grouped cases. The highest predicting variables in descending order were mother's education, friends' and relatives' support, and mother's religiousness.

TABLE 4
Distribution of Breast-Feeding and Bottle-Feeding Mothers According to Homogeneous Versus Mixed Ethnic Marriages in Samples A to D

	Sample A (N = 109)[a]		*Sample B (N = 108)*[b]		*Sample C (N = 465)*[c]		*Sample D (N = 135)*[d]	
Mode of Feeding	*Homogeneous*	*Mixed*	*Homogeneous*	*Mixed*	*Homogeneous*	*Mixed*	*Homogeneous*	*Mixed*
BRSF	56	19	52	12	367	53	99	20
BOTF	21	13	21	3	9	36	4	12

Note. The mothers whose parents were Israeli-born were excluded from the analyses.
[a] $\chi^2 = 1.34$, $df = 1$, $p > .05$.
[b] $\chi^2 = .48$, $df = 1$, $p > .05$.
[c] $\chi^2 = 119.26$, $df = 1$, $p < .001$.
[d] $\chi^2 = 23.29$, $df = 1$, $p < .001$.

DISCUSSION

ne main finding is the failure of the psychological factors to differentiate etween mothers who breast-fed and mothers who bottle-fed. On what might be called an obvious hypothesis, differences in sex-role typing between the BRSF and the BOTF mothers, a significant difference was not found: The BRSF women were just as masculine as their BOTF counterparts, or alternatively, the BOTF women were just as feminine and androgynous as the BRSF women. This is consistent with the findings of two other studies on the effects of sex-role typing on infant interaction (Bem, 1975; Bugen & Humenick, 1983).

What did emerge was that these two groups of women differed only on social factors. The BRSF women were of Asian-African background; less educated; of lower occupational level; more religious; and perceived their husbands, relatives, and friends as supporting them. The discriminant function analysis revealed essentially the same pattern of results except that education, but not country of origin or occupation, was found to be the critical factor in determining the method of feeding behavior. This concurs with other findings from 20 years ago, which showed that despite the large differences in family size between Jews of Asian-African descent and Jews of European descent in Israel, the mother's education is the most important determinant of family size (Matras, 1965).

The major finding of the study that those who breast-feed in Israel are the lower class women resembles the pattern that once existed in the United States. We can briefly point to the historical and cultural similarities and differences that promote breast-feeding in both countries.

Until recently, it was the fashion in developed countries to dispense with breast-feeding. Middle-class women were more reluctant to breast-feed in public because of embarrassment (Carballo, 1977), feelings of modesty (Salber, Stitt, & Babott, 1959), and concern for its effect on their bodies and on their relationship with their spouses (Weichert, 1975). At the turn of the century, when physicians certified the virtues of bottle-feeding over breast-feeding, middle-class women were more receptive to the message due to their proclivity for the scientific approach to mothering. They, more than lower class mothers, could also afford the new bottles and sterilizers.

Although women's emancipation may have been the underlying cause for the overall decline in breast-feeding (Salber et al., 1959), today, having succeeded in American society, middle-class women may feel that by breast-feeding they are fulfilling themselves as women. In a most comprehensive review on the reproductive role of the human breast, Anderson (1983) claims that we have confused the role of the breast as a nurturing agent with its role as an organ of sexual attraction. Accordingly, breast-feeding becomes more attractive to the middle-class, educated, liberated women who wish to deemphasize the erotic nature of the breast, but retain its inherent female sexuality.

Even though many lower class women in Israel work (an economic necessity), this seems to be tolerated, not preferred. For many breast-feeding women, particularly those of Eastern origin, breast-feeding may help justify their not working outside the home. A large proportion of lower class women are orthodox and so are encouraged to breast-feed. And because the use of contraceptives—at least for the male—is forbidden by Jewish law, breast-feeding is one useful way of family planning (Anderson, 1983). Furthermore, many Eastern families eat milk products quite minimally, if at all, and for them breast-feeding is more convenient. Besides saving money by not buying milk, they do not have to purchase dairy dishes, pots, and utensils, which would be required by Jewish custom.

As previously discussed, the combination of country or origin, lower education, and religiosity leads women more to the household role than to higher level occupations. These variables—and more could be added—as to why breast-feeding is prevalent among less educated, more religious Eastern women include those specific to Israeli society as well as those held in common with the United States. There are also influences operating on the middle-class Israeli women not to breast-feed. In spite of the image of the Israeli woman as being sexually equal, the fact is that in many ways she is not. To cite just a few examples, women's income is lower than that of men; in the army, which is compulsory for both men (3 years) and women (2 years), the women are relegated, for the most part, to secretarial work; and even in the kibbutz, women do "women's work." There is no women's movement in Israel to speak of. This is essentially because Israeli women are satisfied with their role as wife and homemaker (Hazelton, 1977). Consequently, today's Israeli middle-class woman is similar to the American middle-class woman before she turned to breast-feeding.

Results of the distribution of BOTF and BRSF mothers in the four samples (Table 4) revealed significant results only in Samples C and D. Women of mixed marriages tended to bottle-feed much more than women of homogeneous marriages. A possible explanation might be related both to the perception of breast-feeding as indicative of educational and cultural sophistication as well as to subtle "status rivalry" characterizing mixed couples relative to homogeneous couples. It is possible to assume that women who perceive breast-feeding as "primitive" and "unsophisticated" and who also feel some strain in regard to their relative status as coming from a different cultural origin might reject breast-feeding as a means, external as it is, to prove their high status. Our research leads us to the conclusion that cultural and historical factors, and not only social class, have an impact on the acceptance or rejection of breast-feeding.

ACKNOWLEDGMENTS

This study was supported by a grant from Bar-Ilan University, Internal Fund for Research.

We thank Ada Merav, Zahava Katz, and Carmela Shmilovitz for their assistance in data collection and Mati Ronen for his help in statistics and computer work. We are indebted to Dr. Sam Cooper for his helpful comments.

REFERENCES

Adams, A. B. (1959). Choice of infant feeding technique as a function of maternal personality. *Journal of Consulting Psychology, 23,* 143–146.

American Academy of Pediatrics Committee on Nutrition. (1973, September 7). Introduction of solid foods. *Medical World News,* pp. 31–36.

Anderson, P. (1983). The reproductive role of the human breast. *Current Anthropology, 24,* 25–45.

Bem, S. L. (1974). The measurement of psychological androgyny. *Journal of Consulting and Clinical Psychology, 47,* 155–162.

Bem, S. L. (1975). Sex-role adaptability: One consequence of psychological androgyny. *Journal of Personality and Social Psychology, 31,* 634–643.

Bramble, D. E. (1978). *Psychological correlates of infant feeding practices.* Unpublished doctoral dissertation, University of Guelph, Canada.

Brown, F., Chase, J., & Winson, J. (1961). Studies in infant feeding choices of primipara. *Journal of Projective Techniques, 25,* 412–421.

Brown, F., Lieberman, J., Winson, J., & Pleshette, N. (1960). Studies in choice of infant feeding by primiparas: I. Attitudinal factors and extraneous influence. *Psychosomatic Medicine, 22,* 421–429.

Bryant, C. A. (1982). The impact of kin, friend and neighbor networks on infant feeding practices: Cuban, Puerto Rican and Anglo families in Florida. *Social Science and Medicine, 16*(20), 1757–1765.

Bugen, L. A., & Humenick, S. S. (1983). Instrumentality, expressiveness and gender effects upon parent-infant interaction. *Basic and Applied Social Psychology, 4,* 239–251.

Carballo, M. (1977). Social and behavioral aspects of breast feeding. *Journal of Biosocial Science, 9*(Suppl. 4), 57–68.

Entwistle, D., & Doering, S. (1981). *First birth: A family turning point.* Baltimore: Johns Hopkins University Press.

Golub, S. (1978). The decision to breast feed: Personality and experiential influences. *Psychology, 15*(2), 17–27.

Hazelton, L. (1977). *Israeli women.* New York: Simon & Schuster.

Heath, H. E. (1976). *Determinants of parental behavior: The effects of support and information of the breast feeding experience.* Unpublished doctoral dissertation, Bryn Mawr College, Bryn Mawr, PA.

Matras, J. (1965). *Social change in Israel.* Chicago: Aldine.

Newton, N. (1955). The relationship between infant feeding experience and later behavior. *Journal of Pediatrics, 58,* 25.

Newton, N., & Newton, M. (1967). Psychologic aspects of lactation. *New England Journal of Medicine, 277,* 1179–1188.

Potter, H. W., & Klein, H. (1957). On nursing behavior. *Psychiatry, 20,* 39-46.

Robertson, W. D. (1961). Breast feeding practices: Some implications of regional variations. *American Journal of Public Health, 51,* 1035-1042.

Salber, E. J., Stitt, P. G., & Babott, J. G. (1959). Patterns of breast feeding in family health clinic: Duration of breast feeding and reasons for weaning. *New England Journal of Medicine, 260,* 310-315.

Switzky, L. T., Vietze, P., & Switzky, S. (1979). Attitudinal and demographic predictors of breast feeding and bottle feeding behavior by mothers of six-week old infants. *Psychological Reports, 45,* 3-14.

Tzuriel, D. (1984). Sex role typing and ego identity in Israeli, Oriental and Western adolescents. *Journal of Personality and Social Psychology, 46,* 440-457.

Weichert, C. (1975). Breast feeding: First thoughts. *Pediatrics, 56,* 987-990.

7

The Age of Transition

Nancy Datan, Aaron Antonovsky, and *Benjamin Maoz*

Researchers who stray too far from the focus of their work are irresponsible, but researchers who ignore the broader implications of their work are no less irresponsible. In this chapter we shall try to avoid either of these two extremes, speculating on the implications of our study within the bounds of good sense, recognizing that we are obliged to address the broader issues of women's lives in a modernizing world, acknowledging in advance that our research is suggestive but far from definitive. If you must hang, choose a tall tree, advises the Talmud; in this chapter we hope to creep cautiously out on one or two limbs.

We shall commence by restating the most important lessons we learned from our study: the strengths and weaknesses of our original hypotheses; middle age as neither loss nor liberation, but transition; the centrality of cultural stability; the significance of the fit between personal aspirations and socially accessible roles; the overwhelming consensus in welcoming the cessation of fertility; the relation of culture to stress. We will go on to review some of the struggles which accompanied our learning. And finally, we shall conclude by suggesting some of the larger lessons we have learned.

At the Israel Institute of Applied Social Research, our study was known by its Hebrew identification: *Gil Hama'avar.* In everyday Hebrew this phrase can refer specifically to menopause; it can also signify middle age, in women or in men. *Menopause:* the cessation of menstruation and of fertility. *Middle age:* no longer young. The literal meaning of *gil hama'avar,* however, is "the age of transition," a meaning we came to appreciate more fully as our study progressed into the final phases of analysis and interpretation. Either of the common translations seemed an incomplete representation of our findings, in which change, more often than loss, was a dominant theme for women in all five subcultures.

Our first glimpse of this understanding came in the pilot study, which led us to begin to think in terms of a net balance of gains and losses and helped us design a questionnaire which opened the way to our first major lesson. This lesson we would now phrase—and it is applicable to all stages of the life cycle, from early infancy through old age—as neither loss nor liberation, but *transition.*

Our study began with competing hypotheses about the relationship between women's responses to the changes of middle age and the degree of modernity characteristic of their ethnic groups. Antonovsky and Maoz anticipated that the traditional woman would welcome the changes of menopause and middle age, which bring an end to childbearing and menstrual taboos, the raised social status of matriarch, and the powerful and meaningful roles of mother-in-law and grandmother. The modern woman, on the other hand, would resist and regret these changes, which signify the loss of youth in a youth-oriented culture and a lost childbearing potential which had never been fully used. These differences, they anticipated, would be expressed as an inverse linear relationship between psychological well-being and the degree of modernity, with the more traditional women the most contented at middle age. Looking back with the wisdom of hindsight, they now wonder whether their scientific hypothesis may have been grounded not only in the dominant literature of psychoanalysis and the observation at a distance of traditional culture, but also in their own identity: they were middle-aged males who were closely familiar with modern women and were living in the cultural climate of the mid-1960s.

Datan rejected this view—influenced by the work of Bernice Neugarten and, it must be admitted, having a personal stake in the outcome of the study herself—and predicted that the modern woman would be best prepared to cope with the changes of menopause and middle age, having coped actively with changes earlier in the life cycle and bringing to her middle age a broader range of coping skills in a predominantly modern culture which, at least in principle, prized these skills. Datan regarded the loss of fertility as inconsequential to the modern woman, who had ceased childbearing years before; it was the traditional woman, she suggested, who would regret her lost fertility, since so much of her identity was bound up with childbearing, leaving her with little besides losses for her later years. Datan expected these differences to be expressed as a direct linear relationship between psychological well-being and the degree of modernity, with the most modern women the happiest in middle age.

If it was our fortune to commence our research with the aid of clear, conflicting hypotheses, it was our exceptional good luck to find our questions answered. Our hypotheses as well as our unstated expectations found answers. As it turned out, each hypothesis was half right. The survey findings yielded a curvilinear relationship between the degree of modernity and self-reported psychological well-being. That is to say, the balance of *naches* and *tsoris,* of joy and sorrow, was most positive for the Central Europeans and the Arabs—the most modern and the most traditional women in our study. Psychological well-being was lowest among the Persian women, who represent the midpoint on our continuum between tradition and modernity. The Turks, midway to modernity, and the North Africans, still close to tradition, were intermediate between the relatively high well-being of the European and Arab women, and the relatively low well-being of the Persians.

Datan, then, had been right—but only about the modern women. Antonovsky and Maoz had also been right—but only about the most traditional women. With the wisdom of hindsight, we learned our second major lesson: the stability of the cultural context, rather than its specific content, may facilitate adaptation to life cycle change. Our European and Arab sub-cultures have the highest measure of cultural stability: the immigrant European women came to a country where the dominant cultural values were European, while the Moslem Arab villagers, living in a stable traditional setting, saw change gradually penetrate their lives. The transitional groups, however—the Turks, Persians, and North Africans—had been socialized into traditional settings and were then transplanted into a modern culture where traditional cues no longer served them. At the same time, the freedoms of modernity were not open to them: they saw no choices for themselves among a plurality of roles, seeing only the broadened horizons open to other women. Self-reported psychological well-being was lowest among the Persians, the group which, by external indicators, such as the degree of traditionalism in the life history and the modernity of the present life context, would appear to have experienced the greatest measure of discontinuity. The Turks, born into a modernizing culture and immigrants to modern Tel Aviv, and the North Africans, born into traditional families and immigrants to towns in which they were the dominant group, experienced less abrupt transitions than the Persian women, born to traditional families and immigrants to modern Tel Aviv.

We found that the content of women's responses to menopause and middle age is shaped by the cultures in which they grew up: the balance of gains and losses seen by women is specific to each culture, a product of earlier life experiences and the resulting resources a woman brings to middle age, as well as the dominant values in her culture. Women in each of the five subcultures of our study viewed menopause as a combination of gains and losses, but this combination differed by subculture. The Europeans, for example, saw a possible decline in emotional health; the Turks, Persians, and North Africans were concerned over a decline in physical health; and the Arabs' responses included pleasure at an end to ritual uncleanliness.

Cultural stability, then, shapes the likelihood of personal adaptation; cultural context, the specific responses to specific concerns. However, the cultural context also specifies the extent to which the social structure makes provision for the fulfillment of the cultural expectations. The modern European woman's psychological well-being may be threatened if her expectations of enhanced companionship with her husband or of a return to work or of voluntary activities are frustrated by the options her social reality makes available to her. The Arab women—and we cite a pattern increasingly frequent since our study—may no longer adapt as well as in the past when her sons marry and, instead of moving into the household with daughters-in-law and grandchildren, move out of the village into town. Successful adaptation requires a fit between the specific cultural expectations and the structural realities. Not all European or Arab women in our study were able to find an ecological niche.

Differences among women in five such different groups were not surprising. What was surprising, however, was the finding that women in all groups welcomed the cessation of fertility, despite large variation in conception control and fertility history, ranging from the Europeans at one extreme, who typically bore one or two children and prevented or aborted unplanned pregnancies, to the Arabs at the other extreme, some of whom were continuously pregnant or lactating between menarche and menopause. That this response is paced by the life cycle and not shaped by prior events in the psychosexual history is suggested by the Europeans' attitudes toward their actual and ideal family size: two-thirds of the European women reported that they would have wanted larger families, but that economic or political circumstances—this cohort bore children at the time of the establishment of the State of Israel, the War of Independence, and a period of economic austerity—prevented larger families. Notwithstanding the desire to have borne more children, often expressed strongly and poignantly, the European women—like women in all other groups—no longer wished to be capable of pregnancy. We have interpreted this finding as suggestive of a developmental change in adulthood, linked—like many earlier developmental changes—to a maturational change.

Finally, our multidisciplinary approach to the question of women's responses to the changes at middle age permitted us to answer the question which originally stimulated the broader study: Is the higher rate of hospitalization of European women for involutional psychosis a consequence of differential rates of stress in different cultures, different modes of expression of stress, or differential diagnosis? From the survey, the medical examination, and the follow-up psychiatric interviews, we were able to provide tentative answers.

There was no support for our first hypothesis, that cultural patterns produced greater stress in more modern cultures, manifest at the extreme as involutional depression. On the contrary, as has been shown, self-reported well-being was greatest at the two poles of the traditionalism-modernity continuum. There was some support for the second hypothesis. That is, there was a greater incidence of psychosomatic complaints on survey responses among the Persian and North African women, while the follow-up psychiatric interviews showed "psychological" symptomatology among the European women and "somatic" symptoms among the women in other groups. The third hypothesis, that involutional psychosis is diagnosed among European but not Near Eastern women, found some support through our follow-up diagnosis of depression among Near Eastern women. The tendency to express stress in psychic symptoms among Europeans and in somatic symptoms among Near Easterners would probably facilitate a diagnosis of depression among Europeans and impede such a diagnosis among Near Eastern women, unless psychiatrists were particularly alerted to consider depression in these ethnic groups. In general, however, our broad-scale study of normal women showed involutional depression to be an extremely infrequent response in any culture. Psychiatrists continue to question the diagnostic label, "involutional psychosis." Whatever their answer, we have no evidence that extreme maladaptation is any more frequent in middle age than other maladaptive responses in other periods of the life cycle.

What, then, have we—the writers and readers of this book, who are far removed from the traditional, transitional, even the modern worlds of the women of our study—learned?

The principal finding of our study is simple. We completed a study of middle-age women in five Israeli sub-cultures, only to discover what Ecclesiastes had said long ago: that to every thing there is a season, a time to sow, and a time to reap. We found that women from cultures selected for their differences responded differently to the changes of middle age—not remarkable, but satisfying findings in the social sciences, where expected differences are not always found and, when found, are sometimes different from what was expected. Nevertheless, our surprising finding was one of similarity: menopause and the loss of fertility did not signify a "closing of the gates"—regardless of a woman's childbearing history. On the contrary, whether a woman had planned and restricted childbearing to only one or two children, or had been bearing children over most of her fertile years, the response to the cessation of fertility was positive.

The significance of this finding, however, is not that it echoes the words of Ecclesiastes, but that the words of Ecclesiastes have gone so long unheeded. The psychoanalytic and psychiatric literature is anchored in themes of loss rather than of change and transition. Indeed, we were no exception; our own expectations about women's responses to menopause were based on culturally shaped differences in the family life cycle, leading in turn to differences in responses to the loss of fertility.

The direction of these differences was a question over which we had argued at length in the early phases of the study. This, then, was the first issue to which we turned our attention when our survey responses had been transformed into computer printout. We discovered, of course, that neither the hypothesis of a positive response varying directly with the degree of modernity, nor its converse, the hypothesis that positive response would vary inversely with modernity, was borne out. Nor did we have a scattering of positive and negative responses across groups, to be traced—if only we had found them—to individual differences in personality, social context, or childbearing history.

Instead, our finding was that women in all cultures responded positively to questions about the loss of fertility at menopause—and our own first response was to suspect computer error, or a failure of the survey technique. Only when we found expectable cultural differences in response to other questions—among them other questions related to menopause—convincing us that neither our computer nor our subjects were fooling us—then and only then did we begin to consider what near-unanimity among nearly twelve hundred women from five very different ethnic groups might signify.

Our interpretation of this finding—that there is a natural rhythm to the seasons of the life cycle—is little more than a restatement of ancient wisdom. The value of our discovery—or rediscovery—is that times have changed greatly since traditional folkways provided a stable culture against which the natural rhythms of the life cycle were highlighted; if traditional wisdom retains its force, it may testify to developmental patterns which transcend culture and history.

The Moslem Arab and North African Jewish women in our study may be among the last generations in Israel to represent a traditional family lifestyle. Folk wisdom guided these largely illiterate women, but their daughters have completed at least eight years of school, often more; the women in our study bore children over most of their fertile years, while their daughters plan families of two or three children. The Turkish women in our study may have come from traditional families similar to those of the Arabs and North Africans, but they, like the daughters of the more traditional women, have grown up in school, and along with literacy came a larger vision of life and fewer children. Yet the Turks feel no regret in middle age over lost fertility, just as the Europeans, for whom these changes are not recent, do not. Times change—in our study we can almost feel the changing times—but the rhythm of the life cycle does not.

The significance of these women's responses reaches beyond the arena of the behavioral sciences into the politics of sexuality and family life. At this writing, abortion is a controversial issue in American politics, while some of the opponents of the Equal Rights Amendment to the American Constitution fear this amendment will threaten family stability. Yet the declaration of the State of Israel guarantees equal rights to both sexes—as well it might, since the three great religious traditions of which the population is comprised do not—and there is no evidence at all to suggest a consequent breakdown of family stability. Most of the European women in our study have aborted at least one unplanned pregnancy, as have many women in other ethnic groups; we have no evidence that abortions in the context of an accepting culture leave emotional scars. On the contrary, there is evidence in our study that bearing too many children with too few resources, whether economic or emotional, can erode both emotional and physical health.

Our study of middle-aged women at a developmental period of transition, against an historical background of transition, permits us a further suggestion. We speculate, remembering that psychological well-being is highest for the Europeans, who are closely followed by the Arabs—two cultures marked by relative stability—and lowest for the Persians, for whom transition is greatest—that the process of transition is costly and painful. This is a speculation with unexpected implications. As we look across the five sub-cultures in our study, it almost seems that we can watch the process of modernization, and with it the changing roles of women. Increased literacy, diminished dependence on traditional rituals, an increased separation between the biological life cycle and the social life cycle, fewer children, the acquisition of political and social rights—these differences, conspicuous in a comparative historical and demographic overview of the five ethnic groups, converge around a common theme. This theme is the liberation of women from the constraints of traditional roles.

Yet our study has taught us that liberation, with its attendant consequences of autonomy and choice, is not a simple progression toward new freedom and prerogatives. On the contrary, liberation, as we see it in a comparative overview of the five sub-cultures of our study, is the exchange of one set of prerogatives for another. It is certainly true that the prerogatives of the modern woman are broader and her constraints fewer; but it is also true that freedom of choice can be accompanied by uncertainty and doubt. The relative certainty of the traditional woman, moreover, seems to us to be bought at the price of ritual constraints; we may fail to see, as outsiders looking into an earlier chapter of our own cultural history, that the traditional woman has confidence in her tradition and rituals. The significance of her confidence will become clear in an examination of our own early assumptions as researchers preparing to explore this area.

Our competing hypotheses about the effects of traditional culture on women's responses to menopause grew out of a shared premise that the traditional woman is fatalistic and passive, while the modern woman copes actively with the changes of the life cycle. Since menopause is an inevitable and universal maturational change, Antonovsky and Maoz reasoned, acceptance is the adaptive response, and is most likely to be seen among women of traditional cultures. Datan rejected the exclusive focus on menopause and reasoned that the family life cycle changes of middle age, such as the departure of children from the home, could best be faced by the active, modern woman, who shapes her life to suit her needs.

Our pilot interviews suggested that we had mistaken tradition for passivity. These findings, together with our survey responses, which showed psychological well-being to be nearly as high for women in the most traditional culture as for women at the modern extreme, encouraged us to rethink the significance of traditional culture.

Our error in equating tradition with passivity was apparent in the responses of one of the Arab women in our pilot study. When we asked whether menopause was a matter of concern to her, she replied that it was, and went on to describe the measures she had taken in response to her concern: free hormone shots at Kupat Holim, the Israel national health service clinic; visits to a gynecologist in Tulkarm, a village just over the Israeli border in what was then the newly opened West Bank, for the sake of the excursion; and finally, the advice of a faith healer. In other words, she employed the full range of medical, political, and spiritual resources, from socialized medicine to magic and witchcraft, in the service of her concern. Through her response, we were helped to remember that what our culture identifies as magic and witchcraft are simply ritual practices which we now know to be ineffective, while scientific measures are those which, as far as we can tell, *do* work—or at least have not yet been proven ineffective.

Magic and witchcraft evolved as means of control over the environment, and we err when we dismiss ritual practices as ineffective and their practitioners as passive. We are equally in error if we identify modernity with active coping. "I don't want menstruation to stop," one of the European women in our pilot study told us, "It stopped in Auschwitz." The machinery of modernity can immobilize the human spirit at least as effectively as any network of ritual and tradition.

Our pilot study also reminded us of the position of women in the traditional family. While formally subordinate in status and power, the traditional woman, like the "woman of valor" described in Proverbs, occupies a pivotal place in the household economy. Thus, while she is formally subordinate, the traditional woman need not necessarily be functionally subordinate. The Arab woman we have quoted was candid about the marital concerns which come with menopause in a traditional culture; she told us she was worried her husband might do as a neighbor had done and marry a younger second wife, over the border in a West Bank town where polygyny, outlawed in Israel, was still practiced. We asked how she dealt with her concerns over her own husband. "Oh, I just keep him at home—I don't let him go to Tel Aviv"—not quite the passive answer we might have expected.

Of course the traditional subordination of the Moslem Arab women cannot be overlooked. Polygyny is legal just over the border, not many miles away from the Israeli villages where our studies were carried out. However, it would also be a mistake to ignore comparable phenomena in modern cultures: a monogamous businessman's affair with his secretary cannot be said to represent progress toward the liberation of women. The secure, pivotal position of the traditional woman makes her vital to the traditional household economy. With transition toward modernity and urbanization, the traditional woman's centrality and security are eroded, as are her stable expectations for a known future.

In place of traditional stability, transition brings change, and with change comes the unknown. The transitional women in our study face the unknown with apprehension—"Don't take me out of my kitchen," says a Persian woman—and look to their broadened potentials, incompletely fulfilled, with regret—"I tasted nothing of life," sighs a Turk. We have speculated that the transitional women, socialized in a traditional culture and then transported to a modern setting where their traditional cues no longer serve them, experience the greatest measure of stress arising from discontinuity.

But in a larger sense we are all in transition. No one in middle age today was reared prepared for today's social climate. Indeed, this is particularly and poignantly apparent for many "modern" middle-aged women. Reared to become wives and mothers, often at the expense of careers, they may be entering the labor force today, when affirmative action programs mandate the hiring of qualified women in preference to men—programs which create new horizons for younger women, but highlight the constricted horizons of older women, whose decisions earlier in the life cycle are likely to leave them at a disadvantage in today's social context.

Yet liberation from traditional role constraints may not inevitably create an easier old age, but rather a different old age. Today's young women may postpone childbearing for a career, and in doing so face the risks of diminished fertility and increasing likelihood of complications during pregnancy and birth—and perhaps some may face a middle age with regret over children not born earlier in the life cycle, while their more traditional counterparts contend with their troublesome grown children.

Many of these observations apply to men as well as to women. But the constraints of biology are more rigorous for women; risk in childbirth is never absent, and it becomes a matter of some concern toward the end of the thirties, while their fertility ends about a decade later. Men do not face the risks of pregnancy and childbirth—a trite statement with nontrivial implications. Moreover, men may remain fertile until the end of life. Thus the outer bounds of egalitarianism and liberation are biological as well as social.

Women seeking both the rewards of family, which we associate with tradition, and the prerogatives of paid work, often considered the prize of modernity, are likely to have to juggle, if not struggle, with the interaction of reproductive biology and the social context. It is clear that our world is moving away from tradition and toward modernity, whatever the particulars of our definitions. The traditional women in our study are a remembrance of the past; even the modern women in our study, housewives more often than not, would not seem modern in the company of a group of young career women. But an overview of our five sub-cultures permits us to anticipate the new directions of modernity—and perhaps to comment on the durability of tradition as well.

Our study suggests that it would be a mistake to assume that certain traditional values are no more lasting than the rituals and folkways of the traditional lifestyle. Women in all five sub-cultures value the companionship of a good marriage and cherish their children, while seeking personal autonomy and the satisfaction of a job well done. Looking across the panorama of social change represented by these five groups, it seems to us that those themes common across cultures may well transcend tradition and modernization, and represent enduring human values, which Freud summed up as the mark of the healthy adult: love and work. Perhaps we might close by suggesting that the task for future generations of women and men is a liberating translation of the best of human tradition.

8

The Association between Health and Retirement: Self-Health Assessment of Israeli Retirees

Yael Kremer

THE PROBLEM

Retirement is considered a potentially stressful life change event. It is counted among the psychological risk factors associated with illness, such as job instability, marital difficulties, death of a spouse, relative or close friend—all critical life transitions demanding modification in the pattern of accustomed life style and requiring adaptive behavior. In most industrialized countries, retirement of females at the age of 60 and males at 65 has become a social norm. For the overwhelming majority it means an abrupt cessation of the accustomed daily routine, abundant leisure time and subtly changed family interactions, initiating a search for time-filling occupations to satisfy psycho-social needs. The transition certainly signifies a drastic shift from lifelong habits [1].

In a number of studies, the elderly of today are illustrated as 'protestant work-oriented' believing in the centrality of the value of work [2–5]. This strongly embedded perception conflicts with the ageing stereotype associated with retirement and puts the individual in a potential psychologically threatening situation. In Israel for example, leisure pursuits and options for the elderly are still too undeveloped to replace work, nor is there any evidence of a compensatory trend among former workers toward a wide range of leisure activities after retirement [5]. Work seems to be a major source of self-identification, occupying a central place in life, while, at the same time, fulfilling other socio-economic needs.

According to a previous survey that encompassed the same sample [6], 54% (136 individuals) of the interviewees anticipated a decline in their health state after their prospective retirement. The majority (70%) was of the opinion that work is a healthy and desirable way of life and stated that they would prefer to continue doing so to some extent after retirement, provided their health would allow it. This evaluation bears out other Israeli studies which indicated a strongly work-oriented conception among both blue and white-collar employees close to retirement [7, 8].

In the Kibbutz society (collective settlement), where retirement is not compulsory, the majority of members remain actively involved in the working process as long as their health condition permits it, often far beyond the age accepted by Western society. We believe this phenomenon to be indicative of the propensity of the older generation toward work, especially among the self employed.

When the meaningful process of work breaks down through mandatory retirement, it is reasonable to assume that work-oriented individuals will be exposed to psychological distress and anomie, a state which, presumably might be expressed in their attitude and be reflected in health deterioration [9–12].

RETIREMENT AND 'DISEASES OF ADAPTATION': THEORIES AND FINDINGS

The accepted explanation for the connection between disease onset and retirement is that the sudden change in daily routine acts as a stimulus interfering with the psychosomatic unity. Many diseases are not the direct result of an external agent, but rather the consequence of maladaptation, particularly when the organism is not capable of coping with anxiety, tension and discontent [12, 13].

Stressors are demands to which there is no readily available adaptive response as opposed to the common daily stimuli that are dealt with successfully [12–14]. They also act as stimuli that disrupt the equilibrium of the natural immunization system and weaken the organism's resistance capacity which, ordinarily, protect the individual's state of integrity [12].

Retirement is a transitional passage in adult life associated with disruption of the accustomed life style, no matter how positively the change is accepted. Nevertheless, the degree of insecurity and emotional disturbance that may accompany retirement depends to a large extent on the interpretation of the retiree regarding his professional and economic loss. Thus, the stronger the pre-retirement work-oriented urge, the higher the predictability of post-retirement obstacles to be coped with [15].

Dissatisfaction with the sudden change in everydays routine may be a critical variable in the, as yet, little understood retirement–disease relationship [16].

Rahe *et al.* [17] showed that there exists a link between a crucial change in life and the onset of disease, two years subsequent to its occurrence.

Holmes and Masuda [18] reviewed the literature concerned with the much used Social Readjustment Scale (SRS) and reported on its employment in a variety of retro- and prospective studies in the U.S.A., addressing the relationship between radical life changes and the manifestation of a wide range of disorders. Retirement was rated 10 on a scale of 42 significant potentially stressful events. On two other life event scales, modified to suit the Israeli context, one specifying 31 items [10] and the other 125 [19], retirement was ranked as 22 and 34, respectively.

Horne and Picard [20] showed that morbidity carries a higher probability among men between 60 and 69 years of age, the curve declining, however, after the age of 70. The latter finding indicates that the act of retirement may be considered a stressor that plays a role in the etiology of morbidity, and therefore meriting the attention of health providers.

On the other hand, studies published in Britain and the United States have attempted to denote job features and elements in work that can be singled out as arduous at an advanced age with a consequent stable phase following retirement [15, 21]. It is possible, therefore, that some retirees may experience a feeling of liberation with, as a result, a—subjective—improved health state.

Correspondence between chronic diseases and age

Epidemiological studies have shown that in developed countries patterns of morbidity have changed from acute diseases to chronic illnesses, impairments or disabilities, a phenomenon inherent in the increased life expectancy [13, 22–24]. Old age is inseparably linked with health deterioration which is, however, controlable by modern health care systems.

In studies carried out in Israel, the age distribution of the population has revealed that almost two-thirds of males over the age of 65 suffer from one or more chronic systemic disorders, among which hypertension, heart disease and diabetes are the three most prevalent ones. The main functional disabilities reported among this age group were hearing problems, impaired vision and impeded locomotion. The subjective feeling of well-being decreased with age with a corresponding increase in visits to the physician [23, 25].

In one of these above mentioned studies [25], it was found that nearly three-quarters of the elderly had visited a physican at least once during the 3 months preceding the survey and that 48% saw a physician at least every 2 weeks. It should be noted here that 95% of the population in Israel is insured by a sick fund. This fact may serve as a partial explanation for the high rate of visits to the health clinic, which is among the highest in the world.

Since, as already stated before, the trend of the health situation is toward chronic rather than acute conditions, a fact which contributes to overall morbidity, health sociologists suggest focusing on health/disease continuum instead of on the traditional pathogenic orientation that dichotomizes the population into healthy and sick [13, 26]. This school of thought encourages research in an effort to elucidate the role of psychosocial stressors, in addition to the conventional pathogenic factors responsible for morbidity. In line with this concept, there is a plea for implementing a scale of factors that promote health rather than of those that cause disease [13].

As already outlined in the previous section, a large volume of studies report that major changes in life serve as the background for stressor situations which demand readjustment capacity. Thus, while on the one hand there may be a possible direct effect of psychosocial stressors on health, on the other, this impact can be moderated—or even eliminated—through anticipatory socialization and availability of social support [27, 28].

Social support as a moderator

The phenomenon of psychosocial support involves pathways that activate the coping and adaptation mechanisms [28]. Consequently, serious attention should be paid to the retiree's self-appraisal of his well-being, which is partly expressed by his ability to cope with the change in his daily routine. In this context, the subjective evaluation rather than the objective health condition (as diagnosed by the professional) is considered important and the interest is focused on understanding the psychological reaction to retirement as a potential risk factor manifested in health change [22, 23, 26, 29].

In the light of this reasoning, it appears that lack of adequate information and unavailability of social support are elements that increase the susceptibility of the organism to various forms of disease. In this respect, social support is viewed as a compensatory factor in situations of stress, when the individual moves away from the ideal state of social homeostasis. Social support may be a meaningful mechanism in helping the individual to master his emotional tensions [12, 14, 19].

Based on the literature which lists retirement among the stressful life events that may have detrimental effects on subjectively evaluated health, it might be expected that (A) the retiree will perceive a deterioration in health and (B) visits to the health clinic will increase post-retirement.

METHODS

The Retirement Planning Society of Haifa, Israel has carried out three studies which followed the attitudes and behaviour of older male workers before and after retirement. The present study is based upon the third and final phase which compares the retrospective self-health assessment and pattern of physician visits pertaining to the pre-retirement period with the same parameters for the post-retirement period.

The accuracy of retrospective reports has received considerable attention from methodologists, without arriving at a firm resolution. Admittedly, the tendency of the individual to have consistent attitudes relating to the past, inevitably carries the risk of bias. Self-image is another source of methodological deficiency in surveys dealing with self reported visits to the physician as opposed to the objective medical records.

However, regarding previous health behavior, recall is considered reliable, and information thus obtained is routinely utilized for medical anamnesis [22, 23, 25].

This affinity for a trustworthy memory regarding health problems and behavior that have occurred in the past, form the basis of this study.

Sample

This study deals with data obtained in 1976 from persons who had retired between the years 1973 and 1975. The sample includes only males, since in these three cycles no female employees were due to retire. Of the 400 individuals contacted in the framework of the survey, 310 (77%) were willing to participate.

The sample constituted a universe of former employees of three industrial plants i.e. a glass works ($N = 50$), an oil-and-soap factor ($N = 33$), a textile mill ($N = 51$), and two public service organizations, i.e. and Electricity Corporation ($N = 99$) and the Haifa Port Authority ($N = 87$). The respondents were between 66 and 70 years of age and had been retired for periods ranging from 6 months to $3\frac{1}{2}$ years. Most of them had been employed at their last place of work for at least 25 years, and quite a few (27%) for 40 years or more. Over two-thirds of the sample (68%) were former blue-collar workers, both skilled (welders, glassware makers, electricians, textile workers) and unskilled (gatekeepers, night watchmen, longshoremen, cleaning and maintenance staff). The remaining 32% included white-collar workers (technicians, production and electrical engineers, bookkeepers, clerks). The majority was of East European origin and had immigrated between the years 1924 and 1935, or after the establishment of the State of Israel in 1948. The remainder had come from Central Europe (9%) or from Middle Eastern countries (13%), while 3% had been born in Israel. Their educational level was distributed as follows: 45% had 8 years of schooling, 35% 12 years, 17% had more than 12 years and 3% had no formal education at all.

Instruments and procedure

A structured interview was conducted with each retiree at his home. The questionnaire included 212 items covering areas such as immediate reaction to the termination of working life, sources of satisfaction, pattern of behavior in the leisure and family domain [5, 30], aspects of health behavior, and self-health assessment before and after retirement. In this study we present data pertaining to the health issue in the context of retirement as a life transitional event which may affect self-health appraisal. The subjects were asked to assess their health state 6 months to $3\frac{1}{2}$ years after and, retrospectively, 1–5 years before retirement.

Responses to the question "Do you consider your state of health nowadays 'very good' (score 5), 'good', 'not so good', 'poor' or 'very poor' (score 1)" were compared with those of the pre-retirement period. The t-test was employed for statistical evaluation of the results. The open question "Did you feel any change in your health state around the time of your retirement" was composed to estimate the timing of perceived changes in the health state prior to or after retirement. The answers were categorized on the basis of the information provided by the retirees. The respondent was then asked to indicate, for the pre- and post-retirement periods, (a) any health problems and (b) pattern of visits to his family physician. The frequency of the visits before and after retirement was classified into three categories: 'do not/did not visit the physician' (score 1), 'infrequent visits' (score 2), 'frequent visits' (score 3). The χ^2 test was used to determine the strength of relationship between pre- and post-retirement health problems, as well as to establish the association between pre- and post-retirement visits to the family physician.

RESULTS

Comparison of self-health assessment during the pre- and post-retirement periods

The findings in Table 1 show a slightly higher value of health state self-assessment for the period of employment than for that of retirement, but remain in the realm of 'good' for both periods ($M = 3.45$ and 2.98, respectively). Although the health gap between the pre- and post-retirement is small (0.47), the t value is statistically significant ($P < 0.001$). Notwithstanding the statistical results, one would hesitate to ascribe this health gap to retirement *per se*.

Change in health state as perceived during retirement

Table 2 presents the retirees' evaluation of the potential change in their health state that might be associated with the interruption in their life and, consequently, with the need to readjust to a new routine: 56.8% did not perceive any change in their health state, while 6.1% even sensed an improvement, possibly due to a better control of diet, relief from strain and/or the ability to rest after so many years of intensive work activity. Of the total sample, 22.2% reported a decline in health, which had already started six to one year before retirement, while 14.2% felt a worsening of their health state immediately upon or during the first year of their retirement.

Table 1. Comparison of self-health assessment between the work period and retirement for sample group of retirees (total sample 308)

Period	Mean	SD	t-value	P*
Work	3.45	1.16		
			6.70	0.001
Retirement	2.98	1.18		

*As determined by a two-tailed paired t-test.

Table 2. Perceived/non-perceived change in health state related to retirement* (total sample 310)

Item	N	%
Improved health state†	19	6.1
No change	176	56.8
Deterioration		
Immediate and up to		
1 year after retirement	44	14.2
1 yr prior to retirement	33	10.6
2 yr prior to retirement	14	4.5
3 yr prior to retirement	7	2.3
4 yr prior to retirement	4	1.3
5 yr prior to retirement	1	0.3
6 yr prior to retirement	10	3.2
Missing	2	0.6

*Categorized open question.
†1–12 months after retirement.

Table 3. Comparison of health problems before and after retirement (total sample 310)

Problems before retirement	Problems after retirement		
	No	Yes	Total
No	92	39	131
	70.2%	29.8%	100.0%
	29.7%	12.6%	42.3%
Yes	23	156	179
	12.8%	87.2%	100.0%
	7.4%	50.3%	57.7%
Total	115	195	310
	31.7%	62.9%	100.0%

$\chi^2 = 104.28$; d.f. $= 1$; $P < 0.001$; Gamma $= 0.88$.

However, none of the participants in this survey incriminated retirement as the responsible factor the the decline in their health state.

The data in Table 3 show that the association between the health state before and after retirement is statistically significant (χ^2 significant at $P < 0.001$). About 50% of the respondents reported on some health problems during the two periods under discussion. This continuity trend of the health state is manifested also by the 29.7% who stated 'no problems' for either period. The notably high gamma coefficient value of the categories (0.88) demonstrated the strong consistency of the health situation in both periods under study.

Visits to physician

Another conventional measure of the health state is the frequency of visits to the family physician. Table 4 presents the distribution of such visits before and after retirement. Of those who did not habitually go to the physician before retirement, 41.8% continued in the same vein after retirement. Also, in this latter period, 38.2% went infrequently and 20.0% made frequent visits to their physician. Further information that may be gleaned from the table is that approx. two-thirds (192/298) of the interviewees revealed a pattern of health behavior that was unaffected by their retirement: the largest group (105 persons) remained consistent in their habit of seldom going to the doctor. The χ^2 value is significant at $P < 0.001$ and the gamma coefficient value is salient (0.509). Analysis of the data for health behavior retirement shows that 87.6% of the retirees (compared with 81.6% before retirement) utilized the services of the physician as opposed to 12.4% (compared with 18.5% before retirement) who refrained from doing so.

A supplementary explanation provided by the interviewees was that they went to the doctor for blood pressure check-up and routine examinations, which complies with the chronic health problems prevalent among this age group.

CONCLUSIONS AND DISCUSSION

Summary of findings

The potential component of stress attached to retirement as reflected by decline in the health state is not reinforced by the findings of this survey. In two previous studies [6, 30], about half of the sample (encompassing the same study population) expressed their concern regarding a deterioration in their health after expulsion from the labor market. However, once retirement had become reality, our population generally revealed reasonable adjustment to this new phase in their lives, which is reflected by the satisfactory self health evaluation for both periods (work vs retirement: $M = 2.98$ vs 3.45). Although these values represent data obtained by self-appraisal, it appears that this subjective indicator is a highly relevant factor regarding the individual's well-being.

The retiree's evaluation of his health condition with respect to the two periods discredits the notion that retirement ensues in a drastically changed health condition. On the contrary, it strongly indicates a trend of unruffled continuity, as is shown by the strikingly similar patterns of health problems and behavior, which are typical for this age group [22, 23]. Streib and Schneider [31], in their often quoted longitudinal study, have found the same results with respect to adjustment to retirement, as have Palmore *et al.* [32] in their recent summary of prominent investigations.

Theoretical and practical implications

The overall picture arising from this study suggests a well adaptive way of coping with retirement among former industrial and service workers. The question whether retirement is considered an etiological factor in disease onset as a result of maladaptation does not receive support by the results of the present study.

These findings may serve as important information

Table 4. Comparison of visits to physician before and after retirement (total sample 298)

Visits before retirement	Visits after retirement			
	None	Infrequently	Frequently	Total
None	23	21	11	55
	41.8%	38.2%	20.0%	100.0%
	7.7%	7.0%	3.7%	18.5%
Infrequently	12	105	40	157
	7.6%	66.9%	25.5%	100.0%
	4.0%	35.2%	13.4%	52.7%
Frequently	2	20	64	86
	2.3%	23.3%	74.4%	100.0%
	0.7%	6.7%	21.5%	28.9%
Total	37	146	115	298
	12.4%	49.0%	38.6%	100.0%

$\chi^2 = 111.94$; d.f. $= 4$; $P < 0.001$; Gamma $= 0.509$.

for pre-retirement education programs that are geared towards the process of socialization. Since a respectable number of such programs have already been initiated in many places [1, 6–8, 15], the incorporation and utilization of reliable information would enhance their success in that they abolish pre-conceived ideas. The insight and knowledge gained by the current investigation strengthens the theoretical point of view that retirement is not necessarily a stressful experience [15, 16, 21, 31, 32]. We were unable to detect supportive evidence for other studies in which retirement was included among the stressors [10, 18–20] that sensitize the retiree and make him vulnerable to 'diseases of adaptation' [12]. Our survey brought to light the weak association between the event of retirement as such and disease onset; it was quite evident that, despite lacking the focus of work, the retiree had come to terms with his new routine.

The fact that retirement does not evoke a crisis situation is due, in all probability, to the existing social support mechanism [27, 28]. Strong support of the spouse, as well as close family ties, assist the retiree in adjusting to the new phase in his life [30]; lacking these supportive elements, the outcome may be entirely different in relation to his self-health appraisal. In another study, in which the same sample participated [6, 30], the satisfaction level of the respondents was mediant, which was explained partly by interaction with the family.

The present study sheds light on the inconsistency of the respondents' pre- and post-retirement concept regarding health consequences. More than half of our subjects foresaw an immediate decline in their health state upon retirement, which is not surprising in view of the stigma attached to mandatory retirement. However, we were unable to discover corroborating evidence—such as frequent visits to the physician—that the retiree assumes the 'ill' or 'sick' role as a psychological reaction to retirement [26]. This is an important aspect, since many health professionals maintain that retirees visit the clinic quite often to exploit their abundant free time.

Further research investigating health problems and health behavior of the retiree is needed to help discard the misconception and stereotypic image of this ever increasing age group.

Acknowledgements—This study was carried out within the framework of the Retirement Planning Society of Haifa, and conducted by the Israel National Insurance Institute.

The author is grateful to Professor Z. Ben-Sira of the Hebrew University of Jerusalem and to Professor A. Antonovsky of the Ben Gurion University in Beersheba for their helpful comments. Thanks are also due to Mr D. Har-Even of the Bar Ilan University in Ramat Gan for his assistance with the computer runs.

REFERENCES

1. Hess B. B. and Markson E. W. *Ageing and Older Age*. Macmillan, New York, 1980.
2. Simpson S. H. and McKinney J. C. *Social Aspects of Ageing*. Duke University Press, Durham, 1972.
3. Kreps J. M. Human values, economic values and the elderly. In *Ageing, Death and the Completion of Being* (Edited by Tassel D. D. V.). University of Pennsylvania Press, Philadelphia, 1979.
4. Kabanoff B. and O'Brien G. E. Work and leisure: a task attributes analysis. *J. appl. Psychol.* **65**, 596, 1980.
5. Kremer Y. and Harpaz I. Leisure patterns among retired workers: Spillover or compensatory trends? *J. vocat. Behav.* **2**, 183, 1982.
6. Kremer Y. and Weiner E. Final report of three surveys among older industrial and service workers, Haifa, Israel. The Retirement Planning Society of Haifa, 1977 (in Hebrew).
7. Perry M. A survey on the issue of retirement in the Israeli aircraft industry: Ben Gurion Airport, Tel Aviv, 1978 (in Hebrew).
8. Bergman S. and Bar Zuri R. *Man in Retirement*. Social and Economic Research Institute, Federation of Labour, Tel Aviv, 1980 (in Hebrew).
9. Ben-Sira Z. Life change and health: An additional perspective on the structure of coping. *Stress* **3**, 18, 1982.
10. Ben-Sira Z. Stress and illness: a revised application of the stressful life events approach. *Res. Commun. Psychol. Psychiat. Behav.* **6**, 317, 1981.
11. Jordan J. and Meckler J. R. The relationship between life change events, social support and dysmenorrhea. *Res. Nurs. Hlth.* **5**, 73, 1982.
12. Appley M. H. and Trumbull R. *On the Concept of Psychological Stress: Issues in Research*. Appleton–Century–Crofts, New York, 1967.
13. Antonovsky A. *Health, Stress and Coping*. Jossey–Bass, San Francisco, 1980.
14. Lasarus R. S. and Cohen J. B. Environmental stress. In *Human Behavior and Environment* (Edited by Altman I. *et al.*), Vol. 2. Plenum Press, New York, 1977.
15. Atchley R. C. *The Sociology of Retirement*. Schenkman, New York, 1976.
16. Minkler M. Research on the health effects of retirement: an uncertain legacy. *J. Hlth soc. Behav.* **22**, 117, 1981.
17. Rahe R. H., Meyer M., Smith M., Kjaer G. and Holmes T. H. Social stress and illness onset. *J. Psychomat.* **8**, 35, 1964.
18. Holmes T. H. and Masuda M. Life change and illness susceptibility, separation and depression. *Am. Ass. advan. Sci.* **94**, 161, 1973.
19. Levav I., Krasnoff L. and Dohrenwend B. S. Israeli PERI life event scale: rating of events by a community sample. *Israel J. med. Sci.* **17**, 176, 1981.
20. Horne R. L. and Picard R. S. Psychosocial risk factors for lung cancer. *Psychosomat. Med.* **41**, 7, 1979.
21. Jacobson D. Fatigue-producing factors in industrial work and pre-retirement attitudes. *Occup. Psychol.* **46**, 193, 1972.
22. Gofin J., Kark E., Mainemer N., Kark S. L., Abramson J. H., Hopp C. and Epstein L. M. Prevalence of selected health characteristics of women and comparisons with men. A community health survey in Jerusalem. *Israel J. med. Sci.* **17**, 145, 1981.
23. Davies A. M. and Fleishman R. Health status and use of health services as reported by the older residents of the Baka neighborhood, Jerusalem. *Israel J. med. Sci.* **17**, 138, 1981.
24. Siegman A. E. and Elinson J. Newer sociomedical health indicators: implications for evaluation of health services. *Med. Care* **15**, 84, 1977.
25. Davies A. M., Lockard J. and Kop Y. (Eds) *Aging in Israel, A Chartbook*. Brookdale Institute for Gerontology, Jerusalem, Israel, 1982.
26. Susser M. Ethical components in the definition of health. *Int. J. Hlth Serv.* **4**, 539, 1974.
27. Kaplan H. B., Cassell J. C. and Gore S. Social support and health. In *Patients, Physicians and Illness* (Edited by Jaco E. G.). Free Press, New York, 1979.

28. Cobb S. Social support as a moderator of life stress. *Psychosomat. Med.* **38,** 300, 1976.
29. Kaplan H. B. Understanding the social and social-psychological antecedents and consequences of psychopathology: a review of reports of invitational conferences. *J. Hlth soc. Behav.* **16,** 2, 1975.
30. Kremer Y. A sociological analysis of retirees' attitudes and activities in the adjustment process to their role. Ph.D. thesis Bar-Ilan University, 1979 (in Hebrew).
31. Streib G. F. and Schneider S. J. *Retirement in American Society.* Cornell University Press, New York, 1971.
32. Palmore E. B., Fillenbaum G. G. and George L. K. Consequences of retirement. *J. Gerontol.* **21,** 109, 1984.

9

Gender Differences in Life Expectancy among Kibbutz Members

Uri Leviatan and *Jiska Cohen*

INTRODUCTION

Research on gender differences in life expectancy (LE) demonstrates two findings which are constantly repeated: (a) the LE of females is longer than that of males; and (b) the longer the LE of a given population, the greater the increase in the LE of females and the wider the intergender difference in LE. These findings are replicated when one compares the LE of males vs females in the same society over a period of time in which LE has increased for that society. This is illustrated by the following examples of gender differences in LE at birth.

In Switzerland the difference in LE between men and women has increased from 2.5 years in 1875 to 5.3 in 1960 [1], while the average LE of males and females has increased from 41.9 to 71.4 years. In Israel this trend is manifested by an increase in the intergender difference in LE from 2.7 years in 1931 to 3.5 years in 1977, while the average LE in that period changed from 61.3 to 73.7 years [2]. The same trend was found in the U.S.A.: from an intergender difference of 2.8 years in 1901 to 7.8 years in 1977 [3], while the average LE of the population has increased from 49.3 to 73.2 years.

This positive relationship between the LE of a population and the size of the intergender differences in LE may also be found in analyses of data across populations which differ from each other in their average LE at a given period. The relationship is so strong that it almost suggests the existence of some sort of law. This is illustrated in Fig. 1. Here, data [4] of 73 societies on two variables is presented in a two-dimensional scatter plot (mean LE of a population and gender differences in LE at birth). In Table 1 the same findings are summarized.

*This study is part of a wider research program on aging in the kibbutz undertaken by the Institute for Research of the Kibbutz, University of Haifa.

As Figure 1 and Table 1 demonstrate, the linear relationship between the two variables at birth is positive and rather strong ($r = 0.75$). The same analysis conducted for LE at age 50 ($N = 64$) reveals a similar relationship between LE and gender differences in LE ($r = 0.59$). The data presented also reveal that females live longer in all societies once LE is not a primary function of infant, child or child-bearing mortality but rather the result of the extension of adult longevity. (In only four societies, for which data are given in the *UN Yearbook*, do males have longer LE at birth. These are all developing countries with relatively low LE and high child mortality.)

These two phenomena relating to gender differences in LE are of great interest and concern to both researchers and policy-makers. Researchers are interested in the causes and explanation of the occurence of such gender differences and why they change in the pattern shown here. The ensuing debate parallels some classical debates in the social sciences, namely, the nature–nurture distinction and what is the relative importance of 'nature' factors as compared to the importance of nurture factors in contributing to the intergender differences found in LE.

Policy-makers have a different perspective. What concerns them is the sexual imbalance in the composition of the aged strata in society. So much so, that in 1978 the U.S. National Institute of Mental Health (NIMH) held a workshop on the subject. The workshop concluded that "Women in the 65 and older age group are the fastest growing segment of the U.S. population with 13.9 million older women in 1977 expected to increase to 33.4 million women by year 2035 . . . By the year 2000 there will likely be ten women for every five men over the age of 75 . . ." and also: "Women now entering their fifties are strikingly different from those now entering their seventies . . . When these women reach 70 . . . they are more likely than those women presently in their

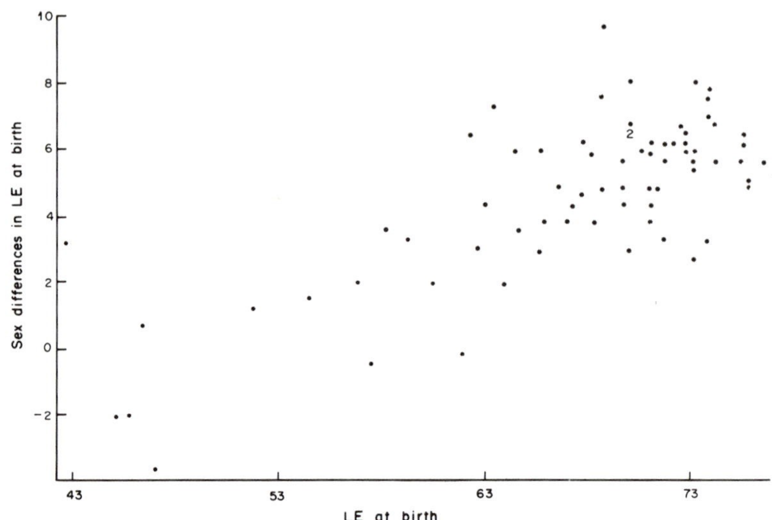

Fig. 1. A scatter plot of 73 societies (source: *UN Yearbook*, 1981) on two variables: (1) LE at birth; (2) sex difference in LE at birth. Both variables are measured by number of years.

seventies to live without husbands because of increasing differences in male/female life expectancy". Hence the report relates to ensuing problems for such single women as regards their well-being, mental health, quality of life and standard of living, as well as the implications for society and its institutions. A similar concern is also expressed in Israel, even though the expected male/female ratio is smaller—in 1990 it is expected to be about 6:5 in favor of women for the 65 and older age group [5].

These two perspectives—that of researchers seeking the *cause* of the gender differences in LE and that of policy-makers concerned about their *social implications*—are of course related to each other: the answer to the first question perhaps paving the way to a solution of the second.

APPROACHES OF EXPLANATION

As already stated, the question of gender differences in LE is another case in point of the debate about the relative importance of 'nature' as compared to 'nurture' in explaining human behaviors. In earlier times the trend of interpretations of gender differences in LE was in favor of the genetic biological (nature) approach. Madigan and Vance [6] summarized and supported this interpretation in their own study. They demonstrated that members of Catholic brotherhoods and sisterhoods devoted solely to teaching had gender differences in LE (expressed in LE ratios) similar to the general U.S. population. This held even though the life style and role expectations of each group were similar.

In more recent years the interpretation pendulum has moved in the direction of attributing the major causes of gender differences in LE to role expectations and role demands of the male in modern societies. Researchers who have investigated gender difference in mortality by cause and by age came to the conclusion that most, if not all, of the major reasons for the gender differences in mortality, and

Table 1. Summary statistics of LE and sex differences (F − M) in LE at birth (73 societies) and at age 50 (64 societies)* in the late 1970s [4]

	At age 50 ($N = 64$)	At birth ($N = 73$)
Males' (M) LE (years)		
Mean	23.5	64.9
SD	2.6	7.2
Females' (F) LE (years)		
Mean	27.3	69.8
SD	3.6	9.0
Average LE $\left(\frac{M+F}{2}\right)$		
Mean	25.4	67.3
SD	3.0	8.0
Sex difference (F − M)		
Mean	3.8	4.9
SD	1.6	2.5
Pearson correlation LE with:		
F − M	0.59	0.75
and Regression:		
B	0.322	0.232
A	−4.399	−10.682
SE	1.341	1.668
Number of societies where:		
LE F < LE M	1	4
LE F > LE M	63	69

*For some societies the data in the *UN Demographic Yearbook* was given only 'at birth' and not at age 50.

hence in LE, are to be found in social definitions of gender roles and expectations of sex-typed behaviors and reactions [e.g. 7–10].

Even Madigan and Vance's conclusion has been criticized [11], suggesting that the 'Brothers' may have smoked more tobacco and drunk more alcohol than the 'Sisters' and that surely each group had different socialization experiences, and therefore different LE, prior to their entering the brotherhood or sisterhood. Nevertheless, the approach suggested by Madigan and Vance [6] is a useful one. The more a research design equates and controls for the role expectations of males and females in a society, the better it allows for conclusions regarding the relative importance of biological factors vs social factors in determining gender differences in mortality and LE. The present paper reports findings based on such a design using the kibbutz society as the data base.

KIBBUTZ SOCIETY AS A RESEARCH SETTING

Kibbutz society in many ways offers a situation where the life experience of males and females is similar. We now present some of the major aspects of this similarity.

(a) The kibbutz society is the only society where *all* men and women are engaged full-time in the labor force outside their homes. That is, all have a worker's role that is defined by given tasks to be performed within a given time framework—and within the job structure of the society. In addition, neither men nor women have a compulsory retirement schedule and in reality both continue to work, at least on a part-time basis, up to the advanced ages of 80 and beyond [12].

(b) Men should not differ from women in the pressures and responsibilities put on them to contribute to maintaining the standard of living of the family and to secure its future. Both are freed from many stresses related to financial burdens and to the prestige race.

(c) Both men and women experience the same community life, similar community social support and similar daily schedules, and more similar involvement in public activities, than do the two sexes outside the kibbutz.

(d) Both men and women are knowledgeable to a similar degree of the experiences of their spouses at work and community domains, hence both can offer similar relevant empathy and social support to their spouses. *More so* than the average person outside the kibbutz; social support has been shown to be negatively related to mortality [13, 14].

(e) Most men and women who were born on a kibbutz have had similar experiences and similar stages in their life cycles: same schooling, a period of military service, work on the kibbutz, family roles etc. Kibbutz members who were not born on the kibbutz but joined it either as founders or as individuals in their youth have had similar stages in their life cycles from the time of joining.

The above characteristics of kibbutz life, which make the sex-typed roles of males and females on the kibbutz in matters related to the determination of LE more similar, should contribute to diminishing the intergender differences in mortality and in LE as compared to those of the society outside the kibbutz, *if* gender differences are mostly due to social and environmental factors. Moreover, the decrease in intergender differences in mortality and LE is hypothesized to be mostly the result of the lowering of the death rate among male members of the kibbutz, as the above factors—reduction of role stress and intensification of social support especially—create a greater difference between males on the kibbutz and in the larger society than between their female counterparts.

GENDER DIFFERENCES IN LE AT DIFFERENT AGES

Sex differences in LE in developed countries are more influenced by death rate differences at older ages than at younger ages. This is so because the number of deaths at older ages is much higher than at younger ages. For instance, out of a total number of deaths among Israeli Jews in 1977, only 15.8% of the male deaths and 11.6% of the female deaths were of 49 years of age or younger, while 84.2% of the male deaths and 88.4% of the female deaths were 50 years of age or older. Observing the different causes of death at different ages, Graney [10] has suggested that intergender differences in mortality at middle age and late adulthood are influenced more by social factors than intergender differences at younger ages. On the basis of these two points, we suggest that a test of the importance of environmental factors in contributing to gender differences in LE is given by comparing societies that differ in their gender role expectations and environments, and on their gender differences in LE at young and old ages. The society with more intergender similarity in roles should have an even smaller gender difference in LE, the older the age at which it is calculated. We should expect, therefore, the observed gender difference in the LE of kibbutz members to be relatively smaller at age 50 that at birth.

The considerations presented in the Introduction thus far relate to three topics. These may be translated into formal hypotheses.

Hypothesis 1. There will be smaller intergender differences in LE among kibbutz members as compared to the expected intergender differences calculated on the basis of the data presented in Fig. 1. and Table 1.

Hypothesis 2. It is the kibbutz males rather than females who gain more from the decrease of the intergender difference in LE.

Hypothesis 3. Sex differences in LE among kibbutz members should be, relative to their expected differences given their LE, smaller at older ages (50) than at younger age (at birth).

METHODS

Population

The data used for calculating LE (number of individuals alive, number of deaths per year, by gender, by age) are taken from the files of the kibbutz federations' statistical departments for the years 1975–1980. Since the purpose of the study was to examine the LE of a particular population—that of kibbutz members—subject to the kibbutz way of life regarding privileges, obligations and role expectations, other persons residing on kibbutz who did not meet this criterion were excluded from the analyses (e.g. parents of members who are not themselves members, volunteers, guests and the like); we used only data pertaining to the population groups of members, candidates for membership and their children.

Due to the different periods of joining the central data file of the kibbutz movement by different federations of kibbutzim, the data consists of a merger of files of the three major federations which are similar in size. The periods covered by the three federations are the years 1975–1980 (Ichud and Dati), 1975–1977 (Meuchad) and 1977–1980 (Artzi).

Computations

For each of the three population groups an average number of members alive and dead for each 5-year age group, by gender, was calculated across the years for which data was available. These averages were then combined across the three population groups and entered into the computation of death rates for the entire membership population. This procedure averages the data, therefore, around the year 1977. The abridged Greville method for calculating LE [15] was then applied to the data.

Death rates of the Jewish population in Israel were included in the formula for two age groups: 80–84 and 85+ since the number of kibbutz members at these ages is minimal (155 in the former and 33 in the latter). This modification of the data results in a conservative measure of LE, since death rates in this small very old kibbutz population were very low.

FINDINGS

The data for the testing of the three hypotheses is given in Table 2. It presents LE calculations for kibbutz males and females at selected ages for 1977. Also shown are the intergender differences in LE and the expected difference according to the regression formula calculated on the basis of the 73 societies for which data was available [4] (See Fig. 1 and Table 1).

Table 2 reveals that the intergender difference in LE is smaller for the kibbutz population than expected on the basis of the regression formula arrived at in Fig. 1 (Hypothesis 1). The expected gender difference in LE at birth is 7.1 years while the actual difference is only 4.5 years, which is 1.60 standard errors of estimate (SE) less than the expected value. The respective results for gender differences in LE at age 50 are: expected difference is 5.1 years, actual difference is 2.7 years which is 1.83 SEs less than the expected value.

A test of Hypothesis 2, as to which gender on the kibbutz gains more in LE, is also given by the data in Table 2 in comparison with the findings in Table 1. The comparison should be made separately for each gender with the LEs of its respective gender groups across all societies. So that we get the kibbutz males' relative standing among the other male groups on a comparable scale with the kibbutz females' relative standing among other female groups. Expressing the positions of the two groups in standardized scores achieves this goal, as it indicates both the relative standing on a continuum as well as the extent of deviation from the mean in scores that are comparable across the two groups. Inspection of the two tables reveals that it is the *men* who gain more from whatever is offered by kibbutz life towards extending LE. Although both male and female members of the kibbutz have LEs which are among the highest of the list given by the UN summaries (cited in Table 1), the men's LE is higher when measured in standardized scores: 1.33 as compared to 1.02 of the women at birth, and 1.85 vs 1.03 at age 50.

Table 2 also shows that the observed kibbutz intergender difference in LE at age 50 deviates from the expected difference in a more pronounced way than at birth. We consider this as direct evidence in support of Hypothesis 3. This finding indicates that the kibbutz intergender differences in LE are smaller at ages beyond which environmental factors are expected to be more pronounced in determining the death rates (hence the LEs) of a population.

Table 2. LE of kibbutz members by age and gender for the year 1977*

Age (years)	Women's LE (years)	Men's LE (years)	F − M difference in LE†		
			Observed	Expected	Deviation in SEs
0	79.0	74.5	4.5	7.1	1.60
10	69.8	65.5			
20	60.0	55.9			
30	50.3	46.6			
40	40.6	37.2			
50	31.0	28.3	2.7	5.1	1.83
60	22.1	19.8			
70	13.9	12.4			

*The data for kibbutz members were calculated from raw data provided by the statistical departments of the kibbutz federations. They are for the years 1975–1980. The data refer to kibbutz members, candidates and their children (see Method for details). These calculations are based on the death rates for kibbutz babies (age 0–1) taken from the Central Bureau of Statistics (since the kibbutz federations' data are unreliable for this age group): males, 11.95 deaths/1000; females, 7.66 deaths/1000.

†The expected F − M difference in LE and the SEs are calculated with the coefficients of the regression formulae given in Table 1.

SUMMARY AND DISCUSSION

The findings presented in the previous section support all three hypotheses: (1) the intergender difference in LE for the kibbutz population is smaller than expected, given this population's average LE; (2) males on the kibbutz, relatively speaking, gain the greatest benefit; (3) the deviation of the observed intergender difference in LE from the expected intergender difference, as expressed in SE scores, is larger at age 50 than at birth, which supports the hypothesis that the environment is an important factor in determining this intergender difference.

Although these findings lead to a conclusion that at least a major part of the gender differences in LE are due to social and environmental causes, some questions remain to be discussed.

(1) We have presented data to the effect that kibbutz members gain in their LE in comparison to members of other societies. We have also shown that kibbutz males are the 'bigger winners': the males' LE at age 50 in standardized scores was found to be 1.85 while the females' LE in standardized scores was found to be only 1.03. This means that whatever factors contribute to the extension of LE for kibbutz members, males gain more than females in comparison to their counterparts in other societies. What remains unanswered at this point is whether the LE of women in the kibbutz is not extended more because: (i) of a 'ceiling effect'; (ii) the relevant added factors that contribute to the extension of LE for women in the kibbutz are fewer; or (iii) the life style of women in the kibbutz adds (compared to women outside the kibbutz) some negative aspects as regards LE (e.g. stressors from their work roles and from their public involvements). Research is needed in order to clarify the alternative interpretations and enable us to choose among them or put them in some order of importance.

(2) Could the reasons for the reduced intergender difference in LE, as reported in this study, be a result of some selection process (self or otherwise) into kibbutz life so that individuals with a higher predisposition for creating small intergender differences in LE, especially at older ages, joined the kibbutzim in higher proportions than others? Is the phenomenon reported here a result of a postselection process so that individuals with a lower potential for contributing to the reduced intergender differences in LE also had a lower probability of staying on a kibbutz because at early ages they either had higher death rates than others or had a lower rate of retention as kibbutz members?

None of these interpretations seems very likely because even though the LE *per se* of kibbutz members as a whole could be attributed to pre- or postselection processes (and we will shortly argue against this), the relatively small intergender difference in LE is a function of opposing trends in the two genders. Our findings show that this reduced intergender gap is a result of the relatively (compared to other male groups) *high* LE of the males on the kibbutz and the *shorter* (compared to other female groups) longevity of the female members. Accepting the possibility of the pre- and/or postselection processes as responsible for these findings suggests that the selection processes had favored males with higher potential for longevity than those not joining kibbutzim but at the same time favored females with lower potential for longevity than those who did not join kibbutzim or those who left them—or died at young ages. (Note that this is a contradiction in itself.)

(3) This paper also presents data that shows the kibbutz membership as a whole to have a very high LE as compared to all other developed societies. What about the pre- and/or postselection processes as explanations for this phenomenon.

The present authors know of no data that bears directly on a test of the existence of the preselection process. Neither can we think of any practical research design to test for its existence in kibbutzim. That is, to test for the existence of a preselection process along the dimension of longevity so that it might be determined whether those who joined kibbutzim had a higher potential for longevity than those who did not join. This leads us to inspection of the possibility of the existence of a postselection process along the dimension of the potential for longevity. A direct test of such a hypothesis would involve a comparison on LE of members who stayed on a kibbutz with members who left kibbutzim after staying on one for a while. Unfortunately, this also is not practically possible. Although the numbers of one time members who eventually left is relatively high (about 40–50% of kibbutz-born members left, as is the case with about 80% of all other joiners), most of those who left (about 80%) did so within the first 5 years of joining and the rest left within the following 5 years. Thus, almost all leavers had left before they reached the age of 35 years. In fact, the statistical departments of the kibbutz movements use in their demographic forecasts a leaving rate of 1 in 1000 per year for the 30–50 age group, and a zero yearly leaving rate for the age group of 50+. This means that it would be next to impossible to trace the population of ex-members, or at least a large unbiased sample of them, in their older ages when most deaths occur and when they had been out of kibbutz life for 30, 40, 50 and 60 years.

As a result of the nonexistence of any direct evidence one has to refer to indirect evidence, deduction and some speculation. First we look at what is known about the differences between stayers and leavers. As said, about 40–50% of the kibbutz-born adults eventually leave their kibbutzim and choose other ways of life [16]. Research into the differences between those who left and those who stayed as kibbutz members [17] has demonstrated that the most important differentiating factor between the two groups is their ideological identification with kibbutz values. Thus, any conclusion that the extent of LE is a result of selection into or out of kibbutz life implies a correlation between ideological convictions (e.g. to Socialist Zionism) and LE. We do not known of any research evidence to support such a claim.

(4) Nevertheless, it is claimed by some that in other groups with high ideological convictions LE was also found to be relatively high and therefore a correlation might exist between a biological tendency for longevity and ideological conviction. But these other ideologically oriented groups (e.g. the Mormons) were

also different in their social arrangements from their surrounding society. These arrangements offered many of the ingredients of kibbutz social life, like social support, public involvement, strong community ties and responsibility, respect for old age etc. Thus, indicating again the importance of environmental and societal factors rather than biological factors in determining LE.

One more point in this regard. Why should the depth of an ideological conviction, which is mostly a result of a process of socialization, be related to any biological disposition. Hence, why should a selection on the basis of ideological conviction (socialization) be correlated with a selection on the basis of a disposition (biology) for longevity? Indeed, in order to test for the validity of the correlation of ideological conviction *per se* and longevity, the best design would be to compare groups of individuals who differ from each other in the depth of their ideological conviction while all other relevant variables are controlled for; a task very difficult to achieve.

We also want to discard the possibility of two other 'weeding out' selection processes being responsible for the high LE of kibbutz members. The first suggests the death of the 'weaker' members during the early periods of the kibbutz existence (before statehood—35 years or more ago) when conditions were harsh and demanding. The second suggests the leaving of the kibbutzim by the 'weakest' of the 50+ age groups.

Had the first possibility been true it would still not have changed the results of the LE to any substantial degree, for it assumes high death rates for the 20–50 age group. But less than 10% of all deaths occur in this age bracket. Death rates in the age category had at least to triple in order to significantly affect the LE of the population. There is no record or any other evidence for such epidemic death in the kibbutzim at any period.

The second possibility does not exist at all because the leaving rate of those over 50 is practically nil. It is also unlikely that the 'weakest' of this age group would leave a secure situation like the kibbutz society.

(5) The kibbutz population in Israel is only 3.5% of the Jewish population in the country. The gender differences in LE of the Jewish population in Israel also seem to be relatively small: 3.5 years at birth as compared to an expected difference of 5.1 years, which is a deviation of 1.74 SEs, while the deviation from the expected value for the kibbutz intergender difference at birth stands at 1.60 SEs. This suggests that the findings reported about the kibbutz population in this study may reflect a phenomenon which is characteristic of the Jewish population in general and not unique to the kibbutz. Our interpretation of the data is different. Although the Israeli data reflect a relatively strong deviation from the expected value, the kibbutz life has something unique that reduces the intergender gap in LE even further.

This is evidenced in two facts:

(i) The deviation of the kibbutz intergender gap in LE at age 50 is 1.82 SEs compared to a deviation of 1.51 SEs for the Jewish population (an observed gap of 2.2 vs an expected gap of 4.2). Accepting the argument that gender differences in LE at older ages are more influenced by environmental factors that at younger ages points to the conclusion that the kibbutz life has a unique contribution to bridging the intergender gap in LE.

(ii) The kibbutz population of both genders have LEs that are in a totally different category to that of the Jewish population of Israel in 1977. At birth the LE for males in Israel was 71.9 years, which in standardized scores is 0.97, for females the figure was 75.4 years, a standardized score of 0.62; at age 50 the figures were 25.7 years (0.85 in standardized scores) for males and 27.9 years (0.17 in standardized scores) for females. These figures are to be compared with the kibbutz data (Table 2) which give standardized scores of 1.33 and 1.85 for males, and 1.02 and 1.03 for females. We contend that one cannot claim the kibbutz population to be so different from the Israeli population in LE and yet view them as belonging to the same population on a variable which is a function of LE.

Incidently, inspection of age-specific death rates of Israeli Jews and the kibbutz population reveals that the death rates of the kibbutz groups is lower for all adult female groups of ages 30+ and for male groups at ages 50+. It is higher for the kibbutz males at ages 20–49. We speculate that this reflects the fact that kibbutz males serve in disproportionally higher percentages in combat units in their military roles, which carry risks to life above the norm at these ages. Calculating the LE for kibbutz males with the Israeli males' death rates for ages 20–49, replacing their actual death rates, does not raise their LE substantially (from 74.5 to only 74.7 years) but the intergender gap in LE is decreased to 4.2 which deviates from the expected value by 1.74 SEs (rather than 1.60 SEs), which is exactly the extent of deviation from the expected shown by the intergender difference of the general Jewish population.

(6) The points raised in the discussion about the possibility of selection processes being the major factors determining for kibbutz members the intergender gap in LE and LE *per se* disputes their likelihood and probability. This strengthens the view that it is the environmental and social situation of the kibbutzim that must be given the major credit for these results.

However, it is important to note that we are in no position to claim that the biological and genetic factors are not important. Even in the current kibbutz population we still find intergender differences in LE that could be related either to the remainder of the differentiated gender roles on the kibbutz *or* to some biological factors. Our findings, however, enable us to say that close to half of the differences in LE found across many societies (the reduction in the gender difference in LE from the expected 7.1 to the actual 4.5 years) are due to social/environmental factors.

(7) To what extent are the findings and conclusions reported here able to be generalized to other societies? The answer to this question hinges upon the validity of the previous argument:

If the kibbutz population does not differ from the rest of society in terms of its biological and genetic predisposition and the gender differences in focus here are the result of societal and environmental arrangements and conduct then, in principle, there should not be any barrier to generalizing from these findings. It might be possible to argue that other societies, by adopting the same principles of conduct (some or all) that guide kibbutz life, would bring about similar results in their intergender differences in LE.

(8) The causal model assumed in this paper thus far has posited two clusters of variables in a causal chain: (a) socially gender-differentiated roles determine (b) the size of gender differences in LE. Clearly, there must be intervening variables that connect the two groups of variables and explain why and how (a) affects (b). This is a task set for further research. The relevant intervening variables are of the kind that represent the gender differences in stress and non-stress situations and in role demands, as well as in the gender differences in strain reactions to those factors. Further research should focus upon sex-typed roles in the kibbutz as compared with sex-typed roles outside the kibbutz. It should also focus upon health-risk indicators such as coffee and tobacco consumption, psychosomatic reactions, blood pressure and paper-and-pencil stress indicators. Finally, research should be done on gender differences in morbidity (type and intensity) and on gender differences in the distribution of causes of death.

Another line of promising research is the comparison of the separate kibbutz movements to each other. Although the similarity among them with regard to the physical, environmental and community conditions is very high, differences do exist in the amount of gender differentiation in the sex-typed roles, as research has reported [18–20]. Preliminary calculations comparing two movements on the relation of intergender differences in LE to the extent of intergender differentiation in sex-typed roles have born out the major hypothesis of this paper but we still refrain from reporting this study as the size of the population upon which the LEs were calculated is still too small to be considered stable (about 1600 deaths in 5 years). A few more years need to pass before a more stable pattern is established and these findings are worthy of publication.

REFERENCES

1. Gillard P. Vieillissement demographique et planification hospitalière Lausanne, Cantan de Vaud, Department de l'Interieur, 1969. (As cited in Rhef H.A. *Human Aging and Retirement*. General Secretariat, International Social Security Association, Geneva, 1974.)
2. Central Bureau of Statistics. *Statistical Abstracts of Israel*, Jerusalem, 1944, 1978, 1979.
3. Verbrugge L. M. Recent trends in sex mortality differentials in the U.S. *Women Hlth* **5,** 17–37, 1981.
4. *United Nations Demographic Yearbook*, New York, 1976, 1981.
5. *Hagil Hachadash* (Hebrew). Israeli Gerontological Association, Nov. 1980.
6. Madigan F. C. and Vance R. B. Differential sex mortality: a research design. *Soc. Forces* **53,** 193–199, 1957.
7. Nathanson C. A. Sex illness and medical care. A review of data, theory and methods. *Soc. Sci. Med.* **11,** 13–25, 1977.
8. Verbrugge L. M. Sex differentials in morbidity and mortality in the U.S. *Soc. Biol.* **23,** 275–296, 1976.
9. Lewis C. E. and Lewis M. A. The potential impact of sexual equality on health. *New Engl. J. Med.* **297,** 863–869, 1977.
10. Graney M. J. An exploration of social factors influencing the sex differential in mortality. *Sociol. Symp.*, 1979.
11. Waldron I. Why do women live longer than men. *Soc. Sci. Med.* **10,** 349–362, 1976.
12. Leviatan U., Am-Ad Z. and Adar G. *Aging in the Kibbutz: Satisfaction with Life and Its Antecedents.* Institute for Research of the Kibbutz, Univ. of Haifa, 1982.
13. House J. S., Robbins C. and Metzner H. L. The association of social relations and activity with mortality. *Am. J. Epid.* **116,** 123–140, 1982.
14. Berkman L. F. and Syme S. L. Social networks, host resistance and mortality: a nine year follow-up study of Alameda County residents. *Am. J. Epid.* **109,** 186–204, 1979.
15. Shyrock H. S. *et al. The Methods and Materials of Demography* (condensed edition by Stockwell E. G.). Academic Press, New York, 1976.
16. Leviatan U. and Orchan E. Kibbutz-born members and their adjustment to new life outside the kibbutz. *Interchange* **13,** 16–28, 1982.
17. Rosner M., Ben David Y., Avnat A., Cohen N. and Leviatan U. *The Second Generation: the Kibbutz between Continuity and Change.* Sifriat Hapoalim, Tel-Aviv, 1978.
18. Tiger L. and Shepher Y. *Women in the Kibbutz.* Harcourt, Brace & Jovanovich, New York, 1975.
19. Leviatan U. *Differences between Male and Female Members of Kibbutzim in Public Involvement and Value Internalization.* Institute for Research of the Kibbutz, Univ. of Haifa, 1983 (Hebrew).
20. Cohen E. and Leinman E. Public participation in collective settlements in Israel. *Int. Rev. Community Dev.* **19–20,** 251–270, 1968.

Part II

Role Behavior in Coping with Health and Illness

10

Coping with Fertility in Israel: A Case Study of Culture Clash

Eileen Basker

INTRODUCTION

The intention of this paper is to describe a lay belief system of symbols and meanings associated with reproduction and to contrast it with the clinical belief system of medical practitioners. The juxtaposition of the two sets of beliefs will serve to point out discrepancies and incongruities in the two culturally anchored systems.

The study reported here fits logically into the ever-growing body of theory and research on medicine as a cultural system (Kleinman 1978) and on lay and professional "explanatory models" for illness or "troubles." We have stretched the concept of EM elaborated by Kleinman (1975, 1980) to give it relevance not only for "illness episodes" (Kleinman 1980: 105) but also for other crises for which medical intervention might be sought – in this instance, unwanted pregnancy.

Redlener and Scott (1979) analyzed the management of a case of pediatric meningitis from the perspective of conflicting ideologies (belief systems) and their resultant explanatory models. They illustrated with this dramatic example that, in the final analysis, the biomedical ideology could not be imposed by force on a resisting family. Despite the scientific knowledge of the medical practitioners, their ideology was not accepted as valid by the patient's family, and mutual ethnocentrism resulted in frustration and lack of satisfactory resolution for all parties concerned. A far cry from patient compliance with medical instructions, this was a case study in non-compliance and finally disengagement.

Meningitis with resultant permanent and serious mental and physical disability is more dramatic than unwanted pregnancy; it is also less common. In the following, I apply the concepts of lay and professional belief systems focused on reproduction and contraception, and explanatory models for conception and its prevention, to a case of unwanted pregnancy. I use for this purpose a case study of a married Jewish woman in Israel who applied for interruption of pregnancy by induced abortion. More specifically, I examine her belief system as it touches upon reproduction; compare it with the belief system of the medical mediators of contraception and abortion; and illustrate how lack of a common belief system impedes communication between the medical practitioners and the client, and puts the woman into a "bind" or "no-win situation" (Laing 1961) where none of the alternatives at her disposal seems correct. The options available for preventing pregnancy are unacceptable or inefficient; having a child is also not acceptable; termination of unwanted pregnancy by abortion is ethically and morally wrong.

The client and the gynecologist in the following study are both victims of their (non-congruent) belief systems regarding sexual intercourse and reproduction. Both are unaware of the incongruities in their beliefs.

By "belief system" I mean both the system of perceptions of "what is" (*culture*: Schneider's (1976) "system of symbols and meanings") and the system of perceptions of "what should be" (social *norms*: Schneider's "models for action").

As background to the basic non-congruence of meaning systems of the authorities on reproduction and their client, I shall also present a picture of interaction between doctor and patient in Israel.

BACKGROUND

The research on which this paper is based was conducted in 1976 in a hospital in Israel. One hundred and two married Jewish women who applied to the hospital's abortion committee for interruption of pregnancy were interviewed as part of a study of abortion and its antecedents.[1] The interviews, accompanied by coffee and cookies, were conducted during the several-hours-long waiting period between the social worker's brief interview of applicants and the committee hearing. The format of my interview was semi-structured, with open-ended questions designed to probe perceptions of the situation. The interviews were taped and transcribed verbatim.

Twenty to thirty women per week applied for abortion to the hospital at which this study was carried out. Nearly ninety percent of the applicants were married. Some data on the women studied are presented in Appendix 1.

In analyzing the verbatim transcripts of the interviews, I found patterns of belief and meaning repeating themselves in numerous interviews. The patterns were not congruent with social or demographic categories, although they tended to cluster in sub-populations. One of the more interesting patterns is that exemplified by the following case; it brings into clear contrast two meaning systems regarding reproduction, and the impact of the discrepancies between them on doctor-patient communication and on contraceptive behavior.

THE CASE EXAMPLE: PNINA

I have chosen here to present a single case from among the 102 interviewees. The case presents characteristics common to many of the women interviewed, and particularly the North-African-born (see Appendix 2). It illustrates several of the cultural dimensions on which one must focus if one is to understand reproductive behavior and the use of abortion in the Israeli setting. It also brings out the apparent contradictions between attitudes toward reproduction and actual behavior, and between symbolic meaning systems of patients and those of doctors.

Pnina was born in Algeria in 1937. She was 39 years old at the time of this study. She immigrated to Israel with her family in 1949, at age 12. She completed eight years of schooling, and married at age 19. Her husband, one year her senior, was also born in Algeria, finished 12 years of schooling, and at the time of the study he served in the standing army. Pnina and her husband had five children, and she had had one induced abortion prior to the study.

Aside from her first pregnancy, which had been desired as soon after marriage as possible, none of Pnina's pregnancies was planned. Her first two children were girls. When she became pregnant immediately after the birth of her second daughter, despite use of *coitus interruptus* by her husband, she weighed the alternative of abortion and decided against it, "because I wanted a son," as she told me. However, when she again became pregnant after the birth of her son, she had an induced abortion privately (i.e., not through a hospital committee), "because we didn't have an apartment," and she felt that her temporary living quarters would not accommodate another child. Thus between 1957 and 1961 she had three births and one abortion. Thereafter she and her husband managed to "be careful" for some two years before she again became pregnant.

The fourth delivery, a second son, was by Caesarean section. Pnina associated the necessity for the Caesarean with the fact of her having aborted the previous pregnancy. In her words, "With all of them I had a normal birth. The fourth being a Caesarean must be because of the abortion I had." Subsequently they were "careful" four and half years until the next unplanned pregnancy, at which point she again considered, and this time rejected, the alternative of abortion. "I watched out [*shamarti*, from the infinitive *lishmor*, to guard, protect, keep, observe]. But if it comes from above [i.e., the will of God], it can stay. I didn't dare to have an abortion." Their fifth child, a daughter, was born in 1969.

About seven months before my interview with Pnina, she underwent surgery for cholecystectomy (removal of the gall bladder). This was the reason she used as medical justification for her application to the hospital for abortion: "I've just had an operation. I'm not allowed [to be pregnant]."

Pnina's interpretation of the process leading to the diagnosis of gall bladder inflammation and the necessity for surgery illustrates the culture clash between Western medicine, as practiced in Israel, and Pnina's expectations and interpretations.

Pnina reported that she began to "feel bad," with headaches and vomiting. She assumed a gynecological problem, because although she had not missed a menstrual period and did not suspect pregnancy, the nausea and vomiting resembled her symptoms at the start of pregnancy. She turned first to Dr. A., the gynecologist at her local clinic, whom she could consult under her medical insurance scheme without extra charge. She said that he had told her, "You don't have anything, just a fungus infection. It's nothing." He had found nothing pathological *as far as his particular specialty was concerned*; however, he did not add this reservation in his communication to Pnina. Pnina, still feeling ill and believing that a private doctor would know better than a clinic doctor what the trouble was, followed a friend's recommendation and turned to Dr. B., a private (female) gynecologist.[2] Dr. B. advised Pnina to use contraceptive pills, and from Pnina's reconstruction of the conversation we deduce that this gynecologist, also attuned to interpreting symptoms in terms of her own medical specialty, attributed Pnina's headaches and vomiting to apprehension lest she get pregnant again. Dr. B., according to Pnina, said, "You must be free [*ḥofshia*]. Take these pills, one each evening, and be free." Pnina reported to me that she took the pills as directed, began to eat and gain weight, and after one month stopped the pills because her family doctor in the sick fund clinic, Dr. C., examined her and said she needed an operation. She did not return to the private gynecologist.

Pnina began with self-diagnosis:

Vomiting + headaches = gynecological disorder.

For a gynecological disorder, the path to treatment began with a gynecological specialist whose fee was paid by her medical insurance. The system in which such a gynecologist functions in Israel encourages attention to a narrow specialty. As Ben-David wrote twenty years ago regarding Israel's medical system:

> [The doctor] . . . feels much less personal responsibility for the patient [than a doctor in private practice], because of the minute division of labour between various specialists and/or because final responsibility rests with the institution [of *Kupat Ḥolim*].
>
> In consequence, there is relatively little direct motivation for 'service,' which creates a lack of congruence between the mutual expectations of the doctor and the patient and generates some feeling of tension. (Ben-David 1958: 266)

Dissatisfied with the gynecologist's handling of her complaint, Pnina faced the choice of returning to her family doctor in the clinic or going outside the clinic framework to a private gynecologist. She chose the latter, consulting a friend rather than a doctor for a referral. In Pnina's words, "The surest is a private doctor and we'll find out what it is."

The path Pnina took to the gall-bladder operation can be diagrammed as shown in Figure 1.

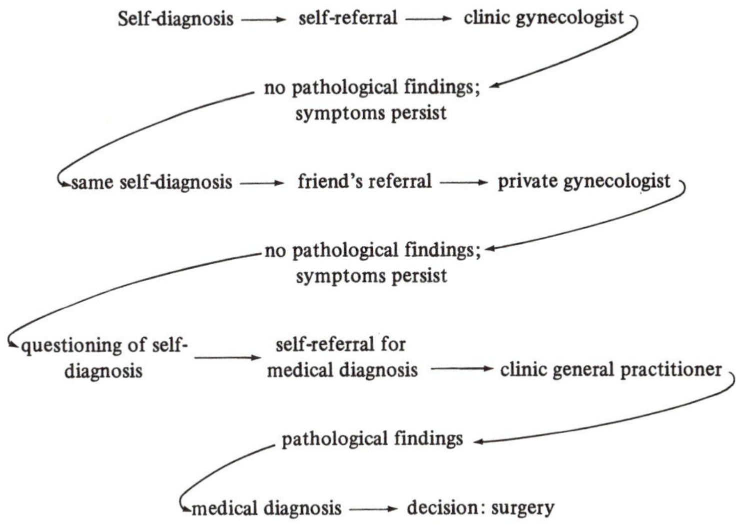

Fig. 1. The Path to Surgery

Into the process went a woman with symptoms of vomiting and headaches. Out came a post-operative patient, minus an internal organ, who saw herself as somehow changed, allowed to take certain liberties with the will of God because of her special circumstances, as illustrated in her handling of her subsequent pregnancy.

Following her operation, and having abandoned contraceptive pills, Pnina and her husband returned to use of *coitus interruptus* to prevent pregnancy. She was accustomed to menstruating regularly every 24 to 25 days. Some six months after the operation her period did not come on time. When she was two days late she began to suspect pregnancy: "I went to my mother's, and she was cooking. The smell made me feel sick, and I said, 'Mother, I'm in trouble. I should have gotten my period and I didn't.'" In order to be certain, Pnina reported, "I tried hot baths, compresses – nothing helped." Some of the friends with whom she discussed her fear of pregnancy suggested that perhaps she was beginning menopause: "Some said, 'Maybe your period is going away.' But that can't be, that at age 38 it stops. Afterwards I said I'd go to the doctor." Her family doctor, Dr. C., sent her for a pregnancy test; the result was negative.

Pnina would not accept this; her nausea and delayed period made her insist on a repeat test. Two weeks later Dr. C. sent her for a repeat test, which indeed showed pregnancy. Pnina told me, "I asked my doctor what would happen – he said, 'Nothing – you're pregnant.' So I said, 'What will I do? You know I'm just after an operation.' 'Ah, yes – right,' so he gave me a slip [referral] to have it out [aborted]." At that point the hospital regulations required written confirmation of the pregnancy by a gynecologist, so the family doctor, Dr. C., referred Pnina to the clinic gynecologist, Dr. A., a process which took another week.

It must be pointed out here that Pnina did not see abortion as an easy way out. She was convinced that her previous abortion had necessitated the subsequent Caesarean. She said she was afraid: "I don't like doing an abortion. I'm scared. It seems to me like I'm taking [literally: *moridah*: to take down, to cause to descend] a soul." Toward the end of the interview, I asked Pnina what she thought she would do after the abortion. She replied, "Maybe they'll turn my womb around [*oolai yahafḫu li et hareḥem*]." She apparently meant tubal ligation, but was not clear about what it was: "Not an operation. To turn the womb." When I explained that it was indeed a minor operation, she expressed concern about possible long-term dangers: "Nothing will happen to me? There's no danger to the body? My health won't suffer?"

ANALYSIS

In a careful reading of the verbatim text of Pnina's interview, one can discern two dimensions along which Pnina ordered her beliefs about reproduction. One dimension is a continuum from "watchfulness [*shmirah*]" to "freedom [*ḥofesh*]." This axis has both a general cultural meaning and a specific reproductive connotation: generally, *shmirah*, in addition to being a euphemism for *coitus interruptus*, is also used to refer to religious observance, while the adjective form *ḥofshi* means non-observant as well as free. Specifically, *shmirah* is associated with preventing pregnancy while *ḥofesh*, freedom from restrictions, will result in pregnancy.[3]

The second axis or dimension along which Pnina's beliefs about reproduction were ordered is a value-dimension of "natural-artificial," with the "natural" or "normal" end of the continuum to be preferred over the "artificial" or "abnormal" end. Interfering with God's will is "artificial." However, interference without resort to artificial means (e.g., *coitus interruptus*) gives God a "fair chance," and is perceived as more natural than using artificial contraception. The abortion which Pnina underwent between her third and fourth births was interpreted by her as unnatural. As punishment for interfering with nature, she was made to undergo a Caesarean section (also "unnatural") in her fourth delivery.

Integrated into Pnina's belief system is also the concept of "foreign body." Pnina and her husband rejected the idea of intrauterine contraception because of her apprehension of a foreign body. This apprehension had two components: the knowledge that the IUD is not "natural," and the belief that an evil influence could pervade her body through the medium of the foreign body. Pnina described her husband as having stated that if she got an IUD he would not touch her; the effect of the evil influence could extend to him as well. This apprehension was supported and reinforced by knowledge of cases where the insertion of an IUD had in fact had serious consequences: Pnina said, "My sister-in-law got a 'coil' and got pregnant outside her womb. She had all sorts of operations and complications."

We can represent the two axes of Pnina's belief about reproduction schematically, as shown in Figure 2. The four squares which result from this schematic representation can be filled with appropriate reproductive behavior.

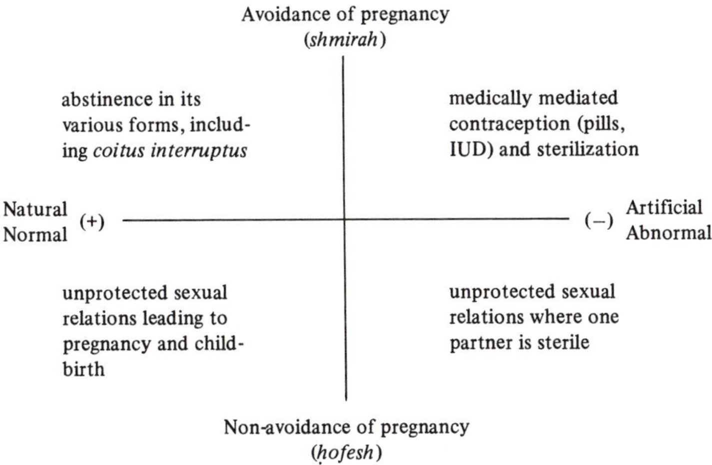

Fig. 2. Reproductive Behavior According to Pnina's Belief System

Pnina's apparently contradictory statements in the course of the interview, that they had used *coitus interruptus* all the time since the birth of their first child, but that she had wanted all of her five children, were not merely "selective remembering." Rather, this juxtaposition illustrates the belief that "natural *shmirah*" does not interfere with God's will. And one dare not admit that one desires other than God's will. Thus pregnancy that comes about despite *shmirah* is by definition desirable and not to be interfered with lightly. El-Hamamsy, writing about family planning in Egypt, explains the symbolic meaning of contraception as follows:

A peasant woman who for overriding reasons does not wish to have any more children will go ahead and use contraception, or even induce abortion. . . . But a contraceptive user may nevertheless harbor the anxiety that she may be pitting her will against God's and live in dread of consequences. (El-Hamamsy 1972: 349)

For the gynecologist whom Pnina consulted, the loaded value dimension was not "natural-artificial," but rather "relaxed-tense," and *ḥofesh* was understood as synonymous not with "non-avoidance of pregnancy" but with "relaxed," as shown in Figure 3.

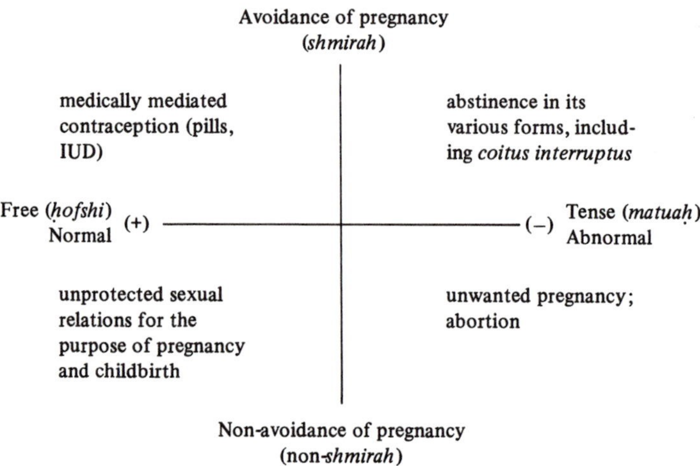

Fig. 3. Reproductive Behavior According to the Gynecologist's Belief System

When the private gynecologist prescribed contraceptive pills for Pnina, that doctor equated taking the pills with "being free." The word "free" connoted, for Dr. B., "freedom from worry," "freedom from tension," "freedom from fear of pregnancy." For Pnina, "free" connoted "unrestrained." Pills to prevent pregnancy had no connotation of freedom for Pnina, who saw them rather as an artificial means of *shmirah* which denied the will of God by excluding the chance of pregnancy.

DISCUSSION

Two features of a study of married Jewish women applying for interruption of pregnancy give it wider significance than "just another study of abortion." First, the women on whom this study focused could each have carried on with her pregnancy without fear of social sanctions, in that they were all married. Yet each had chosen to interrupt her pregnancy instead. Secondly, by the act of applying for abortion, each woman indicated her willingness to interfere with natural fertility; at this point at least she was not passively relying on "fate" or "the powers that be," but was herself taking an active step in controlling her fertility.

As shown in Appendix 1, Pnina's case can be viewed as more than idiosyncratic. She was representative both in background and in belief configuration of one of the dominant patterns which appeared in this population.

In the Introduction, I mentioned that the woman in the case study presented here did not share the belief system of the medical establishment. The gynecologist Pnina consulted, Dr. B., recommended contraceptive pills so that Pnina could be "free" of worry about pregnancy, while Pnina saw being "free" as inviting pregnancy and possibly dangerous. Contraceptive advice in Israel, as elsewhere today, stresses the pill and the IUD; both were perceived by Pnina as "artificial," foreign bodies. In addition to their potential capacity to harm by being vehicles for evil influence, both contraceptives had real objective drawbacks: the pill had made her fat; the IUD could cause extrauterine pregnancy.

From another point of view, the medical establishment had a credibility problem as far as Pnina was concerned. Her experience with the medical world had not always been positive. Neither the clinic gynecologist, Dr. A., nor the private gynecologist, Dr. B., had succeeded in diagnosing her problem as a gall bladder inflammation. And her family doctor, Dr. C., apparently forgot her medical history when she went to him for confirmation of her most recent pregnancy.

A recent paper (Jordan 1977) analyzed the competence of women to diagnose their own pregnancies. The case under discussion here illustrates the length of time needed by medical professionals to confirm the lay diagnosis of pregnancy. The final medical confirmation of Pnina's pregnancy took almost two months from the day she knew she was "in trouble." This time lapse, considered to be a necessary accompaniment to the scientification of medicine, did not help medical credibility for Pnina.

One of the barriers keeping Pnina and her husband from so-called "rational" methods of fertility control was a concern with body integrity, body wholeness – Fisher's (1973) concept of "body consciousness." Artificial interference with natural processes, such as insertion of an IUD to prevent pregnancy, or tubal ligation for sterilization, may threaten body wholeness and ego boundaries. Pulos et al. (1974) describe the body boundary as ". . . concerned primarily with how one's body relates to the environment, as perceived by the person, and includes such assessments as the vulnerability of the body to outside forces and the resiliency of it to protect the individual." (Pulos et al. 1974: 540)

The case of Pnina illustrates the conflicting meaning systems which may underlie communication difficulties and actually contribute to "irrational" behavior. The language of reproduction and contraception carries meanings for all of us, which, in turn, involve a network of associations and experiences. By seeking out and analyzing these meanings, we can reach greater understanding of apparently incomprehensible attitudes and behavior of both participants in the doctor-patient dialogue.

CONCLUSION

I have tried to describe belief systems and their component parts (*cultural* symbols and meanings, and *social* norms for action) as they affect reproduction and fertility control in the Israeli context.

The case of Pnina illustrates a cultural "double bind" (c.f., Weakland 1960) or what Laing (1961) calls a "no-win situation." Pnina and her husband had accepted and assimilated norms regarding interference with natural fertility without changing their cultural perception of artificial intervention as dangerous and wrong. They wanted to limit the size of their family; the options available to them were either unacceptable, given their cultural perceptions, or acceptable but inefficient, leading to other unacceptable consequences. Laing (1961: 125) describes the "no-win situation" as one in which

> The 'victim' is caught in a tangle of paradoxical injunctions, or of attributions having the force of injunctions, in which he cannot do the right thing.

Pnina, in her cultural bind about how to cope with her fertility, is the personification of Liang's "victim."

In this case, as in the Redlener and Scott (1979) study, patient cooperation was thwarted by medical ethnocentrism, and, as in the meningitis study, the result (abortion, feared by the patient and seen as unacceptable birth control by the doctors) constituted a surrender of values by both patient and practitioners.

ACKNOWLEDGEMENTS

This research was supported in part by the Georg Waechter Memorial Foundation. An earlier version of this paper was presented at the annual meeting of the Israel Anthropological Association, Jerusalem, March, 1978; this version was presented at the 80th Annual Meeting of the American Anthropological Association, December 1981. I should like to thank Eric Cohen, Ilse Schuster, Don Handelman and Noel Chrisman for their helpful comments.

NCJW Institute for Innovation in Education
School of Education
The Hebrew University
Jerusalem, Israel

NOTES

1 The study constituted the material for my doctoral dissertation (Basker 1980).

2 A description of the structure of medical practice in Israel, where over 75% of the population is insured through the General Federation of Labor's *Kupat Ḥolim* ("sick fund"), is beyond the scope of this paper (see Ben-David 1958). However, in very brief and general terms we can say that medical specialists, on modest salaries, usually see many patients during short office hours, and both clinic and hospital specialists tend to have private practices in their homes "after hours." The belief that one gets more personal attention from a doctor on a private visit is substantially correct. The belief that one gets "better doctoring" privately is also widely held.

3 There is, to be sure, a certain ambiguity here, an eventuality which Schneider (1976) recognizes as "built-in" to his definition of culture. Among orthodox Jews, "real" *shmirah*, or complete compliance with God's commandments, means not doing anything to prevent pregnancy – freedom from protection against pregnancy – although not freedom from all restrictions, because orthodox Jewish law has many purity proscriptions regarding sexual intercourse.

REFERENCES

Basker, Eileen
1980 Belief Systems, Cultural Milieu and Reproductive Behavior: Women Seeking Abortions in a Hospital in Israel. Ph.D. dissertation, Hebrew University, Jerusalem.

Ben-David, J.
1958 The Professional Role of the Physician in Bureaucratized Medicine: A Study in Role Conflict. Human Relations **11**: 255–274.

El-Hamamsy, L. S.
1972 Belief Systems and Family Planning in Peasant Societies. *In* H. Brown and E. Hutchings, Jr. (eds.), Are Our Descendents Doomed? New York: Viking Press, pp. 335–357.

Fisher, Seymour
1973 Body Consciousness. Englewood Cliffs, N.J.: Prentice-Hall (Spectrum).

Jordan, Brigitte
1977 The Self-Diagnosis of Early Pregnancy: An Investigation of Lay Competence. Medical Anthropology **1**(2): 1–40.

Kleinman, Arthur
1975 Explanatory Models in Health Care Relationships. *In* National Council for International Health: Health of the Family. Washington, D.C.: National Council for International Health, pp. 159–172.

Kleinman, Arthur
1978 Concepts and a Model for the Comparison of Medical Systems as Cultural Systems. Social Science and Medicine **12**: 85–93.

Kleinman, Arthur
1980 Patients and Healers in the Context of Culture. Berkeley: University of California Press.

Laing, R. D.
1961 Self and Others. London: Tavistock.

Pulos, S. M., A. O. Wollitzer, and J. H. Vitale
1974 Body Image Alterations in Adults Due to Cerebrovascular Insufficiency. Journal of Personality Assessment **38**: 540–546.

Redlener, Irwin E. and Clarissa S. Scott
1979 Incompatibilities of Professional and Religious Ideology: Problems of Medical Management and Outcome in a Case of Pediatric Meningitis. Social Science and Medicine **13B**: 89–93.

Schneider, David M.
1976 Notes toward a Theory of Culture. *In* K. Basso and H. Selby (eds.), Meaning in Anthropology. Albuquerque: University of New Mexico Press, pp. 197–220.
Weakland, J. H.
1960 The 'Double-Bind' Hypothesis of Schizophrenia and Three-Party Interaction. *In* D. D. Jackson (ed.), The Etiology of Schizophrenia. New York: Basic Books.

APPENDIX 1

Sociodemographic Data, Hospital Abortion Applicants*
(n = 102)

Current Age		Previous Births	
24 or less	17%	0	–
25–29	22%	1	7%
30–39	47%	2	25%
40+	14%	3	25%
		4	19%
Continent of Birth		5	8%
Europe, America	21%	6+	18%
Africa	37%		
Asia	21%	Previous Abortions	
Israeli-born	22%	0	51%
		1	25%
Years of Schooling		2	13%
8 or less	51%	3+	12%
9–12	34%		
13 or more	12%		
Unknown	3%		

* Totals do not always equal 100%, due to rounding.

APPENDIX 2

Comparative Data on Twenty-One North African-Born Women Aged 30–39

North-African-born women aged 30 to 39 constituted 20.6% of the research population. Selected sociodemographic characteristics of these twenty-one women are:

Characteristic	Mean	Standard Deviation	Pnina
Age	34.7	3.2	39
Age of immigration	15.6	7.2	12
Years of schooling	7.6	2.4	8
Previous pregnancies	7.0	2.0	6
Previous abortions	1.2	1.3	1

Pnina might be considered representative of North African-born women in their 30's who sought abortions at the hospital studied during the period of the study, in that she falls within one standard deviation of the mean on the above characteristics.

The social worker's records indicated that sixteen of these twenty-one women (including Pnina) were using "no contraception." My interviews disclosed that of those sixteen, fourteen (including Pnina) were in fact using *coitus interruptus* to avoid pregnancy.

11

Advice from the Obstetrician and Other Sources: Do They Affect Women's Feeding Practices? A Study among Different Jewish Groups in Jerusalem

Ivonne Mansbach, Hava Palti, Bella Pevsner, Helen Pridan, and *Zvi Palti*

Many studies on breast feeding have shown that advice and support that women receive before and after parturition have a positive effect on their breast feeding practices [1–6]. Advice and support are offered by many sources, among them family members, nurses, general physicians, obstetricians and printed material of a wide range of quality. The purpose of this work is to elucidate the association between the existing support systems in Israel and the practice of breast feeding.

About 50% of pregnant women attend the network of preventive Maternal and Child Health Services during pregnancy and another 50% attend private physicians or hospital clinics. None of the women are without care during pregnancy. All women attend hospital for delivery and 95% attend, with their infants, the preventive MCH services [7]. This high attendance rate exposes the women to many sources of advice. We want to study the effectiveness of their message.

MATERIALS AND METHODS

A population of 402 women who gave birth between January and July, 1979, in Hadassah Mount Scopus Hospital in Jerusalem, Israel, was studied regarding their past and present breast feeding practices. All consecutive cases of women who were delivered of a single birth and who lived within a defined geographical area were included in the study. They were interviewed on four occasions: within 24 hours of parturition in the hospital; before leaving the hospital; between 6 and 7 weeks postpartum at home; and between 4 and 5 months postpartum at home. Sixty-nine percent (276) of the target population answered all four questionnaires. Comparison of those who answered all four questionnaires with those who complied partially indicated that the groups were similar in regard to age, country of origin and educational standard as measured by years of schooling.

A closed questionnaire was filled out on each occasion by an interviewer. In order to detect the sources of information and support we asked the women whether they had received guidance on breast feeding and from whom. The list of sources of advice included reading material, mother, sister, friend, Mother and Child Health Services (MCH) nurse and physician, Sick Fund physician, private physician and hospital physician.

In the fourth interview specific questions on whether the woman had discussed breast feeding with the obstetrician during the postpartum examination were included.

The study population was Jewish and consisted of highly educated women: 52.6% had 13 years or more of schooling and only 5.8% had 8 or less years of schooling. Ethnic background was defined by country or origin of the woman or of her father if she was Israeli born, and we found that 52.5% were of

European or American origin, 21.1% were of Asian origin, 15.7% of North African origin and 10.7% were second generation Israeli. Social class (sc) was classified according to the British Registrar's General Occupational Categories adapted for use in Israel [8] and thus 26.4 and 21% belonged to sc I and II respectively, 17.1% to sc III_2 (white collar workers), 22.1% to sc III_3–IV and V (blue collar and unskilled workers) and 13.2% were wives of students, which is considered a separate category.

Chi square test was used to evaluate the association between different sources of advice and duration of breast feeding, taken in categories such as never breast fed, short term duration (up to 6 weeks) and long term duration (more than 6 weeks). Analysis of variance [9] was used to calculate the separate effects of social class, ethnic origin and advice of obstetrician on the duration of breast feeding, using number of weeks of breast feeding as the dependent variable. Differences resulting in $P < 0.05$ were considered significant.

RESULTS

The prevalence of breast feeding was determined at 4 points: before leaving hospital, at 6 weeks, at 3 months and at 4½ months postpartum. We found that 89.7% of the women were breast feeding when they left the hospital, 62.4% after 6 weeks, 40.3% at 3 months and 27.3% after 4½ months postpartum.

Sixty nine point three percent of women stated that during pregnancy, reading material was a source of guidance and 63.8% mentioned their mother as a source of guidance during that period. Thirty percent of the women reported getting advice from the MCH service nurse and 15% from physicians. The MCH service physician was mentioned by only 2.6% of the total of the women. The women had the possibility to declare more than one source of guidance.

During hospital stay 53.6% of the women reported getting guidance from a hospital nurse especially assigned to this task. A lower percentage of women declared receiving advice from any source after hospital discharge than during pregnancy or during hospital stay (Fig. 1).

Reported guidance on breast feeding by all sources combined indicated that during pregnancy 96.4% of women got advice at least from one source, 53.6% did so during hospital stay, 50.4% mentioned at least one source of guidance in the period after hospital discharge up to 6 weeks and 36.2% of the women declared getting advice from any source between 6 weeks and 4½ months postpartum.

Guidance obtained from reading materials during pregnancy and after hospital discharge, as well as from an educational pre-birth course (Lamaze) were found to be statistically associated with breast feeding practices at 6 weeks and 5 months postpartum, but these associations disappeared when controlling for educational standard or social class. No significant associations were found between other sources of guidance and duration of breast feeding at any specific period, with the exception of advice from the obstetrician during the postpartum examination.

Eighty one point five percent of the women visited the obstetrician around 6 weeks postpartum, 16.3% did not attend this examination and for 2.2% data was not available. In all subsequent analyses that refer to the relationship between the independent variables and breast feeding (i.e. analysis of variance and χ^2 test) are included only those cases who had visited the obstetrician and for which information was complete. The following results are based on these 204 cases.

In order to study the relationship between long-term duration of breast feeding and reported advice from an obstetrician we grouped all women who visited the obstetrician into two categories: those breast feeding at 4½ months and those who had stopped breast feeding before that. We found that 72% were not breast feeding by 4½ months post-partum while 28% still were. Of those breast feeding 66.7% (42) reported discussing breast feeding with the obstetrician during the examination, while among those who were not breast feeding by 4½ months postpartum only 13.6% (22) reported having discussed the subject of breast feeding on that occasion (Fig. 2).

Attendance at the postpartum examination was high among women of sc I and II—88.5% and 91.7% respectively—as well as among women of the lower sc—81.8%—but less among middle class women—72.9%—and wives of students—79.4% (Table 1).

When asked specifically in the last interview 29.4% of the women reported having discussed breast feeding with the obstetrician during the 6 weeks postpartum examination. Of them, the percentage who received advice from each sc was evenly distributed, except for the lower sc in which only 6.7% declared that they received advice ($\chi^2 = 15.21$, $P = 0.004$) (Table 2).

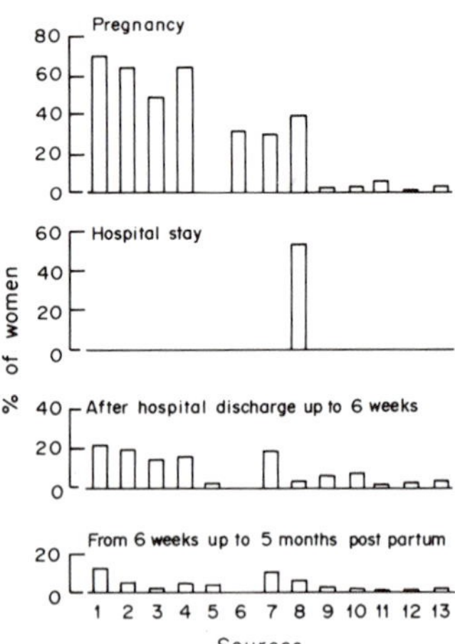

Fig. 1. Percentage of women who received guidance on breast feeding by source of guidance at various stages 1—Reading; 2—mother; 3—sister or sister-in-law; 4—friend; 5—other; 6—Lamaze course; 7—MCH clinic nurse; 8—hospital nurse; 9—MCH clinic physician; 10—Sick Fund physician; 11—private physician; 12—hospital physician; 13—obstetrician.

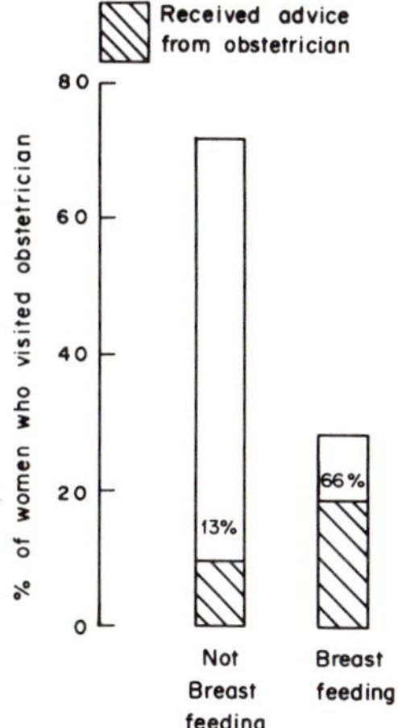

Fig. 2. Percentage of women who received advice from the obstetrician during the postpartum examination by breast feeding practice at $4\frac{1}{2}$ months postpartum.

Among those women who were not breast feeding by the time they visited the obstetrician only 15% reported discussing breast feeding, as compared to 37% among those who were breast feeding at the time of their visit (Table 3). This came to answer whether those women who had stopped breast feeding before they visited the obstetrician actually reported less discussion with him.

We compared all those women who visited the obstetrician (204) with those who still were breast feeding at the time of the postpartum examination (133) by sc in order to see whether those who had stopped breast feeding before that time constituted a distinct group. We found that some women from every sc had stopped breast feeding by the time they visited the obstetrician, although the group which was most affected was the lower sc group in which 49% of its members had stopped breast feeding at 6 weeks postpartum. (Table 4).

We studied the relationship between advice of the obstetrician and breast feeding practice only on those women who were still breast feeding when they had their postpartum exam and excluded those who already had stopped breast feeding by then, as they represented two distinct groups with different probabilities of receiving advice.

A second examination of long-term duration of breast feeding—14 weeks or more—by advice of obstetrician was performed, this time including only those women still breast feeding at the time of the postpartum exam. We found that among those who breast fed less than 14 weeks only 13% reported getting advice from the obstetrician, as compared to 50% among those who breast fed 14 weeks or more. The differences were statistically significant ($\chi^2 = 20.07$, $P = 0.001$) (Table 5).

These results are not very different from those in Fig. 2 which were calculated for all women who had visited the obstetrician for the postpartum exam,

Table 1. Percentage of women who visited the obstetrician in each social class

sc	Visited Yes	Visited No	Total %	Total *n*
Students	79.4	20.6	100	27
I	88.5	11.5	100	54
II	91.7	8.3	100	43
III_2	72.9	27.1	100	35
III_3–V	81.8	18.2	100	45
	83.9	16.1	100	204
Unknown sc	58.2	41.8	100	21
Total	81.5	18.5	100	225

Table 2. Percentage of women who received advice on breast feeding from the obstetrician within each social class

sc	Advice Yes %	Advice No %	Total %	Total *n*
Students	37	63	100	27
I	32	68	100	54
II	40	60	100	43
III_2	37	63	100	35
III_3–V	7	93	100	45
Total	29	71	100	204

$\chi^2 = 15.21$; $P = 0.0043$.

Table 3. Percentage of women declaring advice from obstetrician by breast feeding practice at 6 weeks

		Breast feeding at 6 weeks No %	Breast feeding at 6 weeks Yes %	Total *n*
Advice of obstetrician	No	85	63	159
	Yes	15	37	65
	Total %	100	100	
	Total *n*	79	145	224

$\chi^2 = 10.31$; $P = 0.0013$.

Table 4. Breast feeding practice at the time of visit to the obstetrician for postpartum examination by social class

sc	Breast feeding practice Yes %	No %	Total %	Total *n*
Students	74	26	100	27
I	67	33	100	54
II	74	26	100	43
III_2	66	34	100	35
III_3–V	49	51	100	45
Total	65	35	100	204

$\chi^2 = 7.55$; d.f. = 4, NS.

Table 5. Percentage of women breast feeding for 14 weeks or more by advice of obstetrician*

		Breast feeding for 14 weeks or more No	Yes	Total *n*
Advice of obstetrician	No	87	50	92
	Yes	13	50	52
	Total %	100	100	
	Total *n*	54	98	144

$\chi^2 = 20.07$; $P = 0.00001$.

*Includes only women who were breast feeding at the time they visited the obstetrician.

regardless of feeding practice at the time of the postpartum exam.

The effects of social class, ethnicity and advice of obstetrician upon duration of breast feeding were studied by analysis of variance. Age of mother and parity were also considered and were found not to be associated with duration of breast feeding in our study.

The mean duration of breast feeding for the total population who visited the obstetrician was 13.3 weeks. The mean duration of breast feeding for those women who were still breast feeding by the time they visited the obstetrician for the postpartum examination was 18.8 weeks. The analysis of variance was performed in this second group only. The independent effect of each variable was studied while controlling for all other in the model.

The effect of sc upon duration of breast feeding was statistically significant. The longest duration was observed for students and sc I mothers, whereas the shortest duration was noted in sc III_2 (white collar workers) who had a mean duration of breast feeding of 12.7 weeks.

Differences in duration of breast feeding by ethnic group were statistically significant. Women of European–American origin or Israeli born women from European–American descent had longer breast feeding practices—21.3 weeks and 19.4 weeks respectively, while women from Asian–North African origin or Israeli born from Asian–North African descent had the lowest duration—16.9 weeks and 14.4 weeks respectively—controlling for sc and advice of obstetrician.

Those receiving advice from the obstetrician breast fed 23.1 weeks whereas those not receiving advice only 16.3 weeks. The differences were highly significant.

The model explained 38.6% of the variance. The largest contribution to the explained variance came from the advice of the obstetrician: 12.1%.

DISCUSSION

Winikoff and Baer found that the most significant correlate of successful breast feeding is social class [10]. Martinez and Nalezienski [11] showed that whereas in the 30s and 40s breast feeding was more prevalent among lower sc women, it became an accepted feeding practice in middle and upper classes in the 70s among American women. In our study sc was also associated with breast feeding practices: upper classes and students breast fed more and the duration of breast feeding was longer than in the middle class. We also found more breast feeding women among the lower sc than in the middle class.

Ethnicity was strongly associated with duration of breast feeding practices. Women from Western societies such as Europe and America, breast fed more and longer than those of Asian and North African origin. This is a reversal of the breast feeding pattern described by Thaustein in the 50s in Israel [12]. Women of American and European origin participate in the social movements that intend a return to natural ways of life and to lessen the influence of technology and mechanization on our daily living, whereas among Asian and North African populations, those groups that are on the threshold of modernization want to emulate that 'advanced' and 'easy' way of rearing children and get away from 'primitive' practices. This can very well be appreciated in Israel where many different cultures mingle and although services and guidance and information are basically uniform, breast feeding patterns are distinct for the different groups.

Table 6. The effect of social class, ethnicity and advice of obstetrician on duration of breast feeding*

Grand mean			18.8 weeks			
Factors	Category	n	Mean duration adjusted for the other factors	F	P	% Explained variance
Social class	Students	20	21.0			
	I	36	20.2			
	II	32	18.5	2.719	0.033	5.43
	III_2	23	12.7			
	III_3–V	22	19.3			
Ethnicity	Asian–North African	17	16.9			
	Europe-America	46	21.3			
	Israeli (Asian origin)	25	14.4	3.081	0.019	6.15
	Israeli (European origin)	30	19.4			
	Israeli (2nd, generation)	15	18.8			
Advice of obstetrician	No	84	16.3	24.139	0.01	12.11
	Yes	49	23.1			
Total n		133				
Total explained variance						38.6

*This table includes only those women who were still breast feeding by the time they visited the obstetrician for postpartum examination.

The advice of the obstetrician during the postpartum examination was significantly associated with increased duration of breast feeding of the upper and middle class women. Very few lower sc women declared receiving advice, but among the upper and middle class ones, those who declared receiving advice breast fed longer than those who did not. Newton and Newton [13] reported than an enthusiastic physician can develop a practice in which breast feeding rates are far above the usual in the rest of society. That is, if advice is given and specially by the obstetrician, it has a significant effect on breast feeding rates. Huntingford [14] explains that in the population he studied the mother inevitably looked to the leader of the medical team for advice and guidance. Deutsch and Gerard stress the fact that the normative and informational functions of a reference group, in this case the obstetrician, are usually inextricably linked with one another and occur simultaneously [15]. Information may be supportive in the sense that it makes the woman's task easier and provides more chances of success, while support is in itself informative since it gives the woman a cue to action.

Winikoff and Baer state that minimal expressions of interest by physicians, simply inquiring whether the woman is breast feeding, can make a difference [10]. Even mention of the topic of breast feeding has an informative and supportive effect among some segments of the population. This can be explained in view of the high prestige and status of the specialist within our population and the strong influence he can exert as a result of it. The woman will pay more attention to the informational content of his message than if it came from someone with lower status [16].

Among women of the lower sc, although attendance at the obstetrician's postpartum exam was as high as among other sc, only 6.7% declared that they received advice on breast feeding during that visit, as compared to 31.5, 39.5 and 37.1% among sc I, II and III_2 respectively. We have seen that among those who had stopped breast feeding before they visited the obstetrician fewer women reported receiving advice (15%) than among those who were still breast feeding (37%). More of those who had already stopped belonged to the lower sc—51%—as compared to 33 and 26% in sc I and II respectively. However, this might still not be the only variable which affects reporting of advice from obstetrician by lower sc women. Additional explanations for low reporting could be that the advice was given but the women underestimated it because they expected more, i.e. not only cues but clear and directive information; or that the advice was not given because the obstetrician did not expect these women to breast feed but to follow the usual pattern of 'lower class—bottle feeding'.

It is also possible that the obstetrician did not approach the subject of breast feeding because he did not consider it important or had more appropriate topics to discuss during that short visit. It has been found that obstetricians believe that breast feeding belongs to the domain of the pediatrician and vice versa. Still, these last arguments would not explain the differential advice reported in different social classes but would be relevant to all groups. Huntingford [14] believes that doctors and midwives are indifferent not because they do not believe in the value of breast feeding but for other reasons, such as that the need for breast feeding is less urgent with the availability of artificial milks. Applebaum proposes that the lack of encouragement from the physician stems from his basic lack of understanding of the fundamental principles of breast structure and function [4]. Since the late 70s medical schools have included in their curricula more emphasis on breast feeding and this may have effects which will be felt in the future. However, obstetricians practicing today did not receive this education and may be lacking the skills to promote breast feeding.

There are some general issues which must be considered when our findings rely on reporting on the part of the subjects. Assuming the subject of breast feeding was discussed during the visit to the obstetrician, we must consider the possibility that reporting of it would be contingent upon actual practice at that time. It has been proposed that material which conflicts or is not congenial with existing attitudes is readily forgotten [17]. Eastham *et al.* [18] believe that those who receive undesired advice tend to reject or suppress this information.

Another point to be considered is that interested people request more information than the uninterested [19]. The motivation of a person to seek certain information will depend on the degree of uncertainty, the importance of that information for action decisions and the subjective probability of success of obtaining the information needed. It is possible that women requested information from the obstetrician because they were confronted with specific problems or doubts regarding their feeding practice.

We conclude that there is a strong relationship between discussion of breast feeding with the obstetrician and breast feeding practices among higher social class women in our population. Among lower sc women the discussion of breast feeding with the obstetrician is not related to longer duration of breast feeding practices. This might be explained by a different status perception of the obstetrician by women in different social classes or by the fact that obstetricians really did not relate to the subject of breast feeding with lower social class women. This issue should be further studied as it will give us clues to the optimal way of designing a program of promotion of breast feeding in which the most effective sources will give advice to different target populations.

In Israel most of the care during pregnancy and after leaving the hospital, post delivery, is provided by the nurses of the MCH service. It is with her that the main educational opportunities lie. The MCH staff has frequent contacts with more than half of the women of our population during pregnancy and with over 80% after hospital discharge. During hospital stay—mean duration of hospital stay is only 2.6 days [20]—53% of women received guidance from the hospital nurse. Therefore, although obstetricians should be encouraged to deal with the subject of breast feeding when they care for pregnant women, the initial intervention has to be pursued by the MCH nurse during the first days after hospital discharge in order to prevent the decline of breast feeding at that point. For that purpose she should be taught more effective and appropriate educational techniques.

Acknowledgements—This project was supported by a grant from the Israeli Family Planning Association. We also thank Bela Adler and Eliahu Ben Moshe for their assistance with the statistical analyses.

REFERENCES

1. Ladas A. K. Information and social support as factors in the outcome of breast feeding. *J. appl. Behav. Sci.* **8,** 100, 1972.
2. Jellife D. B. and Jellife E. F. P. *Human Milk in the Modern World.* Oxford University Press, Oxford, 1979.
3. Helsing E. Lactation education: the learning of the "obvious". In *Breast Feeding and the Mother.* Ciba Foundation Symposium 45 (new series), 1976.
4. Applebaum R. M. The modern management of successful breast feeding. *Pediat. Clin. N. Am.* **17,** 203, 1970.
5. Raphael D. *The Tender Gift: Breast Feeding.* Schocken Books, New York, 1976.
6. Smith D. Attitudes to breast feeding. *Br. med. J.* **2,** 695, 1969.
7. Central Bureau of Statistics, Ministry of Health. Survey on Use of the Health Services. Oct-Ce 1977. Special Series No. 639, Jerusalem, 1980.
8. Kark S. L., Peritz E., Shiloh A. *et al.* Epidemiological analysis of the hemoglobin picture in parturient women of Jerusalem. *Am. J. publ. Hlth* **54,** 957, 1964.
9. Nie N. H., Hull C. H., Jenkins J. *et al. Statistical Package for the Social Sciences,* Second Edition. McGraw–Hill, New York, 1975.
10. Winikoff B. and Baer E. The obstetrician's opportunity: translating 'breast is best' from theory to practice. *Am. J. Obstet. Gynec.* **138,** 105, 1980.
11. Martinez G. A. and Nalezienski J. The recent trend in breast feeding. *Pediatrics* **64,** 686, 1979.
12. Thaustein J., Halevy S. and Mundel G. Infant feeding practices in Israel. *Pediatrics* **26,** 321, 1960.
13. Newton N. and Newton M. Psychologic aspects of lactation. *New Engl. J. Med.* **277,** 1179, 1967.
14. Huntingford P. J. Attitudes of doctors and midwives to breast feeding. *Dev. Med. Child Neurol.* **4,** 588, 1962.
15. Jones E. E. and Gerard H. B. *Foundations of Social Psychology,* 309 pp. Wiley, New York, 1967.
16. Raven B. and Rubin J. *Social Psychology: People in Groups,* 199 pp. Wiley, New York, 1976.
17. Murphy G. and Levine J. The learning and forgetting of controversial material. *J. Abnorm. soc. Psychol.* **38,** 507, 1943.
18. Eastham E. D., Smith D. and Neligan G. Further decline of breast feeding. *Br. med. J.* **1,** 305, 1976.
19. Hyman H. and Sheatsley P. Some reasons why information campaigns fail. *Publ. Opin. Q.* **11,** 412, 1947.
20. Diagnostic Statistics of Hospitalized Patients 1974. Published by the Central Bureau of Statistics. Ministry of Health, Jerusalem, 1978.

12

Managing at Home: Relationships between Blind Parents and Sighted Children

Shlomo Deshen and *Hilda Deshen*

The sociocultural ramifications of disability have been studied in several ethnographic monographs, such as Ablon (1984) on dwarfs, Edgerton (1967) on mentally retarded, Estroff (1981) on mentally sick, and Becker (1980) on deaf people. Ever since the seminal work of Goffman (1963), the dominant theoretical approach in these works has been the sociology of stigma. This concerns itself primarily with elucidating the ways in which the physical condition is stigmatized, how disabled people are relegated to social inferiority and how they cope with stigma. But to date some of the major disabling conditions have not been considered in detail, nor have some of the major areas of human interaction pertinent to disability been studied in depth. Thus we know little of the way in which disabled people experience work, family-life or the support system. In this paper we address both these lacuna. We focus on family-life and extend the ethnographic study of disability into the area of blindness, a condition which until now has been described only partially, in Scott's (1969) overview of "the blindness system" and in Gwaltney's (1970) monograph on a Mexican community afflicted with a high incidence of onchocercosis.

In the following sections we dwell on the relationships between blind parents and their sighted children in Israel. These parents must contend with children who are exposed, like anyone else in society, to negative sterotyping of blind people. The latter (as disabled people generally) can to a considerable extent escape the tension of managing in a social environment dominated by the sighted by retreating into the privacy of their quarters. However, when the home is shared by blind and sighted kin, a point is reached that delimits escape. Blind parents, in facing their sighted children, must contend even at home with the problems of stigma. Moreover, in the area of blind parent/sighted children relationships, the disabled person is confronted by an able-bodied person who is clearly of subordinate status in the dimension of generation. In the literature on coping with stigma, there is ample documentation of the doings of the disabled vis-à-vis able-bodied people of superior or equal status, but hardly any concerning disabled people vis-à-vis people who are structurally unambiguously subordinate, and yet naturally form part of the overall sociocultural ambience that stigmatizes. In this particular situation disabled persons are in a position of command and relatively more powerful than they are in studies reported in the literature where they face peers or superiors.

The documentation of coping with stigma in the family-type situation leads us to a new frontier in the sociological study of stigma. In focusing on disabled parent-able-bodied child relationships among the blind, we encounter elements that conceivably might limit the power of stigma, and this paper addresses that possibility.

METHODOLOGY AND THE FIELD. This study is based on anthropological fieldwork of 17 months' duration in the Tel-Aviv area in Israel in 1983–1984.[1] The senior author participated regularly in the activities of several associations of blind people, an advocacy group, an encounter group, a sports and leisure club, and worked daily for about three months in a sheltered workshop. We made numerous informal visits to various local groups and individuals throughout the metropolitan area and beyond. Although we occasionally also visited a support agency and spoke with blindness workers, we devoted relatively little effort to that part of the field. We made the acquaintance of well over 100 legally blind people, but focused only on people of working age who were blinded pre-vocationally, and whose condition does not permit them to be mobile unaided. This precluded people outside the approximate 20 to 60 age bracket. Also, anyone with disabilities in addition to blindness was not included.

Our analysis is based on data from 57 men and women who fitted the limited category selected and with whom we came into contact by "the snowballing technique." Most of them were between 35 and 50 years old, predominantly of Middle-Eastern immigrant background, about equally divided by sex. With eight of the 57 individuals we developed a mutual home-visiting relationship on a family basis, and interacted numerous hours. Twenty other individuals we came to know well, but less than those of the first category. We visited them several times at home and/or often observed and interacted with them in other settings. Twenty-five people we knew only superficially, from single or limited numbers of visits and/or observations in various settings. A final category comprising four individuals whom we never visited, was included, because information of and about them was of particular interest. We also communicated and maintained ties with people by lengthy telephone conversations, as is common among blind people. Our relationships with everyone were informal: visiting, often as a couple, we usually let the talk flow, without much overt direction. The quality of relationship we developed with individuals during the course of the project was the result of mutual personal preferences. The information gathered constitutes about 800 pages of handwritten notes, and forms the data-base of a general ethnography.

The population was employed as follows: telephone switchboard operators (20 individuals), sheltered workshop employees (11), professionals and businessmen (10), homemakers and non-gainfully employed (10), factory workers (3) and students (3). As to family life, 37 individuals are or were married (mostly to blind spouses); most of them have children, all of whom are, to our knowledge, visually healthy.

The basic data of the paper are accounts and analyses of mutual actions of sighted children and youths and their blind parents. These actions are motivated by many forces. One, presumably, is the universal inter-generational clash discussed in psychoanalysis ever since Freud. Another is inter-generational confrontation at specific culture-associated levels, such as the discordance that is common in migration and culture-change situations. Blindness is one element among others that can lead to conflict between family members. We are concerned in this paper to demonstrate the weight of the condition of blindness in the context of other more general factors referred to above. Contrary to popular rhetoric, blindness is neither an all-encompassing fact of life (the stigmatizing position), nor is it trivial (the position of some activists of the rights-for-the-disabled movement). The condition of blindness should be considered within a broad human context, and social interactions involving blind people should be evaluated accordingly. In analyzing our case material, we shall avoid polar positions. A study of inter-generational actions involving blind people should not be reduced only to the factor of blindness, neither should it be reduced exclusively to factors other than blindness.

Blind Parent and Sighted Child. Two crucial processes mold the relationship between blind parent and sighted child: the child's learning the nature of blindness and the parent's learning the nature of sighted childhood. While the trauma of blind children who discover their condition has long been a concern for workers with the blind, the parallel experience of sighted children to whom their parent(s)' blindness is unfolded is virtually unknown.[2] The potential of this experience in molding children's assessment of their parents, and of establishing relative statuses in the family, is weighty. The realization that one has sightless parents is difficult to contend with. In the early stages of this realization, the children view their parents as undifferentiated from other people, but they develop practices towards them that are unique to their condition.

The weight of blind parenthood upon sighted children is exemplified in an incident to which one of us was party. Late one evening the researcher was about to depart from a visit with the Eini family.[3] After starting the farewell preliminaries, the researcher murmured to the hosts that he was going to pick up his coat. Suddenly seven-year-old David Eini, who had been lounging in pyjamas on the settee, half asleep, half listening to the adults, got up and wordlessly led the visitor by the hand to where his coat was and placed his hand on the coat. Evidently, at that late hour, the child was not fully aware of the difference between the visitor and his parents; he behaved to the former with the same anticipatory helpfulness with which he treated his parents. He knew, as his mother Mazal put it, that his parents "see with their hands." Such children, however, tend to become troubled as they eventually become fully cognizant of the distinctiveness of their parents. We proceed with the presentation of a series of situations that document the unsettling quality of that discovery.

A group of blind friends was entertaining each other in the presence of their children with stories of funny situations into which blind people blundered. One was about a blind man who had stepped onto merchandise that a streetwalk hawker had spread on the pavement. The merchandise consisted of plastic toys that squeaked and emitted a cacophony of odd noises when the blind man trod on them. At that point, our informant said, one of the children became frightened and upset at the outlandish doings of the adults and began to cry. On another occasion the researcher was witness to a reaction of apprehension. Rina Sadeh was talking about her mobility problems. Both she and her blind husband work in a busy downtown city street where pedestrian traffic on the narrow sidewalks is heavy. People are inconsiderate; they rush by, oblivious of her need to sweep an arc in front of her with her cane. One day a man accidentally stepped on Rina's cane and broke it. Thoughtlessly, he rushed on without bothering to help or apologize. The note in Rina's voice as she recounted this was one of seething anger, which she had no way of expending. Her nine-year-old son who was sitting with us reacted differently. He was concerned: "Ima, so how did you get home?" The child's reaction expressed anxiety at what might have been the loss of his mother. To an only child in a family with working parents, the absence of parents is a perennial concern. Blindness now intensified the problem.

The behavior of these children clearly attests to the turmoil they experience as they become fully aware of the difference between their parents and other people. On several occasions we observed that young children of blind parents, aged around 7 to 11, made sweeping motions with their hands in front of their parents' faces. Perhaps they may have been effecting primitive vision tests, as if they wished to verify for themselves that their parents did indeed not see anything. Sometimes there was an aggressive quality to the gesture. With a rapid movement the child would extend his/her arm to full length as if about to strike the parent. One might speculate that the distance between verifying whether one's parent is blind and pent-up anger and frustration at this condition is not great. What is not in doubt is the blindness-linked ambiguity of relationships of the sighted child vis-à-vis the blind parent.

In the Sadeh family, the same child whom we had observed exhibiting anxiety and hostility, we saw on another occasion approach his father and attempt to show him a drawing he had made. The boy behaved just like a child with sighted parents. Perhaps he toyed with the idea that his parents had some vision; perhaps he wished to hide their blindness from the researchers by behaving as if they were sighted. Whatever the boy's reasons, the incident attests to the dilemmas such parents pose for their children. Hostile feelings of children towards their blind parent(s) may be rooted in and exacerbated by a number of factors. Parents may use children at a tender age to serve them, particularly as guides. In fact one father who was not adept at using his cane and required help from his young son acquired a guide dog mainly in order to avoid arousing the boy's resentment. Even if they are not being directly exploited, sighted children are prone to developing ambiguous, if not outright negative feelings. Having a blind parent can be profoundly embarrassing to children. They are regarded as unusual, odd by their peers whose parents are sighted. Some of the stigma that is the lot of the blind parents is also that of their sighted children. In addition, poverty is a phenomenon that frequently accompanies disability. Disabled parents are usually not in a position to give their children nearly as many material goods as their peers have. The children of blind parents are unable to share with their schoolmates stories of joint physical activities with their parents, such as camping, outings, going for car rides. The latter deprivation is particularly evident and discomfitting: whereas the children of blind people walk on the street with their slow-moving parents, their schoolmates are picked up from school in the family car.[4] In short, theirs is Goffman's (1963) "courtesy stigma."

The basic condition of blindness is such that it may easily lead to danger, especially street accidents. In fact, several such accidents occurred during our fieldwork. One of the salient goals of mobility and orientation training of the blind is to enable them to operate efficiently under public thoroughfare conditions. Today, due to improved techniques and mobility aids, blind people evince remarkable mobility achievements. However, these are attained only after much effort and frustration. For the children of blind people, the mobility mishaps of their parents arouse deep feelings. This emerged from the account of a blind woman who was taking a three-year-old child to nursery school. She held the child's hand, but he was not able to guide her efficiently. At the same time, his inept guidance disturbed her customary cane-mobility technique and she walked into a pole hurting herself. The woman recalled that at that moment she felt the child's hand "freeze" in her grasp, "it became like a dead limb." Though we have only the adult's version of the event, the incident undoubtedly was very frightening for the child. It is likely that such incidents will have a cumulative disruptive effect on the trust and security of the child in the blind parent.

As children grow and reach the stage of late childhood, their discernment increases and they are able to differentiate their blind parents from other people much more clearly. They begin to introduce stigmatizing behavior into the relationship with their parents. Reuven Ovadia, sorely grieved by the fact that his 11-year-old daughter was ashamed of him, recalled how the problem began:

> At first, as I walked with her in the street holding her hand, she would ask, 'Abba, why does everybody look at you?' Later, when she would see someone on the street whom she knew, she would withdraw her hand and stoop, saying that she had to tie a shoelace.

In this account ambivalence is stark. The child is clearly ashamed of her father, yet she does not admit to him and perhaps also not to herself why she disengaged herself. She fabricates an excuse.

The pressure of society on these children is multifaceted. People in their ambience burden them with "courtesy stigma." But more than emitting a simple stigmatizing message which causes children to dissociate themselves from their parents, the sighted also convey a charitable paternalistic message. People in the sighted environment erroneously assume the blind to be incapable of any achievement above a minimal level. This prompts them to prod self-righteously the sighted child of blind parents into extending unrequired assistance. As a result, parent-child relationships can become painfully convoluted. This was the case in the family of Eliezer Ohayon, a piano-tuner whose work required him to travel familiar and unfamiliar routes to clients. Eliezer exhibited cheerfulness and self-reliance, besides impressive mobility, but he felt that his children were embarrassed by their blind parents. Thus, he recounted, his 11-year-old daughter was particularly troubled. People accosted her, telling her that she should be more helpful to her parents and that she should guide them to places. The blind father said that in fact he was perfectly able to accomplish his work and other errands unassisted. In this family, surrounded by an ambience of do-gooders, the children were highly reserved towards their parents. The oldest left home at the age of 11, insisting on going to a boarding school. The next, though living at home, refused to have her parents visit her at school, saying that she resented having attention drawn to her.

The ability of parents to manage the attitude of their sighted children requires great parenting skills; in their absence blindness-related problems can be compounded. Thus Hava Shmuel, the harassed and sickly mother of three small children, interpreted the pranks of her 7-year-old boy thus: "Sometimes he plays tricks on us. He hides from us when we call him. He exploits our blindness (*menatzel et ha'ivaron shelanu*)!" Obviously, the childish behavior at that age could also be interpreted differently. It is possible that the mother's harsh interpretation was not lost on the child and that his attitude could turn to hostility. Another instance of dubious parenting was voiced in a radio program featuring family problems. A nerve-wracked mother elaborated on her problem: her husband was over-anxious that his children should not lack anything. He was apprehensive lest he be blamed that due to his infirmity he had not provided for his family adequately, and he spoiled the children by giving in to their every whim and wish. The oldest boy made it a practice to scream and make a spectacle of himself in the supermarket whenever he was refused anything while shopping. In addition, when doing small errands for the family, the boy systematically demanded money to buy goodies for himself. All this resulted in financial difficulties and public embarrassment for the family.

While the process of learning to live with blind parenthood and sighted childhood may be flawed in some families, it is successful in others. People do manage to interact to their mutual satisfaction. Thus, Avraham Tzanani's 8-year-old daughter was proud of her father and told her friends about him. Avraham also was happy in his family life. Characteristically, upon elaborating, he specifically singled out the fact that his children had learned to be considerate of some of his particular requirements, namely to avoid keeping drawers and doors half-open, and playing TV or radio at high volume. Such habits hinder Avraham's mobility in the apartment and do not permit him to discern delicate sounds. We were witness to an incident in the Eini home that illustrates socialization to the needs of the blind. Mazal, who was seated with guests at the table, had momentarily risen from her seat to serve refreshments. In doing so she had slightly moved her chair. Her seven-year-old child quietly came, reset the chair so that there would be no chance his mother would falter when regaining her seat.

Barring smooth relations between parent and child, the time of late childhood is one of transition from the complex of feelings that accompany the discovery of parental handicap, to the onset of actual stigmatizing practices in adolescence.

BLIND PARENT AND SIGHTED ADOLESCENT. The results of different socialization processes and contrasting inter-personal relationships become evident as children reach adolescence. In some homes the stigmatization of the disabled parent developed clearly at this stage, with few or no allowances being made for the needs of the blind parent. We were frequently present in homes in which families with teenagers sat around TV sets, without any attempt being made by the youngsters to convey the visual content of programs to the blind person. The latter was relegated to the periphery.

The families that comprised the data base of our research are mainly of Middle-Eastern immigrant background. This implies that factors affecting the disparate cultural changes of young and old, and their relating to practices of the dominant culture (governed by people of Eastern European background) will be significant. Immigrant youth in that situation sometimes disrespect their elders, contending that they are out-of-touch and old-fashioned.[5] The case of the Buskila family affords insight into the contextual weight of blindness in inter-generational friction. The family, composed of three teenage children and their blind mother, was riddled with inter-generational conflict over life-styles, work habits and consumer patterns. The children often held noisy gatherings and parties at home, particularly in their mother's absence. This annoyed her. Therefore, whenever Rivka visited her extended family, which was frequently, she did not inform her children in advance of her intended absences from home. She did this in order to try to prevent her children from planning social events in the home.

Rivka was careful about her outward appearance, dressing neatly with hair well kempt. She participated in a physical fitness group for blind people which featured specially-designed exercises. When she proudly demonstrated some of these exercises to her teenage children, they ridiculed her efforts and called them "exercises for idiots" (*hit'amlut li'mefagrim*). On other occasions, she said, her children vexed her by saying "You are primitive! You have no sense!" Rivka said that she had resigned herself to such behavior in the privacy of the home, but she insisted that it be refrained from in public so as not to cause her embarrassment.

The confrontations revolve around general inter-generational and migration-type issues. Rivka is concerned about the permissive behavior of her children; she would prefer them to conform to traditional mores. She would also like them to be industrious and save money. The children, on the other hand, tend to be light-headed and pleasure-seeking. The conflicts between the two Buskila generations cannot, however, be reduced to general issues only, unrelated to blindness. Clearly the youths are also expressing disdain at their mother's condition. They stigmatize actions that are specific to her as a blind woman. Thus, in addition to the general issues, blindness-related issues also fire the Buskila dissensions. The children's misconception of the nature of blindness dovetails with their mother's lack of empathy for the youth culture of her sighted offspring.

Another type of relationship between blind parent and sighted son is characterized by ambiguity rather than hostility. The Kagans' son had become an Air Force pilot, a signal achievement by Israeli standards. The mother told us that at the time of the October 1973 War, when Israel suffered considerable losses in the air, the parents had gone beyond the call of duty in supporting their son's career. They could have requested that because of their condition the son not be given particularly perilous assignments. The parents had refrained from doing so. The son, however, perceived the situation differently. He felt that he himself had hindered his promotion because of his consideration for his parents, that for their sake he had not accepted particularly dangerous missions.

Ambiguity is not restricted to the sighted youth. Blind parents may also entertain parallel feelings towards their offspring. This became salient in a discussion at a club between Rivka Buskila and Devora Berkovitz, a woman who lived with a daughter in her early twenties. Rivka had been telling tales of woe about the unpleasantness of being guided by her teenage children. She complained that they were inconsiderate, would rush ahead without warning her of impending obstacles, such as steps or a curb. Devora countered by describing her own daughter who, she said, behaved nicely to her and of whom she was proud. She held a good job, respected her mother, and was liked by everyone. However, in the same breath, Devora continued to say that she felt uneasy when walking with her in the street; the daughter was always in command, guiding her. Devora felt inhibited in expressing herself in her presence.

Strikingly, even within the same family one encounters young people whose attitudes towards their parents differ dramatically. Of Miriam Aflalu's children, the eldest daughter, who is in her early twenties, is attached to her parents. So little was she inhibited by her parents' condition that she brought her boyfriend home without warning him of her parents' blindness. Later, so Miriam claimed, the boy's parents made him break up with the girl because of their condition. And again the daughter did not apparently hold it against them. One afternoon we had occasion to observe the girl's behavior and indeed it was engaging. She sailed into the house directly from the hairdresser. Delighted with her new hairdo, the girl came to her seated mother, and crouching, put her mother's hand on her head saying eagerly, "See! How do you like my new hairdo?" The girl's younger brother, on the other hand, evinces diametrically opposite behavior—he avoids being seen in public with his parents and never brings friends to his home. As the sighted youngsters of blind parents grow into adolescence and maturity, the fruit of their parents' efforts are highly variegated. In evaluative terms they are as impressive or as dismal as those of sighted parents. At the time of research, one of the sighted sons was serving a jail sentence for rape, while another made headlines for courageously saving a drowning man. Some adolescents loafed around, out of school and work, and others were productively integrated into society.

While the process of coming of age led many sighted

youngsters to accept the dominant social values with consequent active or implied stigmatization of blind parents, their actions towards their parents were varied. This now brings us to consider the actions of parents.

BLIND PARENTS AND THE ACHIEVEMENT OF STATUS. Parents sometimes find ways to overcome their ambiguous position among the sighted in the family by contributing to the well-being of the latter. This entails actions which effectively make use of resources that blind parents have at their disposal. A number of cases will demonstrate this. Several blind adults, such as David Levi, recounted that they were particularly active in helping their children and other young relatives with homework. The resources of the blind in the sphere of scholarship feature prominently in their families because in Israel the blind are frequently better educated than their sighted relatives (Deshen 1987[a]). Some people exploit this effectively and thus forge an important position for themselves in the family. Another activity which helps the blind attain status in their families was one in which Asher Dalal and his sighted wife engaged. Asher was careful to host his married children and grandchildren hospitably and with largesse when they visited him on Sabbaths. Asher happily noted that his home then "became a nursery school." He continued to say that he hosted with circumspection so that in turn he would be treated respectfully by his children. Mordechai Danino, an uneducated person employed in a sheltered workshop, contributed to his family's welfare in another manner. His married daughter, husband and three children lacked adequate housing. The family was entitled to some public assistance for their housing, but the loan that was offered was insufficient for their needs. Mordechai therefore staged a sit-down strike with his family at the pertinent government office. Mordechai's gesture entailed manipulating his condition so as to move the officials to compassion. At the same time it showed the family that their father's blindness was not only a liability, but also an asset.

David Levi, Asher Dalal and Mordechai Danino assumed disparate roles: that of the scholar, the passive dignified *pater familias* and the afflicted man entitled to compassion. Despite the great differences between them, the common denominator of these roles was the traditional script they followed. Western culture generally offers these roles to the handicapped and David, Asher and Mordechai assumed them. A fourth way that some parents adopted to contribute to the well-being of their sighted offspring, which was not traditional, was the practice of giving public talks in the schools their children attended. In these talks parents would elaborate on the nature of blindness and demonstrate some of the accessories blind people use. Through these lectures the blind parents sought to counteract stigmatizing practices in general, but more specifically to raise their status and that of their children among their peers. In summary, parents chose all these means to assist their sighted children. These were deliberate attempts to break the ambiguity that surrounds blindness in the family.

Lastly, in many families we found overt indications that blind parents command love and respect. Some of our most vivid impressions of interaction among the blind are scenes in the Megidish family. Here we frequently saw their six children, aged 10 to 22, attend their parents, sit around them and listen to their conversation in respectful silence. Another example is that of a mother of six children who was encouraged by her daughter to accept the position of chairperson of the workers' committee in her place of employment. The daughter was confident of her mother's ability to handle the position. Mazal Eini proudly recounted that her children walked in the street hugging her. And a nursery school teacher once complained that Avraham Tzanani's little girl bragged too much about all the wonderful things her blind father could do.

CONCLUSION. The ways of parenting sighted children by blind parents are, as we saw, highly variegated. The differences are rooted in disparate conditions of society and families that are not related to blindness. But there are contingencies, rooted in the peculiarity of the handicap, which do affect the socialization process.

The relationship of the blind parent and sighted child is different from that of the parent-child relationship among the ablebodied, since the superiority of the parent vis-à-vis the subordination of the child is undermined by the physical handicap of the parent. The confrontation of blind parent and sighted child often runs counter to ordinary domestic statuses because of the stigma that pervades relationships between the able-bodied and the disabled. Moreover, since blind parents often make blindness-linked requests of their children, that further underlines the contradiction. These parents face a problem that is particular to the experience of disability, in maintaining the conventional status of generational superiority vis-à-vis their children. In the foregoing accounts we described how blind parents cope with this problem. They maximized blindness-linked elements in their situation in order to benefit their children.

The picture which emerges from our study differs somewhat from that reported in the American literature on the practices of the disabled. Following Goffman, many writers such as Davis (1961) and Levitin (1975), on disabilities in general, Michalko (1982) on visual impairment in particular, and others on various disabilities, have dwelt on a general "disavowal of handicap" theme. They have documented disabled people insisting, in Levitin's words, that "others define them in preferred ways" and not in terms of their specific handicaps. According to the literature, "passing" as able-bodied is a major concern for many disabled people. In the privacy of their homes, however, the Israeli blind parents did not "disavow" their disability vis-à-vis their children. Rather they managed their disability in the terms of a world governed by the sighted, manipulating it as well as they could to their maximal benefit. Thus, some parents succeeded in attaining status in their homes, others did not. Parenting under the conditions that we have outlined requires great skill; it is also contingent on other, non-disability related variables that we have mentioned. We intimate that the variety of parental status in different families derives from that complex domain.

Much of the literature on the ethnography of disability is based on observations made in public settings in the United States. One may surmise that "passing" and "disavowing" would be more common in a public setting that in the intimacy of home. Also, in Israel the rights-for-the-disabled movement is not much in evidence, and the attendant lack of social awareness may account for salient behavioral differences.[6] In order to make cross-cultural comparisons, controls for situation-specific elements must be introduced and only case material drawn from comparable settings should be confronted. Possibly such cross-cultural research might reveal that the issue of generation-superiority emphasized in the present paper is culture-bound and peculiar to the Israeli situation.[7]

Despite the undisputed value of Goffman's influence on the sociology of disability, his approach has lain heavily on the field for many years. For instance, Gussow and Tracy (1968) described the practice of sufferers of leprosy, similar to that of blind parents, lecturing in public about their condition. Gussow and Tracy, however, discussed that in terms of coping with stigma in general. Some time ago Bynder and New (1976) argued that the Goffman paradigm may have exhausted itself, that the time was ripe to study disability in new ways. The present paper suggests that the actions of disabled people need not be viewed solely in the general terms of stigma. We propose that these actions are also linked to specific situational concerns, for example, the desire of parents to fill a superior role vis-à-vis their children. This particular desire is not one that is rooted in disability. We suggest that the sociology and anthropology of disability now face the issue of uncovering the ways that disabled people follow in coping with particular concerns.

NOTES

[1] We are indebted to the Tel-Aviv University Sapir Center for Development, and to the Jerusalem Center for Anthropological Studies who tendered material support. See Deshen 1987a, 1987b for partial accounts.

[2] A recent survey of the social-psychological literature on blindness reflects this imbalance. The survey (Kemp 1981) lists about 150 items, of which 43 focus on blind children. Not one is devoted to the sighted children of blind parents.

[3] The identities of individuals have been conventionally disguised.

[4] In Israel, as in much of the industrialized world, the usage of private cars is of great status significance. Also Edgerton (1967:160–162) reports of the great importance of the lack of automobiles in the lives of the mentally retarded people whom he studied in 1960.

[5] There is a vast literature on these issues in the Israeli setting; for example, see Deshen and Shokeid 1974.

[6] The overt status of blind people in Israel, to evaluate by the Scott (1969) report, does not seem to be inferior to that in the U.S. Concerning employment, probably the crucial index in these matters, the Israeli situation, may in fact be enviable—relatively few blind working-age people in Israel are idle (Deshen 1986, Ch. 1). It would therefore be mistaken to consider the Israeli blind particularly repressed, and to link their actions to that factor. See Goldin 1984 for a more contemporary account of blind people in the U.S.

[7] Eames et al. (1986) have proposed a cross-culturally focused study of blindness.

REFERENCES CITED

Ablon, Joan
1984 Little People of America. New York: Praeger.

Becker, Gaylene
1980 Growing Old in Silence. Berkeley: University of California Press.

Bynder, Herbert, and Peter K. New
1976 Time For a Change: From Micro- to Macro-Sociological Concepts in Disability Research. Journal of Health and Social Behavior 17(1):45–52.

David, Fred
1961 Deviance Disavowal: The Management of Strained Interaction by the Visibly Handicapped. Social Problems 9(2):120–132.

Deshen, Shlomo
1986 Towards an Ethnography of Blindness: The Quest for Dignity. Tel-Aviv: Tel-Aviv University Sapir Center.
1987a Coming of Age among Blind People in Israel. Disability, Handicap and Society 2(2):137–149.
1987b Seeking Dignity and Independence: Toward an Ethnography of Blindness in Israel. Journal of Visual Impairment and Blindness 81(5):209–212.

Deshen, Shlomo, and Moshe Shokeid
1974 The Predicament of Homecoming: Cultural and Social Life of North-African Immigrants in Israel. Ithaca, NY: Cornell University Press.

Eames, Edwin, Shlomo Deshen, and Hannan Selvin.
1986 Blindness as a Focus of Social Science Research: A Programmatic Approach. Paper Presented at the Meeting of the International Sociological Association Conference, New Delhi, India.

Edgerton, Robert
1967 The Clock of Competence: Stigma in the Life of the Mentally Retarded. Berkeley: University of California Press.

Estroff, Sue
1981 Making It Crazy: An Ethnography of Psychiatric Clients in an American Community. Berkeley: University of California Press.

Goffman, Erving
1963 Stigma: Notes on the Management of Spoiled Identity. Englewood Cliffs, NJ: Prentice-Hall.

Goldin, Carol
1984 The Community of the Blind: Social Organization, Advocacy and Cultural Redefinition. Human Organization 43:121–131.

Gussow, Zachary, and S. Tracy George
1968 Status, Ideology, and Adaptation to Stigmatized Illness: A Study of Leprosy. Human Organization 17(4):316–325.

Gwaltney, John L.
1970 The Thrice-Shy: Cultural Accommodation to Blindness and Other Disasters in a Mexican Community. New York: Columbia University Press.

Kemp, N. J.
1971 Social Psychological Aspects of Blindness: A Review. Current Psychological Review 1:69–89.

Levitin, Teresa
1975 Deviants as Active Participants in the Labelling Process: The Visibly Handicapped. Social Problems 22(4):548–557.

Michalko, Rodney
1982 Accomplishing a Sighted World. Reflections: Canadian Journal of Visual Impairment 1:9–30.

Scott, Robert
1969 The Making of Blind Men. New York: Russell Sage Foundation.

13

Family Sense of Coherence and Family Adaptation

Aaron Antonovsky and *Talma Sourani*

The Family Sense of Coherence

The purpose of this paper is dual: (*a*) to consider the possibility of translating the sense of coherence (SOC) construct from the individual to the family level; and (*b*) to test the hypothesis that the family SOC is related to family adaptation. In doing so, we hope to advance the growing link between the different theoretical and research traditions of the fields of family stress and life events and illness, as exemplified in Walker's (1985) paper. It is not our intention to enter into all the theoretical complexity of the work done in this area, but rather, using empirical data from a modest study, to make a contribution toward clarifying this complexity.

The life events literature, from Selye through Holmes and Rahe to the present day, presents an overwhelming emphasis on risk factors as causally related to pathological outcomes. In the mid-seventies, with the appearance of the first Dohrenwend volume (Dohrenwend and Dohrenwend, 1974) and the Rabkin and Struening paper in *Science* (1976), attention was increasingly paid to mediating and buffer variables. The underlying philosophical hypothesis continued to be that life events, stressors, or psychological risk factors eventuate in physical and/or emotional pathology. What was now added was that it was important to see what factors might attenuate this relationship. Occasionally in the more recent papers, especially on social support, a new note is detected: the possibility that such factors might have a direct and positive effect on not getting sick.

The family stress literature, by contrast, tends to show a somewhat different orientation, or at least to be hospitable to one. True, in Hill's classic work (1949, 1965), the dependent variable was crisis. But as this model was developed by Burr (1973) and McCubbin and Patterson (1983), not only was central attention given to the family's resources and its definition of the stressor; regenerative power, reorganization after a period of crisis, and adaptation as fit became central concepts as well.

Starting from a different philosophical orientation than that of the life events literature, Antonovsky, having earlier worked on "resistance resources" (1972), developed a "salutogenic model" (1979). Stressors, he argued, are ubiquitous in human existence; heterostasis is normative; the deviance of illness is far from rare. It is at least of equal importance to seek to explain the origins of health—of successful coping with stressors—as it is to explain the origins of pathology. Moreover, the two questions are seen as radically different. (For a detailed development of this argument, see Antonovsky, 1987, chap. 1.)

The proposed answer to the salutogenic question came to be called the *sense of coherence*. It is derived from a theoretical analysis of what a large variety of "generalized resistance resources" seem to have in common that might explain *how* they work. Briefly put, such resources as social support, money, religious faith, work role autonomy, and cultural stability provide continuing life experiences with three characteristics: consistency (see Cassel's 1974 discussion of feedback); an underload-overload balance; and participation in socially valued decision making. Over the course of time, a person with many such experiences comes to see the world as one that makes sense; or in terms of information theory, one that provides information rather than noise. Formally, this world view, the sense of coherence, is defined as (Antonovsky, 1987: 19)

> a global orientation that expresses the extent to which one has a pervasive, enduring though dynamic feeling of confidence that (1) the stimuli deriving from one's internal and external environments in the course of living are structured, predictable and explicable; (2) the resources are available to one to meet the demands posed by these stimuli; and (3) these demands are challenges, worthy of investment and engagement.

The three inextricably intertwined components of the SOC are called, respectively, comprehensibility, manageability, and meaningfulness. A tendency to expect the world to be ordered, or orderable, facilitates cognitive clarification of the nature of the problems stressors pose. A tendency to expect the demands posed by these problems to be manageable leads one to search out the appropriate resources potentially available to one. And a tendency to see life as meaningful provides the motivational drive to engage in confrontation with the problems. It should be noted that the SOC is not at all a specific coping style, active or otherwise. Its hallmark, rather, is flexibility in selecting coping behaviors that are judged to be appropriate. These may vary radically according to the situation and the culture. This approach proposes that if one has a strong SOC, the motivational and cognitive bases exist for transforming one's potential resources, appropriate to a given stressor, into actuality, thereby promoting health.

The formal definition of the SOC includes the phrase "a global orientation," that is, a general view of the world not limited to this or that area of life. The theory *assumes* that one's view of the world tends to be of whole cloth. When this is not the case, the implication is that one has a weak SOC. Obviously, this assumption will sooner or later have to be tested. In recent work (Antonovsky, 1987, chap. 2) the concept of "boundaries" is introduced, suggesting that what matters is not that *all* stimuli be perceived as coherent, but only those that one defines as important in one's life. For one person, the boundaries might be wide; for another, narrow. But this caveat is qualified by the insistence that no one can so narrow the boundaries as to put beyond the pale of significance four spheres—one's inner feelings, one's immediate interpersonal relations, one's major activity, and existential issues—and yet maintain a strong SOC.

For purposes of the present study, however, we decided to focus on one sphere of life: one's family. The instrument we used to measure the family sense of coherence (FSOC) refers only to this sphere, which brings us to another issue.

In the original formulation of the SOC construct (Antonovsky, 1979), occasional reference was made to the SOC as applicable to the group as well as the individual. But this thought was never seriously developed. It was only with the planning of the present study that the complexity of the problem began to become clear. What does it mean, we asked ourselves, to say that *a family* has a strong, or a weak, SOC? A family has size, structure, division of labor and power, social functions, myths, and so on. But how can a family have a dispositional orientation, a way of seeing the world? We speak of family ambience, morale, atmosphere, and the like, but how do we know such things about a given family?

The clinician, working with the individual person, tends to rest content with obtaining data about the individual's perception of how the family presumably sees things. One can make a case for arguing that this is what matters. Or can one? If the "reality" of how other family members see things is at variance with the individual's perception, this has consequences for what happens to him or her; which brings us back to whether "the family" sees things.

Family researchers, by and large, have ignored the issue. As Walker puts it (1985: 832), "those who study family stress continue to postulate the existence and importance of the family's definition of the event, even though it has yet to be operationalized or measured." (For a detailed discussion of this issue, see Fisher, Kokes, Ransom, Phillips, and Rudd, 1985.) The tendency has been to collect data on the perceptions of reality by different family members. If these perceptions coincide, the problem is "solved." If not, one averages the ratings. When the consistency of family members' perceptions is on the high side, one can reasonably feel that little violence has been done to the data. One can ignore the fact that one has avoided the theoretical problem.

The problem is particularly salient when the issue of concern is a construct like the SOC. Its very essence as a group property requires that there be consensus among family members if one is to speak of a strong family SOC. To use one person's report, or to average data, is to risk the danger that there is dissensus, in itself evidence of a weak family SOC. On the other hand, consensus about seeing the world as incoherent, paradoxically, might hint that there is some order.

Two problems have been raised here with regard to the "family sense of coherence": (*a*) the focus on family life versus the world as a whole as the *object* of the perception of coherence; and (*b*) *who* does the perceiving. The wisdom and problematics of our resolution of these issues in the present study will be considered in the discussion.

Family Adaptation

In the development of the salutogenic model (Antonovsky, 1979), great care was taken to avoid tautology. The SOC was carefully defined, and later operationalized, to avoid any reference to health. Health was specified as referring to one type of "well-being," essentially physical health; thus the slippery concept of mental health was avoided. If a link was indeed found between the SOC and health, one could have some confidence that how a person sees the world of stimuli and how his or her organism functions physiologically are distinct though related variables. But the SOC construct, posited to explain successful coping with stressors or crises, can reasonably be hypothesized to be related to morale, satisfaction, general well-being—or adaptation (see Antonovsky, 1987, chap. 7). Yet how are the two to be measured independently?

Family stress researchers have long wrestled with the problem. However, as Lavee and McCubbin (1985: 1–2) put it in a recent and most significant paper,

> family adaptation is but a descriptive criterion of family post-crisis outcome rather than a purely defined construct with an operationalized set of measures. . . . Specifically, in adopting family adaptation as a dependent variable in family stress research we are faced with the challenge of ensuring the independence of the predictors, such as family resources (e.g., family integration and communication) or family appraisal (e.g., coherence), from the criterion measure of family adaptation.

In the present study, "adaptation" was conceptualized in a way consistent with the literature (McCubbin and Patterson, 1983; Lazarus and Folkman, 1984) and pushed one step further. Specifically, we followed Lavee and McCubbin's (1985: 1) definition of adaptation as "a *fit* at two levels—between the family members and the family unit and between the family unit and the community." We departed, however, from their definition when it came to operationalizing the concept, choosing to measure adaptation by asking about the *satisfaction* with fit (while they chose to operationalize it by asking about general well-being, satisfaction, and family distress). Once again, the wisdom of our decision will be considered in the discussion.

In sum, the present study deals (*a*) with the degree of spouse consensus about the family's perception of the coherence of family life

(FSOC); and (*b*) with the presumed consequences for the perception by spouses of the family's satisfaction with its adaptation to its internal and external environments (FAS).

Sample and Data Collection

Sample

The sample for this study was drawn from the Rehabilitation Branch files of a central Israeli city office of the National Security Institute (Israel's Social Security Administration). All potential respondents who met the following criteria were selected: male, formally recognized disability of at least 40%, disabled from 2 to 10 years, aged 25 to 50 at the time of onset of disability, and married (to the same spouse) with at least one child at home at time of onset and at time of study. These criteria were set in keeping with the purpose of the study, which focused on coping with a family crisis. Of the 65 families identified in the files, 7 refused to be interviewed and 3 could not be traced. The files of an adjacent small community office contained records for another 5 men who met these criteria, and they were included in the sample. The final sample comprised 60 men and their wives.

It should be noted that the sample only includes persons disabled in civilian life. Those disabled while on army duty are registered in the Ministry of Defense Rehabilitation Branch. Among the respondents, then, were persons injured in traffic, at work or in other accidents, or as a result of illness.

The modal male respondent had been disabled for 3 to 5 years (48.3%), had a 51–80% disability (i.e., of sufficient seriousness to warrant institutional assistance in rehabilitation and with reasonable grounds, as the NSI saw it, to anticipate reemployment; 50%), had experienced a decline in occupational status and income after onset (75%), was unemployed and not looking for work (48.3%), had been 41–50 years old at onset (70%), was born in Asia or Africa (53.3%), had had 5 to 8 years of schooling (38.4%), and had three or more children (76.7%). Thus the sample may generally be characterized as a working-class population.

Data Collection

Talma Sourani, an experienced rehabilitation social worker, visited each family at home after an appointment had been made. After the purposes of the study were explained, each spouse was requested to complete the questionnaire, separately and simultaneously. After the forms were collected, any further necessary explanations were given. In nine cases, male respondents were unable to complete the questionnaire by themselves. While the wife was doing so elsewhere, the questions were read aloud and responses recorded. In two of these cases, an adolescent child read the questions to the wife, who was also unable to read and write Hebrew.

Measures

The self-completion questionnaire (see Appendix) opened with a general statement that the items refer to the family's behavior as a whole. The 26-item FSOC measure opened the questionnaire, followed by 9 demographic items. The third part contained the 10-item Family FAS and a single item on overall satisfaction with family life. The questionnaire took, on the average, 20 minutes to complete. Case workers were also asked to evaluate the adaptation of each of "their" families, using a single global 7-point item.

The *Family Sense of Coherence Scale* (FSOC) consisted of 26 semantic differential items, scored from 1 to 7, with extreme anchor phrases. High scores indicate a strong FSOC. Fourteen of the items were phrased so that the higher the number checked, the weaker the coherence; these were reversed in scoring.

The initial basis for constructing the scale was Antonovsky's (1987, chap. 4) questionnaire designed to measure the SOC of the individual as a global orientation. As indicated above, the present study focuses on family life only. Those items that could not easily be adapted to a family context were dropped. Other items referring to issues that come up in everyday life were constructed. In each case, the underlying frame of an item was the extent to which the respondent perceives family life as comprehensible, manageable, or meaningful. Two brief pretests, with 5 and 14 couples, respectively (each with a disabled spouse not included in the sample), led to the construction of the final questionnaire.

The internal reliability of the FSOC was quite high. Cronbach's alpha for the entire sample ($N = 120$) was .921; for husbands separately, .923, and for wives separately, .920. Systematic removal of each item had no impact on the alpha.

The *Family Adaptation Scale* (FAS) consisted of 10 semantic differential items scored from 1 to 7. In each case, the extreme anchor phrases were "completely satisfied" and "dissatisfied." Given the propensity shown in many surveys to give positive answers to such questions, the imbalance was intentional (i.e., the fact that "completely dissatisfied" was not used). Six of the items were phrased so that the higher the number checked, the poorer the adaptation; these were reversed in scoring, so that a high score indicates good adaptation. Five of the items referred to satisfaction with internal family fit (Items 1, 4, 5, 7, and 10); 2 items referred to family-community fit (Items 8, 9); and the 3 others were less specific, covering both facets of fit. Cronbach's alpha for the 10-item scale was .874 for the whole sample (.851 for husbands, .895 for wives).[1]

RESULTS

Preliminary Analyses

Our concern in this study is to test the hypothesis that the *family* construction of family reality is related to the perception of family adaptation. Before doing so, we present data on the individual scores. The mean score on the 26-item FSOC scale was 128.63 ($SD = 33.35$) for husbands and 130.85 ($SD = 33.99$) for wives, or 4.95 and 5.03, respectively, per item. In keeping with many other survey results, these means seem to be on the high, optimistic side, if we consider that 7 is the most positive reply. Since the scale has never been used with any other population, no comparisons can be made. The 29-item individual SOC scale, however, has been used (Antonovsky, 1987, chap. 4). Adjusted mean scores of most of the populations are considerably lower, suggesting that it seems easier for persons to be less optimistic about themselves, at least in survey questionnaires, than about their families. Since many of the items differ on the two scales, however, such a generalization can only be tentative. The important point, for present purposes, is that "high" scores have no inherent meaning, and can only be used for comparative purposes within the same study or across studies when the same instrument is used.

In order to examine the relationship between the FSOC and the FAS, we set cutting points to divide both husbands and wives into three groups as equal as possible on each scale. In each case, the two variables are strongly related. Among men, 46 (77%) of the 60 are in the same third on the two variables, with one extreme deviant (low on FSOC, high on FAS). Among women, 35 (58%) of 60 are in the same third, while 3 are extreme deviants. The correlation coefficient between the two variables for men is 0.89; for women, 0.85 ($p < .001$).

We have, then, initial evidence that does not allow us to reject the FSOC-FAS hypothesis. But this hypothesis relates to the *family's* SOC and the *family's* adaptation, not to the perception by each spouse of the coherence of family life and adaptation. What can the data tell us about this question?

Spouse Consensus on Coherence and Adaptation

To what extent, we now ask, do spouses share a construction of reality, in this case the perception of the FSOC and of the FAS? Many studies ignore the problem by assigning a family score based on the mean spouse score. When few couples in a sample differ substantially—an empirical issue—using mean scores to test hypotheses perhaps does little harm. But when the construct under study bears a very direct relationship to the issue of agreement, as in the present case, it becomes impossible to ignore the matter. The very idea of a family sense of coherence is based on spouse agreement. When spouses disagree, there is by definition a weak SOC.

The correlation between husband's and wife's FSOC is .77 ($p < .001$). As noted, the scores of each gender were trichotomized into groups as nearly equal as possible. Of the 60 couples, 35 (58%) were in the diagonal cells, indicating agreement, whereas only 4 were extreme deviants (husband high—wife low, or the reverse) (chi-square $= 20.9$, 4 df, $p < .001$).

One further way of examining consonance between spouses was taken: examination of the 26 FSOC item-by-item differences. The range of possible mean item differences is from 0 to 6.0. In reality, 19 of the couples (32%) had a mean item difference of less than 1; another 28 (47%), from 1.01 to 2; and the remaining 13 betweeen 2.01 and 4.

Thus it can be concluded that by and large there is a substantial degree of spouse agreement. This proves to be the case on the FAS as well. The correlation between husband's and wife's FAS is .68 ($p < .001$). Again, the scores of each gender were trichotomized into groups as nearly equal as possible. Of the 60 couples, 33 (55%) were in the diagonal cells, indicating agreement, and only 4 were extreme deviants (chi-square = 18.0, 4 *df*, $p < .001$).

Having shown that there is indeed a considerable degree of consensus between spouses, which suggests that, at least in this case, it makes sense to speak of a *family* SOC (as well as of a family perception of adaptation), we may turn to the hypothesis of the study and examine the relationship between the two. But it is of value to analyze the "deviant" cases—in this instance, the spouses whose perceptions of the FSOC are discordant. The correlation between spouses is not perfect; 42% of the couples are not in the same third on the trichotomized scores; 22% of the couples had a mean item difference of 2.01 or more. Most, then, though not all, spouses have a similar construction of family reality. How does this relate to family adaptation? Or, to put the problem in another way: do the separate levels of husband and wife FSOC matter more or less than the fact that they agree or disagree on FSOC?

Family Coherence and Adaptation

Our first way of jointly analyzing the level of FSOC and the extent of spouse agreement as related to FAS was to use the tripartite divisions of spouses on FSOC and on FAS. The small number of cases obviates a very detailed breakdown. Nonetheless, the data, presented in Table 1, are suggestive. There are 13 cases in which both husband and wife had a high FSOC score, that is, they were both high and in agreement with each other. Using the husband's FAS score as criterion, we can see that none of the 13 had a low score. In the wife's perception, only one had a low score. Almost all these husbands (12 of 13) and a majority of the wives (8 of 13) report high adaptation. By contrast, the 13 couples in which both spouses agree that the family has a weak SOC are concentrated in the "poor adaptation" group (11 of the 13 by husband's perception, 12 of the 13 by wife's). The four intermediate groups on FSOC are clearly also intermediate on FAS.

But is the FSOC score more or less important than consensus in relation to the FAS? This issue was examined in two ways. We first compared two sets of two groups from the six in Table 1: the

TABLE 1. DISTRIBUTION OF JOINT SPOUSE FAMILY SENSE OF COHERENCE BY HUSBAND'S AND BY WIFE'S PERCEPTION OF FAMILY ADAPTATION

	Joint Spouse FSOC					
Adaptation	High-High	High-Medium	Medium-Medium	Medium-Low	High-Low	Low-Low
	Husband FAS					
High	92.3%	45.5%	0.0%	20.0%	25.0%	0.0%
Medium	7.7	54.5	77.8	20.0	50.0	15.4
Low	0.0	0.0	22.2	60.0	25.0	84.6
n	(13)	(11)	(9)	(10)	(4)	(13)
	chi-square = 54.3, 10 *df*, $p < .001$					
	Wife FAS					
High	61.5%	36.4%	33.3%	40.0%	0.0%	0.0%
Medium	30.8	54.5	44.4	40.0	50.0	7.7
Low	7.7	9.1	22.2	20.0	50.0	92.3
n	(13)	(11)	(9)	(10)	(4)	(13)
	chi-square = 33.2, 10 *df*, $p < .001$					

medium-high versus the medium-medium FSOC groups; and the medium-low versus the low-low. If the average FSOC level is more important than consensus, then the former in each pair should have a higher adaptation score; if consensus is more important, the opposite should be the case. Using first the husband's FAS and then the wife's FAS as criterion measures, we tested the null hypothesis four times. In all four cases, even though the numbers are small, the mean FAS scores of the discordant FSOC pair are higher than the concordant but lower FSOC average couples. (In three of the four cases, the difference is statistically significant.) Thus, for example, comparing the mean husband's FAS scores of the medium-high and medium-medium couples, $t = 3.15$, $p < .006$.

We next examined the question using the above-noted mean FSOC single-item differences. The 60 couples were trichotomized into low, medium, and high mean differences. Again using the husband and wife FAS scores as criteria, we compared the three mean item difference groups pairwise. None of the comparisons show statistically significant t test differences, though the low-difference group has a bit higher FAS score than the medium, and the medium a higher score than the high-difference group. But even the low-high comparison falls short of significance.

We may conclude, then, that it seems to matter more for adaptation that at least one spouse has a relatively strong FSOC than that the spouses agree. This observation should make those who use average family scores a bit more comfortable. This is not to say that consensus makes no difference. The correlations between the mean item differences and the FSOC of husbands is −.25 ($p < .027$); of wives, −.29 ($p < .012$). The correlations between the differences and the FAS of the husbands and wives, respectively, are −.14 and −.24 ($p < .069$ and .032). Consensus, then, is related to both coherence and adaptation, but it seems less powerful than the average level of coherence.

The Problem of Contamination

Evidence has been provided that the FSOC, whether measured by individual spouse score or joint couple score, is very strongly related to the FAS. In order to confront empirically the question of tautology raised earlier, that is, whether the FSOC and FAS measure the same thing, two steps were taken. First, the individual FSOC items were compared to the individual FAS items in terms of substantive overlap. This subjective comparison led to the identification of 9 FSOC items that seemed to us too close for comfort to FAS items. Thus, for example, FAS Item 7 refers to satisfaction with communication among family members. FSOC Item 1 refers to a feeling of mutual understanding; Item 8 refers to clarifying problems together; Item 14, to others sensing one's feelings. These 9 items (the above 3 and Items 5, 11, 19, 23, 25, and 26) were eliminated and a new scale was constructed on the basis of the remaining 17 items.

Once again, the correlation between husband's and wife's FSOC scores is highly significant (.71, $p < .001$, a bit lower than the .77 of the original scores). Of greater importance, the correlations between the new scores and the FAS scores remain highly significant: .84 ($p < .001$) for husbands and .81 ($p < .001$) for wives. This time, further, we calculated the correlations between husband FSOC and wife FAS scores and vice versa in the attempt to decrease contamination. The correlations were indeed somewhat lower but remained very highly significant (husband FSOC–wife FAS, .57; wife FSOC–husband FAS, .68; $p < .001$ in both cases).

Our final attempt at removing contamination between the two variables seems to be a strict test. We had asked the social workers in the rehabilitation office to provide a global estimate, on a scale of 1 to 7, of each family's level of adaptation. By and large, the worker was most familiar with the disabled husband. We obtained social worker ratings of the overall adaptation of 47 families. The correlations between these and the four major measures of the study are as follows: husband FSOC, .64; wife FSOC, .62; husband FAS, .51; wife FAS, .55 (in all cases, $p < .001$). Thus, even with a totally independent measure of adaptation, which is highly correlated with the respondents' perception of adaptation, there is a strong relationship between the sense of coherence and adaptation. This provides an independent confirmation of our consistent finding.

Discussion

This study was designed to apply the concept of sense of coherence to the level of the family and to test the hypothesis that the family SOC is related to family adaptation. A sample was selected consisting of 60 families who had confronted a severe life stressor or crisis—the disablement of the head of the family—at least two years earlier, an acute event followed by the pileup of stressors involved in the inevitable need to reorganize family life. The data strongly support the hypothesis that those families with a strong family SOC—measured by the perception by spouses that family life is comprehensible, manageable, and meaningful—are more likely to be well adapted, more likely to have reached a high level of reorganization after a period of crisis, as measured by the satisfaction with family fit, internally and vis-à-vis the social environment.

Examination of this brief summary of the study points up a number of conceptual problems that are central to family stress theory. It may well be that the major contribution of this study goes beyond the modest empirical finding and is found in conceptual clarification. These are the issues to which we now turn. We will first consider the meaning of the two central variables of the study, "the family SOC" and "family adaptation." We then will turn to the relationship between the two.

The SOC construct was originally formulated to apply to the individual's perception of the world of stimuli that bombard one. In the present study, we have undertaken to examine whether the construct can be applied to the family. But the word "family" as used in the phrase "the family sense of coherence" has a dual meaning. First, it refers to the *stimuli* generated by interaction among family members and between family members and nonfamily units—to *what* is perceived as more or less coherent. In this sense, the term is narrower than the focus of the original concept. The latter is similar to the focus in Reiss's (1981) concept of "reality." Reiss too encompasses a very broad range and asks how this reality is "constructed" in the minds of the people he studies. The broader scope is also similar to what Lavee and McCubbin (1985: 9) call "family schema," defined as "the family's world view or appraisal of the total situation . . . the most enduring and stable of the family's levels of appraisal." The narrower use of the construct in the present study is analogous to Lavee and McCubbin's Level 3, called "family coherence" and defined as "the family's appraisal of the overall circumstances, particularly, the family's *fit* within the community in which it lives, its sense of manageability about life events, the predictability about circumstances, and the sense of control and trust the family has over present and future events." It also would seem closely related to the Mooses' concept of the family environment (Moos and Moos, 1976).

We have raised these parallels in order to call attention to the distinction between broader and narrower foci, a distinction that has received little attention and is often blurred, particularly when it comes to operationalization. We chose to study the construction of *family* reality, rather than the global orientation of the original SOC concept, following the Moos and Lavee-McCubbin approach. In retrospect, this choice may be regrettable. First, it increased the danger of contamination with the dependent variable (an issue dealt with below). Second, it may have involved the loss of power of the broader concept, which, precisely because it encompasses a global view of the world, promises to be relevant in coping with a wide variety of stressors. On the other hand, limiting the focus of attention to family reality increased the chances that spouses would agree (whereas they are more likely to have divergent views of their major activities, social relations, etc.). Moreover, since coping with family reorganization in the face of the acute and ongoing stressors of disablement is a family issue par excellence, we thought it more appropriate to make the choice we did. Further study would be required to test the hypothesis that global coherence would be a better predictor to adaptation than coherence about family life. A further crucial question for study is the relationship between the global perception of the world as coherent and the perception of family life as coherent. Our important point is that the two should be studied separately. It might be noted that, while Reiss explicitly claims to be studying the construction of all reality, his methodology of observing family interaction in essence compels him to *assume* that how family members interact in coping with problems reflects how they see the world.

The second meaning of "family" refers to the *family* sense of coherence, thus posing the question of what it means to say that "the family" perceives a reality (whether that reality is broader or narrower), or the question of *who* is the perceiver. This question too has been slighted in the literature, the tendency being to assume that the technical device of averaging individual perceptions gives the "family" perception. At the operational level, Moos and Moos (1981) have given attention to this issue in developing and applying the Family Incongruence Score. In a rather different context, Kohn (1983: 6) has also raised the issue, when he writes: "The second issue is so obvious as to be embarrassing to raise, yet it has received surprisingly little attention in the research literature: Mothers and fathers often do not have the same values."

One possibility is to follow Moos and Moos, asking the individual respondent about his or her perceptions. Alternatively, one can, as Reiss (1981) does, obtain data by observing family interaction; the family as a unit, in this case, provides the data directly. In the present study, we sought a solution to the problem by combining the technically easier way of obtaining data from individuals with, in the stage of data analysis, considering spouse consensus as relevant to the SOC. The fact that our data show that consensus is a less powerful predictor of adaptation than is the average perception does not mean that the problem of group perception can be disregarded. We know, however, of no way other than Reiss's method of systematic observation of behavior to get at the orientation of the family as a unit.

We may summarize this issue by proposing a fourfold table of study designs. One may ask, focusing on *who* does the perceiving, about the perceptions of (*A*) individual family members or (*B*) the family as a unit. Second, one may ask, focusing on *what* is perceived, about the extent of coherence in (*a*) family life or (*b*) all of life. In design the present study is of the *Aa* type, asking: To what extent does each spouse perceive family life as coherent? In the analysis, by dealing with the consensus between spouses, we sought to introduce *B*. The fact that we found a high degree of spouse consensus, making it difficult to compare consensual and dissensual families, does not do away with the theoretical problem. This may have been a result of something unique about our sample. These families have all experienced a similar, major, nonnormative stressor and have remained intact. This may have effected a process of greater shared construing as a way to adapt.

The distinctions between *A* and *B*, and between *a* and *b*, may contribute to understanding the rather surprising finding that Moos and Moos's Family Environment Scale and Reiss's Card Sort Procedure showed no empirical association, despite seeming conceptual overlap (Oliveri and Reiss, 1984). The FES represents an *Aa* approach, its scores expressing the average of how individual family members perceive different aspects of family life. The CSP represents a *Bb* approach. Family interactional behavior is observed and scored directly; the focus of attention is on how the "family views the world" (p. 36). In addition to the contribution of methodological differences in obtaining data, Oliveri and Reiss attribute the lack of association to the possibility that "the FES and the CSP are tapping essentially unrelated domains of family functioning. . . . one domain consists of the family processes or properties that govern how individual family members perceive the family and describe it to an investigator and the other domain consists of the family processes or properties that govern how family groups behave in a situation with unclear external demands" (p. 47).

The next issue to which we turn is the conceptualization and operationalization of the "dependent" variable, adaptation. Antonovsky's original work on the coherence-adaptation hypothesis focused on physical health. When this limitation is observed, the problem arises whether it should be measured in terms of "objective" or "subjective" criteria. The former, in practice, comes down to axiomatic acceptance of a medical mode of thinking, which also has its problems of reliability and which poses no less difficulty than the use of self-report. Once one moves to self-report, whether of physical health, psychological well-being, or social functioning, one enters dangerous waters.

On the one hand, one faces the Scylla of determination by the investigator of what is good adaptation, an inevitably value-shaped determination. At the conceptual level, the solution seems to be easy. One can use terms like integration, homeostasis, level of entropy or disorganization, fit among members and between the family and the nonfamily environment, or the balance between demands and capabilities. These are the terms with which the literature is replete. But when it comes down to operationalization, this approach leads to problems. Thus one might ask which of three families is best adapted: when both husband and wife agree that she continue to be a maid-chauffeur? when the wife rebels, against the husband's wishes? or when both agree that the time has come for a radical revision of her role? Residents of Fresno and Berkeley are likely to give quite different answers. Or one might ask about the number of friends spouses have jointly, or how many organizations they both belong to, or how often there are family fights, or whether problems are solved by letting time do its work or by actively discussing them. In each case, the investigator, wishing to rank respondents on adaptation, introduces his or her own values.

On the other hand, one faces the Charybdis of conceptualizing adaptation as satisfaction. Operationally, one can seek to avoid asking directly about satisfaction by asking about physical or psychological symptoms, financial or legal problems, sense of well-being (cheerful, happy, etc.), and so on. But in each case, the underlying question is always one of satisfaction, for it is reasonable to presume that no one is particularly pleased by having symptoms or problems, or by being tense, morose, or miserable. Or one can ask about satisfaction directly, avoiding the investigator's values by the reasonable assumption that a family that is highly satisfied in a variety of life areas is a family that is in dynamic homeostasis.

This latter is the choice we made, in essence asking how well the respondent thought his or her family fitted together and fitted into the community. We have called this choice a preference for Charybdis because it presented the danger of making a valid test of the SOC-adaptation hypothesis impossible. Had we been interested, say, in social class or ethnic differences in adaptation, there would have been no problem. These are zeroing-in variables, not contaminated with the dependent variable, but they are not helpful, except as points of departure, in the task of explaining bon- or maladaptation. Use of the FSOC—or any other presumably explanatory variable, such as perceived resources, definition of the stressful situation, or marital quality—carries the danger of implicitly or explicitly asking about satisfaction with family life.

We tried to avoid this danger by constructing FSOC items that avoid direct reference to satisfaction. In all but a few cases, however, there are clearly desirable answers. But what differentiates the FSOC questionnaire from other measures is that it is constructed on the basis of a theoretical guide. Each item is explicitly constructed to ask about the perception of comprehensibility, manageability, or meaningfulness of a given family issue. On the other hand, the FAS was constructed with the use of the concept of fit.

How, then, are the two variables related? The population selected for study was clearly one whose members had all faced a serious crisis from 2 to 10 years earlier, when the head of the family (in Israeli culture at present, for better or for worse, the husband-father is defined as such) had become seriously disabled because of illness or injury. Though we did not investigate the matter, it is reasonable to assume that, since the onset of disability, there had been a "pileup" of stressors; for example, 75% of the husbands reported a decline in occupational status and income after onset. Was the FSOC, we asked, associated with adaptation?

The data provided strong support for the hypothesis. Whether one looks at husband, wife, or joint perception, the relationship is extremely strong. Correlations of .89 and .85 are not often found in the social sciences. When the FSOC measure was refined by omitting items that seemed overlapping to reduce contamination between the two variables, the correlations were only slightly reduced (to .84 and .81). And when a truly independent measure of adaptation was used, the evaluation by case workers, the correlations remained highly significant (.64 and .62).

These findings are consistent with those of the only other study we know of in which the SOC construct was used to study family adaptation (Lavee, McCubbin, and Olson, 1987, based on Lavee's doctoral dissertation). In a large U.S. national sample of families, the sense of coherence was hypothesized to enhance family well-being. Since the SOC scale developed by Antonovsky was not yet available (Antonovsky, 1983), the researchers used two brief scales that represented the concept: a 4-item scale measuring confidence that problems can be handled by the family, and a 3-item scale measuring acceptance and positive appraisal of stressful situations as part of life. "Well-being" was measured by a scale that "measures family members' satisfaction with various aspects of their lives in areas such as health, work, the family, and the community" (Lavee et al., 1987: 863). "The results show," the authors write, "that sense of coherence has a positive impact upon family well-being [and] acts as a *stress-buffer*" (p. 868).

The study by Lavee et al. (1987) is far more

sophisticated, in plan and analysis, than is suggested by this brief reference. Its importance, in the present context, is that there is a commitment to providing an explanation of the link between SOC and well-being. Their emphasis, in keeping with the original discussion of the SOC construct (Antonovsky, 1979, especially chap. 5), is on the cognitive processes, the factors of appraisal and perception, that facilitate coping with stressors. Our study takes us two steps further, going beyond a strictly cognitive emphasis and incorporating components that are emotional (confidence in the availability of resources) and motivational (viewing the stressor as a challenge).

Neither Lavee and associates nor we have solved the problem of contamination. But we have, we believe, taken a step in the right direction. Some may prefer to see both studies as using two scales that represent a single construct, or as studies of concurrent validity. But the hope is that both contribute to the clarification required for advancing research.

The solution to the problem we would propose at this stage is that a variety of conceptualizations and operationalizations of family adaptation be used. But we would insist, in each case, that it is incumbent on the researcher to specify the *mechanisms* through which the independent variables and one's variant of adaptation are linked. (On this issue, see the exchange between Trost and Spanier in the November 1985 issue of this journal, pp. 1072–1074.) In the present case, such specification provides, we believe, at least some theoretical basis for claiming that the FSOC and the FAS are conceptually distinct and that the hypothesis of the study has been tested.

One final comment is in order. Correlation is not causation. The results of a cross-sectional study cannot demonstrate that a strong SOC is causally predictive of family adaptation. Whatever the plausibility of a theoretical account of a chain of events, the data cannot demonstrate that the SOC indeed precedes adaptation. This can only be tested in a longitudinal study. Moreover, in real life, we would anticipate interactional influence: a strong SOC does foster, by its contribution to successful coping with stressors, a high level of family adaptation; but such adaptation, in turn, leads the family to experiences that reinforce the SOC. To study this process over time is indeed a challenge for research.

Conclusion

Our underlying concern in this study has been to bridge two research traditions that have generally disregarded each other. The SOC construct was developed in the context of life events and coping theory, which primarily seeks to explain physical (and sometimes psychological) illness. Family stress theory, on the other hand, has been concerned with family adaptation (though one of the indices sometimes used is physical distress). Both traditions deal with crises, stressors, coping, and the consequences of the process. There is little doubt that a married couple, experiencing a relatively severe disablement of the husband, confronts both a serious acute stressor and an ongoing stress situation. The study has demonstrated that the levels of the "family sense of coherence" of husband and wife, taken singly and taken jointly, are very closely associated with the extent to which the spouses are satisfied with different aspects of family life. Whether such strong results would have been obtained had an alternative conception of adaptation been adopted remains a matter for future research. Moreover, since the study was cross-sectional, we have no evidence for a causal relationship. The theory proposed points to such causality in that it argues that a strong SOC, particularly one shared by spouses, provides the motivational, perceptual, and behavioral basis for successful resolution of both the instrumental and emotional problems posed by stressors. Such resolution—note, not the absence of stressors, but their successful resolution—should provide one with a sense of satisfaction about family life. Were one to carry on study of the process, one might see that such satisfaction reinforces coherence. But if, at any given time, one wishes to predict which families will resolve crises successfully, the SOC seems to be a promising bet.

Notes

This article is based on an MSW thesis submitted by Talma Sourani to the School of Social Work, University of Haifa, 1983.

1. The inevitable limitations of a one-person endeavor prevented fulfilling the desirable requirement of obtaining data that would test the validity of the FSOC and FAS, for example, by administering the Moos and Moos (1981) Family Environment Scale. Our empirical findings, then, must be treated with

due precaution. But since our major concern in this study was to advance theoretical clarification, we felt justified in using the data at least to illustrate our concepts. Clearly, the scales proposed here will have to be examined further for their psychometric properties before they can be adopted.

References

Antonovsky, Aaron. 1972. "Breakdown: A needed fourth step in the conceptual armamentarium of modern medicine." Social Science and Medicine 6: 537–544.

Antonovsky, Aaron. 1979. Health, Stress, and Coping. San Francisco: Jossey-Bass.

Antonovsky, Aaron. 1983. "The sense of coherence: Development of a research instrument." Newsletter and Research Report 1: 11–22, W. S. Schwartz Research Center for Behavioral Medicine, Tel Aviv University.

Antonovsky, Aaron. 1987. Unraveling the Mystery of Health. San Francisco: Jossey-Bass.

Burr, Wesley, R. 1973. Theory Construction and the Sociology of the Family. New York: Wiley.

Cassel, John. 1974. "Psychosocial processes and 'stress': Theoretical formulation." International Journal of Health Services 4: 471–482.

Dohrenwend, Barbara S., and Bruce P. Dohrenwend (eds.). 1974. Stressful Life Events: Their Nature and Effects. New York: Wiley.

Fisher, Lawrence, Ronald F. Kokes, Donald C. Ransom, Susan L. Phillips, and Pamela Rudd. 1985. "Alternative strategies for 'relational' family data." Family Process 24: 213–224.

Hill, Reuben. 1949. Families Under Stress. New York: Harper and Row.

Hill, Reuben. 1965. "Generic features of families under stress." Pp. 35–52 in H. J. Parad (ed.), Crisis Intervention: Selected Readings. New York: Family Service Association of America.

Kohn, Melvin L. 1983. "On the transmission of values in the family: A preliminary formulation." Pp. 1–12 in A. C. Kerckhoff (ed.), Research in Sociology of Education and Socialization (Vol. 4). Greenwich, CT: JAI Press.

Lavee, Yoav, and Hamilton I. McCubbin. 1985. "Adaptation in family stress theory: Theoretical and methodological considerations." Paper presented at the annual meeting of the National Council on Family Relations, Dallas (November).

Lavee, Yoav, Hamilton I. McCubbin, and David H. Olson. 1987. "The Effect of Stressful Life Events and Transitions on Family Functioning and Well-being." Journal of Marriage and the Family 49: 857–873.

Lazarus, Richard S., and Susan Folkman. 1984. Stress, Appraisal, and Coping. New York: Springer.

McCubbin, Hamilton I., and Joan M. Patterson. 1983. "The family stress process: The double ABCX model of adjustment and adaptation." Pp. 7–37 in H. McCubbin, M. B. Sussman, and J. M. Patterson (eds.), Social Stress and the Family: Advances and Development in Family Stress Theory and Research. New York: Haworth.

Moos, Rudolf H., and Beatrice S. Moos. 1976. "A typology of family social environments." Family Process 15: 357–372.

Moos, Rudolf H., and Beatrice S. Moos. 1981. Family Envircnment Scale Manual. Palo Alto, CA: Consulting Psychologists Press.

Oliveri, Mary E., and David Reiss. 1984. "Family concepts and their measurement: Things are seldom what they seem." Family Process 23: 33–48.

Rabkin, Judith G., and Elmer L. Struening. 1976. "Life events, stress, and illness." Science 194: 1013–1020.

Reiss, David. 1981. The Family's Construction of Reality. Cambridge, MA: Harvard University Press.

Spanier, Graham B. 1985. "Improve, Refine, Recast, Expand, Clarify—Don't Abandon." Journal of Marriage and the Family 47: 1073–1074.

Trost, Jan E. 1985. "Abandon Adjustment!" Journal of Marriage and the Family 47: 1072–1073.

Walker, Alexis J. 1985. "Reconceptualizing family stress." Journal of Marriage and the Family 47: 827–837.

Appendix

The Family Sense of Coherence Scale and the Family Adaptation Scale

In the data-gathering phase of this study, the written questionnaire was introduced to respondents as follows:

> This questionnaire contains questions about the way your family handles various daily problems. The questions relate to your immediate family: spouse and children. In answering, try to think of the behavior of the entire family, and not only of specific individuals. But don't include little children to whom the questions don't apply. There are no right or wrong answers. Each family has its own way of behaving in different situations.

The semantic differential technique was explained next, and the 26 FSOC items were introduced. These were followed by 9 sociodemographic items and the 10 FAS items, again in semantic differential format. The first FSOC item is given here in the format in which it appeared in the questionnaire (translated from the Hebrew). All other items are given with the anchor responses in parentheses, the response appearing under 1 presented first.

In the marginal notations on the FSOC items, "R" shows that the response is reversed for scoring purposes, so that 7 is always a high FSOC. "C," "MA," and "ME" indicate that the item is a comprehensibility, manageability, or meaningfulness item.

Family Sense of Coherence

C 1. Is there a feeling in your family that *everyone* understands everyone else well?

R 1 2 3 4 5 6 7

There's full understanding among all family members. ... There's no understanding among family members.

MA 2. When you have to get things done which depend on cooperation among all members of the family, your feeling is: (there's almost no chance that the things will get done . . . the things will always get done)

R MA 3. Do you have the feeling that it's always possible, in your family, to get help one from another when a problem arises? (you can always get help from all family members . . . you can't get help from family members)

C 4. Let's assume that unexpected guests are about to arrive and the house isn't set up to receive them. Does it seem to you that: (the job will fall on one person . . . all the members of the family will pitch in to get the house ready)

R MA 5. In case an important decision has to be taken which concerns the whole family, do you have the feeling that (a decision will always be taken that's for the good of all family members . . . the decision that will be taken won't be for the good of all family members)

R ME 6. Family life seems to you (full of interest . . . totally routine)

C 7. Does it happen that someone in the family feels as if it isn't clear to him/her what his/her jobs are in the house? (this feeling exists all the time . . . this feeling exists very rarely)

ME 8. When a problem comes up in the family (like: unusual behavior of a family member, an unexpected overdraft in the bank account, being fired from work, unusual tension), do you think that you can together clarify how it happened? (very little chance . . . to a great extent)

R MA 9. Many people, even those with a strong character, sometimes feel like sad sacks (losers). In the past, has there been a feeling like this in your family? (there's never been a feeling like this in the family . . . this feeling always exists)

R MA 10. Think of a situation in which your family moved to a new house. Does it seem to you that (all family members would be able to adjust easily to the new situation . . . it would be very hard for family members to adjust to the new situation)

MA 11. Let's assume that your family has been annoyed by something in your neighborhood. Does it seem to you that (nothing can be done to prevent the annoyance . . . it's possible to do a great deal to prevent the annoyance)

ME 12. Until now your family life has had (no clear goals or purpose at all . . . very clear goals and purpose)

R ME 13. When you think about your family life, you very often (feel how good it is to be alive . . . ask yourself why the family exists)

C 14. Let's say you're tired, disappointed, angry, or the like. Does it seem to you that *all* the members of the family will sense your feelings? (no one will sense my feelings . . . all the family members will sense my feelings)

R C 15. Do you sometimes feel that there's no clear and sure knowledge of what's going to happen in the family? (there's no such feeling at all . . . there's always a feeling like this)

MA 16. When the family faces a tough problem, the feeling is (there's no hope of overcoming the difficulties . . . we'll overcome it all)

ME 17. To succeed in things that are important to the family or to one of you (isn't important in the family . . . is a very important thing for all family members)

R C 18. To what extent does it seem to you that family rules are clear? (the rules in the family are completely clear . . . the rules aren't clear at all)

ME 19. When something very difficult happened in your family (like a critical illness of a family member), the feeling was (there's no point in going on living in the family . . . this is a challenge to go on living in the family despite everything)

MA 20. When you think of possible difficulties in important areas of family life, is the feeling (there are many problems which have no solution . . . it's possible in every case to find a solution)

R C 21. Think of your feeling about the extent of planning money matters in your family (there's full planning of money matters . . . there's no planning about money matters at all in the family)

R MA 22. When you're in the midst of a rough period, does the family (always feel cheered up by the thought about better things that can happen . . . feel disappointed and despairing about life)

ME 23. Does it happen that you feel that there's really not much meaning in maintaining the family framework? (we always have this feeling . . . we've never had a feeling like this in our family)

R C 24. Think of your feeling about the extent of order in your home. Is the case that (the house is well-ordered . . . the house isn't at all ordered)

R ME 25. Let's assume that your family is the target of criticism in the neighborhood. Does it seem to you that your reactions will be (the whole family will join together against the criticism . . . family members will move apart from each other)

R ME 26. To what extent do family members share sad experiences with each other? (there's complete sharing with all family members . . . we don't share our sad experiences with family members)

Family Adaptation Scale

Two anchor replies, printed under scores 1 and 7, were standard for all 10 items: I'm not satisfied . . . I'm completely satisfied. However, to avoid a set, the negative reply was placed under 7 on Items 1, 2, 4, 6, 9, and 10. These items, then, need to be reversed so that a high score represents high satisfaction. Item 11 represents an overall measure of adaptation, scored after reversing.

1. Are you satisfied in belonging to your family?
2. Are you satisfied about the way the children are being raised? (like with their education, their behavior, their activities?)
3. Are you satisfied with the family's way of life?
4. Are you satisfied with the possibility of expressing what you feel in your family?
5. Are you satisfied with the extent to which family members are close to each other?
6. Are you satisfied with how the family spends its leisure time?
7. Are you satisfied with the way family members communicate with each other?
8. Are you satisfied with how your family fits into the neighborhood?
9. Are you satisfied with the social relations your family has?
10. Are you satisfied with the way the family relates to the wishes of all the family members?
11. And now, think of what for you would be an ideal family, one which is perfectly adjusted. Where on the scale would you rank your family compared to the ideal family? (1 = ideally adjusted family; 7 = a family which is not at all adjusted)

14

Self-Care in Israel: Physicians' Views and Perspectives

Judith T. Shuval, Rachel Javetz, and *Diana Shye*

INTRODUCTION AND THEORETICAL BACKGROUND

Self-care by lay persons refers to the set of preventive, diagnostic, curative and rehabilitative actions which lay people take with the aim of preserving or ameliorating their health. The view on which the present paper is based has been stated elsewhere: "Self care and self help are parts of a matrix in the health care system, whereby lay persons can actively function for themselves and/or others to prevent, detect or treat disease and promote health so as to supplement other resources" [1].

There is growing interest among professionals and lay persons in increasing lay autonomy which seeks to decrease dependence on the formal health services and promote independent health-oriented behaviour. Some have suggested that increased self-care by lay persons might result in more rational use of the primary health-care services, in terms of utilization rates and more effective performance by professional personnel. All of these could contribute to reduced costs of running the health-care system [2–6].

Self-care behaviour may occur with or without reference to the formal health-care system. Some self-care is supplementary to, in lieu of, or under the directives of health-care professionals whose views on such lay behaviour are therefore relevant to the lay person. But even when undertaken at lay initiative and with no direct contact with health-care professionals, there is an inherent thread connecting the formal health-care system and the lay person: the connection is through information concerning norms of appropriate health-care behaviour which generally flow from the system to the lay person. While these may be accepted or rejected, it is probably rare for such information and norms to be ignored except by individuals totally insulted in alternative ideologies providing their own health norms.

A comprehensive view of self-care therefore places it in the context of an overall health system, which includes a variety of inter-related actors all of whom play specialized roles: the lay person (whose health is under consideration), the lay person's lay reference groups (family, friends, informal informants), physicians (in primary, secondary or tertiary care settings), other health-care providers (a variety of allied health personnel) and alternative practitioners. Each of these is characterized by goals, norms and values concerning health, and by patterned interaction with others in the system. A lay individual's decisions regarding health are a function of a process of direct and indirect interaction among the above actors at different times and in a variety of situational contexts. The salience and authority of the different actors vary in terms of their expertise, status, legitimation, availability and accessibility to each other.

Physicians occupy a unique position of authority in this system. Indeed, in most Western societies and in many developing societies as well, this group of professionals is structurally dominant in terms of formal authority and control of the professional aspects of the system [7]. This is undoubtedly the case in Israel, where doctors occupy a central and controlling role among the actors in the formal health-care system.

This paper is addreseed to an examination of Israeli physicians' perceptions regarding the potential effects of lay self-care. We assume that changes in the amount, quality or context of lay self-care will effect processes of health-care delivery and the physicians' role in a variety of ways. On the micro-level, relating to the doctor–patient relationship, self-care implies certain shifts in the balance of authority and power which could result in changes in the traditional asymmetry of that relationship and in the physicians' feeling of control in caring for patients [8–11]. On the macro-level, lay self-care could effect clinic utilization rates which in turn effect the cost of health-care delivery and might even change rates of hospitalization. All of these potential effects are relevant to the physician's professional role and therefore to his general attitude toward lay self-care.

The research is designed to explore physicians' perceptions regarding three types of effects of lay self-care. Two are micro-level effects and one, composed of three sub-effects, is on the macro-level.

Micro-level effects:

A. Perceptions of the effects of specific self-care behaviours on the health of the individual.
B. Perceptions of the effect of independence and initiatives by lay persons on the health-care process.

Macro-level effects:

C. Perceptions of the effects of lay self-care on the health-care system in term of utilization, costs and hospitalization rates.

These three perceived effects serve as the dependent variables of the research.

The overall purpose of the research is to examine the three dependent variables in terms of their general distributions and in terms of their inter-relationships, in order to elucidate the structure of physicians' perceptions in the area of self-care. In addition, the research seeks to study differences within the physician population by examining the correlates of these three variables.

Physicians' views regarding lay self-care are far from homogeneous and comprise only one element in their more general complex of attitudes and perceptions regarding health topics. There has been little in-depth scientific research regarding physicians' specific views on self-care. One study carried out in the United States reports physicians to have generally negative attitudes, with many expressing concern about possible damaging effects of self-care [12].

A review of more general research which focuses on related topics indicates considerable variation among physicians in their attitudes and perceptions: these have been found to be a function of their professional training and practice experience, as well as of a variety of personal attributes. An examination of research findings which focus directly or indirectly on physicians' attitudes and perceptions regarding patient self-treatment, lay initiatives in health-care and innovative changes in the organization of medical practice, which could affect physician autonomy, led to the choice of independent variables included in the present study.

Most of the research reviewed was carried out in the United States or in Britain. Thus, the correlates found in these studies may or may not hold in other cultural settings. In seeking appropriate independent variables for the Israeli study we were concerned to include variables that showed a relationship to relevant attitudes in earlier research, but also meaningful variables that showed inconsistent or no relationships in previously studied settings.

Among the personal attributes studied in earlier research, age has shown the most consistent relationship to physicians' attitudes regarding self-care and to departures from traditional forms of medical practice. Younger practitioners generally express more positive views on these topics [12–14]. Age is clearly associated with career stage: medical students and residents tend to be more accepting of newer approaches to health-care [15, 16].

Most studies did not include a sufficient number of women physicians to analyse gender effects. One exception is the study by Heins *et al.* [17] which focused on attitudes toward innovative organization of medical practice. There is some indication that among older physicians, women were more accepting of such innovations. Several studies show Jews to be more accepting of self-care and of changes in the structure of medical practice than are Catholics and Protestants [12, 16, 18, 19].

The effects of a variety of professional and practice characteristics have been examined in previous studies. Specialists have been found to be more accepting of innovation than general practitioners [14, 20]. There is evidence that surgeons may be a particularly conservative group [19, 20]. But several other studies show no relationship by type or level of medical specialization. Physicians whose practice setting departs most from traditional, solo, fee-for-service practice settings are generally more accepting of self-care and of changes in the traditional forms of medical care [14, 15, 19–21]. Physicians' reports of a heavy patient load are associated with negative views on lay self-care [4, 13, 14, 19].

In sum, the selection of independent variables examined in the present study included all of the above but also included additional variables which failed to show relationships in earlier research, but which were thought to be worth examining in the Israeli context.

SETTING THE SCENE IN ISRAEL

Before proceeding to the findings, it is important to make explicit certain cultural and structural characteristics of the Israel health scene, which could be relevant in understanding the findings. A survey of the literature suggests that this is the first study focusing on physicians' views of self-care undertaken outside the United States and Britain.

While Israel does not have a nationalized health-care system, 94.5% of its population is covered by comprehensive health insurance which includes curative and ambulatory care, as well as hospitalization. Only 2% of the Jewish population are not insured. Health-care is organized by a number of sick funds of which the largest is the General Sick Fund (Kupat Holim Klalit) which in 1986 covered 83% of the insured Jewish population. Three smaller sick funds insure an additional 17% of that population. Regional hospitals are located within no more than 30 km of most communities; primary, curative and preventive services are easily accessible on a neighbourhood basis [22].

Israel is characterized by one of the highest physician to population ratios in the world: 36/10,000, i.e. 1/279 [23]. This is a result of the high attractiveness of the profession to Israelis and the policy of admitting and licensing immigrant physicians who constitute a major portion of the primary care doctors [24]. The vast majority of physicians are salaried employees of one of the sick funds or of the Ministry of Health; very few are primarily self-employed in fee-for-service practice, although some engage in part-time private practice in addition to their primary employment.

The high utilization rates in the primary care clinics have resulted in no small amount of frustration among clinic physicians who feel over-burdened by frequent trivial or non-medically relevant complaints [25]. The easy accessibility of primary care physicians has contributed to some erosion of their status. Furthermore, the sharp dichotomy between community and hospital practice also contributes to this process in view of the concentration of high level specialists and sophisticated technology in the hospital system. Indeed, very few graduates of Israeli medical schools opt for community practice if they have a choice. The latter setting ranks lower in prestige than does hospital practice [26].

Health is a central value in the social-cultural context of Israeli society [27]. Jews in many countries have shown heightened awareness and concern for health, relative to other groups [16, 27–30].

In Israel, this orientation is expressed in patterns of health-care which are strongly medically-dependent and take the form of high confidence in physicians, frequent utilization of health services, and high drug consumption, both prescription and non-prescription [31, 32].

The material rewards of salaried medical practice are limited by a strict grading system. The rewards of pratice therefore focus strongly on the intrinsic level: the satisfaction of high quality professional performance and professional fulfillment, which are derived from clinical work and from respect, compliance or deference from their patients. These intrinsic rewards assume special importance when the extrinisc material rewards are perceived as relatively low.

While there is little systematic research on this topic in Israel, observation suggests that the traditional, asymmetrical physician–patient relationship is widespread. Physicians' authority is generally accepted in health matters and there has been little evidence of consumerism among patient populations. Indeed, there appears to be widespread acceptance by lay persons of the appropriateness of the asymmetrical model, although adherence to medical instructions may not be as full as many physicians believe, few voices have yet been raised by patients or other lay persons to overtly question or criticize the style or quality of the doctor–patient relationship.

The structural problems of the Israeli health-care system are such that increased self-care could, under appropriate conditions, make some contribution to their amelioration. A major problem of the primary health-care system is its high consulting rates which reach an average of 12 physicians' visits per year [33]. Among those over 65, this figure is doubled [34]. As noted, it has been suggested that increased lay self-care could reduce clinic utilization rates [30, 35–37].

The Israeli health-care system, like most others in Western societies, is characterized by excessively high costs which it is finding increasingly difficult to meet. A more rational use of the health-care services, with appropriate self-care playing its part in the system, could contribute to some reduction in those costs. On a more general level, it is widely felt in Israel that the highly-developed social welfare services have encouraged patterns of dependency in many areas, among then in health-care. The general goal of lay self-care to strengthen individual independence and autonomy complements a more general goal that is thought by many in Israel to be important.

Israel has been relatively slow to develop consumer consciousness or a formal consumer movement in the health area. These are in the early stages of development relative to many other Western countries. The same may be said of the feminist movement. These two social movements have played important roles in most Western societies in fostering lay self-care [38]. There are few clearly structured pressure-groups seeking to foster self-care as part of an ideological or political goal. Efforts by the major sick fund to promote health-care have taken the form of media messages and some health education programmes. It is unknown what effects these have had on self-care behaviour among lay persons.

In sum, we may say that the Israel context regarding self-care is characterized by underdevelopment and several apparently paradoxical conditions: widespread exercise of physician authority which is most frequently accepted as normative by lay persons; major structural and economic problems of the health-care system which might be ameliorated by increased self-care; little ideologically-based consumer pressure advocating self-care.

DESIGN OF THE RESEARCH

Defining self-care on an empirical level presents major theoretical and practical problems [39]. We view self-care as a multi-dimensional concept, which probably cannot be studied exhaustively in any one research undertaking. As noted, we have chosen to focus on physicians' perceptions of three potential effects of lay self-care. A pilot study based on 60 semi-structured interviews with Israeli physicians provided a rich array of qualitative findings which made it possible to formulate specific questions that would be meaningful in an interview context [40].

The study includes physicians engaged in primary health-care and in hospital practice. In Israel, primary health-care is provided in community clinics by the largest sick fund, General Sick Fund, and by the three small sick funds. The sampling framework therefore was structured in terms of three types of practice setting: the General Sick Fund clinics, the three small sick fund clinics, and the hospitals. In each setting, a systematic sample of physicians was chosen. In addition to general practitioners, doctors in the following specializations were sampled: internal medicine, family medicine, cardiology, gastroenterology and geriatrics. The practice settings included in the study were located in Jerusalem, Haifa, Beer Sheva and metropolitan Tel Aviv. The sample of 258 physicians who participated were distributed in the three practice settings as follows: General Sick Fund clinics—130, small sick fund clinics—53, hospitals—75. Interviewing took place between July 1985 and May 1986*.

The research instrument was a questionnaire composed largely, but not exclusively, of closed questions. In addition to items geared to define the three types of effects of self-care, which served as the dependent

*Details of the sampling procedure are reported in Ref. [41].

variables, it included a set of independent variables of three types:

Personal background characteristics of the physicians: gender, age, country of origin, number of years in Israel, education and occupation of parents and family status.

Professional characteristics of the physicians: date and country of medical education, number of years of practice, specialization, post-graduate training.

Practice characteristics (obtained from the respondent): organizational setting, patient load, hours of work per week, patient characteristics (e.g. perceived proportion of elderly and chronically ill patients).

The full set of independent variables were examined for their relationships to each of the three dependent variables in univariate and multivariate analyses.

PHYSICIANS' PERCEPTIONS OF THREE EFFECTS OF SELF-CARE: FINDINGS

Perceptions of the three effects of self-care will be discussed first in terms of the general distributions of physicians' responses, and then in terms of the relationship of such responses to the personal background, professional and practice setting variables.

Perceptions of the effects of specific self-care behaviours on the health of the individual

A useful taxonomy of self-care skills has been compiled by DeFriese *et al.* from a survey of standard self-care texts and training programmes, and was subjected to review regarding consensus by three panels of health professionals [42]. The self-examination, acute illness care, and chronic illness care items used in the present study, were based on this taxonomy. Self-medication items were derived from studies on this subject by Dunnell and Cartwright [13], as well as from material obtained from the pilot study [40]. Items relating to good preventive health-care, such as proper nutrition, appropriate physical exercise and non-smoking, are so widely accepted by physicians as to be ineffective in their discriminatory power and were therefore excluded, despite their obvious centrality in lay self-care.

Table 1 presents the six health-care behaviours to which physicians were asked to respond. For each they were required to indicate the extent to which they believed it contributed positively, or was likely to damage, an individual's health. The items in the table are ordered in terms of the frequency with which respondents stated that the specific behaviour generally makes a positive contribution to the individual's health.

As expected, there is considerable variation in physicians' views regarding these behaviours, depending on the specific self-care behaviour considered. The figures in Table 1 vary from close to 90% to almost zero.

There was widespread agreement among almost all the physicians that basic self-examination and diagnosis are likely to contribute to health. Over two thirds of the physicians expressed a positive view regarding the health effects of self-monitoring of blood-pressure by hypertensive patients. However, when referring more generally to self-care for medically diagnosed chronic and common acute illnesses, less than half of the population expressed a positive view. At the other end of the spectrum, most doubt was expressed regarding self-medication: only a fifth were prepared to state that use of non-prescription drugs contributes positively to the individual's health, and virtually none accepted self-medication with prescription drugs, when this involves purchase of drugs with prescriptions previously filled, or use of previously prescribed drugs which are still stored in the individual's home.

In addition to observation of the individual items, a composite index was generated after factor analysis of the six items in Table 1 showed that they constitute a single factor which explains 86.2% of the variance. A summary score, ranging from 1 (negative) to 5 (positive), was computed (Cronbach's alpha equals 0.59). The mean score was 3.12 (SD = 0.72).

The Summary Score on the Perceived Effects of Self-Care Behaviour was first examined for relationships to the set of independent variables by means of a one-way analysis of variance. The following significant relationships emerged from that analysis.

Physicians vary in their evaluation of the effects of lay self-care behaviours in terms of their practice settings, the level of their specialization, the number of years in practice and by the country in which they completed their medical education. While the differences are small, they are worth noting. Community clinic practitioners show less favourable attitudes to self-care behaviour than hospital physicians. Complementing this finding is the fact that most positive attitudes are expressed by residents and by younger physicians with least years of experience. The latter two groups are heavily concentrated in

Table 1. Physicians' perceptions of the effects of specific self-care behaviours on the health of the individual ($N = 255$)

Self-care behaviours*	% Indicating a positive contribution to individual's health†
Self-examination and diagnosis, e.g. taking temperature, breast examination, urine tests, etc.	88
Self-monitoring of blood pressure by persons with hypertension	69
Self-care for medically diagnosed chronic illness	48
Self-care for common acute illnesses	40
Self-mediation with OTC drugs	22
Self-medication with prescription drugs‡	3

*The question presented to the physicians was the following: 'To what extent does the following self-care behaviour generally contribute to or damage an individual's health?' Response categories ranged from 1 (is likely to damage health) to 5 (contributes postively to health).

†Those who responded that the given self-care behaviour contributed positively to the individual's health 'in most cases' or 'frequently'.

‡For example, by purchase of prescription drugs with out-dated prescriptions, use of previously provided drugs which are kept at home, etc.

hospital practice. Physicians who completed their medical studies in Israel, in English speaking countries and in western Europe, are characterized by more favourable views on self-care behaviour than those educated in eastern Europe. The other independent variables showed no significant relationship in the one-way analysis of variance.

Since the Summary Score on the Perceived Effects of Self-Care Behaviours is a metric variable, while the independent variables include both metric and non-metric categorical variables, analysis of covariance was used for the multivariate analysis (SPSS ANOVA program). The categorical variables are labelled 'factors' while the metric ones are referred to as 'covariates'. Factor and covariate effects were of equal interest, and no assumptions regarding causal priority between them were held. Therefore, a regression approach was chosen for the analysis, in which the effects of factors, covariates and interactions were assessed together, while controlling simultaneously for all of them. This approach resembles a standard multiple regression analysis involving both metric and dummy variables as predictors.

A preliminary analysis of covariance was carried out using factors and covariates which showed significant, or nearly significant, zero-order correlations with the summary score, as well as other variables which were thought to have conceptual relevance to the dependent variable, e.g. gender. Two-way interactions were assessed at this stage.

The above analysis showed significant interaction between practice setting and gender despite the fact that gender did not show a significant effect in the univariate analysis. A new variable expressing this interaction was created accordingly. Multiple classification analysis was then performed, permitting the assessment of the magnitude of the effects of the factors. Unstandardized partial regression coefficients were computed for the covariates, as well as the percentage of the total variance of the dependent variable which is explained by the factors and covariates included in the model. Table 2 presents the results of the multiple classification analysis and the percentage of the total variance explained by the variables included.

The variables listed in Table 2 explain 27.0% of the variance ($P < 0.001$). All but two of the variables show significant independent effects on the Summary Score on the Perceived Effects of Self-Care Behaviour.

Three of the four variables referred to in the one-way analysis of variance continue to show the same general effects with minor exceptions when controls are introduced.

The role of practice setting noted in the univariate analysis remains in the multivariate analysis among male physicians: hospital practitioners are most positive, the General Sick Fund doctors are next, while the physicians practicing in the small sick funds are least favourable. The female physicians practicing in

Table 2. Summary score on the perceived effects of self-care behaviour by physicians' personal, professional and setting traits: analysis of covariance (summary measure grand mean score = 3.12)

Covariates	Regression coefficient (adjusted for factors and other covariates)	F	P
Number of years in practice	−0.012	7.294	0.007
% Chronically ill patients in practice	−0.005	5.506	0.020
% Elderly among chronically ill patients	0.003	2.581	0.110

Factors	Category	N	Mean score adjusted for factors and covariates	F	P	Beta*
Practice setting × gender	General Sick Fund, men	51	3.11	3.018	0.001	0.063
	Gender Sick Fund, women	72	3.25			
	Small sick funds, men	37	2.97			
	Small sick funds, women	10	2.52			
	Hospitals, men	63	3.18			
	Hospitals, women	8	2.69			
Level of specialization	General practitioners	82	2.90	4.833	0.009	0.044
	Residents	54	3.21			
	Specialists	105	3.22			
Perception of patient load	Optimal	29	3.19	5.653	0.004	0.048
	Acceptable	98	3.28			
	Too heavy	114	2.94			
Percentage of elderly (60+) in practice	⩽25%	56	2.96	3.172	0.025	0.040
	26–44%	59	2.97			
	45–59%	61	3.30			
	⩾60%	65	3.19			
Country of medical studies	Israel	65	3.07	0.716	0.582	0.010
	English-speaking & South Africa	24	3.21			
	Western Europe	45	3.18			
	Eastern Europe	56	3.01			
	U.S.S.R.	51	3.06			
Total N		241				
Total explained variance = 27.0% ($P = 0.001$)						

*Beta and the regression coefficients do not add up to the total explained variance (27%) as they are not fully independent of each other or additive.

the General Sick Fund are more positive in their views on self-care than almost any single sub-groups observed, including male physicians in the same setting. However, in the other two settings, females are less favourable than males, although there are too few cases in these female groups to permit generalization.

The multivariate analysis shows that the least positive views are expressed by general practitioners, while residents and specialists—wherever they practice—are more positive in their views regarding self-care. This analysis also confirms the findings concerning the weak negative effect of years of practice on the Summary Score.

The effect of the country in which medical training took place is shown by the multivariate analysis to be an artifact which is eliminated when controls are introduced.

A number of additional variables are seen in Table 2 to have some effect on physicians' views regarding self-care behaviours when controls are introduced. Most interesting is the finding showing a significant effect of perceived patient load: those who report overload are less positive in their views regarding the effects of self-care.

In addition, it may be seen that physicians who report a greater proportion of elderly persons in their practice tend to express more positive views regarding the effects of self-care behaviours: although the relationship is not fully monotonic, it is clear and significant.

In sum, it appears, that Israeli physicians respond differently to various types of self-care behaviour by lay persons, and their perceptions vary from widespread approval to virtually unanimous disapproval, depending on the nature of the behaviour under discussion. However, their general views on self-care appear to be a function of their length of experience and certain situational characteristics of their practice setting; more positive effects of self-care seen among younger, hospital based, specialists or residents. Conversely, the data show that older general practitioners working in community clinics express less support for self-care behaviours. In addition, work pressures experienced in a heavy patient load, which occur most prominently in the community clinics of the General Sick Fund, are associated with more negative views. Physicians whose practice experience included large numbers of elderly patients express relatively positive views regarding the effects of self-care.

Physicians' perceptions of the effects of independence and initiatives by lay persons on the health-care process

Self-care is often associated with attitudes and behaviour expressing independence and autonomy by lay persons in matters regarding their health. In that context, individuals may pose questions to the physician and lay judgement may be exercised in varying degrees. In some cases, such opinions may also be expressed by reservations regarding physician authority, thus contravening traditional assumptions concerning compliance and acceptance by patients of medical directives. In its most active form, self-care involves a different basic orientation by lay persons to health professionals, which may be perceived by some of the latter as inappropriate or threatening. Traditionally, the normative model of the physician–patient relationship is an asymmetrical one, which fosters dependence and discourages initiatives. The physician is viewed as an expert, responsible in large measure for health-care, and is authorized to make decisions regarding the patient who is expected to comply. From this viewpoint lay initiatives and independence may be viewed by physicians as undesirable in that they challenge the traditional position of professional authority and introduce lay judgement in areas which are ostensibly the physicians' domain. While this traditional model has undergone some modification in recent years, such changes vary between and within societies, and numerous elements of the traditional pattern of relationships persist [8–11].

One of the objectives of the present research is to analyse physicians' perceptions of the effect of expressions of independence and autonomy by lay persons on the health-care process and particularly on the physician–patient relationship [43].

The items selected to address this issue refer to a variety of autonomous behaviours reflecting lay initiatives in health, and may be seen in Table 3. They refer to the use of lay networks as a resource in decision-making in health-care, and to processes of bargaining with physicians as well as modification by lay people of recommended treatment. In addition, items were chosen which describe 'behavioural challenge' of physicians by patients and 'consumerist self-care skills' such as gaining access to medical records and obtaining a second opinion [8, 14, 42, 44, 45].

Physicians were requested to indicate, for each item, whether they believe that the specific behaviour, when it occurs, generally contributes positively to his/her ability to provide good health care or is detrimental to that process. Categories ranged from 1 (negative effect) to 5 (positive effect). Table 3 presents mean scores on the individual items, as well as the percentage of physicians who indicated that the behaviour would generally contribute positively to the health-care process.

On the whole, physicians show considerable reservation regarding patient initiatives of various sorts. No more than a third perceived positive effects of any of the behaviours in Table 3, while several of the items were rejected by almost all the respondents. This contrasts with the findings in Table 1 concerning the perceived effects of specific self-care behaviours on the health of the individual. It will be recalled that there was widespread approval by physicians of some of the types of self-care behaviour referred to. It thus appears that these professionals distinguish between certain *specific self-care behaviours* which are perceived to have positive effects under certain circumstances, and an *attitudinal complex* in which patients express independence and question physicians' authority. There is widespread rejection of the latter.

The mean scores and the percentages in Table 3 show a similar ordering of the items, reflecting physicians' perceptions regarding patients' expressions of autonomy. The items fall roughly into two groups distinguished by the extent to which physicians express acceptance of the consumer's behaviour.

Table 3. Physicians' perceptions of the effects of independence and initiatives by lay persons on the health-care process: response to individual items (means and percentages; $N = 258$)

Patient behaviours*	Mean	SD	% Indicating a positive contribution to the treatment process†
Patient requests a second opinion before accepting your recommended treatment	3.00	1.16	34
Patient states that your recommended treatment is complicated or difficult and requests simpler treatment	2.88	1.32	32
Patient consults family and friends on whether to consult a physician for a health problem	2.81	1.10	21
Patient asks to see his medical record	2.17	1.17	10
Patient states that your recommended treatment is not essential in his case	1.80	1.03	8
Patient consults with family and friends, to obtain their views regarding the treatment you have recommended	1.66	0.94	4
Patient does not carry out your instructions fully, and changes some or all of your recommended treatment	1.30	0.72	2

*The question presented to the physicians was the following: 'How does the following patient behaviour, when it appears, affect your ability to provide good care for that patient?' Response categories ranged from 1 (generally negative effect) to 5 (generally positive effect).

†Those who indicated the two most positive categories.

The most acceptable items of behaviour, which are viewed positively by 20–30% of the respondents, focus on seeking a second opinion, requesting less complicated treatment, and obtaining lay advice about consulting a physician. The remaining four items elicited more negative responses. The behaviours refer to patient requests to see medical records, questioning of the recommended treatment, use of lay referral systems for advice on treatment, and non-compliance with a prescribed regimen. All of these are perceived negatively by 90% or more of the physians; the final item concerning non-compliance and self-initiated modification of treatment, is rejected by virtually all.

In addition to observation of the individual items, a summary score was constructed for physicians' perception of the Effects of Independence and Initiatives by Lay Persons on the Health-Care Process. Factor analysis indicated that the seven items together explain 84.2% of the total variance. Reliability was estimated by Cronbach's alpha = 0.64. Scores range from 1 (negative effects) to 5 (positive effects). The summary score for each respondent was the mean of his scores on all items.

It is of interest that this summary measure was only weakly related to the Summary Score on the Perceived Effects of Self-Care Behaviours discussed above ($r = 0.18$). This indicates general independence of physicians' perceptions regarding these two aspects of self-care: those who tend to perceive positive effects of self-care behaviour by lay persons do not necessarily perceive positive effects from expressions of independence and autonomy among such persons in the course of treatment, and vice versa.

The Summary Measure was examined in relation to physicians' personal background, professional and practice setting variables. One-way analysis of variance showed significant, although small, differences on a number of variables.

There is a difference between male and female physicians regarding perceived effects of independent initiatives. Male physicians are more favourable than females. Physicians' views on lay autonomy are related to their practice setting and specialty status. Least positive effects are perceived by physicians in community clinics of the General Sick Fund and among general practitioners with no specialty status. Physicians who report the most overload regarding patient consulting rates, are also relatively negative. Conversely, those perceiving the most positive effects of patient independence are the hospital practitioners, with specialty status, who report least overload.

Analysis of covariance was used to estimate the joint effect of the independent variables on the summary measure on Independence and Initiatives in Health-Care. Table 4, which presents the findings, includes variables which have a significant zero-order relationship as well as a number of others which seemed conceptually relevant.

The model explains only 12.5% of the variance, and only two of the variables contribute a significant

Table 4. Summary measure of physicians' perceptions of the effects of independence and initiatives by lay persons on the self-care process by physicians' personal, professional and practice setting traits: analysis of covariance (summary measure grand mean score = 2.24)

Covariates			Regression coefficient (adjusted for factors and other covariates)	F	P	
Number of years in practice			−0.008	4.565	0.034	
Factors	**Category**	**N**	**Mean score adjusted for factors and covariates**	**F**	**P**	**Beta***
Practice setting × gender	General Sick Fund, men	54	2.21	1.973	0.083	0.05
	General Sick Fund, women	73	2.11			
	Small sick funds, men	37	2.23			
	Small sick funds, women	11	1.94			
	Hospitals, men	64	2.43			
	Hospitals, women	8	2.17			
Level of specialization	General practitioners	85	2.18	4.186	0.016	0.04
	Residents	54	2.05			
	Specialists	108	2.36			
Perception of patient load	Optimal	29	2.28	1.501	0.225	0.01
	Acceptable	101	2.30			
	Too heavy	117	2.15			
Total N		247				
Total explained variance = 12.5% ($P = 0.001$)						

*Beta and the regression coefficient do not add up to the total explained variance (12.5%) since they are neither fully independent of each other nor additive.

effect. This finding suggests considerable randomness and little structuring of this attitudinal complex in the physician population.

The multivariate analysis generally confirms the picture regarding each of the variables seen in the one-way analysis of variance. Although the effect of the new composite variable (gender and practice setting) is not significant, it may be seen that male physicians consistently tend to express more positive views than females regarding initiatives and autonomy of lay persons; the hospital setting is the most conducive to positive attitudes while both types of community practice settings are less positive.*

The findings regarding level of specialization are partly confirmed when controls are introduced: physicians with specialty status are most positive in their views regarding lay independence and autonomy, but the general practitioners, who are less positive than the latter, are nevertheless somewhat more positive than the residents. All of these differences are small.

The multivariate analysis confirms the effect noted above regarding perceived patient load, but the difference is small and not significant. In addition to the above, length of professional experience has a small significant effect: physicians with more years of experience are somewhat more negative in their perceptions of the effects of lay independence and initiatives on health-care.

Taken together, these findings suggest that a general factor conditioning physicians' perceptions regarding the effects of lay independence in self-care is a situational factor relative to the extent to which he or she feels over-worked or harassed by excessive consulting and trivial complaints. The feeling that many patient visits to the clinic are medically unjustifiable, and the associated sense of overload, may result in lowered willingness by physicians to accept patients' expressions of independence. Affirmation of professional authority may serve as a mechanism to facilitate the handling of excessive numbers of patients.

*The number of female physicians in the small sick funds and in the hospital is negligible and therefore not reliable.

Physicians' perceptions of the effects of increased lay self-care on the health-care system

On the macro-level, a more collectively oriented issue focuses on the possible effects of self-care on the overall health-care system. Physicians were asked whether they believed that increased practice of self-care for acute and chronic illness would have an effect on three aspects of the health-care system: utilization rates of primary care services, costs of running the health-care system, and need for hospitalization. Table 5 presents the distribution of physicians' responses.

Table 5. Physicians' perceptions of the effects of lay self-care on the health-care system ($N = 258$)

Perceived effect*	% of physicians
Regarding consulting rates	
Reduce	61
No effect	16
Increase	23
Total	100
Regarding costs	
Decrease	46
No effect	31
Increase	23
Total	100
Regarding hospitalization rates	
Decrease	35
No effect	65
Total	100

*The question put to the physicians was as follows: 'How would the health-care system be affected if increased numbers of lay persons learned to engage in self-diagnosis and self-care for acute or chronic illness?'

Close to two-thirds feel that increased self-care would reduce the number of consultations. Nearly half feel that it would reduce the costs of health-care and about a third feel that it would reduce hospitalizations. At the same time there is a more pessimistic group of about a quarter of the physicians who believe that increased self-care would have the opposite effects: it would result in increased utilization of primary care services (because people might be sicker as a result of inappropriate and delayed treatment) and would augment costs of the health-care system. Furthermore, two-thirds believe that it would not decrease hospitalization.

The view that increased self-care would reduce utilization rates is most frequent among General Sick Fund clinic physicians who are most exposed to high utilization and frequently for what they view as trivial complaints. Fully 72% of these practitioners state that increased self-care will reduce utilization of primary care services, as compared to 55% of the hospital physicians, and 43% of the small sick fund physicians ($P = 0.000$). No other independent variable showed a significant relationship.

Only one variable among the personal, professional and practice characteristics showed a significant relationship to physicians' attitudes concerning the effects of self-care on the costs of the health-care system: length of professional experience. The less experienced (less than 10 years of practice) are most optimistic in this regard: 56% believe that this would reduce such costs while among those with 10–25 years of experience the percentage is 47% and the veterans (more than 25 years of practice) are least optimistic in this regard with only 36% expressing such hopes. It will be recalled that a similar relationship was found regarding the perceived Effects of Self-Care Behaviour.

None of the independent variables are related to the perceived effects of self-care on hospitalization rates. This indicates that all sub-groups examined show approximately the same distribution as seen in Table 5.

A multivariate analysis of the findings presented in Table 5 was done by means of logistic regression [46, 47]. The system variables were dichotomized for this purpose using the 'positive' category in each case (reduce consulting rates, decrease costs, decrease hospitalizations) against the others. The logistic regression analysis, using the set of relevant background and practice setting variables, indicates that the correlates described above on the basis of the univariate analysis held when controls were introduced, although the total proportional reduction in log likelihood due to the variables in the model is small (13% for effects on utilization rates, 7% for effects on costs and 6% for effects on hospitalization).

The correlations among physicians' perceptions of the three 'system effects' variables are positive and significant. The strongest correlation is between perceived effects on utilization rates and on costs ($r = 0.64$). These two variables are more weakly related to the perceived effects on hospitalization rates ($r = 0.29$ and $r = 0.26$ respectively).

Relationships among the three dependent variables

There is a clear and significant relationship between physicians' perceptions concerning the Effects of Specific Self-Care Behaviours on the Health of the Individual (Summary Measure) and their perceptions concerning the effects of self-care on primary care utilization rates (Table 6). Seventy-nine percent who perceive positive effects of self-care behaviour thought that it would reduce unnecessary clinic visits, while only 47% of those who viewed self-care behaviour negatively thought so. Of those who scored most negatively on this measure, 35% thought self-care would increase clinic utilization, while only 9% of those who scored positively thought so. The health effects variable is more weakly related to physicians' views concerning the effects of self-care on costs and on hospitalization rates.

Table 6. Relationship of physicians' perceptions concerning health effects of self-care behaviours (summary measure) and systemic effects of self-care (%)

	Perceived effects of specific self-care behaviours on health			
Perceived effects of self-care on	Positive effect	No effect	Detrimental effect	Significance
Consulting rates				
Decrease consulting rates	79	61	47	$\chi^2 = 18.9$ $df = 4$ $P < 0.001$
No effect on consulting rates	12	17	18	
Increasing consulting rates	9	22	35	
Total	100%	100%	100%	
Costs				
Decrease costs	57	44	38	$\chi^2 = 8.5$ $df = 4$
No effect on costs	25	37	31	($P = 0.076$)
Increase costs	18	19	31	
Total	100%	100%	100%	
Hospitalization				
Decrease hospitalization rates	45	27	35	$\chi^2 = 6.2$ $df = 2$ $P < 0.05$
No effect on hospitalization rates	55	73	65	
Total	100%	100%	100%	
N	75	94	84	

There is no association between physicians' perceptions of the Effect of Independence and Initiatives by Lay Persons on the Health-Care Process and their perceptions of the three systemic effects of self-care. As already noted, the former variable tends to reflect a separate dimension of self-care, which is not related to the other two dimensions considered here.

SUMMARY AND DISCUSSION

The paper views self-care in systemic terms as part of the overall health-care structure. The study focuses on one group of actors in that system: physicians in Israel. Physicians' perceptions regarding the effects of self-care have been examined in three substantive areas, two relating to the micro-level of clinical practice, and one focusing on the macro-level which concerns the health-care system. More specifically, we have examined perceptions of: (A) the effects of specific self-care behaviours on the health of the individual; (B) the effects of independence and initiatives by lay persons on the health-care process; (C) the effects of lay self-care on the health-care system in terms of utilization, costs and hospitalization rates. General distributions, inter-correlations and correlates of physicians' perceptions of these three variables were examined. Interviews provided data from a sample of 258 physicians employed in two types of primary care settings and in hospitals.

The findings are considered against the background of the Israeli health context which is characterized by the high value placed on health in the culture, widespread exercising of physician authority in the doctor–patient relationship, common acceptance of the latter as normative by most lay persons, the little ideologically-based consumer pressure advocating self-care. In addition, the Israeli health-care system, like many in the world, is troubled by major structural and economic problems.

A central overall finding which sets the scene for the more detailed conclusions stems from the relationships among physicians' perceptions regarding the three types of effects of self-care. Two of these—the first and the third (A and C)—are positively related while the second (B) is related to neither. Subtantively this means that physicians who see positive health effects of self-care behaviours also perceive positive effects of the latter on the health-care system, and vice versa. The association is strongest with regard to the utilization category of C, i.e. self-care by individuals is viewed by physicians as related to the problem of high utilization rates in the primary care system: most believe that self-care behaviour could contribute to the reduction of this disturbing phenomonon which has long plagued the Israeli health-care system. The same general finding is seen with regard to costs of running the system and to hospitalization rates, although the relationship is less pronounced. We may therefore state that substantial groups of physicians perceive a relationship between the micro- and macro-level effects of self-care behaviour and view it in a practical, utilitarian light, as a process that could alleviate some of the real problems characterizing the health-care system.

The attitudinal complex termed 'independence and initiatives by lay persons in health-care' (B) is, as noted, unrelated to either of the above dimensions. It may be viewed as an independent dimension in this area, on which few physicians expressed favourable views. Perceptions concerning independence and initiatives (B) are 'isolated' from other attitudes concerning self-care (A and C). The challenge to the traditional physician–patient relationship, which is reflected in the independence and initiatives variable, is largely rejected in terms of effects on the health care process, and the implied behaviours are perceived as separate from the other two more 'practical' aspects of self-care. This lack of structure probably reflects the 'under-development' of self-care in Israel. Physicians who see the relationship of specific self-care behaviours to certain problematic system-linked issues, do not necessarily perceive 'independence and initiatives' as part of a more general concept of self-care.

Additional evidence for the absence of a general concept of self-care among Israeli physicians is seen in the absence of strong correlates of the views expressed. All the dependent variables regarding the effects of self-care were examined for relationships with personal background, professional and practice setting characteristics. The findings show that physicians' views are distributed somewhat randomly in the population: only weak relationships were found with background and practice setting variables. We view this set of findings as a further indication of the lack of structure in the complex of attitudes examined.

A considerable range of views was expressed by physicians regarding the effects of self-care behaviours on individual health. In general, behaviours perceived as less risky and potentially effective for promoting health were viewed in a favourable light, while those involving potential risk, especially with regard to self-medication, were least favoured. The criteria that physicians seemed to use to evaluate the effects of specific self-care behaviours are pragmatic and focus on the potential contribution and risk to health that these behaviours entail. The relationship noted above to the systemic effects suggests that the physicians may be considering the fact that such behaviours could ameliorate some of the high utilization and cost problems as well.

The physicians who are most likely to perceive positive effects of specific self-care behaviours are the younger, hospital-based specialists and residents who contrast with the general practitioners working in community clinics, who express less positive views. The greater confidence and professional status of the former, as well as their greater exposure to newer views of health-care expressed in the literature and in growing professional or lay circles, are associated with more positive views on self-care [48]. On the other hand, the lower status community clinic practitioners, especially those without a status-giving specialty license, are less willing to relinquish elements of control in health-care to lay persons. Indeed, a heavy patient load, which occurs most prominently in the General Sick Fund community clinics, is associated with more negative views regarding self-care behaviours.

The second aspect of self-care examined physicians' perceptions of the effects of independence and initiatives by lay persons on the health-care process. On the whole, considerable reservation was expressed with regard to the items used to assess views in this area and on some there was almost universal disapproval. This complex of lay behaviours expresses some challenge or scepticism regarding the traditional doctor–patient relationship, and suggests greater control of that relationship by the patients. Although responses varied in terms of the specific items posed, positive responses were never given by more than a third of the physician population and several items were almost unanimously rejected. In the absence of comparative data, we are unable to judge whether this population differs from comparable groups in other countries. Limited data from the United States also shows that physicians express serious doubts regarding self-care initiatives by lay persons [12, 14]. There are few significant correlates of this variable and those found are not strong.

Despite the weak relationships, it is worth pointing to some differentials on this variable in the population of physicians. When controls are introduced, the data show somewhat more positive views regarding the effects of independence and initiative by lay persons among the following sub-groups of physicians: males, those practicing in hospital settings, with specialty status, relatively few years of practice, and reporting relatively less patient load. These subgroups are characterized by relatively higher status than their counterparts (i.e. females in community clinic practice, with no specialty status and greater patient load). It may be suggested that physicians whose professional status is less secure are more likely to be concerned with retention of authority, control and the accompanying power these imply. Such concerns may be expressed in attitudes of scepticism, caution, reservation and in some cases outright objection to lay independence or initiatives in health-care, especially when these are perceived as a potential threat to physician authority on the micro-level. The more harassed community clinic physician may seek certain rewards of practice in exercise of control and authority. These also serve as a mechanism to facilitate the handling of large numbers of patients, many of whom bring what physicians consider to be trivial complaints.

The findings show that physicians distinguish clearly among effects of self-care on various problematic aspects of the health-care system. Thus views differ considerably regarding effects on utilization, cost and hospitalization rates. The most positive effects of self-care are perceived with regard to clinic utilization rates, which over half of the physicians believe will be reduced if self-care is increased. A decrease in the costs of running the health-care system is another widely perceived effect of increased self-care, but less than half the physicians view this effect as likely. Even fewer believe that increased self-care will have the effect of reducing hospitalization rates. What is more, there are non-negligible sub-groups who hold negative views regarding the effects of self-care on these system variables.

In conclusion, it should be recalled that the overall approach of the research is a systemic one and the physicians are only the first set of actors whose views and perceptions regarding self-care have been explored. Research has already been undertaken on a population of allied health professionals [49]; consumers' views and perspectives will complete the systemic picture. Information from these additional groups will help explain the absence of structure in the views expressed by the physicians. We have noted that the Israeli health scene is characterized by the centrality of health in the value system, and by relative underdevelopment of consumer awareness or advocacy regarding self-care. It may be suggested in conclusion that the general lack of structure which characterizes physicians' views on this subject complements the stance of consumers who have been slow or reluctant to take a position regarding self-care. While some forms of self-care are, and always have been, widely practiced, there has as yet been little 'consciousness raising' on the subject in the society.

Acknowledgements—The authors appreciate the support of the Israel National Council for Research and Development and of ESHEL—the Association for the Planning and Development of Services for the Aged in Israel.

REFERENCES

1. U.S. DHEW Publication No. (HRA) 7-3181. Consumer self-care in health. National Technical Information Service, Springfield, Va, 1977.
2. Dean K. Self-care response to illness: a selected review. *Soc. Sci. Med.* **15A,** 673–687, 1981.
3. Dean K. Lay care in illness. *Soc. Sci. Med.* **22,** 275–284, 1986.
4. Levin L. S. and Idler E. L. *The Hidden Health Care System: Mediating Structures and Medicine.* Ballinger, Cambridge, Mass., 1981.
5. Levin L. S., Katz A. H. and Holst E. *Self Care: Lay Initiatives in Health.* Prodist, New York, 1979.
6. Mechanic D. *From Advocacy to Allocation.* Free Press, New York, 1986.
7. Freidson E. *Professional Dominance: The Social Structure of Medical Care.* Atherton Press, New York, 1970.
8. Hayes-Bautista D. E. Modifying the treatment: patient compliance, patient control and medical care. *Soc. Sci. Med.* **10,** 233–238, 1976.
9. Pratt L. V. Reshaping the consumer's posture in health care. In *The Doctor–Patient Relationship in the Changing Health Care Scene* (Edited by Gallagher E. B.), pp. 121–123, U.S. DHEW, Publication No. (NIH) 78-183, 1978.
10. Lazare A., Eisenthal S., Frank A. and Stoeckle J. D. Studies on a negotiated approach to patienthood. In *The Doctor–Patient Relationship in the Changing Health Scene* (Edited by Gallagher E. B.), pp. 119–139. U.S. DHEW, Publication No. (NIH) 78–183, 1978.
11. Katon A. and Kleinman A. Doctor–patient negotiation and other social science strategies in patient care. In *The Relevance of Social Science for Medicine* (Edited by Eisenberg L. and Kleinmen A.), pp. 253–279. Reidel, Amsterdam, 1981.
12. Linn L. S. and Lewis L. E. Attitudes toward self-care among practicing physicians. *Med. Care* **17,** 183–190, 1979.
13. Dunnell K. and Cartwright A. *Medicine Takers, Prescribers and Hoarders.* Routledge & Kegan Paul, London, 1972.
14. Haug M. and Lavin B. *Consumerism in Medicine: Challenging Physician Authority.* Sage, Beverly Hills, Calif., 1983.
15. Goldman L. Factors related to physicians' medical and political attitudes: a documentation of intraprofessional variations. *J. Hlth soc. Behav.* **15,** 177–187, 1974.

16. Mechanic D. Religion, religiosity and illness behavior: the special case of the Jews. *Hum. Org.* **22,** 202–208, 1962.
17. Heins M., Hendricks J., Martindale L., Smock S., Stein M. and Jacobs L. Attitudes of women and men physicians. *Am. J. publ. Hlth* **69,** 1132–1139, 1979.
18. Colombotos J. Social origins and ideology of physicians: a study of the effect of early socialization. *J. Hlth soc. Behav.* **10,** 16–29, 1969.
19. Mechanic D. (Ed.) Factors affecting receptivity to innovations in health-care delivery among primary-care physicians. In *Politics, Medicine and Social Science.* Wiley, New York, 1974.
20. Colombotos J., Kirchner C. and Millman M. Physicians view national health insurance: a national study. *Med. Care* **13,** 369–396, 1975.
21. Mechanic D. General medical practice: some comparisons between the work of primary care physicians in the United States and England and Wales. *Med. Care* **10,** 402–420, 1972.
22. Central Bureau of Statistics. *Statistical Abstract of Israel,* No. 35, 1984.
23. *World Health Statistics Annual, 1986,* WHO, Geneva, 1986.
24. Shuval J. T. Social functions of medical licensing: a case study of Soviet immigrant physicians in Israel. *Soc. Sci. Med.* **20,** 901–909, 1985.
25. Ellencweig A. Y. and Grafstein O. Inequality in health: a case study. Hebrew University-Hadassah Medical School, Jerusalem, 1986.
26. Shuval J. T. *Entering Medicine: The Dynamics of Transition. A Seven Year Study of Medical Education in Israel.* Pergamon Press, Oxford, 1980.
27. Antonovsky A. A model to explain visits to the doctor: with special reference to the case of Israel. *J. Hlth soc. Behav.* **13,** 446–454, 1972.
28. Zborowski M. and Herzog E. *Life is With People.* International Universities Press, New York, 1952.
29. Suchman E. A. Sociomedical variations among ethnic grops. *Am. J. Soc.* **70,** 319–331, 1964.
30. Twaddle A. C. Health decisions and sick role variations: an exploration. *J. Hlth soc. Behav.* **10,** 105–114, 1969.
31. Shuval J. T. Primary care and social control. *Med. Care* **17,** 631–638, 1979.
32. Shuval J. Medical manpower in Israel: political processes and constraints. Paper presented for the *International Conference on the Political Dynamics of Physician Manpower Policy,* London, 24–27 May, 1988. Unpublished.
33. Barell V. and Zadka P. Health care systems in Israel. In *Proceedings of the International Collaborative Effort on Perinatal and Infant Mortality,* Vol. 1. U.S. Department of Health and Human Services, U.S. Public Health Service, National Center for Health Statistics, 1984.
34. Central Bureau of Statistics. *Statistical Abstract of Israel,* No. 37, 1986.
35. Estabrook B. Consumer impact of a cold self-care center in a pre-paid ambulatory care setting. *Med. Care* **17,** 1139–1145, 1979.
36. Zapka J. and Averill B. W. Self-care for colds: a cost effective alternative to upper respiratory infection management. *Am. J. publ. Hlth* **69,** 814–816, 1979.
37. Berg A. O. and Logerfo J. P. Potential effect of self-care algorithms on the number of physician visits. *New Engl. J. Med.* **300,** 535–537, 1979.
38. Ruzek S. B. *The Women's Health Movement: Feminist Alternatives to Medical Control.* Praeger, New York, 1978.
39. Fleming G. V., Sellers C. and Anderson R. Self-care: what are the relevant dimensions for study? Unpublished manuscript, Center for Health Administration Studies, University of Chicago, Ill., 1982.
40. Shuval J. T. and Shye D. Self-care in Israel: a providers' view. Unpublished report, Brookdale Institute of Gerontology and Adult Human Development and The Hebrew University of Jerusalem, 1984.
41. Shuval J. T., Javetz R. and Shye D. Self-care in Israel: physicians' views and attitudes. Brookdale Institute of Gerontology and Adult Human Development, 1987.
42. DeFriese G. H., Steckler A. B., Schiller P. L., Beery W. L., Graham R., Woomert A. and Barry P. Z. An empirical toxonomy of self-care skills. Health Services Research Center, University of North Carolina at Chapel Hill. Paper presented to the *Annual Meeting of the American Public Health Association,* Montreal, Quebec, 1982.
43. Williams T. F. The physicians' viewpoint. In *Elderly Patients and Their Doctors* (Edited by Haug M. R.), pp. 42–46. Springer, New York, 1981.
44. Freidson E. Client control and medical practice. *Am. J. Sociol.* **65,** 374–382, 1960.
45. Stimson G. V. Obeying doctor's orders: a view from the other side. *Soc. Sci. Med.* **8,** 97–104, 1974.
46. Kahn H. A. *An Introduction to Epidemiologic Methods.* Oxford University Press, New York, 1983.
47. Schlesselman J. J. *Case Control Studies: Design, Conduct, Analysis.* Oxford University Press, Oxford, 1982.
48. Javetz R. Conflict and crisis in the health system: the doctors' strike from the profession's point of view. Unpublished, Ford Foundation, 1987.
49. Javetz R., Shuval J. and Shye D. Self-care in Israel: views and perspectives of allied health professionals. Brookdale Institute of Gerontology and Adult Human Development, 1987.

15

The Effects of Latent Social Needs on Physician Utilization by Immigrants: A Replication Study

Tikvah Honig-Parnass

I. INTRODUCTION

The effects of latent social needs on physician utilization constitutes a relatively new and expanding field of inquiry. To be sure, the amount of empirical studies in this field remains slight [1, 2]. But in theoretical writings there has been an increased recognition of latent social needs as a variable with a crucial role to perform in the process of constructing the models aiming at explaining health care utilization by socio-psychological determinants [3–6].

Historically, the new field emerged as part of a wider research tradition which originated with Balint [7]. A concurrent field of inquiry stemming from the same tradition is represented by Mechanic and others, who emphasize emotional problems, and in particular psychological distress as factors of physician utilization [8–12]. Although the two strains deal with different needs, their theoretical orientations are essentially the same. For the underlying notion of both is that turning to a doctor with a complaint may be a mode of coping with problems other than the strictly medical. In such cases the satisfaction of stress-induced needs of a social or psychological nature, constitutes the primary motivation of seeking help from a doctor, regardless of whether it is pursued through the encounter itself with the doctor, or through some secondary gains of illness, like the certification of exemption from daily obligations. It has been recognized that needs influence physician utilization by affecting the health status or by aggravating existing symptoms.

However, the common claim has been that latent social and psychological needs affect the rates of utilization independently of medical needs.

The virtually single systematic attempt to operationalize the concept of latent social needs and empirically examine their impact on physician utilization was made on a population living under rather special conditions, namely, the new immigrant population of Israel. In their insightful study, Shuval *et al.* [13] assumed that new immigrants would undergo a stressful process of 'acculturation', generating certain acute needs, such as the need to cope with failure (i.e. to use illness as a justification for failure) or the need for catharsis (i.e. for social contacts through which one can receive sympathy and support). The authors hypothesized that new immigrants with a high level of need deprivation and a high inclination to 'define oneself as ill' would choose to seek gratification of the needs mentioned above by turning to the health services of the Sick Fund, Israel's largest comprehensive health care scheme, and thus increase the frequency of their physician visits*. Easy access to health services in Israel, as well as the high value attached to health by the Jewish cultural tradition, are seen by the authors as situational factors contributing to the pursuit of the gratification of these needs through medical rather than through other institutional channels [14].

Shuval *et al.* hypothesized that five different latent social needs have an impact upon physician utilization. Two of their hypotheses were not fully confirmed by the findings. As for the remaining three, the

* Comprehensive medical care including ambulatory, hospital, psychiatric and rehabilitative services is provided in Israel on a pre-paid basis to approx. 75% of the population, by the Workers' Sick Fund and to an additional 20% of the population, by a number of smaller sick funds.

hypothesized positive associations held even when (in order to control for the possible effect of needs on illness) the level of general well-being was held constant, and even after the population was broken down by various social background criteria. The latter finding implies that in spite of the differential access to resources for coping with their hardships, immigrants of all socio-cultural backgrounds were exposed to common high stress-inducing experiences responsible for the appearance of similar social needs and of a similar mode of coping with these needs through the 'overutilization' of health services. Hence Shuval *et al.* concluded that the health care system in Israel performs a latent adaptative function in addition to its manifest curative and preventive functions.

In selecting specific latent social needs for investigation, Shuval *et al.* were guided by their presumed relevance to the special conditions of new immigrant life. They considered it plausible to assume that the association between needs and utilization would be strongest during the first years after immigration and would decline thereafter. Therefore, pending further tests, they assumed the existence of an association between the length of stay in the country and the emergence of social needs responsible for increasing the frequency of physician utilization.

The aim of the replication study to be reported in this paper was to submit this assumption to verification on a population of immigrants who had arrived in Israel during the same years as the respondents of Shuval *et al.* The focus of this replication falls on the already mentioned need for catharsis. The specific questions around which the investigation revolved were: (1) does the immigrant's need for catharsis persist 10 years after it was first revealed by Shuval *et al.* to any greater extent than among the natives or veteran settlers? and (2) does it continue to affect physician utilization, independently of the patient's level of health?

The study's point of departure was the hypothesis already put forward by Shuval *et al.*, that with the passage of time the direct effect of need on utilization (i.e. an effect which is not carried via ill-health), would be subject to considerable attenuation. The integration of one-time immigrants into Israeli society would weaken both the intensity of their shared latent social needs and open a wider range of institutional alternatives for them, enabling them to gratify whatever needs for catharsis still persisted. Accordingly, it was hypothesized that even the immigrants whose needs remained high, would turn to the health services only with 'concrete' medical symptoms. In line with this hypothesis, we expect no indirect relationship between the length of residence in the country and physician utilization via the need for catharsis. In short, the higher needs are neither attributable to the immigrant vs old-timer factor, nor do they in turn affect physician utilization.

In Shuval *et al.*'s view, the need for catharsis is a common condition of new immigrants; but, like other needs under investigation, it can also appear in other disadvantaged social groups. The present study attempts to explore this view in some depth. For this purpose it is assumed that the fairly common experiences of the first years after immigration tend to become more differentiated with time due to the unequal access of different social classes and age groups to vital resources. The nature of the life-problems which may or may not be conducive to the emergence of the need for catharsis is here assumed to depend primarily on differential access to resources at the present time. But since the access of the lower classes and of the elderly to vital resources is known to be limited, one can hypothesize that the need for catharsis and, accordingly, the rates of physician visits reach higher frequencies among them, even if the ill-health factor commonly associated with low social class and old age is held constant.

The thus hypothesized relationships between the different variables have been tested within the framework of a path-analytic model that estimates the direct and indirect (i.e. through need for catharsis, well-being and the tendency to define oneself as ill) effects of length of residence in the country, socioeconomic status and age on physician utilization.

II. THE THEORETICAL MODEL

The general model employed here was designed to evaluate the alternative hypotheses described above. It includes the assumptions that the positive association between the need for catharsis and physician utilization is causally related both to length of residence and to social class and age.

As the graphic display of the model shows (Fig. 1), two classes of variables are distinguished: exogenous and endogenous. The following variables are viewed as exogenous: (1) length of residence in the country (i.e. either the immigrants who arrived in the same years as Shuval's respondents or veteran settlers; (2) occupation and (3) education as two components of socio-economic status; and (4) age. Five other variables, i.e. (5) the need for catharsis; (6) emotional disorder and (7) physical illness as two components of well-being; (8) the tendency to define oneself as ill; and (9) the dependent variable (physician utilization), are viewed as endogenous and affected by all the exogenous variables. In addition, physician utilization is also affected by all the other endogenous variables; the tendency to define oneself as ill is also affected by the well-being variables and by need for catharsis; and, the well-being variables are affected by the need for catharsis.

The total effect of need for catharsis consists therefore, of (1) direct effect of that need on utilization; (2) the effect via the two well-being variables (emotional disorder and physical illness); and (3) the effect via the tendency to define oneself as ill. This operationalization seems to conform to Shuval *et al.*'s mode of conceptualizing the need-utilization relationships. The rationale for positing these relationships can be described as follows:

The assumed effects of the need for catharsis on the well-being variables are based on the increasing recognition of social support as an important factor for buffering stress and reducing the risk of illness [15–17]. In particular, the absence of support, as manifesting itself in the need for catharsis, is assumed to aggravate emotional distress; in turn, it either contributes to the susceptibility of the organism to a variety of illnesses, or is responsible for an increased sen-

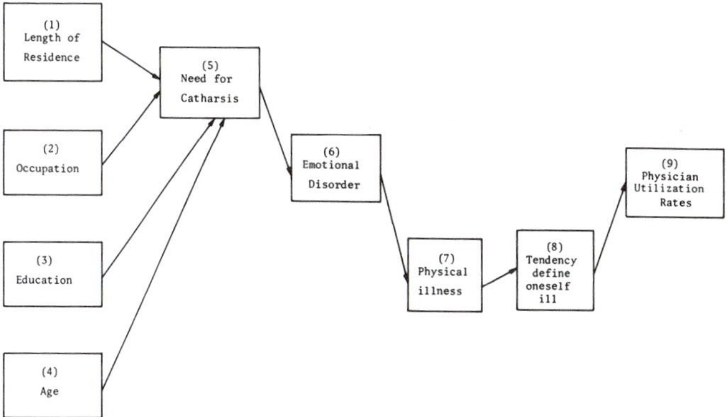

Fig. 1. The causal diagram. The model is fully recursive, i.e. it includes all possible paths between the causally ordered variables. But on the diagram the lines refer solely to links between pairs of variables consecutive in the causal chain.

sitivity to pre-existent symptoms [18–20]. Psychological stress has also been reported to affect some chronic diseases through physiological mechanisms [21–23]. Psychological stress is more than a causal factor in the sense of being antecedent for a sufficient span of time to generate the 'authentic', i.e. diagnostically categorized, diseases; of possibly even greater importance is the fact that physiological disorder may at any point in time aggravate the condition of an individual already afflicted with a physical illness. This is particularly the case in physical chronic illnesses, where the effectuality of remedies depends more on the patient's own efforts and cooperation than on professional expertise [24, 25]. Psychological distress may adversely affect the patient's ability to cope with illness, and thus aggravate the experience with illness and increase dependence on professional medical help [26].

Shuval *et al.* were well aware that people may seek to gratify their needs by turning to social institutions other than medical. Therefore they constructed an overall or summary measure (of the type first elaborated by Mechanic and Volkart) of psychological disposition to seek medical services as a manifestation of the tendency to adopt the sick role. In their design, this tendency was employed as an intervening variable between a social need and clinic attendance. In this way, Shuval *et al.* analyzed each investigated need in relation to this variable. This enabled them to filter out the cases of respondents most predisposed to seek gratification of a given need through the health care system, rather than through an alternative social agency*. The assumption was that respondents who claimed that they would turn to a doctor with non-serious symptoms, and who could therefore be presumed to have a high tendency to adopt the sick role, would also score relatively high on physician utilization. The theoretical explanation of this quite commonly reported association has not yet been fully elaborated. It has been suggested that the tendency in question may indicate a low tolerance of ambiguity in regard to one's own health condition. The low tolerance of ambiguity has, in turn, been alternately attributed to two different sources: either to a high level of general anxiety and low confidence in one's own capability to handle ambiguous situations, or to a 'rationalistic' orientation toward the future, supposed to be descriptive of the Jewish cultural tradition. Implicit in the latter is the notion of the patient's 'understanding' that appropriate measures in cases of clinically non-serious symptoms are those which prevent deterioration, rather than those which bring immediate relief. This orientation, jointly with the high appreciation of health and with the already noted specific characteristics of the health services in Israel are believed to be the major factors responsible for encouraging individuals to define themselves as ill and for using the health services as a means of gratifying their needs [27].

Following the explication of the grounds for assuming that physician utilization is related to the need for catharsis, we can now take up the issue of whether the relationship can still be presumed to hold ten or more years after Shuval's study. The association between the need for catharsis and physician utilization has been assumed to be causally related to the length of residence in the country: it is more descriptive of immigrants than of natives or veteran settlers. The total

* However, the exact nature of the relationship between each need and the tendency to define oneself as ill was not made explicit in Shuval's study. Therefore, as a precautionary measure against the obfuscation of a possible interaction effect between the need for support and the described tendency, a two-way Anova was carried out in the present study, with the two variables in question as independent ones and the Physician Utilization as the dependent variable. Yet no interaction effect was revealed. This finding made it possible to include the tendency variable in the causative model.

effect of the length of residence consists of (1) its direct effect on utilization; (2) the effect via the need for catharsis; (3) the effect via each of the two well-being variables; and (4) the effect via the tendency to define oneself as ill. In agreement with Shuval *et al.*, the exposure to hardships and stressful experiences characteristic of the post-immigration period and the relative social isolation of new immigrants have been assumed to be conducive to the emergence of needs for affiliation and intimacy as a means of winning 'cathartic' support and sympathy. The same factors, conjointly with the burdens of adapting to a new physical setting and new climatic conditions are known to increase the susceptibility of immigrants to symptoms of emotional disorder and physical illness. Furthermore, high levels of general anxiety, common among new immigrants, may well promote a readiness to adopt the sick role. Given the above mentioned cultural and structural aspects of Israeli society and given the limited range of alternatives open to new immigrants, it seems eminently reasonable to expect a positive association between their tendency to define themselves as ill and physician utilization.

Of course, with the passage of time all the referred to attributes of the once-new immigrants may be subject to change. Perforce, this applies to the need for catharsis and to the medical mode of gratifying this need. In a population of former immigrants neither may be typical any more. Instead, the need–utilization relationship may more likely be contingent upon restrictions of access to socioeconomic and psychological resources, prevalent in low socioeconomic status groups and among the elderly. Therefore, occupation, education and age are assumed by the model to have effects parallel to the effects of the length of residence. As is the case with the length of residence, the effects of these exogenous variables consist of the direct effect of each of them on physician utilization, the effect through the need for catharsis, through each of the well-being variables and through the tendency to define oneself as ill.

The literature provides some support for the assumption that the lower classes may have a higher need for catharsis. It has been claimed that the lower classes are deprived not only in terms of 'objective' resources instrumental for coping with life-problems, like money or political power [20], but also of resources requisite for coping with stress-inducing life-events, like access to supportive social relationships or stable community ties [29–31].

The inverse relationship between socioeconomic status and emotional disorder is one of the best documented findings in the literature of psychiatric epidemiology [32–34]. There have been two major explanations for the repeatedly found relationship between socioeconomic status and mild forms of emotional disorder: the first, that sustained exposure to stressful life experiences is responsible for high rates of emotional disorder in the lower classes [35, 36] and the second more recent one, that lower class people are more *responsive* to stress than persons of middle and upper status, and therefore more likely to develop symptoms of emotional disorder when exposed to problematic life experiences [37, 38]. For our purposes, however, the difference between the exposure to stressful experiences and the response to such experiences is not of decisive importance. Both mechanisms can be assumed to be operative, in the sense of contributing to both emotional disorder and physical illness.

The assumption that the socioeconomic variables directly affect the tendency to define oneself as ill is in line with the findings of Shuval *et al.* and others [39]. It has been suggested that lower class people often adopt the sick-role in order to justify their failure in performing socially prescribed roles or in order to relieve their dissatisfaction with the conditions under which they live [40, 41]. Furthermore, some evidence has been adduced to the effect that the lower classes tend to be relatively more concerned with health, since illness shoulders them with a heavier burden [42]. They also have been believed to be more prone to generalized anxieties and to a lack of a 'sense of coherence' contributive to success in coping with ambiguous health situations [43].

Indirect paths leading to the dependent variable has also been posited for age, in the same way as for length of residence and for the two variables of socioeconomic status. The elderly can be expected to be more frustrated in their attempts to win emotional support, to have poorer emotional and physical health, and to display a higher tendency to define themselves as ill. The rationale for the assumed indirect effects of age rests on arguments analogous to the ones concerning the effects of length of residence and of the two socioeconomic variables. The elderly's relative social isolation and higher exposure to stressful experiences are apt to intensify the need for catharsis, emotional and physical health hazards, and the tendency to define themselves as ill. In addition to these indirect paths, a direct path from age to utilization can also be posited. It seems reasonable to assume that the elderly lack sufficient access to alternative social settings in which they could have a chance of gratifying their need for catharsis. It has also been suggested that as people get older they acquire 'free' time, and experience social reinforcement from friends and family in seeking out medical help [44].

III. THE ANALYTICAL MODEL

The causal assumptions that we have built into our model for theoretical reasons, also provide us with an opportunity for using a powerful analytic tool, path analysis, to evaluate the various effects of the need for catharsis on utilization. The advantage of path analysis is that it disaggregates the simple correlation into: (1) total effects; (2) indirect effects; and (3) direct effects. For an explanation of those terms, we'll take the liberty of quoting the definitions of Alwin and Hauser [45, p. 38]: "The total effect of one variable on another is the part of their total association (i.e. that given by their zero-order correlation) which is neither due to their common causes, to correlation among the causes, nor to unanalyzed (predetermined) correlation [46] . . . A total effect tells us how much change in a consequent variable is induced by a given shift in an antecedent variable, irrespective of the mechanisms by which the change may occur. *Indirect effects* are those parts of the variable's total effect which are transmitted or mediated by variables specified as intervening between the cause and effect of interest in a model. That is, they tell us how much of a given effect occurs because the manipulation of the antecedent variable of interest leads to changes in other variables which in turn change the consequent variable. The *direct effect* of one variable on another is simply that part of its total effect which is *not* transmitted via an intervening variable"*.

It is to be acknowledged that in designing the present study, not enough regard was paid to the usual problem of causal enquiries, whether in the field of physician utilization or elsewhere: namely, to the issue of the time-ordering of variables. By definition path analysis implies that the explaining variables are antecedent in time to the dependent variable. But, as will be shown below, the design of the present study is flawed in the sense that both types of variables were obtained from the same household survey. This is to be kept in mind in the following chapters.

IV. DATA

The data for this analysis came from a household survey of 413 adult women (from a sample of 420) subject to interviews of 1–1½ hr duration in their homes between October and December 1977. They were randomly chosen from the complete list of households affiliated with an out-patient clinic belonging to Israel's largest comprehensive pre-paid health scheme, the Sick Fund†. The clinic was selected because the Jerusalem neighborhood it services is inhabited both by immigrants from the same years as Shuval's population, and by 'old-timers' (i.e. either natives or immigrants from earlier periods). The sample was almost evenly split into these two categories. The neighborhood is also socioeconomically heterogenous. Approximately half of the respondents had eight years of schooling or less; nearly a third had completed high school (12 grades), while only 18% were college graduates. In terms of husband's occupation, which is a rough indicator of socioeconomic status, the distribution was quite close to the nationwide distribution of 1976: 40% semi-skilled blue collar workers; 40% foremen, small businessmen, technicians, and clerks; 20% professionals or managers. The age groups of 26–45 and over 45 and the Middle Eastern and European extractions are represented in the sample in roughly equal proportion.

We shall now proceed to describe the ways in which the variables under analysis were operationalized. The categories, means, and standard deviations of the variables are presented in the pertinent notes.

The exogenous variables

Length of residence in the country, occupational status, education and age‡.

The endogenous variables

The following three variables were identical with those used by Shuval *et al.*: the need for catharsis, tendency to define oneself as ill and physician utilization. Ideally, all three should be coterminous. However, while the question about utilization explicitly referred to the twelve months prior to the interview, the time coordinates of the two other measures were less specific. Although the questions on which these measures are based implied a certain duration of the attributes involved prior to the interview, they did not include a specific stipulation to the effect of a 1-year time interval. Regrettably, therefore, the three measures are not exactly coterminous.

The need for catharsis refers to the sense of deprivation of support obtainable through intimate relationships. As noted above, it was one of the five needs which Shuval *et al.* analyzed, and one of the three which they found to be positively related to physician utilization. The reason for its selection was its recognized importance in the literature dealing with class and mental health. The concept is operationalized in terms of a set of questions concerning the feelings of the respondents about whether they usually have sufficient access to people with whom they could talk and feel free and who would listen to them with sympathy and understanding. While, as noted above, the length of time is not specified, the questions do imply that those who score high on need for catharsis have already suffered from deprivation of affiliative intimacy for some amount of time and not just for a short period prior to the interview. The

* The direct effect of A on B is the path coefficient of the path leading from A to B, i.e. the regression coefficient of A in the multiple regression equation, where B is the dependent variable and all the variables preceding B in the Path Diagram (Fig. 1) are independent variables. The following relationships between direct effects, indirect effects and total effects hold: The total effect of A on B is the sum of the direct effect of A on B and the indirect effect of A on B. The Indirect Effect of A on B via C is the direct effect of A on C multiplied by the Total Effect of C on B.

† Shuval *et al.*'s sample also included men. However, the difference between the two studies does not necessarily have to prejudice their comparability. To begin with, Shuval *et al.* found no significant differences between women and men on dimensions of their concern. This is not surprising, since although the literature does provide some inconclusive evidence that behavioral reactions to illness vary with sex, the few studies that have explored this issue demonstrate that the differences are relatively insignificant [47].

‡*Age* was split up into six intervals, ranging from 1 = between 20–29, to 6 = between 70–80; with $\bar{x} = 45$; SD = 12.784; *Residence in the country*. Respondents were broken down into nine categories, ranging from 9 = immigrated before 1948 or born in the country, to 1 = immigrated within the two year span prior to the interview, $\bar{x} = 7.87$ (i.e. 1949–50), SD = 1.653; *Respondent's education* was measured by years of formal schooling; 1 = did not attend school at all; 7 = college graduates; $\bar{x} = 3.6$, SD = 1.808; *Husband's occupational status* was used as a rough indicator of the socioeconomic status of the family. Occupations were graded according to the Hartman Scale of Occupational Status (48) into 9 categories, condensed into five major groups: 1 = unskilled blue collar jobs; 9 = high professions, managers and businessmen; $\bar{x} =$ 2.93; SD = 1.384.

answers to each of these questions indicate the degree of satisfaction with the support obtained. By definition, the lower the satisfaction, the higher the need for catharsis*.

Tendency to define oneself as ill was measured by a number of border-line symptoms presented to the respondent as hypothetical situations with questions about how they would respond, had they themselves been afflicted. Although the questions refer to attitudes as expressed during the interview, it had been assumed that, pending validation, such attitudes indicate a more profound psychological predisposition rooted in their personality structures and/or in specific patterns of their socialization†.

Physician utilization was measured by the self-reported number of visits to the doctor for treatment purposes during the twelve months prior to the interview.

But the measure of health status used by Shuval *et al.* was rejected as rather tenuous and apt to confound physical and mental impairment‡. Instead, two separate measures were adopted, one for mental and the other for physical health status.

Emotional disorder was measured by the Health Opinion Survey (H.O.S.), a symptom check list scale developed in the Stirling Community Study of Psychiatric Disorder and Socio-Cultural Environment [49]. This scale is very similar in content to other 'screening scales' of emotional disorders used in community surveys. It is made up of 20 statements, many of which are about bodily feelings and symptoms and the rest are about behavior. They are interpreted as indicating depression and malfunctioning. Without referring to any specific point in time, the questions clearly imply the recurrence of symptoms prior to the interview. A concurrent appearance of a symptom at the time of the interview is therefore not sufficient to produce a high score on emotional disorder§.

Physical illness was measured by the self-reported number of chronic conditions (e.g. sugar diabetes, arthritis) during the 12 months prior to the interview¶. The recent enormous growth in overall chronic illness rates reached a point at which these illnesses can be presumed to have become a major reason for seeking help from a doctor. The usual alternation between the periods of flare-up and remission makes many of the chronically ill uncertain over whether their symptoms merit a call to a doctor. But unlike in short-term acute conditions, free access to professional medical services is not a sufficient condition for the equality of different social groups in their ability to cope with illness. An earlier analysis of the same data revealed that due to their limited control over social, economic and psychological resources, the prospects of the lower classes and of the elderly for coping with chronic illnesses are also limited. Accordingly, they tend to suffer more from symptoms and to develop a dependency on health services [15].

V. RESULTS

We follow Alwin and Hauser [52] in the tabular presentation of the results of the path analysis which includes the coefficients of the effects of each variable in the model. Table 1 presents the components of the effects of all the independent variables on the dependent variables at each stage of the model and the mechanisms by which the effects come about. For example, Age has an effect of 0.306 on Physical Illness (Dependent Variable 3: Age), of which 0.059 (almost a fifth) is transmitted via Emotional Disorder and 0.243 (almost three-quarters) is direct, i.e. unmediated by other variables in the model.

As Table 1 shows (See Dependent Variable 5: Physician Visits), the best predictors of the frequency of visits to the doctor are both emotional and physical well-being, age and the tendency to define onself as ill (0.334, 0.208, 0.229 and 0.244, respectively). The two dimensions of socioeconomic status, occupation and education, rank lower (−0.133 and −0.161, respectively). The effects of need for catharsis and length of residence are negligible (−0.005 and 0.003).

Even though it has hardly any effect on physician utilization, the need for catharsis is more prominent among the immigrants from the same years as Shuval's respondents than among old-timers. Length of residence ranks highest in accounting for that need and occupational status is next in rank order (Table 1: Need for Catharsis, Dependent Variable 1: −0.111, significant at $P < 0.05$ and −0.080, not significant at $P < 0.05$). Furthermore, the need for catharsis has

* *Need for catharsis.* Respondents giving two or three 'high' answers to the three questions presented to them were scored as having a high need for catharsis (= 2), the rest were scored as having a low need for catharsis (= 1); $\bar{x} = 1.209$; SD = 0.407.

† Three hypothetical situations were presented to respondents: a persistent cold and running nose with temperature, a bad cough without temperature, a temperature of 38° but no other symptoms. Alternative answers for each of them ranged from "I wouldn't do anything", "I would wait until it passes", to "I would go to see a doctor", and "I would ask a doctor to come to my home". Those who responded with the third or the fourth answer to two or all three symptom descriptions were defined as 'high' on the tendency to define themselves as ill (= 2); while those who reported that they would be likely to ignore or to care little about such symptoms were defined as 'low' on the tendency (= 1); ($\bar{x} = 1.361$; SD = 0.481).

‡ Health status is measured by Shuval *et al.* by the answer to a question requesting respondents to define themselves as either generally sick or generally healthy.

§ Each respondent was assigned a total score indicating her general level of psychiatric disorder. The scoring was based on forced multiple-choice answers to twenty questions, such as "Does it happen that you have no appetite?" The 'often' answer to this question was scored 3, and the 'never' response 1: this on the presumption that the latter is 'healthier' than the former. The scoring of other items generally followed the same pattern. A given individual's total score was a simple sum of her single-response scores ($\bar{x} = 11.704$; SD = 6.625).

¶ The measure was used in the Washington Heights Master Sample Survey [50]. Respondents received a list of 30 chronic conditions, among which they were asked to check those from which they had suffered within a 12 month span prior to the interview. The level of health equalled the number of the thus-reported illness conditions. Number of illnesses ranged from 0 to 7 ($\bar{x} = 2.204$; SD = 1.655).

Table 1. Total indirect and direct effects of variables in the explanatory model of physician utilization

Dependent variable	Predetermined variable	Total effect	Indirect effects via				Direct effect†
			Need	Emotional disorder	Physical illness	Tendency	
1 Need for catharsis	Age						0.028
	Length of residence						−0.111*
	Education						−0.009
	Occupation						−0.080
2 Emotional disorder	Need support	0.151					0.151***
	Age	0.126	0.004				0.121*
	Length of residence	−0.019	−0.016				−0.002
	Education	−0.116	−0.001				−0.115
	Occupation	−0.246	−0.012				−0.234***
3 Physical illness	Emotional disorder	0.484					0.484***
	Need support	0.147		0.073			0.074
	Age	0.306	0.004	0.059			0.243***
	Length of residence	−0.029	−0.016	−0.001			−0.011
	Education	0.024	−0.001	−0.055			0.082
	Occupation	−0.188	−0.001	−0.113			−0.062
4 Tendency to define oneself as ill	Physical illness						0.008
	Emotional disorder						0.048
	Need support			0.008	0.000		0.024
	Age		0.001	0.006	0.002		−0.027
	Length of residence		−0.003	0.000	0.000		−0.032
	Education		0.000	−0.006	0.000		−0.094
	Occupation		−0.002	−0.012	0.000		−0.088
5 Physician visits	Tendency	0.244					0.244***
	Physical illness	0.208				0.002	0.206***
	Emotional disorder	0.334			0.101	0.011	0.221***
	Need support	−0.005		0.050	0.015	0.006	−0.077
	Age	0.229	0.000	0.040	0.050	−0.006	0.144***
	Length of Residence	−0.003	0.000	0.000	−0.002	−0.007	0.0006
	Education	−0.161	0.000	−0.038	0.017	−0.023	−0.117*
	Occupation	−0.133	0.000	−0.078	−0.013	−0.021	−0.020

† 0.05 ⩾ * > 0.01; 0.01 ⩾ ** > 0.001; 0.001 ⩾ ***.

some effect on both emotional disorders and physical illness (0.151 and 0.147, see Dependent Variables 2 and 3): the variables which are two major determinants of physician utilization. However, although causally related to the need for catharsis, length of residence was found to have almost no impact on the two well-being variables, neither directly nor via the need for catharsis.

The socioeconomic status variables and age were found to have a significant effect upon the well-being variables, but little of their effect is mediated by the need for catharsis. Occupational status was found to have the strongest effect on emotional disorder (−0.246, thereof −0.234, significant at $P < 0.001$, is not mediated through the need for catharsis. See Dependent Variable 2: Emotional Disorder). The same applies to education and age. Both variables have effects on emotional disorder (Dependent Variable 2: 0.126 and −0.116), little of which is due to a possible inclination of the elderly and the poorly educated to develop a need for support. Likewise, the effects of age and occupation on physical illness are not mediated by this need either (Dependent Variable 3: 0.306 and −0.188). At the same time, no less than almost 60% of the effect of occupational status and one-fifth of the effect of age is transmitted through emotional disorder, frequent among low status occupation and elderly respondents. Neither the need for catharsis nor the length of residence has any significant effect on the tendency to define oneself as ill. The latter is determined mainly by the occupational and educational dimensions of social status, the effects of which are hardly mediated by any other variables in the model (Dependent Variable 4: Tendency to Define Oneself as Ill: −0.104 and −0.098). The lower the social class, the stronger is the tendency to define oneself as ill, but not as a result of the health status, whether emotional or physical.

A substantial part of the effects of the socioeconomic variables and of age upon physician use turns out to be transmitted through the well-being variables. Thus, to take the case of occupational status, about 70% of its effect is due to high levels of emotional disorder and of poor physical condition characteristic of low status occupation respondents. To add to this, about 15% of the effects of occupation are due to the high tendency of low status occupation respondents to define themselves as ill. Thus, with almost 85% of its effect being mediated by other variables, the direct effect of occupational status on utilization cannot but be negligible (−0.020). With the second dimension of socioeconomic status, education, the case is different, however. Even though the total effect of education resembles that of occupation (Dependent Variable 5: Physician Visits: −0.161, −0.133, respectively), the major part of its effect on utilization is direct in the sense of being mediated by no other variables in the model (−0.117, significant at $P < 0.05$). Nonetheless, about a quarter of the effect of education is still due to the higher levels of emotional disorder found among low-education respondents and about a tenth of that effect is due to their high tendency to define themselves as ill. As regards age, about 40% of its effect on physician utilization is due to ill health, thereof roughly one half to emotional and the other half to physical illness. About 60% of the effect of age is direct: 0.144, significant at $P < 0.01$).

VI. SUMMARY AND DISCUSSION

An assumption of Shuval *et al.* that the length of the immigrant's stay in the host country is related to the need for catharsis and physician utilization, has been thereby validated. True, the feeling of deprivation of emotional support and sympathy was found to be more pronounced among our immigrants from the same years as Shuval's sample than among old-timers. Otherwise, the immigrant vs old-timers factor was found to be a quite poor predictor of all the other attributes assumed in the model to affect physician utilization. Moreover, while the need for catharsis was found to be related to both emotional and physical well-being, it failed, by itself, to have any noticeable effect on physician utilization, whether directly, or via the tendency to define oneself as ill.

It seems that with the passage of time the former immigrants have by and large abandoned their previously customary mode of gratifying their need for catharsis through turning to health care services. It can be supposed that they have learned alternative channels of gratification of greater value than modern bureaucratic medicine. It can also be supposed that changes in the health care system tended to preclude the non-medical latent functions it once performed. Hence, even those respondents who were found to keenly experience the need for catharsis tended to refrain from turning to physicians in the absence of 'concrete' symptoms. To be sure, they were relatively more susceptible to physiological and psychophysiological symptoms indicative of psychological distress and to physical illness, but it was the occurrence of the symptoms rather than any affiliative needs which was found to guide their decisions of whether to seek help from a doctor or not.

At the same time, the findings do not fully corroborate the hypothesis that social status and age would at the replication time be the major determinants of the hypothesized chain of events leading to utilization. Nonetheless, while the lower classes and the elderly respondents did not score on the need for catharsis significantly higher than their opposite numbers, they did turn out to have other attributes found to be crucial predictors of physician utilization. Both the lower class and the elderly were found to suffer more from emotional and physical affliction, and the lower class respondents were additionally found to be more prone to adopt the sick role. It seems, then, that it is the differential access to various social resources rather than any persisting communion of the former immigrant's experience which at present sets in motion the chain of variables affecting physician utilization.

Of course, these findings do not preclude the possibility that other measures of need for support or of other social needs may yet turn out to be associated with social class and age and consequently to influence the social class- and age-specific rates of utilization. The data merely show that the need for catharsis, as measured in both the original and the replicated study, tends to remain prominent among the former immigrants even after 10 or more years and even if they no longer opt for coping with it through recourse to the health services. This is why the need for catharsis seems to be more closely descriptive of the new immigrant condition, than of the condition of the lower classes. For the immigrants of any social class are indeed likely to share the experience of hardly having any opportunity for forming support-inducing intimate affiliations.

However, the data give grounds to believe that among the immigrants in the replication sample the need for catharsis may be rather milder than in Shuval's sample. This may be due to the gradually decreasing social isolation of one-time immigrants, but also to the possible 'conversion' of the need into 'real' symptoms and illnesses which the formerly immigrant lower classes and elderly now share with their old-timer opposite numbers. As already noted, the hardships responsible for ill-health among the lower classes and the elderly may have generated other varieties of social needs involving a wide range of modes of coping with them, which are not dealt with by the present study. Therefore, future studies would be well-advised to operationalize social needs so as to make them relevant to social class- and age-determined differential access to social resources. Furthermore, since emotional disorder may be a product of stress-induced social needs, it merits inclusion in the model side by side with physical illness.

However, extraordinary complexities, methodological as well as conceptual, appear in the task of identifying the exact nature of the relationships between the social need and the well-being variables, and between the well-being variables and physician utilization. Future studies will also have to learn to circumvent the pitfalls of the time-ordering of variables. In order to ascertain the effects of needs on physician utilization, follow-up studies are definitely preferable to *post hoc* reports as the sole source of evidence. Furthermore, no solution to the time-ordering problems can be considered successful unless it includes more 'objective' measures in addition to self-reports, so as to prevent contamination.

But the conceptual difficulties inherent in any causal inquiry into the effects of latent needs on physician utilization are no less serious than the methodological ones. The most perplexing among them is perhaps the place of the various dimensions of individual well-being in the theoretical model. Crucial in this respect is the question concerning the direction of the prediction: Is emotional disorder a cause of physical illness or its consequence? In line with the theoretical framework which pervades the entire field of the effects of latent needs on physician utilization, we opted for the first alternative. Hence, in the causal model presented above, emotional disorder was placed before physical chronicity. But we are mindful of the possibility that this choice might have influenced the findings heavily. Its consequence was that while emotional disorder was found to affect utilization both directly and indirectly via physical illness, the effect of physical illness on utilization could not even be found to be mediated by emotional disorder. What adds weight to the problem is the fact that any choice in regard to the direction of this prediction seems to be reflective of some deeper concept of the nature of illness. It seems that contrary to the professed intentions, the very assumption of a one-way causal relationship between emotional and physical disorder reveals the affinity with the clinical and dichotomous model of illness, rather than with the social and processual one. Thus, in line with Mechanics' studies of psychological distress and utilization, the direct effect of emotional disorder on physician utilization as found in this study can well be interpreted as evidence of the impact of some latent, 'non-medical', or 'merely emotional' needs. Likewise, the above-reported association between socioeconomic status and emotional disorder (and the resultant 'overutilization' of services by the lower classes) can well be explained, in the manner of the 'culture of poverty' approach in terms of the life-styles of the poor which are responsible for their over-dependency on the health services, when delivered free of charge.

However, the strong association found between emotional and physical disorders gives us certain grounds to suppose that interpretations of this type may be plain corollaries of the assumptions of the causal model. This is because the association in question does not need to refer to the generation of chronic illness by social needs and psychological distress. Alternatively, psychological disorder may at any point of time contribute to the aggravation of chronic illness and to the resultant dependency of patients on medical facilities. In this respect the poor are at a disadvantage even in various schemes of pre-paid comprehensive health care which are otherwise relatively attentive to their needs. For the poor, equal access to medical facilities is not enough, because they have a limited control over a whole variety of social resources upon which recovery from chronic illness and resumption of independent functioning depends. The repeatedly found susceptibility of the lower classes to psychological disorder is likely to limit their resources even further as well as to aggravate their symptoms, with the effect that their experience of chronic disease is apt to be more painful than the experience of other classes with the same disease. Ultimately, the medical sociologists dealing with the effects of latent needs on physician utilization will have to be concerned not only with the design improvements but also with notions of health and illness which different designs may imply. In particular, those who opt for the social concept of illness as a distinct outlook on medicine may ultimately have to ponder the question: Is the experience of illness any different from illness itself?

The foregoing is not intended to detract from the efforts to describe the emotional problems of the ill for the sake of improving the quality of health care which currently suffers from a pronounced biological bias. Nor is it intended to take a position in the debate on the validity of the distinctions between the physical, mental and social dimensions of health. Rather, the intention is to call the attention of medical sociologists to the intricacies of the relationship between latent social needs, emotional problems as commonly measured, and physical chronic illness, so as to forestall the possible policy decisions which as a result of unclarified preconceptions may be at variance with the real interests of the patient.

REFERENCES

1. Shuval J. T. in collaboration with Aaron Antonovsky and A. Michael Davis, *Social Functions of Medical Practice.* Jossey–Bass, San Francisco, 1970.
2. Mann K. J. *et al. Visits to Doctors.* Jerusalem Academic Press, Jerusalem, 1970.
3. Antonovsky A. A model to explain visits to the doctor: with specific reference to the case of Israel. *J. Hlth soc. Behav.* **13,** 447–454, 1972.
4. Mechanic D. Correlates of physician utilization: Why do major multivariate studies of physician utilization find trivial psycho-social and organizational effects? *J. Hlth soc. Behav.* **20,** 387–396, 1979.
5. McKinlay J. B. Some approaches and problems in the study of the use of services—An Overview. *J. Hlth soc. Behav.* **13,** 115–151, 1972.
6. McKinlay J. B. and Dutton D. B. Social-psychological factors affecting health service utilization. In *Consumer Incentives for Health Care* (Edited by Mushkin S.), pp. 251–303. Prodist, New York, 1974.
7. Balint M. *The Doctor, His Patient, and the Illness.* International Universities Press, New York, 1957.
8. Mechanic D. and Volkart E. H. Stress, illness behavior and the sick role. *Am. Sociol. Rev.* **26,** 51–58, 1961.
9. Mechanic D. Students under stress. *A study in the Social Psychology of Adaptation.* Free Press, New York, 1962.
10. Mechanic D. and Greenley J. R. The prevalence of psychological distress and help-seeking in a college student population. *Social Psychiat.* **11,** 1–14, 1976.

11. Tessler R., Mechanic D. and Dimond M. The effect of psychological distress on physician utilization: A prospective study. *J. Hlth soc. Behav.* **17**, 353–364, 1976.
12. Anderson R. *et al.* Psychologically related illness and health services utilization. *Med. Care* **15**, Supplement, 1977.
13. Shuval J. T. in collaboration with Aaron Antonovsky and A. Michael Davis. *Social Functions of Medical Practice*. Jossey–Bass, San Francisco, 1970.
14. Antonovsky A. A model to explain visits to the doctor: with specific reference to the case of Israel. *J. Hlth soc. Behav.* **13**, 446–454, 1972.
15. Kessler R. C. Stress, social status, and psychological distress. *J. Hlth soc. Behav.* **20**, 259–272, 1979.
16. Liem R. and Liem J. Social class and mental illness reconsidered: The role of economic stress and social support. *J. Hlth Behav.* **19**, 139–156, 1978.
17. Cobb S. Social support as a moderator of life stress. *Psychosom. Med.* **38**, 300–314, 1976.
18. Mechanic D. Correlates of physician utilization: why do major multivariate studies of physician utilization find trivial psychosocial and organizational effects? *J. Hlth soc. Behav.* **20**, 387–396, 1979.
19. Caplan R. D. Organizational stress and individual strain: a social-psychological study of risk factors in coronary heart disease among administrators, engineers and scientists. Dissertation Abstracts International 32, 6706b–6707b (University Microfilms No. 72-14822) 1972.
20. Antonovsky A. *Health, Stress and Coping*. Jossey–Bass, San Francisco, 1979.
21. Sparer P. (Ed.) *Personality, Stress and Tuberculosis*. International University Press, New York, 1956.
22. Travis G. *Chronic Disease and Disability*. University of California Press, Berkeley, 1961.
23. Rahe R. H. Social stress and illness onset. *J. Psychosom. Res.* **8**, 35–44, 1964.
24. Gallagher E. B. Lines of reconstruction and extension in the Parsonian sociology of illness. *Soc. Sci. Med.* **10**, 207–218, 1976.
25. Honig-Parnass T. Lay concepts of the sick-role: An examination oi the proiessionalist bias in Parson s model. To be published in *Soc. Sci. Med.*
26. Honig-Parnass T. The relative impact of status and health variables upon sick-role expectations. Presented in ASA 76th Annual Meeting, Toronto, 1981.
27. Antonovsky A. A model to explain visits to the doctor: with specific reference to the case of Israel. *J. Hlth soc. Behav.* **13**, 454–466, 1972.
28. Antonovsky A. *Health, Stress and Coping*. Jossey–Bass, San Francisco, 1979.
29. Dohrenwend B. S. and Dohrenwend B. P. Class and race as status-related sources of stress. *Social Stress* (Edited by Levine S. and Scotch N. A.), pp. 111–140. Aldine, Chicago, 1970.
30. Kessler R. C. Stress, social status, and psychological distress. *J. Hlth soc. Behav.* **20**, 259–272, 1979.
31. Liem R. and Liem J. Social class and mental illness reconsidered: The role of economic stress and social support. *J. Hlth Soc. Behav.* **19**, 139–156, 1978.
32. Dohrenwend B. S. and Dohrenwend B. P. Class and race as status-related sources of stress. *Social Stress* (Edited by Levine S. and Scotch N.), pp. 111–140. Aldine, Chicago, 1970.
33. Myers J. K., Lindental J. J. and Pepper M. P. Social class, life events, and psychiatric symptoms: a longitudinal study. *Stressful Life Events: Their Nature and Effects* (Edited by Dohrenwend B. S. and Dohrenwend B. P.), pp. 191–206. Wiley, New York, 1974.
34. Kessler R. C. Stress, social status, and psychological distress. *J. Hlth Soc. Behav.* **20**, 259–272, 1979.
35. Dohrenwend B. S. and Dohrenwend B. P. Class and race as status-related sources of stress. *Social Stress* (Edited by Levine S. and Scotch N. A.), pp. 111–140. Aldine, Chicago, 1970.
36. Myers J. K., Lindental J. J. and Pepper M. P. Social class, life events, and psychiatric symptoms: A longitudinal study. In *Stressful Life Events: Their Nature and Effects* (Edited by Dohrenwend B. S. and Dohrenwend B. P.), pp. 191–206. Wiley, New York, 1974.
37. Kessler R. C. Stress, social status, and psychological distress. *J. Hlth Soc. Behav.* **20**, 259–272, 1979.
38. Brown G. W., Ni Brol-Chain M. and Harris T. Social class and psychiatric disturbance among women in an urban population. *Sociology* **9**, 225–254, 1975.
39. McKinlay J. B. and Dutton B. B. Social-psychological factors affecting health service utilization. *Consumer Incentives for Health Care* (Edited by Mushkin S.), pp. 251–303. Prodist, New York, 1974.
40. Cole S. and Lejeune R. Illness and the legitimation of failure. *Am. Sociol. Rev.* **37**, 347–356.
41. Twaddle A. C. Health decisions and sick-role variations: An exploration. *J. Hlth soc. Behav.* **10**, 105–115, 1969.
42. McKinlay J. B. and Dutton B. B. Social-psychological factors affecting health service utilization. *Consumer Incentives for Health Care* (Edited by Mushkin S.), pp. 251–303. Prodist, New York, 1974.
43. Antonovsky A. *Health, Stress and Coping*. Jossey–Bass, San Francisco, 1979.
44. Rundall T. G. and Wheeler J. R. C. The effects of income on use of preventive care: An evaluation of alternative explanations. *J. Hlth soc. Behav.* **20**, 397–406, 1979.
45. Alwin D. F. and Hauser R. M. The decomposition of effects in path analysis. *Am. Sociol. rev.* **40**, 37–47, 1975.
46. Duncan O. D. Path analysis: sociological examples. *Am. J. Sociol.* **72**, 1–16, 1966.
47. Levine Sol and Kozloff M. A. The sick role: assessment and overview. *A. Rev. Sociol.* **4**, 317–343, 1978.
48. Hartman M. *Occupation as an Indicator of Social Status in Israeli Society*. Institute of Labour and Social Studies, Tel Aviv (in Hebrew), 1927.
49. Leighton D. C. *et al. The Character of Danger*, p. 441. Basic Books, New York, 1963.
50. Gell C. and Elinson J. The Washington heights master sample survey. *Millbank Mem. Fund Q.* **47**, 1966.
51. Honig-Parnass T. The relative impact of status and health variables upon sick-role expectations. Presented in ASA 76th Annual Meeting, Toronto, 1981.
52. Alwine D. F. and Hauser R. M. The decomposition of effects in path analysis. *Am. Sociol. Rev.* **40**, 37–47, 1975.

16

The Effect of Ethnic Origin on Personality Resources and Psychophysiological Health in a Chronic Stress Situation: The Case of Spouses of Dialysis Patients

Varda Soskolne

Introduction

Chronic physical illness in the family has long ago been recognized as a major source of stress for the physical, psychological and social well-being of each family member (1). Yet, more research has been carried out on the deleterious effects on the patient rather than on other family members.

In Israel, the investigation of the reactions of family members to physical illness is even more complicated considering the different cultural background of Jewish ethnic groups which determine their attitudes to health, their perception of illness and their adjustment in times of stress.

This paper presents some of the results from a study on the impact of dialysis on the patient's spouse. The study attempts to show that chronic dialysis is as stressful for the spouse as for the patient, with harmful impacts on the spouse's psychological and social coping resources and on his health. It was further assumed that ethnic origin plays an important role in determining these reactions.

The effects of dialysis treatment

In the last decade, chronic dialysis has become a common mode of treatment for terminal renal failure and many papers, written by psychiatrists working in dialysis units, described the patient's reactions and adjustment to dialysis (2–4). While the general impression has been that the patient's adjustment may be influenced by the response of the family, information about the impact of dialysis on other family members is nevertheless limited.

Most of the studies on families of dialysis patients examined relatively small samples and focused on selected topics. These studies reported changes in financial conditions, reallocation of roles within the family, decline in social activities and decline in sexual functioning (5–7).

The few studies that have investigated the psychopathological responses of the patient's spouse to these changes, have reported depression, guilt, hostility, denial and regression (8–10). These studies have tended to be descriptive and little attempt has been made to understand either the sources of stress specific to the spouses, or the potentially significant demographic and psychosocial factors. Absence of a comparison group of spouses of healthy people has been another shortcoming of most studies.

It is this gap that the present study attempts to narrow through the application of the concepts of stress research.

Stress and health

In general, stress research in the behavioral and medical sciences during the last decade has brought a multiplicity of evidence to light which indicates that many minor and major health disturbances are related not only to physical, but also to psychological and social factors. Many studies reveal that people who experience social or cultural change (11), a sudden crisis (12), a series of stressful life events, or a prolonged state of stress (13), are more vulnerable to health problems (14).

It is also widely accepted now that the association between stressful situations and health disturbances is mediated by the individual's psychological and social coping resources (15), or 'generalized resistance resources' as termed by Antonovsky (16). These mediating variables and the health outcomes are directly influenced by situation variables (defining the stress condition) and by socio-demographic factors (17, 18), such as sex, age, ethnic origin or race, education and socio-economic status.

The main hypothesis of the present study was that the prolonged stress of dialysis severely impairs the spouse's psychosocial resistance resources with a resultant deterioration in his general health, as compared to matched controls of spouses of healthy people. The findings confirming this hypothesis were reported previously (19). The present report will focus on the modifying effects of ethnic origin on these differences between spouses of dialysis patients and healthy spouses, controlling for other socio-demographic variables.

Ethnicity and health, and personality resources

Ethnic origin was found to have a direct effect on health and on personality variables. Cochrane et al (20) showed that Asian immigrants to Britain have lower symptoms score than British natives. In the United States, most of the studies report lower scores of psychological disturbances for Blacks than for Whites (controlling for socio-economic status (21)), with intermediate scores for Mexican Americans (22), or, at least, similar scores for the overall population (23).

In Israel, Levav et al (24) showed that Israelis and European-born (Western) respondents score significantly lower than the Afro-Asian-born (Oriental) respondents using the shortened version of the CMI. However, in reanalyzing the data, the differences in symptoms scores were explained mainly by education level and not by ethnicity (25).

The confounding effect of education was also found elsewhere when the 'degree of somatization' was examined in relation to several variables, including ethnic origin (26). The Oriental patients tended to complain more of somatic symptoms, but this association disappeared when controlling for education level.

Coping style, which was found to be an important variable mediating between stress and health (15), was investigated in Israel in the general population, and in selected patient groups. In general, it has been shown that people of Western origin tend to be better copers than people of Oriental origin (27), especially when the joint effects of ethnic origin and education are examined (28). However, ethnic origin has no significant effect on the coping style of dialysis patients (29).

Internal–External Locus of Control is another personality variable which was investigated as a mediating effect between stress and health; it has previously been found to change in different racial or ethnic groups. In the United States, Blacks tended to be more external than Whites (30). In Israel there are contradicting reports. Most studies showed that people of Oriental origin had higher (more external) scores than those of Western origin (31–33), but this association was not always found (34).

The question raised in the present study was whether ethnicity has a modifying effect as well as a direct effect on health and on psychological resources; i.e. whether the symptoms and psychological resources scores not only change according to ethnic origin (direct effect), but whether the *differences* in these scores between spouses of dialysis patients and controls change as well according to ethnic origin. As ethnic origin in Israel is still confounded with education, these possible modifying effects were to be examined controlling for education level.

Methods

Measurement of variables

Health status. Psychophysiological symptomatology was measured using the Langer 22 Item Scale (35). Early investigators used this scale as a unidimensional measure of mental health. More recent studies argue that it is more appropriate to use it as a measure of demoralization (36), or psychophysiological stress (37, 38) but there are contradictory reports on its dimensionality (37, 39, 40). In order to resolve this controversy over the scale's construct validity before proceeding with the data analysis, the spouses' responses to the scale were subjected to Smallest Space Analysis (SSA). Two clear sub-scales emerged: Physiological symptoms and psychological symptoms, each containing 11 symptoms (41). This is similar to the division made by Seiler and Summers (42). For the purpose of comparison to other works, the total score for the 22 items is given in addition to the separate scores in each sub-scale.

Ethnic origin was defined as the country of birth and was further categorized as Oriental origin — referring to Israelis born in Asia (excluding Israel) and North Africa — and as Western origin — refering to people born in Europe or in the Western hemisphere. The ethnic origin of people born in Israel was defined by the country of birth of the father.

Personality variables. Coping style and Locus of Control measures were included. Coping style was evaluated using the Shanan's Sentence Completion Test (SSCT), a semi-projective technique developed in Israel for the study of coping style (43); its validity and reliability have been established. The test contains 40 items (sentence stems) divided into four categories with 10 items in each category. The categories refer to: 1) perception of aims and goals, 2) perception of sources of fear and frustration (internal vs. external), 3) readiness to cope actively with novel and/or complex situations, and 4) self-perception (positive vs. negative) (29). Higher scores indicate more active coping. Other scoring possibilities of the test (e.g. direction of energy investment and rejection) are not reported here.

Internal–External Locus of Control Test (30) was given in its Hebrew translation. It had previously been examined for validity and reliability. The scale consists of 29 forced-choice items including six nonscoring filler items to make the purpose of the test more ambiguous. The total score represents the number of items answered in the external direction.

Study population

Spouses of all Jewish patients from 13 dialysis centers in Israel were considered for inclusion in the study based on the following criteria: 1) patient had been on dialysis for at least 6 months, 2) the patient was neither hospitalized nor suffered any other illness, 3) there was no other severe illness in the family, 4) the spouse spoke Hebrew, and 5) the family resided in an urban area.

In total, 166 dialysis spouses fitted the above criteria: 140 (84%) were interviewed, 8 (5%) were not located, and 18 (11%) refused to be interviewed.

Jewish, married controls were selected by individual matching procedure for age, ethnicity and residence from a random list drawn from the Israel Population Register. Education was not a matching criteria as no information was available from the Population Register. Absence of any severe illness in the family was a further criteria for inclusion in the study established at interview. One hundred and forty-four control spouses (from those located) fitted the criteria, 120 (83%) were interviewed and 24 (17%) refused. All data analyses were therefore limited to 120 matched pairs.

All the spouses were interviewed at home by trained interviewers, using a pre-coded closed ended questionnaire.

In both groups, 45 spouses were men and 75 were women. The mean age was 48 years. As to ethnic origin, 43% were of Oriental origin and 57% of Western origin. While only 51% of the dialysis spouses had more than 8 years of schooling, 65% of the control spouses fitted into this education level. Special statistical technique was used to examine the possible confounding effect of education prior to all data analyses.

Statistical analysis

A one-tailed *t*-test for matched pairs was used to compare between spouses of dialysis patients and control spouses on the mean scores of each of the variables in the two ethnic groups. Multiple regression analyses of the differences between the spouses of dialysis patients and control spouses as dependent variables followed in order to examine the modifying effects of ethnic origin, controlling for other background variables. The number of matched pairs varied in the data depending on the number of responses to each scale.

Findings

1. *t-test comparison*

a) Psychophysiological state of health. The elevated symptoms scores of the spouses of dialysis patients are evident in both ethnic groups. Only the items testing physiological symptoms of spouses of Western origin did not reach statistical significance (Table 1). It is also interesting to note that the mean score of psychological symptoms is higher than for the physiological symptoms even though each sub-scale contains 11 symptoms.

b) Active coping. (Shanan's Sentence Completion Test). The shift to a more passive coping style by the spouses of dialysis patients seem to be more marked for those of Western origin. Their scores in all four categories and in the total score were significantly lower than those of their controls. Spouses of Oriental origin manifested only a significant shift to negative self-perception (category 4) and a tendency for lower scores in category 1 (the readiness to realistically identify aims and goals (Table 2)).

TABLE 1. *Comparisons of scores of physiological symptoms, psychological symptoms, and total symptoms of spouses of dialysis patiets vs control spouses, of Oriental and Western ethnic origin*

Symptoms		Oriental Origin (N=52 pairs) mean scores ±SD*		Western Origin (N=65 pairs) mean scores ±SD*	
Physiological Symptoms	D	2.0±1.9	($p < 0.05$)	1.2±1.5	(NS)
	C	1.4±1.8		1.0±1.1	
Psychological Symptoms	D	4.8±2.8	($p < 0.01$)	3.6±2.3	($p < 0.01$)
	C	2.6±2.1		2.0±1.6	
Total 22 items Score	D	6.7±4.2	($p < 0.01$)	4.7±3.1	($p < 0.01$)
	C	4.0±3.7		3.0±2.2	

* One-tailed *t*-test for matched pairs.
D—Dialysis spouses, C—Control spouses.

c) Locus of Contol. Even though no significant differences were found between the spouses of dialysis patients and control spouses in either ethnic group (Table 3), the results indicate a slight shift towards externalization of spouses of dialysis patients in the Western origin group. This tendency can be better clarified if we turn to Table 4 which shows the direct effect of ethnic origin, separately, for the spouses of dialysis patients and for the control spouses. No significant difference was found in the general population (control group) but the scores are similar to previous findings that showed a tendency for a higher (external) score for Oriental respondents. A very different picture emerges in the dialysis group. The spouses of Western origin have significantly more external scores than the Oriental spouses. This finding should be regarded with caution as the spouses of dialysis patients of Oriental and Western origins were not matched for other background variables.

2. Multiple regression analyses

Tables 5–7 shed more light on the modifying impact of ethnicity on the above differences. It appears to be the best predictor among the background variables, accounting for most of the variance (R^2), even though in most of the regression equations the cumulative R^2 was very low and insignificant.

a) Psychophysiological state of health. The results here, as in Active Coping, show negligible modifying effects of the background variables on the differences in physiological and psychological symptoms between the two groups. Ethnic origin accounted for all the variance in the differences in physiological symptoms, falling short of significant effect (p=.09), which indicated that spouses of dialysis patients of Oriental origin have more symptoms compared to their matched controls than do spouses of dialysis patients of Western origin (Table 5). No such effect was found for the differences in psychological symptoms, but again ethnic origin accounted for at least half of the variance.

b) Active coping. The background variables together seem to have low and insignificant modifying effects on the differences in Active Coping categories (Table 6). They account for between 2.5% of the variance in category 1, to 9% of the variance in category 2. Ethnic origin does account for most of these variances, even more than education level, reaching statistically significant

TABLE 2. *Comparisons of scores of Active Coping (SSCT) categories of spouses of dialysis patients vs control spouses, of Oriental and Western ethnic origin*

SSCT Variables		Oriental Origin (N=39 pairs) mean scores ±SD*		Western Origin (N=41 pairs) mean scores ±SD*	
1) Perception of aims and goals	D C	4.6±2.1 5.2±2.5	(NS)	4.6±1.9 5.4±2.5	(p⩽ 0.01)
2) Perception of sources of fear and frustration	D C	3.8±1.7 4.0±1.9	(NS)	3.6±2.0 4.7±2.3	(p⩽ 0.01)
3) Readiness to cope actively with novel or complex situations	D C	2.1±1.7 2.3±1.8	(NS)	2.6±1.7 3.4±2.1	(p⩽ 0.05)
4) Self-perception	D C	4.2±1.9 6.3±1.7	(p⩽ 0.01)	4.6±2.2 5.5±1.5	(p⩽ 0.05)
Total score	D C	14.9±4.5 17.8±4.6	(p⩽ 0.01)	15.5±4.5 19.1±4.9	(p⩽ 0.01)

* One-tailed *t*-test for matched paris.
D—Dialysis spouses, C—Control spouses

TABLE 3. *Comparison of scores of Rotter's Locus of Control Scale of spouses of dialysis patients vs control spouses of Oriental and Western ethnic origin*

Group	Oriental Origin (N=30 pairs) mean scores ±SD*		Western Origin (N=23 pairs) mean scores ±SD*	
Dialysis	10.1±3.0	(NS)	11.2±2.9	(NS)
Control	10.1±3.4		9.9±3.7	

* One-tailed *t*-test for matched pairs

TABLE 4. *Comparison of scores of Rotter's Locus of Control Scale of Oriental vs Western ethnic origin in spouses of dialysis patients and control spouses*

Ethnic Origin	Dialysis Spouses mean scores ±SD*			Control Spouses mean scores ±SD*		
Oriental	9.3±2.9	(N=27)	(P=0.01)	10.3±3.1	(N=29)	(NS)
Western	11.2±2.9	(N=42)		9.7±3.9	(N=38)	

* One-tailed *t*-test for independent samples

TABLE 5. *Standardized regression coefficients,* individual and cumulative R-squares of background variables on the differences in physiological symptoms, psychological symptoms and total symptoms scores between spouses of dialysis patients and control spouses (N=75 pairs)*

Background Variables	Differences in Symptoms** Physiological		Psychological		Total	
	β	R^2change	β	R^2change	β	R^2change
Age	.027	.000	.028	.007	.03	.004
Sex	-.019	.000	.08	.007	.05	.003
Ethnicity	.244 (p=.09)	.063	.07	.022	.16	.047
Education	.018	.000	.12	.009	.10	.005
R^2		.063		.045		.059

* Positive coefficients represent larger differences in older age, men, Oriental origin and lower education.

** Scores of the dialysis spouses minus the scores of the control spouses.

influence on the differences in category 2 — the perception of sources of fear and frustrations. However, the directions of the effects are not consistent. The shift to a more passive coping is greater in spouses of dialysis patients of Western origin only in categories 1 to 3, and the shift to a more negative self-perception (category 4) is greater in spouses of Oriental origin.

c) Locus of Control. First, it is important to point out that the modifying effect of education could not be examined here because only 34 matched pairs of those who completed the Locus of Control test were also fully matched for education; only one pair was matched for lower education level (8 years). Therefore, the regression equation included all 53 pairs that completed the test, controlling for possible differences in education level between spouses of dialysis patients and control spouses (see study population).

The modifying effect of ethnicity was high and significant. It accounted for about 12% of the 16% variance in the differences between spouses of dialysis patients and control spouses. It confirms the direction which was manifested previously (Tables 3 and 4) of spouses of Western origin being more negatively effected than spouses of Oriental origin. They showed a significantly greater shift towards external Locus of Control.

Discussion

The findings in the present study indicate that the prolonged stress of chronic illness has deleterious effects on the spouses of dialysis patients. A clear trend emerges which indicates that the magnitude of these effects is modified by ethnic origin, even though they do not reach statistical significance in all variables. These modifying effects were far beyond the influences of other background variables, all of which hardly accounted for the variances in the differences between the spouses of dialysis patients and control spouses.

The comparison of the results from this work with previous studies which used the same psychological measures is almost impossible. Most of the other studies examined the direct effects of ethnic origin, as well as other background variables, on the reactions of the general population or patient groups and did not look at the modifying effects of ethnic origin.

The direct effects of ethnic origin on coping style showed a greater tendency among people of Oriental origin towards passive coping; this usually did not reach statistical significance (27, 29, 44). This tendency was found in the first three categories of the SSCT but not in category 4, the perception of the self. The scores in the general population were higher (more positive self-perception) in the group of Oriental origin (27). The same directions were found in the control group of the present study but not in the spouses of

TABLE 6. *Standardized regression coefficients,* individual and cumulative R-squares of background variables on the differences in Active Coping categories (SSCT) between spouses of dialysis patients and control spouses (N=60 pairs)*

Background Variables	Differences in Coping**									
	Category 1		Category 2		Category 3		Category 4		Total score	
	β	R^2 change	β	R^2 change	β	R^2 change	β	R^2 change	β	R^2 change
Age	−.002	.000	.083	.015	.064	.001	−.134	.009	.032	.000
Sex	.068	.005	−.011	.000	−.018	.000	−.063	.004	.001	.000
Ethnicity	−.100	.016	−.312 ($p < 0.05$)	.068	−.188	.049	.200	.061	−.150	.025
Education	−.080	.004	.111	.007	−.067	.002	.120	.008	−.030	.001
R^2		.025		.090		.052		.082		.026

* Positive coefficients represent larger differences in older age, men, Oriental origin and lower education.
** Scores of the control spouses minus the scores of the dialysis spouses.

TABLE 7. *Standardized regression coefficients,* individual and cumulative R-squares of background variables on the differences in Locus of Control scores between spouses of dialysis patients and control spouses (N=53 pairs)*

Background variables	Differences in Losus of Control Scores**	
	β	R^2change
Age	−.14	.000
Sex	.15	.014
Ethnicity	−.37 ($p < 0.05$)	.119
Differences in education***	−.18	.027
R^2		.160 (p=.07)

* Positive coefficients represent larger differences in older age, men, Oriental origin and larger differences in education.

** Scores of the dialysis spouses minus the scores of the control spouses.

*** Education level of control spouses minus education level of dialysis spouses.

dialysis patients. Therefore, the shift toward a more negative self-perception was greater in spouses of dialysis patients of Oriental origin than in Western spouses, as their self-perception could have been even more positive than that of Western spouses.

Shanan (28) notes that in certain groups the self-perception (category 4) acts as a counter tendency to the readiness to cope actively (category 3). This may be a partial explanation for the present findings which show qualitative differences due to ethnic origin. In spouses of dialysis patients of Western origin, the ability to perceive aims and goals (category 1), sources of threat (category 2), and the readiness to cope actively (category 3) are more negatively effected than their self-perception. In the Oriental spouses, the dialysis does not bring many changes in the first three categories of coping, but it shakes their self-perception. As the SSCT is based on the conception of active coping as a parameter of ego functioning, it may be concluded that these several aspects of coping change differently according to ethnic origin. This lends further support to Shanan's conclusion (28) that it is not sufficient to evaluate the overall coping (total score), but it is important to investigate the different aspects of coping.

Similar results were found for the second ego-functioning parameter, Locus of Control. The marked, significant shift to externalization of spouses of Western origin may be due in part to a greater use of defence mechanisms that promote externalization (e.g. projection, displacement, regression) which may not have been so frequently used by them before the onset of dialysis. Another expression of this use of defence pattern were shown in the Western spouses' greater rejection of the SSCT, reported elsewhere (41).

In contrast to the above findings the spouses of Oriental origin are those who have a greater increase in symptoms, mainly physiological symptoms. (The greater difference in total symptoms score is largely accounted for by the greater differences in physiological symptoms.) However, these directions are not striking if they are explained by the differences between Western and Oriental Jews in expressing their difficulties in somatic or psychological terms. A greater degree of somatization was present among Oriental psychiatric patients (26), while Western patients reported more psychological symptoms. These may also be the different patterns in reaction to the stress of illness in the family. The psychological resources of Oriental spouses are less undermined than those of Western spouses but they tended to express their stress in somatic terms. The Western spouses are more vulnerable psychologically and the increase in their physiological symptoms was smaller than that of Oriental spouses.

These findings indicate that even though spouses of dialysis patients of all ethnic groups bear the risk of the deterioration of their personality resources and psychophysiological state of health, the magnitude of these effects and the areas in which they are manifested differ according to their ethnic origin. This influence is far beyond that of other background variables. The overall small effects of the background variables suggests that other factors, possibly dialysis-related and psychosocial factors, account for the differences in symptoms scores between the dialysis spouses and their matched controls.

References

1. Croog Sh. The family as a source of stress. In: Levine S, Scotch NA, eds. Social stress. Chicago: Aldine Press, 1970.
2. Levy NB, ed. Living or dying: adaptation to hemodialysis. Springfield: Thomas, 1974.
3. Levy NB. Psychonephrology 1: Psychological factors in hemodialysis and transplantation. New York: Plenum, 1981.
4. Kaplan De-Nour A. The hemodialysis unit. Adv Psychosom Med 1980; 10:132–50.
5. Friedman EA, et al. Psychosocial adjustment of family to maintenance hemodialysis. Part II. NY State J Med 1970; 70:767–74.
6. Levy NB, Wynbrandt GD. The quality of life on maintenance hemodialysis. Lancet 1975; 1328–30.
7. Maurin J, Schenkel J. A study of the family unit's response to hemodialysis. J Psychosom Res 1976; 20:163–8.
8. Holcomb JL, Macdonald RW. Social functioning of artificial kidney patients. Soc Sci Med 1973; 7:109–19.
9. Shambaugh PW, et al. Hemodialysis in the home — emotional impact on the spouse. Trans

Am Soc Artif Int Organs 1967; 13:41–5.
10. Steele TE, et al. Hemodialysis patients and spouses. J Nerv Ment Dis 1976; 162:225–37.
11. Kark SL. Epidemiology and community medicine. Ch 10. Applenton-Centry Crafts 1974.
12. Maddison D, Viola A. The health of widows in the year following bereavement. J Psychosom Res 1968; 12:297–306.
13. Dohrenwend BS, Dohrenwend BP, eds. Stressful live events: Their nature and effects. New York: John Wiley & Sons, 1974.
14. Najman JM. Theories of disease causation and the concept of a general susceptibility: A review. Soc Sci Med 1980; 14A:231–7
15. Pearlin LI, Lieberman MA, Menaghan EG, Mullan JT. The stress process. J Health Soc Behav 1981; 22:337–56.
16. Antonovsky A. Health, stress and coping. San Francisco: Jossey Bass, 1979.
17. Cassel J. The contribution of the social environment to host resistance. Am J Epidemiol 1976; 104:107–23.
18. Dohrenwend BS, Dohrenwend BP. Some issues in research on stressful life events. J Nerv Ment Dis 1978; 166:7–15.
19. Soskolne V. The impact of dialysis treatment on the patient's spouse. In: Levy NB, ed. Psychonephrology. Vol. 3. Kidney substitution: Psychological complications and their treatment. Plenum Publ Co (in press).
20. Cochrane R, Hashmi F, Stopes-Roe M. Measuring psychological disturbance in Asian immigrants to Britain. Soc Sci Med 1977; 11:157–64.
21. Dohrenwend BP. Sociocultural and social-psychological factors in the genesis of mental disorders. J Health Soc Behav 1975; 16:365–92.
22. Antune G, et al. Ethnicity, socioeconomic states, and the etiology of psychological distress. Social Soc Res 1974; 58:361–92.
23. Roberts RE. Prevalence of psychological distress among Mexican Americans. J Health Soc Behav 1980; 21:134–45.
24. Levav I, Arnon A, Portnoy A. Two shortened versions of the Cornell Medical Index — A new test of their validity. Int J Epidemiol 1977; 6:135–41.
25. Abramson JH, Levav I. Use of symptom inventories as measures of emotional ill-health in epidemiological studies. Letter to the Editor. Int J Epidemiol 1978; 7:381.
26. Lerner J, Noy P. Somatic complaints in psychiatric disorders: Social and cultural factors. Int J Soc Psychiatry 1968; 14:145–50.
27. Shanan J. Psychological changes at mid-life. Final report. Social Security Institute, Jerusalem, 1968 (in Hebrew).
28. Shanan J. Life beyond the 'peak': Psychological changes at mid-life. Social Security, June 1972 (in Hebrew).
29. Shanan J, Kaplan De-Nour A, Garty I. Effects of prolonged stress on coping style in terminal renal failure patients. J Hum Stress 1976; 2:19–28.
30. Rotter JB. Generalized expectancies for internal versus expectancies for external control of reinforcement. Psychol Monographs 1966; 80:605–15.
31. Kagan V. Locus-of-Control of children. M.A. thesis. Tel-Aviv University, 1980 (in Hebrew).
32. Yaar-Yuchtman E, Shapira R. Sex as a status characteristic: An examination of sex differences in Locus-of Control. Sex Roles 1981; 7(2):149–62.
33. Gutman J, et al. Locus-of-Control and moral judgement: a cross cultural study in Israel. J Moral Educ 1981; 10(3):186–91.

34. Merdix S. The relationship between Locus-of-Control, psychological differentiation and creativity in Sepharadic and Ashkenazi children. M.A. thesis, Haifa University, 1979 (in Hebrew).
35. Langner TS. A twenty-two item screening score of psychiatric symptoms indicating impairment. J Health Hum Behav 1962; 3:269–76.
36. Link B, Dohrenwend BP. Formulation of hypotheses about the true prevalence of demoralization in the United States. In: Dohrenwend BP et al, eds. Mental illness in the United States: Epidemiological estimates. Preager, 1980.
37. Seiler LH. The 22-item scale used in field studies of mental illness: A question of method, a question of substance, and a question of theory. J Health Soc Behav 1973; 14:252–64.
38. Garrity TF, Somes GW, Markes MB. The relationship of personality, life change, psychophysiological strain and health status in a collge population. Soc Sci Med 1977; 11:257–63.
39. Roberts RE, Forthoffer RN, Fabrega H. Further evidence on dimensionability of the index of psycho-physiological stress. Soc Sci Med 1976; 10:483–90.
40. Cochrane R. A comparative evaluation of the Symptom Rating Test and the Langner 22-term Index for use in epidemiological surveys. Psychol Med 1980, 10:115–24.
41. Soskolne V. The impact of dialysis treatment on the patient's spouse. Unpublished Ph.D. thesis. The Hebrew University, Jerusalem 1982 (in Hebrew).
42. Seiler LH, Summers GF. Toward an interpretation of items used in field studies of mental illness. Soc Sci Med 1974; 8:459–67.
43. Shanan J. Active coping. Behavior 1967; 16(2–3):188–95 (in Hebrew).
44. Shanan J, Adler H, Adler E. Coping style and rehabilitation. Bitahon Sociali (Social Security) 1975; 9–10:53–66 (in Hebrew).

17

The Effect of Cultural Conceptions on Therapy: A Comparative Study of Patients in Israeli Psychiatric Clinics

S.D. Minuchin-Itzigsohn, R. Ben-Shaoul, A. Weingrod, and *D. Krasilowsky*

INTRODUCTION

This article deals with cultural influences on conceptions of mental illness and the treatment process among the Jewish population of Israel.[2] The analysis is the result of comparative research carried out in public psychiatric clinics[3] with patients from three *edot*, or groups based upon country of origin: "Moroccan," "Persian," and "Ashkenazi" Jews.[4] As a multidisciplinary team working in the field of mental health, we aimed in this study to clarify how the cultural differences among *edot* are expressed in their conceptions of illness, and how these in turn influence the therapeutic encounter in the clinic.

It is useful to sketch briefly the general and theoretical background to the study. Within Israel there is a common denominator for all Jews: for example, the national framework includes a common language, legal apparatus and health and educational systems. Moreover, the strong historical identification with the Jewish people and religion also provides broad universal links.

Nonetheless, the Jewish population of Israel is strikingly heterogeneous. It is frequently observed that a cultural dichotomy separates the "Oriental" (Middle-Eastern and North African) and "Ashkenazi" (European-derived) country-of-origin groups. The *edot* are also identified according to specific origins as "Yemenite," "Persian," "Russian" and so forth (Eisenstadt 1955; Weingrod 1965; Deshen and Shokeid 1974). In regard to stratification, the dominant culture is fundamentally Western, and the European-origin Ashkenazim tend to hold the more prestigious and powerful social, economic and political positions.

According to Eaton, Lasry and Sigal (1979), social inequality among Jewish ethnic groups in Israel affects mental health for four reasons: (1) persons from lower-status *edot* may have low self-esteem, which in turn is linked to psychological disorders, neuroticism, alienation and fatalism; (2) they have increased vulnerability to crises that originate in the economic system, increased mortality and morbidity, which are accompanied by an increment in stress and resultant mental disorders; (3) they have lessened social and economic resources to deal with crisis situations; and (4) they have more hostility, open or covert, directed against the dominant group (or against other minority groups), which may lead to depression or anti-social behavior. Mental health in Israel is hence likely to differ among *edot* depending upon their relative disadvantage and place on the stratification scale (Eaton and Levav 1982).

These phenomena may also be analyzed within the context of immigration and acculturation. A large proportion of the Israeli Jewish population are recent immigrants whose social and cultural systems are undergoing rapid changes. Among the consequences of these changes may be a lack of synchronization between members of a particular *edah* (singular of *edot*) and the dominant Ashkenazi culture. These trends are likely to affect all aspects of life; however, existential features such as illness, in which emotional involvement is especially high, are particularly sensitive. Putting it broadly, within the context of social change, lack of clear meaning plus disorientation may accentuate emotional reactions and cause disorganized experiences. Indeed, "facts" themselves may be a source of confusion or *angst* (Bastide 1978). Devereux's (1973) observation is relevant in this regard: different cultures encourage contrasting forms of releasing tension, and specific forms of expression are accepted or forbidden because the culture reinforces particular defense mechanisms.

Our research was based upon these theoretical perspectives. We wish to understand how knowledge and beliefs relating to illness, as well as behavior regarding illness, influence the therapeutic encounter. More specifically, we argue that "knowledge and beliefs" are composed of segments of traditional and religious wisdom, passed on as group tradition by families and traditional healers, as well as knowledge acquired from the wider society by means of personal networks, educational contexts and the mass media. In addition, contact with modern medical agencies also leads to conceptions of illness. Stemming from different sources, these theories may be organized in parallel systems which do not clash, or alternatively, in contradictory patterns. With this in mind we studied how patients from three different *edot* conceptualize the problems from which they suffer, and what their expectations are regarding treatment. We also wished to discover how this knowledge affects the atmosphere in which the initial contact with the therapist takes place, as well as the length of time the patient continues in therapy. Our objective, in other words, was to analyze how "culture" influenced the course and outcome of the treatment process.

METHODOLOGY

The material presented in this article is part of a larger study carried out in three public psychiatric outpatient clinics in Jerusalem, Israel, during 1979–1981. We chose to work in outpatient clinics rather than in hospitals in order to avoid the influence of a total institution and of psychotic states on patients' conceptions. For this reason we also chose patients who had not been hospitalized during the five years prior to the study and who were not psychotic. Following a preliminary survey of those who attend the clinics, we selected members of three *edot* most frequently represented:[4] "Ashkenazim" born in Israel of Eastern or Middle European origin; "Moroccans," Moroccan-born or first-generation Israeli-born of Moroccan-born parents; and "Persians," Persian-born or first-generation Israeli-born of Persian-born parents.

Eighty-four patients aged 18–60 were interviewed; these included each new patient who had the proper criteria and came to an outpatient clinic during the period of the study. Consent to be interviewed was first obtained from both the patient and the staff member treating him/her. The population included 52 women and 32 men, approximately equally distributed among the three *edot*. Most were interviewed twice: they were interviewed first at the start of treatment, in order to minimize the influence of treatment on knowledge and beliefs, and a second time (for 51 of these patients) to ascertain changes in "knowledge" and modifications in behavior connected with treatment. The second interview took place from twelve to eighteen months after the first. In addition, we interviewed 25 family members in order to learn more about norms in the social networks of the patients.

The interviews were conducted in the clinics or in the patients' homes. They followed a standard question format and were open-ended. Interviews took from 3 to 20 hours to complete.

RESEARCH RESULTS

As a means of depicting the distinctive features of each group, we have chosen to present the data mainly in the form of case studies. That is, for each *edah* we present a single case study in considerable detail. It is important to emphasize that in each instance there are idiosyncratic features which must be accounted for. For this reason we also stress how each case differs from or resembles others in the *edah*. Table I to IV below summarize relevant background features according to *edah* membership.

TABLE I
Sex, age and place of birth of 84 patients from three *Edot*

	Number of Interviews	Sex		Age		Birthplace	
		Male	Female	18–40	41–60	Israel	Outside of Israel
Persian	27	41%	59%	74%	26%	40%	60%
Moroccan	29	34%	66%	83%	17%	45%	55%
Ashkenazi	28	32%	68%	82%	18%	100%	–

TABLE II
Mean number of living children in families of origin

Persian	Moroccan	Ashkenazi	
		Except ultra-orthodox	Ultra-orthodox
7.0	6.9	3.0	10.3

TABLE III
Educational background of 84 patients

	Primary school		High school		Post-high school	Total
	1–7	8	9–11	12	13+	
Persian	15%	22%	26%	15%	22%	100%
Moroccan	14%	21%	38%	10%	17%	100%
Ashkenazi	–	7%	7%	32%	54%*	100%

* 21% of the Ashkenazi patients had yeshiva education.

TABLE IV
Self-classification of religious observance

	Ultra-orthodox	Religious	Traditional	Secular	Total
Persian	11%	29%	41%	19%	100%
Moroccan	–	28%	51%	21%	100%
Ashkenazi	18%	25%	14%	43%	100%

1. *The Persian Patients*

Persian Jews in Israel number 110,314 and comprise approximately 3.5% of the Jewish population (Central Bureau of Statistics 1980). A small Persian community had existed prior to the establishment of Israel in 1948; large numbers of Persian Jews immigrated at about that time, and since then the immigration has proceeded at a slow pace. Persian Jews tend to live near each other and to preserve traditional patterns of occupation. There is also a tendency to marry within the *edah* as well as within the extended family. Generally speaking, they tend to identify themselves with other Israelis of Persian origin, as well as with the specific town or city in Iran from which they or their parents immigrated. Unlike several other *edot* (notably Moroccans and Yemenites), the Persians in the past have tended to have "low" social, cultural and political visibility; in recent years, however, and especially since the revolution in Iran, the organizational links among them have been strengthened and they have attracted greater public attention.

Dina is one of the 27 patients of Persian origin whom we interviewed. She is 35 years old, was born in Jerusalem and grew up in a neighborhood populated by many families of Persian origin. Her parents were born in Mashad, Iran, and immigrated to Israel some 40 years ago. Dina is the youngest of three children; although her parents received little formal education, Dina and her siblings completed a state religious primary school in Israel. At age 16 she began working as a clerk. Dina was married when she was 29; her husband is of Sephardi-Turkish origin, with a primary school education, and is employed as a policeman. Within four years following their marriage Dina gave birth to three children, a daughter and two sons. Both sons have had problems in motor and verbal development. Dina remained at home with her small children for a number of years, but recently she resumed working. She speaks Persian with her parents and Hebrew with her husband and children.

Although she was born in Israel, Dina identifies herself with the Persian *edah* and specifically with the community originating in Mashad. She speaks of life in Iran nostalgically as if she herself had been there. Dina describes herself as "traditional" and her family of origin as "religious." She observes the Sabbath (does not travel or turn on lights), *kashrut*, and rituals of family purity.[5] She considers *kashrut* and purity of the family important for health.

Dinah was first referred to the clinic by a gastroenterologist. In the psychiatric clinic she was diagnosed as suffering from a crisis with depressive-conversive symptoms. Her main complaints included stomach pains, constipation, gases, headaches, dizziness, weakness, fear and depression.

Dina explains her situation in the following terms: "I compared myself to an earthquake. In the earth there are poisonous gases and that's what I have in my body. I lose my balance like an earthquake and have weakness in my legs. I feel dizzy and nearly faint. When my stomach is full, my head hurts. Something in my digestive system shrivelled. I used to eat a lot of hot (spicy) food and it affected my stomach, which is sensitive. The stomach has all the energy of the body; it warms the body. I am worried about what exactly I have: it gives me bad thoughts, all sorts of *pahadim* (fears) about *dika'on* (depression). I am afraid that in a minute I'll die, in a minute they'll put me in a mental hospital. I explain exactly what I have and the doctors don't grasp. When they tell me 'psychological, psychological,' I have the feeling that I'm mentally ill."[6]

Dina describes the reasons for her conditions as follows: "I had three babies, one after the other, and it was *Pesach* (Passover) and I didn't have help, and I worked day and night until I collapsed, and I didn't eat as I should, so apparently my body shrivelled. After birth a woman is weak; she has everything open, as they say. The womb isn't closed. In our community in Persia, a woman who comes home after childbirth does not touch anything for 40 days. Everyone serves her and gives her medicines which slowly, slowly strengthen her. For forty days she doesn't hang the baby's laundry and she is not allowed to leave the house. No one can sit on her bed, because it can harm the child's development. Sexual relations are forbidden for forty days after the birth of a son, and for sixty days after the birth of a daughter." (see note 5.)

Worried about her state of health, Dina consulted with a series of doctors. "I went to my family doctor, then to an even bigger internist because he (the family doctor) didn't help me, then to a bigger specialist privately. I go from doctor to doctor, doctor to doctor, and all the tests come out, thank God, all right." In addition to these consultations, she also simultaneously went to an Iraqi-Jewish rabbi healer who treats patients according to religious tradition. At a later stage she was referred to the psychiatric clinic. "I was sent (to the clinic) by the gastro-doctor for intestinal problems. He said I need a psychologist because I don't let my feelings out of my heart and my belly." This is the second time that Dina came to the clinic. A year earlier she was referred by an endocrinologist. In both instances she dropped out of treatment after a few sessions.

Dina is pessimistic about the possibility of curing psychological problems and illnesses. She had expected to receive clear explanations and instructions. In her words, "Like a small child, who one tells what to do, they should calm me, they should give me medicine so I'll get over it." (It should be noted that she hardly took the medicine she was given.) She sees no connection between her condition and the therapist's emphasis on her past, and it makes her angry. She says, "I explain everything to her (the therapist), and she asks about everything from the start, the family, relationships when I was young, and I said, "What's past is past. My stomach just isn't right; maybe the muscles in my belly have contracted. What do I come for? To have you ask about the past? Now it's different, it's family and problems. I don't want all this nonsense; it makes me angry. Okay – I'm nervous and I have reason to be nervous."

In her richly-detailed remarks Dina places particular emphasis upon her inability to fulfill the ideal behavioral norms that were followed by "her community" in Persia. The main features of these norms include strong support from one's extended family, correct behavior during the delicate post-partum period, care in removing magical threats to mother and child during this period, as well as eating natural, fresh foods. Without entering into questions of Dina's clinical condition, it is clear that she takes these factors to be critical for understanding her state of health. The considerable gap between these norms and her real situation in Israel provided Dina with one explanation of her unsatisfactory health condition. However, this interpretation was not closely connected or integrated with the message she continued to receive from the health professionals with whom she consulted. This led Dina to worry over her health, and these worries grew even stronger when she compared herself with her neighbors who appeared to be objectively like her. As she puts it, "With them there are no reactions like mine – physical – and it's as if I'm different from everyone, I already have bad thoughts that I'm mentally ill." During her frequent medical consultations no organic reasons were found for her health problems. Being referred to the psychiatric clinic provoked additional fears and worry, because she interprets the doctor's message of "psychological problems" to mean "mental illness."

There are many similarities between Dina and the other Persian patients. She is among the 40% of Persian interviewees who were born in Israel; 95% of the foreign-born Persians immigrated in the 1950's. She resembles most of them in her identification with the community of origin; although they identify, many of the younger persons also complained about overprotection and conservatism within their *edah*. With regard to religion, 70% define themselves as traditional or religious (see Table IV). They observe the same religious commandments and see a connection between *kashrut*, family purity and health. In these respects we did not find important differences between the Israeli-born or educated and the Persian-born interviewees.

Like Dina, the Persian patients tend to come to mental health clinics following referral by a doctor rather than on their own initiative; they previously or simultaneously had also consulted other doctors and reported having had various clinical tests. The majority also reported having gone to rabbi healers for these problems (see Table VIII).

Among the Persian patients 44% described their problems as if they were mainly physical. There is a quantitative difference in the number of psychosomatic symptoms reported by members of this group in comparison with the others; indeed, what stands out among the Persians is an emphasis upon somato-psychic along with psychological symptoms. As shown in Table VII, the proportion of psychosomatic or somato-psychic to psychological complaints was the highest among members of this group. The Persian patients also described disturbances in bodily functioning in rich metaphoric language and with considerable symbolism. (Parenthetically, it is interesting to note that our findings in this regard are similar to those reported by Good (1977) in his studies in Iran, although in contrast with Good the focus of complaints was not the heart but rather the digestive system.[7]) Fully half of our Persian patients reported that they suffered from symptoms connected with the digestive system: common complaints included eating problems, upset stomach, vomiting, stomach aches and constipation. As Dina, they explained that health is connected with eating habits and that improper foods may be a cause of illness. Proper eating demands selecting healthy, natural foods that were more available in Iran.

Many Israeli therapists have recognized a culture-bound syndrome informally labelled "Parsitis" that is thought to be prevalent among Persian patients.[8] This syndrome consists of hypochondria expressed as preoccupation with physical problems and pains accompanied by fear of serious illness (Basker et al. 1982). As can be seen in Table V, in comparison with the two other groups, the Persians show a higher prevalence of fear of illness, as well as fear of illness accompanied by pains and other bodily complaints. These findings tend to support the therapists' informal diagnosis of "Parsitis."[9]

TABLE V
Patients with complaints relevant to "parsitis" (in %)

	Persian	Moroccan	Ashkenazim
Fears about illness	41%	11%	11%
Fears about illness with pains	19%	7%	0%
Fears about illness with bodily complaints	30%	11%	4%

The Persian patients we interviewed made no clear distinction between physical illness, psychological problems and mental illness (Table VI). The causes of mentall illness and psychological problems are either located within the person or, alternatively, are both within and outside of the person, and there is no mention of interaction between the two.

The tendency of the Persians not to differentiate between physical and mental problems causes difficulty in choosing suitable health services since these are designed to be differentiated by specialties. Even when they come to psychiatric clinics, the Persians present their problems in keeping with the non-differentiated conception. An unclear message is frequently transmitted: a combination of fear with a psychological content, plus pains and various somatopsychic symptoms; in short, "Parsitis." We suspect that this label may *a priori* create the impression that Persian patients are "difficult to treat." This may, in turn, foster a negative atmosphere which is sensed by the patient. Together with the patients' difficulty in choosing the proper place to request help, this leads them to pursue complicated paths including simultaneous and successive visists to various specialists, among them psychotherapists. Insofar as these visits do not result in successful solutions, they tend to increase the patients' fear and worries and lead to additional visits; a closed circuit is, in effect, created. Especially evident is the strong desire to receive explanations and advice in order to clarify all of the unorganized information gathered in the course of many visits to different agencies. Explanations become problematic since in order for them to be acceptable they must conform to cultural conceptions.

Many of the Persian patients do not connect their current condition with the past; indeed, they interpret the message of the therapist and translate it in their own terms so that it appears absurd. We suppose that the clinic personnel also have special problems in translating the Persian patients' message so that it conforms with their own therapeutic model and allows them to arrive at a diagnosis.

Finally, the social stigma surrounding psychological problems and mental illness is especially strong among the Persians. It seems to us that their emphasis upon physical ailments is utilized as a device to guard themselves against their fears of mental illness. Moreover, as members of a small, inward-focused *edah* their concern regarding stigma prevents them from consulting with members of their social network or recommending psychiatric treatment to others. The majority (74%) told us, furthermore, that they would not recommend psychological treatment to others; they did not "wish to hurt other persons," they explained, and besides they did not want others to suspect that they themselves were in treatment. Indeed, in the clinic they tend to be apprehensive regarding other patients, neighbors and acquaintances.

We were impressed by the fact that the Persians found it important to believe that they would recover "on their own." When we interviewed them after an interval of a year or so, several reported sensing changes in their lives, feelings or symptoms; they explained these changes as stemming from "their own power," from the help they received in therapy, or from a rabbi or neurologist. Their typically pessimistic view of the chances of curing psychological problems and mental illness (Table VI) also lowers their motivation, and this too contributes to difficulties in the therapeutic interaction. All of these factors combine to influence the psychiatric process; they lead, in effect, to their dropping-out of treatment. Nearly 74% of the Persian patients did not continue in treatment, did not attend regularly and dropped out before completing ten visits. Many of them later returned to the clinic.

2. *Ashkenazi Patients*

The Ashkenazim immigrated to Israel from different countries and continents (mainly from Europe and America). They number 1,294,831, and comprise 41.5% of the Jewish population of Israel (Central Bureau of Statistics 1980). In this study we selected patients who were at least second generation Israelis of Eastern or Central European origin. This group occupies a high status in Israel, and they continue to be the main social model. As measured by their places of residence, education and occupational status, most of the Ashkenazim are middle class or higher. Persons in this category do not see themselves as an *edah*, but rather as "citizens of the country."

Among the Ashkenazim there also are ultra-orthodox sub-groups which are strikingly different. We were able to interview only a small number of ultra-orthodox patients, and consequently our analysis relates primarily to the majority of Ashkenazim who do not belong to these groups.[10]

David, one of the 28 Ashkenazi patients we interviewed, is 42 years old. He is a third generation Israeli, and was born and has always lived in the same Jerusalem neighborhood. He is the youngest of three children. His mother died several years ago; his brother and sister are married, and he is single and lives at home with his father, a 75–year-old pensioner. The family is of Russian-Polish origin. David's mother completed primary school; his father graduated from high school (*gymnasia*). David and his siblings have had some post-high school education. He attended a state school, presently works at a white-collar occupation, and has written and published several books. He began working at age 16, and remained at the same place for 17 years; he has been at his current job, in the same field, for 9 years.

David does not especially identify with any *edah*, and believes in a process of *mizug galuyot* (blending or mixing of the *edot*). He describes his family and himself as "traditional." While not observant, his family nonetheless maintains a certain religious ambience – for example, lighting Shabbat candles and attending synogogue on special occasions. For him religious tradition is principally a matter of aesthetics and logic; he sees it as functional to society.

David came to the psychiatric clinic as a consequence of a crisis accompanied by anxiety and depression. The crisis was caused by changes in his life and the need to make decisions in several areas – family, social and occupational. This frightened him, and he became anxious and depressed. At the clinic he was diagnosed as suffering from obsessive neurosis, personality disorders and post-encephalitis.

He describes himself as follows: "I was born and raised and still live in the same place. This is typical of my psychological condition. I don't adapt to new situations. I even always choose to walk on the same streets." According to David, the quality of his obsessiveness aids him in his work, and, in turn, his occupation strengthens his obsessiveness. "New demands put me into stress, which makes me blush and my hands begin to tremble. I lose weight when I feel bad psychologically." He describes himself as shy, isolated and sensitive. David continues, "I feel different because I didn't serve in the army, and I didn't finish the university because of my problems."

David went to the clinic on his own initiative since he was already familiar with the procedure. During adolescence he had been in both individual and group therapy for several years. He suffered then from headaches, depression and anxiety. The depression passed, but the anxiety persisted.

On this occasion David discussed his problems with his father, sister and brother. He did not ask them for their advice since, as we have noted, he had already recognized his own situation. He also did not consult with a rabbi, since he "does not believe." David has a rational explanation for the ability of rabbis, "like witch-doctors," to cure those who turn to them: the psychological influence of faith cures them. When David came to the clinic he knew how to describe his problems in the psychological terms he had learned from past experience in treatment, from reading, and from his cultural milieu.

For David, mental and physical illnesses are two categories which affect one another. He attributes problems and psychological illnesses to the interaction between character related factors and external "triggers." Psychological problems are curable by treatment, he says, but his problems can only be alleviated and not completely cured. "What does 'completely' mean?" he asks, philosophically.

David faithfully attended a total of twenty-two therapy sessions. He believes that the therapy was positive and that it helped him to return to the condition he had been in before his crisis. He was critical of the lack of flexibility in public services that work according to "standards" and do not adjust the intensity of treatment to the patient's condition. He thinks that given the crisis he was undergoing when he first came, he should have had more intensive treatment at the start, and less later, in order to prevent dependence on therapy. Despite his criticism, David faithfully maintained the therapeutic contract and believed that the treatment helped him.

Comparing David with the other Ashkenazim whom we interviewed, they too do not define themselves as belonging to an *edah* and tend to express an egalitarian ideology. In this regard a discrepancy exists between their ideal norms and their descriptions of actual social relationships; for example, most expressed a sense of superiority and a feeling that "Israel was theirs." It is interesting to note how Ashkenazi patients use their ethnic superiority to solve idiosyncratic problems; several stated explicitly that they feel more comfortable in the company of people of other *edot*, since they themselves have "inferiority complexes."

Most of the Ashkenazi patients chose to observe some religious customs (such as fasting on Yom Kippur and lighting Shabbat candles), without stressing religious faith. They did not relate especially to *Kashrut* or to family purity, nor did they see any connection between these rituals and health. Fifty-seven percent described themselves as secular or traditional, and there was no marked difference between the two (see Table IV).

Nearly three-fourths of the Ashkenazim came to the clinic on their own initiative, including those patients who had no prior therapeutic experience (Table VIII). In most cases persons in their social network advised them to turn to the clinic; in some instances the treatment was a topic of informal social conversation. With the exception of the ultra-orthodox, none of the Ashkenazim consulted a rabbi or a rabbi-healer. However, many enrolled or attended agencies which are fashionable in Israel today, such as Yoga, meditation and astrology. They attended the psychiatric clinic and these agencies simultaneously and for the same reasons.

Relative to other *edot*, the Ashkenazim we interviewed mentioned few symptoms when they described their problems. In checking the list of symptoms we elicited from all patients, we find that their symptoms do not cluster together, but are rather distributed throughout most of the categories. There is a tendency to mention depression, insecurity, and a "weak character." Relative to other *edot*, most of the Ashkenazim mentioned many more psychological than psychosomatic symptoms, and the proportion of psychosomatic to psychological complaints was lower than the other two groups (Table VII). They describe their condition in psychological terms, attribute their psychosomatic symptoms to a psychological source, and expect that their psychosomatic complaints will be "cured" as a result of psychological treatment. They typically describe the causes of their problems as an interaction between internal personality traits (such as "character" and "heredity") and external factors such as early childhood socialization or family and social problems. Eighty-three percent attributed equal weight to internal and external features as the cause of psychological problems and mental illness. Indeed, the mutual interaction among the different features stands out in their explanations (Table VI).

Sixty-three percent of the Ashkenazim are not certain that it is possible to completely cure their psychological problems; some character traits or external factors are likely to persist. However, they maintain that it is possible to improve one's situation by undergoing psychological treatment that would increase their self-awareness and provide tools to deal with the problems.

The Ashkenazi patients perceive mental and physical illness as two separate categories and emphasize the interaction between them. This differentiation allows them to more readily accept the specialization that exists in Israeli medical services. As patients in psychiatric clinics, they emphasize psychological symptoms and tendencies; thus they relegate psychosomatic symptoms to psychological sources and expect to be relieved of them by treatment in the clinic. They also use concepts or terms that are common in psychology and medicine and that are often used by staff members – such terms as "socialization," "internalization of early childhood experiences," or "the interplay between nature and nurture." They tend to distinguish between mental illness as an unusual condition and psychological problems as a common situation; as a consequence they are also less sensitive to stigma or social pressures regarding psychological problems. It follows as well that it is easier for them to consult with members of their social networks regarding their problems and to accept the fact that they are in psychological treatment.

These patients expect to receive tools that will enable them to be aware of their problems and cope with them more successfully. On the other hand, they do not expect to be entirely cured. They also imagine treatment to be a lengthy process, and some are therefore disappointed when the clinic staff decides upon short-term psychotherapy for them. A kind of "popularized" medicine and psychology is an integral feature of their symbols and understandings. In the clinic this is evidenced by the ways in which they readily accept interpretations and understand the language of treatment, the consistency between their expectations and those of the staff members, and their faithfully maintaining the "therapeutic contract" with the clinic staff.

Most of the Ashkenazim completed treatment or were continuing in regular therapy a year later. Those who dropped out during the year had attended about twenty therapy sessions (Table VIII). When we interviewed them a year later, the patients tended to describe positive changes in their feelings and behavior. They attributed these changes to tools that they acquired during therapy, and saw a potential for additional changes via continuing or future treatment.

3. *The Moroccan Patients*

There are 443,901 Moroccan Jews in Israel, and they constitute 14.6% of the Jewish population (Central Bureau of Statistics 1980). They are the largest non-Ashkenazi *edah*. Moroccan Jews who immigrated to Israel are a heterogeneous population whose exposure in Morocco to the influence of French culture was not uniform. A number of studies (Weingrod 1960a, 1960b, Bar-Yosef 1970), have described the consecutive processes of acculturation of Moroccan Jews to French culture in Morocco and subsequently to Israel after immigration. They conclude that this was a kind of double cultural shock, and suggest that it may, at least in part, explain the special position of Moroccans in Israel. The Moroccan *edah* is described as having a negative social stereotype (Shuval 1956). Given this stereotype, Moroccans have tended to emphasize their own ethnic identity. Members of this *edah* are prominent in ethnic-class struggles in which they see themselves as representative of all the non-Ashkenazi groups. Moroccans have recently become more upwardly mobile, and some have achieved positions of political power.

Shula is one of twenty-nine clinic patients of Moroccan origin whom we interviewed. She is nineteen years old and was born in Fez, Morocco, where her family had lived for many generations. Shula is the eighth of twelve children. When she was one year old, her family immigrated to Israel by way of France. During the first year they lived in an outlying development town populated mainly by Moroccan immigrants; they then moved to Jerusalem and made their home in a low-income neighborhood. Shula was married at age 17; she gave birth a year later and is pregnant again. After her marriage she and her husband lived in a low income neighborhood, but more recently they moved to a new and attractive apartment.

Her father completed several years of school in Morocco. There he had a fruit and vegetable store; while in Israel he is employed as an unskilled wage laborer. Her mother had no schooling and is a housewife. She and her older siblings completed religious primary school, and her younger siblings attend high school. In her family of origin Moroccan Arabic is mainly spoken; she converses in Hebrew with her siblings and in her own nuclear family.

Shula's husband is twenty-five-years-old and was born in Israel of "Oriental" (but not Moroccan) parents. He has a primary school education. Recently he has not been working steadily. Prior to her marriage Shula had also worked, but she is presently unemployed. She and her family manage economically with the help of welfare payments.

In common with the other Moroccan patients, Shula has ambivalent, contradicatory feelings regarding her *edah*. She often contrasts the positive situation of Moroccan Jews in Morocco with their negative position in Israel. Her description mirrors the negative stereotype of Moroccans in Israel as "aggressive" and "primitive"; she accepts the stereotype as accurate, but since they were different in Morocco she blames Israeli society for having caused these negative features. Shula (who left Morocco when she was a year old) says: "It was better there. Here it's bad, all the hardship, income tax, discrimination. Here there are thieves and criminals. We Moroccans are hot tempered and nervous. In Morocco there was proper education, there were no divorces, no rabbinate (in Israel divorce is determined by religious courts), no police, and parents kept peace at home." At the same time she also interprets her family's behaviour in Morocco as "primitive," basing this on her father's stories of how parents demanded "too much respect – without limits" from their children.

She defines herself and her family of origin as "traditional" and says: "I keep the commandments, light candles, observe *mikveh* (ritual bath), maintain family purity." She believes that *kashrut* and family purity are important for health reasons.

Shula came to the clinic on her own initiative. According to her own diagnosis she was suffering from "*pahad*" (fear) and "*dika'on*" (depression). She was diagnosed by the clinic staff as having an "immature personality." Her principal complaints included "heart attacks," absence of desire, fear and worry.

She describes her condition in the following terms: "I felt problems, I'm shaking, I'm deathly afraid, it's as if I have heart attacks. Before I only had thoughts. All the thoughts started after the wedding, and the *dika'on* (depression) started after the birth. Many times I got angry, fell down, and couldn't breathe – as if I was finished. They called an ambulance; I had tests and they gave me injections. They, the doctors, know what I have; they say, 'nerves,' 'depression.' I have no patience, I'm fed up with everything, I have no desire to do anything, not food, not my husband, not movies, no desire."

Shula has serious problems with her family of origin and within her own nuclear family. She claims that her family of origin threw her out of the house at a young age and pays no attention to her; she is alone. She also feels that her husband does not meet her expectations. Before marriage her goals in life conformed to a "model" that she saw as the norm in Israeli society. They included a tall, blond, educated and wealthy husband, a social circle in which people talk about politics, and a new apartment in a good "cultured" neighborhood. In fact, as she describes her situation, she is married to a short, dark man – in her words, "The black I caught, a card shark, full of hashish and debts, in a 'primitive' neighborhood where we live like beasts." (This refers to their first apartment.) Later, when we met for the second interview in her new apartment, she described her hopes that she would learn from her neighbors how to organize her household, set an elegant table and carry on a proper conversation.

She began to see herself as different from her neighbors due to her different life-style which, as she explained, was the result of her economic circumstances: "If I could go to a movie once a week, I'd develop and wouldn't need a psychologist!" She attributes her depression to the rift with her family of origin, disappointment with her husband and lack of financial resources.

According to Shula, her psychological problems were expressed in acute attacks. She suffered from *pahad* (fear) and *dika'on* (depression) as well as apathy, nervousness and worry; all these precipitated crises such as heart attacks, lack of breath, loss of consciousness, shaking and blanching. She explained too that the causes of her problems were external to herself and resulted from her family and economic situation. She believed that psychological problems can be prevented or cured: "it depends on life – psychological problems are only in life."

Shula attended the psychiatric clinic ten times, often alone and at other times with her husband. She then dropped out of treatment without informing the staff. Shula says that she was disappointed by the clinic. She had expected that the treatment would consist of advice, guidance, calming and financial help. Instead, the psychiatrist "asks me all sorts of questions and it isn't pleasant. They should give advice about what to do." She blames the therapy for causing her fear of death. She says: "I also had *pahadim* (fears) before, but without cause, and they would ask me if the fear is fear of death, and if the depression is connected with my daughter, and it 'took' (literally: 'came into me') – it's psychological" Shula also complained that she didn't receive financial help, because "they didn't understand her."

In addition to attending the clinic, Shula also went on several occasions to consult with rabbis who deal in cabalistic healing. She explains that she turned to the two sources for different reasons: "*Dika'on* (depression) is for the psycholgoist; it isn't shameful, it's the brain. The rabbi treats *pahad* (fear) and not *dika'on*".

Bilu (1978), who studied illnesses with demonic etiology among Moroccans from the Atlas Mountains living in small Israeli villages, describes the concept "fear" (*pahad*) as having roots in Moroccan tradition. *Pahad* is a cause, not an effect; it is related to many symptoms of an acute or "attack" nature, like choking, heart illness, fainting, crying, and paralysis of hands and feet. Other symptoms which he found resulting from *pahad* were *dimayon* (imagination), a traditional concept referring mainly to excessive thoughts, and *dika'on* (depression), a more modern concept acquired through contact with western medicine. *Dika'on* appears as a response secondary to *pahad* and *dimayon*.

There are many parallels between Shula's remarks and those of the other Moroccan patients in our population. Like Shula, they also identify strongly with their *edah*; moreover, they attribute their low social status to immigration and put the blame upon Israeli society. The conflict between their *edah* and the wider society also affects them as individuals. For example, among some of the patients there is an expressed desire to achieve in order to prove to the society that Moroccans can be "good" and "successful." This is also true of those better educated Moroccans who immigrated to Israel more recently; despite the fact that their social status is higher they feel that the stereotypes applied to Moroccans damage them as well.

Most of the Moroccans observe the same religious commandments as Shula, and some also see a link between *kashrut*, family purity and health. Indeed, they tend to define themselves as traditional and religious (Table IV).

We found a tendency for the Moroccan interviewees to describe psychosomatic symptoms as attacks: "heart attacks," fainting, body shaking, "black-out" (*Shahor b'eynayim*), a "catch" in the throat, binding of hands and feet. The descriptions were acute and dramatic. Although they described all of the psychosomatic "attacks" extensively and in detail, they nonetheless stressed the psychological symptoms and define their problems as psychological. "Nervousness" appears as the most common symptom accompanying these "attacks"; other psychological complaints described were "disquiet", "crying", "*dika'on*" (depression), and "extensive worries and thoughts" (Table VII).

Eighty-one percent of the Moroccan patients located psychological problems and mental illness in the "head" or the "brain" and not in the body. They clearly distinguished between physical and mental disease and the place in which each type is located (Table VI).

The symptoms presented by our Moroccan interviewees also resembled those found by Bilu, even though our patients represented less traditional segments and came from other parts of Morocco. Less mention was made of *pahad*, perhaps because the population is less traditional. Unlike Bilu's findings, in our population there are only a few traces of demonic and magic etiology – primarily evil eye – and little mention of demons and witchcraft as causes of illness.

Seventy-eight percent of the Moroccans defined the onset of disease in "external circumstances" (Table VI). Among the main external facts were economic or family problems, or broadly, "the society." The Moroccan patients believed in the possibility of curing psychological problems or illnesses; half of them made the cure conditional on external factors, since they considered these to be the source of the problem (Table VI).

About half of the Moroccan patients came on their own initiative, while the other half were sent by doctors or, in some cases, by social service agencies (Table VIII). Seventy-three percent of those who came on their own differed from Shula in that they were advised by others to turn to treatment. By relating their problems to difficult life circumstances, the Moroccan patients are able to explain their reaction as unavoidable: the fault or blame is in the environment. This has the effect of lessening the social stigma regarding psychological problems and/or mental illness, and they are therefore ready to discuss their problems with others (Table VI). This includes members of their own generation – friends and family – although, like Shula, they tend to hide the topic from parents, who in their opinion do not understand psychological matters and will consider them to be "crazy."

Like Shula, about half of the Moroccans turned to rabbi healers with the same problems they brought to the clinic (Table VIII). Others went to rabbis with problems of infertility, birth, illness in the family, a wedding or a trip abroad.

Shula's critical response to therapy was typical of most of the Moroccans we interviewed. They too had expected to receive advice, guidance and help (Table VI); like Shula, they did not make a connection between actual and external problems, on the one hand, and the past or psychological interpretations, on the other. The psychodynamic approach forced them to dwell on matters that made them less calm. The expectations and reactions of Moroccan patients with more education were closer to the conceptions of treatment held by the therapists. Nonetheless, their symptomatic expressions were in most ways similar to the other Moroccans in our population.

Shula's behavior resembles that of 69% of the Moroccans who did not continue in regular treatment and left after less than ten sessions (Table VIII). The rest completed psychological treatment or were still in treatment a year later. These patients tended to be from among those with higher education. It should also be noted that the patients we interviewed a year later (including some of those who dropped out of treatment) described changes that had taken place in themselves regarding their work, residence and "feeling." Those who had dropped out entirely attributed the changes not so much to therapy but to changes in their situation.

While there is an almost equal emphasis upon both psychological and psychosomatic symptoms, the Moroccans tend to define their problems as psychological and make use of psychological terminology. For the therapists, this may create the impression that beyond these concepts there is a potential for psychological insight, and they may instill expectations regarding the patient's ability to accept explanations. Typically, however, the interpretative message of the therapist is not accepted and even arouses opposition; transferring problems from the past to the present creates a situation exacerbating pain and fear.

The onset of dramatic, acute attacks among the Moroccan patients leads them to expect rapid solutions from the clinic staff. They await advice that will relieve the pressures from the life areas that are seen to be the source of the problem. They tend to believe that it is possible to be completely cured of mental disease by altering the source of the problem – that is, changing the external circumstances. On their part, the clinic staff tends to see these requests as instrumental or attempts at secondary gain. Even in those instances in which the patients' circumstances are clearly problematic, the clinic's ability to solve problems stemming from social circumstances is limited at best. Taken as a whole, there is thus a considerable gap between the Moroccan patients' view and that held by the clinic staff. The accord between them is typically unstable and the patients tend therefore to drop out of treatment.

CONCLUSIONS

A summary of the data is present in Table VI to VIII below. The data are arranged according to *edot* and review our major findings. In this final section we wish to place special emphasis upon the relevance of our research for the treatment process.

The Persian patients were sent to the psychiatric clinic after the health system failed to find any organic basis for their somatic complaints. Their experiences at the clinic must be seen as one more in a series of contacts with health practitioners of various kinds. In turning to many different experts, they magnify their own anxiety and confusion. In addition, because of the stigma of mental illness and psychological problems, coming to the psychiatric clinic may arouse considerable fear. Consequently, they tend to reject the clinic as a solution and emphaszie the symptoms that provide a legitimate interpretation of their condition as physical. They are prepared to accept the doctor's role, but not that of the other professionals in the psychiatric clinic. However, the clinic staff does not make this distinction. When the Persians receive psychotherapy, they tend to reject the therapist's interpretation as irrelevant to their condition. These factors, together with somatization on the part of the Persian patients, cause uneasiness and embarrassment to the staff. The staff's attitude, in turn, may reinforce the Persians' desire to quit treatment and to deal with their condition on their own or with the help of other doctors.

The Moroccans emphasize the view that social or economic problems are at the source of their difficulties. This allows them to blame society and to see the clinic as part of the welfare system. They expect the staff to give them instrumental help and take an active interest in their life situation. There are contradictions between this view and the way in which the clinic staff defines its tasks: on the one hand, the clinic may intervene in a patient's situation if it is seen to damage his or her mental health to a serious degree; on the other hand, the therapeutic model strongly emphasizes the notion that treatment must enable the patient to deal with his situation by himself. As a result of the conflicting view of therapy, many of the Moroccan patients ultimately reject the clinic's attitude and interpretation. Nevertheless, their view of themselves as suffering from objectively difficult life circumstances reduces the stigma they might otherwise feel and tends to ease their return to the clinic.

The Ashkenazi patients have a certain cultural familiarity with the clinic's staff and consequently tend to accept the role of the therapist and the therapeutic contract. Psychological interpretation is not foreign to them, although this may reflect popular knowledge rather than deep psychological understanding. Among the Ashkenazim (with the exception of the ultra-orthodox), stigma is related mainly to mental illness, as distinct from psychological problems.

TABLE VI

Conception of mental illness and psychological problems in the three *Edot*

	Categories of physical and mental illness		Site of physical and mental illness			Location of cause	Possibility of curing	Expectation from treatment		Group stigma regarding mental illness and psychological problems	
			One	Two							
	One	Two		Separated	Interaction			Short-term	Long-term	Strong	Weak
Persians	27%	73%	58% Body	42% Body and Head or Brain		36% Internal 24% External 36% Internal and External	22% depends on illness	Explanation and advice		For both	
Moroccans		100%	8%	92% Body and Head or Brain		85% External	52% depends on external factors	Advice and practical assistance			For both
Ashenazim		96%	20%		80% Body and Soul or Head or Brain	81% Internal and External	37% depends on psycho-logical treatment		Psycho-logical awareness Medicine treatment for ultra-orthodox	For mental illness	For psycho-logical problems

TABLE VII
General Map of Complaints in the Three *Edot*

	Focus of complaints	Proportion of physical psychological complaints	Relevant symptoms
Persian	Physical	0.62	Fear 48% Excessive worries 48% Digestive problems 48% Nervousness 44%
Moroccan	Psychological and physical	0.41	Nervousness 74% Depression 44% No desire 41% Excessive worries 41%
Ashkenazim	Psychological	0.31	Distribution rather than focusing on particular symptoms

Indeed, psychological treatment may enhance rather than damage one's social status. The Ashkenazi patients often refer to their problems openly in social situations, and they are also prepared to interpret the behavior of others in psychological terms.

These points reflect contrasting understandings among the three *edot*. However, some views are common to Persian and Moroccan patients. For example, members of both groups held to the traditional belief that supernatural powers can cause illness. Another belief common to both groups is the relation of health with *kashrut* and family purity. These traditional beliefs are reinforced by the rabbi healers to whom members of these *edot* tended to turn.

In the data we presented, we saw that most of the Persian and Moroccan patients dropped out of treatment after a few sessions. In contrast, the Ashkenazim continued, and those who dropped out did so after a longer time in therapy. While at first glance it appears that this is another instance of differences between Ashkenazi and "Oriental" *edot*, the reality is much more complex: all three of the groups differ in their understanding of their problems and their expectations from treatment. Both the Persian and the Ashkenazi patients considered themselves to be the focus of treatment, but each emphasized different causes of illness: the Persians stressed organic sources, while the Ashkenazim emphasized psychological features. This contrasts, in turn, with the Moroccans who tended to interpret the cause of mental illness and the locus of treatment as external. To cite another example, Moroccan as well as Ashkenazi patients defined their problems as psychological, but while the Ashkenazim translate

TABLE VIII

Tendencies of behavior concerning the problems and treatment in the three *Edot*

	Advice from the social network to consult psychological therapists	Traditional Agencies consulted	Source of referral to the clinic	Not continue treatment	Recommend psychological treatment to others
Persian	26%	54%	Medical – 48% Self – 27%	74%	33%
Moroccan	52%	48%	Self – 52% Medical – 34% Welfare Agency – 14%	69%	93%
Ashkenazim	59%	22%*	Self – 71% Medical – 22%	21%	79%

* Nearly all were ultra-orthodox.

"psychological" to mean internalized personality factors, the Moroccan meaning is related more to a reaction to external features.

In regard to expectations from treatment, both the Moroccans and the Persians thought that they would receive brief treatment and advice. Yet each sought different advice: the Persians wanted an explanation of their medical situation, while the Moroccans expected instrumental advice to help with their daily problems. In constrast, the Ashkenazim expected to broaden their psychological knowledge regarding their own problems, and they frequently were insistent about wanting to remain in treatment.

These cultural differences can also be seen in the patients' own definitions of their problems. In each of the cases presented the patient arrived at the clinic with the same self-diagnosis: depression and fear (or anxiety). At the same time, each described his or her symptoms and the source of the problems in terms of his or her own cultural norms. Dina, the Persian patient, felt ill since her physical symptoms distinguished her from her neighbors who lived in similar circumstances. The diagnosis of her problems as psychological led her to suspect that she was mentally ill. David, the Ashkenazi patient, accepted his limits and defined himself as a person with psychological problems. His sense of difference arose from the fact that his problems limited his ability to perform roles expected by members of his *edah*. Shula, the Moroccan patient, began to feel different when she contrasted her life-style and living conditions with those of her neighbors in her new neighborhood. She did not define herself as ill, but maintained that her difficult economic situation affected her psychological state.

Finally, this research raises problems for future study. To what extent is it possible to map distinctive symptoms for each *edah*? To what extent are such symptoms used to organize behavior when the individual is in a situation of conflict? It would also be valuable to look at verbal utterances and analyze the terms used by members of each *edah* in describing their problems.

It is hoped that the data we have presented here, as well as data from additional studies, will help to expand our understanding of the "clinical reality" (Kleinman et al. 1978). In multi-cultural situations such as Israel, understanding the patient's mental health concepts is a basic requirement for effective treatment. The point is not that certain types of therapy are "better suited" to particular populations: as we see it, the patients' beliefs and understanding regarding illness and health should be built into the therapists' approach irrespective of the therapeutic treatment he or she employs.

Talbieth Hospital, Jerusalem

NOTES

1 The research was conducted by a multidisciplinary team including a psychiatrist (Krasilovsky) and three anthropologists (Minuchin-Itzigsohn, Ben-Shaoul, Weingrod). It was initiated and sponsored by Talbieh Hospital, Jerusalem, a psychiatric hospital belonging to the General Federation of Labor's "Sick Fund". We are grateful to the Jerusalem Center for Anthropological Studies and its director, Dr. Edgar Siskin, for generous support. We should like to thank Dr. Eileen Basker and Prof. Virginia R. Dominguez for their extensive assistance in editing and translating. We also wish to thank Dr. Ram Aronson, director of the clinic at Talbieh Hospital, Dr. Jose Itzigsohn, director of the clinic at Ezrat Nashim Hospital, and Dr. Shlomo Litman, director of the clinic at Eitanim Hospital, and to express our appreciation to the staffs of all the clinics for their understanding of the significance of the research and for their help. We thank all of the patients who participated in this study. Finally, we wish to express our thanks to the editor of CMP and the anonymous readers for their many helpful suggestions.

2 The public health system in Israel treats Arabs as well as Jews. However, in this research project, it was only the Jewish population which was the object of study.

3 The public psychiatric out-patient clinics in Israel accept patients without charge, according to geographic catchment area. Each clinic accepts patients from specified neighborhoods, and the divisions by *edah* are therefore ecological and not indicative of the size of the group or its rate of treatment.

4 *Edah* (plural: *edot*) is a Jewish socio-cultural unit. In Israel, the term is used both in scientific work and in popular and political usage. *Edah* is similar to the notion of "ethnic group", although it is not a "clean" category of classification. Generally there is congruence between *edah* and country of origin, but not always. It is customary in Israel to refer to Ashkenazim as one *edah*, although they immigrated from many different countries. We chose to interview only Ashkenazim from Middle or Eastern European backgrounds who were born in Israel because they belong to the group which represents the dominant culture.

5 *Kashrut* is the ritual observance of dietary laws in Judaism. "Purity of the family" is a concept in Judaism governing the taboo on women during "pollution" connected with the menstrual cycle and the puerperal period. The belief that these two commandments are important for health was widespread in the ancient world, and is reflected both in the Talmud (in which edicts concerning menstruation and the post-partum period are grounded in medical and physiological arguments) and in the writings of Maimonides (who connects forbidden food with sickness).

6 In Hebrew the word *nefesh* (soul, spirit) has many meanings. Psychiatric clinics are formally called "clinics for the health of the *nefesh*" (mental health). In the adjective form, *nafshi* may mean "psychological", as in *ba'aya nafshit* (psychological problem), or "mental", as in *mahala nafshit* (mental illness), the latter carrying connotations of craziness.

7 a. The differences may be explained as deriving from the fact that the two studies are based upon different populations. Good studied a Muslim, mainly Kurdish population that was centered in a rural area in Iran. Our population is composed of immigrants to Israel who, while Iranian, are urban and Jewish. b. It is interesting to note that the Persians in Israel frequently make use of the term "Dehl" (and not "Qualb"). This term has two meanings – heart and belly. In both senses it is used as a metaphor for emotion.

8 The term "Parsitis" is derived from Parsi, the Hebrew term for Persia. This is not a formal label, but rather a kind of oral tradition among therapists. Good (1977) and Langsley et al. (1983) describe analogous symptoms, such as fear, worry and somatization in Iranian populations. They also describe "fright" as a culture-bound

disorder. We did not find "fright" to be characteristic of this population, although "fear" was associated with health problems.

9 Our conclusions in this regard contrast with Basker et al. who did not find support for "Parsitis". The differences in the findings may be related to two factors. First, the method of data collection differs; as noted by Basker et al, their data were gathered from case records which are the end result of a filtration of the patient's presentation. In our study there was no such filter since we directly recorded everything said by the patient. Second, the size of the sample also differs. Basker et al. examined a large sample of records (196) compared to our smaller sample size (27).

10 We were only able to interview a small number of ultra-religious patients since they typically arrived at the clinic in a psychotic state (as diagnosed by the staff). Members of these groups live in homogeneous, tightly organized communities that are directed by religious leaders. They have distinctive ideologies emphasizing religious learning and ritual practices; indeed, the status of males depends heavily upon their reputation as "learned". Members of these groups sometimes relate their psychological problems to failure in study. At the clinic most receive follow-up care, and they also get spiritual support from rabbis. Ultra-orthodox patients tend to accept the patient role and maintain the "therapeutic contract" with the assistance of close family members and their rabbi.

REFERENCES

Bar-Yosef, R.
1970 The Moroccans. Background to the Problem. *In* Eisenstadt, S. N., Bar-Yosef, R. and Adler, C. (eds.), Integration and Development in Israel. Jerusalem: Israel Universities Press, pp. 419–429.

Basker, E., Beran, B. M. and Kleinhauz, M.
1982 A Social Science Perspective on the Negotiation of a Psychiatric Diagnosis. Social Psychiatry 17: 53–58.

Bastide, R.
1968 Sociologie des Maladies Mentales. Paris: Flammarion.
1978 Le Prochain et le Lointain. Paris: Cuyas.

Bilu, Y.
1978 Traditional Psychiatry in Israel: Moroccan-Born Moshav Members with Psychiatric Disorders and Problems in Living and their Traditional Healers. Thesis for the degree Doctor of Philosophy (submitted to the Senate of the Hebrew University, Jerusalem) (in Hebrew).

Central Bureau of Statistics
1980 The Demographic Characteristics of the Population in Israel 1977–1978. Jerusalem: Government Printing Office.

Deshen, S., and Shokeid, M.
1974 The Predicament of Homecoming. Ithaca: Cornell University Press.

Devereux, G.
1973 Essais d'Ethnopsychiatrie Generale. Paris: Gallimard.

Eaton, W. W., Lasry, J. C., and Sigal, J.
1979 Ethnic Relations and Community Mental Health among Israeli Jews. The Israel Annals of Psychiatry and Related Disciplines 17: 165–174.

Eaton, W. W., and Levav, I.
1982 Schizophrenia, Social Class and Ethnic Disadvantage: A Study of First Hospitalization Among Israeli-Born Jews. The Israeli Journal of Psychiatry 19(4):

Eisenstadt, S. N.
1955 The Absorption of Immigrants. Glencoe: Free Press.

Good, B. J.
1977 The Heart of What's the Matter. The Semantic of illness in Iran. Culture, Medicine and Psychiatry 1: 25–58.
Kleinman, A., Eisenberg, L., and Good, B.
1978 Culture, Illness and Care. Annals of Internal Medicine 88: 251–258.
Langsley, D. G., Barter, J. T., and Amir-Moshiri, A.
1983 Psychiatry in Iran and China. Social Psychiatry 29: 39–47.
Shuval. J.
1956 Patterns of Inter-group Tension and Affinity. International Social Science Bulletin, Vol. VIII, pp. 75–126.
Smooha, S.
1978 Israel: Puralism and Conflict. Berkeley: University of California Press.
Weingrod, A.
1960a Moroccan Jewry in Transition. Megamot 10: 193–208 (Hebrew).
1960b Change and Continuity in a Moroccan Immigrant Moshav. Megamot 10: 322–335 (Hebrew).
1965 Israel: Group Relations in a New Society. London: Pall Mall.

Part III

The Health Services and Professional Socialization

18

Politics and Medicine: The Case of Israeli National Health Service

Yael Yishai

Medical policy of which the system of national health insurance is one of its basic elements, is determined by a variety of factors. It is an outcome of economic considerations and availability of resources [1]; it is affected by prevailing values and social norms [2]; and it also results in political struggles and conflicts over powerholds. Previous studies of National Health Insurance (NHI) explained its introduction in terms of group politics [3] or class struggle [4]. The Israeli case of the NHI presents another dimension of medical policy—the utilization of medical policy by political parties as an instrument for acquiring political power.

The debate on the introduction of the NHI is as old as the state itself, and to date has not been resolved. Several times throughout the 32 years of Israel's existence the NHI issue has been on the top of the political agenda, attracting public and elite attention. However, its proponents were never powerful enough to surmount objections, which in effect hindered any change. The NHI continues to be viewed as the 'brightest star' in welfare statism [5]. Hence it is rather surprising that Israel remains one of the welfare states [6] in which NHI has not been introduced. This paper purports to examine the development of the NHI proposals in the Israeli history, to identify the actors involved in the struggle over its adoption and to explain the factors (in terms of power relations) which prevented the acceptance of any scheme, thus creating a stalemate in the provision of health services.

THE PROBLEM

The Israeli health care system presents a paradox: on the one hand a great majority (96%) of the population is covered by a voluntary health insurance and medical care is provided by one major and four small nonprofit sick funds. On the other hand the system suffers from a serious malaise of proliferated services which put a heavy financial burden on the state's budget and render their inefficiency [7]. The search for organizational remedies for these problems dates back to the early days of statehood. These may be summarized in two major proposals: one to make insurance compulsory but at the same time to retain the 'pluralism' of health services, i.e. the existing multiple medical institutions. This opinion was held by the left wing parties and their affiliated organizations, which had a strong vested interest in the prevailing health care structure. The other proposal favored the concentration of health facilities in one central organ under state control and the nationalization of health services regardless of organizational affiliation. Surprisingly the supporters of nationalizing the medical services have been those who are usually identified with free enterprise and social decentralization—the right wing parties. The explanation of this paradox lies in Israel's power structure and in the nature of the political processes which determine the allocation of national (including the medical) resources.

POLITICAL ACTORS: WHO WANTS WHAT, WHEN AND HOW?

The actors who played a role in the formulation of the NHI policy may be divided into three categories: (a) medical organizations consisting of the sick funds and the ministry of health; (b) political parties with which the sick funds are affiliated and (c) interest groups, the chief of which is the Israeli Medical Association (IMA).

MEDICAL ORGANIZATIONS: THE SICK FUNDS

The Israeli sick funds are the prominent actors in the formulation of the NHI policy since, as previously noted, the majority of the population is in effect insured by them. Most of the sick funds have a rather distinct socio-political basis which is manifested either by affiliation with a political party or by a linkage with a social group.

The general workers sick fund (KH)

KH is the largest and the oldest sick fund in Israel covering approx. 70% of the state's population. It was established in 1912 by a group of 150 Jewish settlers in order to cope with the medical hardships encountered by them in their new country. In 1920, with the founding of the Histadrut (the General Federation of Workers) KH became officially affiliated with it in terms of membership and financial resources [8]. This affiliation fitted well into the Histadrut's functions. While being a federation of trade unions the Histadrut was (and to a large extent still is) engaged in various enterprises such as construction, farming, banking and cultural activities. Provision of medical services was regarded as a national imperative geared to the fulfillment of the Histadrut comprehensive functions. Since the Histadrut is dominated by the Labor parties the health issue became highly politicized and subject to power contests and rivalries.

With the passage of time KH has grown into a medical empire encompassing a variety of health services. It owns about one-third of the general hospital beds (3931) located in 15 medical institutions. Ambulatory services are provided in 1225 clinics throughout the country. In development towns and remote peripheries KH is the only provider of health care services, a fact which has bearing on its mode of budgeting. KH is financed by three sources: membership dues, which are part of the Histadrut's fees and are calculated on a percentage rate from the members' income with a ceiling regardless of the insured age or family size [9]. The members' dues provide only about a half of KH's budget.

Second, employers' funds which comprise an amount equal to 3.7% of the workers' salary (42% of the budget) [10]. Last, but by all means not least, KH is financed by the government in a variety of ways: its hospital services are subsidized in recognition of its central role in the provision of health care. There is also direct funding which amounted to one-third of KH's budget during the Labor's control of government and fell to approx. 13% in 1977 when the Likud ascended to power. Even then half of the Ministry of Health's budget was due to finance the sick funds [11] of which KH gets the lion's share. The membership of KH is made up primarily of the Histadrut's members whose affiliation with KH is obligatory. As a rule, one cannot enjoy the benefits of the sick fund without being a union member, nor can one be a Histadrut member without having to pay for KH. In addition, other individuals such as elderly poor people, disabled and welfare recipients are insured under a number of governmental programs. KH also provides health services for members of the religious parties (the National Religious Party—NRP and Agudat Israel) who are affiliated with it through their organizations and not as individuals. Hence with total insurees of 2,890,000 and 29,397 employees KH became one of the most powerful organizations not only in the health domain but in the country at large.

The other sick funds

Beside KH four other sick funds provide health services to the Israeli populace, however on a much smaller scale. The National Sick Fund, covering 6.3% of the population, is affiliated with the right wing Herut and was established (1933) by its political antecedents for people who could not obtain, for political reasons, medical care from the Histadrut.

The deep animosity between the two political wings of the Israeli establishment rendered the separation of health services. However in contrast to KH the National Sick Fund distinguished between membership in the medical organization and in the trade union. This separation exists to date even though the Likud (including Herut) joined the Histadrut (1964). The National Sick Fund still appeals to Herut's adherents although many of them have joined the Histadrut and concomitantly KH.

The people's Sick Fund was established (in 1930) as a medical service for the members of the former General Zionists (at present also part of the Likud) who were dwellers of larger rural settlements. This sick fund, whose membership consists of 8% of the insured population, attracts mainly a middle class constituency and self employed people. Currently the political affiliation of the People's Sick Fund is rather tenuous. The same applies to Maccabi, which was the outcome of a private enterprise of unemployed physicians (1941) mainly from Central Europe, who sought a solution to their occupational problems. Maccabi appeals mainly to professionals and the affluent segments of the urban population. Following amalgamation with another small sick fund (Asaf) it comprises approx. 12% of the insured population.

In contrast to KH the smaller sick funds do not maintain hospitals and their medical services are dispensed in the physicians' private clinics. Hospitalization is obtained in governmental and voluntary institutions. They, like their big counterpart, also enjoy governmental subsidy for their operations which are concentrated mainly in the big urban centers.

The introduction of the plans for NHI has become a major concern for all sick funds and especially for KH, whose attitudes toward the issue remained unchanged. It totally rejected the proposal to nationalize the health services in which case it would turn into 'provider of services' under the auspices of the state. The opposition of KH to this proposal rests on three grounds: ideological, political and economic.

As a carrier of socialist ideas and as an extension of a socialist movement KH promotes the ideology of mutual aid, regarding the provision of health care services as one of the major functions of a social organization. Since its inception the Histadrut viewed medical treatment as the very essence of mutual responsibility and self help. The physician, as his counterpart the teacher, was not evaluated on the basis of his professional skill and achievements but rather on the merit of his contributions to the collective goals. The medical doctor was a pioneer just as those who ploughed the soil [12]. Reminiscence of this attitude may be traced even in the present era where the salience of collective goals has sharply declined and the Histadrut has become an all-powerful organization promoting the interests of its members, especially those with a strong pressure capacity. Yet, a genuine 'pioneer' is still expected to follow the rules of mutual aid and to be a member of both the Histadrut and its KH. The Labor Movement still promulgates ideological symbols although in practice it hardly adheres to them.

There is another ideological aspect of objection to the nationalization of health services, grounded in the notion of voluntary participation [13]. KH is presumably the expression of public will and therefore should not be nationalized to become a state organ. Being a voluntary organization (i.e. not owned by the state) KH is the epitome of social pluralism on which democratic society rests, and is in sharp contrast to government controlled enterprises. Hence, in an ostensible paradoxical manner it was the left oriented Labor and its affiliated sick fund which promoted free enterprise in terms of autonomy to each voluntary organization in the field of health care.

The political argument against the nationalization of NHI is almost obvious and is manifested in the makeup of KH institutions. The supreme KH organs are the conference and the supervisory council, both of which are composed on the basis of political affiliation [14]. The Board of Directors (including its chairman) is also politically rather than functionally oriented [15]. In fact appointments of directors of KH are usually a political act, quite often even without consulting the Histadrut. Hence one of KH's major concerns is to serve as a base of the political power of the Labor Party. This party, which until 1977 controlled the government and to date dominates the Histadrut, utilized KH in providing patronage and increasing its power resources. It was not only the financial assets of KH which would have been threatened in case nationalization was to take place, but also the dependency of the majority of the Israeli populace on the Histadrut's (and through it—on the party's) services. It is precisely the Likud's attempts to curb the Labor's power by dissociating the link between the sick fund and the Histadrut that generated blatant objections. The political source of opposition had another aspect: since the state's inception KH has been the major actor in setting up the health care agenda. It also had veto power thus determining the forces which exert influence on medical decision-making. The nationalization of health services and the introduction of NHI according to the Likud's version could have undermined KH central position in the medical power arena.

As for the economic basis of objection, this is linked to KH's position within the Histadrut. The sick fund is not only one of the country's largest organizations, employing nearly thirty thousand workers (including 5261 physicians) it is also the economic stronghold of the Histadrut. Since the fees to both organizations are united, KH actually finances the labor movement. The importance of KH in the Histadrut's budget is explained by the ratio of KH in the trade union's membership fees. KH's share in the 'united tax' paid by the Histadrut membership is approx. 60%. The rest is devoted to the maintenance of the Histadrut's expanding bureaucracy. Hence the Labor Union is dependent on KH for the operation of its administrative functions and objects to any infringement of its rights. The Labor Party also has a direct stake in maintaining the present financial arrangements. Part of the Histadrut taxes are termed 'party activities tax' which are distributed according to the proportionate strength of the various parties at the Histadrut elections. The nationalization of the health services would entail a heavy financial loss not only to the Histadrut but also to its dominant party—the Labor Party. As an alternative to the nationalization scheme KH proposed its own plan whereby health insurance would be compulsory but carried out by the existing sick funds. The sick fund's major objective was to ensure its organizational and budgetary autonomy after the enactment of NHI law. Hence KH opposed any leeway in the selection of a sick fund. It also opposed any proposal to ensure, by law or any other official decree, that the dissident would not be subject to any form of sanctions. Quite the contrary, the Histadrut declared that any of its members choosing sick fund other than KH would be expelled. The proposal to have fees collected by the National Insurance Institute was also totally rejected by KH for fear of losing control of the budgets.

Most of the other sick funds also rejected the attempt to nationalize the health system although from different reasons. The only sick fund which supported the NHI in its Likud version is, not surprisingly, the People's Sick Fund which is affiliated with Herut. For this organization, headed for the past two decades by the present Minister of Health (Mr Eliezer Shostak) 'statehood' is both an ideology and a political imperative. Needless to say, the power considerations overshadow the sick fund's vested interest. The nationalization of health insurance could curb the power of all sick funds, including that of Herut. This seemed a reasonable price of an organization which was always been in the periphery of both medical and political centers of power. Its gains, in terms of influence and resources, would outbid its losses.

The other sick funds, namely United and Maccabi, followed KH in their objection to the proposed NHI. The minor sick funds were apprehensive lest they be swallowed up by the all encompassing bureaucratic organization to be set up upon the affirmation of the Likud's bill. Naturally these sick funds have their own staff, both medical and clerical, who were suspicious of any proposed change.

THE MINISTRY OF HEALTH

Although Israel spends 7.5% of its GNP on health services [16] the ministry responsible for their administration does not rank high in terms of political power and importance. In fact the Ministry of Health was always headed by minor members of the coalition party (the religious partners from 1948–52; 1961–66; the General Zionists from 1952–55 and Mapam from 1955–61; 1966–77). Surprisingly as it may sound, during the nearly thirty years of Labor control the Ministry did not play a major role in the formulation of health policy. Instead, power was vested in extra-governmental institutions, the chief of which was KH.

POLITICAL PARTIES

Being such a politicized issue in a society in which parties predominate [17], it is not novel that all parties express, in their electoral platforms, their preferences regarding the NHI. Limits of space preclude discussion of the history of partisan attitudes, however, no major changes have been noticeable, hence, partisan positions exhibited in the Ninth (1977–1981) Knesset would present the major trends.

Israeli parties are divided between those in favor of a fully nationally administered NHI, including its financial aspects and those advocating NHI on the basis of the existing sick funds with an implicit predominance to KH. Generally speaking the supporters of the respective proposals are aligned with the right-left spectrum. There are, however, some exceptions to this rule. One of the extreme left wing parties (Shelli—a Zionist variation of the Communist party which failed to secure representation in the Tenth Knesset) demanded full nationalization of health services and their administration by the state, in accordance with the Socialist creed. This view was also shared by the so called center parties (Ratz—the Movement for Civil Rights, the Democratic Movement for Change and the Progressive Party) which were concerned with civil and individual liberties and promoted the idea of equal, universal treatment regardless of political affiliation. Needless to say the Likud, including its four parties, advocates full nationalization for political rather than ideological reasons. The only parties which adhere to the second, state free version are the Labor party and its affiliated (within the Alignment) Mapam. These parties regard the attempts of the Likud to advance NHI on the basis of their preferences as a naked political device, aimed at striking Labor in the core of its power. The religious parties have refrained from explicit attitudinizing toward NHI. The more extreme, Agudat Israel, owing perhaps to a lack of interest, the more moderate NRP—owing to its ambivalent position. The NRP has turned into a hawkish party sharing with the Likud its positions on foreign policy and is, at present, an enthusiastic coalition member. On the other hand, as earlier noted, most of the NRP's membership enjoy the services of KH. In fact, the party wishes to enter the Histadrut, however one of the Labor's conditions for its inclusion is linked with the NRP's position toward the NHI. The upshot of this ambivalence has been a non-accidental silence in public forums on the NHI issue. Only recently, with the introduction of the bill in the Knesset, the NRP joined the opposition and voted against it. Its defection from a government supported bill has not caused a political crisis since it was granted in the coalition agreement that the party has a right to veto the legislation of NHI if and when it wished to do so [18].

Political parties have not sufficed with articulating the issue in their platforms. They also may be regarded as the chief promoters of the issue to the political agenda and as those predominantly involved in the struggle over its implementation.

THE ISRAELI MEDICAL ASSOCIATION (IMA)

The IMA, founded in 1912, embraces approx. 95% of the physicians in Israel. At present, it consists of 6800 doctors, 85% of whom are salaried workers employed by two major institutions—KH and the government. The IMA is a professional association which promotes its members' interests rather than the general, national objectives. It is often engaged in militant labor disputes and is almost incessantly involved in wage negotiations. While its leaders have been publicly linked to political parties, the association as such refrains from explicit identification with any party. The dissociation between the IMA and the centers of power limited the former's potential influence, aside from wage negotiations. Professional control was accounted by Ivan Illich to be a major source of power [19]. In Israel the impact of the IMA on health policy making has been rather meagre. Only two legislative processes attracted the IMA's attention and induced its activity and involvement—the Anatomy and Pathology Law [20] and the NHI bill.

The interest of medical associations in NHI is universal and not surprising. Not only professional–economic interests are at stake, but the whole system of medical service is determined by such legislation. The IMA, in contrast to some of its counterparts, has been, by and large, in favor of NHI. Its position may be summarized as follows:

(1) NHI should cover the whole population and be state administered. Fees should be centrally collected by the National Insurance.

(2) The NHI should be freed from any political linkage either to political parties or to politicized trade unions.

(3) Freedom of choice should be ensured both for the patients—to join and quit any sick fund according to their preference, and to the physician to establish sick funds or to administer health services in accordance with his professional concience.

(4) The physicians, through their association, the IMA, should be the major carriers of the NHI and should be consulted previous to any act of legislation.

Evidently the IMA preferred the Likud's version on that of the Labor. However, under no circumstances was it willing to circumscribe the physicians' role in the administration of the NHI. As will be further indicated the demand of the IMA for consultation has not been responded. Moreover, the alternative proposal for the organization of health services is Israel, recommended by the Mann Committee which was set out by the IMA [21] had been shelved and disregarded by policy makers. Hence, the IMA rejected the two proposals of the NHI in their extreme version although it tilted toward that which favored central administration of health services. The attitude of the IMA may be attributed to economic and political factors. Undoubtedly the medical association has a vested interest in the promotion of a pluralist health system in which the pecuniary benefits of its members would not be harmed. On the other hand, one has to bear in mind the organizational and political heterogenity of the IMA, which is divided between hospital and clinic doctors (one-third and two-thirds respectively) and KH and state-employed doctors (40 and 60% respectively), let alone the political dissent within each group. The only basis for consensus within the framework of this plurality is the advocacy of professional and medical interests. While ambiguously defined this loose consensus enabled the IMA to act in a manner which, as will be further described, had under special circumstances, a decisive impact on the formulation of the NHI policy.

THE PROCESS OF LEGISLATION: THE STRUGGLE FOR POWER AND INFLUENCE

The struggle on the NHI evolved in four consecutive phases: first (up to 1969) when the issue was elaborated mainly in public committees whose recommendations were shelved, ignored and not translated into political action. In the second phase (1970–1974) legislative measures were initiated by the government. In the third phase (1976), when the bill was about to become a law, the struggle between the contenders reached its peak and the legislative process was temporarily halted. In the fourth phase (1977 onwards), power relations have been altered, and the Likud tried to push its version of the NHI through the legislative machinery, so far to no avail.

From 1948 to 1969 four committees laid down proposals regarding the organization of the health system and the introduction of NHI. The first, which prepared the blueprint for the administration of social services in the state, recommended that the government should assume the supreme responsibility for medial and social affairs. A similar recommendation was adopted by the second interdepartmental committee for Social Insurance, headed by the chairman of KH (Kanev Committee), which envisaged the establishment of one government sponsored sick fund, administered by the insurees. Although one of the major outcomes of these recommendations has been the formation of the general National Security System, the section pertaining to health policy was carefully evaded. The recommendations of the two other committees (the second Kanev Committee—1958 and the Hushi Committee—1967) also called for a plan for general health insurance preserving the multiplicity of the sick funds and the autonomous management of the insurees organizations. Since these recommendations were adopted by a marginal majority the stymie of opposition to their implementation could not be surmounted.

At the same period several attempts were made to raise the NHI issue on the Knesset's agenda. The major proponents of change, i.e. of expropriating of the health services out of KH were the opposition parties whose representatives submitted Private Member Bills to this effect [22]. Following the second Kanev Committee the government took the initiative and its Minister of Labor (not Health!) encouraged 'public debate' on the issue [23]. Neither public debate nor legislative measures ensued the Minister's statement. Even the inclusion of an explicit commitment in the coalition's agreement, following the pressures of the Progressive Party, did not precipitate the legislative process. In fact, in 1964 the deputy Minister of Health admitted in the Knesset that NHI had reached a stalemate. During the year 1966–1967 three more Private Bills were introduced to the Knesset proposing to establish NHI. The politicization of the health system evoked feeling of uneasiness among MKs. "Its about time", claimed one of them "that the state should be established also in the health domain" [24]. Following the Hushi Committee's report an interdepartmental committee was nominated by the Ministers of Labor and Health in order to formulate legislation. A friction between the two ministers over the distribution of authority halted the process. Only in March 1971 was the bill drafted within the 'smoke-filled rooms' of the administration. None of the interested parties was involved. The IMA heard about the planned move in a radio interview. Not only the IMA was evaded, but also the top officials of the Ministry of Health were not consulted. The issue was elaborated and concluded by the political elite, with the exclusion of medical professionals, included those employed as government officials. "Is medicine too serious a business to be handled by the medical profession?" exclaimed the IMA's chairman [25], demanding to be incorporated in the process of formulating the bill.

In July 1973 the NHI bill was introduced for the first Knesset hearing. It included service provision by the sick funds, collective membership and dues collection and a division of responsibility between the (powerful) Minister of Labor and the (weak) Minister of Health. Although the IMA was assured it would be accorded access to the legislative process, it remained a non-participant. The grounds for its exclusion were the formal adherence to Knesset procedure, granting the legislative Committee full discretion as to those appearing in its hearings. Moreover, an appeal by the IMA to the Premier, Mr Rabin, requesting his personal interference was rejected also on formal grounds [26]. The IMA, on its part, publicly advocated its right to be involved in the legislative process. It insisted that as a legitimate sectional group promoting its members' interests its inclusion in the decision-making process should be imperative. It is precisely the democratic creed, which according to the Knesset Committee deemed the exclusion of the IMA, which necessitated the involvement of the interested public. These arguments proved to be futile in face of ruling decision-makers determined to advance their cause. The only effective way to halt the legislative process was to ally with parties, preferably within the coalition, which could threaten to withhold support from the government in the event that the Knesset would affirm the NHI bill. Indeed, two of these parties—the NRP (to some extent) and the Progressive Party supported the IMA's cause. The road to these parties went through public opinion and media attention. The IMA launched an intensive campaign to mobilize support. The Progressive Party remained reluctant, despite its electoral commitment, anticipating possible political sanctions which it could hardly endure. The change occurred following a public attack of the Minister of Health on the IMA. In a televized interview the Minister accused the physicians for being greedy, and of being seekers of easy profit. These allegations brought the NHI issue to the forefront of the political agenda. Public opinion, usually in favor of the attacked physicians, was unequivocally against the proposed bill. Under the circumstances the Progressive Party followed suit and threatened to invoke a governmental crisis should the bill not be withdrawn. Surprisingly opposition to the bill was joined by Histadrut leaders fearing that the proposed law would lead to an increase in the sick fund's membership and autonomy. The last straw was broken when the PM himself, realizing the political (and economic) price the law would entail gave in and decided to halt the legislative process.

Hence, in one of the rare cases in Israeli politics,

the government retreated from its legislative intentions owing to surmounting pressures which it could not withstand. Labor proved to be strong enough for the initiation of the bill and its introduction to the Knesset. At the same time it was too weak to complete the process and materialize its goals. Opposition, within and outside the Knesset, had been too strong and pervasive to be resisted or ignored.

In the fourth phase the actors of the NHI changed roles: it was the opposition party, the Likud which gained control of the government. Being faithful to its electoral commitment, it reintroduced the NHI in its own version, aiming to nationalize the health system, i.e. emasculating KH [27]. The bill was drafted in accordance with the recommendations of the Zohar Committee which was appointed by the Minister of Health. The leading principles of the new bill were organizational unification and administrative regionalization of health services. Each resident in Israel would be entitled to receive all health care in his region by vitue of his being insured by the National Insurance. Once again the IMA was left out of the picture neither being consulted nor informed of the legislative process. However, it could spare its resources since KH carried a blatant campaign against the bill. Although the Alignment was outstripped of its ruling position, it still maintained control of the Histadrut and its powerful resources. KH employed two methods in its struggle against the bill. First, it threatened to apply sanctions such as strikes and cutting off medical services. Second, it mobilized the support of the major trade unions within the Histadrut (known as the 'Thirteen Unions') [28] which, in effect, control the Israeli economy. The opposition was joined by the NRP which already had in mind the prospects of recoalescing with the Alignment which scored high in public opinion polls [29]. In addition, the general weakness of the Likud government, which suffered a serious decline in its popularity and legitimacy, also contributed to the anti-bill mood. Yet, on the verge of its termination, on the same day that the Knesset decided to advance the elections, the NHI bill was introduced for a first Knesset hearing, and was affirmed by the parliamentary majority (56:47) despite the NRP's objection [30]. KH withheld its medical services for a day, however it ceased to take further measures fearing negative public reactions. The Alignment, on its part, declared that it would abolish the bill on its return to government. The IMA remained totally silent, withdrawing from the arena that became virtually monopolized by the parties and their proxies. Thus it seems that the NHI turned into a campaign issue dissociated from medical needs and objectives. The fact that the bill deals with one of the essential aspects of the health system seems to have been ignored by those responsible for this domain of public policy.

CONCLUSIONS

To date, neither of the two major political blocs in Israel has been successful in changing the status quo which dates back to the pre-state era. None was able to establish a NHI system in accordance with its priorities. The analysis of the Israeli case of the NHI highlights aspects which are specific to this political system and to politics of health in general as follows:

(1) Although Israel is a parliamentary democracy in which the majority prevails, the power of this majority does not suffice to overcome strong opposition if and when it occurs. Small parties, in spite of their marginality, may exert influence when (a) supported by public opinion and (b) taking advantage of a specific constellation in which their power far exceeds their numerical strength.

(2) The political elite tends to exclude the participation of 'nonpolitical' actors from the processing of politicized issues disregarding their expertise. Influence thus can be obtained only by employing political channels, i.e. by securing the support of actors within the political arena rather than by direct public pressure.

(3) It is common knowledge that medical agenda is not merely or even mainly determined by health needs. Rather it manifests a host of political, economic and personal interests which seek to be advanced through the medical issue. Put differently the medical issue is in some cases no more than an instrument for the articulation of other pressing needs.

(4) Health problems are deeply interwoven into the social and political fabrics. Their multidimensional facet also determine the manner in which medical resources are allocated. The struggle over an issue, which ostensibly is grounded in health rationale, may be imbued with competition on power and resources.

(5) Lastly, it seems that there is no one road to the heaven of an optimal provision of health services. Rather, there is a variety of medical options tainted by political colours. Health issues are subject to bargaining and power struggles in an open political market in which each of the contenders trades his resources for desired objectives. As noted elsewhere, consensus barely exists except on the most abstract 'welfare of the patient' level [31]. Who is to determine the contents of this 'welfare' and the means for its attainment?

The futile introduction of the NHI in Israel thus demonstrates that in a society in which politics ranks as prime, health services cannot be isolated from the mainstream. In fact, the case presents one of the most politicized health service systems among the democratic nations.

REFERENCES

1. On this aspect, especially in developing countries see Sorokin A. L. *Health Economics in Developing Countries*, Lexington Books, Lexington, MA, 1976
2. Yishai Y. Abortion in Israel: social demands and political responses. *Polit. Stud. J.*, **7**, 270–289, 1978.
3. Klein R. Policy Making in the National Health Service, *Polit. Stud.* **22**, 1–14, 1974; Satran W. *Veto Group Politics: The Case of Health Insurance Reform in West Germany*, Chandler, California, 1967; Eckstein H. *Pressure Group Politics: The Case of the British Medical Association*, Allen & Unwin, London, 1960.
4. Navarro V. *Class Struggle, The State and Medicine*, Martin Robertson, London, 1978. Also Navarro V. Social class, political power and the state and their implication in medicine *Soc. Sci. Med.* **10**, 437–454, 1976.

5. Gregg P. *The Welfare State*, p. 48. Harrap. London, 1967.
6. On arrangements in other countries see Fulcher D. *Medical Care Systems* ILO, Geneva, 1974; Simanis J. G., *National Health Systems in Eight Countries* SSA, 75-11924, U.S. Department of Health, Education & Welfare, 1975.
7. See Halevi H. S. The pluralist structure of health services in Israel. *Soc. Secur.* **17,** 5–50, 1979 (Hebrew).
8. On the development of KH see Kanev I. *Mutual Aid and Social Medicine in Israel* Kupat Holim, Tel Aviv, 1965; and Histadrut Sick Fund, Tel Aviv, 1979 (Hebrew).
9. The percentage for the fiscal year 1980 is 4.6 up to a salary of 2700 IS and 5.6 for a higher salary up to a ceiling of 4500 IS.
10. As of 1973, the employees contribution has been paid to the National Insurance Institute, which apportions it among the different sick funds.
11. See Bureau of Budget (1978–1979), The Ministry of Health, Vol. XI.
12. Ben David J. Professionals and unions in Israel. In *Integration and Development in Israel* (Edited by Eisenstadt S. N. *et al.*). Jerusalem University Press, Jerusalem, 1970; Eisenstadt S. N. *Israeli Society*. Weidenfeld & Nicolson, London, 1967.
13. The problems of participation in health services is discussed by Brown R. G. S. *Reorganizing the National Health Service*, pp. 214–216. Basil Blackwell, Oxford, 1979.
14. The composition of the 501 delegates Conference is as follows: Labor—254; Likud—129; NRP—45; Agudat Israel—6. *Haaretz*, December 21, 1979.
15. On the politicized process of electing the chairman of the Board of Directors in KH see Pizam A. and Meir J. The management of health care organizations—medical vs administrative orientations: the case of Kupat Holim. *Med. Care* **12,** 682, 1974.
16. The figures for other selected countries are: U.S.—8.4%; Canada—7.1%; Sweden—8.7%; U.K.—5.6%; West Germany—9.7%, Russell L. B., Medical Care. In *Setting National Priorities: Agenda for the* 1980s (Edited by Pechinan J. A.), p. 181. The Brooking Institution, Washington, DC, 1980.
17. Akzin B. The role of parties in Israeli democracy, *J. Polit.* **17,** 507–545, 1955.
18. *Maariv*, May 16, 1980.
19. Illich I. *Medical Nemesis: The Expropriation of Health*. Caldar & Boyars, London, 1975.
20. Yishai Y. Autopsy in Israel, political pressures and medical policy. *Ethics Sci. Med.* **6,** 11–20, 1979.
21. On this committee see Margolis. E. National health planning and the medical model: the case of Israel. *Soc. Sci. Med.* **11,** 181–186, 1977.
22. One was Rafi, Ben Gurion's party that split from Mapai, the second was Gahal—the predecessor of the Likud. Both bills proposed to establish a NHI under the auspices of the government rather than the sick funds.
23. *Minutes of the Knesset*. **26,** 1948, 1959 (Hebrew).
24. *Ibid.* **47,** 4121, 1966.
25. Dr Kaplinski in the IMA's Council, *A Letter to the Member*, 2.2. 1971.
26. The Office of the PM to the IMA, March 30, 1976.
27. On this process see Arian, A. Health Care in Israel: Political and Administrative Aspects. *Int. Polit. Sci. Rev.* **2,** 43–56, 1981.
28. These include the most powerful unions such as the electricity, air and port workers.
29. In June, 30, 1981 the Likud regained its electoral majority and will probably renew its efforts to introduce the NHI bill, encountering, probably, the same difficulties and objections.
30. *Haaretz*, February 11, 1981.
31. Barnard K. and Lee K. (Eds) *Conflicts in the National Health Service*. Croom Helm, London, 1977.

19

Nurses' Autonomy and Job Satisfaction

Sara Carmel, Ilana S. Yakubovich, Leah Zwanger, and *Tsila Zalcman*

INTRODUCTION

Autonomy at work is recognized as an essential element in the definition of a profession. The nursing literature shows that autonomy at work is related to job satisfaction [1–6]. Theoretically, autonomy is defined in various ways [7–10]. Practically, when people on-the-job were interviewed they referred to freedom from close supervisory attention as "the key aspect of experiencing autonomy at work" [10, p. 524].

Nurses' autonomy at work is limited on the one hand by regulations and laws which define the range of nurses' activities, and on the other hand, by physicians' traditional close supervision and control over nurses' daily role performance. Among themselves nurses are still debating issues pertinent to the definition of a nurse's role and autonomy [11–14]. However, nurses do complain about gaps between professional socialization and actual role performance due to structural constraints [11, 15], and feel that major changes should take place in their work relationship with physicians [16].

Nurses in Israel experienced an unusual work situation when for 3 months they had to provide primary care services without physicians. This occurred in 1983, when physicians were on strike. During the strike physicians abandoned the primary care clinics all over the country and nurses had to carry on and work in the clinics without them. Usually nurses are responsible for the work organization in the clinics but physicians have the highest authority and the major part of nurses' work is to carry out physicians' orders. The absence of physicians from the clinics during the strike created a structurally new work setting for nurses, where the immediate constraints on autonomy in the work place were significantly reduced. Nurses thus had the opportunity, within legal constraints, to function in a more autonomous way; they could now regulate their own allocation of time and efforts in the performance of routine tasks and could freely initiate new ones.

The purpose of this study is to examine nurses' perceptions of autonomy and job satisfaction after this temporary experience of autonomy at work, when they returned to their usual work conditions.

METHODS

Data collection

Data were collected 2 to 4 weeks after the physicians' strike was over. Self-administered questionnaires were sent to all the clinics and distributed to the nurses. Questionnaires were returned within the following 2 weeks.

Study population

Participants in this study are 1144 nurses in primary health care clinics operated by the Sick-Fund (Kupat-Holim) in Israel. Eighty-five percent of the Israeli population are insured in this health care system. The primary care clinics are located in every neighborhood. Sixty one percent of the nurses responded to the questionnaire (1144/1876). Respondents are predominantly female (93%); the mean age is 32.5. About half (46%) are registered nurses, the other practical nurses. Twenty percent of the questionnaires were returned unanswered due to nurses being on vacation. Others were not filled out due to language problems. Another 72 completed

Table 1. Distribution of age, sex and professional status in a sample of 1144 primary care nurses and in the total population of Kupat-Holim community nurses (%)

	Sex		Age				Professional status	
	Female	Male	<29	30–39	40–49	>50	RN	Other
Kupat-Holim	94	6	11	29	31	29	51	49
Sample	93	7	11	31	31	27	53	47

questionnaires were not processed for technical reasons.

To assess the degree to which our study population is representative of the primary health clinics' nurse population, we compared the demographic and professional characteristics of our sample to data published by Kupat-Holim describing all community nurses ($n = 3343$), including both primary health care nurses and nurses working in secondary health services (not hospitals). The data are shown in Table 1. As can be seen in Table 1 the demographic and professional characteristics of our sample are similar to these of the target population.

Questionnaires

The questionnaire, pre-coded and self-administered, was designed for this study. It took about 20 min to fill out. It was pre-tested on 45 nurses and several corrections were made. Participation was voluntary and participants were not asked to identify themselves. All completed questionnaires were sent to the researchers in Ben-Gurion University to be processed.

Measures

Changes in role performance during the strike. Nurses were asked to compare their work activities during the strike and in regular work conditions. A series of questions asked about increase, decrease, or no change in performing traditional nurse's tasks in the clinic. A measure of increase in workload during the strike was constructed by summing up the number of activities reported to have increased (range: 0–11). A separate measure of special initiatives was based on responses to two questions: whether nurses undertook or initiated special programs in the clinic and whether special programs were initiated in the community during the strike.

Autonomy. The items measuring autonomy were adapted from Leatt and Schneck [17]. Nurses were asked to rate on a 5 point scale (1 = strongly agree to 5 = strongly disagree) their agreement to the following statements with regard to: (1) their usual work conditions and (2) the strike situation:

a. Very few activities can be carried out by nurses without doctor's orders.

b. Even in cases where nurses would like to decide by themselves on a nursing treatment they face immediate opposition.

c. Even minor decisions regarding patients' care have to be referred to physicians for final approval.

The intercorrelations among the three variables in each of the two sets (one referring to the time of the strike and the other to usual work conditions) were computed and found to be statistically significant (Pearson's $r = 0.36$–0.41). The mean scores of each set of the three responses were used as measures of perceived autonomy for the two periods of time. The difference between these two scores was used as a comparative measure of perceived autonomy in the two work settings (usual working conditions and during the strike period).

Job satisfaction. Two questions were asked to assess job satisfaction:

1. Generally, to what extent are you satisfied or not satisfied with your job? Five categories of answers were given, from 'very satisfied' to 'not at all satisfied'.

2. During the strike, were you more or less satisfied with your job than during nonstrike conditions? The possible answers were: (1) much more satisfied, (2) more satisfied, (3) similarly satisfied, (4) less satisfied, (5) much less satisfied.

RESULTS

The pattern of change in nurses' role performance during the strike is shown in Table 2, which presents the proportions of nurses reporting increase or decrease in various activities. As can be seen, on all but one activity, many more nurses reported an increase than the number who reported a decrease. The main change is observed in two of the more autonomous activities; triage and referrals, and patients' instruction (87% and 85%, respectively). Other activities are reported by fewer nurses to have increased (23%–75%). The only function which showed a substantial decrease during the strike is direct patient care (20% of the nurses report a decrease in such activities vs 1%–9% reporting a decrease in other activities). A sizeable proportion of the nurses (67%) reported that during the strike they carried out and/or initiated special programs in the clinic, and 51% reported undertaking such initiatives in the community. Nurses were also asked by an open ended question to specify their initiated activities. Those who answered this question, mentioned mainly community screening for cardiovascular risk factors, re-evaluations of diets, explanations about drugs, blood tests to diabetic patients, and home visits.

Although most nurses are satisfied with their jobs in nonstrike conditions (34%—very satisfied, 44%—satisfied, 15%—quite satisfied, 6%—not so satisfied, 1%—not satisfied, 0%—not at all satisfied), 31% reported an increase in job satisfaction during the strike (14% of the nurses reported being much more satisfied, 17% more satisfied, 39% equally satisfied and 24% less satisfied).

The mean score of the perceived autonomy index under usual work conditions is 3.4 (on a scale from 1 = low perception of autonomy to 5 = high perception of autonomy), and during the strike the mean

Table 2. Reported changes in nurses' activities during the strike (%)

A. Changes in regular activities		Increased	Decreased
1.	Triage and referrals	87	3
2.	Instructing and giving consultation to patients	65	1
3.	Routine tests (blood, urine, etc.)	75	2
4.	Keeping nurse's logbook	69	1
5.	Home visits	64	2
6.	Updating patients' records	64	5
7.	Reports to supervisors	52	3
8.	Prescriptions	49	9
9.	Administrative work	42	7
10.	Contacting other agencies (e.g. welfare services)	39	3
11.	Direct patient care (injections, dressing, etc.)	23	20
B. Special programs initiated or carried out			
1.	In the clinic	67	
2.	In the community	51	

score is 4.0. The difference was found to be statistically significant ($P < 0.01$) by a paired t-test.

To examine the possibility that differences in perceived autonomy and in job satisfaction in strike and in nonstrike conditions are associated with changes in role performance during the strike, the two measures of job satisfaction and perceived autonomy were compared across varying levels of extended activity during the stike (Table 3). The proportion of nurses whose autonomy scores are higher in the strike period than in nonstrike conditions gradually increases with the degree of extended activity during the strike (from 28.9% among nurses who reported no change in the studied activities to 70.9% among nurses who reported increase in most activities).

A similar trend is seen when nurses who did not initiate special programs in the clinic or in the community, are compared with nurses who had initiated and/or carried out such programs. The differences are highly significant. The reported change in job satisfaction was also found to be significantly associated with the extent of increased activities during the strike and with the extent of special initiatives undertaken by the nurses during the strike. The proportion of nurses who reported an increase in job satisfaction ranges from 12.2% among nurses, who did not increase their activities during the strike, to 40.9% among nurses who expanded most of their activities. A similar trend is seen when the change in job satisfaction is examined with relation to the extent of initiated special programs.

Table 4 shows the associations between role performance during the strike and perceived autonomy and job satisfaction in nonstrike conditions. A gradual, statistically significant decrease is seen in autonomy scores, with the increase in activity during the strike. (From 4.00 among nurses reporting no increase in activities to 3.29 among nurses who reported increase in most activities.) Statistically significant contrasts at the 0.05 level (by the Duncan multiple range test) were found between each of the first two groups (with none or 1–3 increased activities) and the two groups with 4–6 or 7+ increased activities.

Similarly, nurses not involved in special programs have higher autonomy scores in usual work conditions than those who were involved in special pro-

Table 3. Changes in perception of autonomy and job satisfaction by increase in workload and initiatives during the physicians strike (%)

	Perception of autonomy				Job satisfaction			
Increase in workload	Higher in strike	Same	Lower in strike	Total	Higher in strike	Same	Lower in strike	Total
0	28.9	60.0	11.1	100% (45)	12.2	63.3	24.5	100% (49)
1–3	40.5	48.0	11.5	100% (131)	12.3	55.9	31.8	100% (154)
4–6	63.7	28.3	8.0	100% (336)	27.8	40.4	31.8	100% (381)
7+	70.9	19.0	10.1	100% (457)	40.9	29.8	29.3	100% (508)
	Chi-square = 73.8, $P < 0.001$				Chi-square = 71.59, $P < 0.001$			
Initiatives								
None	49.5	40.3	10.2	100% (236)	21.0	46.7	32.3	100% (257)
Clinic or community	69.9	22.4	7.7	100% (196)	35.2	36.0	28.8	100% (222)
Clinic and community	68.5	22.3	9.2	110% (349)	39.8	31.9	28.3	100% (385)
	Chi-square = 39.55, $P < 0.001$				Chi-square = 26.80, $P < 0.001$			

Table 4. Perception of autonomy and job satisfaction in nonstrike condition, by work change during the strike (mean scores)

Increase in workload	Mean score of autonomy in nonstrike conditions	Mean score of job satisfaction in nonstrike conditions
0	4.00	1.83
	(49)	(54)
1–3	3.86	1.86
	(141)	(156)
4–6	3.37	1.98
	(361)	(382)
7+	3.29	1.96
	(496)	(505)
	$F = 16.20$	$F = 0.99$
	$P < 0.001$	$P = 0.398$
Initiatives		
None	3.62	1.91
	(247)	(266)
Clinic or community	3.33	2.01
	(211)	(220)
Clinic and community	3.33	1.93
	(378)	(383)
	$F = 6.18$	$F = 0.98$
	$P = 0.002$	$P = 0.375$

grams. The difference is statistically significant. No associations, however, were found between job satisfaction in nonstrike conditions and role performance during the strike.

Job satisfaction and perception of autonomy in nonstrike conditions were found to be positively correlated, but the association, although statistically significant, is rather weak ($r = 0.15$, $P < 0.01$). The two measures comparing autonomy and job satisfaction (in strike vs nonstrike conditions) are also positively correlated ($r = 0.22$, $P < 0.01$).

DISCUSSION

During the 1983 physicians' strike, Israeli doctors abandoned the primary care clinics for about 3 months. This unique situation created a vacuum in health services and presented a challenge for nurses. Nurses had an opportunity to exercise self-control over their own work and, to some extent to go beyond the traditional role of physician's aide. The purpose of this study was to examine nurses' perceived autonomy and job satisfaction at the end of this unique experience in relation to changes in role performance, perceptions of autonomy and job satisfaction during the strike.

The special circumstances of the strike put the main burden of providing primary care services on the nurses. The fact that primary care clinics continued to provide services throughout the strike period is reflected in nurses' reports that almost all types of their activities had increased during the strike. The expansion in autonomous activities was expressed mainly in special projects initiated and carried out by a majority of the nurses. Among such activities were community screening for cardiovascular risk factors, explanations about drugs, reevaluation of diets, etc.

Job satisfaction and perceived autonomy were reported by nurses to be higher during the strike than in usual work conditions. These changes were found to be associated with the degree of extended activity during the strike period; the more extra work they had, and the more the nurses took advantage of the strike conditions to initiate special clinic and community activities, the higher the likelihood of a positive change during the strike both in job satisfaction and in perceived autonomy.

With regard to nonstrike work conditions, the findings indicate that nurses are usually satisfied with their jobs and perceive them as rather autonomous. This is consistent with previous reports about nurses' job satisfaction [6]. While no association was found between change in activities during the strike and job satisfaction in usual conditions an inverse relationship was observed between the extent of change in role performance during the strike and perception of job autonomy during usual work conditions. This finding suggests that the strike experience is associated with nurses general perception of autonomy, but not with their general job satisfaction, and is consistent with the weak correlation found between job satisfaction and perceived autonomy.

Since our study is cross sectional, it is not possible to determine whether nurses with low perception of autonomy were more likely than others to take advantage of the strike situation to expand their role, or whether nurses who, for various reasons had experienced significant change in role performance during the strike became more aware of their lack of autonomy in usual work conditions. During the strike, however, the findings suggest that the general increase in activity and responsibility, and possibly the freedom from close supervision by physicians positively affected both job satisfaction and perceived autonomy. These unique work conditions during the physicians' strike seem to have been a positive professional experience for the nurses in primary care clinics, but this experience of contextual autonomy was probably viewed as a temporary and unusual situation rather than a model for change in professional status.

To the best of our knowledge, when physicians called off the strike and returned to work there was no attempt on the part of the nurses to preserve any of the changes which occurred during the strike. Since the physician strike in 1983 nurses were involved in several labor disputes. Redefinition of roles and a call for more work autonomy were never an issue in these disputes. It seems that when presented with a challenge in the delivery of primary care, nurses can stand up to it; but they are not yet ready or willing to take the initiative and publicly struggle for additional professional autonomy. This seems to be the case at least among primary care nurses in Israel for the present.

REFERENCES

1. Sluyter G. V. and Cleland C. C. Self actualization among institutional personnel. *Traing Schl Bull.* **69,** 83, 1972.
2. Stamps P. L. *Ambulatory Care Systems.* Lexington Books, Massachusetts, 1978.
3. Weisman C. S., Alexander C. S. and Chase G. A. Job satisfaction among hospital nurses: a longitudinal study. *Hlth Serv. Res.* **15,** 341, 1980.
4. Carlsen R. H. and Malley J. O. Job satisfaction of staff registered nurses in primary and team nursing delivery systems. *Res. Nurs. Hlth* **4,** 251, 1981.
5. Weisman C. S. and Nathanson C. A. Professional satisfaction and client outcomes: a comparative organizational analysis. *Med. Care* **23,** 1179, 1985.
6. Hale C. Measuring job satisfaction. *Nursg Times* **82,** 43, 1986.
7. Goode W. Encroachment, charlatanism and the emerging profession: psychology, sociology, and medicine. *Am. Soc. Rev.* **25,** 902, 1960.
8. Friedson E. *The Profession of Medicine.* Dodd, Mead, New York, 1970.
9. Wolinsky F. D. Nurses and the para-professions. In *The Sociology of Health: Principles, Professions and Issues.* Little, Brown, Boston, Mass., 1980.
10. Schwalbe M. L. Autonomy in work and self-esteem. *Sociol. Q.* **26,** 519, 1985.
11. Lurie E. E. Nurse practitioners: issues in professional socialization. *J. Hlth soc. Behav.* **22,** 31, 1981.
12. Milne D. 'The more things change the more they stay the same': factors affecting the implementation of the nursing process. *J. Adv. Nursg* **19,** 39, 1985.
13. Celentano D. D. and Anderson S. E. Conflicting perceptions of the health provider domain by new health professionals. *Soc. Sci. Med.* **14A,** 645, 1980.
14. Perry J. Has the discipline of nursing developed to the stage where nurses do 'think nursing'? *J. Adv. Nursg* **10,** 31, 1985.
15. Rosenow A. M. Professional nursing practice in the bureaucratic hospital-revisited. *Nursg Outlk* **3,** 34, 1983.
16. Keddy B., Jones Gilis M., Jacobs P., Burton H. and Regers M. The doctor–nurses relationship: an historical perspective. *J. Adv. Nursg* **11,** 745, 1986.
17. Leatt P. and Schneck R. Work environments of different types of nursing subunits. *J. Adv. Nursg* **7,** 581, 1982.

20

Disability, Stress, and Readjustment: The Function of the Professional's Latent Goals and Affective Behavior in Rehabilitation

Zeev Ben-Sira

INTRODUCTION

Readjustment in the wake of a traumatic irrevocable, eventually stigmatizing, impairment, is generally recognized as a crucial indicator of successful rehabilitation [1–3;6, p. 98; 9;10, p. 218]. Yet recent studies [2, 3] which focused on the development and empirical verification of a multivariate *paradigm of readjustment of disabled* highlighted an evidently serious barrier to readjustment. The data revealed a consistent pattern suggesting that assistance by rehabilitation agencies is more likely to result in dependence on these agencies, rather than in readjustment. The data further ascertained that dependency on rehabilitation agencies is detrimental to successful readjustment [2–4]. These findings give rise to a crucial issue: what are the factors underlying the eventual failure of apparent competent professional agencies to promote the readjustment, in particular, of those who are in the greatest need for such assistance? Relating to this question seems particularly crucial in light of the eventual indispensability of professional expertise for facilitating a disabled person's successful reintegration into normal social life.

Traditional models of the professional-client relationship, highlighting the clients' inferiority *vis-à-vis* 'powerful' professionals may allude to a possible direction for furthering the understanding of the issue. According to these approaches, the professionals' power is basically a result of their control of indispensable resources [11, p. 22; 12, pp. 72–80]. Yet, it is exactly their resource deficiency which motivated the disabled persons' turning to professional help. Why then should resource-inequality *per se* be detrimental to the clients' readjustment?

Accumulating evidence about the eventual failures and frustrating—occasionally conflict arousing—episodes [13, pp. 120–150] throughout the laborious process of 'resource enhancement' which is indispensable for readjustment [14] may suggest a possible explanation. Overcoming the eventually adverse consequences of such frustrating yet evidently unavoidable episodes requires trust in the professional. Trust, according to classic functionalism, implies belief in the professionals' collectivity orientation, i.e. that the professionals place their clients well-being above their self-interest [15, pp. 343–347, 434–436]. The belief in the professionals' adherence to the norms of collectivity orientation [16, p. 131], in turn, may lead clients to bring into the interaction expectations regarding the satisfaction of their subjectively defined needs [17, p. 2[illegible]]. Yet, inherent in the professionals' behavior are characteristics that may shatter the clients' trust in their helpers. Thus, for instance, dismissing the clients' demands as irrelevant due to their lacking of professional expertise or stressing the necessity for compliance may eventually arouse such doubts. Indeed, as Zola [18, p. 57] rightly points out, inherent in the traditional notion of help is dependence on providers who often "contend that their years of experience and lack of personal involvement permit them to understand disabled people's needs more clearly than they do themselves" [18, p. 55]. In fact, Zola concludes in his book on his own career as a disabled person that "... society has created many avenues for some people to determine what *other* people need, but few channels for those in need to easily ask for what they need" [19, p. 229]. Thus, the nature of the "care or treatment relationship which requires the disabled person to accept the imposition of values and attitudes [and to] assume the role of status inferior to the professional" [20, p 234] may lead to the growing suspicion as to whose interests are actually being served and who is the ultimate beneficiary of the service—the professional or the client [21–24]. In other words, do professionals, under the guise of professionalism, pursue a *latent*, though predominant, goal of promoting their self-interests rather than those of their clients?

Monopolization of 'esoteric professional expertise' [16, pp 112–114; 26, p. 2; 26, p. 51] and an ideology assuming the "superiority of specialized knowledge and expertise [and] well-defined role distance between practitioner and client" [27, p. 149], may give rise to suspicions that power enhancement is indeed the professional's *predominant latent* goal [28, pp. 73–88; 29, pp. 70–72]—a goal to be satisfied through the interaction with clients. Inferentially, then, perpetuating the client's dependence may be suspected to serve as a means for maintaining professional dominance. Consumerist activities [30–32] or ideologies, such as the Movement for Independent Living [33–35] reflect the public's reaction to the professional's suspected latent goals Eventual reservations of professional rehabilitation workers against 'Self-Help' and 'Independent Living' movements on grounds of their alleged adverse consequences for successful rehabilitation [36, pp 10 11] may be interpreted by the public as support to their suspicions.

However, the crucial question for the issue at hand is *not* whether disabled persons suspect that the professionals seek to satisfy their self-interests by interacting with persons in need The question is actually as to the extent to which this suspicion is detrimental to a needy persons' readjustment Furthermore, if such suspicion indeed affects readjustment, how can the deleterious consequences be overcome? Professional expertise is evidently inevitable for assisting disabled persons in overcoming the obstacles placed in their way of daily social functioning. Under these circumstances of neediness, even a behavior according to Zola's suggestion, where "Caregivers . act as advocates assisting their clients to act for themselves" [18, p. 57], carries the risk of being interpreted as a demonstration of professional power.

Insights regarding a possible approach to overcoming this evidently vicious circle may be inferred from suggestions that stress the importance of generating a feeling of being sincerely understood by the helping agent [39, p. 172]. Accumulating evidence on the function of the physicians' "*affective*" (humane, person-oriented) behavior in promoting the patients' well-being [37, 38, 40, 41] may give rise to the question as to the extent to which such types of behavior may contribute to the generating of such a feeling of sincere understanding

The aim of the present study, then, is to further develop the recently established *paradigm of readjustment* of disabled persons [2, 3] by focusing on two crucial issues: (a) the extent to which the eventually detrimental outcomes of a rehabilitation agency's assistance may be understood as a consequence of clients' inclination to attribute to the professional the latent (though predominent) goal of furthering his own self-interest; and (b) the eventual function of the professional's *affective* behavior in reducing the deleterious consequences.

ANALYTICAL FRAMEWORK

The structure of readjustment

In the recently developed paradigm [2. 3], *readjustment* is conceptualized, on the basis of prevailing approaches to stress and breakdown [42–44]. as restoration of psychological homeostasis which has been disturbed by unmet *demands* following a traumatic irrevocable, eventually stigmatizing change in one's life. Such demands, which, in Lazarus and Cohen's words "exceed the resources of the system or to which there [are] no readily available responses" disturb the individual's psychological homeostasis, i.e. become *stressors* [44, p. 109]. A prolonged failure in restoring homeostasis, conceptualized by Antonovsky [42] as 'stress', may result in 'breakdown', disease or further deterioration of the afflicted person's condition being one of its expressions [45].

The concept of demand: a further explication

Recent studies [2. 3] a ude that evidently the severity of impairment *per se* does not make disability a stressor Following Lazarus [46], it seems reasonable that it is to a great extent the subjective interpretation of any single demand of daily life through the lenses of the disabled person's perception, that make that demand a stressor Jones *et al.* argue that, as a consequence of the possible self-conception of now being a different. stigmatized person, "each decision to connect with the social world will involve a special effort, a conscious decision of whether the contact is worth the possible humiliation and further negative reaction" [47 p 111]. Inferentially. then. the self-conception of now being a different person may have the potential of making demands, which under ordinary conditions are easily met, to be sensed as unsurmountable.

A traumatically disabled person may subjectively feel unable to confront the usual societal demands of work or leisure, or unable to maintain social or family relations—a feeling that is a consequence of self-conception or sense of being stigmatized, rather than of 'objective' physical barriers. Under such circumstances 'normal' demands may become stressors. *Successful coping*, by definition then. implies *perceived* success in meeting demands, resulting in emotional homeostasis. Successful coping, in turn, is enhanced by resources that the individual has at his disposal [2, 3, 42, 43, 48, 49]. Inferentially, then, the greater an individual's control of resources, the better are his/her chances of successful coping. And vice versa, the less the control of own resources, the greater the chances of either being unable to meet demands, or having to mobilize resources from the environment. As indicated earlier, recent studies [2, 3] clearly showed the greater efficacy of support by the primary environment (spouse, friends) than that of assistance from the formal secondary environment (e.g. rehabilitation agency).

The problematics of attributed latent goals

The above brief conceptualization of the recently

developed basic rehabilitation paradigm [2, 3] in terms of the coping–stress relationship [42–49] brings us back to the central question underlying the present study, namely, why does professional assistance that is overtly aimed at the readjustment of disabled persons often have detrimental consequences?

As Reid and Gundlach suggest, one of the ultimate goals of welfare assistance is to enhance needy individuals self-esteem and sense of power [50]. Yet self-esteem is "a construction based on one's own thoughts, feelings and behavior with respect to oneself and the perception of the thoughts, feelings and behavior of *other people* with respect to the self" [47, p. 116]. Considering this *a priori* disadvantageous situation of the disabled, the rehabilitation process aimed at enhancing the individual's resources [14], may result in failures and consequent frustrations, thus arousing adverse feelings towards the rehabilitation worker [13, p. 127]. These feelings may further be reinforced by the professionals' dominance, stressing their knowlege regarding the disabled persons' needs [18, p. 55], and to assume the role of status inferior to the professional [20, p. 234]. As a result, in addition to their *a priori* disadvantageous condition, the clients may feel further "objectified or dehumanized by being treated as a case . [whereas] professionals may come to resent their patients. [and even develop] negative attitudes toward the disabled or infirm over time" [47, pp. 289–290]. On the other hand, responding to eventual demands of the clients, such as allocation of direct material assistance ('resource compensation') instead of engaging in the laborious, eventually frustrating, efforts of motivating the disabled toward reintegration into productive life ('resource enhancement'), may initially be satisfying for the recipient, but, at the same time, perpetuate his/her dependence [14]. Furthermore, in the long run, the rehabilitation workers may be blamed for having allocated resource compensation with the deliberate intention of perpetuating the disabled's inferior position in order to enhance their own power. Thus, the disabled may feel exploited for promoting the professional's *latent goal* of power enhancement—a feeling gaining support from the increasing suspicion against welfare professionals as to whose interests they actually promote: those of the professionals, or of the clients [22–24].

Thus, whatever the actual goal of rehabilitation workers, chances are that those in need for professional assistance may come to attribute to the professionals the *latent goal* of pursuing their self-interests. The inherent distrust regarding the rehabilitation worker's aim may affect adversely the rehabilitant's motivation to cooperate, and, as Germain argues, may "show [itself] in verbal and nonverbal expressions of anger toward the worker...or in silence or in acting-out behaviors ranging from missed appointments impulsive and even dangerous actions, particularly of a self-destructive nature (for example, flouting a diabetic diet, overactivity in a cardiac patient). Such resistance. .effectively blocks motivation to move ahead on coping efforts" [13, p. 127]. Thus, perceiving rehabilitation workers as pursuing predominantly, though latently, their self-interest, may express itself in lack of cooperation or conflict—a behavior impeding the laborious efforts of 'resource enhancement' hence ultimately leading to maladjustment and consequent dependence.

Affective behavior

What, then, are the means that a rehabilitation worker has at his disposal for overcoming such a dysfunctional relationship? Germain suggests that such "negative feelings toward the worker should be met with an empathic comment on their presence" [13, p. 127]. It seems highly important to generate a feeling of being sincerely understood by the helping agent [39, p. 172] and, following Zola, explicitly acting as "advocates assisting their clients to act for themselves" [18, p. 57]. Taking these suggestions a step further, I propose that, similar to evidence from studies in the physician–patient relationship [37, 38, 40, 41], *affective behavior* also in the rehabilitator–rehabilitant relationship may fulfill a crucial function in preventing such dysfunctional relationship. Evidence from doctor–patient relationship suggests that the physician's affective behavior toward the patient fulfills an anxiety alleviating function and consequently contributing to recovery, both through its inherent supportive nature and by providing 'lay intelligible clues' by which patients tend to judge the quality and efficacy of the doctor's essentially *esoteric* medical (instrumental) activities [37, 38, 40, 41].

The rationale and content of rehabilitation workers' intervention activities, though doubtless differing in their 'esotericity' [38] from the physician's may frequently not be overtly evident, and their outcome may often be uncertain. Affective behavior, which comprises among others sincere interest in, and attention to the client's problems (even if irrelevant from a purely professional viewpoint), allocating sufficient time, patience, giving explanations and demonstrating devotion [37, 38, 40], in addition to its basic supportive nature, may serve as a *bridge over the status gap*—a means for counteracting the client's propensity of attributing to the professional the latent goal of power enhancement.

Summary

In summary, a further development of a previously suggested paradigm of readjustment of disabled [2, 3] is proposed:

(a) readjustment of disabled persons will be greatly enhanced by successful coping with demands, the surmountability of which is a product of the afflicted person subjective perception;

(b) successful coping is facilitated predominantly with the help of own resources, to some extent with resources from the primary environment, and to a lesser extent from the secondary environment (rehabilitation agency);

(c) resources from the secondary environment seem to be less efficacious than those from the primary environment, eventually may lead to dependence and thus be detrimental to readjustment;

(d) the eventual detrimental nature of the rehabilitator's assistance is to a great extent a consequence of the rehabilitant's propensity of attributing to him the latent goal of enhancing his own interests;

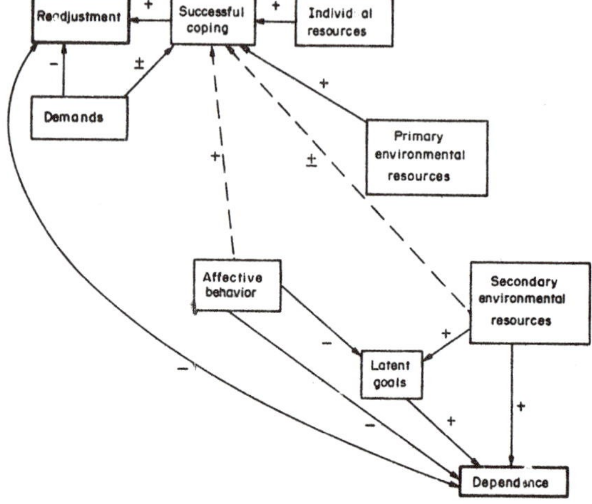

Fig. 1. Hypothesized structure of readjustment (the + and − indicate positive and negative correlations).

(e) affective behavior toward the client will counteract the rehabilitant's perception of that latent goal;

(f) counteracting the perception of the latent goal will reduce the adverse consequences of assistance from rehabilitation agencies, thus enhancing the chances of successful coping.

A revised structure of coping with disability is hypothesized, which is schematically displayed in Fig. 1.

METHOD

This paper is based upon a survey carried out among a stratified sample of disabled Israeli war veterans.

Sample and fieldwork

Sample: In order to achieve proper representation of disabled persons according to degree of impairment* and age groups†, a stratified systematic sample was drawn from the registers of the Department of Rehabilitation of the Ministry of Defense. A reserve sample comprising potential respondents having identical characteristics was prepared in order to substitute dropouts.

Data collection. Field work was carried out from July to December 1978. Interviews with 545 disabled persons were conducted using a closed questionnaire presented by interviewers in the respondents' homes. Dropout rate from initial sample was 30%. For each dropout, a substitute respondent having identical characteristics (age, degree of impairment and area of residence) was interviewed. (For characteristics of final sample, see Appendix A.)

Measures

Readjustment. Emotional homeostasis was applied as an indicator of readjustment. As in previous studies on readjustment [2, 3, 45], Langner's [51] MHI scale was applied as a valid composite measure of emotional homeostasis. This scale is of particular relevance for the present issue, considering that it focuses on prolonged disturbance (or maintenance) of homeostasis. It has been found valid in a large array of studies in differentiating among groups according to their level of emotional homeostasis [52–56].

Demands. Following Jones *et al.*'s [47, p. 111] line of reasoning, the herein investigated concept of 'demand' will focus on subjectively perceived impediments in interacting with the social environment, impediments which are allegedly a consequence of disability. The demands herein investigated will be in the areas of leisure, social relations, work, and relations with children as well as a general feeling of

*Degrees of impairment are defined by percentages ranging from 5 to 100% (total disability). The number of disabled persons decreases with the increase in degree of disability. A systematic random sample would not have allowed for a proper representation of the severely handicapped.

†Age groups were substituted for the date of the incident which was not noted in the register. We were interested in an equal representation of the disabled from all combat periods since the Isaeli War of Independence in 1948 and up to the Yom-Kippur War of 1973.

being ashamed (shame)* In addition to that, the objective degree impairment was applied.

Successful coping was measured, as in previous studies on rehabilitation and readjustment [2, 3, 45] by the respondent's satisfaction in various life areas, satisfaction implying, by definition, a feeling of successfully meeting the demands in those life areas (e.g. "to what extent are you presently satisfied with your social relations?" 1—Very satisfied 6—Very dissatisfied)

Resources Any attempt to operationalize the concept of resource is confronted by the problem of a conceptual differentiation between *initial resource* and *outcome* measures† Income, education, or occupational status. may be both a resource and the outcome of coping with the help of other resources. Thus, as in previous studies [45, 56], an item was defined as a measure of resource if it indicated either a potential of enhancing coping or a product of coping. Resources were classified, as in other studies [2, 3, 45, 56] according to the *source* of the resource, own resources vs those from the primary or secondary (in our case rehabilitation agency) environments. Based on this classification, the following resource items were applied: with respect to *own resources*, the focus was on resources which are concerned predominantly with the individual's SES, such as employment occupational status and power, and housing density, considering them as the basic factors for coping successfully with the demands of life [57, 58], and for the achievement of other resources (e.g. [59, pp. 309, 327–347]). In addition, leisure activities and the extent of interaction with spouse were considered, being a basic means for meeting emotional demands. Regarding resources from the primary environment, the focus was on the 'affective' (emotional) aspect of social support, considering its generally recognized, predominantly emotional function [60, 61]. Thus, the study asked about the extent to which the respondent obtained emotional support (herein defined as 'catharsis') from wife and friends at present and at the time of discharge from the medical institution. With respect to resources from the secondary environment, the schedule asked about the following types of assistance received from rehabilitation agencies: (a) *material compensation* (monetary allowances for various needs such as unemployment, apartment, car); (b) *resource enhancement* (vocational training); and (c) *emotional* ('catharsis') (see list in Appendix C).

Rehabilitator's affective behavior was defined as the respondent's perception of the rehabilitator's humane behavior toward him (i.e. showing interest in his personal problems, attention, giving explanations, showing devotion, moral support in times of crisis and reassurance). A composite measure comprising 12 variables, belonging to the same underlying factor as ascertained by factor analysis was established (For items comprising this measure see Appendix B.)

Rehabilitator's instrumental behavior was defined as the respondent's perception of the rehabilitator's direct efforts for promoting his rehabilitation (e.g. attempting to solve difficult problems, offering quick solutions, finding satisfactory alternatives. proficiency, making necessary inquiries) A composite measure was established comprising six items relating to the same underlying factor as ascertained by factor analysis.

Rehabilitator's domineering behavior was defined as the respondent's perception of the rehabilitator's manifestation of power (e.g. treating the respondent as an 'object'). Two pairs of open-ended questions at the end of the interview asked about the respondent's general feelings and evaluation about the rehabilitator's activities in the framework of the agency (2 questions) and professional attitude (2 questions). For each pair of questions, responses were classified into four categories (1—assessment of 'domineering' behavior on both questions; 2—'domineering' behavior on one question; 3—neither helpful nor domineering; 4—helpful). One additional open question asked about reasons for *hesitance* in seeking rehabilitator's help for emotional problems (1—incompetent/wrong person; 2—unable; 3—did not hesitate).

Latent functions. A composite measure comprising six statements was intended to elucidate the extent to which respondents perceived the goals of the rehabilitator as satisfying aims other than those of the respondent himself. The items were as follows (factor analysis ascertained that items related to the same underlying factor; factor loading of items indicated in parentheses): (1) responding to pressures rather than promoting rehabilitation (0.64); (2) helping mainly the powerful (to avoid trouble for the rehabilitator) (0.63); (3) causing injustice (0.66); (4) causing dependence (0.63); (5) giving things just to get rid of the respondent (0.57); (6) giving material benefits and not rehabilitating (0.51) (1—definitely agree... 6—definitely disagree).

Manifest functions. A composite measure comprising four items (included in the same battery of items as the latent functions) was intended to elucidate the extent to which respondents perceived the goals of rehabilitator as predominantly promoting readjustment: (1) assistance facilitating reintegration of the respondent into appropriate social roles (0.76); (2) rehabilitator's activities enhance respondent's motivation to succeed in meeting the demands of life (0.51); (3) rehabilitator's activities help live a decent life (0.44); (4) rehabilitator helps overcome psychological crises (0.47).

Dependence was measured by the respondent's report of feeling dependent on the rehabilitation

*The following is an illustration of the wording of a question: "To what extent do the limitations due to your impairment hinder your spending leisure time as you would like to?" (1—to a very great extent...5—Not at all).

†Pearlin and Schooler's [48] comprehensive study on coping may serve as an illustration of the difficulty of differentiating between resource and outcome measures. They defined "Marriage does not give me the opportunity to become the person I'd like to be" as an *outcome measure*, while "A feeling of control over things" as a *resource*, and "How would you compare your marriage to that of most people like yourself" as a coping response [48, pp. 18–21]. I think that each of these items could serve equally as a resource or outcome measure.

agency for satisfaction of needs. With regard to 'affective' needs, the schedule related to 'catharsis' (now, and at time of discharge from medical institution) with regard to leisure and relations with children. As to instrumental needs, the schedule asked about dependence in the areas of economic, employment (now and at time of discharge) and housing. One additional question asked about a general feeling of dependence on the agency (1—very dependent.... 6—not dependent at all).

For a complete list of variables see Appendix C.

Data analysis

Correlations. In accordance with the aim of the study, which is to elucidate the extent to which the variables are predictive of readjustment of dependence of recipients of rehabilitation assistance, the strength of the relationships among the items was deemed an appropriate indicator of their predictive power. A weak monotonicity correlation coefficient (μ_2)—which is especially appropriate in conditions such as ours where linearity is not assumed—was used [62, 63]. The formula for μ_2 is as follows: given n pairs of observations on numerical variables (x, y), (x_i, y_i) $(i = 1,2,\ldots,n)$, then

$$\mu_2 = \frac{\sum_{h=1}^{n}\sum_{i=1}^{n}(x_h - x_i)(y_h - y_i)}{\sum_{h=1}^{n}\sum_{i=1}^{n}|x_h - x_i||y_h - y_i|}.$$

SSA (*smallest space analysis*). The logic of our framework requires a technique that facilitates inferring conclusions from the *overall* structure of the interrelationships among the variables in a multivariate content universe. Such a technique should enable a simultaneous perception of the predictive power of each variable *vis-a-vis* all the other variables, thus enabling to arrive at conclusions regarding the factors involved in predicting readjustment or dependence, hence resulting in an empirical verification of the suggested paradigm in Fig. 1. A practical technique is smallest space analysis [64, 65], which is a graphic display of the interrelationships among the variables, reflecting the relation of each variable *vis-à-vis* all the others. In the SSA technique, the computer locates the variables as points on a map according to the strength of the correlations among them: the stronger the positive correlation between two variables, the smaller the distance between the points representing them; the weaker the positive correlation (or the stronger the negative correlation) between two variables the greater the distance between the points representing them. The extent of accuracy to which the spatial distances on the map reflect the actual relationships is expressed by the Coefficient of Alienation (COA): the smaller the coefficient of alienation the more accurate the fit. A coefficient of 0.15 is considered an almost accurate fit [66]. (In the present study COA = 0.19—still considered a satisfactory reflection of the actual relationships).

Conclusions are derived from the relative proximity among all variables (and not merely from specific pairwise relations), namely, from the entire structure of interrelations. (For an extensive discussion on the value of this method and illustration of its application, see [67, 68].)

RESULTS

The structure of readjustment

The SSA-1 (Fig. 2) which displays graphically the interrelations among the variables* reveals a structure which greatly supports the hypothesized paradigm (Fig. 1). As hypothesized, demands threaten the disabled's emotional homeostasis whereas successful coping enhances homeostasis (i.e. readjustment). Successful coping, in turn, is predicted predominately by the individual's own resources, and somewhat less by resources from the primary environment. Assistance from rehabilitation agencies, on the other hand, predicts dependence rather than successful coping, vocational training being an exception. Perception of rehabilitators' latent goals and domineering behavior predicts dependence and hesitance in seeking his help for emotional problems. Affective behavior, on the other hand, predicts satisfaction with instrumental behavior, which in turn predicts the enhancement of individual resources, and finally, readjustment. Affective behavior also predicts belief in the rehabilitator's sincerity regarding the manifest goal of aiding the rehabilitant rather than pursuing latent functions of self-interest.

These conclusions are derived from the location of the variables on the SSA map (Fig. 2). On the extreme left is located the variable denoting *readjustment* (variable 1), while on the extreme right are the dependence variables (variables 42–50) (in accordance with the strong negative correlation with readjustment—μ_2 varies from -0.74 to -0.37). The closer an item is to the right, the greater its power to predict (i.e. the stronger it is correlated with) dependence and *maladjustment*—in accordance with the strong correlation between them and its negative correlation with readjustment. The location of the variables on the map forms six consecutive regions containing the variables as classified in the analytical framework. Moving from left to right, closely surrounding the *readjustment* variable (i.e. most strongly correlated with it) are the *success* variables, followed by the region of *individual resources.* Next comes the region of *primary group support*, in turn followed by *rehabilitation assistance*, which borders with the region of *dependence*. Farthest from readjustment (i.e. strongly negatively correlated with it) lies the region of 'demands' which partly overlaps (i.e. closely correlated with) the region of dependence (μ_2 between *readjustment* and *dependence* items varies: -0.73, -0.61, -0.49, -0.20 and -0.36 according to their order in Appendix C).

In the region of *rehabilitation assistance*, at the bottom of the map and close to the region of *dependence*, are located the variables comprising *latent functions*; these are relatively remote from (i.e. negatively correlated with) both affective and instru-

*Because of space economy, matrix of correlation coefficients not included but can be obtained from the author.

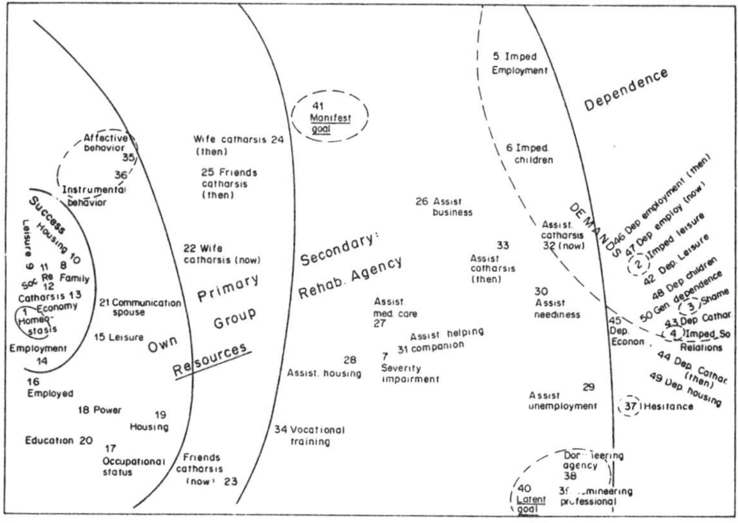

Fig. 2. The empirical structure of readjustment: two-dimensional smallest space analysis (SSA-1) of the intercorrelations (μ_2) among the variables (see Appendix C).

mental behavior (μ_2 varies from -0.81 to -0.66), yet positively correlated with *hesitance* to seek the rehabilitator's emotional support ($\mu_2 = 0.43$). The variables of manifest functions, on the other hand, also in the *rehabilitation assistance* region, are located close to the *success* region.

Attribution of latent goals

An in-depth analysis of the data highlights the function of attributing to the rehabilitator pursuit of latent goals (variable 40). First, its strong relationship with the rehabilitator's domineering behavior (variables 38 and 39—$\mu_2 = 0.53$ and 0.59 respectively) suggests the significance of the rehabilitator's behavior with respect to the suspected latent interests of the rehabilitator. Second, the negative correlations of both latent goals and domineering behavior with all of the *successful coping* items allude to their detrimental function in furthering successful coping—a function ascertained by their positive correlations with all *dependence* (variables 42–50). This implies that the more a rehabilitant perceives the rehabilitator as pursuing latent goals, the greater the rehabilitator's dependence on the service.

These findings bring us back to the crucial question of the study, namely: to what extent is the perception of the rehabilitator as pursuing latent goals associated with the relationship between rehabilitation assistance and dependence? In relating to this question, respondents were divided into two groups—those highly inclined to suspect the existence of latent goals (Hi: $N = 261$), and those with a low inclination to do so (Lo: $N = 267$). The cutting point between the two groups was the median.

In Table 1, correlation coefficients (μ_2) between dependence items and high (Hi) inclination to suspect latent goals are compared with those between dependence and (Lo) low inclination. Except for a few exceptions, for which we have at present no explanation, the data greatly support the hypothesis that association between receiving assistance and dependence is a product of the attribution of latent functions. The data follow a consistent pattern, in which the positive coefficients are weaker in the Lo group than in the Hi group, and some of the relationships are even weakly negative. The grand average of the correlations at the right bottom corner of the table ($\bar{\mu}_2 = 0.26$ in the Hi group goes down to 0.12 in the Lo group) evidently highlights the overall finding that rehabilitants who are highly inclined to attribute to their helpers the inclination of satisfying predominantly their self-interests (latent goals), are also relatively highly susceptible to perpetuated dependence. Conclusions as to the types of assistance whose consequences are most likely to be negatively affected by perception of latent goals may be derived from a comparison of the average correlations ($\bar{\mu}_2$) at the bottom row of Table 1: monetary assistance for employing a helping companion (0.22 to -0.02), unemployment payments (0.45–0.24), payments during medical treatment (0.12–0.02), and monetary help for establishing a business (0.13 to -0.03). Also with respect to emotional support, the efficacy of the rehabilitator's assistance regarding 'catharsis' is contingent on the perception of his goals (0.44–0.31). On the other hand, the consequences of vocational training and monetary allowance for housing seem to be unaffected by perception of latent goals.

Table 1. Correlations (μ_2) between receiving rehabilitation assistance and dependence, by extent of the rehabilitant's perception of rehabilitator's pursuance of latent goals (decimal point omitted)

Dependence on rehabilitation agency regarding:	Correlation (μ_2) between dependence and receiving rehabilitation assistance regarding:																			
	Business		Medical treatment		Housing		Unemployment		Neediness		Companion		Catharsis (now)		Catharsis (then)*		Vocation training		Average	
	Perceived latent goals of rehabilitation worker																			
	Lo	Hi	Lo	Hi	Lo	Hi	Lo	Hi	Lo	Hi	Lo	Hi	Lo	Hi	Lo	Hi	Lo	Hi	Lo	Hi
Leisure	−17	05	−25	19	05	17	32	35	41	56	−16	24	52	48	38	33	05	−03	13	26
Catharsis (now)	−10	−01	−23	08	−08	−03	29	52	37	50	−16	11	42	64	30	44	−15	02	07	25
Catharsis (then)*	11	−04	−05	04	−11	−01	22	28	06	31	−18	04	15	37	51	63	−11	−25	07	15
Economy	−19	43	43	43	21	25	26	69	85	62	41	67	44	57	42	35	11	02	33	45
Employment (then)*	−11	37	02	−01	−04	01	41	48	16	40	−19	29	18	37	38	45	10	02	10	26
Employment (now)	−09	42	08	12	−11	−07	18	39	44	78	−06	−01	14	48	41	33	01	−04	13	27
Children's needs	25	−20	−01	−16	−21	15	−18	17	−09	29	05	−13	33	11	54	29	−31	−13	04	04
Housing	−02	−16	−13	06	−27	07	32	47	13	54	−20	21	17	34	18	19	−18	08	00	20
In general	−09	35	32	35	06	20	31	66	77	74	30	55	40	58	13	44	−15	−14	23	41
Average (all areas of life)	−03	13	02	12	−05	08	24	45	34	53	−02	22	31	44	36	38	−07	−05	12	26

*'Then' = at the time of discharge from medical rehabilitation institution.

The function of the rehabilitator's affective behavior

The power of the rehabilitator's affective behavior in counteracting the inclination to attribute to him latent goals seems evident from its strong negative correlation with such goals ($\mu_2 = -0.66$). Concomitantly, affective behavior enhances the rehabilitant's belief in the rehabilitator's sincere intentions of promoting his readjustment (μ_2 with manifest goals = 0.52) and encourages turning for help in coping with emotional problems (μ_2 with hesitation to turn for help for emotional problems = 0.52) Furthermore, perception of affective behavior evidently promotes a feeling of successfully coping with demands (μ_2 with successful coping varies from 0.49–0.28) and contributes to decreasing dependence (μ_2 varies from −0.43 to −0.14).

DISCUSSION AND SUMMARY

The present study contributes to the understanding of the factors involved in promoting or impeding readjustment in the wake of impairment. By further developing the paradigm of readjustment which has been suggested and empirically verified in earlier studies [2, 3, 45], the contribution of the present study is specifically in the understanding of the detrimental outcomes that may result from rehabilitation assistance. Attributing to rehabilitators the *latent*, though predominant, goal of pursuing self-interest rather than the rehabilitant's, greatly explains the resulting dependence. The detrimental consequences of perceived latent goals are particularly evident with regard to direct monetary compensations (e.g. monetary assistance for neediness, unemployment, establishing a business). These findings may lend further support to the conclusion, delineated in a recent article [14], that *resource compensation*, though immediately rewarding, may in the long run be perceived as having been aimed at perpetuating the rehabilitant's inferior position. The effect of attributing latent goals on the negative outcome of the search for 'catharsis' may serve as an additional support of this line of reasoning: in this type of assistance, in which a close interaction between the rehabilitator and the rehabilitant is needed, the former's demonstration of dominance may result both in reluctance to seek his emotional support ('hesitance') and in an increasing sense of inferiority, hence being detrimental to readjustment of the rehabilitant.

On the other hand, demonstration of affective—i.e. humane person-oriented—behavior, greatly counteracts these deleterious consequences. It evidently fulfills an important function in bridging over the dominance-gap by opening a two-way channel of communication, giving the rehabilitant a sense of cooperation in a common task and reducing his sense of being merely an object for satisfying the rehabilitator's self-interest. In fact, the close association of the rehabilitator's affective behavior with the rehabilitant's successful coping suggests that this type of behavior apparently constitutes a resource by its own merit. Thus the study reveals that the significance of affective behavior in client satisfaction, as ascertained in studies on physician–patient relationship [37, 38, 40, 41], applies also to this type of needy population.

It will be recalled that readjustment has been conceptualized as successful resolution of stress, which is a consequence of unmet demands. Thus, the study contributes to the understanding of the demand–stress relationship. In particular, it clearly supports Lazarus' [44, 46] contention that it is not the demand *per se*, but rather its *subjectively* perceived implications, that makes it a stressor. This we infer from the lack of correlation of emotional homeostasis with the severity of the impairment *vis-à-vis* its relatively strong negative correlations with *perceived implications* of impairment.

These conclusions, however, should be considered with caution, in light of several weaknesses.

First, the study is unable to ascertain causality. In this respect, however, the present study does not differ from any other field study in the social sciences which has to use personal interviews for data collection. (Controlled experiments which allow for establishing causality are evidently irrelevant for the present type of study. Ascertaining causality merely by data analysis methods is seriously questioned today [69].)

Second, the fact that the study has no longitudinal followup, may be considered a further shortcoming. However, in view of the great difficulties involved, the present study may at least provide important, empirically-based insights regarding the factors involved in the readjustment of disabled persons, thus lending further contribution to evidence from other recent empirical studies in the field of rehabilitation [2–5]).

However, some confidence regarding the direction of the prediction may be obtained from the time sequence: whereas the reporting about receiving rehabilitation assistance relates mostly to the past, the respondents' condition regarding successful coping and readjustment relates to the present.

The fact that this study is confined to the Israeli society, is doubtlessly a limitation on the external validity of the findings for other societies. Further research is needed for validating the paradigm in other cultural contexts.

However, despite these limitations, I think that the study may provide insights regarding the eventual deleterious consequences that rehabilitation assistance may have. The association between dependence and attributing latent functions on the one hand, and that between successful coping and affective behavior on the other, may allude to the importance of the rehabilitator's behavior toward his client and sensitivity to his needs, conforming with Wright *et al.* [27, p. 168] who urge "welfare workers...to revive a humanistic orientation in the welfare bureaucracy [and]...at least...to increase their level of sensitivity and awareness of cultural differences between themselves and their clients".

The findings bring up the question that has been raised in a recent paper [14] regarding the problematics of *resource compensation* activities in rehabilitation, and the efforts that should be devoted to *resource enhancement* activities: direct assistance may be immediately rewarding, but in the long run it may lead to feelings of deprivation, with its deleterious consequences. Of course, rehabilitation assistance is occasionally concerned with highly impaired persons who may lack the most basic resources. The question, however, is whether efforts are being made to identify and determine the limit up to which resource compensation is indispensable, and from there start the laborious effort of *resource enhancement* activities. The study may at least draw attention on the one hand to some of the deleterious consequences of relinquishing such efforts. On the other hand, it highlights the necessity of promoting the disabled persons' belief in the caregivers' aim to act as their advocates assisting them to act for themselves [18, p. 57].

Acknowledgements—This study is part of a project on the 'Achievements of Rehabilitation', commissioned by the Department of Rehabilitation of the Israeli Ministry of Defense and conducted by the author in the framework of the Israel Institute of Applied Social Research. My gratitude is expressed to the Department of Rehabilitation, and specifically to Dr E. Lahav, Chief of Research and Planning in that department, for their cordial assistance in rendering any required information and clarification, their helpful remarks and cooperation throughout all stages of the entire project, and for their permission to use the data for this paper. However, the responsibility for the analysis, interpretation of the data, and conclusions rest entirely with the author. My gratitude is expressed to Mrs Haya Gratch for her indispensible assistance and advice in editing this paper.

REFERENCES

1. Russel R. Concepts of adjustment to disability: an overview. *Rehab. Lit.* **42,** 330–337, 1981.
2. Ben-Sira Z. The structure of readjustment of the disabled: an additional perspective on rehabilitation. *Soc Sci. Med.* **15A,** 565–581, 1981.
3. Ben-Sira Z. Loss, stress and readjustment. *Soc Sci. Med.* **17,** 1619–1632, 1983.
4. Smith R T. and Midanik L. The effect of social resources on recovery and perceived sense of control among disabled. *Sociol. Hlth Illness* **2,** 48–63, 1980.
5. Albrecht G. L. and Higgins P. C. Rehabilitation success: the interrelationship of multiple criteria. *J. Hlth soc. Behav.* **18,** 36–45, 1977.
6. Cull J. G. and Hardy R. E. (Eds) Understanding the psychological aspects of disability. In *Understanding Disability for Rehabilitation Services*, pp. 97–111 Thomas, Springfield, Ill., 1973
7. Goldin G. S., Perry S. L., Margolin R. S. and Stotsky B. A. *Dependence and its Implications for Rehabilitation.* Heath, Lexington, Mass., 1972.
8. Stotsky B. A. Social psychological factors in dependency. *Rehab. Rec.* **4,** 8–9, 1963.
9. Levitin T. E. Deviants as active participants in the labeling process: The visibly handicapped. In *Health, Illness and Medicine* (Edited by Albrecht G. L. and Higgins P.). Rand–McNally, Chicago, 1979.
10. Safilios-Rothschild C. *The Sociology and Social Psychology of Disability and Rehabilitation.* Random House, New York, 1970.
11. Blau P. M. *Exchange and Power in Social Life.* Wiley, New York 1969.
12. Freidson E. *Profession of Medicine.* Dodd, Mead, New York, 1972.
13. Germain C. B. *Social Work Practice in Health Care* Free Press, New York, 1984.
14. Ben-Sira Z. Societal integration of the disabled: power struggle or enhancement of individual coping capacities. *Soc. Sci. Med.* **17,** 1011–1014, 1983.
15. Parsons T. *The Social System.* Glencoe, New York, 1964.

16. Elliot P. *The Sociology of Professions*. Macmillan, London, 1972.
17. Albrecht G. L. (Ed.) Socialization and the disability process. In *The Sociology of Physical Disability and Rehabilitation*, pp. 3–38. The University of Pittsburgh Press, Pittsburgh, 1976.
18. Zola I. K. Developing new self images and interdependence. In *Independent Living for Physically Disabled People* (Edited by Crewe N. M. and Zola I. K.) pp 49–59. Jossey–Bass, San Francisco, 1983.
19. Zola I. K. *Missing Pieces: A Chronical of Living with Disability*. Temple University Press, Philadelphia, 1982.
20. Sussman M. R. The disabled and the rehabilitation system. In *The Sociology of Physical Disability and Rehabilitation* (Edited by Albrecht G. L.), pp. 223–246. The University of Pittsburgh Press, Pittsburgh, 1976.
21 Ben-Sira Z. The doctor–patient relationship: collectivism or exchange. Unpublished Ph.D. thesis (Hebrew), Hebrew University, Jerusalem, 1972.
22. Betz M. and O'Connel L. Changing doctor–patient relationships and the rise in concern to accountability. *Social Problems* **31**, 84–95, 1983.
23. Burnham J. C. American medicine's golden age: what happened to it? *Science* **215**, 1475–1478, 1982.
24. Cihlar C. Consumer views. *Hospitals* **48**, 189–191, 1974.
25. Jackson J. A. (Ed.) Professions and professionalization. In *Professions and Professionalization*. Cambridge University Press, London, 1970.
26. Johnson T S. *Professions and Power* Macmillan, London, 1972.
27 Wright R., Salleby D., Watts T and Lecco P. *Transcultural Perspectives in Human Services*. Thomas, Springfield, Ill., 1983.
28. Goffman E. *Asylums*. Penguin, Harmondsworth, 1968.
29. Perrow C the analysis of goals in complex organizations. In *Readings on Modern Organizations* (Edited by Etzioni A.). Prentice–Hall, Englewood Cliffs, N.J., 1969.
30. Haug M. R. The erosion of professional authority: a cross cultural inquiry in the case of the physician. *Milbank meml Fund Q.* **54**, 83–105, 1976.
31. Haug M. R. and Sussman M. B. Professional autonomy and the revolt of the client. *Social Problems* **17**, 153–161, 1969.
32. Haug M. R. and Lavin B. Practitioner or patient—who's in charge? *J. Hlth soc. Behav.* **22**, 212–229, 1983.
33. De Jong G. *Environmental Accessibility and Independent Living Outcomes: Directions for Disability Policy and Research*. Michigan State University, Michigan, 1981.
34 De Jong G. *The Movement for Independent Living: Origins, Ideology and Implications for Disability Research*. Michigan State University, Michigan, 1979.
35. Williams G. H. The movement for independent living: an evaluation and critique. *Soc. Sci. Med.* **17**, 1003–1010, 1983.
36. De Jong G. Defining and implementing the independent living concept. In *Independent Living for Physically Disabled People* (Edited by Crewe N. M. and Zola I. K.). pp. 4–27. Jossey–Bass, San Francisco, 1983.
37. Ben-Sira Z. Lay evaluation of medical treatment and competence: Development of a model of the function of the physician's affective behavior. *Soc. Sci. Med.* **16**, 1013–1019, 1982.
38. Ben-Sira Z. Stress potential and esotericity of health problems: the significance of the physician's affective behavior. *Med. Care* **20**, 414–424, 1982.
39. Saxton M. Peer counseling. In *Independent Living for Physically Disabled People* (Edited by Crewe N. M. and Zola I. K.), pp. 171–186. Jossey–Bass, San Francisco, 1983.
40. Ben-Sira Z. Affective and instrumental components in the physician–patient relationship: an additional dimension of interaction theory. *J. Hlth soc. Behav.* **21**, 170–180, 1980.
41. Ben-Sira Z. The function of the professional's affective behavior in client satisfaction: a revised approach to social interaction theory. *J. Hlth soc. Behav.* **17**, 3–11, 1976.
42. Antonovsky A. Breakdown: A needed fourth step in the conceptual armamentarium of modern medicine. *Soc. Sci. Med.* **6**, 537–544, 1972.
43. Antonovsky A. *Health, Stress ana Coping*. Jossey–Bass, San Francisco, 1979.
44. Lazarus R. S. and Cohen J. B. Environmental stress. In *Human Behavior and Environment* (Edited by Altman I and Wohlwill J. F.), Vol. 2. Plenum Press, New York, 1977.
45. Ben-Sira Z. Chronic illness, stress and coping. *Soc. Sci. Med.* **18**, 725–736. 1984.
46. Lazarus R. S. *Psychological Stress and the Coping Process*. McGraw–Hill, New York, 1966.
47. Jones E. E., Amerigo F., Hastorf A. H., Markus H., Miller D. T. and Scott R. A. *Social Stigma*. Freeman, New York, 1984.
48. Pearlin L. I. and Schooler C. The structure of coping. *J. Hlth soc. Behav.* **19**, 2–21, 1978.
49. Pearlin L. I., Lieberman M. A. Menaghan E. G. and Mullin J. T. The stress process. *J. Hlth soc. Behav.* **22**, 337–356, 1981
50. Reid N. P. and Gundlach J. H. A scale for the measurement of consumer satisfaction with social services. *J. soc. Serv. Res.* **7**, 37–54, 1983.
51. Langner T. S. A twenty-two item screening score of psychiatric symptoms indicating impairment. *J. Hlth Hum. Behav.* **3**, 1982, 269–276, 1962.
52. Abramson J. H The Cornell Medical Index as an epidemiological tool. *Am. J. publ. Hlth* **56**, 287–298, 1966.
53. Cochrane R. A comparative evaluation of the symptom rating test and the Langner 22-Item Index for use in epidemiological surveys. *Psychol. Med.* **10**, 115 124, 1980.
54. Wildman R. C and Johnson D. R. Life change and Langner's 22-Item Mental Health Index: a study and partial replication. *J. Hlth soc Behav* **18**, 197 198, 1977.
55. Johnson D. R. and Meile R. L. Does dimensionality bias in Langner's 22-Item affect the validity of social status comparisons? *J. Hlth soc. Behav.* **22**, 415–437, 1981.
56. Ben-Sira Z. Potency: a stress-buffering link in the coping–stress–disease relationship. *Soc. Sci. Med.* **21**, 397–406, 1985.
57. Kohn M. L. Class, family and schizophrenia. *Social Forces* **50**, 1972, 295–302, 1985.
58. Dohrenwend B. S. and Dohrenwend B. P. Class and race as status related sources of stress. In *Social Stress* (Edited by Levine S. and Scotch N. A.), pp. 111–140. Aldine, New York, 1970.
59. Musgrave P. H. *The Sociology of Education*. Methuen, London, 1972.
60. Thoits P. A. Conceptual methodological and theoretical problems in studying social support as a buffer against life stress. *J. Hlth soc. Behav.* **23**, 145–156, 1982.
61. Lin N., Simeon R. S., Ensel W. M. and Kuo W. Social support, stressful life events, and illness: a model and an empirical test. *J. Hlth soc. Behav.* **20**, 108–119, 1979.
62. Guttman L. and Levy S. Structure and dynamics of worries. *Sociometry* **38**, 448–473, 1975.
63. Rave A. Finding periodic patterns in time series with monotonic trend: a new technique. In *Theory Construction and Data Analysis in Behavioral Sciences* (Edited by Shye S.), pp. 371–390. Jossey–Bass, San Francisco, 1978.
64. Ben-Sira Z. and Guttman L. *A Facet Theoretical*

Approach to Research. Institute of Applied Social Research, Jerusalem, Israel, 1971.

65 Bloombaum M. Doing smallest space analysis. *J. Conflict Resolut.* **14,** 409–416, 1970.

66. Brown J. An introduction to the uses of facet theory. In *Facet Theory: Approaches to Social Research* (Edited by Canter D.), pp. 17–57. Springer, New York, 1985.

67. Canter D. (Ed.) *Facet Theory: Approaches to Social Research*. Springer, New York, 1985.

68. Borg I. (Ed.) *Multidimensional Data Representations. When and Why*. Mathesis Press, Ann Arbor, Mich., 1981.

69. Guttman L. What is not what in statistics. *Statistician* **26,** 81–107, 1977.

APPENDIX A

Sample Characteristics

1. All respondents were male	
2. Degree of impairment:	%
19% and less	17
20–29%	17
30–39%	18
40–49%	8
50–79%	20
80–100%	20
	100%
N	(540)
3. Year of birth	
1923 and before	11
1924–1928	10
1929–1933	10
1934–1938	11
1939–1943	11
1944–1948	18
1949–1953	21
1954–1959	7
	100%
N	(541)
4. Year of impairment	
1947 and before	3
1948–1949	15 (War of Independence)
1950–1956	10 (1956: Sinai campaign)
1957–1966	9
1967	9 (Six Day War)
1968–1970	14 (War of Attrition)
1971–1972	7
1973	21 (Yom Kippur War)
1974–1977	12
	100%
N	(543)
5. The decisive damage which affected the degree of impairment	
Upper extremities (not incl. amputation)	13
Lower extremities (not incl. amputation)	21
Spine (no paralysis)	4
Chest/abdomen/back (not incl. spine)	11
Eyes (no blindness)	3
Blindness of one eye	4
Complete blindness	2
Head	18
Amputation of one or both legs	5
Amputation of one or both arms	3
Paralysis of lower extremities (paraplegia)	3
Quadriplegia	1
Other (incl. mental and other chronic illnesses)	11
	100%
N	(543)

APPENDIX B

Measure of Affective Behavior

Wording of the introduction to the battery of questions in the questionnaire was as following: "When you turned to the rehabilitator for help in a problem relating to your condition, to what extent was his behavior toward you, in the following aspects, sufficient, in accordance with your expectations?" (1—entirely sufficient...6—entirely insufficient).

Behavior item (question)	Factor loading
Devoted sufficient time	0.75
Showed interest in personal problems	0.80
Paid careful attention to my problems, whatever they were	0.80
Related to me as human being and not as a number	0.80
Made an effort to explore and detect problems and needs	0.84
Made an effort to seek the most appropriate solution to my needs	0.86
Showed the same attitude to all clients	0.68
Explained rationale of his/her judgements and decisions	0.77
Gave a feeling that he/she represented the disabled's interests	0.85
Gave a feeling that his/her job was to *serve* the disabled	0.86
Encouraged in times of breakdown	0.85
Gave reassurance	0.84

APPENDIX C

List of Variables

Domain	Variable
Readjustment	1. Psychological homeostasis
Demands	2. Impediment: leisure
	3. Shame
	4. Impediments: social relations
	5. Impediment: employment
	6. Impediment: relations with children
	7. Severity of impairment
Successful coping with demands of:	8. Family life
	9. Leisure
	10. Housing
	11. Social relations
	12. Catharsis
	13. Economy
	14. Employment
Own resources	15. Spending leisure
	16. Employment
	17. Occupational status
	18. Power (no. of subordinates)
	19. Housing density (Lo–Hi)
	20. Education
	21. Communication with spouse
Primary environmental resources (primary socials support)	22. Spouse catharsis (now)
	23. Friends catharsis (now)
	24. Spouse catharsis (then)*
	25. Friends catharsis (then)
Secondary environmental resources (assistance from rehabilitation agency)	26. Monetary assistance for establishing business
	27. Monetary assistance during medical treatment
	28. Monetary assistance for housing
	29. Monetary assistance for unemployment
	30. Monetary assistance for general neediness
	31. Monetary assistance for employing companion
	32. Catharsis (now)
	33. Catharsis (then)
	34. Vocational training
Behavior toward rehabilitant	35. Affective
	36. Instrumental
Rehabilitant's hesitance	37. Hesitance in turning for emotional support
Latent goal	38. Domineering agency
	39. Domineering professional
	40. Latent goal
Manifest goal	41. Sincere assistance
Dependence on rehabilitation agency regarding:	42. Leisure
	43. Catharsis (now)
	44. Catharsis (then)
	45. Economy
	46. Employment (then)
	47. Employment (now)
	48. Children's needs
	49. Housing
	50. In general

*Then = at time of discharge from medical rehabilitation institution.

21

Soviet Immigrant Physicians in Israel

Judith T. Shuval

Since the early 1970s, over 162,000 Jews have migrated to Israel from the Soviet Union. Among these have been more than 1,250 physicians. Between 1970 and 1980 they comprised 45 percent of all immigrant physicians to Israel. This chapter presents selected findings from a sociological study that examined the entry processes of these physicians into a new occupational structure (Shuval 1983). It may be viewed as a case study in professional migration that attempts to elucidate more general patterns that are not idiosyncratic to Israel.

An influx of trained immigrant labor most often represents an asset for a host country, which thereby gains skills without having directly invested in educational expenses or training. At the same time, some effort is needed to utilize fully the contributions that can be made by people trained in a diversity of occupational skills, often in traditions differing from those of the host society. Thus, it may take time for long-term benefits from immigrant labor to become apparent, while short-run dysfunctions may be considerable.

For a professional group such as physicians, characterized by the norms of that profession in the host society, acculturation seems comparativley simple. In the case considered here, modern, Western-style medicine is practiced in both the Soviet Union and in Israel; however, since the general cultural context and the values of the social system, as well as the history and structure of professional practice, affect the nature of role performance, professionals are likely to perform somewhat differently in the two societies.

The migration of professionals has been a widespread phenomenon in recent years and has been encouraged by many countries principally in order to augment inadequate manpower in certain fields. Medicine has been prominent among these. (Fortney 1970; Mick 1975; Stevens, Goodman, and Mick, 1978). The European Common Market has been

---

Some of the material in this chapter has appeared in "Soviet Immigrant Physicians in Israel" in *Soviet Jewish Affairs* 14, no. 2 (1984). Unattributed quotations in this chapter are comments by interviewees.

actively concerned with physician mobility among its member countries and particularly with problems of licensing (Commission of the European Communities 1974; Orzack 1980). In the 1970s, one-fifth of all physicians practicing medicine in the United States and Canada were trained in foreign medical schools (Mick 1975). Limitations on the admission of immigrants have recently been imposed by a number of countries largely because of changes in the number of locally educated professions and economic cutbacks. Indeed in virtually all countries with the exception of Israel, migration policies have been geared to reflect labor needs of the economy.

The acceptance of immigrants, who may have been forced to leave their homes or who may have opted to come, has been one of the high priorities of Israeli society. Despite the fact that Israel is characterized by the highest doctor-to-population ratio in the world—1 to 351 (World Health Organization 1978)—there has never been any reservation about the importance of admitting immigrant physicians and integrating them into the medical care system, albeit this has not always been easy.

This chapter presents four aspects of this process with regard to Soviet immigrant physicians: licensing procedure and its social function; social and professional background; medical practice in Israel; and feelings of Soviet immigrant physicians about their professional work in Israel. More comprehensive details on these and related topics have been presented elsewhere (Shuval 1983).

Study Population

In 1972, 31,652 immigrants arrived in Israel from the Soviet Union, among whom were 405 physicians. In 1975 it was decided to examine how the 1972 arrivals had entered the medical care system. A three-year period allows newcomers time to acquaint themselves with the system and to deal with early problems of adaptation; however, newness and immigrant status are still clearly evident to the individual and to relevant reference groups.

By 1975, 19 (5 percent) of the physicians who arrived in 1972 had left Israel (Israel Ministry of Absorption 1979). There were 386 immigrant physicians in 1975 who were eligible for the study; 298 were contacted and interviewed either in their homes or clinics. These do not constitute a sample but rather 77 percent of the total population under consideration. After several attempts, the remainder were not interviewed because addresses were wrong or the physicians were unavailable. Eight persons (2 percent) refused to be interviewed. The data presented here are drawn from the 298 physicians interviewed. In addition, qualitative data were gathered from interviews with 25 Israeli physicians who had served as supervisors of immigrant doctors during their early period in the country.

Medical Licensure in Israel and Its Social Functions

The mechanism for licensing immigrant physicians in Israel parallels the more general procedure for medical licensure. It involves a two-stage process: to establish formal professional qualifications for general medical practice and to establish qualifications for specialty practice.

At the first stage, after the immigrant physician has shown competence in the Hebrew language, the Licensing Authority of the Ministry of Health examines the physician's credentials. If these demonstrate completion of studies at one of the medical schools listed by the World Health Organization, a one-year license is granted for general practice. Documents are subjected to cautious scrutiny, and, in the case of Soviet immigrants, a work card listing occupational history (dates and job description) may serve as additional verification for medical status. If there is doubt about the validity of these documents, the Ministry of Health rechecks the claimant's medical school diploma, requiring in some cases confirmation from the Soviet authorities. This is the same general procedure as was used to validate the credentials of refugee physicians after World War II (Holborn 1956).

Since all immigrant physicians are employed in one of the medical care organizations, they are all subject to collegial evaluation. At the end of one year, the immigrant physician's supervisor is required to evaluate professional performance. If this evaluation is positive, the immigrant is granted a license for general practice. Almost all of the Soviet immigrant physicians who received a one-year license were eventually licensed for general practice.

This first stage of licensure should be viewed in the context of the Israeli health care system. Israel does not have a national health insurance system; however, almost the entire Jewish population is covered by comprehensive health insurance through sick funds: 80 percent are covered by Kupat Holim of the General Federation of Labor, and an additional 10 percent are covered by a number of small sick funds. Virtually all physicians are salaried. Although there is private practice, it is used by a relatively small proportion of the population. The few physicians who practice privately do so on a part-time basis in addition to their full-time salaried posts. The licensure system must be viewed in terms of a medical care system in which virtually all physicians are employed by Kupat Holim, by one of the hospitals run by the Ministry of Health, or by one of the other health care organizations. Therefore, there is maximum exposure to collegial scrutiny and evaluation (Grushka 1968; Davies 1972; Medalie 1972; Doron 1979; Shuval et al. 1970, 1983).

At the second stage, qualification for licensure in a medical specialty is determined by the Scientific Council of the Israel Medical Association. The gatekeeping process involves a critical scrutiny of the immigrant physician's qualifications and training to ascertain whether he or she reaches the local standard. In the case of Soviet immigrant physicians, the process is complicated by the multitiered system of specialization in the Soviet Union and the different forms of training required for each. The immigrant physician may have to take extra courses, which are individually tailored to his or her background or, depending on the physician's experience, an examination may be required.

Comparative Structure of Medical Education and Specialization

In this study of Soviet immigrant physicians in Israel, the social functions of licensing need to be viewed against the medical education and training for specialization that prevail in the two societies. These differ considerably.

There are ninety-two medical schools in the Soviet Union, of which only nine are attached to universities. On the whole there is a preference in the USSR for teaching applied studies at institutes rather than at universities, and graduates are granted a diploma rather than a degree (Ryan 1978). Thus there is a practical emphasis in medical education, which is less oriented to the pure science background or research component of medical practice.

The medical school course lasted five years until 1955, when it was lengthened to six years. In 1966 a further year of mandatory internship was added. Fewer than 20 percent of the immigrant physicians in this study were trained after 1966. Forty-six percent completed their training before 1955, when the curriculum lasted only five years. The upheavals of World War II and its aftermath were felt by 40 percent who underwent their medical training during that period. On the whole, then, the immigrant physicians' training was somewhat shorter than that of many of their Israeli colleagues.

Students in the USSR are admitted to medical school on completion of eleven years of primary and secondary school. Admission is highly competitive, and admission ratios range from one in five applications to one in fifteen, depending on the medical school. Preference is given to people who worked in allied health professions. Twenty percent of medical students are former *feldshers*, or assistant physicians mostly in rural areas (Muller et al. 1972). An additional 10 percent are foreigners from developing countries (Ryan 1978). Groups that receive preference vary from time to time (Cooper 1971; Fry 1969; Fry and Crome 1972).

A major effort has been exerted in the Soviet Union to augment the physician population rapidly by admitting large numbers of students to medical school. In the late 1960s the average entering class numbered 330 as contrasted to 88 in the United States and 64 in Britain (Fry 1969). Such large classes necessarily limited the quality of teaching. A group of Western visitors to the USSR noted that students in laboratories were only able to observe rather than participate. Furthermore, because research is conducted primarily in special institutes rather than in the medical schools, students have little exposure to basic research during their training.

A high proportion of Soviet physicians are women (70 percent in 1975). This percentage will decrease in the future because a deliberate attempt is being made to increase the proportion of males in the medical student population (Ryan 1978). In 1976 only 56 percent of the medical students were women.

After completing their training, graduates of Soviet medical schools are required to practice for three years in areas in need of medical personnel. In fact, many apparently evade this obligation or succeed in influencing the location of their post. These are often married women graduates who do not want to be separated from their spouses during their service (Ryan 1978).

Specialization begins early in the Soviet system of education. When entering professional school, the Soviet student chooses one of four career lines in health: general medicine (therapy), pediatrics, public health, or dentistry (stomotology). During the first two years the curricula for these programs are similar, including chemistry, biology, physics, anatomy, histology, physiology, and Marxism. Beginning with the third and fourth years of study, the curriculum differs for each of these areas. During the sixth year, students specialize in a specific area of practice, which they continue during internship. Before the introduction of a compulsory internship, graduates were licensed to practice after six years, when they would be considered first-level specialists. More recently graduates go through an additional year of specialized study during their internship before starting practice as first-level specialists. This is called the *subordinatura* level of specialization and is based on an early streaming process during medical school training. Large numbers of physicians practice as specialists after the *subordinatura*.

After completing three years of service, physicians may attain specialty status by attending postgraduate courses in a specialty field. They receive time off from their regular job for additional training, and specialty status may be attained over a period of several years. Alternatively, young physicians may enter a formal program of specialization, the *ordinatura*, a two-year program of supervised clinical training in one of the specialty areas.

An alternative, more ambitious formal specialization program is the *aspirantura,* which can also be entered after the three-year service period. The *aspirantura* is three years of intensive clinical work in a specialty area, a research project, a thesis, and an examination. It is geared to physicians seeking senior posts or academic careers. On completion of the *aspirantura,* specialists are accorded the title candidate for medical science (Fry, 1969).

An even higher level of specialization can be acquired after several years of additional specialization and completion of a much more elaborate thesis. This highest level is the doctor of medical science.

Four percent of the immigrant physicians in the present study had completed the *aspirantura,* 11 percent the *ordinatura,* 7 percent had some other form of specialization, and 59 percent reported that they had attained a specialty through postgraduate courses. Nineteen percent of the immigrant doctors stated that they had no recognized specialty status in the Soviet Union. The latter group may have responded in terms of the perceived system of specialization in Israel since virtually all physicians in the Soviet Union are considered specialists. In its effort to upgrade the level of medical care, the Soviet Union structured its entire medical care system according to specialty practices, in effect eliminating the role of generalist in medicine (Fry and Crome 1972).

The general trend in the Soviet Union toward narrow specialization was reflected in the excessive splintering and proliferation of specific areas of medical practice, which numbered 173 in 1969. The Soviets realizing that this trend was excessive, recognized 51 specialties in 1970 (Popov 1971; Ryan 1978). But many of the immigrant physicians in the study had entered practice prior to the 1970 consolidation of specialties and continued to view themselves as specialists.

An interesting example of an area that is highly developed in the Soviet Union but is only marginal in Israel is balneology: the curative use of spas and baths for prevention and therapy. There is widespread use in the USSR of therapeutic mud and mineral waters for both baths and drinking. Rest homes and sanatoriums are available and widely recommended by physicians for a great variety of ailments. Some observers suggest that these forms of treatment are, at least to some extent, functional equivalents of tranquilizers, which are widely prescribed in Western countries (Forster and Benton 1966).

Furthermore, some of the specialty areas recognized in the Soviet Union are defined or categorized differently in Israel. In some cases they do not exist. Among these unfamiliar medical specialties, Ryan (1978) lists infectious diseases, dietetics, physiotherapy, laboratory medicine, and general or communal hygiene. While some of these areas of practice exist in the West and in Israel, physicians do not generally engage in them.

The Israeli system of medical education presents a different picture. Basic medical education in Israel is a seven-year process. Students are admitted on the basis of their average grade on the nationally administered secondary school matriculation examinations; only top achievers are permitted to apply. Stringent selection from this pool is carried out by each of the four medical schools by means of a variety of intelligence and personality tests. Over a thousand young people apply each year for about 230 places; the ratios of admission vary among the schools depending on the number of applicants to each (Shuval 1980).

All medical schools are affiliated to universities. Students are exposed to a rigorous science-based academic program, as well as considerable ongoing research by teaching staff, both preclinical and clinical.

The seven-year period is divided into four subperiods: one premedical year during which basic sciences and some social science are taught; two preclinical years during which subjects include anatomy, physiology, biochemistry, pharmacology, pathology, growth, and development and epidemiology; and three clinical years during which students rotate in small groups through different clinical departments. During the sixth clinical year, they take the final examinations and, upon passing them, are given the title doctor and a temporary license to practice. (A somewhat different curriculum exists at the Beersheba Medical School.) In order to obtain a permanent license, they must complete a final year of internship in a recognized hospital. The internship is structured on a rotating basis: three months of internal medicine, one additional month in a subspecialty of internal medicine, two months in general surgery, one month in orthopedic surgery, one month in traumatology, two months in pediatrics, and two (sometimes three) months in elected departments. The deliberately designed rotating system is not intended to produce specialists at the end of internship.

On completion of the internship, students receive a license to practice but no specialty status. Specialization begins after internship and involves between three and a half to five and a half years of additional clinical training in a specific field under the supervision of senior specialists. National examinations (boards), which the physician must pass before being recognized as a specialist, have been required since 1973 and are controlled by the Israel Medical Association. Prior to that date, competence was determined by the supervising specialist. Specialty status is conservatively controlled by the profession, and every effort is made to maintain high standards. There are no intermediate levels of specialization, although some fields require longer periods of training than others. Virtually no graduates of Israeli medical school start practice without continuing their training in a residency program. Moreover, many Israeli physicians travel and take postgraduate training in

Western countries. Their exposure to the professional literature and to recent medical developments is considerable.

In Israel the proportion of women in the medical schools has consistently been about 20 percent. The pool of applicants has also included about 20 percent women, so there is no evidence of the overwhelming feminization of the medical profession from new recruits (Shuval 1980). Although the newest medical school, in Beersheba, has tended to admit relatively more women, their small classes are unlikely to contribute markedly to the general sex ratio in the professional population.

In sum, it would seem that the general level of medical education in the Soviet Union was shorter, less science based, and less research oriented than medical school training has been in Israel since medical schools were opened there in the early 1950s. Compared to graduates of Israeli medical schools, most Soviet physicians have been trained in larger classes, have had less direct laboratory experience, and have experienced less individually oriented teaching. However, those who worked in central, elite medical institutions were more likely to be exposed to newer techniques and equipment than the majority, who worked at the local or district level.

Perceived Quality of Soviet Medical Care

Observers of the Soviet medical care system note that some Soviet physicians are comparable to the best anywhere in the world, particularly in such fields as orthopedics and ophthalmology. Certain facilities—for example, the Bakuley Institute of Cardiovascular Surgery—use the most sophisticated medical equipment and enjoy unrivaled reputations in their fields. At the same time primary and hospital medical care in many cases is characterized by low-level equipment, chronic shortages of basic medical necessities, inadequate pharmaceuticals, and poor physical facilities. The system ranges from superior practices and facilities for selected, privileged sectors, to mediocre or below standard, depending on the setting and the population being served (Hyde 1974; Smith 1976; Kaser 1976; Field 1967, 1971). Immigrant physicians in Israel have practiced in a wide variety of such settings in the Soviet Union, and their experience was naturally conditioned by the nature of the specific medical institutions in which they worked.

Most of the Israeli doctors interviewed during the course of the research expressed doubts concerning the quality of medical practice in the Soviet Union and felt that these immigrant physicians generally did not measure up to the level of medical practice in Israel. One expressed this common attitude: "They've got to change the medicine they learned in the Soviet Union. . . . We've got to bring them up-to-date. . . . Very few are up to the standards of our practice here."

Most Israeli physicians interviewed showed some awareness of regional and institutional variation in the Soviet Union and admitted that this could be relevant to the quality of the professional background of the immigrant physicians. But on the whole, Israeli practitioners believe in a negative stereotype concerning the quality of Soviet medicine. Like other stereotypes, this one contains a kernel of truth, although there is no systematic empirical evidence in Israel for lower-quality practice among Soviet immigrant physicians. In one of the few empirical studies in this general area, U.S. medical graduates were compared with foreign medical graduates working in the United States in terms of their supervisors' ratings. The foreign physicians were rated lower in all specialty training programs except surgery (Halberstom and Dacso 1966; Halberstom, Rusk, and Taylor 1970; Darbyshire 1969; Margulies, Bloch, and Cholko 1968). Margulies, Bloch, and Cholko (1968) also reported lower-quality practice among foreign medical graduates in the United States. On the other hand, Knobel (1970) points out that the quality of immigrant physicians' professional performance is a function of the level of development and Westernization of their country of origin. In general, there is little consensus concerning the criteria for evaluation, nor can the evaluators' preconceptions be separated out.

Although the evidence in Israel is based on a small sample, the stereotype appears to be widely held, with little scrutiny of the empirical evidence that is available—the practice and knowledge of the immigrant practitioner. Stereotyping tends to block the consideration of contrary evidence and inevitably affects the evaluation process (Butter and Grenzke 1970; Stevens, Goodman, and Mick, 1978; Kunz 1975). Instead of judging individual immigrants on their personal merits, there is a tendency to apply the stereotype first and seek empirical evidence for its confirmation.

Licensing of Immigrant Physicians

Recognition of their professional status is a prominent issue for all immigrant physicians and especially for those from the Soviet Union. Voronel (1976) has discussed the centrality of work in Soviet culture and its unique salience for professionals. Smith (1976) and Shipler (1983) note that there is a long history in the Soviet Union of sensitivity to the nuances of the pecking order. Its egalitarian ideology has not prevented the Soviet system from differentiating and emphasizing gross and minute differences of rank, which are expressed in power, title, privileges, and prestige (Shipler 1983). This tradition has heightened the sensitivity of immigrant physicians to the recognition of their occupational status in Israel.

In 1975, three years after their arrival, all of the immigrant physicians were practicing, but only 33 percent were licensed to practice in their specialty. This is a lower percentage than that reported among immigrant scientists to Israel, 76 percent of whom reported that they were employed in their field of specialization (Orzack 1980).

Those whose specialty status was not recognized frequently found it difficult to comprehend how they could be licensed for general practice but not for the field in which they perceived themselves to excel. Indeed there was a good measure of exasperation among practitioners as they tried to make their way in the Israeli medical care system, which on the one hand provides them with professional employment but at the same time shows reluctance or delay in recognizing their specialty status. "Why don't they recognize my specialization? I've been in practice for over twenty years." "Why do they delay giving me an answer? . . . They asked for all the documents; I sent them in but still no answer." "If they recognize us as doctors, why don't they recognize us as specialists? I've taken specialty courses and have worked in my field for ten years . . . "

Table 6–1 presents the specialties practiced in the Soviet Union by immigrant physicians in the population under study. Several specialties listed do not exist as such or as separate areas of practice in Israel: physiotherapy (not practiced by physicians), traumatology, laboratory medicine, and infectious diseases. There were also ten tuberculosis specialists, who are grouped with the internists in the table. Only 19 percent declared that they had not been recognized as specialists before immigrating, but these physicians may be responding in terms of their perception of Israeli standards of practice since virtually all Soviet doctors tend to view themselves as specialists.

It is of interest to observe the licensing of specialists in Israel by specialty in the Soviet Union even though the small numbers in each category require caution in interpretation. This is also shown in table 6–1. Over half of those who had practices in anesthesiology, dermatology, neurology, psychiatry, and eye, ear, nose, and throat specialties were licensed as specialists by 1975. To some extent this may reflect more positive evaluation by the Israeli authorities of the level of practice in these fields in the Soviet Union. In some cases, however, such as anesthesiology, it reflects a shortage in the medical care system of specialists in this field. Recognition was granted relatively infrequently to physicians who were specialists in obstetrics-gynecology and in various internal medicine specialties, which tend to be saturated.

Table 6–1
Medical Specialities of Soviet Immigrant Physicians in the Soviet Union and Percentage Licensed as Specialists in Israel, 1975

Specialty in the USSR	*Number*	*Percentage among Specialties*	*Percentage Licensed as Specialists in Israel*
Internal medicine	79	27	19
Medicine	47		21
Endocrinology	11		18
Cardiology	8		13
Tuberculosis	10		
Surgery	27	9	37
Urology	12		33
Neurology	8	3	
Psychiatry	18	6	56
Pediatrics	27	9	19
Obstetrics-gynecology	18	6	11
Eye, ear, nose, and throat	18	6	56
Ophthalmology	10	3	30
Dermatology	7	2	71
Anesthesiology	5	2	80
Roentgenology	12	4	25
Specialities not recognized in Israel	13	4	
Physiotherapy	1		
Traumatology	1		
Laboratory medicine	6	2	
Public health	1		
Infectious diseases	2	1	
Legal medicine	2	1	
No specialty	53	19	
No information	3	1	
Total	298	100	33

The specialty backgrounds of the immigrant physicians are, of course, not necessarily attuned to specific needs of the medical care system. Israel has the highest doctor-to-population ratio in the world. As in other countries, however, there is poor geographical distribution, with the nonurban areas understaffed; furthermore the community clinics are staffed by relatively old physicians, while the younger graduates of Israeli medical schools generally seek hospital positions (Doron 1979).

Sixty percent of the immigrant physicians were employed at the time of the study in community clinics. On the whole these physicians were less frequently licensed as specialists than their colleagues employed in hospitals. Most important, despite the large absolute number of physicians in Israel, certain areas of specialization were characterized by shortages of physicians. Such shortages normally would be quickly filled in a small country where the total number needed in any one field is relatively small. In 1975, however, the following areas of practice lacked physicians: roentgenology, geriatrics, physical medicine, family medicine, and anesthesiology. Retraining courses were offered in these fields in an attempt to channel immigrant physicians to areas of practice in which there were shortages of medical personnel. Some of these areas have been traditionally shunned by graduates of Israeli medical schools, so the immigrants fill a real need by retraining for them (Shuval 1980). In 1975 5 percent of the immigrant physicians reported that they had participated in courses that changed their specialty. Twenty-two percent participated in other retraining courses geared toward upgrading their medical background.

Licensure of immigrant physicians for specialty practice is strongly correlated with the form and rank of the specialty practices in the Soviet Union. Because of variation in titles of specialties and their excessive differentiation, table 6–2 makes use of the formal ranks used in the Soviet Union. Forty percent of the immigrant physicians in the population studied hold one of the two highest ranks of specialization in the Soviet Union. This rank order is recognized by the Israel gatekeepers; there is a sharp decline in licensing from those of the highest rank, 83 percent of whom were licensed as specialists, to the first rank, only 40 percent of whom received that recognition during the first three years in Israel. The sharp and systematic decline in the percentages licensed

Table 6–2
Licensing of Specialty Status in Israel by Rank of Specialty in the USSR
(N = 298)

Specialty Rank in USSR[a]	*Percentage in Rank*	*Percentage in USSR Rank Licensed as Specialists in Israel in 1975*
Highest	10	83
First	30	40
Second	12	27
Third	9	14
Specialty practice without formal rank	20	8
No specialty	19	

[a]These are formal ranks in the Soviet system.

reflects some doubts among the Israeli gatekeepers about the quality of Soviet medicine.

Recognition of specialty status serves as a stringent control mechanism on the quality of medical practice in Israel. Although general practitioners play a major role in the primary care system, they are limited to practicing in community clinics, and their professional status is relatively low. Thus the two-stage licensure procedure fulfills two social functions: to enable prompt professional employment for immigrant physicians and to control the quality of medical practice.

Social and Professional Background

Personal Background

What is the social and professional background of Soviet physicians who have immigrated to Israel? What was their work experience before immigrating, and where do they fit into the medical care system of the host society? A comparative structural analysis of the two medical care systems has been presented elsewhere (Shuval 1983); here, selected data provided by the physicians themselves are discussed. (See table 6–3.)

Sixty-four percent of the immigrant physicians were women. This was somewhat less than the proportion of women physicians in the Soviet Union, about 70 percent at the time of the study. The small disparity most likely stemmed from selective factors in the decision to emigrate. Indeed, 76 percent of the Soviet Jewish physicians who migrated to the United States at this period were women (HIAS 1978).

The overall proportion of women physicians in Israel is 25 percent, but it is 35 percent among the doctors employed by Kupat Holim and reaches 42 percent in the community clinics. Regardless of their place of employment in Israel, however, female immigrant physicians from the Soviet Union generally find themselves in a less feminized setting than is present in their country of origin.

Compared to the age distribution of Israeli physicians, immigrant physicians from the Soviet Union tend to be relatively young. About 40 percent of Israeli doctors are under the age of 47 compared to 66 percent of the immigrant physicians. Israel community clinic physicians tend to be older than hospital physicians; 44 percent of the physicians employed by Kupat Holim in community clinics will reach retirement by the end of the 1980s. Thus the Soviet physicians in such clinics find themselves working with older professional colleagues more often than do immigrants employed in hospital settings.

The Soviet Union is characterized by considerable regional variation in terms of cultural traditions as well as levels of medical education

Table 6–3
Personal Background of Soviet Immigrant Physicians

Characteristics	*Percentage (N = 298)*
Sex	
Women	64
Men	46
Age	
Under 28	5
28–47	61
48–65	33
over 65	1
Geographic area of residence in USSR	
Baltic republics (e.g., Latvia, Lithuania, Estonia, Moldavia)	47
Asian republics (e.g., Georgia, Siberia)	5
Central European republics (e.g., RSSR, Ukraine, Belorussia)	48
Knowledge of languages at time of immigration (self-reported)	
Hebrew	
None	89
Speak only	
Read only	4
Speak and read	7
English	
None	40
Speak only	3
Read only	42
Speak and read	15
Yiddish	
None	28
Speak only	48
Read only	
Speak and read	24

and services. The Baltic areas (Latvia, Lithuania, Estonia, Moldavia), annexed to the Soviet Union between 1939 and 1941, demonstrate a relatively high level of medical education, which is still influenced by the period before they came under Soviet domination. They are also characterized by a comparatively active Jewish cultural life when compared to other parts of the USSR, largely because a tradition of such activity and religious identification persists from the period preceding World War II.

Immigrants to Israel from the Asian regions of the Soviet Union (Georgia, Ubekistan, Siberia) come from an Eastern cultural and religious tradition (as contrasted to Ashkenazic), which markedly differentiates them from other Soviet immigrants. The Central European republics (RSFSR, Ukraine, Belorussia) have the weakest tradition of Jewish cultural life because of the prolonged influence of Soviet policy and ideology since 1921 (Gitelman 1972, 1982). Among the immigrant physicians to Israel, 47 percent came from the Baltic region, only 5 percent from the Asian republics, and 48 percent from the Central European areas of the Soviet Union.

Language skills were mixed among the immigrant physicians (Weinshall and Raveh 1980). Eighty-nine percent stated that they knew no Hebrew at all on arrival. The 11 percent who reported any knowledge of Hebrew were generally referring to acquaintance with written prayers rather than to modern spoken Hebrew. After two years in Israel, however, 42 percent of the sample of Soviet immigrants said that they could speak Hebrew fluently, and 41 percent felt that their knowledge of the language was sufficient for their needs at work (Israel Ministry of Absorption 1976).

English is also needed for professional work in Israel. Scientific work is based on published material in English, little of which is translated into Hebrew. Fifty-seven percent of the immigrant physicians state that they can read English, although it is not clear whether such knowledge is sufficient to permit reading of scientific literature in all cases; but 43 percent cannot read English.

In contrast to the critical importance of English reading skills, the importance of Yiddish is essentially as a spoken language. Seventy-two percent of the immigrant physicians, largely from the Baltic region, stated that they could speak this language. Yiddish is necessary to communicate with some patients, notably older people of European origins, and with some colleagues or other medical personnel.

Professional Background

Only 6 percent of the immigrant physicians received their medical degrees before the start of World War II, but a large group 40 percent) went through medical training during or immediately after World War II. This was a period of unrest, and the formal educational system presumably reflected the disorder of the times. The medical school curriculum in the USSR lasted only five years until 1955, when it was lengthened by a year. Thus the group that received its medical degrees between 1956 and 1965 (32 percent) was exposed to six years of training; the extra year of internship affected only the most recently educated group, which obtained degrees after 1966 (22 percent).

Seventy-four percent of the immigrant physicians reported that they had been employed in hospital settings. Some of these physicians worked in the outpatient polyclinics maintained by most hospitals in the Soviet Union, in addition to the inpatient services. There is a considerable dif-

Table 6–4
Professional Background of Soviet Immigrant Physicians

Characteristics	*Percentage (N = 298)*
Year received first medical degree	
Before 1939	6
1939–1947	12
1948–1955	28
1956–1965	32
1966 or later	22
Professional work setting in USSR	
Hospital, city level	21
Hospital, district (*oblast*) level	14
Hospital, republic level	19
Hospital, other	20
Polyclinic, neighborhood level	7
Polyclinic, higher level	5
Institute, medical school	4
Institute for medical research	2
School, kindergarten, other educational institution	1
Emergency service	2
Sanitarium	1
Public health service	2
Other	2
Professional behavior in USSR	
Frequency of use of medical library (average number of times a month)	
10 or more	28
5–9	18
2–4	39
Once	8
Less than once	7
Number of professional journals read more or less regularly	
4 or more	37
2–3	53
One	6
None regularly	3

ference in the quality of medical care in hospital and community polyclinics. There is also a major status difference between the two settings, with hospitals generally viewed as more prestigious. Furthermore, the quality of medical practice in the Soviet Union is thought to be correlated with the organizational level of the practice setting; those employed in a republic-level hospital are likely to have worked with better equipment and more sophisticated technology in a professional atmosphere characterized by more updated knowledge than those working at the district or city level. It is therefore noteworthy that 19 percent stated that they had been employed in hospitals at the republic level (Field 1967, 1971; Fry 1969; Fry and Crome 1972; Hyde 1974; Kaser 1976; Navarro 1977; Ryan 1978).

When asked about their professional behavior in the Soviet Union, we may assume that some nostalgia or wishful thinking may distort the reporting of what it was like in the old country. But even reducing the reported frequency of use of medical libraries and regular reading of professional journals before migration, the immigrant physicians clearly perceived themselves as conforming to professional norms of reading current journals and using updated reference materials. Thus the problem of reading English was serious for substantial numbers of immigrant physicians who were accustomed to keeping themselves informed about the profession through Soviet literature.

Practice in Israel

All of the immigrant physicians were employed as doctors, most as general practitioners. (See table 6–5.) They moved relatively quickly into a professional job. By the time they had been in Israel for five months, 62 percent had been placed. It took nine or more months to establish only 10 percent of the immigrant physicians in jobs. Despite the fact that a special committee composed of representatives of all the major employers, as well as the Ministry of Absorption, was established to assist immigrant physicians in job placement, the vast majority located their job with little apparent help from this official body. Only 27 percent were assisted by this committee. Twenty-one percent stated that informal assistance of friends, relatives, and acquaintances helped them locate their job, and half stated that they accomplished the task themselves. This points to the familiar sociological generalization concerning the usefulness and importance of informal networks and the relative absence of impact made by bureaucratically structured mechanisms.

Most physicians (60 percent) were employed by Kupat Holim of the General Federation of Labor, the largest sick fund, which runs most of the community clinics for ambulatory care and some of the hospitals. The Ministry of Health employed 23 percent, and 10 percent were employed by smaller sick funds.

The data on places of employment indicate that approximately 39 percent of the immigrant physicians work in hospitals and 55 percent in a variety of community clinics delivering primary care. The latter are in many ways the most problematic in terms of the quality of their professional performance. When given a choice, few young graduates of Israeli medical schools seek practice in the primary care clinics of Kupat

Table 6–5
Job Setting in Israel of Soviet Immigrant Physicians

	Percentage (N = 298)
How long did it take after your arrival to obtain your job?	
Less than a month	2
1–2 months	8
3–5 months	52
6–8 months	28
9 or more months	10
Employer	
Ministry of Health	23
Kupat Holim of the General Federation of Labor	60
Kupat Holim Leumit[a]	7
Other sick funds	3
Other	7
Professional work setting	
Small hospital (up to 150 beds)	6
Large hospital (over 150 beds)	33
Community clinic (neighborhood setting)	48
Community clinic (district setting)	4
Rural clinic	3
Other	6
Location of job (region)	
Tel Aviv	49
Jerusalem	9
Haifa	21
Other urban setting	16
Nonurban setting	5
How did you locate your job?	
Through the Committee for Placement of Physicians[b]	27
Through friends, relatives, acquaintances	21
By myself	50
Other	2
Average number of patients you care for during a week	
1–35	11
36–80	12
81–149	10
150–199	11
200–259	16
260–399	19
400 or more	13
Not in clinical practice	8

[a]Kupat Holim Leumit (National Sick Fund) is the largest employer among the smaller sick funds.

[b]A committee composed of representatives of the Ministry of Absorption, Kupat Holim, the smaller sick funds, the Ministry of Health, the Israel Medical Association, and other potential employers. The purpose of the committee was to assist immigrant physicians in job placement.

Holim (Shuval 1980). The concentration of immigrant doctors in community clinics exacerbates the sensitive issue of the quality of their practice since that setting is not structured to encourage the highest-quality professional performance (Medalie 1972; Shuval 1979). Stevens and Vermeulen (U.S. Department of Health 1972) note that placing immigrant physicians in such less desirable work places tends to reinforce their professional weaknesses, providing a self-fulfilling prophecy.

High physician utilization is prevalent in both Israel (Israel Central Bureau of Statistics 1983) and the Soviet Union (Ryan 1978). Immigrant physicians employed in Israeli community clinics raise this issue repeatedly, and they are obviously disturbed (as are most Israeli physicians) by it.

Table 6–5 shows the number of patients reportedly cared for by Soviet physicians in their Israeli practices. The data are provided by the physicians themselves. The feeling that they are swamped with patients is important. Close to half the physicians report that they see more than 200 patients a week; this represents more than 6 patients an hour for a 6 hour, 6 day work week. Thirteen percent state that they see 400 or more patients a week; this is probably an exaggerated figure that is more expressive of the overwhelmed feelings of the practitioner than of objective reality.

Work norms in the Soviet Union require that 12 minutes on the average be spent with patients in polyclinics. But Hyde (1974), in reporting on a survey done in the USSR in the mid-1960s, states that the average time is less: 7.4 minutes by pediatricians, 8.8 minutes by obstetricians, and 1.0 minute by neuropathologists. The workday in the Soviet Union is 6.5 hours long. But the *uchastock* (local neighborhood) physician is supposed to spend half of the time visiting patients, and half an hour each day should be spent in health education. It would therefore seem that officially a patient load could range from a maximum of 200 a week to a minimum of about 100, depending on the physician's conformity to the 12 minute norm and the number of his or her home visits (Ryan 1978; Fry 1969). However, giving patients less than the official 12 minutes and cutting down on house calls could considerably increase the total patient load. Indeed, the utilization figures from the Soviet Union, which show 11.12 annual consultations with a physician in urban areas, are similar to the Israeli figures, which range between 9 and 12 visits per year to ambulatory clinics of Kupat Holim (Ryan 1978; Shuval, Antonovsky, and Davies 1970; Israel Central Bureau of Statistics, 1983).

We must therefore conclude that many Soviet physicians, notably those who worked in primary care clinics, have previously experienced high utilization rates by patients. Those who have been overwhelmed by the phenomenon in Israel probably were not employed in the primary care delivery before immigrating.

Feelings about Work in Israel

The centrality of work for persons of Soviet origin has been spelled out by Voronel (1976), who has referred to it as the professional cult. It has been empirically documented by Toren, Grifel, and Portnoy (1979) and Toren (chapter 5 of this book). It is therefore of interest to determine how immigrant physicians feel about their jobs in the host society. Do they gain satisfaction from it? Are current difficulties seen in perspective as part of the short-term adjustment process, or are they viewed as inherent in the work situation?

Two dimensions of this issue will be considered: present feeling about their job and future job orientation. This distinction between present patterns and future orientations is of special importance among immigrants whose problems of entry into the occupational system may be a function of time.

Present feeling about job was estimated by means of the following question: "Are you interested in changing your present job in the near future?" Four categories of response were provided. Future job orientation was measured by three items:

1. "How do you feel about your chances for advancement at work?"
2. "How do you feel about your opportunities for advancement at work?" "How do you feel about your chances for realizing your professional expectations in the near future?"
3. "In the light of your experience, would you recommend that other physicians in your field immigrate to Israel?"

After establishing the unidimensionality of this set of questions, mean scores based on four categories of response were calculated for future job orientation (Shuval, 1983). The two dimensions are only weakly correlated: $r = .24$. This correlation is stronger among physicians employed in community clinics ($r = .28$); among hospital physicians the correlation is only .12, indicating that the present and future dimensions of effect in the occupational sphere are more independent of each other.

Half the immigrant physicians state that they do not wish to change their present job, but a third say they are interested or very much interested in changing jobs. These percentages do not differ from comparable samples of Soviet immigrants or academically trained immigrants from a variety of countries who have been in Israel for three years

(Shuval, Markus, and Dotan 1975). We may assume that immigrant populations undergoing occupational change and entry into a new social system inevitably include a group characterized by low job satisfaction. But this proportion is no larger among the Soviet immigrant physicians than in a comparable sample.

Concerning the future, feelings were mixed in the population. Thirty-two percent felt their chances for advancement were poor, while 29 percent were more optimistic, stating that their prospects were excellent or good. Half stated that the likelihood of realizing their occupational expectations in Israel was not so good or poor, but the remaining half was more optimistic. Both of these affective variables showed more positive scores among immigrant physicians who were employed in hospital settings.

Do these feelings about work vary among immigrant physicians with different past experience, among those practicing in various settings in Israel, or by those with specific personal characteristics? Are these feelings a function of interpersonal relations among the immigrant and his or her colleagues or of other experiences in Israel? In an attempt to explore these issues, a mutiple regression analysis was carried out using the two dimensions of feeling about work in Israel as dependent variables.

Three types of independent variables were examined in this analysis: characteristics of physicians' work setting in Israel, personal background and demographic characteristics considered relevant to professional performance, and immigrants' professional background and experience in the Soviet Union.

1. Characteristics of work setting in Israel: Type of employer; setting of practice; professional rank, number, social characteristics and attitude of patients under his or her care; social characteristics of colleagues and supervisors; extent of informal and professional contacts with colleagues and supervisors; similarity of present job to work in the Soviet Union; perceived attitude of Israeli physicians and patients to immigrant physicians from the Soviet Union; length of time that elapsed until job was located; participation in retraining program.
2. Personal and demographic background characteristics: Age; sex; marital status; occupation of spouse; knowledge of languges (Hebrew, English, Yiddish); Jewish background; identification with Israeli society; expectations concerning life in Israel; satisfaction with non-work-related areas (housing, leisure activities, education of children, social life); tolerance for ambiguity; suspicion toward others.

3. Professional background in the Soviet Union: Job status; specialty status; rank, locus, and setting of work; normative behavior with patients; relations with colleagues and supervisors; rewards from patients and colleagues.

Table 6–6 presents the findings and includes only those independent variables that show a significant relationship to one of the "feeling" variables ($p < .05$). None of the physicians' specific work-setting characteristics in the USSR is related to either of the "feeling" variables; however, the overall similarity of the immigrants' previous work to the job now held is related to both variables: the greater the similarity between the present job and the one held prior to migration, the more positive the immigrant's feelings about the former.

The findings in present feeling about job show an inverse relationship between the size of the physician's patient load and the present feeling about his or her job. The high rate of clinic utilization appears repeatedly as a source of frustration to immigrant physicians, especially among those employed in community clinics where this problem is endemic. Although utilization rates in the Soviet Union are also high and remarkedly similar to the rates in Israel, many immigrant physicians are distressed by the pressure of large numbers of patients and their inability to devote the time they consider necessary to each.

Women physicians tend to be more satisfied with their present jobs than men, despite the fact that they are more frequently placed in community clinics. Indeed, many of the women physicians have experience in clinics at the *uchastock* (local community level) in the Soviet Union and therefore may have been somewhat more familiar with the problems of primary care delivery. There is also the possibility that women physicians may have lower expectations and may therefore be relatively more content in situations that cause dissatisfaction among their male colleagues.

Future job orientation is linked to immigrant physicians' relations with colleagues, both supervisors and peers. The great importance placed by Soviet immigrants on the entire occupatonal sphere makes it clear why the relationship with their supervisors is so vital: they are dependent on them for approval and promotion, but the employer also determines working conditions and the availability of professional equipment. Another correlate that probably taps the same issue is the extent of similarity in the cultural and social backgrounds between the immigrant and his or her professional colleagues. For example, if the latter are Russian or Yiddish speaking, informal as well as professional relations will more likely be established with them. Other research concerning immigrant physicians also notes a positive correlation between

Table 6–6
Regression Coefficients (Standard Form) of Feeling about Work on Independent Variables

	Present Feeling about Job		*Future Job Orientation*	
Independent Variables	*Beta*	*Significance*	*Beta*	*Significance*
Characteristics of Israeli work setting				
Similarity of work to job in USSR	.29	.001	.15	.01
Number of patients under physician's care	−.18	.03		
Quality of personal relations with supervisors			.19	.01
Similarity in social background of physician and colleagues			.11	.03
Physician's perception of patient's evaluation of USSR doctor			.09	.05
Socioeconomic background of patients			.11	.03
Personal and demographic characteristics of immigrant physician				
Satisfaction with nonwork rewards	.17	.01	.14	.02
Sex[a]	.17	.01		
Identification with Israeli society			.31	.001
Characteristics of work setting in the Soviet Union				
None				
R^2 for all independent variables	.36	.001	.52	.001

Note: All independent variables were introduced into the regression analysis. Entries in the tables are limited to those variables in which $p < .05$.

[a]More positive feeling by women.

satisfaction with work experience and contact with host colleagues (Dacso, Antler, and Rusk 1968).

Another reference group that plays a role in immigrant physicians' future job orientation comprises patients with whom they have contact. Those who perceive patients as less accepting of Soviet physicians are more negative about the future. To the extent that patients are middle class and of European origin, future orientation tends to be more positive. Treatment of patients of North African or Near Eastern origins, with whom there are language barriers and whose cultural background is different, is associated with a less positive orientation toward the future.

An important predictor of future job orientation is a variable concerning a more general attitude toward the host society: To the extent that immigrant physicians positively identify with Israeli society and gain satisfaction from areas outside the occupational sphere, they are also likely to be positive in their future job orientation. As in the case of all other attitude studies, it is possible only to establish the interrelatedness of these attitudes rather than determine the direction of the relationship.

Conclusion

The migration of professionals is an increasingly widespread phenomenon. In recent years, economic cutbacks, unemployment, and changes in labor needs have caused many countries to limit the entry of professionals. But in the long run, professionals whose skills are readily transferable to different settings will continue to be among the more mobile occupational groups. In a sample of immigrant physicians in the United States, 72 percent stated that medicine is a profession that can be practiced anywhere (Stevens, Goodman, and Mick 1978). Furthermore, the many professionals who migrated during the 1960s and 1970s are frequently still identified as strangers in their adopted countries. The integration process is a gradual one. Thus the sociology of professionals' migration is of more than passing interest.

The entry of migrant professionals into a society requires control mechanisms for the quality of practice. With regard to physicians, it is of particular societal concern to ensure an adequate standard and quality of practice for persons trained in a system different from the local one. Medical licensure seeks to meet these needs, but it fulfills other social functions as well (Orzack 1980). The research in Israel demonstrates licensure procedures that reflect certain values and situational constraints of that society. These may be a means of reconciling two fundamental values: a need to provide prompt employment for immigrants in jobs that will be acceptable to them and a need to maintain high-quality professional practice in accordance with the standards of the best available scientific knowledge. Neither of these values can be compromised too far, and the research points to some, albeit unobtrusive, tension in the system in its efforts to meet the needs of both. Indeed there is evidence of cross-pressures exerted by various interested parties—the medical profession, the official bodies concerned with absorption of immigrants, and the immigrant physicians themselves—to bring together these conflicting themes. Some conflict has been observed in the system, although it has remained unobtrusive. Protests by immigrant physicians and demands for recognition of their specialty status or of their years of experience have periodically caused such conflicts to erupt (Weinschall and Raveh 1980; Shuval 1983).

The licensure mechanisms in Israel reflect the open-door policy that admits Jewish immigrants from many countries, regardless of their occupational or other qualifications, and seeks to integrate them economically and socially into the society. It is based on a long history of immigration that has consistently admitted large numbers of professionals trained in widely different cultural traditions, for whom a uniform system of examinations would be problematic. Examinations could serve as a major deterrent to entry into the occupational system, particularly when such professionals emigrate at mid- or late-career stages. The requirement of a degree from a recognized medical school, although it undoubtedly causes some unevenness in professional backgrounds, serves as a functional mechanism to deal with this issue. It is a universalistic criterion, providing employment opportunities, ensuring a basic standard of practice skills, and thus affording protection to the patient population. But at the same time it limits the practitioner to general practice and therefore to a lower status in the system. Furthermore it relegates immigrant physicians to community practices, which are viewed as less desirable by Israeli medical graduates and are often located in less attractive geographical settings otherwise not provided with medical personnel.

Some quality control is exercised at this stage of licensure by collegial supervision. The basic license for general practice is granted quickly in most cases but is provisional for one year during which time the immigrant physician is supervised by an Israeli colleague. Only after one year, when that supervisor indicates approval of the immigrant physician's standard of medical practice, is a license for general practice granted.

This stage of licensure (which most closely expresses the general societal value of the open door for immigrants) is implemented by the Ministry of Health. Thus this policy reflects a general societal value rather than one associated with a given sector or professional group. The division of authority with regard to the two stages of licensing parallels the two themes referred to. At the first stage the emphasis is on the first theme, critical to the very raison d'être of the society. To some extent the quality issue is compromised in the interests of the value theme, but that compromise is controlled by the allocation process.

The second stage, licensure for specialty practice, is perceived as the heart of the quality issue. Here the medical profession acts as the gatekeeping authority. After the demands of the first basic value are met, the profession takes upon itself stringent control of licensure for specialty status. Critical quality control is exercised at this stage, and licensure is granted with extreme caution and restraint. This contrasts sharply with the almost automatic licensure for general practice granted at the first stage, when formal completion of medical studies is the criterion. Since the nature of specialty practice in the Soviet Union is so different from that practiced in Israel, examination of credentials and experience is a painstaking process characterized by conservatism. Extra training is frequently required, as are examinations. The profession encourages no compromises and little flexibility at the second stage.

But there is some evidence that the reverse may be the case. The widespread stereotyping with regard to Soviet physicians may be interpreted in this light. Such a pattern is not unique to Israel (Butter and Grenzke 1970; Kunz 1975; Stevens, et al., 1978; U.S. Department of Health 1972). As in the case of all other stereotypes, attitudes are polarized, overgeneralized, and rigidly structured so that qualities contrary to the stereotype are either ignored or viewed as idiosyncratic. Analysis of the medical care system of the Soviet Union indicates that there is a central core of truth in this negative evaluation, but in many cases it is generalized beyond the level of objective judgment. Medical education in the Soviet Union is generally less science based than current medical education in Israel; it takes place in large classes with less clinical instruction, and for many of the immigrants it was shorter than the program now in use. Furthermore, many of the physicians in the Soviet Union are less exposed than their Israeli colleagues to contemporary developments in medical science, newer drugs, medical technology, and sophisticated innovations in equipment. There are extreme contrasts in the quality of Soviet medical care, depending on its setting and on the population it serves.

There is, however, frequently little consideration by Israeli gatekeepers of the considerable differences in the level and experience of Soviet immigrant physicians, especially their positions in the hierarchy of the Soviet medical care delivery system. Moreover, in demanding the highest standards of performance for immigrant physicians, there is a tendency to ignore the prevailing variation in quality of medical care among veteran Israeli practitioners themselves. In fact, some have medical training from schools similar to those in the Soviet Union.

More general consideration of the functional role of stereotypes indicates that they serve important needs for both professionals and laypersons. They reinforce an image of the high quality of medical care in the society. In this manner they assert the superiority of the veteran practitioner regarding newcomers and reassure the lay population that they have been receiving the best possible medical care. From this viewpoint, the stereotype is a protective mechanism that reveals as much or more about those who hold it as about the group it describes.

Stereotyping appears to be a general response of host groups to newcomers and can be expected in most migration situations. By highlighting negative qualities and blocking perception of positive ones, stereotypes serve the needs of those who hold them but impede the entry of newcomers into the social system, placing them on the defensive with a constant need to demonstrate professional competence.

This study does not include measurement of the quality of clinical practice. We are therefore unable to judge the objective quality of medical care delivered by Soviet immigrant physicians. But given the social and psychological bases for stereotyping, we may assume that on the whole the quality of care is likely to be better than is suggested by the stereotype. The implicit nature of the stereotyping process is such that the situation is likely to be less negative than the stereotype suggests.

Immigrant physicians from the Soviet Union provided an injection of young blood into the population of practicing physicians in Israel. On the average they were several years younger than their Israeli colleagues; however, younger immigrant physicians were more likely than older ones to be placed in hospital settings while the older were employed in community clinics. This pattern reflects the feeling of many Israeli practitioners that younger immigrant physicians are less set in their ways and more receptive to retraining. They are also more likely to have been trained during the period when Soviet medical schools required a year of internship as part of the physician's training. In all cases hospital-based physicians expressed more positive feelings about their professional work than did community practitioners.

This overall pattern may be a self-fulfilling prophecy. Immigrant physicians tend to be placed in less desirable practice settings, where few young Israeli graduates agree to work. The same pattern is reported in other countries and generally pertains when immigrant physicians are perceived as less competent (Stevens, Goodman, and Mick 1978). On the other hand, when immigrant physicians arrive in Israel with strong professional reputations from prestigious institutions, they are usually employed in senior hospital posts. Thus the generalization described does not apply to immigrant stars but to the majority of immigrant physicians.

Sixty percent of the immigrant physicians from the Soviet Union are women, a considerably higher proportion than is found among Israeli doctors, 25 percent of whom are female. Two-thirds of the women among the Soviet immigrant physicians are employed in community clinics as contrasted to only half the men. Women physicians also tend to be heavily concentrated in primary care settings in the Soviet Union, far outnumbering their male colleagues in such clinics. There is also a relatively heavy concentration of Israeli women physicians in community clinics as a result of specialty choices, situational constraints associated with spouses' employment, and the rigorous demands of hospital practice, which often do not mesh well with female physicians' lateral roles as wife and/or mother.

Thus Soviet women physicians in Israeli community clinics are more likely to find themselves working with female Israeli colleagues than are those employed in hospitals, where the collegial population is predominantly male. But regardless of their place of employment, female immigrant physicians in Israel find themselves in a less feminized professional setting than is present in the Soviet Union.

The differential distribution of physicians by gender in the community clinics and the hospitals must be viewed in the context of the relative prestige and quality of medical care associated with each of these settings. In both Israel and the Soviet Union, there is an invidious difference that favors hospital practice over community clinics. Although this differential distribution may be prominent among immigrant physicians, it occurs among veteran Israeli doctors as well and apparently reflects deeper social processes than those simply associated with migration and entry into a new system of practice. In allocating medical personnel to practice settings, weaker groups include immigrants and women. In other societies the criteria for distinguishing better from worse practice settings may be diffrent—for example, inner city settings versus suburbs, university hospitals versus community hospitals, and lower-class versus middle- or upper-class patients.

Whatever adjustment problems are endemic to community clinics as contrasted to hospital settings are therefore more likely to be encountered by immigrant physicians and, more specifically, by the women among them. Women are particularly disturbed by the divided workday with a long noon break between the morning and afternoon shifts. In the Soviet Union there are certain institutionalized mechanisms to assist in child care: a longer school day than that prevalent in Israel and low cost or free crèches and nursery school services.

At the same time, it is interesting that immigrant physician women express a higher level of job satisfaction than do men. Women physicians may have somehat lower expectations than their male colleagues and are therefore less demanding in their professional needs.

The problem of high clinic utilization rates has long perturbed Israeli physicians and health planners (Shuval, Antonovsky, and Davies 1970). Although the rates are not too different in the Soviet Union, frequent comments indicate that the doctors feel overwhelmed by the large number of patients they are obligated to see in ambulatory care clinics. We may surmise that part of the problem is a cultural one, with immigrant physicians reacting to factors such as the less formal behavior that often characterizes the clinic setting. Although large numbers of patients utilize the clinics in the Soviet Union as well, they may accept the physician's authority more than many Israeli patients. Furthermore, physicians whose knowledge of Hebrew is weak during their early period in the country could have difficulty communicating with many Israeli patients.

The larger the number of patients under a physician's care, the more likely he or she is to express a desire to change place of employment. Therefore high physician utilization reduces job satisfaction. Job satisfaction is also a function of immigrant physicians' relations with colleagues and patients, which depend to a considerable extent on cultural distance and communication. The findings demonstrate the importance of informal relations in the occcupational sphere.

Finally—and perhaps most important—the work sphere is not dissociated from other spheres of social life. In fact, it is perhaps more closely associated for Soviet immigrants than for others. Thus the findings show a positive relationship concerning immigrant physicians' feelings about their professional work, their more general identification with Israeli society, and their satisfaction with the nonoccupational aspects of their life in Israel.

References

Butrov, V.N., and Nekrasov, V.P. 1971. *Advanced Training of Doctors in the USSR by Two-Part Formal and Correspondence Courses*. WHO/EDUC 71.143. Geneva: World Health Organization.

Butter, Irene, and Brenzke, Janet. 1970. "Training and Utilization of Foreign Medical Graduates in the U.S." *Journal of Medical Education* 45 (August): 607–617.

Butter, Irene, and Sweet, R.G. 1977. "Licensure of Foreign Medical Graduates: An Historical Perspective." *Milbank Memorial Fund Quarterly, Health and Society* (Spring):315–340.

Commission of the European Communities. Directorate-General for Research, Science, and Education. 1974. *Report of a Hearing Concerning the Mutual Recognition of Professional Qualifications in Relation to the Freedom of Establishment of Doctors, Brussels, 22–25 October, 1973* (Brussels). XII/52/74-E.

Cooper, John A.D. 1971. "Education for the Health Professions in the Soviet Union." *Journal of Medical Education* 46 (May):412–418.

Dacso, M.M.; Antler L.; and Rusk, H.A. 1968. "The Foreign Medical Resident Training in the United States." *Annals of Internal Medicine* 68:1105–1113.

Darbyshire, R.C. 1969. *Medical Licensure and Discipline in the U.S.* Baltimore: Johns Hopkins Press.

Davies, A. Michael. 1972. "The Health of Israel: Preventive Medicine in a Developing Society." *Preventive Medicine* 1:121–140.

Doron, Haim. 1979. "Kupat Holim: Its Principles, Services and Development of New Facilities." Unpublished Kupat Holim report. Tel Aviv.

European Communities. 1975. *Official Journal, Council Directives.* 18, no. L. 167. Brussels: European Communities.

Field, Mark G. 1967. *Soviet Socialized Medicine.* New York: Free Press.

———. 1971. "The Russian Health System." In *Medicine and Society: Contemporary Medical Problems in Historical Perspective.* Philadelphia: American Philosophical Library Society.

Forster, Sigmund, and Benton, Joseph G. 1966. "Spas in the Soviet Union." *Archives of Physical Medicine and Rehabilitation* 47 (January):62–66.

Fortney, Judith A. 1970. "International Migration of Professionals." *Population Studies* 24, no. 2:217–232.

Fry, John. 1969. *Medicine in Three Societies: A Comparison of Medical Care in the USSR, USA and UK.* Aylebury Bucks: MPT.

Fry, John, and Crome, L. 1972. "Medical Care in the USSR." In *International Medical Care.* Edited by J. Fry and W.A.J. Farndale, pp. 172–203. Oxford and Lancaster: Medical and Technical Publishing Co. Ltd.

Gitelman, Zvi. 1972. *Jewish Nationality and Soviet Politics.* Princeton: Princeton University Press.

———. *Becoming Israelis: Political Resocialization of Soviet and American Immigrants.* New York: Praeger.

Grushka, T., ed. 1968. *Health Services in Israel.* Jerusalem: Ministry of Health.

Halberstom, Jacob L., and Dacso, Michael. 1966. "Foreign and United States Residents in University Affiliated Hositals: An Investigation of U.S. Graduate Medical Education." *Bulletin of the N.Y. Academy of Medicine* 42: 82–208.

Halberstom, Jacob L.; Rusk, H.A.; and Taylor, E.J. 1970. "Foreign Surgical Residents in University-Affiliated Hospitals." *Annals of Surgery* 171:485–500.

Hebrew Immigrant Aid Society. 1978. *Statistical Abstract* 19, no. 1.

Holborn, Louise. 1956. *The International Refugee Organization.* London: Oxford University Press.

Hyde, Gordon. 1974. *The Soviet Health Service.* London: Lawrence and Wishart.

Israel Central Bureau of Statistics. 1983. *Statistical Abstract of Israel, 1982.* Jerusalem.

Israel Ministry of Absorption. 1976. *Immigrant Absorption, 1975*. Jerusalem.

——— . 1979. *Immigrant Absorption, 1978*. Jerusalem.

Kaser, Michael. 1976. *Health Care in the Soviet Union and Eastern Europe*. Boulder, Colo.: Westview Press.

Knobel, R.J., Jr. 1970. "A Study of the Variable Distribution of Foreign Medical Graduate Residents in U.S. Teaching Hospitals." Ph.D. dissertation, University of Michigan.

Kunz, Egon F. 1975. *The Intruders: Refugee Doctors in Australia*. Canberra: Australian National University Press.

Lopuchin, J.M. 1970. "Basic Principles of Higher Medical Education in the Soviet Union." Paper presented to the World Health Organization Conference on Medical Education, November 16–20, Rabat.

Margulies, H.; Bloch, L.S.; and Cholko, F.K. 1968. "Random Survey of U.S. Hospitals with Approved Internships and Residencies: A Study of the Professional Qualities of Foreign Medical Graduates." *Journal of Medical Education* 43:706.

Medalie, J.H. 1972. "The Present and Future of Primary Medical Care in Israel." *International Journal of Health Services* 2:285–295.

Mick, Stephen S. 1975. "The Foreign Medical Graduate." *Scientific American* 232, no. 2 (February):19–21.

Muller, James E.; Abdellah, Faye G.; Billings, F.T.; Hess, Arthur E.; Petit, Donald; and Egeberg, Roger O. 1972. "Soviet Health System: Aspects of Relevance for Medicine in the U.S." *New England Journal of Medicine*, March 30, pp. 693–702.

Navarro, Vincente. 1977. *Social Security and Medicine in the USSR*. Lexington, Mass.: Lexington Books, 1977.

Orzack, Louis H. 1980. "Educators, Practitioners, and Politicians in the European Common Market." *Higher Education* 9:307–323.

Petrovskig, B.V. 1967. "New Trends in Medical Education in the USSR." *Medical Education Bulletin* (WHO Regional Office for Europe), no. 2.

Popov, G.A. 1971. "Principles of Health Planning in the USSR." *Public Health Papers*, no. 43.

Ryan, Michael. 1978. *The Organization of Soviet Medical Care*. Oxford: Basil Blackwell and London: M. Robertson.

Shioshvily, A.P., and Prorokov, N.N. 1971. *Specialization and Advanced Training of Therapeutists in the USSR*. WHO/EDUC/71.150. Geneva: World Health Organization.

Shipler, David K. 1983. *Russia: Broken Idols, Solemn Dreams*. New York: Times Books.

Shuval, Judith T. 1979. "Primary Care and Social Control." *Medical Care* 17, no. 6 (June):631–41.

——— . 1980. *Entering Medicine: The Dynamics of Transition*. Oxford: Pergamon Press.

——— . 1983. *Newcomers and Colleagues: Soviet Immigrant Physicians in Israel*. Houston: Cap and Gown Press.

Shuval, Judith T.; Antonovsky, A.; and Davies, A.M. 1970. *Social Functions of Medical Practice*. San Francisco: Jossey Bass.

Shuval, Judith T.; Markus, E.J.; and Dotan, J. 1975a. *Patterns of Integration over Time: Soviet Immigrants in Israel,* No. JS/521/6. Jerusalem: Israel Institute of Applied Social Research.

Shuval, Judith T.; Markus, E.J.; and Dotan, J. 1975b. "Age Patterns in Integration of Soviet Immigrants in Israel." *Jewish Journal of Sociology* 2:151–163.

Smith, Hedrick. 1976. *The Russians.* Quadrangle: New York Times Book Company.

Stevens, Rosemary; Goodman, L.W.; and Mick, S.S. 1978. *The Alien Doctors: Foreign Medical Graduates in American Hospitals.* New York: Wiley.

Storey, Patrick B. 1971. "Continuing Medical Education in the Soviet Union." *New England Journal of Medicine* 285:437–442.

Toren, Nina; Grifel, Avi; and Portnoy, Grasiela. 1979. *Immigrant Scientists in Israel.* Jerusalem: Ministry of Immigrant Absorption.

U.S. Department of Health, Education and Welfare. 1972. *Foreign Trained Physicians and American Medicine.* Report prepared by Rosemary Stevens and Joan Vermeulen. DHEW Publication No. (NIS) 73-325. Washington, D.C.: Government Printing Office.

Voronel, A. 1971. "The Aliyah of the Russian Intelligensia." *Midstream* 22, no. 4.

Weinschall, T.D., and Raveh, Y.A. 1980. *Absorption of Immigrant Scientists in Research and Development Groups.* Tel Aviv: Tel Aviv University, Faculty of Management.

World Health Organization. 1978. *World Health Statistics. Vol. 1: 1978.* Geneva: WHO.

22

A Transcultural Review of Israeli Psychiatry

Yitzhak Levav and *Yoram Bilu*

Israel houses many ethnocultural groups within its small geographic confines. These groups differ both in their original characteristics and in their rates and patterns of adaptation to the sociocultural mould provided by the Israeli state (Eisenstadt 1967). Transcultural psychiatry in Israel must therefore identify and describe the components of a mosaic which includes contributions from traditional Jewish sources, from diverse ethnic groups which brought knowledge, attitudes, and practices from their respective countries and from the Zionist pioneers who gave birth to the Israeli state and whose dominant ideology has had many implications for mental health. It must also attempt to discover how these elements have interacted with Western-oriented psychiatry (Miller 1970). While other ethnocultural groups such as Arabs, Druzes, and Samaritans also exist in Israel, to try to discuss all these groups in one article would be to risk losing coherence for the sake of comprehensiveness. The availability of studies published in the psychiatric literature and in the literature of related fields dictated the framework for the following review.

ATTITUDES TOWARD MENTAL ILLNESS AND THE MENTALLY ILL

Psychiatry was regarded by the early Zionist pioneers "not only as an esoteric profession, but also as an unnecessary one" (Palgi 1963). They felt that self-realization through work, along with the enthusiasm (Rosen 1969) created by rebuilding the old-new homeland would free the people from the anguish of their existence and, most specifically, from the psychological consequences of their hazardous lives in anti-semitic countries. Palgi wrote in 1963:

> In Israel there was a tendency, which still lingers on today, to place exaggerated faith in the therapeutic powers of the Jewish State as such . . . There are without a doubt, objective sociopsychological grounds for this belief. However, the real roots of this belief may be found in Jewish traditions and mysticism associated with the concepts of the Holy Land. This belief was an additional factor

which made it possible for the country to maintain a certain *denial* of emotional and mental problems until they became intolerable for the public.

New social and cultural elements were incorporated into this initial ideological setting after the creation of the State of Israel in 1948. Independence led to the absorption of former inmates of the concentration camps of Nazi Europe with their severe psychological scars. European immigration was almost immediately followed by mass immigration to Israel from Oriental countries (Miller 1977). The new social scene, which contained many people in need of mental health care, hastened the development of community psychiatric services. This process is well documented in a relatively recent and comprehensive historical review by Miller (1977). The powerful effects of the social processes which have occurred in Israel since these beginnings, such as the consequences of war and related stress (Milgram 1978), must be considered in dealing with this subject.

A brief outline of the sociocultural backgrounds of four empirical studies of public attitudes conducted in Israel follows. These studies attempted to elucidate the attitudes of different population groups toward mental illness and toward the mentally ill. The first study, conducted by Hes (1966–67), contrasted the knowledge and attitudes of the husbands of former psychiatric inpatients of East European (Polish) origin with those of Oriental (Moroccan and Yemenite) origin. The group from Poland was at the vertex of the high exposure scale while the Moroccan group was placed toward the middle because, as is argued by Hes, "They have lived in the proximity of the French culture and were acquainted . . . with medical services." The group from Yemen came "from a socially backward and economically deprived country" (Hes 1966–67) where there was no familiarity with psychiatry. The respondents consisted of 143 husbands of former inpatients ranging in age from 20 to 60 years who had stayed in the hospital for not less than six months. The field study was conducted in 1962.

In general, results indicated that the respondents had a relatively negative attitude toward psychiatry. All three groups of respondents had kept the patient-wife at home for some length of time from the moment the first signs of illness became evident until admission to hospital although, as expected, this time period varied according to diagnosis. (Those wives who were eventually diagnosed as schizophrenic were taken to the hospital earlier.) All respondents believed that the mental hospital need not be considered "the last alternative for a person in need of psychiatric care" (Hes 1966–67). Basically, the mental hospital was not favourably regarded. Fifty-two percent of the Oriental respondents sought consultations with rabbis and native healers while their wives were hospitalized, apparently in an attempt to find a support system similar to the one they had known in their native countries. Only a minority (17 per cent) of the Europeans did the same. This latter group also differed in the husbands' feelings of shame over the illness that had afflicted the spouse: 73 percent of the Polish-born respondents concealed their wife's hospitalization in contrast with 48 percent of the Yemeni-Moroccan group.

Two community-based studies complete the information that is available on this subject. One study consisted of a relatively small survey in a Jerusalem neighbourhood (Levav and Minami 1974); the other, much larger study, took place in Tel-Aviv (Zohar, Floro, and Modan 1974). The field work for the first study was conducted in 1972; that for the second probably took place during the same time period.

The Jerusalem study (Levav and Minami 1974) surveyed the attitudes of about 50 mothers of mixed European and Asian origin and the attitudes of their eldest daughters. On the average, the daughters had more years of education than their mothers and those of Western origin were more educated than those of Oriental ancestry. The interviewers relied on the clinical vignettes designed by Shirley Star. Although the findings were not statistically significant, a clear trend existed throughout: the respondents did not perceive the cases in psychopathological terms. Interestingly, the daughters, despite their relatively higher education levels, more often failed to judge the descriptions as psychiatric syndromes. The respondents tended not to favour the mental hospital as a locus of treatment. This negative attitude toward the mental hospital had a halo effect for the former patient: the overall acceptance of former patients was low and almost homogeneous throughout the groups. Unexpectedly, those of Western origin were only slightly less rejecting in their attitudes than those of Eastern origin. Although the group of daughters was also less rejecting of hospitalization, their overall level of acceptance was low considering their education level (mean, approximately 12 years). This study gives the impression that the small population investigated tended to deny mental illness and to react negatively towards former mental patients.

These findings were further supported by those obtained in the Tel Aviv study which questioned 504 people selected from a stratified city sample. Respondents were of both sexes, ranged in age from 31 to 60 years, and had immigrated from Europe (USSR, Poland, Romania, and Western Europe), Asia (Yemen and Iraq), and North Africa. Native Israelis were also included. The authors used the techniques described above to investigate knowledge and attitudes (Zohar, Floro, and Modan 1974). On the layman's appraisal of cases of paranoid behaviour, simple schizophrenia, and alcoholism, identification of these cases as requiring psychiatric care was 71 percent, 55 percent, and 21 percent respectively. This level of recognition was lower than that obtained in a household survey conducted by Dohrenwend and Ching-Shong (1967) in New York City where the corresponding levels for these same cases were 90 percent, 67 percent, and 41 percent.

The data on attitudes toward ex-patients showed that friendship with a former patient was accepted by 52 percent of the respondents in the Tel Aviv study; in New York it was accepted by 72 percent. Working in the same place as a former patient was accepted by 57 percent of the Israeli respondents and by 62 percent of New York respondents. Finally, regarding a closer-to-the-self life situation—marriage—only 10 percent of the respondents in the Tel Aviv study accepted marriage to a former patient while 37 percent of those in the New York study stated that they would allow their children to marry a former patient. In brief, the Israeli authors concluded, and the reviewers concur, that the Israeli public showed little understanding of mental illness.

A tangential confirmation of the relatively negative attitude toward mental illness that seems to characterize all population groups in Israel society comes from an incomplete report on the attitudes of kibbutz members. The interest of such a study is twofold: first, because the kibbutz is a relatively closed and egalitarian society and, second, because of the strong impact of the kibbutz ideology on the emerging pioneer Israeli society (Leon 1969). It is noteworthy that the central role played by the kibbutz movement is not grounded on the extent of its membership—which now accounts for only 3 percent of the total Jewish population of the country—but on the centrality of its ideology. Kaffman (1967), a psychiatrist and also a kibbutz member, presented data on the attitudes toward mental illness of kibbutz members which do not seem to indicate a marked difference from the attitudes of urban populations. This report refers to an analysis of a subsample of 200 respondents in a large unpublished study that included 600 respondents.

The open-mindedness of kibbutz respondents toward psychiatry was generally limited to their recommendations of mental health care for children with behavioural disturbances (68 percent made such a suggestion), and to their acceptance of a former patient in a work situation. (Notice should be taken of the fact that the work situation in a kibbutz carries greater emotional charge than work in the city because of the central place work holds in kibbutz life.) In contrast to the above recommendations, the willingness to recommend treatment falls to 38 percent in the case of severe and prolonged depressive reaction. Twenty-five percent of respondents answered that the ill member should try to overcome his emotional state alone, bringing to mind the self-reliance of the pioneer; 8 percent suggested consulting a friend, and 15 percent suggested taking a vacation. No sick role with secondary benefits was accorded to such a member. In other words, there was no room for illness with privileges; the overriding attitude was to negatively sanction any condition that affected work (Kaffman 1967).

Problems related to methodology indicate the need for other studies to clarify issues previously raised as well as to update information since these studies were conducted prior to 1973. The Yom Kippur War, by bringing emotional problems to public attention, may well have provoked interest in psychiatric problems which had previously been denied (Milgram 1978).

A SELECTIVE LOOK AT PSYCHIATRIC EPIDEMIOLOGY IN ISRAEL

A number of epidemiologic studies have been conducted in Israel. Seven of these were community surveys: Maoz, Levy, Brand, and Halevi (1966); Hoek, Moses, and Terespolsky (1965); Abramson (1966); Polliack (1971); Wamoscher (1972); Levav and Arnon (1976); and Menkes (unpublished data). (Another study (Schlosberg 1977) is completed but results are not yet available.) All other studies were based on the national case register of the ministry of health where all admissions and discharges at every inpatient psychiatric facility in the country are listed on a cumulative basis. This register was started in 1952—only four years after Israel became a state. A rather large number of publications have come out based on data from the national case registry (e.g. Mandel, Chesler-Gampel, and Miller 1971). These studies are of limited value for this review, in so far as it focuses on ethnic origin and mental disorders, because of the differential use of psychiatric services by different ethnic groups. The number of disorders treated reflects, to a greater or lesser extent, the idiosyncratic use of psychiatric services by a given population rather than providing a true picture of the mental health status of that population. Although the seven community surveys provide a more accurate picture of the mental health status of groups within the population, studies based on the case register provide interesting information on the overall admissions rates by place of origin and on specific disorders, e.g. schizophrenia and affective disorders.

In addition to being community-based, the seven surveys have a number of common characteristics. All were restricted to single localities (city, town, village, *moshav*, or kibbutz). Four were based on general practice populations (Hoek, Moses, and Terespolsky 1965; Polliack 1971; Wamoscher 1972; Levav and Arnon 1976). In none of these studies was the population concerned directly examined by a psychiatrist, although in one a psychiatrist reviewed all the medical records of the studied population (Levav and Arnon 1976).

Most case findings were based on the use of the Cornell Medical Index (CMI), either in its complete version of 195 questions (Abramson 1966; Polliack 1971; Wamoscher 1972), or in its shortened version (Levav and Arnon 1976). In one study (Menkes) the 22 Item Scale, developed by Langner in the USA, was utilized. In two (Wamoscher 1972; Levav and Arnon 1976), case findings were based both on the general practitioner's appraisal of the mental health status of the population and on the CMI. Five of these studies were comprehensively reviewed by Aviram and Levav (1975) who expressed grave reservations based on methodology.

Two of the studies are of an analytic nature (Abramson 1966; Menkes). The latter work is of interest to us because Menkes compared two villages with the same ethnic constitution (Kurdistan origin) but a contrasting degree of social organization and discussed their respective rates of mental disorders. The overall objective of this study was to contribute to the nature-nurture issue. Menkes's research strategy was to locate similar ethnic villages settled on a non-selective basis under almost identical environmental circumstances, and then to relate the level of organization-disorganization with the prevalence of disorders. The author found that the disorganized village had a mean of 6.1 symptoms on the Langner scale whereas the mean for the organized village was 4.2 symptoms.

In all of the community surveys, women exhibited higher rates of symptoms than men did, especially in those studies where case identification relied only on the CMI. Of greater interest was the reported higher prevalence of emotional disorders among immigrants than among native Israelis. Thus Abramson (1966), studying a Jerusalem neighbourhood, found a prevalence rate for emotional disorders of 4 percent for native Israeli men in the 20 to 29 year age group and 28 percent for native Israeli women of the same age. The rates for foreign-born men and women were 15 percent and 53 percent respectively. Abramson (1966) used the CMI to establish his rates. This report is of interest because he controlled for social status when he compared the populations. A year earlier, Hoek, Moses, and Terespolsky (1965) had very similar findings for a section of the same neighbourhood using a different method of identification, that of the general practitioner's appraisal. Hoek, Moses, and Terespolsky also found higher rates of symptoms for men of Afro-Asian origin than for native Israeli men. They suggested that the breakdown of traditional institutions in the immigrant population caused stress and, therefore, emotional difficulties. However, Aviram and Levav (1975) in their review wrote, "We feel, based on methodological grounds, that the assumption made in the study is premature since the number of Israeli-born included . . . was too small."

Most community studies did not break down the rates of symptoms by country of origin, thus "limiting the potential depth of the analysis" (Aviram and Levav 1975). An exception was the study by Levav and Arnon (1976); in this study the prevalence of emotional disorders was highest for Moroccans. However, no control was made for levels of education although the authors mentioned that the Moroccans came from villages with the lowest average level of educational attainment. The only study where ethnic origin as well as social status was controlled for was conducted by Abramson (1966). Unfortunately, in his study the breakdown by origin was only by continent of birth and not by country.

Gershon and Liebowitz (1975) conducted a study of the Jewish population in Jerusalem based on the case register. Their objective was to study the association between affective disorders and sociocultural and demographic characteristics. In view of the results of American studies (Malzberg 1973) which claim that affective disorders are more common among Jews than among other ethnic groups, they examined this issue in Israel by comparing the rates between Oriental and Ashkenazi Jews. The treated incidence (first admissions) for the Ashkenazi was higher, although ethnic origin per se explained less of the variance than factors such as demographic characteristics. They also found that first admissions in Jerusalem for the years 1969–72 were higher for Western than for Eastern Jews. However, their findings were limited to that city; rates for first admissions in 1966 for the whole country were the same for both ethnic groups (Mandel, Chesler-Gampel, and Miller 1971). Treatment statistics showed that the rate of first admission for native Israelis, for all diagnoses, was 188/100,000 for the population 15 years of age and older; the respective rate for foreign-born was 213/100,000 (Mandel, Chesler-Gampel, and Miller 1971).

Comparison of both community and case register studies shows that foreign-born have higher rates of disorders in terms of both prevalence rates in the community surveys and in treated incidence rates (admissions) in the registry studies. There is a different association for the treated disorders; while those of European-American origin showed higher rates for affective disorders, those of Afro-Asian origin had higher rates for schizophrenia as well as for personality disorders, alcoholism, and drug addiction. Two main issues need to be raised. In most of the studies there was no control for social class. Thus ethnic origin could be said to express primarily a social class effect since Israelis of Oriental origin are generally disadvantaged. The other issue is of a more restrictive nature—to lump together such different groups as Moroccans, Yemenites, and Iraqis and call them Orientals may be creating a group whose main common denominator is the fact that they are not Westerners. More carefully designed studies are necessary to clarify the picture of descriptive epidemiology. Only then can analytic insights be attempted.

TRADITIONAL BACKGROUND OF FOLK PSYCHIATRY IN ISRAEL

It seems that the ethnopsychiatric systems of various Jewish groups in their countries of origin have been shaped by integrating indigenous customs and practices with fervently preserved Jewish traditions although it is difficult today to estimate the differential contributions of both uniquely Jewish sources and those belonging to indigenous traditions. The two systems were not subjected to systematic investigation either in the countries the Jews came from or in Israel itself, at least not in the critical period of mass immigration in the early 1950s. In Jewish sources, the interest in mental disturbances, including attempts at classification, diagnosis, and therapeutic interventions, can be traced back to the Bible (Hes and Wollstein 1964). Later sacred writings, such as the Talmud, include sophisticated statements and conclusions concerning many aspects of human nature and behaviour which today might be considered part of the domain of psychiatry. For example, one may find in a tractate (*Berakhot*: Blessings) a detailed discussion of the nature and interpretations of dreams that partly anticipated Freudian notions (Bakan 1958; Cohen 1932; Lorand 1957).

The preoccupation with psychopathology and its remedies was especially marked in Jewish cabalistic literature which viewed these subjects from a religious-mystical perspective. Some techniques and devices of Jewish mysticism may be seen as having clearly therapeutic purposes. Cases of possession may serve as an illustration here. These altered states of consciousnes were explained by the mystical doctrine of transmigration (*Gilgulim*), a contribution of the Cabala to Judaism (Scholem 1976). According to this theory, the possessing agent was considered to be the soul of a deceased person who had been suspended from entering the other world. This soul, through possession of a living human being, could gain reparation and amendment and so obtain permission to enter the heavenly world. "Clinical" cases of possession thus appear in cabalistic literature from the sixteenth century on, although no attempt has been made to analyse them from a psychiatric perspective—a fascinating and intriguing task.

Some important, although not completely relevant, references to the subject under discussion are worthy of further mention. The monumental study by Trachtenberg (1939), *Jewish Magic and Superstition*, still constitutes a unique attempt to encompass the beliefs and practices which he titled folk-religion—the majority of which is closely related to folk-psychiatry—among the German Jews in the Middle Ages (eleventh to sixteenth centuries). This work focused primarily on pure Jewish sources, although some examples of local customs and practices which the Jews had adopted were mentioned. Only one chapter is directly related to medicine, but there is no problem in translating other chapters into psychiatric-medical language in order to learn about etiologic agents of problems and diseases (e.g. spirits of the dead, demons), diagnostic devices (e.g. divining lots), and therapeutic interventions (e.g. amulets, incantations).

Other works, which usually focus on one aspect of folk-psychiatry, are not as voluminous as that of Trachtenberg. Bezek (1968) described various magical practices from ancient Jewish sources, emphasizing the ambivalent attitude of the rabbinic establishment towards them. A fine documentation of the use of Jewish amulets, the major curing element in the traditional context, was made by Schrire (1966). It seems that these works almost exhaust the studies in this area.

Some researchers in Israel have attempted to reconstruct ethnographically elements of traditional psychiatry that were used by various groups before their immigration to Israel. Major etiological agents of problems of living according to the beliefs of Moroccan Jews have been described in detail. Ben-Ami (1969) presented the Jewish Moroccan version of demonic beliefs, describing the essence and nature of demons, the human situations considered vulnerable to demonic attack, and the customs and practices destined to appease or expel demons. In a second study, Ben-Ami (1972) also described certain magical practices among the Moroccans, called *tkaf* in Arabic, which consist of sorcerous devices charaterized by symbolic acts of inhibiting, binding, or blocking. These devices were mainly employed to make women barren and men impotent. The belief in the evil eye among Moroccan Jews was the subject of a detailed review by Stillman (1970) who described the typical problems caused by the evil eye as well as the characteristics of both offenders and victims, and the therapeutic techniques used against it. All the above mentioned etiological factors were mentioned in Willner and Kohls's (1962) partial reconstruction of Jewish life in the Atlas mountains of Morocco. Based on interviews with Jewish Yemenite rabbi-healers (*mori*), Hes (1963), a leading Israeli social psychiatrist, reconstructed the major patterns of somatic and mental problems and their explanations and therapies among Jews in Yemen.

These ethnographic studies are important for two reasons. First, if information is available concerning the beliefs and practices of the indigenous population in the countries from which the Jewish groups under study migrated to Israel, there exists a possibility of examining and estimating the relative contribution of each source to Jewish ethnopsychiatry. For example, the characteristics of the Jewish Moroccan demon previously mentioned (Ben-Ami 1969) are very similar to those of the Moslem demon (Westermarck 1926; Crapanzano 1973). Nevertheless, an interesting difference can be discerned concerning the conception of a demonic double, or twin who, symmetrical to his human fellow, accompanies him from birth to death. This particular belief, although very popular among the Jews, was not mentioned by Westermarck or Crapanzano, suggesting a possible uniquely Jewish tradition. Second, ethnographic reconstructions may be employed as a baseline against which changes in folk-systems in Israel since immigration can be evaluated. These changes are evident considering the pressures that the modern "core" culture in Israel has exerted on the traditional groups; unfortunately, studies using this baseline are yet to be done.

CULTURAL ASPECTS OF PSYCHOPATHOLOGY

The ability to evaluate mental symptoms in relation to the appropriate ethnic and cultural context in which they were shaped is an asset that mental health practitioners in Israel must possess. Yet sociocultural components of psychopathology have been underemphasized by Israeli psychiatrists. Palgi, an anthropologist, has contributed more than anyone else to making these components understandable. She has shown how seldom psychiatrists took such cultural factors into account. Thus, in the past, bizarre items of behaviour were judged according to Western standards and, when it was impossible to ignore behavioural differences, they were related to differences in social status and educational attainment. The classical dilemma of psychiatrists in a multicultural setting soon manifested itself in Israel:

> In view of the association of psychosis and belief in devils and witchcraft in Europe, psychiatrists in Israel found themselves in a new situation when dealing with patients from the Moslem orbit whose beliefs in spirits are an integral part of their life. As a result, diagnosed hallucinatory behaviour among Middle-Eastern patients, on closer examination, sometimes turned out to be culturally acceptable magical beliefs, intensely activated by a person under stress (Palgi 1963).

Empirical evidence of the above view comes from a study conducted in the early 1960s in the only university hospital psychiatric clinic in Israel at that time. The findings showed that the illnesses of a relatively high percentage of patients of Oriental origin remained undiagnosed. It was the authors' conviction that this "indicated lack of understanding of the psychopathology showed by those patients on the part of the psychiatrist" (Moses and Shanan 1961).

On the other hand, Palgi properly warned against a naive cultural relativism which would relate all differences in behaviour to the variable of cultural background. It is her conviction—shared by us—

that an integrated approach must be established which would enable the identification of genuine patterns of psychopathology, even if these are coloured by cultural factors and channelled into traditionally acceptable ways of behaviour. Given the culturally heterogeneous background of Israeli society, it is important to formulate clear criteria indicating when a belief in demons and sorcery, which is still accepted by certain groups in the population, ceases to be a normative behaviour and becomes a sign of psychopathology. Some guidelines for such criteria can be found in Bilu's (1978) study of Moroccan-born village members. One-time encounters with demons, if short and abrupt in nature, perceived as the result of suspected sorcery, and kept well hidden in a private context (i.e. the family) were not perceived as deviant by significant others. These behavioural patterns serve as a legitimate resource to be used in certain crisis situations. However, the new social reality in Israel dictates an economical and limited use of these patterns which, if they go beyond a quantitatively low threshold, are considered invalid (and indicative of mental disturbance) by the traditional group presently under discussion.

Until the past few years it had been quite clear that the bias toward "psychiatric imperialism" was much more dangerous than that toward the more naive approach of "cultural relativism." It now seems that this situation is undergoing rapid changes because of the increasing awareness by mental health practitioners of the important role played by cultural factors in a society as ethnically pluralistic as Israel. Several case studies that refer to the role of cultural aspects in shaping behavioural patterns of psychopathology among Jews in Israel have recently been published. Before briefly reviewing these cases and some generalizations drawn from them, it is worth pointing out that these cases lack a unifying theoretical frame of reference and are presented with a differential emphasis on the cultural components. All the cases described are those of patients of Oriental origin (Morocco, Tunisia, Libya, Yemen, Iraq, Turkey, and the USSR–Georgia), none of whom had refrained from seeking medical or psychiatric treatment in modern agencies. It would be a mistake to conclude that these cases represent rare, exotic, and rapidly disappearing disturbances. Unexpectedly, most of the patients described were young, in their twenties or thirties, and on the average had lived in Israel for 15 years. Some were infants when their families arrived, suggesting that the influence of the cultural heritage unique to certain ethnic groups is preserved with remarkable tenacity.

Accusation of sorcery is the most frequently presented cultural theme among these cases, reflecting the psychiatric dilemma in a culturally pluralistic society. On the one hand, the intensity and popularity of the belief in sorcery among Oriental Jews in Israel is emphasized throughout these case studies, but, on the other hand, the diagnoses given to most of the patients described included the label of paranoia or some of its derivatives.

Arieli (1970) analysed three cases involving beliefs in sorcery and the evil eye from a psychoanalytical perspective. He found that the magical thinking underlying these beliefs contained the two basic mechanisms which Freud called "omnipotence of thought" and "projection of a wish." Aggressive envy of others in the vicinity, sexual desires towards a mother-in-law, and homosexual wishes towards a brother-in-law were all manifested and projected into the conviction that these important others had bewitched the patient. Arieli (1970) pointed out that the first tendency to see this conviction as paranoid thought is not objective: "This way of thinking, being very primitive, has to be considered as a regressive symptom which points to the gravity of the patient's state. Nonetheless, one must say that the magical thought is frequent in the cultural environment in which the patient grew up and lived in, and especially in the bosom of the family."

How is one to decide whether the patient is exhibiting a symptom or culturally accepted behaviour? Arieli argued for some kind of a quantitive answer. "We found that the patients were not alone in their magical beliefs. . . . But with the families, the main thought remained in any case rational, according to objective reality, while with the patient, the magical thought rules exclusively. This proves that a weak ego, in its struggle against strong demands which do not allow repression or solution by other means of defence, needs a technique of omnipotence of thought" (Arieli 1970). In any case, the point was made that these patients are not by definition psychotic. The fact that their bizarre ideations stemmed from culturally shared beliefs does, in some way, alleviate the gravity of their disturbances.

Anthropologists who analysed cases of sorcery were less concerned with the validity of the psychiatric diagnosis given to these patients than with the use of such cultural patterns as coping mechanisms. Such mechanisms may be activated in the situations of stress and crisis often caused by a discrepancy between traditional norms and modern ways of life in Israel.

Shokeid (1971) presented the case of a woman, living in a village (*moshav*) where most of the inhabitants were from Morocco, who, having suffered from somatic symptoms, accused some of her neighbours and friends of sorcery. Without paying much attention to this woman's mental status, Shokeid focused on the conflict between traditional norms concerning division of labour between men and women and the new economic reality in the *moshav*. The woman's family was economically backward; the husband had refused to maintain a farm but, at the same time, he also refused to allow his wife to work and earn money. The woman, in spite of her religious background, had worldly (economical) aspirations and, ironically, she succeeded in fulfilling them through her breakdown which involved a temporary hospitalization. Her husband accepted a job as a night watchman and agreed that she could work. All of the neighbours claimed that she had "won the battle." It was no accident that her suspicions of sorcery were aimed at those modern women neighbours of whom she was jealous but towards whom she was also ambivalent because of their permissiveness concerning religious prohibitions.

Ornet (1977), an anthropologist, presented three cases involving outpatients at the Mental Health Center of Jaffa (a southern neighbourhood in Tel Aviv), all of whom had claimed to be victims of sorcery. He demonstrated that individuals tend to explain crisis situations caused by intrafamilial conflicts as the result of sorcery and to stress the immoral behaviour of the suspected sorcerer. Such accusations allow the accusers to avoid feelings of guilt and inadequacy. In this sense the accusations served as a method of socioeconomic adaptation. Ornet, though not psychoanalytically oriented, was nonetheless sensitive to the fact that all of his cases included a strong sexual component.

Two generalizations may be drawn from these cases. First, the varied problems allegedly caused by sorcery belong to three main categories: (1) romantic, marital, and sexual problems, which include the breaking or weakening of romantic or marital relations, failure in finding a spouse, infertility, pregnancy complications, and impotence; (2) interpersonal conflicts and struggles, mainly intrafamilial in nature; and (3) somatic problems, mainly pains. The other generalization is that suspicions of sorcery are directed towards people living in the close vicinity, mainly relatives. Accusations within the nuclear family are relatively infrequent and typically involve the husband accusing the wife, not vice versa. Within the extended family those accused of sorcery are usually relatives via marriage; the main targets are mothers-in-law. (As in other traditional societies, women are considered specialists in the magical realm.) The alleged sorcerer's motivation is understood to be a combination of envy and frustration, generated by marked discrepency in achievement between the victim-accuser and the assumed offender (and enhanced by physical proximity), or by a pre-existing conflict between them, usually in the context of a romantic involvement. In traditionally oriented families, one's most intensive contacts in day-to-day life are with neighbours and relatives. These relationships, although positively valenced, may at times develop into an arena for conflicts and struggles, thus rendering these people particularly vulnerable to accusations of sorcery.

Descriptions of clinical cases involving some form of demonic attack are less frequent than those of sorcery. Bilu (1978) described several cases of "demonic diseases" among Moroccan Jews. Palgi, some years before (1966), discussed one case of spirit possession in a newcomer from Turkey. However, several other cases such as those of Aleksandrowitz (1972) involved a more covert demonic intervention.

In contrast with this small number of cases, Bilu (1978) found that among Moroccan-born *moshav* members who employed traditional healers' services, demonic attack was still the most prevalent etiologic explanation of disease although pure cases of possession were vanishing. The belief in the existence of demons still prevails in the *moshavim*, even among young people, and almost every one is acquainted with the basic notions and customs concerning the nature of *jnun* (Arabic for demon), as well as the places, times, statuses, and situations considered to be haunted by demons and therefore dangerous.

On the basis of these demonic beliefs, a specific etiology is likely to be produced in cases of ailments involving mental symptoms. This etiology is an ordered sequence, integrating factors from both reality and demonic beliefs. The first element is a harsh event with a traumatic quality (i.e. a sudden and unexpected death in the family or coming to blows with neighbours), followed by an emotional derivative (affective expressions of fright, anger, or both). The second component in the explanatory sequence relates to the damaging act. Many of the interviews identified specific behaviour patterns which brought demonic retaliation. Those patterns most frequently identified were those which included hitting others (as in the context of a fight) or physical damage occurring to the self (as in the context of a sudden disaster). The patients were usually conscious of these real components, but the explanatory sequence became meaningful only with the healers' contributions. The healers emphasized the vulnerability of the situation to demonic intervention, strengthening the demonic factors by explication: the onset of the disease was explained by them as having characteristics of location, timing, specific activities, and personal status which created the arena for a demonic attack. This rich specificity made the demonic explanation appear plausible and convincing. The healers usually supplied information concerning the attacking demon (specifying characteristics or even personal identity) and the body location of the demonic blow. Thus the explanatory system was completed and the empirical occurrences were channelled to a specific set of symptoms.

Demon-caused diseases of Moroccan Jews, considered by Bilu (1978) to be valid examples of culture-bound syndromes, were developed along an external-internal dimension. *Tsira* is a generalized term for a group of diseases allegedly caused by a demonic attack from the outside, while *aslai* relates to various states of possession in which the demon controls the victim from within. In its moderate form, which is the most prevalent, *tsira* is a short-term disturbance, episodic or cyclic by nature, with a very clear and abrupt onset. The syndrome has two major components, one of which includes somatic complaints about pain and bodily dysfunction while the other is a "fright" syndrome with ideational as well as somatic aspects.

In the *aslai* group, the "evil spirit disease" is the Jewish Moroccan version of classical possession. The attack begins with a short period of falling and unconsciousness, followed by a violent and uncontrolled dissociative phase. The patient, usually a woman, becomes very powerful and aggressive, often harming herself and others. Her activities are ascribed to the demon and he speaks through her mouth in strange voices and expressions, sometimes in a strange language. The presence of the demon endows the patient with a supernatural power of divination and revelation. The attack is marked by total or partial amnesia.

Both *tsira* and *aslai* are culture-bound disturbances, but the cultural significance of the first is focused on the etiologic, demonic aspect while the symptoms are, to a large extent, traditionally neutral. *Aslai* is a traditional syndrome from both etiologic and symptomatic points of view. Here a complicated repertoire of behaviours is enacted only by a patient who is deeply involved in the traditional culture and demonic beliefs and who has had models for identification with this culture. These conditions, which are necessary if the disturbance is to take on the specific pattern of "evil spirit disease," are not easily attained in Israel. All of the patients who suffered from this kind of possession brought their disease with them from Morocco. No "Israeli" cases were located in the two *moshavim* where the study was conducted (Bilu 1978).

Two cases of *koro* were identified in Israel (Hes and Nassi 1977). This syndrome consists of anxiety attacks accompanied by the idea that the patient's penis is withdrawing into the abdominal cavity and by the fear that this condition will ultimately lead to death. *Koro* is considered to be a culture-bound syndrome specific to Southeast Asia. Of the two Israeli cases, one was a male Yemenite Jew who could not obtain sexual gratification because of religious prohibitions. Given the emphasis on the negative consequence of masturbation and sexual overindulgence in Jewish religious literature, his resulting preoccupation with masturbation resulted in castration fears which the so-called *koro* anxiety served to alleviate. But, like many other neurotic mechanisms, this means of diminishing anxiety generated new fears—in this case, fears of sexual impotence.

Even though the traditional ideas of Chinese physiology (the yin-yang equilibrium) which may shape the *koro* syndrome (Yap 1964) do not exist in Judaism, it seems that divergent cultural constellations may create similar symptoms and syndromes. However one must question whether the term *koro* is applicable to a patient of any cultural background other than Chinese who expresses anxious feelings about a shrinking penis. The fact that neither of the two Israeli patients expressed the idea that their condition would ultimately lead to their death supports this reservation.

A fine analysis of psychopathology from a cultural perspective was done by Palgi, Goldwasser, and Goldman (1955) who related certain patterns of withdrawal from the female role among young Iraqui women to the socialization and sociocultural milieu in their country of origin. These women displayed a clinical picture of depression, accompanied by a strong tendency to engage in fantasy and the withdrawal from close relationships with men. The analysis showed that the process of maladjustment underlying these patterns had begun in Iraq and was further aggravated in Israel.

Since the British mandate began in Iraq, Jewish girls have had the opportunity to attend schools, thus gaining access to some external expressions of Western culture (e.g. social conventions, etiquette, dress, etc.). These were radically different from traditional values and patriarchal family patterns according to which women were expected to be "ideal maids," submissive and obedient to their husbands or, if they were not married, to their fathers and brothers. As a result of this exposure to two different cultures, these girls experienced an ongoing conflict between the Western values and attitudes they acquired at school and the tradition-oriented patterns of their families. This conflict was further aggravated when the girls reached marriageable age, generally 16 years, and learned that the bridegroom who had been chosen for them by the parents was disappointingly remote from their romantic ideals because he was Oriental and represented values they had learned to despise. The typical defensive solution adopted by these girls was to strictly isolate themselves from contacts with males. The conflict of cultures in Iraq had created the seeds that developed into psychopathology in Israel: in some cases the girls and their families had experienced a drastic loss in socioeconomic status in moving to Israel and realized that their desired ideal image of a non-Oriental male was unrealistic or unattainable.

The Palgi, Goldwasser, and Goldman study is much more significant than the former case studies: not merely an individual case but a disturbance characteristic of a certain subgroup, ethnically discerned, is analysed and the underlying factors in the sociocultural milieu of that group in the past and at present are exposed. This study is a step toward the type of research required in this multidisciplinary field, research that combines more rigorous methodology with both psychiatric sensitivity and anthropological skill.

Another contribution to the field of cultural psychiatry in Israel was made by Perez (1977) who described the clinical picture of "the messianic psychotic patient." This term applies to paranoid schizophrenic male patients with delusions characterized by the belief that they have been elected by a superior power for the execution of a special task and have been endowed with supernatural powers. This special task is almost always redemptive and usually has two main objectives: the attainment of universal peace and the resurrection of the dead. This delusional configuration is coloured by the religious-cultural beliefs and notions concerning the messianic idea in Jewish mystical traditions as indicated by the fact that Jewish (as well as Moslem) patients do not present delusions of identification with God, in contrast to Christian patients with similar symptoms who often have such delusions. This finding is consistent with the fact that a process of humanization (transformation of God in man) exists in Christianity but does not occur in the Jewish and Moslem religions.

The Perez (1977) study is based on a fairly large sample (57 Jewish and 20 Moslem patients) but, unfortunately, some important information is conspicuously lacking, particularly concerning the Arab group. A general profile of the majority of the Jewish patients is offered: "a young male with narcissistic premorbid personality . . . of religious or notably traditional familial extraction, of lower middle class, average age between 20 to 30 years, suffering serious conflicts with the parental figures and who has repeated in two or three psychiatric breakdowns the messianic delusional picture" (Perez 1977). No data are presented concerning the ethnic extraction of the parents of these patients.

The interplay between ethnic origin and psychopathology has been investigated not only through case studies but also epidemiologically in a number of different studies. Some of the work was triggered by the clinician's impression that patients from Oriental countries complained in somatic terms more often than other patients —which, parenthetically, meant that clinicians did not offer psychotherapy to such patients since the somatic language "is the type of communication with which the psychiatrist is least able to deal" (Hes 1968). In his review of 360 psychiatric outpatients, Hes (1968) found that 15 percent were diagnosed as "hypochondriacs." Hypochondriac concerns were not limited to any single nosologic entity. Although 56 percent of the case load was of Oriental origin, the proportion of those of Oriental origin among the hypochondriacs reached 80 percent. The most relevant finding of the study was that years of education (and not ethnic origin) was the factor that most often accounted for hypochondriasis. Since Orientals are more educationally disadvantaged, it is no surprise that they suffered from such psychopathology more than other ethnic groups. Additional evidence of the spurious effect of ethnic origin in such studies is drawn from another patient survey conducted at almost the same time. This study (Lerner and Noy 1967) consisted of a review of nearly 500 charts of outpatients at a university hospital clinic over a 30 month period. The population included only first-contact patients who were less than 60 years of age and who had been diagnosed as suffering from any disorder other than psychosomatic. (The use of the latter criteria, totally unexplained by the authors, raises an issue of method in an otherwise flawless research design.) The authors studied the association between the "degree of somatization" and a number of variables, particularly ethnic origin. Their findings repeated the findings described above: "somatization" was higher among Oriental-born patients. However, such associations faded when education was held constant. The authors argued "that indeed it is the low level of education that explains the high degree of 'somatization' in the Oriental group" (Lerner and Noy 1967).

The tendency for patients from ethnic groups of Oriental origin to present more somatic complaints was explored by Wamoscher (1972) and by Levav, Arnon, and Portnoy (1977) in two separate community studies which used almost identical research strategy. Wamoscher compared prevalence rates obtained by two methods, one based on a review of his own medical records and a second based on the administration of the CMI (Cornell Medical Index). Although, based on his records, the rates were identical in contrasting ethnic groups (35.4 percent for Orientals, 35.7 percent for the European-American), the rates differed when based on the CMI (7 percent higher among those of Oriental ancestry). Interestingly, native Israeli respondents showed inverse prevalence rates: rates were higher if based on the records, lower if based on the CMI. Levav, Arnon, and Portnoy (1977) used a psychiatric appraisal—degree of "caseness" (Leighton, Harding, Macklin, MacMillan and Leighton 1963) to determine prevalence rates. They relied on the review of records, complemented by the CMI. They found that when the study was controlled for sex, Israeli and European-born respondents consistently answered negatively to the CMI questions, even those who were rated as "cases" by the psychiatrists, whereas Asian and African-born respondents more often replied positively, even those who were rated as "non-cases" by the psychiatrist. However a recent re-analysis of the same data (Abramson and Levav 1978) showed that the variance explained by ethnic origin was of a lower order than was that explained by educational attainment.

Although ethnic background and psychopathology are only spuriously related in these studies, the interplay of both factors is present in other studies. One example of this is a survey of a child guidance clinic which is of interest because it also suggests the role of socialization in the psychopathology of different ethnic groups (Skea, Draguns, and Phillips 1969). Oriental boys (actually of Iraqi and Yemeni descent) showed a clearly different type of psychopathology from those of European descent (Polish, German). While the Oriental children showed more outwardly directed psychopathology

(Yemenites were more passive-aggressive, while the Iraqis were more active-rebellious), those of European ancestry showed more affective and intrapsychic disturbances. Undoubtedly, research concerning ethnic origin and the modes of expression of psychic distress based on epidemiologic inquiry is necessary, especially studies which could integrate diverse approaches.

TRADITIONAL HEALERS AND THERAPIES

Israel has a number of folk healers from various ethnic groups, Jewish as well as non-Jewish, who represent heterogeneous traditions. Although, in our opinion, they constitute significant psychiatric resources, they have not been the subject of systematic and thorough research. Hence mental health practitioners generally have little information concerning their practices and skills.

Only three studies have dealt directly with Jewish folk healers. Hes (1964a) and Bilu (1977, 1978) studied male healers (Yemenites and Moroccans respectively) while Aleksandrowitz (1972) presented a case study of a female curer of Kurdistan origin. There are striking similarities between the Yemeni healers—or *mori*—and their Moroccan counterparts. Both groups are respectfully given the title of Rabbi although only a few deserve it according to the formal criteria of religious scholarship. In their countries of origin, these healers played a vital role in preserving Jewish traditions and ways of life being, among other things, ritual slaughterers, teachers of the *Torah*, performers of the act of circumcision, and prayer leaders at the synagogue. "One can hardly think of a situation in which the advice of a *mori* could not be sought" (Hes 1964a). As Jewish religious healing in both Yemen and Morocco was at least partly based on the manipulation of sacred names and verses, healing was considered to be a natural part of the role of the religious practitioners in places where physicians were not found.

Both of the studies mentioned above provide data on the process of becoming a healer. In Yemen, a person was chosen and prepared for the manifold tasks that he would eventually have to perform by becoming an apprentice to another *mori* or by attending classes in a school for higher education. For Moroccan healers, rabbis and *hachamim* (wise men) played a vital role in teaching the basic attributes of religious healing. Healing attributes were acquired primarily through the *Zechut Avot* (the right of the elders) which gave an ascribed and unconditional merit of holiness and hence of healing power. In addition, apprentices followed their ancestors' path by engaging in religious scholarship. Some of these religious studies may have been necessary prerequisites for the skills of name manipulation which are important in healing. In the families of healers, one could often find old books of lots and medical formulas which might have been used by a young healer, at least in his first studies. All the healers had a role model in their near vicinity, usually a rabbi-teacher, although at times a Moslem sheikh filled the role of model (Hes 1964a).

Moroccan healers attained their role mainly through self-selection although this process was accelerated by supernatural elements such as receiving an approving hint from a saint or a holy father in dreams. It is interesting to note that six out of the eight healers interviewed by Bilu (1977, 1978) had lost a parent at a very young age. The fact that in all cases the deceased parent was the father may indicate that the motivation to become a healer was related to certain personality dynamics shaped by the effects of growing up without a father. The curing role might then be seen as the enactment of an omnipotent wish, compensating for early experiences of frustration and helplessness (D'Andrade 1961).

Yemenite *mori* were divided into two groups: a minority of more scientific, organically oriented healers who were interested in precise diagnosis and appropriate treatment with herbs and drugs, and a larger group of healers with a magic-mystical orientation who believed in demons and evil eyes as the causes of disease and used complicated rituals against these (Hes 1964a). The division into magical versus scientific orientation does not hold true for Moroccan healers who use various types of name manipulation, usually accompanied by the application of different herbs, to cure disease (Bilu 1978). Healers from both ethnic groups treated the same type of problems, including a wide spectrum of mental disturbances, some somatic ailments (i.e. pain), romantic, marital and sexual problems, interpersonal conflicts and struggles, and material difficulties. Their clientele were recruited mainly from within their own ethnic group although they did have clients from other groups such as Orientals (mainly of Middle Eastern extraction). Ashkenazi patients were rare in the waiting rooms of these healers.

Although the Yemenite *mori* and the Moroccan rabbi have lost some of their functions in Israel, their healing role has been tenaciously kept. Hes's (1964) appraisal of the *mori* in Israel seems applicable to his Moroccan counterpart as well: "The *mori* in Israel still provide an important source of psychotherapeutic help for persons suffering from emotional problems and troubles in living. This kind of help is adapted specifically to the needs of his fellow men and could not be easily supplied in more effective ways from another source."

The vast array of female healers in Israel, most of whom use special diagnostic tools (coffee and cards for divination are used almost exclusively by women), is represented by a single case study (Aleksandrowitz 1972). In this study Aleksandrowitz described Um-Razzia, an old woman of Kurdistan origin. Her healing was based on contact with demons which appeared to her in dreams and guided her in treating her patients. (There are other healers, mostly Arabs, who are allegedly aided in their therapeutic work by demons.) Aleksandrowitz described several cases treated by this healer and provides a psychodynamic formulation of her personality. She concluded, based on the old woman's Rorschach, that Um-Razzia had an oral personality and used fantasies of grandeur and eternity to defend herself against depression and fear of death. This was, according to Aleksandrowitz, a pathological motivation for her becoming a healer. It could be argued that such a judgement is somewhat ethnocentrically biased, based as it is on the analysis of Rorschach determinants. Thus it is questionable whether a reduced F+ percentile is indicative of poor reality testing in the case of an old woman from a purely traditional background. In the two studies discussed previously (Hes 1964a and Bilu 1978) there were no major hints of psychopathology in the healers.

Attempts to describe and classify various diagnostic and therapeutic methods used by folk healers in Israel have been made only in the studies by Hes and Bilu. Thus data are again drawn from Jewish Yemenite and Moroccan sources. Bilu (1978) found that the healers in his sample employed a rich repertoire of tools as diagnostic devices. These could be divided into three main categories: casting tools, organic diagnostic materials, and demonic aids. Lots are based on sophisticated formulas for transforming some identifying details, such as the patient's name and the name of his mother, into an elaborate system of numbers, letters, or figures which provides etiologic or prognostic information. Organic diagnostic materials (e.g. oil and eggs) may be manipulated in various ways to produce a set of signs, the interpretation of which leads to useful diagnostic conclusions. The healers may use demonic power for specific aims such as divination and discovery of the source of the problems they were asked to cure.

In a Jewish folk context, healing was primarily based on skillful manipulation of sacred names and formulas taken from old handwritten books which were at the disposal of the rabbi-healers. The healer wrote down the relevant formula for the patient. Most of these healing formulas are derived from the Jewish mystical tradition (Cabala) although some of the Jewish healers employ Moslem versions. Although these Moslem versions are called "profane names" in their Hebrew equivalents, many people are convinced of their therapeutic power.

The prototype of traditional treatment in the Jewish Moroccan context has two objectives: prevention and curing (symptom removal). To protect the patient from future calamities, the healer prepares an amulet to be carried under the patient's clothes. Curing may be achieved by an active transformation of name manipulations, e.g. erasing the written formula by water or by burning. The most effective of these manipulations involves bringing the formula into concrete physical contact with the patient's body (the water which erased the formula is drunk, the smoke of its burning is inhaled). There is no doubt that this treatment involves a powerful element of suggestion which contributes to its therapeutic effectiveness (Bilu 1978).

Some of the curing methods used by the Yemenite *mori* are similar to those previously mentioned. Hes (1964) maintained the division of healers into naturalistic-organic versus magic-mystical and described various plant remedies used by the naturalistic-organic group. Important techniques among the magic-mystical group were those of *fashta* and *makwa*—physical interventions which involved scratches and burns on various parts of the body. The rationale behind such techniques may be magical (i.e. expelling an evil spirit).

ENCOUNTERS WITH MODERN MEDICINE AND PSYCHIATRY

In Israel, the supremacy of modern Western-type medical agencies is generally acknowledged, at least by the socioculturally and politically dominant Ashkenazi Jews. It seems, however, that significant segments of Israeli society, particularly those of Middle-Eastern origin, employ traditional therapeutic resources of healing. The fact that the latter population belongs predominantly to the lower socioeconomic strata tends to lead to these traditional resources being regarded as primitive, even dangerous, and hence illegitimate. What is the nature of the contacts between patients and therapists from both sides of this modern-traditional division?

Although many medical practitioners have become increasingly aware of the importance of sociocultural factors in shaping the behaviour patterns (including patterns of psychopathology) of ethnically different individuals, medical practitioners as a whole are not yet completely free from stereotypical, ethnocentric attitudes toward traditional healers and patients. According to Shuval (1970), physicians in her research sample appeared concerned about traditional practices and wanted to prevent patients from using traditional medical remedies, even when this practice was in no way damaging from a medical point of view. The doctors "believed that Western medicine cannot tolerate parallel systems of therapy based on a different cultural rationale" (Shuval 1970).

Patients who use traditional medicine are favourably oriented toward modern agents of therapy (Epstein 1977; Rosenfeld 1956; Shuval 1970). This recurrent finding, explained by Shuval (1970) as an attempt to solve the "magic-science conflict" by transferring to the physician magical skills previously attributed to the healer, suggests that the two systems of treatment are mutually complementary, not mutually exclusive.

Bilu (1978) found that the positive attitude toward modern therapeutic methods also expressed itself in the priority given to them. In his sample, 89 percent of the problems allegedly caused by demons were treated by a physician before the patient consulted a healer. Only a frustrating experience with modern treatment methods motivated the patient to turn to a healer. This pattern, mentioned in other studies as well (Aleksandrowitz 1972; Deshen and Shokeid 1974) may reflect an "acculturative sequence" indicating readiness to accept modern medical practices in a traditional society undergoing acculturation (Romanucci-Ross 1969).

In his previously reviewed study, Hes (1968) examined referrals to traditional healers made by families of psychiatric inpatients belonging to three Jewish groups—Yemenites, Moroccans, and Poles. His findings indicate that a positive orientation toward Western medicine was present at the same time as a need for support from traditional healers. Motivation to use traditional healers increased with the length of hospitalization, suggesting that a longer hospital stay was interpreted as indicating that the modern system had failed to treat these patients effectively. This perception of the failure of modern medicine, especially prominent in psychiatry, becomes a central criterion in defining "traditional diseases" (i.e. demon possession). Thus, the borderline between the areas of modern and folk medicine is empirically determined (Bilu 1978). Most traditional healers encouraged their patients to use modern agencies. By doing so, they have consciously contributed to the attenuation of their curing role (Landy 1974) but, simultaneously, they remain as a positive recourse for the patient whenever modern medicine fails to provide a cure.

Why have physicians and psychiatrists failed to treat traditional patients effectively? Cohen (1959), who studied a community of Yemenite newcomers in the early fifties, offers a devastating answer.

> An irreversible opportunity to acquire the people's trust in the first period had been missed. They had an enormous confidence in the physician and this positive orientation could have been employed for planning changes in their approach . . . but in those days, as well as today (1959), they have continually suffered degrading attacks on their self-dignity. They were considered ignorant and primitive by some, childish and easy-going by others. In any case, an attempt to ask for their help in planning ways to improve their situation has never been made. Even those customs which could be preserved have been the target of mockery and contempt. . . . The result is that these people have negatively reacted to physicians and nurses who took care of them. Being omnipotent in the beginning, every failure cast doubt on their work-system as a whole . . .

The patients in Bilu's sample (1978) who used traditional healers complained that many physicians and psychiatrists had failed to explain to them what was wrong. Often this was because the Western doctors had not found any clear-cut causes for their symptoms, but sometimes it was because the doctors did not believe that a modern explanation would be understood by such patients. When an explanation was given to the patient, it was often given in a rather laconic manner and without any intelligible rationale. The typical treatment that a patient experienced was purely organic—"needle and pills"—which was considered by the patient to be a "symptomatic" treatment, in contrast with treatment by the traditional healer which followed a lucid rationale and was coherently related to an etiologic explanation.

What are the attitudes of traditional healers toward their modern colleagues? Bilu (1978) found that the healers tend to emphasize encounters with representatives of modern medicine in which the healers' superiority is clearly manifested. This boastful approach actually masks a marked ambivalence toward modern health practitioners. This ambivalence is clearly displayed through the continual use of medical terms and images by traditional healers in their practice, indicating that the medical professional serves as a reference group for them. By using metaphors from the medical field, they stress their closeness to it, thus adding to their prestige. It appears that healers respect their modern colleagues and acknowledge their skill although they try to exclude a relatively small area of human disease from the field of responsibility of these colleagues (mainly demon-caused diseases). The curing role of the traditional healer has been sufficiently attenuated in Israel to permit the stable co-existence of both systems of medicine.

REFERENCES

ABRAMSON, J. H. 1966. Emotional disorder, status inconsistency and migration. A health questionnaire in Israel. *Milbank Memorial Fund Quarterly* 44: 23.

ABRAMSON, J. H. and LEVAV, I. 1978. Use of symptom inventories as measures of emotional ill-health in epidemiological studies. *International Journal of Epidemiology* 7: 381–82.

ALEKSANDROWITZ, M. 1972. The art of native therapy. *Bulletin of the Menninger Clinic* 36: 596.

ARIELI, A. 1970. Certain magical beliefs in mental diseases. *The Israel Annals of Psychiatry and Related Disciplines* 8: 3.

AVIRAM, U. and LEVAV, I. 1975. Psychiatric epidemiology in Israel—an analysis of five community studies. *Acta psychiatrica scandinavica* 52: 295.

BAKAN, D. 1958. *Sigmund Freud and the Jewish Mystical Tradition*. Princeton: Van Nostrand.

BEN-AMI, I. 1969. The presence of demons in the Jewish-Moroccan house. Paper presented at the Fifth World Congress for Judaism, Jerusalem. (In Hebrew)

———. 1972. Magic rituals among Moroccan Jews. *Zhor Le'Avraham 195-2-5, va'ad Adat Hama'araviim*, Jerusalem.

BEZEK, Y. 1968. *Beyond the Senses*. Tel Aviv: Dvir.

BILU, Y. 1977. General characteristics of referrals to traditional healers in Israel. *The Israel Annals of Psychiatry and Related Disciplines* 15: 245.

———. 1978. Traditional Psychiatry in Israel: Moroccan-Born Moshav Members with Psychiatric Disorders and "Problems in Living" and Their Traditional Healers. Ph.D. diss. Hebrew University, Jerusalem.

COHEN, B. 1932. Uber Traumdentung in der Judischen Tradition. *Imago* 18: 117.

COHEN, P. 1959. *Community and Stability in a Town of Immigrants*. Jerusalem: Ministry of Social Welfare. (In Hebrew)

CRAPANZANO, V. 1973. *The Hamadsha: A Study in Moroccan Ethnopsychiatry*. Berkeley: The University of California Press.

CUMMINGS, E. and CUMMINGS, J. 1957. *Closed Ranks*. Cambridge: Harvard University Press.

D'ANDRADE, R. G. 1961. Anthropological studies of dreams. In E. K. Hsu, ed., *Psychological Anthropology*. Homewood: The Dorsey Press, Inc.

DESHEN, S. A. and SHOKEID, H. 1974. *The Predicament of Homecoming: Cultural and Social Life of North African Immigrants in Israel*. Ithaca: Cornell University Press.

DOHRENWEND, B. P. and CHIN-SHONG, E. T. 1967. Social status and attitudes toward psychological disorder: The problem of tolerance of deviance. *American Sociological Review* 32: 3.

EISENSTADT, S. N. 1967. *Israeli Society*. London: Weidenfeld and Nicholson.

EPSTEIN, G. 1977. Culture, personality and behavior: A field study in Jerusalem. *Mental Health and Society* 4: 36.

GERSHON, E. S. and LIEBOWITZ, J. H. 1975. Sociocultural and demographic correlates of affective disorders in Jerusalem. *Journal of Psychiatric Research* 13: 37.

HES, J. P. 1963. Treatment of mental ailments among the Jews in Yemen. *The Hebrew Medical Journal*, American Edition, 2.

———. 1964a. The changing role of the Yemenite Mori. In A. Kiev, ed., *Magic, Faith and Healing*. New York: The Free Press.

———. 1964b. From native healer to modern psychiatrist. *The Israel Annals of Psychiatry and Related Disciplines* 2: 192.

——— and WOLLSTEIN, S. 1964. The attitude of the ancient Jewish sources to mental patients. *The Israel Annals of Psychiatry and Related Disciplines* 2: 103.

———. 1966. From native healer to modern psychiatrist. *Social Psychiatry* 1: 117.

———. 1966–67. From native healer to modern psychiatrist. Afro-Asian immigrants to Israel and their attitudes toward psychiatric facilities. Part II: Attitudes of relatives toward the hospital. *The International Journal of Social Psychiatry* 13: 1.

———. 1968. Hypochondriacal complaints in Jewish psychiatric patients. *The Israel Annals of Psychiatry and Related Disciplines* 6: 134.

——— and NASSI, G. 1977. Koro in a Yemenite and a Georgian Jewish Immigrant. *Confinia Psychiatrica* 20: 180.

HOEK, A., MOSES, R., and TERESPOLSKY, L. 1965. Emotional disorders in an Israeli immigrant community. *The Israel Annals of Psychiatry and Related Disciplines* 3: 213.

KAFFMAN, M. 1967. Survey of opinions and attitudes of kibbutz members toward mental illness. Preliminary report. *The Israel Annals of Psychiatry and Related Disciplines* 5: 17.

LANDY, D. 1974. Role adaptation: Traditional curers under the impact of Western medicine. *American Ethnologist* 1: 103.

LEIGHTON, D. C., HARDING, J. S., MACKLIN, D. B., MACMILLAN, A., and LEIGHTON, A. H. 1963. *The Character of Danger*. New York: Basic Books.

LEON, D. 1969. *The Kibbutz—A New Way of Life*. London: Pergamon Press.

LERNER, J. and NOY, P. 1967. Somatic complaints in psychiatric disorders: Social and cultural factors. *International Journal of Social Psychiatry* 14: 145.

LEVAV, I. and MINAMI, H. 1974. Mothers and daughters diagnose mental illness. *The Israel Annals of Psychiatry and Related Disciplines* 12: 319.

——— and ARNON, A. 1976. Emotional disorders in six Israeli villages. *Acta psychiatrica scandinavica* 53: 387.

———, ARNON, A., and PORTNOY, A. 1977. Two shortened versions of the Cornell Medical Index—A new test of their validity. *International Journal of Epidemiology* 6: 135.

LORAND, S. 1957. Dream interpretation in the Tálmud. *The International Journal of Psychoanalysis* 38: 92.

MALZBERG, B. 1973. Mental disease among Jews in New York State. *Acta psychiatric scandinavica* 49: 479.

MANDEL (POPPER), M., CHESLER-GAMPEL, J., and MILLER, L. 1971. Cases That Were Admitted to the Psychiatric Hospitals in Israel, 1966. Jerusalem: State of

Israel, Ministry of Health. (In MAOZ, B., LEVY, S., BRAND, N., and HALEVI, H. S. 1966. An epidemiological survey of mental disorders in a community of newcomers to Israel. *Journal of the College of General Practitioners* 11: 267.)

MENKES, A. Psychiatric disorders in two comparable Kurdistan communities in Israel. Unpublished manuscript.

MILGRAM, N. A. 1978. Psychological stress and adjustment in time of war and peace: The Israeli experience as presented in two conferences. *The Israel Annals of Psychiatry and Related Disciplines* 16: 327.

MILLER, L. 1970. The mental health of immigrants in Israel. In A. Yarus et al., eds., *The Child and Family in Israel.* New York: Gordon and Beach.

———. 1977. Community intervention and the historical background of community mental health in Israel. *The Israel Annals of Psychiatry and Related Disciplines* 15: 300.

MOSES, R. and SHANAN, J. 1961. Psychiatric outpatient clinic, an analysis of a population sample. *Archives of General Psychiatry* 4: 60.

ORNET, A. 1977. *Israel—Three Studies in Urban Anthropology.* Haifa: University of Haifa.

PALGI, P., GOLDWASSER, M., and GOLDMAN, H. 1955. Typical personality disturbances found among immigrant women from Iraq. *Megamoth* 3: 236. (In Hebrew)

———. 1963. Immigrants, psychiatrists and culture. *The Israel Annals of Psychiatry and Related Disciplines* 1: 43.

———. 1966. Cultural components of immigrants' adjustment. In H. P. David, ed., *Migration, Mental Health and Community Services.* Switzerland: American Joint Distribution Committee.

PEREZ, L. 1977. The messianic psychotic patient. *The Israel Annals of Psychiatry and Related Disciplines* 15: 364.

POLLIACK, M. R. 1971. The relationship between Cornell Medical Index scores and attendance rates. *Journal of the College of General Practitioners* 21: 453.

ROMANNUCCI-ROSS, L. 1969. The hierarchy of resort in curative practices: The Admiralty Islands, Melanesia. *Journal of Health and Social Behavior* 10: 201.

ROSEN, G. 1969. *Madness in Society.* Chicago: Chicago University Press.

ROSENFELD, H. 1956. *Taiy'ba: An Analysis of its Patterns of Authority and an Investigation of Basic Health Conditions and Attitudes.* Jerusalem. Ministry of Health.

SCHLOSBERG, A. 1977. Personal communications.

SCHOLEM, G. 1976. *Basic Lectures in Cabala and its Symbolism.* Jerusalem: Mosad Bialik. (In Hebrew)

SCHRIRE, T. 1966. *Hebrew Amulets: The Decipherment and Interpretation.* London: Routledge and Kegan Paul.

SHOKEID, M. 1971. *The Dual Heritage: Immigrants from the Atlas Mountains in an Israeli Village.* Manchester: Manchester University Press.

SHUVAL, J. T. 1970. *Social Functions of Medical Practice.* San Francisco: Jossey-Bass Publishers.

SKEA, A., DRAGUNS, J. G., and PHILLIPS, L. 1969. Ethnic characteristics of psychiatric symptomatology within and across regional groupings: A study of an Israeli child guidance clinic population. *The Israel Annals of Psychiatry and Related Disciplines* 7: 31.

STILLMAN, Y. 1970. The Evil Eye in Morocco. In D. Noy and I. Ben-Ami, eds.,

Folklore Research Center Studies, Volume I. Jerusalem: The Magness Press, The Hebrew University.

TRACHTENBERG, J. 1974 (1939). *Jewish Magic and Superstition: A Study in Folk-Religion.* New York: Atheneum.

WAMOSCHER, Z. 1972. The relationship of emotional disorders to the attendance rate in family medicine. *Harefuah* 32: 1. (In Hebrew)

WESTERMARCK, E. 1926. *Ritual and Belief in Morocco.* London: McMillan & Co.

WILLNER, D. and KOHLS, M. 1962. Jews in the High Atlas Mountains of Morocco: A partial reconstruction. *Jewish Journal of Sociology* 4: 207.

YAP, P. M. 1965. Koro—a culture-bound depersonalization syndrome. *British Journal of Psychiatry* 111: 43–50.

ZOHAR, M., FLORO, S., and MODAN, B. 1974. The image of mental illness and the mentally ill in the Israeli society. *Harefuah* 86: 8. (In Hebrew)

23

Formation of Professional Images among Israeli Student Nurses

Orit Ichilov and *Mirit Dotan*

Preparation for a professional role has been regarded as a complex process consisting of the acquisition of knowledge and skills (role socialization), on one hand, and the development of values, attitudes, beliefs and behaviors (status socialization), on the other (Merton *et al.*, 1957; Becker *et al.*, 1961).

This study has focused on the value dimension of the professional socialization process of Israeli student nurses. More specifically, the study has examined changes in the characteristics that students attribute to nursing at different stages of their training, and the extent to which such characteristics become part of their professional self-concept. The role teachers and nurses play in the formation of students' professional images has also been examined.

Theoretical discussion

Socialization in the nursing profession

The literature concerning professional socialization in general tends to emphasize several outcomes of the socialization process. First, students tend to dispose of incompatible or inadequate notions, and adopt legitimized professional values and perspectives. Secondly, students resolve inner conflicts and uncertainties concerning the particular profession, and achieve greater congruence between their perception of the profession and their professional self-concept (Sarbin, 1954). These outcomes are usually related to the influence of both faculty and peers during the socialization process (Merton *et al.*, 1957; Becker *et al.*, 1961). At each stage values and skills are acquired as the student is exposed to new experiences. Throughout the process, changes in the perception of nursing and in the students' self-image occur.

One would expect that first-year students would show great similarity concerning motivations, expectations and perceptions of nursing. They probably would be characterized by altruistic and philanthropic orientations expressed in a desire to help others, to serve humanity, etc. Such professional notions reflect the lay image of nursing which is idealistic, expressive and humanitarian (McPortland *et al.*, 1957; Hughes *et al.*, 1958; Meyer, 1960; Levitt *et al.*, 1962; Adler, 1969).

During their clinical training, which in Israel starts after six months of schooling, students get acquainted with the hierarchical structure of the hospital staff. They come to realize that nurses are distinguished from nursing aides and practical nurses by their possession of advanced professional skills (Becker and Carper, 1958). Clinical experience in the hospital reinforces a technical orientation which among first-year students is expressed by a shift in focus from the patient to the mastery of technical skills (Gail and Collins, 1971).

It is generally agreed that first-year students are motivated by external rewards more than by internalized values and norms (Kelman, 1961). They are characterized by compliance in an attempt to win professional recognition and approval. This task orientation and compliance can be viewed as the first phase of professional identification (Becker and Carper, 1958).

During the second stage, from the end of the first year on, trained nurses come to play an increasingly more important role in the student's professional socialization. The students learn to perform as members of the medical and nursing staff at the hospital, and adopt nurses as models for identification and imitation. According to Kelman (1961), this identification becomes an important step in the formation of a professional self-concept.

The encounter with the reality of nursing sometimes results in crises which lead to the discarding of romantic and idealistic notions about the profession. Studies report that second-year students tend to describe nurses in negative terms such as impatient, tyrannical, hasty, preoccupied with paper work, etc. (McPortland *et al.*, 1957; Hughes *et al.*, 1958). Others report an increase in cynicism and a decrease in humanitarism at this stage (Brooks, 1960; Eron, 1967). It is possible that this cynicism helps the students to cope with the emotional stress resulting from their encounter with human suffering, death, unaesthetic situations and hard work.

Among graduating students, advanced professional characteristics of nursing are emphasized. Graduating students describe the nurse's role as one demanding empathy, responsibility, independence, initiative and participation in teamwork with the patient as the focal point.

At this stage the internalization of professional values and norms has already taken place, and the students are motivated by internal, as well as external, rewards. Davis (1966) argues that a stable internalization of values and norms is related to the students' ability to integrate and achieve congruence among the different perceptions, values and concepts related to the profession. The professional images of graduating students are not unidimensional, and reflect a mixture of idealistic, realistic, emotional and technical orientations.

So far, the professional socialization process has been described here as fairly uniform for all students. Olesen and Davis (1964, 1966) challenge the assumption that professional socialization results in a greater similarity among students regarding their outlooks about their chosen profession. One might surmise that the outcomes of the socialization process will vary depending on the interaction among notions, motivation and personality traits of the students, their sociocultural background, their experiences during training, and the structural characteristics of the nursing school.

Teachers and nurses as agents of socialization

The training of nurses takes place at the nursing school and at the hospital simultaneously. These two frameworks represent two distinct subcultures of the nursing profession. For the students, these two subcultures are represented by the academic staff of the school, on one hand, and by the nurses in charge of their clinical experiences in the hospital, on the other.

Nursing students start clinical practice at an early stage in their training compared with students of law, medicine or teaching, for instance (Mauksch, 1963). They enter the hospital prior to the acquisition of a solid theoretical and practical foundation, and without an understanding of the professional norms of behavior expected of them. This situation of uncertainty increases the students' dependency on the nurses, who serve as a source of information and as a model for imitation and identification (Simpson, 1967; Olesen and Whittaker, 1968; Parry-Jones, 1971).

Studies show that differences often exist between teachers in nursing schools and practicing nurses concerning educational goals and professional outlooks. Smith (1965) reports that when evaluating students, nurses tend to emphasize criteria related to their relations with other staff members (obedience and collaboration, for example), while teachers emphasize cognitive and affective orientations concerning patient care (sensitivity, leadership, emotional support and decision making, for example). In Israel it was found that nurses treat students as helping hands, while teachers view them as trainees (Ron and Kav-Venaki, 1971).

Differences concerning the importance of teachers and nurses as role models were found among students at different stages of their professional training. Martin and Katz (1961) report that first-year students view teachers as their main role-model, while for second- and third-year students nurses become more staff-oriented. However, among graduating students teachers again become the main role-model. In Israel it was found that although second- and third-year students identified with nurses, their professional concepts were shaped by, and were congruent with, those of the nursing school's educational staff (Shuval, 1974).

It should also be noted that studies show that the greater the consensus among socialization agents concerning their educational goals and professional outlooks, and the greater the clarity of messages conveyed to the students, the easier it is for the students to form a consonant and stable professional self-concept (Wheeler, 1966; Rosen and Bates, 1967; Sherlock and Morris, 1967).

Hypotheses

Changes in students' images over time

(1) Graduating students will score higher than first-year students on 'traditional', 'advanced' and 'bureaucratic' factors concerning the perception of nursing, and on 'lay', 'traditional' and 'occupational' factors concerning professional self-image. On all other factors, for both dimensions, graduating students will score lower than first-year students.

(2) Among graduating students, greater congruence will be found than among first-year students between perception of the nursing profession and professional self-concept.

(3) Group consensus concerning the relevance of characteristics for the profession and self will be greater among graduating students than among first-year students.

Relationships between student and faculty images

(1) Significant differences will be found between first-year students on one hand and teachers and nurses on the other concerning both perception of the profession and self-image. These differences will decrease steadily over the years.

(2) Graduating students will be similar to practicing nurses with respect to a 'traditional' factor and similar to their teachers with respect to an 'advanced' factor.

(3) The greater the group consensus is found to be among teachers and nurses concerning professional outlooks, the greater will be the group consensus among students.

The study

The research sample

The study sample consisted of 239 first-, second- and third-year students, and of 31 teachers and 41 nurses representing the educational staff in two nursing schools in Israel.

The schools selected were similar with respect to several structural characteristics. Both schools were considered large, were located in highly populated areas, and had similar curricula with respect to theoretical and practical studies. Also, both schools had undergone a process of academization two years before, meaning that they both employed university-trained staff, had relatively greater autonomy concerning curricula, and were able to plan clinical experiences according to educational goals rather than according to the needs of the hospital in which they trained.

The student sample was quite homogeneous with respect to major background variables. Most of the students were Israeli-born, half of them were of an European or American origin, and most of them had come from middle-class urban families. The distribution of these variables was similar for first-, second- and third-year students. This similarity was important for our study since it was based on a cross-sectional rather than a longitudinal approach. Hence we were able to assume that differences among students at different stages of their schooling were related to the socialization process more than to background variables.

Concerning the educational staff, most of the teachers and nurses were Israeli-born. Most of them had completed their training in the same school or hospital in which they were working at the time of the study. Almost half of them had participated in additional professional courses since their graduation from nursing school.

Differences between teachers and nurses existed, however, with respect to age, number of years of schooling and number of years in the profession. The nurses tended to be older than the teachers; most of them (over ¾) had been working in the profession for more than ten years, while more than half of the teachers had been working in their profession for less than ten years. Two-thirds of the teachers had university training and the rest had completed secondary education. In comparison, two-thirds of the nurses lacked a high school matriculation certificate, and only a few had completed secondary and/or higher education.

The research instrument

The research instrument consisted of 18 descriptive statements representing different aspects and images of the nursing profession (see Table 1). Each statement was rated on a scale ranging from 1 (unimportant) to 8 (very important). This instrument was based on Davis-Olesen Characteristics of Nursing Questionnaire (Oleson and Davis, 1964, 1966), also used by Siegel (1968). Additional items which were regarded as relevant to the nursing context in Israel were included, while some items were deleted.

Validation of the research instrument was carried out in several steps. First, 16 nurses who teach in the Nursing Department at Tel-Aviv University were selected as judges. They were asked to evaluate the accuracy of the Hebrew translation of the statements, to suggest a better translation if necessary, and to propose additional items relevant to the Israeli nursing context. The judges were also requested to classify each item into one of the following categories of images: advanced, traditional, bureaucratic and lay. The judges reached full agreement concerning the classification of items into advanced and bureaucratic categories, and a great consensus was found among them concerning lay and traditional images. The judges' classification was congruent with that of Olesen and Davis and Siegel.

Secondly, a factor analysis (using principle factor method and oblique rotation) was performed on the 18 items from the data collected on the research sample. The analysis was carried out twice, once concerning the perception of the profession, and once concerning self-image. Items were assigned to a particular factor on the basis of a factorial loading of 0.25 or greater. Items belonging to more than one factor by this criterion were assigned to a particular factor according to their content.

Factor analysis yielded five factors similarly structured for self-perception and perception of the profession, as can be seen from Table 1. In addition to the four images commonly mentioned in the literature, a fifth image which has been termed 'occupational' was found.

The five factors were as follows:

(1) Lay or altruistic image, consisting of four items representing the emotional aspects of nursing prevailing in the public.

(2) Advanced image, consisting of four items representing intellectual and creative aspects of nursing.

(3) Occupational image, consisting of two items representing socioeconomic aspects of the profession.

(4) Traditional image, consisting of five items representing aspects concerning the actual performance of nursing.

(5) Bureaucratic image, consisting of three items representing organizational and managerial aspects of nursing.

Cronbach's alpha coefficient of reliability (Cronbach, 1951) was calculated for each factor. Table 1 shows that the alpha values are higher than or approach 0.60, the minimum value set by Cronbach for scale homogeneity. The subject's score and group scores were calculated for each factor.

On the basis of the validation process the instrument was concluded to be suitable for use in the Israeli nursing context, and for differentiating between different professional images.

Data collection

The research instrument was administered twice. The first time the respondents were asked to rate each item with reference to how important they considered it for the profession. The second time they were asked to specify how important it was for them personally. In order to minimize the influence the first measurement might have on the second, a week's interval was made between the two administrations.

Findings

Changes in students' professional images throughout the years

Changes of students' professional images over the years was examined, focusing on three central aspects. First, the emphasis given to each factor as expressed by its mean score was examined (the higher the score, the more emphasized the factor). A respondent's mean score was computed as follows:

$$\frac{\text{sum of scores of a respondent for items comprising the factor} \times 10}{\text{maximum score that can be obtained}}$$

Secondly, congruence between the perception of the profession and professional self-image was examined. Congruence was defined as a situation in which the difference between the mean scores of the two dimensions were of no statistical significance. Thirdly, group consensus as measured by the standard deviations of the mean scores was examined. An increase in the standard deviation over the years marked a decrease in group consensus, and vice versa.

Table 1. Images of the nursing profession—factor analysis summary

Statistical tests	Lay			Advanced			Occupational			Traditional			Bureaucratic		
	Items	Perception of profession	Self-image	Items	Perception of profession	Self-image	Items	Perception of profession	Self-image	Items	Perception of profession	Self-image	Items	Perception of profession	Self-image
Factor loading	Dedicated service to humanity	0.46	0.48	Originality and creativity	0.48	0.48	Occupation highly respected in the community	0.43	0.52	High technical skill	0.32	0.30	Clearly defined work tasks	0.21	0.24
	Sense of inspiration and calling	0.44	0.55	Exercise of imagination and insight	0.41	0.56	Angel in white	0.43	—	Meticulousness	0.25	0.32	Close supervision and direction	0.29	0.36
	Human drama and excitement	0.29	0.30	Innovative approach to solution of problems	0.39	0.69	Job security	—	0.36	Job security	0.35	—	Clear cut lines of authority	0.26	—
	Emotional control	0.32	—	Solid intellectual content	0.49	0.39				Order and routine	0.25	—	Order and routine	—	0.50
	Angel in white	—	0.35							Emotional control	—	0.50			
										Hard word	—	0.50			
Eigen value		3.11	0.94		1.33	1.72		0.65	3.49		0.79	0.46		0.36	0.56
Percentage of explained variance		49.88	13.1		21.2	24.0		10.5	48.7		12.7	6.4		5.7	7.9
α*		0.60	0.68		0.69	0.74		—	—		0.42	0.56		0.37	0.52

*Alpha scores cannot be computed for the occupational image which consists of two items only.

Table 2 presents the mean scores of first-, second- and third-year students on each factor, for both the perception of the profession and self-image. In addition, the statistical significance of the differences between scores are shown.

As hypothesized, differences were found in the emphasis students place upon the different images throughout the years. However, these differences were not always linear or significant.

Concerning the perception of the profession, it was hypothesized that graduating students would score higher than first-year students on the traditional, advanced and bureaucratic images, and would score lower on the rest. This hypothesis won partial support. No significant differences were found between graduating and first-year students, with the exception of the advanced image on which graduating students scored significantly higher. Concerning professional self-image, graduating students scored lower than beginners on the traditional image, as hypothesized. However, contrary to our hypothesis, the score for the lay image also decreased significantly. Concerning all other images, no significant differences were found between first-year and graduating students.

We expected that greater congruence would be achieved between self-image and perception of the profession throughout the years. The data shows that congruence concerning most of the professional images was achieved only among graduating students. It was also expected that group consensus would increase over the years. This was the case for the perception of the profession where the standard deviations of the mean scores decreased over the years. However, concerning self-image, group consensus decreased over the years.

Findings concerning the images of the educational staff

The professional outlooks of teachers and nurses were examined with respect to the emphasis they place upon the various images, group consensus and congruence between perception of the profession and self-images. A comparison was made between the images of the educational staff and those of the students.

Table 3 presents teachers' and nurses' mean scores and standard deviations for the various images. Also, the statistical significance of the differences between students and each of the two socialization agents is indicated.

Table 3 shows that teachers tended to stress the advanced image concerning self-image, and lay and traditional images in the perception of the profession. Among teachers, congruence between the two image dimensions was found concerning advanced, traditional and bureaucratic images, while lay and occupational images showed incongruence. Greater consensus was found among teachers concerning perception of the profession than concerning professional self-image. Group consensus was especially high for advanced and traditional images.

Nurses stressed the traditional image for both dimensions. Concerning the perception of the profession, advanced and bureaucratic images were also stressed. As among teachers, congruence was found between self-image and perception of the profession for all images except lay and occupational images. Also, nurses, like teachers, exhibited greater group consensus concerning perception of the profession than concerning professional self-image. The greatest group consensus was found concerning both dimensions of the bureaucratic image, and in the dimension of perception of the profession with respect to the traditional image.

Generally speaking, the professional outlooks of teachers and nurses were shown to be very much alike. Teachers, however, scored significantly higher than nurses on the advanced

Table 2. Means and standard deviations of students' scores

		Image and dimensions									
		Lay		Traditional		Bureaucratic		Occupational		Advanced	
		Perception of profession	Self-image	Perception of profession	Self-image	Perception of profession	Self-image	Perception of profession	Self-image	Perception of profession	Self-image
First-year	Mean	67.5	59.4	63.4	70.0	54.3	55.4	50.4	60.8	55.0	65.1
	S.D.	12.0	13.4	11.0	8.8	15.6	11.7	18.3	17.2	15.3	12.4
	Significance of differences between image dimensions	$P<0.001$		$P<0.001$		N.S.		$P<0.001$		$P<0.001$	
Second-year	Mean	65.0	53.6	66.7	63.6	48.2	53.7	40.9	58.4	57.4	62.7
	S.D.	10.8	17.8	9.8	19.6	13.3	17.8	18.2	20.6	14.0	20.1
	Significance of differences between image dimensions	$P<0.001$		N.S.		$P<0.022$		$P<0.001$		$P<0.030$	
Third-year	Mean	65.2	51.1	65.1	59.9	56.0	52.7	46.9	54.7	61.7	59.2
	S.D.	7.7	19.7	7.7	21.3	14.0	19.9	15.6	21.2	14.8	21.3
	Significance of differences between image dimensions	$P< 0.001$		N.S.		N.S.		$P<0.016$		N.S.	
Significance of differences between:	First- and second-year students	N.S.	$P<0.023$	$P<0.046$	$P<0.015$	$P<0.009$	N.S.	$P<0.001$	N.S.	N.S.	N.S.
	Second- and third-year students	N.S.	N.S.	N.S.	N.S.	$P<0.002$	N.S.	N.S.	N.S.	N.S.	N.S.
	First- and third-year students	N.S.	$P<0.006$	N.S.	$P<0.001$	N.S.	N.S.	N.S.	N.S.	$P<0.007$	N.S.

Table 3. Faculty scores and a comparison of students' and faculty scores

		Image and dimensions									
		Lay		Traditional		Bureaucratic		Occupational		Advanced	
		Perception of profession	Self-image	Perception of profession	Self-image	Perception of profession	Self-image	Perception of profession	Self-image	Perception of profession	Self-image
Teachers	Mean	60.0	49.2	61.1	60.8	50.1	45.9	41.0	54.2	60.6	65.6
	S.D.	14.2	17.7	10.0	17.8	14.9	16.0	17.4	20.4	11.5	17.4
	Significance of differences between image dimensions	$P<0.001$		N.S.		N.S.		$P<0.004$		N.S.	
Nurses	Mean	60.7	49.1	67.4	64.4	52.8	56.6	41.7	55.0	51.7	56.4
	S.D.	13.4	17.9	8.2	14.2	12.9	12.9	14.2	18.4	16.0	17.4
	Significance of differences between image dimensions	$P<0.001$		N.S.		N.S.		$P<0.001$		N.S.	
Significance of differences between:	Teachers and nurses	N.S.		$P<0.004$	N.S.	N.S.	$P<0.002$	N.S.		$P<0.007$	$P<0.015$
First-year student and:	Teachers	$P<0.002$	$P<0.003$	N.S.	$P<0.005$	N.S.	$P<0.002$	$P<0.009$	N.S.	$P<0.048$	N.S.
	Nurses	$P<0.003$	$P<0.001$	$P<0.019$	$P<0.023$	N.S.	N.S.	$P<0.006$	N.S.	N.S.	$P<0.005$
Second-year students and:	Teachers	$P<0.051$	N.S.	$P<0.007$	N.S.	N.S.	$P<0.002$	N.S.		N.S.	
	Nurses	N.S.		N.S.		N.S.		N.S.		$P<0.053$	N.S.
Third-year students and:	Teachers	N.S.		$P<0.035$	N.S.	N.S.		N.S.		N.S.	
	Nurses	N.S.		N.S.		N.S.		N.S.		$P<0.002$	N.S.

image, while the nurses scored significantly higher than teachers on the traditional and bureaucratic images.

A comparison between the images of students and faculty reveals that first-year students differ from both teachers and nurses in that they scored significantly higher concerning both dimensions of lay and occupational image, and on the self-image dimension of the traditional image. First-year students scored lower than nurses on the perception of profession dimension of the traditional image, and scored higher than nurses and lower than teachers on the self-image dimension of the advanced image.

The differences between the educational staff and second- and third-year students were significant, for the most part. However, second-year students scored higher than teachers on the perception of profession dimension of the traditional image, and on the self-image dimension of the bureaucratic image. Third-year students scored higher than teachers on the traditional image, and scored higher than nurses on the perception of profession dimension of the advanced image.

Concerning congruence, we have seen that first-year students achieved congruence concerning the bureaucratic image only, and for second-year students only the traditional image showed congruence. Among third-year students the same level of congruence as that of teachers and nurses was found, namely, all images were congruent with the exception of lay and occupational images.

Concerning group consensus, greater consensus with respect to the self-image dimension of the various images was found among first-year students than for the perception of the professional dimension. For second- and third-year students the situation is reversed, and becomes similar to that found among teachers and nurses.

The general trend that can be seen from the data is that in the three year nursing program, student nurses' images come to resemble those of the educational staff with respect to emphasis, congruence and group consensus. The findings also lend support to our hypothesis that when the images of teachers and nurses are consistent with each other, the students become closer to both socialization agents in their professional outlooks. This was the case, for example, concerning lay and occupational images. However, when differences occur, the students got closer to the agent which emphasized most strongly that particular image. Thus, for example, students showed greater resemblance to teachers concerning the advanced image, and greater resemblance to nurses concerning traditional and bureaucratic images.

Discussion and conclusions

This study examined the formation of professional outlooks among student nurses, focusing on their perception of the profession and on their professional self-image. The study also examined the role played by teachers and nurses in the formation of professional images among students. The formation process was examined via reference to the degree of emphasis of each image, group consensus, and congruence between the perception of the profession and professional self-image.

For the lay image, which represents affective aspects of nursing, the emphasis remained over the years relatively high and unchanged for the perception of profession dimension. However, concerning self-image, the lay image decreased in importance between the first and second years, and thereafter remained stable until graduation. In other words, the importance of altruistic aspects for students' self-perception diminishes between the time a student enters nursing school and graduation.

The traditional image, representing performance aspects of nursing, stabilizes for both dimensions in the second year. However, while traditional characteristics gain in importance as descriptive of nursing, they become less important for students' self-image.

For the bureaucratic image expressing organizational and managerial aspects of nursing, changes occur throughout the years for the dimension of perception of the profession. Emphasis decreases between the first and second years, and increases again in the third year. However, for the self-image dimension, emphasis does not significantly change over the years.

The occupational image, representing economic and stratificational aspects of nursing, remains unchanged throughout the years.

The advanced image, which stresses intellectual and creative aspects, gains in importance as characterizing the nursing profession, and stabilizes in the third year. However, concerning self-image, emphasis remains relatively great and unchanged over the years.

In their emphasis upon the various images, graduating students come to resemble both teachers and nurses. However, like the nurses and unlike the teachers, graduating students emphasize traditional and bureaucratic images. At the same time they emphasize the advanced image like teachers and unlike nurses.

These findings correspond to those of May and Hardi (1970) and O'Neill (1973), who have reported that first-year students tend to emphasize religious values, corresponding to the lay image in our study, and that this emphasis remains high throughout the years. The emphasis upon economic and political values, corresponding to our occupational and bureaucratic images, remains low throughout the years, while theoretical values, corresponding to our advanced image, gain in importance.

It was found that congruence between what students consider important for the profession and what they consider important for them personally is achieved in the last year of schooling, concerning most images. The lay and occupational images, which remain incongruent among graduating students, were found to be incongruent among teachers and nurses as well. This finding could be explained by the fact that congruence, as an important aspect of the formation of professional outlooks and self-identity and as an indicator of the internalization of values, can be achieved only during the advanced stages of the professional socialization process. At this time students become capable of organizing the various perceptions and concepts related to their profession, and accept them as part of their self-definition (Davis, 1966).

Concerning group consensus it was found that differences concerning perception of the profession decrease over the years and that students come to view their profession in a more uniform way. However, group consensus concerning professional self-image was found to decrease over the years. It is possible that consensus among first-year students concerning self-image reflects similar expectations and motivations concerning their chosen profession. Differences concerning the perception of the profession among first-year students may be attributed to different sources of information and different experiences prior to entering the school. During their studies and clinical experience the students develop a more uniform perception of the profession, but apparently develop different expectations concerning their professional careers and their self-realization in the profession. These changes also reflect a growing resemblance between the students and the educational staff.

The findings concerning group consensus lend support to the contention of Olesen and Davis (1964, 1966) that the outcomes of the professional socialization process are not as uniform as suggested by the literature. However, contrary to their findings which show that students achieve greater consensus concerning self-image than concerning perception of the profession, we have found greater group consensus concerning the perception of the profession.

The present study shows that teachers and nurses play an important role in the formation of professional outlooks and concepts among students. It also shows that the greater the consensus among teachers and nurses concerning professional images, the greater their joint influence. In cases of inconsistency between teachers and nurses, students are influenced more strongly by the socialization agent that emphasizes more strongly that particular image.

In spite of the above-mentioned differences between teachers and nurses, which might reflect differences in their education and professional status (Smith, 1965), a wide common base exists among them concerning professional outlooks. This great similarity is surprising if one considers the fact that the teachers are more educated than nurses and teach in schools which have recently gained professional autonomy.

References

Adler, S. P. (1969). Swedish student nurses: a descriptive study. *Nursing Res.* **18,** 363-365.

Becker, H. S. *et al.* (1961). *Boys in White.* University of Chicago Press, Chicago.

Becker, H. S. and Carper, J. W. (1958). Development of identification with a profession. *Am. J. Sociol.* **61,** 289-298.

Bergman, R. and Sterolowitz, N. (1969). Social and demographic attributes of students in schools for certified nurses in Israel. Tel Aviv University, Kupat Cholim, Tel Aviv.

Bergman, R. (1970). Nursing teaching staff in Israel: selected demographic data about nursing teachers in school for certified nurses 1966, 1968. Tel Aviv University, Kupat Cholim, Tel Aviv.

Bills, R. E., Vance, E. L. and McLean, O. S. (1951). An index of adjustment and values. *J. consult. Psychol.* **15,** 257-261.

Brim, O. and Wheeler, S. (1966). *Socialization After Childhood: Two Essays.* John Wiley, New York.

Brooks, B. R. (1960). Students attitudes: how they change. *Nurs. Wld.* **13,** 24-27.

Cronbach, L. Y. (1951). Coefficient alpha and the internal structure of tests. *Psychometrica* **16,** 297-333.

Davis, F. (1966). Professional socialization as subjective experience: the case of student nurses. University of California, San Francisco, Mimeograph.

Davis, F., Olesen, V. L. and Whittaker, E. W. (1966). Problems and issues in collegiate nursing education. In *The Nursing Profession.* F. Davis (Ed.). pp. 138-175. John Wiley, New York.

Davis, F. and Olesen, V. (1965). Career outlook of professionally educated women. *Psychiatry* **28,** 334-335.

Eron, L. D. (1967). The effects of nursing education on attitudes. In *Research Process in Nursing.* D. J. Fox and R. L. Kelly (Eds.). pp. 224-234. Appleton-Century-Crofts, New York.

Fox, D. J., Diamand, L. K. *et al.* (1967). Satisfying stressful situations in basic programs in nursing education. In *Research Process in Nursing.* D. J. Fox and R. L. Kelly (Eds.). pp. 248-260. Appleton-Century-Crofts, New York.

Hughes, E. C. *et al.* (1958). *Twenty Thousand Nurses Tell Their Story.* J. B. Lippincott, Philadelphia.

Kelman, H. C. (1961). Process of opinion change. *Public Opinion Quarterly* **25,** 57-78.

Kramer, M. and Benner, P. (1972). Role conception and integrative role behavior of nurses in special care and regular hospital nursing units. *Nurs. Res.* **21,** 20-29.

Levitt, E. *et al.* (1962). The student nurse, the college woman and the graduate nurse: a comparative study. *Nurs. Res.* **11,** 80-82.

Mauksch, H. O. (1963). Becoming a nurse: a selective view. *Ann. Am. Acad. polit. soc. Sci.* **346,** 88-98.

Martin, H. W. and Katz, F. E. (1961). The professional school as molder of motivation. *J. Hlth Human Behav.* **2,** 106-112.

May, T. and Hardi, R. L. (1970). Change and stability of values in collegiate nursing students. *Nurs. Res.* **19,** 359-362.

McPortland, T. S. *et al.* (1968). Formal education and the process of professionalism. In *The Student Nurse.* J. Psaths (Ed.). pp. 82-83. Springer, New York.

Merton, R. K. *et al.* (1957). *The Student Physician.* Harvard University Press, Cambridge, MA.

Meyer, G. R. (1960). *Tenderness and Technique.* Institute of Industrial Relations, University of California, Los Angeles.

Meyer, G. R. (1959). Conflict and harmony in nursing values. *Nurs. Outlook* **7,** 398-399.

Miller, M. H. (1974). A follow-up of first year nursing student dropouts. *Nurs. Forum* **13,** 32-47.

Olesen, V. L. and Davis, F. (1964). Baccalaureate students' images of nursing. *Nurs. Res.* **13,** 8-15.

Olesen, V. L. and Davis, F. (1966). Baccalaureate students' images of nursing: a follow-up report. *Nurs. Res.* **15,** 151-158.

Olesen, V. L. and Whittaker, E. (1968). *The Silent Dialogue.* Jossey-Bass, San Francisco.

O'Neill, M. F. (1973). A study of baccalaureate nursing student values. *Nurs. Res.* **25,** 437-443.

Parry-Jones, W. L. (1971). Roles in nursing 1: the student. *Nurs. Times* **67,** 30-31.

Ron, R. and Kav-Venaki, S. (1971). The significance assigned to concepts related to nursing by two groups of certified nurses (unpublished manuscript, in Hebrew).
Rosen, B. C. and Bates, A. P. (1967). The structure of socialization in graduate school. *Social Inquiry* **37**, 71-84.
Rosenberg, M. (1957). *Occupations and Values.* Free Press, Glencoe.
Sarbin, T. R. (1958). Role theory. In *Handbook of Social Psychology.* G. Lindzey (Ed.). pp. 448-567. Addison-Wesley, Cambridge, MA.
Sherlock, B. J. and Morris, R. T. (1967). The evolution of the professional. *Social Inquiry* **37**, 27-45.
Shuval, J. (1962). Social factors conditioning the recruitment of nurses in Israel. *J. Hlth Human Behav.* **3**, 109-120.
Shuval, J. (1963). Perceived role components of nursing in Israel. *ASR* **20**, 37-46.
Shuval, J. (1974). A comparative study of nursing and medical students' attitudes and changes taking place within them. School of Medicine, Jerusalem (in Hebrew).
Siegel, H. (1968). Professional socialization in two baccalaureate programs. *Nurs. Res.* **17**, 403-407.
Simpson, I. H. (1967). Patterns of socialization into professions: the case of student nurses. *Social Inquiry* **37**, 47-54.
Smith, K. M. (1965). Discrepancies in the role-specific values of head nurses and nursing educators. *Nurs. Res.* **14**, 196-202.
Super, D. E. (1953). A theory of vocational development. *The American Psychologist* **8**, 185-190.

(*Received* 27 *February* 1980; *accepted for publication* 5 *March* 1980)

24

Trait-Anxiety Differences among Medical Students

Judith Bernstein and *Sara Carmel*

The purpose of this study was to investigate whether trait-anxiety remains stable over time, as measured by age and year of study in a population of medical students over six years of medical studies, and whether anxiety scores vary by sex and marital status. The analyses presented here are derived from data collected in the first wave of a longitudinal panel study.

Trait-anxiety theory, as developed by Spielberger (15, 16), posits that trait-anxiety is a relatively stable personality characteristic which differentiates among individual tendencies to appraise specific situations as threatening. Most empirical studies of the stability of trait-anxiety over time, using the State-Trait Anxiety Inventory (18) provide support for this theory. These studies, however, generally compare trait-anxiety scores before and after respondents' exposure to a short stressful event such as an operation (3, 17) or a course examination (8, 19). Newmark (12) measured trait anxiety among students in an introductory psychology course four times over a ten-month period and found it relatively stable as well.

While investigations on the stability of trait-anxiety over a long period of time have not been reported in the literature, two cross-sectional studies of general adult populations have investigated age differences in trait-anxiety. Ray (14), in Sydney, Australia, did not find a significant correlation between age and trait-anxiety. The long-term stability of trait-anxiety is questioned, however, by the findings of Knight, Waal-Manning, and Spears (10), who measured trait-anxiety as part of a general health survey conducted in England among 1173 adults aged 16 to 89 yr., and found an inverse relationship between age and trait-anxiety. Although this was a cross-sectional study, data suggest that trait-anxiety declines with age.

Spielberger (16) suggests that individuals who frequently face stressful situations may develop coping responses or defense mechanisms which serve to reduce their reactions (state-anxiety) to such situations. The question arises as to whether a decrease in objective stressors or the development of coping mechanisms are manifested over time not only in a decline in state-anxiety but also in trait-anxiety.

Many studies on the stressful nature of medical school have been reported in recent years (4, 5, 11). While each year of study apparently has its own unique stressors, there seems to be consensus that stress declines over the years of medical school (7, 9, 13). In an unpublished study of the perception of stress of the same medical students who participated in this study,[2] which replicated work of Coburn and Jovaisas (5) and used their questionnaire, an inverse but statistically nonsignificant relationship was found between perception of stress and year of study. Discussing the findings that stress declines over the years of medical education, Adsett (1) suggests that medical students, particularly in the first years of study, not only are confronted with the rigorous demands of medical education, but they are also facing the social and psychological challenges of young adulthood.

In light of Adsett's (1) suggestion, it was hypothesized that trait-anxiety would decline with year of study, as medical school stressors decline. It was also hypothesized that trait-anxiety would decline with age, as students develop coping mechanisms to deal with the developmental challenges of young adulthood. Furthermore, it was expected that women would have higher trait-anxiety scores than men. This sex difference has been found in many studies of trait-anxiety (2, 18). Finally, as a result of Coombs and Fawzy's (6) findings of a beneficial effect of marital status on perceived stress in medical school, it was hypothesized that married students would have lower trait-anxiety scores than single students.

Method

This study was undertaken in the Medical School of the Ben-Gurion University of the Negev in Beer Sheva, Israel, where medical studies last six years. While the optimal method to investigate changes in trait-anxiety over time is a panel longitudinal research design, the second best is a cross-sectional study of populations similar on relevant characteristics. The students who participated in this study are from the first-, second-, fourth-, and sixth-year classes. All were selected by identical admissions criteria, and the curriculum of study did not change significantly over the six years. There is no reason to expect, therefore, that upperclassmen started their medical school careers

[2]S. Carmel, & J. Bernstein, Associations between different sources of medical school stress and trait anxiety. (Unpublished manuscript)

with lower trait-anxiety scores than the current first year class. While 20% of the students at this medical school begin their training immediately after graduating from high school and a few have had some university level education before entering medical school, the vast majority start medical studies after two years (for women) or three years (for men) of army service. Most students are in their early twenties when they enter the first year of medical school. The 131 students (94 men and 37 women) who participated in this study have an average age of 23.2 yr., with ages ranging from 18 to 30 yr. The average age of the male and female respondents was similar, and they were equally likely to be married. Married respondents were older than single respondents; most of them (65%) were in the sixth year of study. The over-all response rate was 76%; and respondents were representative of the total population on age, sex and marital status.

Respondents filled out a questionnaire which included the Hebrew translation[3] of the State-Trait Anxiety Inventory (18), questions on perceived medical school stressors, and questions on such demographic characteristics as age, sex, marital status, and year of study.

RESULTS

The mean trait-anxiety score of this sample is 35.8. Table 1 presents mean trait-anxiety scores by sex, marital status, and year of study. Women students have significantly higher trait-anxiety scores than their male peers;

TABLE 1

TRAIT ANXIETY SCORES BY SEX, MARITAL STATUS AND YEAR OF STUDY

Characteristics	*n*	Trait-Anxiety levels		*t*
		M	*SD*	
All Students	131	35.8	7.2	
Sex				
Women	37	39.2	8.0	
				–3.43†
Men	92	34.6	6.4	
Marital status				
Married	26	32.8	6.2	
				–2.41*
Single	102	36.6	7.3	
Year of study				
1	44	36.6	7.5	
2	31	38.1	7.9	
4	27	35.2	6.1	
6	29	32.9	5.7	
Preclinical	75	37.2	7.7	
				2.59*
Clinical	56	34.0	5.9	

$*p < .05$. $\dagger p < .01$.

[3]Y. Teichman, & C. Melanik, Hebrew Version, Spielberger's (1970) State Trait Anxiety Inventory. (Unpublished test manual, Univer. of Tel Aviv, 1977)

and married students have lower levels of trait-anxiety than single students. Trait-anxiety scores are lower over successive years of study. Significant differences are found, in addition, between the trait-anxiety scores of students in the first two preclinical years versus those in the clinical years. A negative linear relationship was found between age and trait-anxiety score (Pearson $r = -.32, p < .001$).

Multivariate analysis was undertaken to determine the relative contribution of each of the independent variables to explain differences in trait anxiety; see Table 2. Together these variables explain 17% of the variance in trait-anxiety. This table indicates that sex is the best predictor of trait-anxiety of the four independent variables. Although there is a strong correlation be-

TABLE 2

STANDARDIZED REGRESSION COEFFICIENTS PREDICTING TRAIT ANXIETY

Independent variables	Beta	F
Age	–.226	3.89*
Year of study	–.044	.16
Sex	.254	9.04*
Marital status	.048	.22
	$R^2 = .17, F = 5.91, p < .001$	

$*p < .05$.

tween age and year of study (Pearson $r = .62$) and both are significantly correlated with trait-anxiety, the multiple regression analysis shows that, when year of study is controlled, age still contributes significantly to the variability in trait-anxiety.

DISCUSSION

As reported previously, our data also indicate that women score higher on trait-anxiety than men. Single students have higher trait-anxiety scores than married students. While it has been reported (6), that married students perceive medical school as less stressful than single students, the relationship between marital status and trait-anxiety has not been discussed in the literature. Perhaps those students who choose to get married are less anxious than those who remain single; perhaps marriage, by providing social support, serves to reduce trait-anxiety. These two alternative or complementary explanations will be tested in a prospective research study. It was also found, as expected, that trait-anxiety declines with year of study and age.

Multivariate analysis shows that the best predictor of trait-anxiety is sex and that age is a better predictor than year of study. It should be recalled that the age range of the studied population is 12 yr. (18 to 30 yr.). It is suggested that during the period of young adulthood, individuals are confronted with crucial challenges which affect the crystallization of their psychological, interpersonal, and professional identity. Resolution of developmental challenges over time may contribute to the decline in trait-anxiety found among the young adults in this study. One important developmental stage for young Israelis is army service. In every year of this medical school, twenty percent of the students have not yet served in the army, so they are at least two or three years younger than their classmates. It is possible that this crucial difference in life experience is expressed in the dominance of age over year of study in the prediction of trait-anxiety in this population.

The explanations suggested for the findings reported here are clearly limited by the cross-sectional research design. To measure whether and to what extent trait-anxiety changes over a long period of time and to provide well-grounded evidence for the effects on trait-anxiety of the factors studied here, a population must be followed up over several years. A longitudinal panel study of this population is in progress to address the theoretical issues raised in this study.

REFERENCES

1. ADSETT, C. S. (1968) Psychological health of medical students in relation to the medical education process. *Journal of Medical Education*, 43, 728-734.
2. BANDER, R. S., & BETZ, N. E. (1981) The relationship of sex and sex role to trait and situationally specific anxiety types. *Journal of Research in Personality*, 15, 312-322.
3. BOEKE, S., DUIVENVOORDEN, H., & BONKE, B. (1984) Agreement for surgical patients on two situations for the Trait Anxiety Inventory. *Psychological Reports*, 54, 278.
4. BOYLE, B. P., & COOMBS, R. H. (1971) Personality profiles related to emotional stress in the initial year of medical training. *Journal of Medical Education*, 46, 882-888.
5. COBURN, D., & JOVAISAS, A. V. (1975) Perceived sources of stress among first year medical students. *Journal of Medical Education*, 50, 589-595.
6. COOMBS, R. H., & FAWZY, F. T. (1983) The effect of marital status on stress in medical school. *American Journal of Psychiatry*, 139, 1490-1493.
7. GAENSBAUER, T. J., & MIZNER, G. L. (1980) Developmental stresses in medical education. *Psychiatry*, 43, 60-70.
8. JOESTING, J. (1975) Test-retest reliability of STAI in an academic setting. *Psychological Reports*, 37, 270.
9. KILPATRICK, D. G., DUBIN, W. R., & MARCOTTE, D. B. (1974) Personality, stress of the medical education process and changes in effective mood state. *Psychological Reports*, 34, 1215-1223.
10. KNIGHT, R. G., WAAL-MANNING, H. J., & SPEARS, G. F. (1983) Some norms and reliability data for the STAI and the Zung Self-rating Depression Scale. *British Journal of Clinical Psychology*, 22, 245-249.
11. MURPHY, J. M., NADELSON, C. C., & NOTMAN, M. T. (1984) Factors influencing first-year medical students' perceptions of stress. *Journal of Human Stress*, 10, 165-173.
12. NEWMARK, C. S. (1972) Stability of state and trait anxiety. *Psychological Reports*, 30, 196-198.

13. NICHOLS, E. J., & SPIELBERGER, C. D. (1967) Effects of medical education on anxiety in students. *Mental Hygiene*, 51, 74-79.

14. RAY, J. J. (1984) Measuring trait anxiety in general population samples. *The Journal of Social Psychology*, 123, 189-193.

15. SPIELBERGER, C. D. (1966) Theory and research on anxiety. In C. D. Spielberger (Ed.), *Anxiety and behavior*. New York: Academic Press. Pp. 3-20.

16. SPIELBERGER, C. D. (1972) Anxiety as an emotional state. In C. D. Spielberger (Ed.), *Anxiety: recent trends in theory and research*. Vol. 1. New York: Academic Press. Pp. 23-49.

17. SPIELBERGER, C. D., AUERBACH, S., WADSWORTH, M., DUNN, M., & TAULBEE, E. (1973) Emotional reactions to surgery. *Journal of Consulting and Clinical Psychology*, 40, 33-38.

18. SPIELBERGER, C. D., GORSUCH, R. I., & LUSHENE, R. I. (1970) *Manual for the State-Trait Anxiety Inventory*. Palo Alto, CA: Consulting Psychologists Press.

19. WADSWORTH, JR., A. P., BARKER, JR., H. R., & BARKER, B. (1976) Factor structure of the State Trait Anxiety Inventory under conditions of variable stress. *Journal of Clinical Psychology*, 32, 576-579.

Accepted September 2, 1986.

25

Sex Differences in Persistence and Alternative Occupational Choice of Unsuccessful Applicants to Medical School

Dafna N. Izraeli and *Netta Notzer*

INTRODUCTION

Accumulated research suggests that there are systematic sex differences in occupationally relevant attitudes and behaviour, (for a review see Fitzgerald and Crites, 1980). At the same time, studies comparing men and women *within* occupations, show them to be very similar in a wide range of role relevant variables. For example, when occupation was held constant, no significant sex differences were found in job satisfaction, motivation to work, job involvement, job outcome preferences, leader behaviour, communication style and perceived abilities (for a review see Donnell and Hall, 1980; also Birsdall, 1980; Kaufman and Feathers, 1980). Although the results are not always consistent, the general thrust of the research supports the theory of person–environment fit (Holland, 1973), according to which self-selection for professions has a 'homogenizing effect'.

Studies of intra-occupational sex differences to date, have focused almost exclusively on either student populations, already engaged in academic studies, or on professionals practising in the field. Unsuccessful applicants to professional schools constitute a relatively large population which has received very little attention (AAMC, 1976). This category is theoretically interesting because it permits the examination of such variables as sex differences in persistence in the face of initial rejection and in alternative occupational choices, generally overlooked in studies of students and practitioners.

The present study compares the behaviour of men and women, unsuccessful applicants to an Israeli medical school, along three dimensions: (1) persistence in reapplications; (2) ultimate career choice; and (3) long-term academic achievements. Stretching the definition somewhat all three dimensions may be treated as aspects of persistence: persistence in getting in; persistence in the health field; persistence in academic investments.

1. Persistence in reapplications

The few studies of unsuccessful medical school applicants reveal that many have the necessary qualifications for entry (Becker *et al.*, 1973; Johnson, 1971) and a high proportion of repeaters of both sexes eventually enter medical school (Gordon, 1979). There are a number of reasons to expect, however, that women would persist less than men in attempting to gain acceptance. These include the smaller proportion of female than male role models in medicine (O'Leary, 1974), the greater support and encouragement men receive for their medical career ambitions (McLure and Piel, 1978), and the constraints of family life created for women when entry is postponed. Furthermore, girls who aspire to non-traditional occupations were found to have lower expectations of achieving their occupational goal than boys with similar aspirations (Marini and Greenberger, 1978). It is reasonable to expect that persistence will be less when expectations for success are lower.

2. Ultimate career choice

Becker *et al.* (1973), the only detailed study of ultimate career choice of unsuccessful medical school applicants, found that of those who did not enter medicine, a greater proportion of women than men remained in the health field. Among those who left the health field, the majority of men selected male dominated occupations (law and business), while the majority of women selected female dominated occupations (teaching). This study examines whether similar patterns occur in the Israeli sample.

3. Long-term academic investments

Studies show that women aspiring to non-traditional careers are more prepared to make long-term investments in training than are women planning traditional careers (Spitze and Waite, 1980). The high scholastic quality of medical school applicants, furthermore, make women, like men, attractive candidates for other faculties with a higher application to acceptance ratio than medicine.

Research questions

1. Do women persist less than men in reapplications to medical school?
2. Do more women than men remain in the health *situs*? Do women not in medicine opt for female dominated occupations? Do more men than women exchange occupational *situs* for occupational status?
3. Are there sex differences in long-term academic investments?

METHOD

Population and social context

The population under study consists of unsuccessful applicants to the Tel-Aviv Sackler School of Medicine in the year 1970 ($n=800$). A representative sample of 300 applicants was randomly drawn. Of these 224 were located at the time of the study (1979). Eleven refused to participate and in 25 cases data were obtained from a spouse or parent of the respondent who was not in the country. The final sample of 213 comprised 179 males and 34 females. With only very few exceptions, first application was submitted following compulsory army service (3 years for males and 2 for females). In 1970 women comprised approximately 23 per cent of all applicants and 18 per cent of all those accepted to the Medical School.

Admissions were based on high school matriculation marks, the Raven Aptitude test and a personal interview. Women in general scored somewhat higher than men on matriculation marks and somewhat lower on the Raven test, although differences were not significant. The university was known to prefer offspring of medical doctors but was not reputed to discriminate against women. The proportion of women accepted annually since 1970 has been consistently between 5 and 10 per cent less than the proportion of female applicants. For example, in 1978 women comprised 44.4 per cent of the applicants and 35.3 per cent of those accepted.

The MD in Israel is a 7-year programme requiring no preliminary undergraduate degree. Until 1971 Israelis had the choice of only two local medical schools. Alternatively they could study abroad. Because of citizen and/or preliminary language requirements in most foreign countries, those who did go abroad, with only few exceptions, studied in Italian schools where admission is non-selective. For Israelis, studying in Italy is expensive, entails acquiring a new language, considerable social isolation and learning in a non-supportive academic structure built largely on self study. For these reasons, as well as because of the inferior job opportunities of Italian graduates, Israelis who begin studies in Italy prefer to complete their MD degree in Israel and persist in reapplying to Israeli schools. Of our sample, 38 per cent of the women and 32 per cent of the men began medical school in Italy.

Procedure

Information was obtained by means of a telephone interview conducted by a small number of specifically trained interviewers using a structured questionnaire.

Dependent variables

(a) Persistence in application: respondents were asked how many times they reapplied to medical school after the first rejection. In some cases the modal year (1970) was not the first application.

(b) Ultimate career choice: respondents were asked about their current occupation, whether and where they were employed and what their job role was.

(c) Academic investments: respondents were asked which academic degree(s) they had obtained or were in the process of obtaining.

RESULTS

There are several indications that the unsuccessful female applicants were 'non-typical'. At the time of the follow-up, 100 per cent were employed compared to 75 per cent for Israeli women with 13+ years of schooling. Only 47 per cent were married compared to 78 per cent of the men in the sample of comparable age. Of the marrieds, only 4 had at least one child; the only 4 who had married prior to beginning their university education.

On the average men are more persistent than women. Of the 179 males in the sample, 7.2 per cent reapplied once, 36.9 per cent twice, 30.2 per cent three times, 16.2 per cent four times and 9.5 per cent five times. Of the 34 females, 23.6 per cent reapplied once, 44.1 per cent twice, 20.6 per cent three times, 8.8 per cent four times and 2.9 per cent five times. The difference between the sexes is significant ($X^2 = 11.5, p < 0.05$). This finding is consistent with that reported by Becker *et al.* (1973, p. 995).

Table 1 details the career choice of men and women as reported in 1979. Although the numbers in Table 1 are too small to permit any conclusive statement, a number of apparent trends suggest hypotheses worthy of further research. First, women

Table 1. Ultimate career choice by sex (absolute numbers)

Occupation		Men		Women	
Health	Total	120	67.0%	25	73.5%
Medicine		95		18	
Dentistry		13		1	
Veterinary		1		—	
Medical engineering		—		1	
Clinical psychology		1		1	
Research psychology		4		—	
Physiological research		3		3	
Pharmacy		1		—	
Medical biology		2		—	
Laboratory technician		—		1	
Hard sciences	Total	19	10.6%	3	8.8%
Biology		3		1	
Chemistry		2		1	
Engineering		13		1	
Agronomy		1		—	
Other	Total	40	22.4%	6	17.7%
Teaching (high school science)		2		3	
Adminst/bus/economic		15		—	
Law		5		1	
Military and Police (officers)		6		—	
Social Sciences		2		—	
Computers (systems analysis)		3		—	
Accountancy		3		—	
Tourism		2		1	
Clerical Work		—		1	
No information		2		1	

appear to make a greater commitment to the health field than men. If we discount those who entered medicine and dentistry, 40 per cent of the women compared to 16.9 per cent of the men selected alternative occupations within the health *situs*. A second finding is that only one-third of the women not in medicine selected female dominated occupations (teaching, clerical work, tourism); the remainder gravitated to what, in Israel, are male-dominated or mixed-sex occupations (Izraeli and Gaier, 1979). Even those in teaching (a female occupation) specialized in high school sciences (a mixed-sex specialization). Third, more men than women who failed to enter medicine opted for high status male dominated occupations such as engineering, business, accountancy, law and the military. It appears that men more than women exchanged occupational *situs* for high occupational status.

An examination of the highest academic degree actually or almost completed in 1979 reveals that men and women do not differ significantly in the extent of their long term academic investments. Of the 179 men and 34 women respectively highest degree achieved was as follows: M.D. 60.9 per cent and 55.9 per cent; Ph.D. 5.6 per cent and 5.9 per cent; M.Sc./M.A. 12.8 per cent and 14.7 per cent; B.Sc./B.A. 17.9 per cent and 23.5 per cent; no degree 2.8 per cent and 0.0 per cent. It is interesting to note that none of the women had failed to complete at least the B.A. degree.

DISCUSSION

This study addresses the general issue of sex differences *within* an occupation. It found that after initial rejection from medical school, men were more persistent in reapplications than women; a greater proportion of men than women left the occupational field in favour of higher occupational status but women did not revert to traditionally female occupations. No sex differences were found in the extent of long-term academic investments.

The sex difference in persistence cannot be explained by the deterring effect of growing family responsibilities, which typically takes place among women in their 20s. Less than half the women in our sample had married and most who had, were in medicine. It may be suggested that the relatively lower expectations that women who aspire to non-traditional fields have about achieving their goal may have a depressing effect on persistence behaviour. These expectations may be influenced, furthermore, by the weak support given to women compared to the encouragement given to men, for non-traditional occupational aspirations which in turn may have a similar depressing effect.

An interesting additional possibility relates to sex differences in perceived equity. Becker *et al.* report that 'women were significantly more likely than men to perceive their own rejection as reasonable, despite their relatively better college grade–point averages' (1973, p. 997). It may be suggested that people who view their rejection as equitable are less motivated to persevere than those who do not. On the other hand women who view the admissions procedure as inequitable, that is, as biased in favour of men, are less likely to believe that perseverence will be effective. It may be hypothesized that the belief that one's own rejection was not equitable but that the system as whole is, are conditions conducive to perseverence. Perceived equity may also be a significant factor in observed sex differences in other types of persistence behaviour such as asserting one's demands for promotion, or a better job.

The alternative occupational choices of those not in medicine suggest that men and women may be initially attracted to the profession for different reasons. Becker *et al.* (1973), for example, found that a significantly higher proportion of males than females unsuccessful applicants rated prestige and high income as important reasons for entering medicine. Job outcome preferences, however, are also shaped by perceived opportunities in the work setting (Kanter, 1977). Occupations that rank high in prestige and income are also those with fewest female role models and least welcoming of women. Bartol and Manhardt (1979) who studied sex differences in job outcome preferences of college graduates entering business, a week after their appointment, found that over a nine-year period, the job outcome preferences of women had converged towards that of men. They explain that women in 1974 attributed greater importance to career aspects of their jobs than in 1966 because affirmative action legislation had expanded career opportunities for women. In the early 1970s in Israel, the other high status occupations such as law and engineering, were even more male dominated than was medicine (in which women then comprised approximately 25 per cent of the practitioners) (Central Bureau of Statistics, 1976). The fact that fewer women than men in our study left the health *situs* for other high prestige and income occupations may in part be reflective of sex differences in anticipated job opportunities in other male dominated occupations.

Achievement generally requires persistence especially in the face of initial failure. Sex differences in persistence behaviour among adults have not been adequately explored. Although our sample was small and the nature of the available data limited, our study suggests that future research into intra-occupational sex differences needs to examine the moderating effects of such variables as perceived equity of rejection and opportunity structure on the relationship between sex and persistence behaviour as well as between sex and alternative occupational choice, respectively.

REFERENCES

AAMC (Association of American Medical Colleges) (1976). U.S. Department of Health, Education and Welfare, *The Medical School Admissions Process*, U.S. Department of Commerce: National Technical Information Service.

Bartol, K. M. and Manhardt, P. J. (1979). 'Sex differences in job outcome preferences: trends among newly hired college graduates', *Journal of Applied Psychology*, **64**(5), 477–482.

Becker, M. H., Katasky, M. E. and Seidel, H. M. (1973). 'A follow up study of unsuccessful applicants to medical schools', *Journal of Medical Education*, **48**, 991–1001.

Birsdall, P. (1980). 'A comparative analysis of male and female managerial communication style in two organizations', *Journal of Vocational Behavior*, **16**(2), 183–197.

Central Bureau of Statistics (1976). 'Employed persons in Annual Labor Force, 1972', *Monthly Bulletin*, Supplement XXVII, No. 7, Jerusalem, Israel, 76–103.

Donnell, S. M. and Hall, J. (1980). 'Men and women as managers: a significant case of no significant difference', *Organizational Dynamics*, Spring, 60–77.

Fitzgerald, L. F. and Crites, J. O. (1980). 'Toward a career psychology of women: What do we know? What do we need to know?', *Journal of Counselling Psychology*, **27**(1), 44–62.

Gordon, T. L. (1979). 'Study of U.S. medical school applicants, 1977–78', *Journal of Medical Education*, **54**, 677–702.

Holland, J. L. (1973). *Making Occupational Choices: A Theory of Careers*, Prentice-Hall, Englewood Cliffs, New Jersey.

Izraeli, D. N. and Gaier, K. (1979). 'Sex and interoccupational wage differences in Israel', *Industrial Relations: A Journal of Economy and Society*, **18**(2), 227–232.

Johnson, L. (1971). 'A comparison of the social characteristics and academic achievement of medical students and unsuccessful medical school applicants', *British Journal of Medical Education*, **5**, 260–263.

Kanter, R. M. (1977). *Men and Women of the Corporation*, Basic Books, New York.

Kaufman, E. and Feathers, M. L. (1980). 'Work motivation and job values among professional men and women: A new accounting', *Journal of Vocational Behavior*, **17**, 251–262.

Marini, M. M. and Greenberger, E. (1978). 'Sex differences in occupational aspirations and expectations', *Sociology of Work and Occupations*, **5**(2), 147–179.

McLure, G. T. and Piel, E. (1978). 'College-bound girls and science careers: perceptions of barriers and facilitating factors', *Journal of Vocational Behavior*, **12**(2), 172–183.

O'Leary, V. E. (1974). 'Some attitudinal barriers to occupational aspirations in women', *Psychological Bulletin*, **81**, 809–825.

Spitze, G. D. and Waite, L. J. (1980). 'Labour force and work attitudes: young women's early experiences', *Sociology of Work and Occupations*, **7**(1), 3–33.

Author's address:
Dr Dafna N. Izraeli, Department of Labour Studies, Tel Aviv University, Tel Aviv, Israel.

A Selected Bibliography

Prepared by Avishai Antonovsky

An attempt has been made here to overcome the restrictions imposed by the criteria for selection of papers included in this volume (only papers which appeared since 1980 and no more than one by any individual senior author) as well as by space limitations. An extensive computer search was conducted, curricula vitae and references cited in papers submitted for publication were reviewed, and members of the section on medical sociology of the Israel Sociological Society were canvassed. The bibliography, it is to be hoped, includes the largest part of the published social science research on health and health care in Israel in English. Undoubtedly some references have been missed; our apologies are extended to their authors.

It is always difficult to determine the precise boundaries of a research field. We have had to use our judgment to exclude items that are unlikely to interest sociologists, without being too restrictive. Again, the reader should be reminded that, as in the contents of the volume itself, the bibliography does not include reference to work by Israeli sociologists that does not bear directly on Israel.

Adler, I., and Kandel, D.B. "Cross-Cultural Perspectives on Developmental Stages in Adolescent Drug Use." *Journal of Studies on Alcohol* 42 (1981): 701-15.

Adler, I., and Shuval, J.T. "Cross Pressures during Socialization for Medicine." *American Sociological Review* 43 (1978): 693-704.

Anson, J. "Mortality and Living Conditions: Relative Mortality Levels and their Relation to the Physical Quality of Life in Urban Populations." *Social Science and Medicine* 27 (1988): 901-10.

Anson, O., Antonovsky, A., and Sagy, S. "Gender, Family and Attitudes toward Retirement." *Sex Roles*. (In press)

Anson, O., Bernstein, J., and Hobfoll, S. "Anxiety and Performance in Two Ego-Threatening Situations." *Journal of Personality Assessment* 48 (1984): 168-72.

Antonovsky, A. "Breakdown: A Needed Fourth Step in the Conceptual Armamentarium of Modern Medicine." *Social Science and Medicine* 6 (1972): 537-44.

______. "Changes in Attitudes about Mental Health among Second Year Medical Students." *International Journal of Health Education* 20 (1977): 259-70.

______. "Conceptual and Methodological Problems in the Study of Resistance Resources and Stressful Life Events." In *Stressful Life Events*, 245-58, eds. B.A. Dohrenwend and B.P Dohrenwend. New York: Wiley, 1974.

______. "The Fluctuating Fortunes of the Behavioral Sciences." *Israel Journal of Medical Sciences* 23 (1987): 1022-26.

______. "The Image of Four Diseases Held by the Urban Jewish Population of Israel." *Journal of Chronic Diseases* 25 (1972): 375-84.

______. "A Model to Explain Visits to the Doctor: With Specific Reference to the Case of Israel." *Journal of Health and Social Behavior* 13 (1972): 446-54.

______. "The Professional-Proletarian Bind: Doctors' Strikes in Western Societies." In *Cross-National Research in Sociology*, ed. M.L. Kohn. Beverly Hills: Sage (ASA Presidential Series), 1989.

______. "The Sense of Coherence: Development of a Research Instrument." Newsletter and Research Report, W.S. Schwartz Research Center for Behavioral Medicine, Tel Aviv University 1 (1983): 11-22.

______. "Social and Cultural Factors in Coronary Disease: An Israel-North American Sibling Study." *Israel Journal of Medical Sciences* 7 (1971): 1578-83.

______. "Student Selection in the School of Medicine, Ben-Gurion University of the Negev: A Case Study." *Medical Education* 10 (1976): 219-34.

______. "Teaching a Social Medicine Orientation to Medical Students." *Journal of Medical Education* 41 (1966): 870-76.

______. "Training Mental Health Care Manpower: The Medical Student." *Israel Annals of Psychiatry and Related Disciplines* 15 (1977): 268-76.

______. "The Utility of the Breakdown Concept." *Social Science and Medicine* 7 (1973): 605-12.

Antonovsky, A., Adler, I., Sagy, S., and Visel, R. "Attitudes toward Retirement in an Israeli Cohort." *International Journal of Aging and Human Development*. (In press)

Antonovsky, A., Alter, M., and Leibowitz, U. "Age Cohort Analysis: A Method of Estimating Frequency Changes in Multiple Sclerosis." *Acta Neurologica Scandinavica* 44 (1968): 241-50.

Antonovsky, A., and Anson, O. "Factors Related to Preventive Health Behavior." In *Cancer: The Behavioral Dimension*, eds. J.W. Cullen, B.H. Fox, and R.N. Isom. New York: Raven Press, 1976.

Antonovsky, A., Anson, O., and Bernstein, J. "Interviewing and the Selection of Medical Students: The Experience of Five Years of Beersheba." *Programmed Learning and Educational Technology* 16 (1979): 328-34.

Antonovsky, A., and Glick, S. "The Beer Sheva Experiment: An Assessment of the First 13 Years: Content and Purpose of the Volume." *Israel Journal of Medical Sciences* 23 (1987): 939-44.

Antonovsky, A., and Katz, R. "The Life Crisis History as a Tool in Epidemiologic Research." *Journal of Health and Social Behavior* 8 (1967): 15-20.

Antonovsky, A., and Katz, R. "The Model Dental Patient: An Empirical Study of Preventive Health Behavior." *Social Science and Medicine* 4 (1970): 367-80.

Antonovsky, A., Leibowitz, U., Medalie, J.M., Smith, H.A., Halpern, L., and Alter, M. "Epidemiological Study of Multiple Sclerosis in Israel. III. Multiple Sclerosis and Socioeconomic Status." *Journal of Neurology, Neurosurgery and Psychiatry* 3 (1967): 1-6.

______. "Reappraisal of Possible Etiologic Factors in Multiple Sclerosis." *American Journal of Public Health* 58 (1968): 836-48.

Antonovsky, A., Leibowitz, U., Smith, H.A., Medalie, J.M., Balogh, M., Katz, R., Halpern, L., and Alter, M. "Epidemiologic Study of Multiple Sclerosis in Israel. I. An Overall Review of Methods and Findings." *Archives of Neurology* 13 (1965): 183-93.

Antonovsky, A., Maoz, B., Dowty, N., and Wijsenbeek, H. "Twenty-five Years Later: A Limited Study of the Sequelae of the Concentration Camp Experience." *Social Psychiatry* 6 (1971): 186-93.

Antonovsky, H., and Ginath, Y. "Changes in Attitudes of Medical Students to Psychiatry: An Evaluation of a Clerkship in Psychiatry." *Journal of Psychiatric Education* 8 (1984): 218-26.

Antonovsky, H., and Sagy, S. "The Development of a Sense of Coherence and Its Impact on Responses to Stress Situations." *Journal of Social Psychology* 126 (1986): 213-25.

Antonovsky, A., and Shuval, H. "An Evaluation of the Effect of Mass Media in a Health Education Programme." *International Journal of Health Education* 9 (1966): 58-68.

Antonovsky, A., and Sourani, T. "Family Sense of Coherence and Family Adaptation." *Journal of Marriage and the Family* 50 (1988): 79-92.

Arian, A. "Health Care in Israel: Political and Administrative Aspects." *International Political Science Review* 2 (1981): 43-56.

Aviram, U. "Community Mental Health in Israel: An Interim Policy Assessment." In *Evaluating the Welfare State: Social and Political Perspectives*, 217-31, eds. S.E. Spiro and E. Yuchtman-Yaar. Orlando, FL.: Academic Press, 1983.

______. "Facilitating Deinstitutionalization: A Comparative Analysis." *International Journal of Social Psychiatry* 27 (1981): 23-32.

Aviram, U., Ben-Sira, Z., Shoham, I., and Stern, I. "Bodily Complaints with No Identified Organic Cause Among Women: Psychosocial Resources as a Buffer." In *Social Psychiatry*, 821-41, ed. V. Hudolin. New York: Plenum, 1984.

Baider, L., and Abramovitch, H. "The Dybbuk: Cultural Context of a Cancer Patient." *Hospice Journal* 1 (1985): 113-19.

Baider, L., and Abramovitch, H.H. "Enuresis in Cross-Cultural Perspective: A Comparison of Training for Elimination Control in Three Israeli Ethnic Groups." *Journal of Social Psychology* 129 (1989): 47-56.

Barell, V. "Risk Factor Assessment/Outcome in Israel: The National Program for Reduction of Infant Mortality." In *Proceedings of the International Collaborative Effort on Perinatal and Infant Mortality* II (1988): 1-47. Hyattsville, Md.: National Center for Health Statistics.

Barell, V., and Kaplan, G. "Health in the Elderly: The Kiryat Ono Census." *Israel Journal of Medical Sciences* 21 (1985): 254-59.

Barell, V., Wax, Y., and Ruder, A.M. "Analysis of Geographic Differentials in Infant Mortality Rates: The Or Yehuda Community." *American Journal of Epidemiology* 128 (1988): 218-30.

Barnoon, S., Carmel, S., and Zalcman, T. "Perceived Health Damages During a Physicians' Strike in Israel." *Health Services Research* 22 (1987): 141-55.

Basker, E. "Coping With Fertility in Israel: A Case Study of Culture Clash." *Culture, Medicine and Psychiatry* 7 (1983): 199-211.

Basker, E., Beran, B., and Kleinhauz, M. "A Social Science Perspective on the Negotiation of a Psychiatric Diagnosis." *Social Psychiatry* 17 (1982): 53-58.

Baumatz, S. "The Importance of a Mental Health Center in the Community in Israel." *Israel Annals of Psychiatry and Related Disciplines* 1 (1963): 79-87.

Ben-David, J. "The Professional Role of the Physician in Bureaucratized Medicine." *Human Relations* 11 (1958): 258-73.
Ben-Sira, Z. "Affective and Instrumental Components in the Physician-Patient Relationship: An Additional Dimension of Interaction Theory." *Journal of Health and Social Behavior* 21 (1980): 170-80.
______. "Disability, Stress, and Readjustment: The Function of the Professional's Latent Goals and Affective Behavior in Rehabilitation." *Social Science and Medicine* 23 (1986): 43-55.
______. "The Function of the Professional's Affective Behavior in Client Satisfaction: A Revised Approach to Social Interaction Theory." *Journal of Health and Social Behavior* 17 (1976): 3-11.
______. "Chronic Illness, Stress and Coping." *Social Science and Medicine* 18 (1984): 725-36.
______. "The Health Promoting Function of Mass Media and Reference Groups: Motivating or Reinforcing of Behavior Change." *Social Science and Medicine* 16 (1982): 825-34.
______. "Interethnic Cleavage, Stress, Coping and Compensatory Mechanisms: The Case of Israel." In *Current Selected Research in Human Stress*, vol. I, ed. J.H. Humphrey. New York: A.M.S. Press, 1986.
______. "The Interrelationship and Dynamics of the Symptoms of Psychological Distress: An Additional Approach to the Theory of Readjustment and Breakdown." In *Research in Psychology and Medicine*, 117-29, eds. D.S. Oborne, M.M. Gruneberg and J.R. Eiser. London: Academic Press, 1979.
______. "Involvement with a Disease and Health Promoting Behavior." *Social Science & Medicine* 11 (1977): 165-73.
______. "Involvement with a Disease and Primary Care Utilization." *Sociology of Health and Illness* 2 (1980): 247-76.
______. "Latent Fear-Arousing Potential of Fear-Moderating and Fear-Neutral Health Promoting Information." *Social Science and Medicine* 15E (1981): 105-12.
______. "The Latent Functions of Welfare and Need-Satisfaction of the Disadvantaged." *Journal of Sociology and Social Welfare* 13 (1986): 418-44.
______. "Lay Evaluation of Medical Treatment and Competence: Development of a Model of the Function of the Physician's Affective Behavior." *Social Science and Medicine* 16 (1982): 1013-119.
______. "Lay Perceived Legitimacy of Presenting Emotional Complaints." *Medical Care* 21 (1983): 1128-30.
______. "Life Change and Health: An Additional Perspective on the Structure of Coping." *Stress* 3 (1982): 18-27.
______. "Loss, Stress and Readjustment." *Social Science and Medicine* 17 (1983): 1619-32.
______. "The Plight of Primary Medical Care: The Problematics of Committedness to the Practice." *Social Science and Medicine* 22 (1986): 699-712.
______. *Politics and Primary Medical Care: Dehumanization and Overutilization.* Aldershot, England: Gower, 1988.
______. "Potency: A Readjustment-promoting Link in the Rehabilitation of Disabled Persons." *Sociology of Health and Illness* 11 (1989): 41-61.
______. "Potency: A Stressbuffering Link in the Coping-Stress-Disease Relationship." *Social Science and Medicine* 20 (1985): 397-406.

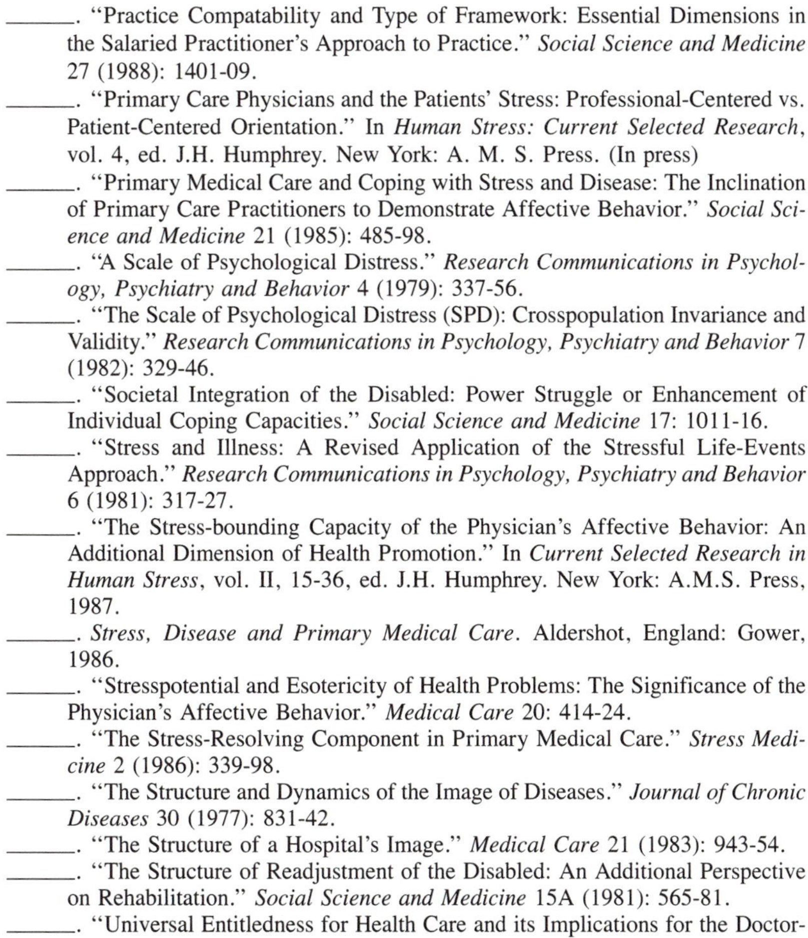

______. "Practice Compatability and Type of Framework: Essential Dimensions in the Salaried Practitioner's Approach to Practice." *Social Science and Medicine* 27 (1988): 1401-09.

______. "Primary Care Physicians and the Patients' Stress: Professional-Centered vs. Patient-Centered Orientation." In *Human Stress: Current Selected Research*, vol. 4, ed. J.H. Humphrey. New York: A. M. S. Press. (In press)

______. "Primary Medical Care and Coping with Stress and Disease: The Inclination of Primary Care Practitioners to Demonstrate Affective Behavior." *Social Science and Medicine* 21 (1985): 485-98.

______. "A Scale of Psychological Distress." *Research Communications in Psychology, Psychiatry and Behavior* 4 (1979): 337-56.

______. "The Scale of Psychological Distress (SPD): Crosspopulation Invariance and Validity." *Research Communications in Psychology, Psychiatry and Behavior* 7 (1982): 329-46.

______. "Societal Integration of the Disabled: Power Struggle or Enhancement of Individual Coping Capacities." *Social Science and Medicine* 17: 1011-16.

______. "Stress and Illness: A Revised Application of the Stressful Life-Events Approach." *Research Communications in Psychology, Psychiatry and Behavior* 6 (1981): 317-27.

______. "The Stress-bounding Capacity of the Physician's Affective Behavior: An Additional Dimension of Health Promotion." In *Current Selected Research in Human Stress*, vol. II, 15-36, ed. J.H. Humphrey. New York: A.M.S. Press, 1987.

______. *Stress, Disease and Primary Medical Care*. Aldershot, England: Gower, 1986.

______. "Stresspotential and Esotericity of Health Problems: The Significance of the Physician's Affective Behavior." *Medical Care* 20: 414-24.

______. "The Stress-Resolving Component in Primary Medical Care." *Stress Medicine* 2 (1986): 339-98.

______. "The Structure and Dynamics of the Image of Diseases." *Journal of Chronic Diseases* 30 (1977): 831-42.

______. "The Structure of a Hospital's Image." *Medical Care* 21 (1983): 943-54.

______. "The Structure of Readjustment of the Disabled: An Additional Perspective on Rehabilitation." *Social Science and Medicine* 15A (1981): 565-81.

______. "Universal Entitledness for Health Care and its Implications for the Doctor-Patient Relationships: A New Perspective on Medical Care." In *Advances in Medical Sociology*, ed. G.L. Albrecht. Greenwich, Conn.: JAI Press, in press.

Ben-Sira, Z., Aviram, U., Stern, I., and Shoham, I. "A Facet Theoretical Approach to Psychosomatic Complaints." *Israel Annals of Psychiatry and Related Disciplines* 16 (1978): 219-30.

Ben-Sira, Z., and Padeh, B. "Instrumental Coping and Affective Defense: An Additional Perspective in Health Promoting Behavior." *Social Social and Medicine* 12 (1978): 163-8.

Benor, D.E., and Hobfoll, S.E. "Prediction of Clinical Performance in Medicine: The Role of Prior Experience." *Journal of Medical Education* 56 (1981): 653-8.

______. "Prediction of Clinical Performance of Medical Students: An Integrative Approach to Evaluation." *Medical Education* 18 (1984): 236-43.

Benor, D.E., Notzer, N., Sheehan, T.J., and Norman, G.R. "Moral Reasoning as a Criterion for Admission to Medical School." *Medical Education* 18 (1984): 423-28.

Bergman, R. "Interpersonal Relations in Health Care Delivery." *International Nursing Review* 24 (1977): 104-7.

Bernstein, J., and Carmel, S. "Trait Anxiety and the Sense of Coherence." *Psychological Reports* 60 (1987): 1000-1.

______. "Trait-Anxiety Differences among Medical Students." *Psychological Reports* 59 (1986): 1063-68.

Biderman, A., and Antonovsky, A. "The Submerged Part of the Iceberg and the Family Physician." *Family Practice* 5 (1988): 101-3.

Bilu, Y. "Demonic Explanation of Disease among Moroccan Jews in Israel." *Culture, Medicine and Psychiatry* 3 (1979): 363-80.

______. "General Characteristics of Referrals to Traditional Healers in Israel." *Israel Annals of Psychiatry and Related Disciplines* 15 (1977): 245-52.

______. "The Moroccan Demon in Israel: The Case of 'Evil Spirit Disease'." *Ethos* 8 (1980): 24-38.

Bilu, Y., and Abramovitch, H. "In Search of the Saddiq: Visitational Dreams among Moroccan Jews in Israel." *Psychiatry* 48 (1985): 83-92.

Bilu, Y., and Levav, Y. "A Transcultural Review of Israeli Psychiatry." *Transcultural Psychiatric Research Review* 17 (1980): 7-56.

Carmel, S. "Hospital Patients' Responses to Dissatisfaction." *Sociology of Health and Illness* 10 (1988): 262-81.

______. "Satisfaction with Hospitalization: A Comparative Analysis of Three Types of Services." *Social Science and Medicine* 21 (1985): 1243-49.

Carmel, S., Barnoon, S., and Zalcman, T. "Social Class Differences in Coping with a Physicians' Strike in Israel." *Journal of Community Health*. (In press)

Carmel, S., and Bernstein, J. "Identifying with the Patient: An Intensive Programme for Medical Students." *Medical Education* 20 (1986): 432-6.

______. "Perceptions of Medical School Stressors: Their Relationship to Age, Year of Study and Trait Anxiety." *Journal of Human Stress* 13 (1987): 39-44.

Carmel, S., Yakubovich, I.S., Zwanger, L., and Zalcman, T. "Nurses' Autonomy and Job Satisfaction." *Social Science and Medicine* 26 (1988): 1103-07.

Datan, N., Antonovsky, A., and Maoz, B. "Love, War and the Life Cycle in the Family." In *West Virginia University Life Span Developmental Psychology: Historical and Generational Effects*, 143-59, ed. by K.A. McCluskey and H.W. Reese. New York: Academic Press.

______. *A Time to Reap: The Middle Age of Women in Five Israeli Subcultures*. Baltimore: John Hopkins University Press, 1981.

______. "Tradition, Modernity, and Transitions in Five Israeli Subcultures." In *In Her Prime: A New View of Middle Age Women*, 173-79, eds. J.K. Brown and V. Kerns. South Hadley, Mass.: Bergin and Garvey, 1985.

Davies, A.M., and Fleishman, R. "Health Status and Use of Health Services as Reported by Older Residents of the Baka Neighborhood, Jerusalem." *Israel Journal of Medical Sciences* 17 (1981): 138-44.

Deshen, S. "Coming of Age among Blind People in Israel." *Disability, Handicap and Society* 2 (1987): 137-49.

______. "Seeking Dignity and Independence: Toward an Ethnography of Blindness in Israel." *Journal of Visual Impairment and Blindness* 8 (1987): 209-12.

Deshen, S., and Deshen, H. "Managing at Home: Relationships between Blind Parents and Sighted Children." *Human Organization* 48 (1989): 386-410.

______. "On Social Aspects of the Usage of Guide-dogs and Long Canes." *Sociological Review* 37 (1989): 89-103.

Doron, A. "Ailing Health Services." *Jerusalem Quarterly* 14 (1980): 82-93.

______. "Health and Social Security Services in Canada and Israel." In *Canada-Israel: Comparative Perspectives*, 27-33, ed. A. Shachar. Jerusalem: IACS-Academon, 1988.

______. "The Struggle for National Insurance in Israel: 1948-1955." *Social Welfare and Social Work Series* 10 (1975): 7-12.

Doron, H., and Ron, A. "The Organization of Primary Care in Israel." In *Getting Better: A Report on Health Care from the Salzburg Seminar*, ed. H.C.P. Gleason. Cambridge, Mass.: Oelgeschlager, Gunn and Hain, 1981.

Dowty, N., Maoz, B., Antonovsky, A., and Wijsenbeek, H. "Climacterium in Three Cultural Contexts." *Tropical and Geographical Medicine* 22 (1970): 77-86.

Eli, I., and Shuval, J.T. "Professional Socialization in Dentistry." *Social Science and Medicine* 16 (1982): 951-55.

Elizur, A., Neumann, M., and Bawer, A. "Interdependency of Attitudes, Diagnostic Assessments and Therapeutic Recommendations of Medical Students toward Mental Patients." *International Journal of Social Psychiatry* 32 (1986): 31-40.

Ellencweig, A.Y. "The New Israeli Health Care Reform." *Journal of Health Politics, Policy and Law* 8 (1983): 366-86.

Factor, H., and Habib, J. "Role of Institutional and Community Services in Meeting the Long-Term Care Needs of the Elderly in Israel: The Decade of the 1980's." *Israel Journal of Medical Sciences* 21 (1985): 212-8.

Fleishman, R., Peritz, E., and Leibel, B. "Quality of Care for an Elderly Population: The Case of Hypertension." *Comprehensive Gerontology*. (In press)

Fleishman, R., Rosin, A., Tomer, A., and Schwartz, R. "Cognitive Impairment and the Quality of Care in Long-term Institutions." *Comprehensive Gerontology* 1 (1987): 18-23.

Fleishman, R., and Shmueli, A. "Patterns of Informal Social Support of the Elderly: An International Comparison." *The Gerontologist* 24 (1984): 303-12.

Galinsky, D., Cohen, R., Schneiderman, C., Gelper, Y. and Nir, Z. "A Programme in Undergraduate Geriatric Education: The Beer Sheva Experiment." *Medical Education* 17 (1983): 100-4.

Gofin, J., Kark, E., Mainemer, N., Kark, S.L., Abramson, J.H., Hopp, C., and Epstein, L.M. "Prevalence of Selected Health Characteristics of Women and Comparisons with Men. A Community Health Survey in Jerusalem." *Israel Journal of Medical Sciences* 17 (1981): 145-59.

Goldbourt, U., and Kark, J.D. "The Epidemiology of Coronary Heart Disease in the Ethnically and Culturally Diverse Population of Israel: A Review." *Israel Journal of Medical Sciences* 18 (1982): 1077-97.

Goodman, A.B., Rahav, M., and Popper, M. "A Social Area Analysis of Jerusalem: Implications for Mental Health Planning and Epidemiologic Studies." *Israel Journal of Psychiatry and Related Sciences* 19 (1982): 185-97.

Greenberg, D.S. "Health Care in Israel." *New England Journal of Medicine* 309 (1983): 681-4.

Greenfield, S.F., Borkan, J., and Yodfat, Y. "Health Beliefs and Hypertension: A Case-Control Study in a Moroccan Jewish Community in Israel." *Culture, Medicine and Psychiatry* 11 (1987): 79-95.

Grushka, T., ed. *Health Services in Israel*. Jerusalem: Ministry of Health, 1968.

Guttman, L., and Levy, S. "Worry, Fear and Concern Differentiated." *Israel Annals of Psychiatry and Related Disciplines* 14 (1976): 211-28.

Halevi, H.S. *The Bumpy Road to National Health Insurance: The Case of Israel*. Jerusalem: JDC-Brookdale Institute of Gerontology and Adult Human Development, 1980.

______. "Frequency of Mental Illness among Jews in Israel." *Journal of Social Psychiatry* 9 (1963): 268-82.

Hes, J.P. "From Native Healer to Modern Psychiatrist. Afro-Asian Immigrants to Israel and Their Attitudes towards Psychiatric Facilities. II. Attitudes of Relatives towards the Hospital." *International Journal of Social Psychiatry* 13 (1966): 21-27.

Hobfoll, S.E., Anson, O., and Antonovsky, A. "Personality Factors as Predictors of Medical Student Performance." *Medical Education* 16 (1982): 251-58.

Hobfoll, S.E., and Benor, D.E. "Prediction of Student Clinical Performance." *Medical Education* 15 (1981): 231-36.

Hobfoll, S.E., Lomranz, J., Eyal, N., Bridges, A., and Tzemach, M. "Pulse of a Nation: Depressive Mood Reactions of Israelis to the Israel-Lebanon War." *Journal of Personality and Social Psychology* 56 (1989): 1002-12.

Holtzman, E., Goldbourt, U., Rosenthal, T., Yaari, S., and Neufeld, H.N. "Hypertension in Middle-Aged Men: Associated Factors and Mortality Experience." *Israel Journal of Medical Sciences* 19 (1983): 25-33.

Honig-Parnass, T. "The Effects of Latent Social Needs on Physician Utilization by Immigrants: A Replication Study." *Social Science and Medicine* 16 (1982): 505-14.

______. "Lay Concepts of the Sick Role: An Examination of the Professionalist's Bias in Parsons's Model." *Social Science and Medicine* 15A (1981): 615-23.

Ichilov, O., and Dotan, M. "Formation of Professional Images among Israeli Student Nurses." *International Journal of Nursing Studies* 17 (1980): 247-59.

Izraeli, D.N., and Notzer, N. "Sex Differences in Persistence and Alternative Occupational choice of Unsuccessful Applicants to Medical School." *Journal of Occupational Behavior* 4 (1983): 229-35.

Javetz, R., and Shuval, J.T. "A Syndrome of Social Vulnerability." *Youth and Society* 16 (1984): 171-93.

______. "Vulnerability to Drugs among Israeli Adolescents." *Israel Journal of Psychiatry and Related Sciences* 19 (1982): 97-119.

Kandel, D.B., Adler, I., and Sundit, M. "The Epidemiology of Adolescent Drug Use in France and Israel." *American Journal of Public Health* 71 (1981): 256-65.

Kaplan, G., Barell, V., and Lusky, A. "Subjective State of Health and Survival in the Elderly Adults." *Journal of Gerontology* 43 (1988): S114-20.

Katz, E., Gurevitch, T., Peled, T., and Danet, B. "Doctor-Patient Exchanges: A Diagnostic Approach to Organizations and Professions." *Human Relations* 22 (1969): 309-24.

Kremer, Y. "The Association Between Health and Retirement: Self-Health Assessment of Israeli Retirees." *Social Science and Medicine* 20 (1985): 61-66.

Lazin, F.A. "Comprehensive Primary Care at the Neighborhood Level: An Israeli Experiment That Failed." *Journal of Health Politics, Policy and Law* 8 (1983): 463-79.

Leibowitz, U., Antonovsky, A., Katz, R., and Alter, M. "Does Pregnancy Increase the Risk of Multiple Sclerosis?" *Journal of Neurology, Neurosurgery and Psychiatry* 30 (1967): 354-7.

Leibowitz, U., Antonovsky, A., Medalie, J.M., Smith, H.A., Halpern, L. and Alter, M. "Epidemiological Study of Multiple Sclerosis in Israel. II. Multiple Sclerosis and Level of Sanitation." *Journal of Neurology, Neurosurgery and Psychiatry* 29 (1966): 60-68.

Levav, I., Krasnoff, L., and Dohrenwend, B.S. "Israeli PERI Life Event Scale: Ratings of Events by a Community Sample." *Israel Journal of Medical Sciences* 17 (1981): 176-83.

Levav, Y., and Bilu, Y. "A Transcultural Review of Israeli Psychiatry." *Transcultural Psychiatric Research Review* 17 (1980): 7-56.

Levi, S. "Can Social Worker Students Change the Agencies?" In *Issues and Explorations in Social Work Education*, ed. S. Spiro. Israeli Association of Social Work, 1978.

______. The Involvement of Social Workers as Professional Volunteers in Wartime Bereavement Casework." In *Stress and Anxiety*, vol. 8, eds. C.D. Spielberger, E.G. Sarason, and N.A. Milgram. Washington, D.C.: Hemisphere Press, 1981.

______. "Research on the Severely Retarded Infant Population in the North of Israel." In *The Development of Community Services for the Retarded in Haifa*, ed. Y. Ginegar. Haifa, Israel: University of Haifa, 1979.

______. "Triggering Change, a Case Study in Innovation." *Social Work in Health Care* 2 (1977): 319-28.

Levi, S., Elad, N., and Weiss, Y. "Theoretical Empirical Issues in Continuity of Care for the Chronically Ill." *Proceedings of the Second Biannual Conference of the European Society of Medical Sociology*, Zagreb 1988.

Leviatan, U., and Cohen, J. "Gender Differences in Life Expectancy among Kibbutz Members." *Social Science and Medicine* 21 (1985): 545-51.

Lewin-Epstein, N. "Employment and Ill-Health among Women in Israel." *Social Science and Medicine* 23 (1986): 1171-79.

______. "Work Characteristics and Ill Health: Gender Differences in Israel." *Work and Occupation* 16 (1989): 80-104.

Machnes-Caspi, Y. "Consumption of Private Medical Services by Israeli Households with Full Coverage of Health Insurance." *Public Health* (London) 94 (1980): 89-94.

Mann, K.J., Medalie, J.H., Lieber, E., Groen, J.J., and Guttman, L. *Visits to Doctors*. Jerusalem: Academic Press, 1970.

Mansbach, I., Palti, H., Pevsner, B., Pridan, H., and Palti, Z. "Advice from the Obstetrician and Other Sources: Do They Affect Women's Feeding Practices? A Study among Different Jewish Groups in Jerusalem." *Social Science and Medicine* 19 (1984): 157-62.

Maoz, B., Antonovsky, A., Apter, A., Datan, N., Hochberg, J., and Salomon, Y. "The Effect of Outside Work on the Menopausal Woman." *Maturitas* 1 (1978): 43-53.

Maoz, B., Antonovsky, A., Apter, A., Wijsenbeek, H., and Datan, N. "Ethnicity and Adaptation to Climacteriuva." *Archir fur Gynakologie* 223 (1977): 9-19.

______. "The Perception of Menopause in Five Ethnic Groups in Israel." *Acta Obstetrica Gynecologia Scandinavica* (suppl.) 65 (1977): 69-76.

Maoz, B., Dowty, N., Antonovsky, A., and Wijsenbeek, H. "Female Attitudes to Menopause." *Social Psychiatry* 5 (1970): 35-40.

Maoz, B., Stern, J., and Spenser, T. "Developing Psychosocial Sensitivity among Family Doctors—a Content Analysis of Balint Seminar Discussions." *Israel Journal of Psychiatry and Related Sciences* 23 (1986): 205-13.

Margalit, M. "Perception of Parents' Behavior, Familial Satisfaction, and Sense of Coherence in Hyperactive Children." *Journal of School Psychology* 23 (1985): 355-64.

Matras, H. "Wholeness and Holiness in *Sifrei Segulot*." *Korot* (Jerusalem) 9 (1988): 96-107.

Mikulincer, M., and Solomon, Z. "Causal Attribution, Coping Strategies, and Combat-related Post-traumatic Stress Disorder." *European Journal of Personality*. (In press)

Miller, A.E. "The Expanding Definition of Disease and Health in Community Medicine." *Social Science and Medicine* 6 (1972): 573-81.

Miller, L. "An Approach to Psychiatric and Mental Health Research in Israel." *Israel Annals of Psychiatry and Related Disciplines* 1 (1963): 3-10.

______. "Community Intervention and Historical Background of Community Mental Health in Israel." *Israel Annals of Psychiatry and Related Disciplines* 15 (1977): 300-309.

______. "The Mental Health of Immigrants in Israel." In *The Child and Family in Israel*, ed. A. Yaros. New York: Gordon and Beach, 1970.

______. "Social Change, Acculturation and Mental Health in Israel." *Israel Annals of Psychiatry and Related Disciplines* 4 (1966): 1-15.

Minuchin-Itzigsohn, S.D., Ben-Shaoul, R., Weingrod, A., and Krasilowski, D. "The Effect of Cultural Conceptions on Therapy: A Comparative Study of Patients in Israeli Psychiatric Clinics." *Culture, Medicine, and Psychiatry* 8 (1984): 229-54.

Moses, R., and Kligler, D.S. "A Comparative Analysis of the Institutionalization of Mental Health Values, the United States and Israel." *Israel Annals of Psychiatry and Related Disciplines* 4 (1966): 162-67.

Notzer, N., Lebran, D., Mashiach, S., and Soffer, S. "Effect of Religiosity on Sex Attitudes, Experience and Contraception among University Students." *Journal of Sex and Marital Therapy* 10 (1984): 57-62.

Notzer, N., and Soffer, S. "Determination in Rejected Medical School Applicants: a 10-Year Follow-Up." *Medical Education* 21 (1987): 405-9.

Notzer, N., Soffer, S., and Aronson, M. "Traits of the 'Ideal Physician' as Perceived by Medical Students and Faculty." *Medical Teacher* 10 (1988): 181-9.

Notzer, N., Soffer, S., and Yadgar, O. "The Role of Senior Teachers in Students' Achievements." *Medical Education* 20 (1986): 13-16.

Noy, S., Nardi, C., and Solomon, Z. "Battle and Military Unit Characteristics and the Prevalence of Psychiatric Casualties." In *Stress and Coping in Time of War: Generalizations from the Israeli Experience*, ed. N.A. Milgram, pp. 73-77, New York: Brunner/Mazel, 1986.

Oren, H., and Epstein, L. "Sociological Intervention in Communication and Interactional Processes among Nurses in an Obstetrics Unit." *Social Science and Medicine* 15A (1981): 73-76.

Palgi, P. "Immigrants, Psychiatrists, and Culture." *Israel Annals of Psychiatry and Related Disciplines* 1 (1963): 43-58.

______. "Mental Health, Traditional Beliefs, and Moral Order among Yemenite Jews in Israel." In *The Anthropology of Medicine*, 319-35, eds. L. Romanucci-Ross, D.E. Moerman and L.R. Tancredit. South Hadley, Mass.: J.F. Bergin, 1983.

______. "Persistent Traditional Yemenite Ways in Dealing with Stress in Israel." *Mental Health and Society* 5 (1978): 113-40.

Palgi, P., and Abramovitch, H. "Death: A Cross-Cultural Perspective." *Annual Review of Anthropology* 13 (1984): 385-417.

Pelz, S.L., Levy, S., Tamir, A., Spenser, T., and Epstein, L.M. "A Measure for Family Functioning in Israel." *Journal of Comparative Family Studies* 15 (1984): 211-30.

Pilpel, D., Carmel, S., and Galinsky, D. "Self-rated Health among the Elderly: A Comparative Analysis of Health Status Measures, Leisure Activities and Social Involvement in Age-sex Groups." *Comprehensive Gerontology* B (1988): 110-16.

Pilpel, D., Naggan, L., and Sarov, B. "Coping with Health Services Disruption: Perceiving Need and Utilizing Available Services During a Doctors' Strike." *Medical Care* 23 (1985): 1372-80.

Priel, B., and Rabinowitz, B. "Teaching Social Sciences in the Clinical Years through Psychosocial Conferences." *Journal of Medical Education* 63 (1988): 555-8.

Rahav, M. "Labelling the Mentally Ill through Psychiatric Records: The Israeli Case Register." *Social Science and Medicine*. (In press)

Rahav, M., Goodman, A.B., Popper, M., and Lin, S. "Distribution of Treated Mental Illness in the Neighborhoods of Jerusalem." *American Journal of Psychiatry* 143 (1986): 1249-54.

Rahav, M., Struening, E.L., and Andrews, H. "Opinions on Mental Illness in Israel." *Social Science and Medicine* (In press).

Reinharz, S., and Mester, R. "Israeli Culture and the Emergence of Community Mental Health Practices: The Case of the West Jerusalem Mental Health Center." *Mental Health and Society* 5 (1978): 241-51.

Ron, A., Karsh, D., Ziplin, A., and Kahan, M. "Use of Medical Care by Children During a Physicians' Strike." *Medical Care* 23 (1985): 89-98.

Roskin, M., and Edelson, J.L. "A Research Note on the Emotional Health of English-Speaking Immigrants in Israel." *Jewish Journal of Sociology* 26 (1984): 139-44.

Segal, S.P., and Aviram, U. *The Mentally Ill in Community Based Sheltered Care: A Study of Community Care and Social Integration*. New York: Wiley, 1978.

Shanan, J., Kedar, H., Eliakim, M., Oster, Z.H., and Prywes, M. "Evolution of Selection Methods for Admission to Medical School. III. Psychological Tests in the Selection of Medical Students." *Israel Journal of Medical Sciences* 6 (1970) 132-44.

Shiloh, A. "The Interaction of Middle Eastern and Western Systems of Medicine." In *Peoples and Cultures in the Middle East*, 373-86, ed. A. Shiloh. New York: Random House, 1969.

Shoham, I., Carmel, S., Zwanger, L., and Zalcman, T. "Autonomy, Job Satisfaction and Professional Self-image among Nurses in the Context of a Physicians' Strike." *Social Science and Medicine*. (In press)

Shoham, I., Yakabovich, I., and Barell, V. "Maternal Education as a Modifier of the Association between Low Birthweight and Infant Mortality." *International Journal of Epidemiology* 17 (1988): 370-77.

Shokeid, M. "The Emergence of Supernatural Explanations for Male Barrenness among Moroccan Immigrants." In *The Predicament of Homecoming: Cultural and Social Life of North African Immigrants in Israel*, 122-50, eds. S. Deshen and M. Shokeid. Ithaca, N.Y.: Cornell University Press, 1974.

Shuval, J.T. "Autobiographical Notes of a Medical Sociologist in Israel." In *Medical Sociologists at Work* 271-88, eds. R.H. Elling and M. Sokolowska. New Brunswick. N.J.: Transaction Press, 1978.

______. "A Comparison of Israeli and American Dentists." *International Dental Journal* 20 (1970): 690-703.
______. *Entering Medicine: The Dynamics of Transition: A Seven Year Study of Medical Education in Israel*. Oxford: Pergamon Press, 1980.
______. "Ethnic Stereotyping in Israeli Medical Bureaucracies." *Sociology and Social Research* 46 (1962): 455-65.
______. "From 'Boy' to 'Colleague': Processes of Role Transformation in Professional Socialization." *Social Science and Medicine* 9 (1975): 413-20.
______. "Health in Israel: Patterns of Equality and Inequality." *Social Science and Medicine*. (In press)
______. "Levels of Professionalism: A Dual System of Dental Care." *Medical Care* 10 (1972): 50-59.
______. "Manpower Pools for Three Health Professions in Israel." *Social Science and Medicine* 7 (1973): 893-910.
______. "Medical Manpower in Israel: Political Processes and Constraints." In *The Political Dynamics of Physician Manpower Policy*, eds. I. Butter, M. Field and M. Rosenthal. London: Kings Fund Press, in press
______. "Methods of Assessing Public Attitudes toward Health." *International Dental Journal* 17 (1967): 63-74.
______. "Migration and Stress." In *Handbook of Stress* 677-91, eds. L. Goldberger and S. Breznitz. New York: Free Press, 1982.
______. *Newcomers and Colleagues: Soviet Immigrant Physicians In Israel*. Houston, Tex.: Cap & Gown Press, 1983.
______. "Occupational Interests and Sex Role Congruence." *Human Relations* 16 (1963): 171-82.
______. "Patterned Ambivalence in Orientation to Medical Professions: General Practitioners and Dentists." *Social Science and Medicine* 5 (1971): 127-36.
______. "Perceived Role Components of Nursing in Israel." *American Sociological Review* 20 (1963): 37-46.
______. "Preventive Dental Behavior in Israel: Some Contrasts between a Professional Population and its Clients." *Medical Care* 9 (1971): 345-51.
______. "Primary Care and Social Control." *Medical Care* 17 (1979): 631-8.
______. "Sex Role Differentiation in the Professions: The Case of Israeli Dentists." *Journal of Health and Social Behavior* 11 (1970): 38-44.
______. "The Sick Role in a Setting of Comprehensive Medical Care." *Medical Care* 10 (1972): 40-49.
______. "Social Factors Conditioning the Recruitment of Nurses in Israel." *Journal of Health and Human Behavior* 3 (1962): 109-20.
______. "Social Functions of Medical Licensing: A Case Study of Soviet Immigrant Physicians in Israel." *Social Science and Medicine* 20 (1985): 901-9.
______. "Socialization of Health Professionals in Israel: Early Sources of Congruence and Differentiation." *Journal of Medical Education* 50 (1975): 443-57.
______. "Some Issues in Cross National Research on Socialization of Medical Students." In *Cross-National Sociomedical Research: Concepts, Methods, Practice*, eds. M. Pflanz and E. Schach. Stuttgart: Georg Thieme, 1976.
______. "Some Persistent Effects of Trauma: Five Years after the Nazi Concentration Camps." *Social Problems* 5 (1957-58): 230-43.
______. "Soviet Immigrant Physicians in Israel." In *New Lives: The Adjustment of Soviet Jewish Immigrants in the United States and Israel* 119-50, ed. R.J. Simon. Lexington, Mass.: Lexington Books, 1985.

______. "Soviet Immigrant Physicians in Israel." *Soviet Jewish Affairs* 14 (1984): 19-40.

Shuval, J.T., and Adler, I. "Health Occupations in Israel: Comparative Patterns of Change During Socialization." *Journal of Health and Social Behavior* 20 (1979): 77-89.

______. "Processes of Continuity and Change During Socialization for Medicine in Israel." *Journal of Health and Social Behavior* 18 (1977): 112-24.

______. "The Role of Models in Professional Socialization." *Social Science and Medicine* 14A (1980): 5-14.

Shuval, J.T., Antonovsky, A., and Davies, A.M. "The Doctor-Patient Relationship in an Ethnically Heterogeneous Society." *Social Science and Medicine* 1 (1967): 141-54.

______. "Illness: A Mechanism for Coping with Failure." *Social Science and Medicine* 7 (1973): 259-65.

______. *Social Functions of Medical Practice: Doctor-Patient Relationships in Israel.* San Francisco: Jossey-Bass, 1970.

Shuval, J.T., and Gilbert, L. "Attempts at Professionalization of Pharmacy: An Israel Case Study." *Social Science and Medicine* 12 (1978): 19-25.

Shuval, J.T., Javetz, R., and Shye, D. "Self-Care in Israel: Physicians' Views and Perspectives." *Social Science and Medicine* 29 (1989): 233-44.

Slater, P.E. "The Israel Doctors' Strike [letter]." *New England Journal of Medicine* 310 (1984): 660-1.

Slater, P.E., Ellencweig, A., Goldstein, L., Dresner, R., and Fink, T.R. "Quality of Emergency Room Care During the Israel Doctors' Strike." *Public Health* (London) 98 (1984): 354-60.

Slater, P.E., and Ever-Hadani, P. "Mortality in Jerusalem During the 1983 Doctors' Strike [letter]." *Lancet* 2 (1983): 1306.

Slater, P.E., Steinberg, A.L., and Stern, Z. "Effects of a Doctors' Strike on Emergency Room Utilization in a Jerusalem Hospital." *Public Health* (London) 97 (1983): 331-5.

Solomon, Z. "Post-traumatic Stress Disorder and Social Functioning: A Three-year Prospective Study." *Social Psychiatry*. (In press)

Solomon, Z., Avizur, E., and Mikulincer, M. "Coping Resources and Professional and Interpersonal Functioning Following Combat Stress Reaction: A Longitudinal Study." *Journal of Social and Clinical Psychology*. (In press)

Solomon, Z., and Flum, H. "Life Events, Combat Stress Reaction and Post-traumatic Stress Disorder." *Social Science and Medicine* 26 (1988): 319-25.

Solomon, Z., Kotler, M., and Mikulincer, M. "Combat-related Post-traumatic Stress Disorder among the Second Generation of Holocaust Survivors: Preliminary Findings." *American Journal of Psychiatry* 145 (1988): 865-68.

Solomon, Z., Mikulincer, M., and Avizur, E. "Coping, Locus of Control, Social Support and Combat-related Post-traumatic Stress Disorder: A Prospective Study." *Journal of Personality and Social Psychology* 55 (1988): 279-85.

Solomon, Z., Mikulincer, M., Freid, B., and Wozner, Y. "Family Characteristics and Post-traumatic Stress Disorder: A Follow-up of Israeli Combat Stress Reaction Casualties." *Family Process* 26 (1987): 383-94.

Solomon, Z., Mikulincer, M., and Hobfoll, S. "Effects of Social Support and Battle Intensity on Loneliness and Breakdown during Combat." *Journal of Personality and Social Psychology* 51 (1986): 1269-77.

Soskolne, V. "The Effect of Ethnic Origins on Personality Resources and Psychophysiological Health in a Chronic Stress Situation: The Case of Spouses of Dialysis Patients." *Israel Journal of Psychiatry and Related Sciences* 21 (1984): 137-50.

Soskolne, V., and Kaplan-DeNour, A. "The Adjustment of Patients and Spouses to Dialysis Treatment." *Social Science and Medicine*. (In press)

______. "The Psychosocial Adjustment of Patients and Spouses on Home Hemodialysis, CAPD and Center Dialysis." *Nephron* 47 (1987): 266-73.

Stockler, R.E. "Development of Community Health Services for the Arab Village Population in Israel." *Nursing R S A Verpleging* (S. Africa) 6 (1983): 33-40.

Tabory, E., and Weller, L. "The Impact of Cultural Context on the Mental Health of Concentration Camp Survivors." *Journal of Holocaust and Genocide Studies* 2 (1987): 299-305.

Tzuriel, D., and Weller, L. "Social and Psychological Determinants of Breast-feeding and Bottle-feeding Mothers." *Basic and Applied Social Psychology* 7 (1986): 85-100.

Warner, E. "Israel's Troubled Health Care System." *Canadian Medical Association Journal* 130 (1984): 454-63.

Weller, L., and Aminadav, C. "Attitudes toward Mild and Severe Retardation." *British Journal of Medical Psychology*. (In press)

Weller, L., and Grunes, S. "Does Contact with the Mentally Ill Reduce Prejudice?" *British Journal of Medical Psychology* 61 (1988): 277-84.

Weller, L., Harrison, M., and Katz, Z. "Changes in the Self and Professional Images of Student Nurses." *Journal of Advanced Nursing* 13 (1988): 179-84.

Yishai, Y. "Politics and Medicine: The Case of Israeli National Health Insurance." *Social Science and Medicine* 16 (1982): 285-91.

Zuckerman-Bareli, C. "Effects of Border Tensions on Residents of an Israeli Town." *Journal of Human Stress* 5 (1979): 29-41.

______. "The Effect of Border Tension on Adjustment of Kibbutzim and Moshavim on the Northern Border of Israel." In *Stress and Anxiety*, vol. 8, 81-91, eds. C.D. Spielberger and I.G. Sarason. New York: McGraw-Hill, 1982.

Zuckerman-Bareli, C., and Ronen, M. "Folk Medicine in Israel." In *Social and Cultural Integration in Israel*, ed. A. Deutsch and G. Tules, pp. 11-35. Ramat Gan, Israel: Bar-Ilan University, Sociological Institute for Community Studies, 1988.

Contributors

Henry Abramovitch is in the Department of Behavioral Science, Sackler School of Medicine, Tel-Aviv University

Aaron Antonovsky is in the Department of Sociology of Health, Faculty of Health Sciences, Ben-Gurion University of the Negev, Beersheba

Avishai Antonovsky is a graduate student in psychology at the Hebrew University, Jerusalem

Lea Baider is in the Department of Clinical Oncology and Radiotherapy, Hadassah University Hospital, Jerusalem

Eileen Basker (deceased) was in the Community Mental Health Center, Ministry of Health, Jaffa

R. Ben-Shaoul is in the Talbieh Psychiatric Hospital, Jerusalem

Zeev Ben-Sira is in the Baerwald School of Social Work, Hebrew University, and the Israel Institute of Applied Social Research, Jerusalem

Judith Bernstein is in the Department of the Sociology of Health, Faculty of Health Sciences, Ben-Gurion University of the Negev, Beersheba

Yoram Bilu is in the Department of Psychology, Hebrew University, Jerusalem

Sara Carmel is in the Department of the Sociology of Health, Faculty of Health Sciences, Ben-Gurion University of the Negev, Beersheba

Jiska Cohen is in the Institute for Study and Research of the Kibbutz and the Cooperative Idea, University of Haifa

Nancy Datan (deceased) was in the Department of Psychology, University of Wisconsin at Green Bay, U.S.A.

Hilda Deshen is in the Department of Sociology and Anthropology, Tel-Aviv University

Shlomo Deshen is in the Department of Sociology and Anthropology, Tel-Aviv University

Mirit Dotan is in the Department of Nursing, School of Education, Tel-Aviv University

Tikvah Honig-Parnass is in the Department of Labour Studies, Faculty of Social Sciences, Tel-Aviv University

Orit Ichilov is in the Department of Nursing, School of Education, Tel-Aviv University

Dafna N. Izraeli is in the Department of Labour Studies, Faculty of Social Sciences, Tel-Aviv University

Rachel Javetz is in the Department of Medical Ecology, School of Public Health and Community Medicine, Hebrew University-Hadassah Medical School, Jerusalem

David Krasilowsky is in the Talbieh Psychiatric Hospital, Jerusalem

Yael Kremer was in the School of Nursing, Hebrew University-Hadassah Medical School, Jerusalem

Yitzhak Levav is in the Department of Social Medicine, School of Public Health and Community Medicine, Hebrew University-Hadassah Medical School, Jerusalem

Uri Leviatan is in the Institute for Study and Research of the Kibbutz and the Cooperative Idea, University of Haifa

Noah Lewin-Epstein is in the Department of Sociology and Anthropology, Faculty of Social Sciences, Tel-Aviv University

Ivonne Mansbach is in the Department of Social Medicine, School of Public Health and Community Medicine, Hebrew University-Hadassah Medical School, Jerusalem

Benjamin Maoz is in the Division of Mental Health, Faculty of Health Sciences, Ben-Gurion University of the Negev, Beersheba

S.D. Minuchin-Itzigsohn is in the Talbieh Psychiatric Hospital, Jerusalem

Netta Notzer is in the Department of Medical Education, Sackler School of Medicine, Tel-Aviv University

Phyllis Palgi is in the Department of Behavioral Sciences, Sackler School of Medicine, Tel-Aviv University

Hava Palti is in the Department of Social Medicine, School of Public Health and Community Medicine, Hebrew University-Hadassah Medical School, Jerusalem

Zvi Palti is in the Department of Social Medicine, School of Public Health and Community Medicine, Hebrew University-Hadassah Medical School, Jerusalem

Bella Pevsner is in the Department of Social Medicine, School of Public Health and Community Medicine, Hebrew University-Hadassah Medical School, Jerusalem

Helen Pridan is in the Department of Social Medicine, School of Public Health and Community Medicine, Hebrew University-Hadassah Medical School, Jerusalem

Diana Shye is in the Department of Medical Ecology, School of Public Health and Community Medicine, Hebrew University-Hadassah Medical School, Jerusalem

Judith T. Shuval is in the Department of Medical Ecology, School of Public Health and Community Medicine, Hebrew University-Hadassah Medical School, Jerusalem

Varda Soskolne is in the Department of Social Work, Hadassah Medical Organization, Jerusalem

Talma Sourani is a rehabilitation social worker in Petach Tikva

David Tzuriel is in the School of Education, Bar-Ilan University, Ramat Gan

Alex Weingrod is in the Department of Behavioral Sciences, Faculty of Humanities and Social Sciences, Ben-Gurion University of the Negev, Beersheba

Leonard Weller is in the Department of Sociology, Bar-Ilan University, Ramat Gan

Ilana S. Yakubovich is in the Department of Epidemiology, Faculty of Health Sciences, Ben-Gurion University of the Negev, Beersheba

Yael Yishai is in the Department of Political Science, University of Haifa

Tsila Zalcman was in the Department of the Sociology of Health, Ben-Gurion University of the Negev, Beersheba

Chaya Zuckerman-Bareli is in the Department of Sociology, Bar-Ilan University

Leah Zwanger is in the Recanati School of Community Health Sciences, Faculty of Health Sciences, Ben-Gurion University of the Negev, Beersheba and in Kupat Holim Klalit